management

theory

process

and

practice

RICHARD M. HODGETTS

The University of Nebraska—Lincoln

1975

W. B. SAUNDERS COMPANY • Philadelphia • London • Toronto

W. B. Saunders Company: West Washington Square
Philadelphia, PA   19105

12 Dyott Street
London, WC1A   1DB

833 Oxford Street
Toronto, Ontario M8Z 5T9, Canada

Library of Congress Cataloging in Publication Data

Hodgetts, Richard M

Management: theory process and practice

1. Management.   I. Title.

HD31.H556   658.4   74–6687

ISBN 0–7216–4708–1

Management—Theory Process and Practice   ISBN   0-7216-4708-1

Last digit is the print number: 9   8   7   6   5   4   3   2   1

To SALLY and STEVEN

PREFACE

Man's progress in this century may be measured by his technical and scientific prowess, but it is accounted for by his managerial expertise. Without the ability to formulate objectives, to draw up plans and to coordinate men and materials in a synergistic fashion, Henry Ford would never have built his production line and Neil Armstrong would never have walked on the moon. In many undertakings, management, the process of getting things done through people, is the key to success or failure.

The purpose of this book is to familiarize the reader with basic modern management concepts and to acquaint him or her with the present status as well as the future of this growing field. It is assumed that the reader is either a newcomer or a practitioner with little formal training in management. As such, this book can be used effectively in the first management course in undergraduate or junior colleges. It can also be employed in professional training courses and should prove useful to the practicing executive who wishes to update his knowledge in the field.

DISTIN-GUISHING FEATURES I have attempted to present the concepts of modern management in an interesting, easy-to-read style through the use of the following special features:

Organization. This book is organized into three major parts. Part I covers the history of management thought and provides the reader with a basis for understanding the evolution of modern management. Part II examines modern management theory and practice, emphasizing and explaining many of the concepts important to the practicing manager. Part III reviews new developments on the management horizon, from computer technology to modern organization structures and from transactional analysis to behavior modification.

Exhibits. A large number of tables, charts and illustrations are employed in this text, both to highlight important concepts and to present them in an easy-to-understand manner.

Historical Pictures and Biographical Sketches. In Part I, a number of important contributors to early management thought are discussed. In order to provide the reader with a better understanding of these individuals, a picture and a brief biographical sketch of many of them have been included.

Short Cases. All too often students learn theories without ever understanding their practical application. For this reason, I have included four short cases at the end of each chapter, providing the reader with an opportunity to apply the principles, processes and practices presented in the chapter, and thus reinforcing the major concepts introduced.

Glossary of Terms. At the end of the text the reader will find a glossary of terms that identifies or describes many of the concepts presented in the book. This glossary is more comprehensive than that contained in any other basic management text and should provide the reader with a definition or explanation of the most important topics contained herein.

SUPPLE-MENTS AND TEACHING AIDS

The following supplements and teaching aids have been designed to accompany this text:

Readings Book—contains selections related to each of the parts of this text and provides readings on some of the most relevant concepts in modern management.

Student Workbook and Study Guide—contains fill-in, true-false and multiple choice questions as well as work projects for each chapter. The study guide is designed to review and expand the important concepts in each chapter.

Teacher's Manual—contains a synopsis of the goals and material in each chapter. In addition, there are answers to the review and study questions at the end of each chapter, questions associated with the cases at the end of each chapter and a large pool of true-false and multiple choice questions for testing purposes.

ACKNOWL-EDGMENTS

There are many individuals who have played a decisive role in helping me write this book, although I accept full responsibility for all errors of omission and commission. In particular, I would like to thank Dr. Fred Luthans, University of Nebraska, who provided me with many helpful suggestions and ideas, which I have incorporated into the book. I would also like to thank those who have read, reviewed and commented on portions of the text. In particular, Professor T. P. Appleton, Point

Park College; Dr. John C. Athanassiades, Georgia State University; Drs. Robert Blake and Jane Mouton of Scientific Methods, Inc; Dr. Richard T. Hise, Virginia Commonwealth University; Dr. A. Thomas Hollingsworth, University of South Carolina; Professor Richard Howe, Orange Coast College; Dr. Ronald Johnson, Northeast Louisiana University; Dr. John M. Larsen, Jr., University of Tennessee; Dr. Cheedle Millard, University of Dallas; Dr. Russell Morey, Western Illinois University; Ms. Pat Rogers, Clarkson Memorial Hospital; Dr. Gary Schwendiman, University of Nebraska; Dr. Dumitru Teodorescu, Youngstown State University; Dr. Stewart Tubbs, General Motors Institute; Dr. A. K. Wickesberg, University of Minnesota; and Dr. Daniel Wren, University of Oklahoma. I would also like to thank Dr. Henry Albers, University of Nebraska, for his assistance and encouragement in writing this text; Mr. John C. Neifert of the W. B. Saunders Company for his many helpful suggestions on format and approach; Mr. Kenneth Atwood, Wayne Koch and Gail Huggins, also of the W. B. Saunders Company. Finally, thanks go to Jeanne Maynard for her assistance in typing the manuscript.

Richard M. Hodgetts

CONTENTS

PART I: THE DEVELOPMENT OF EARLY
         MANAGEMENT THOUGHT............................ 1

CHAPTER 1

FROM ANTIQUITY TO THE INDUSTRIAL
REVOLUTION 5

    Sumerians 6
    Babylonians... 6
    Chinese.. 8
    Romans.. 9
    Roman Catholic Church 9
    Niccolò Machiavelli...................................... 11
    The Industrial Revolution............................. 12
        Richard Arkwright.............................. 14
        Adam Smith 14
    Case: A Giant Edifice 17
    Case: Organization of the Legion 17
    Case: Same Old Stuff 18
    Case: A Matter of Participation................. 19

CHAPTER 2

THE SCIENTIFIC MANAGEMENT MOVEMENT.............. 21

    Early Scientific Management........................ 21
        Boulton & Watt Soho Foundry 22
        Owen's New Lanark Experiment........... 23
        Charles Babbage 24
        William S. Jevons.............................. 25
        Early American Forerunners 26
            Henry R. Towne 26
            Frederick Halsey 27
    Scientific Management Movement 28
        Frederick Taylor................................. 28
        The Gilbreths.................................... 33

Henry L. Gantt... 34
Harrington Emerson..................................... 34
Case: White Collar Output............................ 37
Case: Let's Face the Music........................... 38
Case: Fighting the "Blahs"........................... 39
Case: A Matter of Efficiency........................ 39

CHAPTER 3

CONTRIBUTORS TO EARLY MANAGEMENT THEORY

CONTRIBUTORS TO EARLY MANAGEMENT
THEORY... 41

Henri Fayol... 42
James D. Mooney and Alan C. Reiley 49
Lyndall F. Urwick 51
Chester I. Barnard...................................... 56
Case: Technicians and Managers 60
Case: A Call for Formal Training...................... 61
Case: Getting It All Together......................... 62
Case: Who is in Charge Here? 63

CHAPTER 4

THE HUMAN ELEMENT IN THE WORK PLACE: EARLY RESEARCH

THE HUMAN ELEMENT IN THE WORK PLACE:
EARLY RESEARCH.. 65

Hugo Münsterberg.. 66
Mayo's Mule Spinning Inquiry 71
Hawthorne Studies 72
Case: A Matter of Intelligence 82
Case: The Firefighter................................. 83
Case: A Big Influence................................. 84
Case: I've Gotta Be Free.............................. 86

CHAPTER 5

EARLY MANAGEMENT THOUGHT IN PERSPECTIVE

EARLY MANAGEMENT THOUGHT IN
PERSPECTIVE.. 87

Scientific Management Shortcomings...................... 87
Classical Management Deficiencies 89
Inadequacy of the Human Relations Approach 91
The Positive Side of the Picture 92
Case: My Boss Doesn't Understand Me................ 97
Case: For a Few Dollars More 98
Case: The New Assembly Technique.................... 99
Case: Use Me Well 100

**PART II: MODERN MANAGEMENT THEORY
          AND PRACTICE**................................... 103

SECTION A: The Development of Modern
            Management Theory........................ 105

CHAPTER 6

MODERN SCHOOLS OF MANAGEMENT THOUGHT....... 106

Management Process School 107
Quantitative School 112
Behavioral School 115
Toward a Unified Theory?................................. 117
The Weaknesses of the Schools............................ 118
A Conceptual Framework 121
Case: The Manager's Job................................. 122
Case: The Advertising Budget 123
Case: A State of Confusion 124
Case: One Out of Three................................. 125

SECTION B: The Management Process School................. 127

CHAPTER 7

THE PLANNING PROCESS 128

Comprehensive Planning................................... 128
Strategic Planning 130
Developing A Propitious Niche 138
Long- and Intermediate-Range Objectives.................. 140
Operational Planning 141
Use of a Planning Organization 148
Advantages of Planning................................... 150
Planning Is No Guarantee................................. 151
Case: Just Leave Us Alone 154
Case: A Better Mousetrap 156
Case: Milking the Cow 157
Case: Pruning the Product Line........................ 158

CHAPTER 8

THE ORGANIZING PROCESS 161

From Strategy to Structure............................... 161
Common Forms of Departmentalization..................... 162
Committee Organizations.................................. 167
Span of Control.. 169
Authority-Responsibility Relationships.................... 171
Decentralization of Authority 178
The Art of Delegation.................................... 180
The Informal Organization................................ 182
Case: I Did It My Way................................. 186
Case: A New Switch.................................... 187
Case: A Matter of Opinion 189
Case: Hospital Business................................ 190

CHAPTER 9
THE CONTROLLING PROCESS 193

The Basic Controlling Process 193
Requirements for an Effective Control System 196
Traditional Control Techniques 198
Specialized Control Techniques 203
Controlling Overall Performance 209
Case: Safety Margins 217
Case: Efficiency vs. Profitability 218
Case: A Possible Compromise 219
Case: The Dean's Dilemma 221

SECTION C: The Quantitative School 223

CHAPTER 10
FUNDAMENTALS OF DECISION MAKING 224

Decision-Making Process 224
Rationality and the Means-End Hierarchy 225
Personal Values and Decision Making 226
Types of Decisions 228
Decision-Making Conditions 230
Decision-Making Techniques 236
Case: I'll Be Home for Christmas 245
Case: One, Two or Three 246
Case: The Profitable Pen 247
Case: The Car Dealer's Dilemma 248

CHAPTER 11
MODERN QUANTITATIVE DECISION-MAKING
TOOLS AND PROCESSES 249

Operations Research 250
Inventory Control 251
Linear Programming 254
Game Theory 260
Queuing Theory 266
Monte Carlo Technique 267
Decision Trees 267
Heuristic Programming 269
Case: An Economic Approach 272
Case: A Little of This and a Little of That 273
Case: Half and Half 274
Case: The Big Payoff 275

SECTION D: The Behavioral School 277

CHAPTER 12

INTERPERSONAL AND ORGANIZATIONAL COMMUNICATION... 278

Interpersonal Communication 278
Common Barriers to Effective Communication........... 281
Communication Channels.. 288
Communication Media.. 294
Toward Effective Communication.............................. 296
Case: Good Work Is Expected.................................... 303
Case: A Big Production Number 305
Case: A Two-Way Experiment................................... 306
Case: Speed and Comprehension 309

CHAPTER 13

MODERN MOTIVATION THEORY.............................. 311

Needs and Behavior.. 311
Maslow's Need Hierarchy... 312
McGregor's Assumptions.. 318
Argyris' Immaturity-Maturity Theory 322
Herzberg's Two-Factor Theory of Motivation............. 323
Expectancy Theory and Learned Behavior.................. 327
Vroom's Theory 328
Porter and Lawler's Model... 330
Equity or Social Comparison Theory.......................... 332
Case: Take the Money and Run 336
Case: The Great Escape 337
Case: Join Us 338
Case: A New Deal... 339

CHAPTER 14

LEADERSHIP EFFECTIVENESS.................................. 341

The Nature of Leadership 341
Leadership Behavior... 344
   A Leadership Continuum 344
   Likert's Management Systems 345
   Two-Dimensional Leadership........................... 350
   Fiedler's Contingency Model............................ 354
   Three-Dimensional Leadership......................... 355
   Life Cycle Theory of Leadership...................... 357
The Adaptive Leader... 359
Case: A Matter of Style 361
Case: Old Habits 362
Case: The Fast Gun... 364
Case: Contingency Chaos... 365

SECTION E: **The Future of Management Theory**.............. 367

CHAPTER 15

MANAGEMENT THEORY: CURRENT STATUS AND FUTURE DIRECTION 368

The Systems School.. 370
The Organization As An Open System 373
Totally Adaptive Organization Systems 376
Managerial Systems 379
The Systems Point Of View 382
Management Theory In The Future 383
Case: A Great Big Secret... 386
Case: Input-Output 387
Case: Modifications, Modifications........................ 388
Case: A Systems View... 389

PART III: RECENT DEVELOPMENTS IN MANAGEMENT 391

CHAPTER 16

MANAGEMENT INFORMATION SYSTEMS AND THE ROLE OF THE COMPUTER 394

Management Information Systems 395
    Designing an MIS 395
    MIS and the Impact of Change 398
The Role and Impact of Computers.......................... 403
    Modern Computers.. 403
    Computer Programming................................... 404
    Computer Uses.. 406
    Drawbacks to Computers 410
    Impact of the Computer.................................. 411
Case: We Told You So 417
Case: The Old Ways Are Best................................. 418
Case: What If?... 419
Case: Just Around the Corner 420

CHAPTER 17

TECHNOLOGY, MANAGEMENT AND THE ORGANIZATION 422

Technology: An Historical Perspective 423
Modern Technological Advances: Opportunities and Challenges.. 424
Technological Forecasting 428
Technology and the Personnel 433
Technology and Structure.. 438
Case: Faster Than a Speeding Bullet 444
Case: The Next Best Thing to Being There 445
Case: 1985: An Early Look...................................... 446
Case: More Order, Not Less 448

CHAPTER 18
MODERN ORGANIZATION STRUCTURES.................... 449

The Decline of Bureaucratic Structures.................... 449
The Project Organization 450
The Matrix Structure 452
Free-Form Organizations 459
Contingency Organization Design 463
Case: New Times, New Structures 468
Case: The Glorified Coordinator 470
Case: Fly Me to the Moon....................................... 471
Case: A Team Approach.. 472

CHAPTER 19
THE MANAGEMENT OF HUMAN ASSETS:
TOOLS AND TECHNIQUES... 473

The Great Jackass Fallacy 473
Human Resources Accounting................................. 474
Job Enrichment 479
Management by Objectives 483
Sensitivity Training.. 484
Transactional Analysis... 485
Organization Behavior Modification......................... 490
Case: A Liquidation of People................................. 495
Case: Doing Your Own Thing.................................. 496
Case: Turning People On.. 497
Case: A Case of Eligibility 498

CHAPTER 20
SOCIAL RESPONSIBILITY: A
DEVELOPING CHALLENGE..................................... 500

Enlightened Self-Interest 500
Equal Opportunity.. 502
    Legislation.. 502
    Hiring of the Hard-Core Unemployed............. 503
    Minority Capitalism.. 504
    Female Discrimination 506
Ecology... 508
    Pesticides.. 509
    Air Pollution 510
    Water Pollution.. 513
    Noise Pollution 514
    Ecological Legislation 516
Consumerism... 517
    Consumer Information and Assistance............. 517
    Product Safety 518
Case: Male Chauvinist Pig 523
Case: Let the Seller Beware................................... 524
Case: Show and Tell... 525
Case: A Case of Discrimination?............................. 526

CHAPTER 21

INTERNATIONAL MANAGEMENT: CHALLENGES
AND OPPORTUNITIES 528

Entering Foreign Markets... 529
Identifying the Firm's Basic Mission 530
Evaluating the Possible Advantages 530
Evaluating the Possible Disadvantages............ 532
Understanding the Joint Venture 535
Making the Final Decision............................ 536
Management of Foreign Operations......................... 537
Organization Structure................................. 537
Control 539
Staffing.. 540
The Multinational Corporation.............................. 543
International Economic Power........................ 543
Becoming Truly International........................ 544
Case: Twenty Questions.. 549
Case: Yankee Go Home 549
Case: Developments From Abroad 550
Case: A Big Windfall 551

CHAPTER 22

MANAGEMENT IN THE FUTURE 553

The Past is Prologue 553
The Future of Modern Management Theory 555
Other Developments on the Horizon 557
Corporate Democracy..................................... 557
Scramble for Young Executive Talent............. 561
Continuing Trend Toward Professionalism 564
Just a Beginning.. 566
Case: One Man's Opinion..................................... 569
Case: The Nonconformists 570
Case: Executive Recruiting..................................... 571
Case: Telling It Like It Is 572

GLOSSARY OF TERMS.. 573

NAME INDEX 589

SUBJECT INDEX... 595

PART I

THE DEVELOPMENT OF EARLY MANAGEMENT THOUGHT

The purpose of this book is to present a systematic approach to the study of modern management. There are three major parts in all. In this first part, an examination of early management thought will be undertaken for the purpose of providing the reader with the requisite background for understanding how modern management theory evolved. After all, how can one truly understand where the field of management is, or where it is going, without some knowledge of where it has been?

Chapter 1 is a historical view of management, beginning with the Sumerians and continuing through the Industrial Revolution. Many "modern" management principles and practices are merely different applications of the very same concepts employed by organizations in antiquity. Of course, today it is being analyzed more systematically than ever before, and there is greater emphasis on textbook education in contrast to simple trial and error. Yet in short, management has been practiced effectively for thousands of years.

In Chapter 2 an examination of the scientific management movement is undertaken. The Industrial Revolution brought about the factory system, and with it came a tremendous interest in developing tools and techniques for increasing worker productivity. The individuals who, through the use of time and motion study, work analysis and incentive wage payment plans, helped to attain these efficiency increases are known as scientific managers. Their basic ideas and contributions to management will also be reviewed in Chapter 2.

In Chapter 3 the focus is on the early management theorists. As worker productivity rose, organizations found they needed more managers to handle their operations. Scientific management helped to bring about an increase in the manager-worker ratio. This, in turn, led to interest in the role of the manager, eventually culminating in investigations of such questions as: What is management? What are the functions of a manager? What general administrative guidelines should an effective manager employ? The people who sought to answer these questions, and in so doing formulated the basis of modern management thought, are often known as early management theorists. Some of their major contributions are reviewed in Chapter 3.

Then, in Chapter 4, an examination is made of early human behavior research in the work place. The scientific managers and early management theorists were greatly interested in the management of work. It was inevitable, however, that attention would also be focused on the management of people. What are the norms and values to which workers subscribe? What makes people tick? How can this information be employed for the benefit of both workers and the organizations? Individuals who are known today as human relations researchers provided some important early insights in this entire area.

Finally, in Chapter 5, the contributions of these three groups—scientific managers, management theorists and human relationists—to early management thought are examined in perspective. Many of these writers and researchers made valuable contributions to management. However, some of their work had very serious shortcomings. In order to evaluate their contributions and to place them in proper perspective, it is also necessary to examine their weaknesses.

Thus, the overriding goal of Part I is to familiarize the reader with some of the important management developments that occurred prior to modern times. Today the horizons of management are expanding, but virtually all of these new areas had their genesis somewhere in early management thought. To understand and appreciate recent developments in the field, a grasp of the past is necessary.

CHAPTER 1

FROM ANTIQUITY TO THE INDUSTRIAL REVOLUTION

GOALS OF THE CHAPTER

Management has been popularly defined as "getting things done through people," and for thousands of years this has been the key to success for individuals and civilizations alike. Effective management practices have helped to raise the United States to a position of world power in this century. Such practices have also played key roles in the success and development of giant corporations such as General Motors, American Telephone & Telegraph and IBM. Today, as the free and communist countries seek detente, effective management will be needed to bring both sides together. Thus, whether one is examining the prerequisites for world prominence, corporate growth or international peace, management must be considered.

The concept of management is not new; it has been practiced for thousands of years. The Sumerians employed it. So, too, did the Babylonians, the Romans and all other civilizations that ever rose to prominence and power. But one need not turn to antiquated ruins and ancient documents to verify this statement. The Roman Catholic Church has survived to this day, owing in no small part to its outstanding administrative abilities.

The primary goals of this chapter are to examine some of the institutions and individuals that contributed to management thought from the dawn of civilization to the Industrial Revolution. Particular attention will be focused on:

a. the management control process developed by the Sumerians;
b. the management significance of Hammurabi's code;
c. the contribution of the Chinese to military management;
d. Diocletian's massive reorganization of the Roman Empire;
e. the management significance of the Roman Catholic Church;
f. Machiavelli's four broad principles of leadership;

    g. the importance of the Industrial Revolution in the development of man-
       agement thought;
    h. the contributions of Richard Arkwright to the practice of managment; and
    i. Adam Smith's writings on the division of labor.

Throughout this examination one point should be noted; most of the basic concepts of management being used by modern organizations were employed in some form by their predecessors in antiquity.

SUMERIANS

One of the earliest civilizations known to man is that of the Sumerians, famous for their development of a written language. From 3000 B.C. onward, priests in the city of Ur kept business, legal and historical records on clay tablets. Some of these tablets relate the management practices of Sumerian priests, the most influential class in the civilization.

One of the ways in which the priests attained their high position was by refashioning religious doctrine. For example, initially the gods demanded human sacrifice. However, over time this changed, and the priests announced to the people that the deities would also be willing to accept substitutes such as money, oxen, goats, chickens, butter, oil and cakes. Enriched by this beneficence, the priests soon became the wealthiest and most powerful class in Sumer. They also collected taxes and managed revenues and estates, but they did not squander these riches. Instead, they wrote down all transactions so that an account of their stewardship could be made to the chief priest. In fact, it is highly likely that the Sumerians developed a written language in response to their need for a *managerial control process*. As Will Durant, the historian, writes,

Managerial control process was developed.

"For centuries writing was a tool of commerce, a matter of contracts and bills, of shipments and receipts; and secondarily, perhaps, it was an instrument of religious record, an attempt to preserve magic formulas, ceremonial procedures, sacred legends, prayers and hymns from alteration or decay."[1] Thus, some of the earliest writings in existence provide illustrations of managerial control.

BABYLONIANS

Another early civilization that made important contributions to management thought was that of the Babylonians.

Code of Hammurabi

The most significant contribution of the Babylonians was Hammurabi's code, which contained 285 laws, ranging in topic areas from personal property to real estate and trade to family and personal matters. Some of the laws applicable to business were:

---

[1]Will Durant, *The Story of Civilization*, Part 1, *Our Oriental Heritage* (New York: Simon and Schuster, 1954), p. 131.

On Control

If a merchant lend to an agent and the agent return to the merchant whatever the merchant had given him; and if the merchant deny [receiving] what the agent has given to him, that agent shall call the merchant to account in the presence of god and witnesses and the merchant, because he has had a dispute with his agent, shall give to him sixfold the amount which he obtained.[2]

On Responsibility

Managerial guidelines were set forth.

If a man hire a man to oversee his farm and furnish him the seed-grain and intrust him with oxen and contract with him to cultivate the field, and that man steal either the seed or the crop and it be found in his possession, they shall cut off his fingers.[3]

On Minimum Wage

If a man hire oxen, a wagon and a driver, he shall pay 180 KA of grain per day.[4]

Hammurabi's code is of great management significance because it provided guidelines from which to administer an empire. If Hammurabi had done nothing else, he would be assured a place in management history. However, the king also deserves mention for his leadership style. Hammurabi realized that his kingdom would fall to pieces if he could not maintain the requisite law and order, and he therefore attempted to develop an image of himself as a guardian and protector of his people. In one of his inscriptions that has survived he relates how he provided water, security and government to many tribes. He also spent countless hours coddling the clergy, for he was aware of the role that religion played in his society; and he built temples for the gods, including a gigantic sanctuary for the national deities at Babylon. In return for the laws he provided to the people and the attention he lavished on the clergy, he demanded and received the obedience of his people. Hammurabi not only provided *management guidelines* through his code but also left a clear illustration of the importance of *effective leadership style.*

Nebuchadnezzar Following Hammurabi's death, the Babylonian empire crumbled, and it was over 1500 years before the Babylonians regained their former glory. When that time arrived, Nebuchadnezzar was their king. His use of effective management practices was evidenced by the construction projects he sponsored and by the production control he employed in his textile mills and granaries.

Construction Projects. During Nebuchadnezzar's reign the

---

[2]Robert F. Harper, *The Code of Hammurabi, King of Babylon* (Chicago, Illinois: University of Chicago Press, 1904), p. 37.
[3]*Ibid.*, p. 89.
[4]*Ibid.*, p. 93.

famous Hanging Gardens were built. The feat was a phenomenal one for its time. One historian has described it as follows:

> The topmost terrace was covered with rich soil to the depth of many feet, providing space and nourishment not merely for varied flowers and plants, but for the largest and most deep-rooted trees. Hydraulic engines concealed in the columns and manned by shifts of slaves carried water from the Euphrates to the highest tier of the gardens.[5]

Magnificent structures were erected.

Another of the magnificent buildings of Babylon was an immense and lofty zuggurat 650 feet high. The structure, taller than any of the pyramids of Egypt, is believed by historians to be the famed Tower of Babel. In addition to these, there were many other great construction feats, including the gigantic Temple of Marduk and the beautiful Ishtar Gate.

Production Control. An even more explicit illustration of effective management is seen in the production control methods used by the Babylonians. In their textile mills they used colored tags to identify the yarn entering the mill each week. On the basis of the color they were able to determine how long each batch of raw materials had been in the mill. Nebuchadnezzar used this very same concept in the granaries, where the produce was stored in large earthenware jars and a colored reed was placed in the seal of each. In this way it was possible to determine how long the grain had been in the warehouse. These same basic concepts of production and inventory control are employed in industry today, although, of course, in a more sophisticated form.

Production and inventory control was employed.

Nebuchadnezzar made Babylon the unrivaled capital of the Near East, yet all of his accomplishments would have been impossible without effective planning, organizing and controlling. The Babylonians, therefore, must have known and employed management concepts.

CHINESE

The Chinese also made contributions to management thought. One of the most famous is found in Sun Tzu's *The Art of War*, written around 500 B.C. It is the oldest military treatise in the world, but the principles and guidelines put forth by the author are still applicable today, as the following excerpts from the book indicate:

On Strategy

Military guidelines were set forth.

> Thus the highest form of generalship is to baulk the enemy's plans; the next best is to prevent the junction of the enemy's forces; the next in order is to attack the enemy's army in the field; and the worst policy of all is to besiege walled cities.[6]

---

[5]Durant, *op. cit.*, p. 225.

[6]Thomas R. Phillips, *Roots of Strategy* (Harrisburg, Pennsylvania: Military Service Publishing Company, 1941), p. 26.

On Tactics

The general who is skilled in defense hides in the most secret recesses of the earth; he who is skilled in attack flashes forth from the topmost heights of heaven. Thus on the one hand we have ability to protect ourselves; on the other, a victory that is complete.[7]

On Maneuvering

To refrain from intercepting an enemy whose banners are in perfect order, to refrain from attacking an army drawn up in calm and confident array— that is the art of studying circumstances.[8]

ROMANS

The Romans have provided numerous illustrations of effective management. Perhaps the most famous is Diocletian's reorganization of the empire.

Empire structure was reorganized.

Assuming his position A.D. 284, Diocletian soon realized that his empire was unmanageable in its present form. There were far too many people and matters of importance for the emperor to handle himself. He therefore abandoned the old organization in which the provincial governors reported directly to him and designed a new structure. First, he divided the empire into 100 provinces. Each of these was then grouped into one of 13 dioceses. In turn, the dioceses were grouped into four major geographical divisions. Three individuals were appointed to administer three of these divisions while Diocletian kept the last one for himself. By interposing two levels of management between himself and the province governors the emperor increased his control over the empire, and the province as a unit of government was reduced in importance. Under this new organization it was extremely difficult for anyone to defy imperial authority. To further enhance his power the emperor delegated only civil governmental authority to the governors, and thus the military forces stationed in their provinces were no longer under their control. These basic concepts employed by Diocletian are still used today by organizations attempting to stabilize their centralized authority.

During the time of the Roman Empire another great organization was coming into existence. However, unlike the empire, the Roman Catholic Church has survived the test of time.

ROMAN CATHOLIC CHURCH

In terms of longevity, "the most effective formal organization in the history of Western civilization has been the Roman Catholic Church."[9] This institution has made some significant

[7]*Ibid.*, p. 29.
[8]*Ibid.*, p. 40.
[9]Harold Koontz and Cyril O'Donnell, *Principles of Management: An Analysis of Managerial Functions*, 5th edition (New York: McGraw-Hill Book Company, 1972), p. 20.

contributions to management theory in the areas of the hierarchy of authority, specialization of activities along functional lines, and the staff concept.

Functionalism

Job descriptions were developed.

Long before the great corporations of modern times were faced with the challenge of managing their far-flung operations, the Catholic Church had solved similar problems. An organizational structure had been designed and a *scalar chain of command* established from the Pope, through the bishops, to the priests and the laity. The Church had also employed *functionalism*, assigning certain tasks to specific individuals. For example, in distinguishing between the functions of the bishop, presbyter, and deacon in the second century, two management historians have noted that "the bishop was the pastor, the presbyters constituted his council, and the deacons had under their special supervision the care of the poor and the sick."[10]

Staff Principle

The use of the staff principle was also widely employed in the Catholic Church. Advisory services were performed by various individuals and committees. However, the Church also made use of what can be termed *compulsory staff service.*

. . . Under this rule the abbot of a Benedictine monastery must consult the elder monks about him before rendering decisions, even on minor matters. On matters of more vital importance he must consult everyone, even the youngest. The subordinates are not merely free to express their opinions. These opinions must be sought and solicited. This rule in no way abridges the line authority of the abbot in making the final decision. He is simply prohibited from rendering *any* decision until the rule is complied with.[11]

Use of advisors was encouraged.

In addition, the concept of *staff independence* was employed. For example, in the Jesuit order the head of the Society does not choose his own advisors, although he is required to listen to them. These advisors are chosen for him, thereby avoiding the "yes man" pitfall. Mooney and Reiley explain:

. . . These councilors are chosen by the general congregation. They are not appointed by the general of the Society and they are not removable by him. They are literally imposed upon him. Here we have something more than compulsory staff service. We have another principle, if possible, even more significant—that of *staff independence.*[12]

Today, many subordinates feel that their boss does not listen to them. Others openly admit that the superior expects them to conform to the image of the organization man. Over a thou-

---

[10]James D. Mooney and Alan C. Reiley, *Onward Industry!* (New York: Harper & Brothers Publishers, 1931), p. 246.
[11]*Ibid.*, p. 266.
[12]*Ibid.*, p. 268.

sand years ago the Roman Catholic Church was developing management practices for sidestepping these very pitfalls.

The Bettman Archive Inc.

Niccolò Machiavelli

One of the most important individual contributors to the development of early management thought was Niccolò Machiavelli. Born in 1469 in Florence, Machiavelli secured employment in the city-state at the age of 29, eventually serving as unofficial emissary to every important city-state in Italy as well as to several outside countries. However, in 1512 the Medici family returned to power and Machiavelli lost his job and was exiled. The remainder of his life was spent in a vain effort to be reinstated.

During his time in exile he wrote extensively. Some of his best known works include *The Prince* and *The Discourses.*[13] Throughout the former work he presented several broad management principles to which he believed leaders should subscribe. First, he emphasized the importance of relying upon *mass consent*. Machiavelli felt that the prince or leader's authority emanated from the bottom. No one was a leader unless the followers agreed. Five hundred years later some management theorists would be treating this concept as newly discovered, failing to realize that Machiavelli had identified and described it long before. Second, the leader must strive for *cohesiveness* in the organization. He must reward his friends and maintain their

Four principles of leadership.

allegiance. In addition, the people should know what they can expect of their leader and understand what he expects of them. This is of the greatest importance in maintaining cohesiveness. Third, the prince must have a *will to survive*. This will keep him alert and prepared. Then, if some overthrow of his regime is attempted, he will be in a position to respond quickly and forcefully. Machiavelli believed that under these conditions the prince was justified in taking harsh steps. There need be no pretense of virtue or justice on his part. Fourth, the prince has to be a *leader*. He should be capable of setting an example for the people. This calls for wisdom, kindness and justice, traits which should be exercised at all times, except when his survival is placed in jeopardy.

Machiavelli made a systematic analysis of the prince's (manager's) job and from it derived *practical* principles that are as useful today as they were 500 years ago. No wonder a recent writer has concluded that Machiavelli's works are "bursting

---

[13]Niccolò Machiavelli, *The Prince* and *The Discourses*, (New York: The Modern Library, Inc., 1940).

with urgent advice and acute observations for top management of the great private and public corporations all over the world."[14]

THE INDUSTRIAL REVOLUTION

Although early civilizations and the writings of select individuals provide illustrations of effective management practices, the technological innovations of the Industrial Revolution had a more dynamic impact on managerial thinking than anything that had occurred previously. This is clearly seen in Great Britain between the years of 1700 and 1785, when major changes occurred in the basic organization of production. These changes, in chronological order, are commonly referred to as the domestic system, the putting-out system and the factory system.

Domestic System

The *domestic system* was predominant during the early eighteenth century. A family having enough labor to provide for its own survival would begin to turn out a product for sale by specializing in some area. For example, a loom or a spinning wheel might be purchased; then the group would buy raw materials, fabricate the textiles, and sell them at the local fair for whatever they would bring. The system was very successful and remained in existence for quite some time for two basic reasons. First, it was easy to set up this kind of operation because a loom or spinning wheel was not very expensive; there was ease of entry into the field. Second, transportation systems were inefficient, and it was therefore impossible for outside competition to provide fabricated textiles to the local people. This domestic system was basically a family operated enterprise with business being conducted at an informal, unsophisticated level. Little concern was given to the development of efficient management practices or skills.

Family entre-preneurship emerged.

Putting-Out System

The domestic system was doomed, however, because of its inefficiency. As one might have guessed, it was not long before enterprising individuals at these local fairs began underwriting the entire risk themselves, agreeing to take all the goods a family could manufacture at a fixed price. This transition continued further, to the point where the individuals became willing both to provide the family with the raw materials it needed and to pay them a fixed amount for each unit of output they provided. The domestic system thus came to an end and the *putting-out system* emerged. The family was no longer an entrepreneurial enterprise. Now its members who processed the material were merely workers operating on a piece-rate basis.

Workers oper-ated on a piece-rate basis.

The new system had advantages for both sides. On the one

[14]Antony Jay, *Management and Machiavelli* (New York: Holt, Rinehart and Winston, 1967), p. 4.

hand, the workers no longer had to concern themselves with either the purchasing of raw materials or the selling of finished goods. On the other hand, the dealer who was trying to fill orders from many buyers was able to insure himself of many supply sources. In addition, there was an impetus toward the development of faster and more efficient production tools for insuring that the orders would be filled on time; one result was the invention of the spinning jenny. Moreover, this putting-out system proved to be slightly more management-oriented than the old, resulting, for example, in a greater concern for materials control. There was, however, one aspect of the entire system that proved very disconcerting:

The piece rates paid to workers under the putting-out system were not notably high, and hard-pressed workers were not above withholding materials and selling them on the sly. Although the merchants realized what was going on, they could not prove it because they lacked objective standards of material usage, and they lost control of the material when they gave it to the artisan. To protect themselves from such practices, the merchants appealed for laws.... Yet despite these rigorous laws and rights, the practice of stealing was too widespread to be stopped by statute. The result of this failure appears to be one of the major factors that contributed to the breakdown of the putting-out system and to the rise of the factory system.[15]

Factory System

Management now controlled all operations.

The invention of power-driven machinery drastically revised the entire production process, for, unlike the loom, this new machinery was far too expensive for the average worker to purchase; capital costs and capital requirements were beyond his means. As a result, the *factory system* came into existence. Machines were placed under one roof and the employees now came to a central location to work. The putting-out system was dead. Under these new conditions the management was finally able to control the labor force and to direct it toward the goal of increased output.

This control was accomplished in a number of ways. First, management cracked down hard on theft by the employees. Second, financial controls were introduced via double-entry bookkeeping. Third, traces of explicit planning began to appear, such as the location planning of the Carron Ironworks (1759) in Scotland. Initially, however, managerial practices were crude and undeveloped. Production control was primitive, the only apparent principle being that individuals working on a piece-rate basis were much more likely to produce at higher levels than those being paid on a day-rate basis.

Gradually, however, managerial practices began to improve. Managers started to do more planning, organizing and controlling. One of the foremost examples is found in the case of Richard Arkwright.

[15]Claude S. George, Jr., *The History of Management Thought*, 2nd edition (Englewood Cliffs, N. J.: Prentice-Hall, 1972), pp. 51–52.

The Bettman Archive Inc.
Richard Arkwright

Richard Arkwright is credited with providing the managerial know-how that greatly accelerated the advent of large-scale enterprise in the cotton industry in England. He did this by centralizing all cotton textile production under one roof, introducing division of labor and then devoting his time and attention to the coordination of all these interrelated activities. In addition, he spent considerable time on plant-site planning. He was also interested in the human side of enterprise, cutting the work day in his factories to 12 hours while everyone else was working their people a minimum of 14. He maintained strict discipline among the workers, but all considered him to be a fair man. Of him one management historian has written:

Efficient managerial principles gradually emerged.

His contributions of continuous production, plant site planning, coordination of machines, materials, men, and capital, factory discipline, and division of labor mark him as a pioneer in the use of efficient management principles. If he had written a principles book on good management practice he would probably rank as one of the true leaders in the field. Why, we might ask ourselves, did not he or some other industrialist of the period do so? The answer, it seems, is that they were too busy coping with the new problems evolving from large-scale production to be bothered with advancing a formalized, written analysis of correct managerial principles.[16]

One of the concepts upon which these early managers relied very heavily was *division of labor*, a subject made famous by Adam Smith.

The Bettman Archive Inc.
Adam Smith

Adam Smith was a Scottish political economist and philosopher. His book The Wealth of Nations (1776) had a tremendous influence on the development of economic and political theory and practice. However, his contributions were not limited to these areas. He also, in the same book, made an important contribution to the development of management thought when he described the impact that division of labor was having on manufacturing. Using the production of pins as his illustration, he described the process as follows:

To take an example, therefore, from a very trifling manufacture; but one in which the division of labour has been very often taken notice of, the trade of the pin-maker; a workman not educated to this business (which the division of labour has rendered a distinct trade), nor acquainted with the use of the machinery employed in it (to the invention of which the same division of

[16]*Ibid.*, p. 58.

Specialization led to increased efficiency.

labour has probably given occasion), could scarce, perhaps, with his utmost industry, make one pin in a day, and certainly could not make twenty. But in the way in which this business is now carried on, not only the whole work is a peculiar trade, but it is divided into a number of branches, of which the greater part are likewise peculiar trades. One man draws out the wire, another straights it, a third cuts it, a fourth points it, a fifth grinds it at the top for receiving the head; to make the head requires two or three distinct operations; to put it on, is a peculiar business, to whiten the pins is another; it is even a trade by itself to put them into the paper; and the important business of making a pin is, in this manner, divided into about eighteen distinct operations, which, in some manufactories, are all performed by distinct hands, though in others the same man will sometimes perform two or three of them. I have seen a small manufactory of this kind where ten men only were employed, and where some of them consequently performed two or three distinct operations. But though they were very poor, and therefore but indifferently accommodated with the necessary machinery, they could, when they exerted themselves, make among them about twelve pounds of pins in a day.[17]

This was made possible, in Smith's words, because of three factors:

...first, to the increase of dexterity in every particular workman; secondly, to the saving of the time which is commonly lost in passing from one species of work to another; and lastly, to the invention of a great number of machines which facilitate and abridge labour, and enable one man to do the work of many.[18]

Thus managers of the eighteenth century were most interested with what can be called the mechanical side of the job: division of labor, work flow, coordination of activities and control of operations. This would be true for most of the nineteenth century as well.

SUMMARY

In this chapter some early management practices and concepts were examined. Although terms such as management principles or management theory may not have been used, successful organizations in antiquity were well aware of the importance of effective management practices. And as mankind progressed and moved into the Industrial Revolution era, management gained in importance. The factory system, for example, placed greater demands on managers than did the putting-out system because the manager was now in direct control of operations and responsible for far more activities than previously. With these new job demands came an increasing interest in effective management practices as reflected by division of labor, work simplification and plant-site planning. In Chapter 2, an examination will be made of the nineteenth-century managers. In particular, attention will be focused on the development of what is known as scientific management.

[17]Adam Smith, *The Wealth of Nations*, (New York: The Modern Library, 1937), pp. 4–5.
[18]*Ibid.*, p. 7.

REVIEW
AND
STUDY
QUESTIONS

1. What contributions did the Sumerians make to early management thought? Put them in your own words.

2. Why is the Code of Hammurabi considered an important contribution to early management thought?

3. Are the principles and guidelines put forth by Sun Tzu in his book, *The Art of War*, still applicable today? Explain.

4. How did Diocletian reorganize the Roman Empire? Be specific.

5. What were some of the contributions made by the Roman Catholic Church that merit it a place in the annals of management history?

6. Identify and describe the four broad principles to which Machiavelli felt all leaders should subscribe.

7. What brought about the Industrial Revolution?

8. What was the domestic system? Putting-out system? Factory system? Explain.

9. Why is Richard Arkwright so important to the history of management thought? Explain.

10. What is Adam Smith's contribution to management thought?

11. What management concepts do you think were of most interest to the manager in the Industrial Revolution era? Explain.

**SELECTED
REFERENCES**

Bagley, F. R. C. trans., *Ghazali's Book of Counsel for Kings (Nasihat al-Muluk)*, London: Oxford Press, 1964.

Brand, C. E. *Roman Military Law*. Austin, Texas: University of Texas Press, 1968.

George, C. S., Jr. *The History of Management Thought*. Englewood Cliffs, N.J.: Prentice-Hall, Inc., 1972.

Hammon, R. *The Philosophy of Alfarabi*. New York: The Hobson Book Press, 1947.

Jay, A. *Management and Machiavelli*. New York: Holt, Rinehart and Winston, 1967.

Machiavelli, N. *The Prince* and *The Discourses*. New York: The Modern Library Inc., 1940.

Mooney, J. D. and A. C. Reiley, *Onward Industry!* New York: Harper & Brothers, Publishers, 1931.

More, Sir T. *Utopia*. Edward Surtz, ed. New Haven, Conn.: Yale University Press, 1964.

Phillips, T. R. *Roots of Strategy*. Harrisburg, Penn.: Military Service Publishing Company, 1941.

Ramaswamy, T. N. *Essentials of Indian Statecraft*. London: Asia Publishing House, 1962.

Roman Farm Management, The Treatises of Cato and Varro. trans. by a Virginia Farmer. New York: The Macmillan Company, 1913.

Smith, A. *Wealth of Nations*. New York: The Modern Library, 1937.

Wren, D. A. *The Evolution of Management Thought*. New York: The Ronald Press, 1973.

CASE: A GIANT EDIFICE

The Egyptians built numerous funerary edifices, the most famous of which is the Great Pyramid. The dimensions of the tomb provide some indication of their engineering abilities. Almost perfectly square, the pyramid, when intact, covered an area slightly over 13 acres and was approximately 147 meters high. The sides rose at an angle of 51° 52' and were accurately oriented to the four cardinal points. In all, approximately 2,300,000 blocks, each weighing an average of 2.5 tons, were used in the structure. Modern engineers have calculated that the inside of the pyramid is so vast that the Cathedral of Florence, the Cathedral of Milan, St. Paul's in London, West Minster Abbey, and St. Peter's in Rome could all be grouped within it.

The physical dimensions of the structure, however, should not be allowed to overshadow the managerial skill that was required to build it. Stones had to be cut at the quarries, transported down river, removed from the raft, carried to the construction site, and then put in place. In addition, Herodotus, the Greek historian, reports that it took the Egyptians ten years to build the road from the river to the construction site and twenty years to actually erect the edifice using a work force of 100,000 men.

Questions

1. How much management expertise would the Egyptians have needed in building this pyramid? Defend your answer.

2. Do modern construction firms use the same basic management concepts in building skyscrapers as the Egyptians used in erecting the Great Pyramid? Explain.

3. Could modern construction firms build the Great Pyramid with less men in a shorter span of time than the Egyptians did? Why or why not? What does your answer reveal about modern management methods?

CASE: ORGANIZATION OF THE LEGION[1]

In the prime of the Roman Republic, legions contained approximately 4200 foot troops divided into "lines." One historian has described them as follows:

[1] The data in the case can be found in C. E. Brand, *Roman Military Law* (Austin, Texas: University of Texas Press, 1968), p. 48.

First Line

1200 *hastati* or spearmen. These were the average, medium-armed, line-of-battle soldiers, forming the first line of resistance to meet the enemy.

Second Line

1200 *principes* or leaders. These were mature men in their prime, the best armed and equipped in the legion. They formed the main line of resistance.

Third Line

600 *triarii* or "third" men. These were the oldest and most experienced soldiers, employed as a tactical reserve.

Supernumeraries

1200 *velites* or skirmishers. These were young men, lightly armed, and not organized as a separate line or arm, but distributed among the entire sixty centuries of the legion to fill out their strength.

Each of these lines, in turn, was organized into smaller groups, the equivalent of companies, platoons and squads.

Questions

1. Are modern armies organized in a fashion similar to that used by the Roman legions? Explain.

2. What basic ideas do modern businesses use in organizing their companies that are similar to those used by the Roman legions?

3. In managing the legion, the Romans had a chain of command from the consul on down to the noncommissioned officers and the men. Do modern business firms have a similar chain of command? Explain.

CASE: SAME OLD STUFF

As part of honors convocation week, Bill Whitling, vice president of a large computer firm, had been asked to talk to a group of graduating seniors in the College of Business at State University. Bill was delighted to do so. He decided to speak about the dynamic environment in which his firm operated and the challenges facing the managers. At one point in his talk, he said:

Today, our management people are being confronted with new problems and we have to come up with brand new solutions. Managers in our company find that while a business education is helpful, there's a tremendous adjustment that has to be made in moving from the halls of academia to those of industry. Quite frankly, we've never before faced a similar situation; the challenges and problems are brand new.

During the question and answer session that followed, one

student asked Bill, "Aren't the basic problems confronting the modern manager the same ones that his counterpart in antiquity had to face? The way I see it, whether we're building the Great Pyramid or the Hoover Dam, the management problems are virtually the same. Oh sure, the problems or issues may be more complex, but our forebears in the Roman Empire or some other early civilization probably wrestled with similar problems."

Questions

1. Are modern managers facing totally new problems or are they confronting the same old ones? Explain.

2. How can a knowledge of management history be of value to the practicing manager? Explain.

3. What problems do today's universities create for managers? Have these problems changed with time? Explain.

CASE: A MATTER OF PARTICIPATION[1]

Many writers in the field of management contend that the effective leader is one who allows his people to have a voice in what goes on. He is a participative decision maker. However, the question arises: What are the characteristics of participative leadership? In an attempt to answer this question, a group of 157 managers were recently given a questionnaire survey containing 39 leadership characteristics. They were asked to rate each characteristic on a scale from 1 to 7. A "one" meant low participation and a "seven" indicated high participation. The highest five participation characteristics were:

Rank	Average scale-rating (1 to 7)
1. Gives subordinates a share in decision making.	6.08
2. Keeps subordinates informed of the true situation, good or bad, under all circumstances.	5.69
3. Stays aware of the state of the organization's morale and does everything possible to make it high.	5.45

[1]The data in this case can be found in Larry E. Greiner, "What Managers Think of Participative Leadership," *Harvard Business Review*, March–April 1973, pp. 111–117.

4. Is easily approachable.   5.38

5. Counsels, trains and develops
    subordinates.   5.34

In addition, the respondents indicated that a participative leader maintained free flowing and honest communication and expressed consideration and support for his people.

Questions

1. Ancient organizations and civilizations could not have been successful unless they too employed participative management. Do you think this statement is true or false? Explain.

2. Did ancient organizations actually attempt to counsel, train and develop their subordinates? Give your reasoning.

3. How important was participative management to a factory owner during the early Industrial Revolution? Explain.

CHAPTER 2

THE SCIENTIFIC MANAGE-
MENT MOVEMENT

GOALS OF THE CHAPTER

As was shown in Chapter 1, the Industrial Revolution had a tremendous impact on business operations. The putting-out system eventually gave way to the factory system, in which all the workers were located under one roof. With this change came new challenges and new opportunities. The goals of this chapter are to examine the management developments that took place between the late eighteenth and early twentieth centuries. Particular attention will be focused on:

a. Boulton and Watt's use of the scientific approach in managing their Soho foundry;
b. Robert Owen's New Lanark experiment;
c. William Jevons' early writings on labor and fatigue;
d. Henry Towne's gain sharing payment plan;
e. Frederick Halsey's premium plan;
f. Frederick Taylor's famous Bethlehem Steel experiments;
g. Taylor's four principles of scientific management;
h. the contribution made to time and motion study by the Gilbreths;
i. Henry Gantt's task-and-bonus system; and
j. Harrington Emerson's twelve principles of efficiency.

EARLY SCIENTIFIC MANAGE-MENT

The basic challenge facing management in the early years of the Industrial Revolution was that of developing rational, scientific principles for handling men, materials, money and machinery. This challenge took two forms: (a) how to increase productivity (output/input) by making the work easier to perform; and (b) how to motivate the workers to take advantage of these new methods and techniques. The men who developed approaches for meeting this challenge helped lay the foundation for what was to become known as scientific management. Boulton and Watt were two of these individuals.

**Boulton &
Watt Soho
Foundry**

One of the earliest applications of the scientific approach to
management took place in 1800 in England at the Soho Engineering Foundry of Boulton, Watt, & Company. The firm had
been founded originally by Matthew Boulton and James Watt to
manufacture Watt's steam engine. By 1800 their two sons were
in charge of the foundry and had begun making drastic changes
in the company's management practices.

*Forecasts were
conducted.*

First, major emphasis was placed upon forecasting and production planning. Company representatives on the European continent kept the home office informed of information that might
affect the demand for steam engines.

Second, with additional information on demand, the owners
were able to finalize their plans for a new factory. In this new
building, operations were designed and laid out according to
the flow of work. In addition, the speeds of each machine were
studied in an attempt to determine how much output could be
expected. This was broken down further into a series of minor

*Time and motion
study was em-
ployed.*

operations so that each worker's job could by systematically analyzed. Thus, there were the rudiments of modern time and motion study.

Third, wage payment systems were devised for each job. A
piece-rate approach was used on those tasks that were standardized and could be easily classified into groups. Then a standard or expected output was determined for each job. Anyone

*Work standards
were established.*

who produced more than the standard received a bonus for this
production. Workers who did not have jobs that permitted a
piece-rate payment plan were hired for a weekly wage. However,
interestingly enough, Boulton & Watt paid the foreman of these
workers on a piece-rate basis, the logic being that the man
should encourage his work group to increase its output. These
payment plans, especially the piece-rate ones, were worked out
in such great detail that one management historian has reported:

> With many piece rates at Soho it was found that the time it took to make dif-
> ferent-size items varied more nearly in proportion to the diameter of the part
> than to any other factor. A formula was therefore developed to express this re-
> lationship and was used for setting standards and piece rates—an example of
> management's use of standard data a century ahead of other firms. Soho mana-
> gers, however, took great pains to make the system simple and easily under-
> stood by the workers. In all, three wage scales were used: (1) a flat piece rate
> for each article, (2) a piece rate varying according to size or diameter, and (3) a
> piece rate varying with the horsepower of the engine for fitting working gears.[1]

Fourth, in attempting to maintain high morale, keen attention
was paid to the human element. The foundry walls were white-
washed to provide a cheerful environment, and, on occasion,
special entertainment was presented to the employees. At
Christmas time, presents were given to them and their families
and wage raises were announced. The company also provided

[1]Claude S. George, Jr., *The History of Management Thought*, 2nd edition (Englewood Cliffs, N.J.: Prentice-Hall, Inc., 1972), p. 61.

Fringe benefits were provided.

a kind of paternalistic protection for the men. Houses were built for them, with part of their wages being received in the form of rent, and a mutual insurance society for the benefit of the employees was established. Each person, on the basis of his earnings, contributed to this plan with benefits that varied according to contribution. Then, each year Boulton brought in an independent accountant to audit the fund.

Cost accounting was used.

Fifth, the company employed an elaborately detailed accounting system. Raw material costs, labor charges and finished goods inventory were all recorded. In addition, indirect costs were kept. With these records the management was able to pinpoint inefficiencies and waste, ascertain productivity changes and job costs, and determine new wage scales based on the results.

The Bettman Archive Inc.

Robert Owen

At the same time that Boulton and Watt were devising their scientific approach to management, Robert Owen was achieving dynamic results in the cotton mills of New Lanark, Scotland. Having attained great success as manager of a large cotton mill in Manchester, Owen eventually became a manager and partner in the Chorlton Twist Company of Manchester and persuaded his partners to buy the New Lanark Mills. Owen's theory was that he could operate this company more successfully and on higher principles than other commercial mills in the country.

Owen's New Lanark Experiment

At the time Owen took over, the New Lanark Mills had two thousand employees, 25 per cent of whom were children from poorhouses and charities. Although the children had been well treated by the former owner, conditions of the people in general were unsatisfactory. Owen set about changing all this; he improved the housing and through his own personal influence taught thrift, cleanliness and order. He opened a store where goods could be bought at little more than cost, but he placed the sale of liquor under strict supervision.

Work reforms were instituted.

In the mills he instituted similar reforms. No children under ten were employed; instead, they were sent to school. Those who were permitted to work had their day limited to 10¾ hours, and punishment of employees was forbidden. Meanwhile, if any workers in the factory had a complaint, Owen's door stood open. He believed that attention to the human element was of maximum importance, and he was right. Although the workers initially viewed him with suspicion, he soon won their confidence, and the New Lanark Mills proved to be highly profitable.

Owen explained his basic managerial philosophy and formula for success to a group of manufacturers in the following way:

Human resources are important.

> . . . you will find that from the commencement of my management I viewed the population (the labor force) . . . as a system composed of many parts, and which it was my duty and interest so to combine, as that every hand, as well as every spring, lever, and wheel, should effectually cooperate to produce the greatest pecuniary gain to the proprietors. . . . Experience has also shown you the difference of the results between a mechanism which is neat, clean, well-arranged, and always in a high state of repair; and that which is allowed to be dirty, in disorder, without the means of preventing unnecessary friction, and which therefore becomes, and works, much out of repair. . . . If, then, due care as to the state of your inanimate machines can produce such beneficial results, what may not be expected if you devote equal attention to your vital machines [the human resource], which are far more wonderfully constructed?[2]

Boulton and Watt's scientifically designed factory and Owen's human relations approach to management were both successful because they combined the "production" and "people" sides of management. This was no easy task, because it required managers to identify and synthesize physical and human laws of operation and from them construct a leadership style that would elicit the greatest efficiency from all the workers. Unfortunately, with the exception of Boulton, Watt, Owen and a handful of others, most were unable to meet the challenge, treating their workers less as human beings and more as factors of production. When human considerations were afforded the employees, it was usually in the name of higher productivity. For example, managers who permitted rest breaks did so because they realized a fatigued worker needed to regain his strength if he was to produce higher levels of output. These basic ideas are found in the writings of numerous individuals of the time such as Charles Babbage.

The Bettman Archive Inc.
Charles Babbage

Charles Babbage is best known for his pioneering work on the first digital computer. However, he was also a mathematician, scientist and author, and is credited with contributing more than any other writer in the first half of the nineteenth century to the development of the scientific approach to the study of management.[3]

Babbage was particularly interested in formulating laws and generalizations that could be useful to managers. In so doing, he traveled extensively throughout England and the Continent,

---

[2]Robert Owen, *The Life of Robert Owen* (London: Effingham Wilson, 1857), Appendix B, p. 260.
[3]George, *op. cit.*, p. 75.

acquainting himself with all sorts of manufacturing problems and noting the methods used for solving them. As a result of his experiences, he encouraged managers to use division of labor, time study and cost analysis. In his best-known work, *On the Economy of Machinery and Manufactures*, he offered the following recommendations to managers:

1. Analyze manufacturing processes and cost.
2. Use time study techniques.
3. Use printed standard forms for investigation.
4. Use the comparative method of studying business practices.
5. Study the effects of various tints of paper and colors of ink to determine which is least fatiguing to the eye.
6. Determine how best to frame questions.
7. Determine demand from statistics based on income.
8. Centralize the production processes for economy.
9. Inaugurate research and development.
10. Study factory location relative to the proximity of raw materials, considering whether the raw material gained weight or lost weight relative to the finished product.
11. Use a beneficial suggestion system because "every person connected with it should derive more advantage from applying any improvement he might discover."[4]

Babbage's recommendations for managers.

Babbage was concerned with the management of work. So, too, were others, such as William S. Jevons, whose writings contain some important insights into the intensity of labor and fatigue.

Historical Pictures Service, Chicago

William S. Jevons

William S. Jevons was a leading British economist and logician who is perhaps best known for his writing on the utility theory of value. However, his most famous work, The Theory of Political Economy, *also contained some very important passages on the subject of labor and fatigue:*

Improved work tools can reduce fatigue.

Let us take such a simple kind of work as digging. A spade may be made of any size, and if the same number of strokes be made in the hour, the requisite exertion will vary nearly as the cube of the length of the blade. If the spade be small, the fatigue will be slight, but the work done will also be slight. A very large spade, on the other hand, will do a great quantity at each stroke, but the fatigue will be so great the labourer cannot long continue at his work. Accordingly, a certain medium-sized spade is adopted, which does not overtax a labourer and prevent him from doing a full day's work, but enables him to accomplish as much as possible. The size of a spade should depend partly upon the tenacity and weight of the material, and partly upon the strength of the labourer. It may be observed that, in excavating stiff clay, navvies use a small spade; for ordinary garden purposes a larger spade is employed; for shovelling

[4]Charles Babbage, *On The Economy of Machinery and Manufactures* (London: Charles Knight, 1832), p. 250.

loose sand or coals a broad capacious shovel is used, and still a larger instrument is employed for removing corn, malt, or any loose light powder.[5]

These findings were very similar to those obtained some years later by Frederick Taylor in America when he conducted his now famous coal shoveling experiment.

Another of Jevons' citations related to the effect of marching on fatigue:

Work speed and fatigue are related.

In different cases of muscular exertion we shall find different problems to solve. The most advantageous rate of marching will greatly depend upon whether the loss of time or the fatigue is the most important. To march at the rate of four miles an hour would soon occasion enormous fatigue and could only be resorted to under circumstances of great urgency. The distance passed over would bear a much higher ratio to the fatigue at the rate of three, or even two and a half miles an hour. But, if the speed were still further reduced, a loss of strength would again arise, owing to that expended in merely sustaining the body, as distinguished from that of moving it forward. The Economics of Labour will constantly involve questions of this kind. . . . In a regular and constant employment the greatest result will always be gained by such a rate as allows a workman each day, or each week at the most, to recover all fatigue and recommence with an undiminished store of energy.[6]

These findings were similar to those obtained by scientific managers in America who studied the problems of work load and fatigue in industrial settings.

Early American Forerunners

Until now the entire focus has been on British contributions to scientific management. America, however, also had its advocates. Managers of industrial complexes were, for the most part, engineers by training, and many belonged to the American Society of Mechanical Engineers (ASME). At the ASME meetings these men would describe techniques they were using to increase worker output. Two of these early scientific managers were Henry R. Towne and Frederick Halsey.

Henry R. Towne was president of the Yale & Towne Manufacturing Company for 48 years. During this time period he introduced many modern management methods in his firm. In his paper, "The Engineer as an Economist," presented to the ASME in 1886, he pointed out that shop management was as important to a firm as engineering management. He also stressed the need for a vehicle by which information collected by shop managers could be exchanged with managers in other companies, so as to keep everyone up-to-date on the latest methods. Only through such an exchange, he believed, could businessmen benefit from one anothers' experience.

Culver Pictures

Henry R. Towne

---

[5]W. S. Jevons, *The Theory of Political Economy* (New York: The Macmillan Company, 1888), p. 204.
[6]*Ibid.*, p. 208.

Three years later, in 1889, Towne presented a second paper, "Gain Sharing," to the ASME. In this paper he pursued a topic that was as important to management as time and motion study or cost analysis, namely, the method for paying the workers. In Towne's view, each individual should be given a guaranteed wage. Then, a standard of work should be set for each department and the costs of production determined. If any department had a gain because of increased efforts, this should be shared between the workers in the department and the management on a fifty-fifty basis. In this way, only productive departments would be rewarded. Towne insisted on calling his plan gain sharing and not profit sharing, since the latter shared all profits between management and the workers, and what one department saved through hard work another could lose through inefficiency. In Towne's view, gain sharing sidestepped this inequity.

Gain-sharing re-warded depart-mental efficiency.

Frederick Halsey

Frederick Halsey's contribution to management, as Towne's, was along the lines of payment plans. He presented his ideas to the ASME in 1891 in a paper entitled "The Premium Plan of Paying for Labor." He began by outlining the three most common plans in use. First, there was the day-work plan, whereby the worker is paid for the number of hours spent on the job. The problem, of course, is that any increases in efficiency accrue solely to the em-ployer, so there is no incentive to work hard. Second, there was the piece-work plan, in which the individual is paid in proportion to the amount of work done. The problem here is that eventually the employer begins lowering the price paid per item because he is unwilling to let the worker make too much money and there-by, in Halsey's words, "he kills the goose that lays the golden egg." Third, there was the profit-sharing plan, under which increases in pro-ductivity were shared between employers and employees. Halsey, as Towne, opposed this ap-proach because it rewarded the workers as a group and not individually. However, Halsey disagreed with Towne's gain-sharing idea be-cause within a department there might be high- and low-producing workers, and gain sharing gave everyone equal reward. In addition, both profit- and gain-sharing plans gave these re-wards too long after they had been earned. Halsey's solution was a premium plan.

The premium plan guaranteed everyone a daily wage. Then, using the individual's past performance, a premium was offered for all work that exceeded this amount. For example, if a man was paid 30¢ an hour to do a job that should take him ten hours, his daily earnings would be $3.00. If, however, he did

Premium plan re-warded individual efficiency.

the job in half the time, he would receive payment for five hours, or $1.50. In addition, he would be given a premium 33⅓ per cent of what he had saved the company in wages, or 50¢. Thus, he would be averaging 40¢ an hour for the first five hours and would have an additional five hours left to earn more money.

Benefits of premium plan.

Halsey felt that this plan had several advantages over the others in use at that time. First, a day rate was paid regardless of performance, thereby reducing some of the old worker-management friction brought on by other incentive plans. Second, wages would not be excessive, since the worker was only getting one-third of all savings. There was, therefore, no incentive to cut the premium. Third, the plan did not concern itself with how fast the job could actually be done; it merely encouraged the worker to do more than he had done previously. Halsey felt, in fact, that it was impossible to ascertain precisely how fast a job could be done. Thus, the worker competed against his old performance and not some standard set by a time and motion study.

SCIENTIFIC MANAGEMENT MOVEMENT

By the late 1800's many changes were occurring on the management scene. In particular giant corporations were coming into existence and two industrial groups were emerging—management and labor. The growth of this industrial managerial class helped further the development of management thought as the focus of attention shifted from a day-to-day, short-run operating philosophy to a more unified, systematic, long-run orientation. The early scientific managers helped create this environment and set the stage for the entry of their most prominent colleague, Frederick Winslow Taylor.

Historical Pictures Service, Chicago

Frederick W. Taylor

Frederick W. Taylor, often referred to as the Father of Scientific Management, is the best known of all the scientific managers. Born in Germantown, Pennsylvania in 1856, many of his early years were spent attending school in Germany and France and traveling on the European continent. In 1872 he enrolled in Phillips Exeter Academy to prepare for Harvard College. However, although he passed the entrance exams with honors, poor eyesight prevented him from attending that institution. In late 1874 he entered the pattern making and machinist trades, finding work in a small company owned by family friends.

In 1879, with employment in the machinist trade difficult to obtain, he went to work at the Midvale Steel Company as a laborer. His rise in Midvale was swift. Within eight years, one of the biographers relates, he had risen from ordinary laborer to time keeper and then on to machinist, gang boss, foreman, assistant engineer and, finally, chief engineer of the works. Meanwhile, continuing his education through correspondence courses and home study, he managed to complete all requirements for a mechanical engineering degree at Stevens Institute.[7]

Taylor's success at Midvale must be attributed in large part to his production record; he knew how to get the work out. Initially, however, as gang boss he encountered stiff opposition from the men because he used pressure to achieve this increased output. He then realized that such pressure could be eliminated if management would determine what a proper day's work was for every position in the shop. Lacking such information, management relied upon past performance, and the men, realizing this, deliberately kept output low. Such "systematic soldiering" on their part was recognized by Taylor. When he became foreman he attempted to eliminate as much of it as possible by determining exactly how much could be done by each man in the shop. He started his systematic study in the area of lathe operations. Employing time and motion study, he attempted to identify the specific tasks involved in this work and to calculate the time required to complete each one. Such time and motion experimentation was to be characteristic of his work from this point on, although his most famous experiments were later conducted at Bethlehem Steel.

Work standards were determined via time and motion study.

Bethlehem Steel Experiments.   In 1898 Taylor went to work for the Bethlehem Steel Company. While there, he conducted important studies in the areas of pig iron handling, shoveling and metal cutting.

The first of these experiments, *pig iron handling,* involved a group of about 75 men who were loading ingots or "pigs" of iron into an open railroad car. Their job entailed picking up the pig of iron, which weighed about 92 pounds, carrying it up an inclined plane and dropping it into the railroad car. At the time Taylor arrived at Bethlehem Steel, each man was loading an average of 12½ long tons[8] a day. Taylor decided to experiment with the job to see if he could increase the output. His research showed that a worker ought to be able to load 47 long tons a day, working 43 per cent of the time and, because of the heavy work load, resting for the remainder. This rest was based on his own law of heavy laboring, which stated that for all energy exerted under load there had to be recuperating time. In order to test the validity of his theory, Taylor chose one of the workers, to whom he gave the pseudonym Schmidt, and began supervising the man very closely. He was told when to work and when to rest. The basic concept was explained by Taylor himself:

[7]Frederick Winslow Taylor, *Scientific Management* (New York: Harper & Brothers Publishers, 1911), p. ix (Foreword by Harlow S. Person).
[8]A long ton weighs 2240 pounds.

Work instruc-
tions were pro-
vided.

Perhaps the most prominent single element in modern scientific management is the task idea. The work of every workman is fully planned out by the management at least one day in advance, and each man receives in most cases complete written instructions, describing in detail the task which he is to accomplish, as well as the means to be used in doing the work. And the work planned out in advance in this way constitutes a task which is to be solved . . . not by the workman alone, but in almost all cases by the joint effort of the workman and the management. This task specifies not only what is to be done but how it is to be done and the exact time allowed for doing it.[9]

By early evening of the first day, Schmidt had loaded the 47½ long tons. Other men in the group were then gradually trained to load this amount.

It should be noted that Taylor kept only one-eighth of the gang on this job because the rest of the men were not physically able to do this much work. Such action was in line with his philosophy of scientifically selecting and training each of the workers. To load 47½ long tons, Taylor concluded, the worker had to be built like an ox, and only one-eighth of the crew fit into this category. Most of the remainder of the crew were given jobs elsewhere in the company.

The second of Taylor's Bethlehem Steel experiments was concerned with the *shoveling of iron ore and rice coal*. At the time of Taylor's arrival, each of the workers was bringing his own shovel. When they shoveled iron ore, the weight per scoop would be very great, for the ore was quite heavy. Conversely, when they shoveled rice coal, the weight per scoop would not be very great, for the coal was quite light. Taylor's experiments indicated that an average scoop load of 21 pounds would result in maximum output. Thus, for heavy coal there should be a shovel with a small scoop, whereas for light coal the shovel should have a large scoop. In order to implement this approach, Taylor did away with everyone's bringing his own shovel. Instead, the company built a tool room to stock shovels, all designed to carry a 21-pound load, for handling various types of material. In addition, Taylor conducted time and motion stud-

Work tools were
provided.

[9]Taylor, *op. cit.*, *Principles of Scientific Management*, p. 39.

TABLE 2–1   Results of Shoveling Experiments

	Old Plan	New Plan Task Work
The number of yard laborers were reduced from between	400 to 600	140
Average number of tons per man per day	16	59
Average earnings per man per day	$1.15	$1.88
Average cost of handling a ton of 2240 pounds	$0.072	$0.033

Source: Frederick Winslow Taylor, *Principles of Scientific Management* (New York: Harper & Brothers Publishers, 1911), p. 71.

Taylor estimated the first year's saving with the new plan to be over $36,000, and during the next six months, when all the yard was on task work, the annual saving was estimated to be $75,000 to $80,000.

The third area in which Taylor conducted experiments at Bethlehem Steel was that of *metal-cutting*. Actually, this was a continuation of work he had begun at Midvale. Through these experiments, Taylor gathered a wealth of data about the proper speeds and feeds needed for various machines. One of the results was a patent for high-speed steel, with which machine shops were able to decrease the average cutting time to one third of what it had formerly been. The patent proved so valuable that Taylor and his partner sold the rights for its use in England for $100,000.

Taylor's Writings and Philosophy. In 1885 Taylor joined the ASME and presented two papers before the membership. The first, presented in 1895, was entitled "A Piece Rate System." In this paper, Taylor expressed concern over incentive schemes such as Towne's gain-sharing plan and Halsey's premium plan, claiming that such cooperative endeavors, in which management and the employee divide cost-savings or share profits, had not really worked. As an alternative, Taylor recommended a *differential piece rate system*. For each job in which it was to be employed, a time and motion study was first conducted. On the basis of the results, a standard (a fair day's work) would be ascertained. If the worker produced less than standard, he would receive a certain price for each piece produced. If standard were reached or surpassed, a higher per piece rate would be paid. For example, if standard were 100 pieces a day, with the low rate being 1.1¢ per piece and the high rate being 1.8¢ per piece, an individual producing 90 pieces would receive 99¢, whereas a person turning out 102 pieces would receive $1.84.

Salary was tied to output.

One of the bases of this plan was Taylor's belief that the workmen in nearly every trade could (and would) materially increase their present output if they were assured of a greater permanent return for their time. Yet although Taylor placed great importance on the value of money, he also stressed the need for a systematic approach on the part of management in conducting its business. This idea went unnoticed by his followers, who devoted their attention to the mechanics of his payment plan.

In 1903 Taylor presented a second paper, entitled "Shop Management." This time, emphasis was on his *philosophy of management*. Taylor pointed out the need to provide high wages and attain low per unit production costs. This, he felt, entailed the scientific selection and training of workers coupled with management-employee cooperation. As before, his managerial philosophy was not understood.

Once again, in 1911, he put forth his ideas, this time in a book entitled *Principles of Scientific Management*. In this book Taylor enunciated four principles, the scope of which was far more than time and motion study. They represented a combination of mechanical, conceptual and philosophical ideas:

Principles of sci-
entific manage-
ment.

First. Develop a science for each element of a man's work, which replaces the old rule-of-thumb method.

Second. Scientifically select and then train, teach, and develop the workman, whereas in the past he chose his own work and trained himself as best he could.

Third. Heartily cooperate with the men so as to insure all of the work being done in accordance with the principles of the science which has been developed.

Fourth. There is an almost equal division of the work and the responsibility between the management and the workmen. The management take over all work for which they are better fitted than the workmen, while in the past almost all of the work and the greater part of the responsibility were thrown upon the men.[10]

Although his papers and writings brought him acclaim, Taylor's fame and his title Father of Scientific Management were probably accounted for more by the publicity he received at a Congressional hearing in 1912 than by anything he had previously done. Speaking before the United States committee that was investigating systems of shop management, he related what he felt scientific management was *not*, as well as what it was.

Scientific management is not an efficiency device, not a device of any kind for securing efficiency; nor is it a bunch or group of efficiency devices. It is not a new system of figuring costs; it is not a new scheme of paying men; it is not a piecework system; it is not a bonus system; it is not a premium system; . . .

Now, in its essence, scientific management involves a complete mental revolution on the part of the working man engaged in a particular establishment or industry — a complete mental revolution on the part of these men as to their duties toward their work, toward their fellow men, and toward their employers. And it involves the equally complete mental revolution on the part of those on the management's side — the foremen, the superintendent, the owner of

A mental revo-
lution.

the business, the board of directors — a complete revolution on their part as to their duties toward their fellow workers in the management, toward their workmen, and toward all of their daily problems. And without this complete mental revolution on both sides scientific management does not exist.[11]

As a result of these hearings, his fame spread. Scientific management and Frederick Taylor became synonymous terms. In some quarters, the system of shop management that he advocated became known as the Taylor system. However, as he stated in his testimony before the House, he was only one of

[10]*Ibid.,* pp. 36–37.
[11]*Ibid.,* Taylor's Testimony Before the Special House Committee, pp. 26–27.

many people instrumental in developing this system. Another, to whom he gave specific credit, was Frank Gilbreth.

Frank Gilbreth

Frank Gilbreth, born in 1868, passed the entrance exams for the Massachusetts Institute of Technology, but decided instead to go into the contracting business. Beginning as an apprentice bricklayer, his attention was quickly aroused by the different sets of motions that were used in training bricklayers. First, the man was taught how to lay bricks; then he was taught how to work at a slow pace; finally, he was trained to work at a fast pace. Gilbreth wondered which of these three sets of motions was best.

The Gilbreths

As a result, he began studying the motions used by bricklayers. Were there any extraneous motions that could be eliminated, thereby reducing the time and effort necessary to lay bricks? After much experimentation, he was able to reduce the number of hand motions required to lay exterior brick from 18 to 4½ and interior brick from 18 to 2. He also developed an adjustable stand to eliminate the need for stooping to pick up the bricks. Likewise, mortar of proper consistency was employed to eliminate "tapping." As a result, he was able to increase the number of bricks a man could lay in an hour from 120 to 350.

Bricklaying techniques were developed.

In 1904 Gilbreth married Lillian Moller. With her background in management and psychology, the two combined their talents for the purpose of developing better work methods. One of their most famous techniques was the use of motion pictures. By filming the individual at work and then playing back the film, they could analyze the person's motions and determine which, if any, were extraneous. Since the cameras in those days were hand cranked, Gilbreth invented the microchronometer, a clock with a large sweeping hand that records time to 1/2000 of a minute, and placed it in the field of work being filmed. (Today, unless the camera contains constant-speed electric motors, the microchronometer is still used in photographing time and motion patterns.) In this way, he could analyze the individual's motions while determining precisely how long the work took. In addition, the Gilbreths went so far as to categorize all hand motions into 17 basic motions such as "grasp," "hold" and "position," which they called therbligs, Gilbreth spelled backwards with the "t" and "h" transposed. Having made such monumental contributions to the area, it is no wonder that Frank Gilbreth is known as the Father of Motion Study.

Standard hand motions were categorized.

Historical Pictures Service, Chicago

Henry L. Gantt

*Daily wage was
guaranteed.*

Another famous scientific manager of this period was Henry L. Gantt. Both a contemporary and protégé of Frederick Taylor, Gantt worked with Taylor at the Midvale Steel Company in 1887 and was impressed with his concepts. Gantt, however, had a far better understanding of the human element in the work environment than did his teacher. This is seen in the task-and-bonus system that he developed. In contrast with Taylor's differential piece rate plan, Gantt's system guaranteed each worker a day's wage. In addition, if the man accomplished the task assigned to him for that day, he received a bonus, a result of Gantt's recognizing that job security was a powerful incentive. Like Taylor, Gantt was also aware of the need for instruction of the workers by management. In a paper presented to the ASME in 1908, "Training Workmen in Habits of Industry and Cooperation," he put forth these ideas, but he was ahead of his time. It was to be years before management agreed that training workers was one of its responsibilities.

*The Gantt chart
is a planning and
controlling de-
vice.*

The contribution for which he is most famous is the Gantt chart, developed in 1917. Along the horizontal axis time, work scheduled and work completed are measured. The vertical axis identifies the individuals and machines assigned to these work schedules. Simple in nature, the chart provides an effective planning and control technique. By the late 1950's the concept was being employed by the United States Navy in its Polaris Missile Project. Although the Navy's application involved much greater sophistication than did the original chart designed by Gantt, the basic concept was the same in that it stressed efficiency, a topic made famous by another early scientific manager, Harrington Emerson.

From Human Life, April 1911

Harrington Emerson

Harrington Emerson is best known for his appearance before the Interstate Commerce Commission in 1910. The railroads wanted a rate increase while shippers opposed it. Speaking on the shippers' behalf, Emerson told the committee that if the railroads would adopt scientific management principles, they could save one million dollars a day. His major concepts were set forth in his book The Twelve Principles of Efficiency.[12] These principles were:

---

[12]Harrington Emerson, The Twelve Principles of Efficiency (New York: The Engineering Magazine Company, 1924).

1. *Clearly defined ideals.* By this Emerson meant that the organization should formulate objectives and familiarize everyone in the company with them.
2. *Common sense.* In employing common sense, the manager should adhere to ideals, survey problems at a distance so they can be seen in their entirety, and seek good advice.
3. *Competent counsel.* The manager should look for qualified counsel whenever and wherever it can be found. Of course, it will not all come from one man. However, by obtaining the best from each person, competent counsel, on a collective basis, can be obtained.
4. *Discipline.* There must be strict adherence to rules. In Emerson's view, discipline brings about allegiance to the other eleven principles.
5. *Fair deal.* In essence, this requires three managerial qualities: sympathy, imagination and, most of all, justice.
6. *Reliable, immediate, adequate, and permanent records.* Records provide a basis upon which intelligent decisions can be made. Unfortunately, too many companies keep poor records for cost control while accumulating other reports that are of no value.

Twelve principles of efficiency.

7. *Despatching.* By this term Emerson meant that organizations should formulate effective production scheduling and control techniques.
8. *Standards and schedules.* There must be a method and a time schedule for performing tasks. This can be accomplished through the use of time and motion studies, the establishment of work standards and the proper placement of each worker on the job.
9. *Standardized conditions.* A standardization of conditions will reduce waste by conserving both effort and money. This standardization can be applied to both individuals and the work environment.
10. *Standardized operations.* A standardization of operations, whenever and wherever possible, will greatly enhance efficiency.
11. *Written standard-practice instructions.* Written, standardized instructions that are continually updated can result in rapid progress toward the objective.
12. *Efficiency reward.* Efficiency should be rewarded. Emerson noted that "Efficiency constitutes 9 out of the 18 elements of cost-efficiency of quality and quantity and overhead for materials, for labor and for fixed charges. It has been found exceedingly satisfactory and convenient to base efficiency rewards on the cost of efficiencies, the method being so flexible as to be applicable to an individual operation of a few minutes' duration, or to all the work of a man for a long period, or to all the work of department or plan.[13]

As a result of his work, Emerson became known as the High Priest of Efficiency. In placing him in historical perspective, one historian has credited him with "codifying a set of principles to guide management, and this attempt, along with the soundness of his principles, served to reemphasize the growing awareness of the distinct nature and universality of management."[14]

SUMMARY

Two areas of prime interest for the scientific managers were ways of increasing productivity (output/input) by making the work easier to perform, and methods for motivating the workers

[13]*Ibid.,* p. 365.
[14]George, *op. cit.,* p. 109.

to take advantage of these labor-saving devices and techniques. The former was characterized by time and motion studies, and the latter led to the development of many different wage payment plans.

For the most part, the scientific management movement was concerned with the management of workers. The interests of Taylor and his colleagues rested squarely at the lower levels of the organization. However, there were people coming on the management scene who were interested in operations at the middle and upper levels of the hierarchy. These individuals, known as the early management theorists, will be the focus of attention in the next chapter.

REVIEW AND STUDY QUESTIONS

1. Boulton and Watt's Soho Foundry provides an excellent illustration of the scientific approach to management. Explain this statement.

2. Why was Robert Owen successful in his New Lanark experiment?

3. How did Henry Towne's gain-sharing plan work? Explain.

4. Explain Frederick Halsey's premium plan.

5. Why is Frederick Taylor known as the Father of Scientific Management?

6. What were Taylor's principles of scientific management?

7. Why is Frank Gilbreth known as the Father of Motion Study?

8. Henry Gantt was a humanistic-scientific manager. Explain this statement.

9. What was Harrington Emerson's contribution to management? Explain.

10. What contribution to management thought did the scientific managers make?

SELECTED REFERENCES

American Economic Association. *The Adjustment of Wages to Efficiency.* New York: The Macmillan Company, 1896.

Babbage, C. *On the Economy of Machinery and Manufactures.* London: Charles Knight, 1832.

Cook-Taylor, R. W. *Introduction to a History of the Factory System.* London: Richard Bentley and Sons, 1886.

Emerson, H. *Efficiency as a Basis for Operation and Wages.* New York: The Engineering Magazine Company, 1900.

Emerson, H. *The Twelve Principles of Efficiency.* New York: The Engineering Magazine Company, 1924.

Gantt, H. L. *Work, Wages, and Profits,* New York: The Engineering Magazine Company, 1910.

Gilbreth, F. B. *Bricklaying System.* New York: The Myron C. Clark Publishing Company, 1909.

Gilbreth, F. B. *Motion Study.* New York: D. Van Nostrand Company, Inc., 1911.

Gilbreth, L. M. *The Psychology of Management.* New York: Sturgis and Walton Company, 1914.

Gilman, N. P. *Profit Sharing Between Employer and Employee, A Study in the Evolution of the Wage System.* New York: Houghton Mifflin Company, 1889.

Hoxie, R. F. *Scientific Management and Labor.* New York: D. Appleton and Company, 1915.

Kakar, S. *Frederick Taylor: A Study in Personality and Innovation.* Cambridge, Mass.: MIT Press, 1971.

Metcalfe, H., *The Cost of Manufactures and the Administration of Workshops Public and Private.* New York: John Wiley & Sons, Inc., 1885.

Scott, W. D. *Increasing Human Efficiency in Business.* New York: The Macmillan Company, 1913.

Spriegel, W. R., and C. E. Myers, eds. *The Writings of the Gilbreths.* Homewood, Illinois: Richard D. Irwin, Inc., 1953.

Taylor, F. W. *Scientific Management.* New York: Harper & Brothers Publishers, 1911.

Wright, C. D. *Report on the Factory System of the United States.* Washington, D.C., Government Printing Office, 1884.

CASE: WHITE COLLAR OUTPUT[1]

Quite a lot has been written about increasing productivity among blue collar workers. However, there is currently a push to improve the efficiency of white collar workers as well, and there may be a need for it. William G. O'Brien, president of Science Management Corporation, a consulting firm that specializes in work-measurement programs, certainly seems to think so. According to him, manpower utilization in most offices rarely exceeds 60 per cent. As a result, as much as $800 million a day is lost to the United States economy, half of this resulting from inefficiency in white collar and service jobs. Mr. O'Brien attempts to recoup part of these losses for companies through the use of work measurement.

While "work measurement" suggest platoons of stern-faced engineers standing around with stopwatches in hand, Science Management officials say such tactics aren't necessary. The firm's staff does observe the work flow but relies mainly on massive tables prepared over the years to calculate "target times" for performing clerical jobs. These studies cover everything from the time it takes to prepare a first-class mailing label (24 seconds) or make a phone call (slightly over 25 seconds to notify someone that a duplicating order is ready) to the time required for a telephone-company draftsman to draw up a street conduit system 1,220 feet long (one hour).

[1]The data in this case can be found in James C. Hyatt, "Productivity Push," *Wall Street Journal,* April 25, 1972, pp. 1, 30.

With such figures in hand, the firm's staff determines the amount of work to be done and the amount of time needed to do it.

Many companies in the white collar and service fields who have tried work measurement say that employees respond favorably to the system because it lets them know what is expected of them.

Questions

1. Is scientific management as applicable to white collar jobs as it is to blue collar jobs? Explain.

2. Is Mr. O'Brien a scientific manager? In what way is his approach similar to that of the scientific managers? How does it differ? Explain.

3. Why would employees favor work measurement? Why would they oppose it? Explain.

CASE: LET'S FACE THE MUSIC[1]

The Cincinnati Symphony Orchestra has signed a new labor contract. Under the latest terms, Saturday rehearsals will be limited to seven a year. At the same time, however, the musicians have agreed to extend rehearsal times, in certain circumstances, from the usual $2\frac{1}{2}$ hours to 3 hours. Thomas Schippen, the music director, contends that a three-hour rehearsal is often more productive than two $2\frac{1}{2}$-hour sessions.

The new contract also permits the orchestra to be divided into smaller groups for the purpose of rehearsing complicated numbers. According to an orchestra official, these new procedures will allow for increased productivity and decreased costs.

Questions

1. What analogy exists between the conditions that existed before and after the new orchestra contract and those that existed at Bethlehem Steel before and after Frederick Taylor conducted his experiments?

2. Can the concepts of time and motion study be applied in reducing the number of people needed in a symphony orchestra?

3. Do Taylor's four principles of scientific management have any application to an orchestra? Explain.

---

[1]The data in this case can be found in "Orchestras Face the Music and Raise Their Efficiency," *Wall Street Journal*, April 25, 1972, p. 26.

CASE: FIGHTING THE "BLAHS"[1]

In the early hours of the morning, giant presses set up a deafening roar as they print *The New York Times*. However, thanks to Muzak, Inc., a division of the TelePrompter Corporation, a number of the pressmen are completely oblivious to the noise. This is because they are wearing plastic earmuffs wired for sound that allow them to go about their work while listening to old and new tunes, including *Stranger in Paradise, The Magnificient Seven* and many other hits.

Muzak's studies indicate that worker productivity usually reaches its low point in midmorning and midafternoon and picks up just before people go to lunch or leave for the day. To boost productivity when the "blahs" set in, Muzak pipes in music. Is this approach really beneficial to productivity? "Bing" Muscio, president of Muzak, seems to think so. He claims that music has definite physiological and psychological effects on people. "It affects," he said, "the heartbeat and blood pressure, and moderates tenseness and anxiety." And an AT&T division manager agrees, pointing out that telephone operators report they are more relaxed with music by Muzak than they were prior to its installation. And there are many other companies using Muzak's services, including Black & Decker and American Machine & Foundry Inc., who support these findings. However, the company does not confine its services exclusively to business; Muzak speakers are even installed in the White House.

Questions

1. Is not music by Muzak another variation of scientific management, i.e., a change in some environmental condition designed to bring about increased productivity? Explain.

2. Can music actually cause greater work efficiency? Give your reasoning.

3. How could this approach be made more "scientific"?

CASE: A MATTER OF EFFICIENCY[2]

Harrington Emerson was very interested in developing principles and concepts that companies could use to increase their efficiency. In particular, he concentrated his attention on the railroads.

---

[1]The data in this case can be found in "Muzak's Earmuffs For Noisy Jobs," *Business Week*, January 13, 1973, p. 62c.

[2]The data in this case can be found in Harrington Emerson, *The Twelve Principles of Efficiency* (New York: The Engineering Magazine Company, 1924.)

In applying one of his principles, common sense, to railroad operations, Emerson related the story of the railroad superintendent who sent one of his locomotives to a central shop a few hundred miles away for repairs. Rather than let it go under its own steam, the superintendent put the locomotive in a freight train and had it hauled to its destination. This improved the superintendent's tonnage record, but, as Emerson noted, common sense should have revealed to the manager the foolishness of his decision.

In the case of a second efficiency principle, "despatching," Emerson noted that railroads dispatched their trains very efficiently in meeting timetables. Why, then, could they not dispatch work in their repair shops with equal efficiency? In attempting to accomplish this goal, Emerson recommended that locomotives be scheduled for repair based on the extent of work needed and then immediately returned to service. For minor repairs, the engine should be operational again in 12 days; for intermediate repairs, 18 days; major repairs, 24 days. He also suggested that each separate step in the repair work be scheduled in proper sequence, thereby completing the job in the shortest possible time.

Questions

1. Are these two efficiency principles still of value to modern railroads? Explain.

2. Are the two principles also applicable to other business organizations? Give an illustration.

3. How can a business firm make certain that its managers use these principles?

CHAPTER 3

CONTRIBUTORS TO EARLY MANAGEMENT THEORY

GOALS OF THE CHAPTER

As seen in Chapter 2, the scientific managers concentrated on the operational level of the organization. Their scope of activities encompassed the workers and the foremen, but little else. It was inevitable, however, that attention would gradually be focused further up the hierarchy as the scientific management movement led to changes in the composition of the worker-manager ratio. Henry K. Hathaway, vice president of the Tabor Manufacturing Company, explained:

> At the Tabor Manufacturing Company we have succeeded through the application of the Taylor principles of Scientific Management in increasing our production to about three times what it formerly was, with the total cost approximately the same and approximately the same total of men; of course with a very much smaller proportion of men in the shop, and a very much increased proportion of men in the planning department, or on the management side.[1]

With more and more people entering the management ranks, it was not long before the study of management began to receive attention. Questions such as What is management? What are the principles of organization? How can the manager be more effective in his job? began to be raised. The people who devoted attention to answering these questions helped formulate the basis of modern *management theory*. Many of them worked independently of each other, unaware that elsewhere someone was raising similar questions and arriving at virtually the same conclusions.

The goals of this chapter are to examine some of the works of these individuals. Naturally, it is impossible to cover everyone

---

[1] *First Tuck School Conference on Scientific Management*, October 12–14, 1911 (Hanover, N.H.: The Amos Tuck School of Administration and Finance, Dartmouth College, 1912), p. 339.

who contributed to early management theory. Nor is the following discussion intended to be complete on all points, for this would require volumes. However, a cursory view will be taken of five major contributors. In particular, attention will be focused on:

a. Henri Fayol's view of the possibility of teaching management in the classroom;
b. Henri Fayol's fourteen principles and five functions of management;
c. the concept of functional foremanship;
d. James Mooney and Alan Reiley's principles of organization;
e. Lyndall Urwick's synthesis of the writings of the early classical theorists; and
f. Chester Barnard's psychological-sociological analysis of organizational structure.

Henri Fayol

Henri Fayol is commonly referred to as the Father of Modern Management Theory. Receiving his degree from the National School of Mines at St. Etienne at the age of 19, he entered the employ of a mining combine known as the Commentry-Fourchambault. Here he remained for his entire career, attaining the position of general manager in 1888 and holding it until 1918, when he became a director of the firm. Throughout these years, he proved himself an outstanding administrator, as evidenced by the fact that when he assumed the position of general manager the firm was in critical condition, but by 1918 its financial stability was excellent.

Definition and Teaching of Administration

In 1916 Fayol wrote a monograph entitled *Industrial and General Administration*,[2] in which he sought to synthesize his managerial experience and knowledge into a four-part book. The first part, dealing with the possibility and necessity of teaching management, and the second part, describing the principles and elements of management, were the only parts ever published. Fayol's overall goal was to elevate the status of administration by providing an *analytical framework for management.* One of the most important sections of the book dealt with the definition and teaching of administration.

In his definition of administration, Fayol wrote that all activities and business undertakings could be divided into six groups. These were:

1. Technical operations (production, manufacture)
2. Commercial operations (purchases, sales, and exchanges)
3. Financial operations (finding and controlling capital)

[2]Henri Fayol, *Industrial and General Administration* (Translated from the French edition by J. A. Coubrough, Geneva: International Management Institute, 1929).

4. Security operations (protection of goods and persons)
5. Accounting operations (stocktaking, balance sheet, costing, statistics)
6. Administrative operations (planning, organization, command, coordination, and control)[3]

Managers need administrative ability.

In addition, he made an analysis of these six operations, noting that the workman's chief characteristic is technical ability, but as one goes up the organizational hierarchy, the relative importance of this ability declines while that of administrative ability increases.

Technical ability is the chief characteristic of the lower employees of a big undertaking and the heads of small industrial concerns; administrative ability is the chief characteristic of all the men in important positions. Technical ability is the most important quality at the bottom of the industrial ladder and administrative ability at the top.[4]

In contrasting Fayol with Taylor, it is evident that the former was far less concerned with the operational level and much more interested in approaching the subject from a general management point of view. In so doing, he made one of his greatest contributions to management, namely, the identification of the administrator's activities or functions: planning, organizing, commanding, coordinating and controlling, If a manager could carry out these functions properly, he would be effective. Yet Fayol believed that insufficient attention was given to these functions. Many people recognized them as important, but believed they could only be learned on the job, as technical skills are. With this he disagreed, pointing out that administration could be taught in a scholastic setting, if only a *theory of administration* could be formulated.

Management can be taught.

This teaching will not make all its pupils good administrators any more than technical teaching makes every pupil a first-class technical man. . . . Its main objective would be to enable young people to understand and make use of the lessons of experience. At present, a man who is starting his career has neither theory nor methods of administration to help him, and many people remain in that condition all their lives.

It is, therefore, necessary to distribute administrative knowledge among all classes of the population, and the school has evidently a large part to play in this work.[5]

Principles of Administration

In Part II of his book, Fayol discussed principles of administration. Noting that the administrative function was concerned only with the human part of an undertaking, he hastened to explain that he employed the word "principles" and not laws or rules because of the flexibility required in applying them to people. Since these principles are hardly ever used twice in the same way because of changing conditions, the administrator has

[3]*Ibid.*, p. 8.
[4]*Ibid.*, p. 15.
[5]*Ibid.*, p. 17.

to adapt them to his needs. The fourteen principles that Fayol felt he had occasion to use most frequently were:

Fayol's 14 princi-
ples of adminis-
tration.

1. *Division of Labor.* By employing the classic concept of specialization of labor, increases in efficiency can be achieved. One illustration was provided in Chapter 1 with Adam Smith's description of the production process in a pin factory. However, Fayol believed that division of labor need not be confined to technical work; it could be applied to managerial tasks also.

2. *Authority and Responsibility.* According to Fayol, authority and responsibility went hand in hand. Authority was "the right to command and the power to make oneself obeyed."[6] Responsibility was a reward or penalty accompanying the use of this power. In later years this principle would be called parity of authority and responsibility, indicating that the two should always be equal. Naturally, this is a utopian view, in light of the fact that many administrators seem to desire authority but shun responsibility. Fayol understood this, pointing out that as one moves up an organizational hierarchy, it becomes more difficult to establish an individual's degree of responsibility. Operations become more complex, and cause and effect are more widely separated. For this reason, he concluded that "The best safeguard against abuse of authority, and against weakness on the part of a leader, is personal character, and particularly, high moral character."[7]

   Of more importance, however, was the distinction he drew between statutory and personal authority. *Statutory authority* comes with a position; anyone holding a specific job has some statutory authority. *Personal authority* derives from the individual's intelligence, knowledge, moral character and ability to command, oftentimes called informal authority or power. A good leader must have both statutory and personal authority.

3. *Discipline.* The essence of discipline is "obedience, diligence, energy, correct attitude, and outward marks of respect, within the limits fixed by the agreement between a concern and its employees."[8] This alone, however, will not guarantee good discipline. An organization must also have effective leaders who are capable of enforcing penalties in the case of insubordination. In Fayol's words, discipline is what leaders *produce.* When discipline is poor, people have a tendency to blame the rank and file. Actually, bad discipline usually comes from bad leadership.

4. *Unity of Command.* Everyone should have one and only one boss. Fayol believed so strongly in this guideline that he

---

[6]*Ibid.*, p. 20.
[7]*Ibid.*
[8]*Ibid.*

referred to it in his book as a rule and not as a principle. In support of this idea, he even went so far as to oppose Frederick Taylor's concept of functional foremanship, illustrating in the process that he was aware of Taylor's work in America.

Functional foremanship was an organizational concept devised by Taylor. He proposed that there should be eight foremen supervising each worker. He arrived at this number by breaking down the foreman's job into its basic subfunctions. Four of these men (route clerk, instruction card clerk, cost and time clerk, and shop disciplinarian) would be in the planning room. The other four (speed boss, inspector, repair boss and gang boss) would be out on the shop floor managing the actual production operations. Figure 3–1 presents a simplified illustration of the concept. Although Fayol praised Taylor's contributions to time and motion study, he disagreed with the concept of functional foremanship, contending that "it is dangerous to allow the idea to get about that the principle of unity of command is unimportant and can be violated with impunity. We ought to retain the old scheme of organization, in which unity of command is respected. . . ."[9]

5. *Unity of Management.* Not to be confused with unity of command, this principle calls for one manager and one plan for all operations having the same objective. In this way, resources can be intelligently coordinated and all efforts directed toward the common goal. Unity of management is provided by a sound organizational structure.

6. *Subordination of Individual Interests to the Common Good.* The goals of the organization must take precedence over those of individuals or groups of employees. Factors such as ignorance, ambition and egotism tend to make people

[9]*Ibid.,* p. 52.

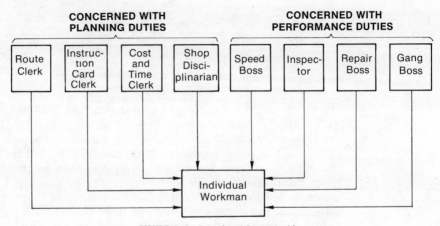

FIGURE 3–1   Functional Foremanship

put their interests ahead of the common good. Constant vigilance and good example on the part of the manager are two ways of reconciling these differences.

7. *Remuneration of the Staff.* Fayol believed that a payment plan should: (a) insure fair remuneration; (b) encourage keenness by rewarding successful effort; and (c) not lead to rewards beyong a reasonable limit. After reviewing such remunerative payment plans as timework, taskwork, piece-work, bonuses and profit sharing, he concluded that each had advantages and disadvantages, but no payment plan could substitute for competent management.

8. *Centralization.* In and of itself, centralization of authority is neither good nor bad, but it is always present to some degree. The challenge is to ascertain what degree is best for the organization. This will depend on the quality of the management and the staff as well as environmental conditions in general. Since these factors are always in a state of flux, the "right" degree of centralization-decentralization will also be changing.

9. *The Hierarchy.* The hierarchy, or *scalar chain* as it is often called, is the order of rank that runs through the organization from top to bottom. In order to preserve the integrity of the hierarchy and to insure unity of command, communications should follow this formal channel. However, Fayol was also cognizant of the red tape involved in a large organization and the inadvisability of always taking the long formal route. In Figure 3–2, for example, to get a message from E to K it is necessary, if one is to follow the scalar chain, to go up the hierarchy to A and then down to K.

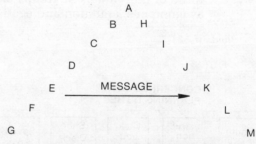

FIGURE 3–2   Fayol's Gangplank Principle

To overcome this problem, Fayol prescribed his "gangplank principle." People at the same level of the hierarchy should be allowed to communicate directly, provided they have permission from their superiors to do so and they tell their respective chiefs afterwards what they have agreed to do. In this way, the integrity of the hierarchy is never threatened. Furthermore, noted Fayol, if A made his subordinates B and H use the gangplank principle and they did likewise for their subordinates C and I, much greater efficiency would be introduced into the organization. Although it is an error to leave the hierarchical chain without a good reason, it would be greater mistake to follow it when such a procedure would prove harmful to the undertaking.

10. *Order.* "A place for everything and everything in its place" was the way Fayol described this principle, and he applied it to both material and human resources. He noted that perfect human order requires both effective organization and careful employee selection.

11. *Equity.* Equity results when friendliness is combined with justice. The effective manager sets a goal for himself of insuring that equity permeates all levels of the hierarchy.

12. *Stability of Staff.* It takes time for an able employee to settle down to a job and perform satisfactorily. For this reason, successful organizations are generally those whose managerial personnel have been on board for a long time. In fact, a mediocre administrator who has been in his position for some time is infinitely preferable to a host of competent managers who have quickly moved on to other jobs, because none of the latter have been around long enough to do the job well. As Fayol noted, in general terms, "the managerial staffs of successful enterprises are stable, while those of unsuccessful ones are unstable."[10] Thus, organizations should encourage the long-term commitment of their employees.

13. *Initiative.* Fayol defined initiative as the power to conceive and execute a plan of action. Such activity increases both the keenness and the energy of employees. For this reason, it should be encouraged and developed as fully as possible within, of course, the limits imposed by respect for authority and discipline.

14. *Esprit de Corps.* This spirit depends upon harmony and unity among an organization's staff. In Fayol's view, the most effective way of achieving this is through unity of command and oral, as opposed to written, communication.

Elements of Administration

In concluding this section of his book, Fayol pointed out that he had made no attempt to be exhaustive in his coverage of principles. He had merely described some of those he had used most often.

The second part of Fayol's book was devoted to a description of the five functions, or "elements" as he called them, of administration: planning, organizing, commanding, coordinating and controlling. He elaborated upon each.

---

[10]*Ibid.,* p. 31.

Functions of management: planning, organizing, commanding, coordinating and controlling.

Planning requires a forecast of events and, based on the forecast, the construction of an operating program. These forecasts should extend as far into the future as the needs of the organization demand, although ten-year forecasts should be redrafted every five years.

Organizing entails the structuring of activities, materials and personnel for accomplishing the assigned tasks. This calls for effective coordination of all the firm's resources. In attempting to accomplish this objective, Fayol set forth the following guidelines:

1. Ensure that the plan of operations is properly prepared and executed.
2. See that the organization structure is consistent with the firm's resources and objectives.
3. Establish a competent vigorous management that has a singleness of purpose.
4. Harmonize and coordinate operations and efforts.
5. Make clear and precise decisions.
6. Carefully select all personnel.
7. Define duties clearly.
8. Encourage initiative and responsibility.
9. Reward employees fairly and judiciously.
10. Employ appropriate sanctions to correct errors.
11. Maintain discipline.
12. Assure that individual interests do not supersede those of the organization.
13. Employ unity of command.
14. Ensure order among human and non-human factors alike.
15. Maintain control over everything.
16. Avoid excessive red tape.

Commanding encompasses the art of leadership coupled with the goal of putting the organization into motion. Setting a good example, making periodic examinations of the organization, eliminating incompetent personnel and not getting bogged down with detail were some of the suggestions Fayol made for effectively carrying out this function.

Coordinating provides the requisite unity and harmony needed to attain organizational goals. One way of accomplishing this, Fayol believed, was through regular meetings of managers and subordinates. If this function were properly implemented, everything would flow smoothly.

Controlling entails seeing that everything is done in accord with the adopted plan. This function must be applied to all segments of an activity—men, materials and operations alike.

Fayol's Contribution

Fayol's contribution to management theory cannot be understated. First, he provided a conceptual framework for analyzing the management process. In the post-World War II era, when colleges of business in America began to flourish, it was Fayol's conceptual framework that provided the guidelines along which many management texts were written. Writers would identify a number of managerial functions and then describe each in depth. Some even went so far as to provide specific principles of management at the end of each section, e.g., principles of planning and principles of organizing. Known as the *management process school*, there is no doubt that the basic framework originated with Fayol.

Second, the attention Fayol focused on the need and possibility of teaching management via the development of a theory of administration put him in the forefront of classical management theoreticians. Much of what was to follow constituted an extension and development of his basic ideas. Two individuals who complemented his work were James D. Mooney and Alan C. Reiley.

James D. Mooney

James D. Mooney was a General Motors executive. Joining the firm in 1920, he worked his way up the organization ranks to become president of the General Motors Export Corporation. During the late 1930's, President Franklin Roosevelt selected Mooney as his personal secret emissary to Hitler in a vain attempt to end the war before America became involved. During World War II, Mooney helped convert General Motors to defense production and then left the firm to head the United States Navy Bureau of Aeronautics. After the war he became president and chairman of the board of Willy Overland Motors.[11] His cohort, Alan C. Reiley, was advertising manager of the Remington Company (currently the Remington Rand Division of the Sperry Rand Corporation) from 1900 to 1928. He was highly knowledgeable in the area of typewriters, authoring "The Story of the Typewriter" and serving as the contributor of the section on typewriters in the Encyclopaedia Britannica.[12]

James D. Mooney and Alan C. Reiley In 1931, James D. Mooney and Alan C. Reiley authored a book entitled *Onward Industry!*,[13] later revised and called *Principles of Organization*.

The book complemented the work of Fayol while adding a new dimension via a rather complex conceptualized framework of

---

[11]Daniel A. Wren, *The Evolution of Management Thought*, (New York: The Ronald Press, 1972), p. 346.
[12]Henry H. Albers, *Principles of Management: A Modern Approach*, 3rd edition (New York: John Wiley & Sons, 1969), p. 46.
[13]James D. Mooney and Alan C. Reiley, *Onward Industry!* (New York: Harper & Brothers Publishers, 1931). The authors revised the book in 1939 and changed the title to *Principles of Organization*. In 1947, Mooney revised the book again and Reiley's name was dropped.

management. The major thesis set forth in the text was that an efficient organization had to have formalism, which in turn had to be based on principles. To prove the thesis, the two men attempted to uncover, identify, define and correlate the principles of organization.

For them, a principle applied to any fundamental truth that could be shown to be universal within its province. Using personal business experience and the examination of the military, government, church, and industry, they constructed their model. Before examining their principles of organization, however, it should be noted that the framework for the analysis followed the order of the basic laws of logic employed by Lewis F. Anderson.[14] This logic postulates that every principle has a process and an effect and each process and effect, in turn, has its own principle, process and effect. Mooney and Reiley's framework, shown in Table 3–1, was based on the following thesis:

Mooney and Reiley's principle-process-effect thesis.

A. The first principle of organization is *coordination*,[15] which entails the orderly arrangement of group effort to provide unity of action in the pursuit of a common objective. This statement expresses the principles of organization in their entirety, and all other principles are subordinated to it. In turn, the principle is implemented by the *scalar process,* the chain of authority which runs from top to bottom in the organization. The result is the *functional effect* which is the definition of the duties of each person in the scalar chain. Thus, the principle (coordination) has a process (scalar) and an effect (functional.) And each of these three, in turn, has its own principle, process and effect, as seen in B–D, which follow.

B. For completeness, coordination must have its own principle, process and effect. The foundation of the coordinating principle is *authority,* the supreme coordinating power. This authority is put into process by *processive coordination* which refers to all activities designed to bring about unity and direction of activity. The result is *effective coordination.*

C. The determining principle of the scalar process is *leadership.* This is put into process through *delegation* of authority to subordinates. The result is *functional definition,* or the assignment of the duties to be performed.

D. *Functional effect,* as seen in A above, is the end result of the coordinating principle and refers to the duties and responsibilities of individuals in the organization. The principle, process and effect of *functional effect* are *determinative, applicative* and *interpretative functionalism.* By determinative functionalism (principle) is meant the function of identifying broad objectives. Applicative functionalism (process) refers to the actual executing of the requisite activity. Interpretative functionalism (effect) deals with the analysis of what was accomplished in comparison to what was expected. Mooney and Reily felt these three functions were similar to those carried out by the executive (determinative), legislative (applicative) and judicial (interpretative) branches of government.

---

[14]Lewis F. Anderson, *Das Logische. Seine Gesetze und Kategorein* (Leipzig: Felix Meiner, 1929).
[15]Mooney and Reiley, *op. cit.,* p. 19.

TABLE 3-1 Logical Framework of the Principles of Organization

	Principle	Process	Effect
The Coordinating Principle	Authority or coordination *per se*	Processive coordination	Effective coordination
The Scalar Process	Leadership	Delegation	Functional definition
The Functional Effect	Determinative functionalism (legislative)	Applicative functionalism (executive)	Interpretative functionalism (judicial)

Source: James D. Mooney and Alan C. Reiley, *Onward Industry!* (New York: Harper & Brothers Publishers, 1931) p. 542. Reprinted with permission.

Mooney and Reiley's Contribution

Although their thesis is very difficult to follow unless read and reread several times, *Onward Industry!* was a major contribution to the development of early management theory. Mooney and Reiley attempted to show the causal relationships of fundamental organization principles. They also stressed the applicability of these principles to any activity or objective, refusing to be confined, as were other writers of the day, merely to industrial or production organizations. For them, the principles were universally applicable to all organized human effort.

Although Mooney and Reiley arrived at their findings independent of Fayol, their work was similar to his in that it provided a basis from which to understand the management of organizations. This similarity was made clear through the writings of Lyndall F. Urwick.

Lyndall F. Urwick was educated at Oxford and served with distinction in the British Army during both world wars. From 1928 until 1933 he was Director of the International Management Institute in Geneva and Chairman of Urwick, Orr and Partners, Ltd., a management consulting firm in London, until his retirement.[16]

Lyndall F. Urwick

---

[16]Wren, *op. cit.*, p. 357.

A synthesis of current management knowledge was attempted.

In 1943 Urwick wrote a book entitled *The Elements of Administration*,[17] in which he sought to integrate the theories of Taylor, Fayol, Mooney, Reiley and other early management writers. While conceding that management was a social science that lacked the rigor and precision of the physical sciences, he also noted that there was a very large body of management knowledge available. It was his contention that if these ideas and concepts could be brought together in composite form, management would be shown to be a much more scientific field of endeavor than it appeared to be. Urwick's goal, therefore, was to gather together in a logical framework principles of administration that had been formulated by different authorities.

The main point...is that it focuses in a logical scheme various "Principles of Administration" formulated by different authorities. The fact that such "Principles"—worked out by persons of different nationalities, widely varying experience and, in the majority of cases, no knowledge of each other's work—were susceptible to such logical arrangement, is in itself highly significant.[18]

In pursuing this goal, Urwick placed Fayol's elements of administration within Mooney and Reiley's principle-process-effect framework. The first part of this analysis incorporated the planning function.

Planning

Principles of administration.

Urwick began his analysis by refining Fayol's administrative functions of planning, organizing, commanding, coordinating, and controlling and by pointing out that Fayol's use of the word *prevoyance* meant more than "to plan"; it also entailed forecasting. Thus, there are six aspects of administration that can be related according to process and effect. In Urwick's view: forecasting (process) leads to planning (effect); organization (process) results in coordination (effect); command (process) brings about control (effect). It can now be seen how Urwick began to integrate Fayol's ideas and those of Mooney and Reiley. There is, however, one concept still missing: what are the three principles that precede the above three processes? Urwick saw the principle underlying the whole art of administration as being that of *investigation*, which is as necessary to the administrator as it was to Taylor in his time and motion studies. Thus:

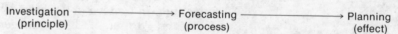

Investigation ————————→ Forecasting ————————→ Planning
   (principle)   (process)   (effect)

FIGURE 3–3   Principles Underlying Entire Administrative Process

Forecasting, in turn, has its own principle namely, *appropriateness*. The human and material organization must be consistent with the firm's resources and objectives. Likewise, planning

---

[17]L. Urwick, *The Elements of Administration* (New York: Harper & Brothers Publishers, 1943).
[18]*Ibid.*, p. 7.

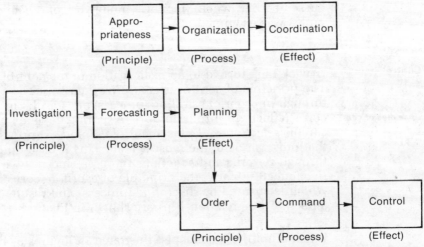

FIGURE 3-4   The Principles of Administration (Adapted from L. Urwick, *The Elements of Administration,* New York, Harper & Brothers, 1943, p. 19.)

finds its principle in *order*. Combining these ideas together into a conceptual framework results in Figure 3–4. Urwick then moved on to describe the principles of coordination and control.

Coordination

Principles of coordination.

In Urwick's view, the foundation of coordination is *authority,* which is implemented by the *scalar process,* resulting in the definition of individual duties (assignments and integration of functions). The remainder of the logic is presented in Figure 3–5 and represents a mere recapitulation of what was dis-

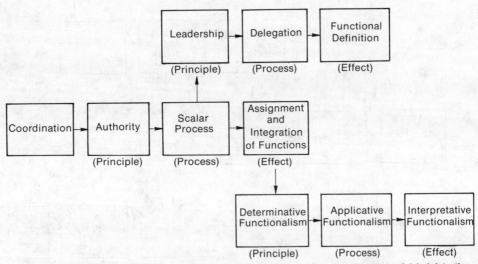

FIGURE 3-5   The Principles of Coordination (Adapted from L. Urwick, *The Elements of Administration,* New York, Harper & Brothers Publishers, 1943, p. 43.)

cussed earlier, when Mooney's framework of organization principles was examined.

Control

Principles of control.

Urwick then turned to an examination of the control function. The principle of control is *centralization*, which is accomplished through *appropriate staffing* (process) and results in *esprit de corps* (effect). In turn, appropriate staffing depends upon the careful *selection and placement of employees* (principle) so that they can be of the most benefit. This is accomplished through *rewards* and *sanctions* (process) and results in *initiative* (effect). Finally, the principle of *esprit de corps* is *equity*, which is ensured by *discipline* (process) and results in *stability* (effect). These relationships are shown in Figure 3–6.

When all of these concepts illustrated in Figures 3–4, 3–5 and 3–6 are brought together into a conceptual framework, Figure 3–7 results.

Urwick's Contribution

Urwick did an excellent job of combining the work of Fayol, Mooney, Reiley and other early management theorists into composite form. As seen in Figure 3–7, the ideas of the men, as tempered by Urwick, fit together into a logical scheme. There was indeed much agreement among the theorists of the day regarding administrative principles.

Thus, although Urwick did not make an original contribution to management thought in terms of new input, he did synthesize the writings of many of the early theorists and accomplished his

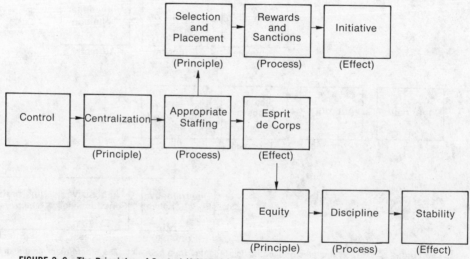

FIGURE 3–6 The Principles of Control (Adapted from L. Urwick, *The Elements of Administration,* New York, Harper & Brothers Publishers, 1943, p. 78.)

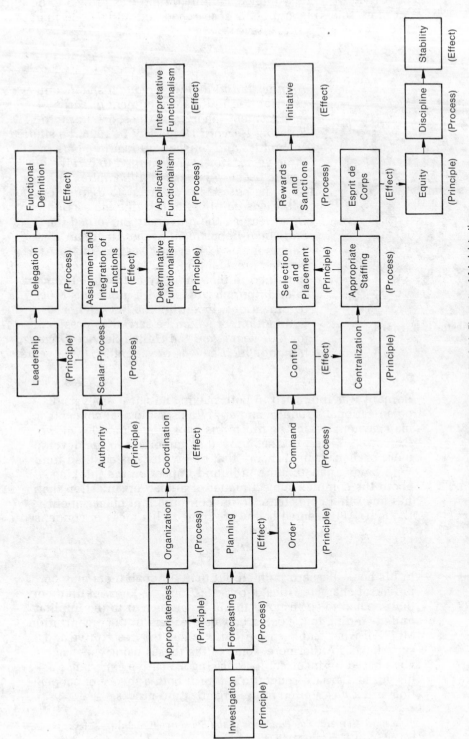

FIGURE 3-7 Conceptual Framework of Urwick's Elements of Administration

objective. As a consequence, administration was proved to be far more scientific and better researched and understood than had previously been believed.

Chester I. Barnard

Another individual who made a significant contribution to the development of early management theory was Chester I. Barnard. Entering Harvard University in 1906, he studied economics and finished all requirements in three years. However, he failed to receive his degree because he lacked a laboratory science. Since he passed the course with distinction, he felt it was pointless to take the lab section. Upon leaving the university, he joined the Statistical Department of the American Telephone and Telegraph system. In 1927 he became president of New Jersey Bell and remained in that capacity until his retirement. In addition, he worked with numerous other organizations, including the Rockefeller Foundation, of which he served as president for four years, and the United Service Organization, of which he was president for three years.

Barnard was interested in both making a logical analysis of organizational structure and applying sociological concepts to management, which he did in his book *The Functions of the Executive*.[19] His work has proved so important to the development of management theory that one writer has credited him with having had "a more profound impact on the thinking about the complex subject matter of human organization than has any other contributor to the continuum of management thought."[20] Presented below are some of his ideas in condensed form.

Functions of the Executive

In his book, Barnard pointed out that although there may be universal characteristics of organizations, he knew of no theory that seemed to correspond to his experience or to the implicit understanding that existed between leaders in the organization. Much of what had been written was just too descriptive and superficial. Furthermore, some of the theses being espoused were based on incorrect logic. Using *executive experience* as his guide, Barnard sought to set forth both a theory of cooperation and a description of the organization process.

[19]Chester I. Barnard, *The Functions of the Executive* (Cambridge, Mass.: Harvard University Press, 1950).
[20]Claude S. George, Jr., *The History of Management Thought*, 2nd edition (Englewood Cliffs, N.J.: Prentice-Hall, Inc., 1972), p. 140.

He defined the formal organization as *a system of consciously coordinated activities or forces of two or more persons.*[21] Within this structure the executive is the most strategic factor; it is up to him to maintain a system of cooperative effort. The entire process is carried out through three essential executive functions: (a) providing a system of communication; (b) promoting the acquisition of essential effort; and (c) formulating and defining the purposes and objectives of the organization.

Establish and maintain a communication system.

The first of these functions, establishment and maintenance of a *communication* system, is the executive's *primary* job. It requires a coalescence of executive personnel and executive positions, and it is accomplished through careful employee selection, the use of positive and negative sanctions, and the securing of the informal organization. This informal organization plays a key role in communication because it helps to reduce the necessity for formal decisions while minimizing what Barnard called "undesirable influences."

Promote acquisition of essential effort.

The second of the functions, to promote the acquisition of *essential effort* from organizational personnel, requires two main steps. First, the people have to be brought into a cooperative form of relationship with the organization; they have to be recruited in some way. Then, when this is accomplished, the organization must get them to identify with the firm. This requires the establishment of inducements and incentives.

Formulate the purpose and objectives of the organization.

The third executive function, formulating the *purpose and objectives* of the organization, requires the delegation of authority. Everyone is given a piece of the overall master plan to implement. Then, by means of communication feedback, obstacles and difficulties can be noted and the plan changed appropriately. In light of such changes, new responsibilities can be assigned.

The Theory of Authority

Throughout his book, Barnard emphasized the importance of *inducing* the subordinate to cooperate. Merely having the authority to give orders is insufficient, for the subordinate may refuse to obey. In fact, stated Barnard:

A person can and will accept a communication as authoritative only when four conditions simultaneously obtain: (a) he can and does understand the communication; (b) *at the time of his decision*, he believes it is not inconsistent with the purpose of the organization; (c) *at the time of his decision*, he believes it to be compatible with his personal interest, as a whole; and (d) he is able mentally and physically to comply with it.[22]

---

[21]Barnard, *op. cit.*, p. 73.
[22]*Ibid.*, p. 165.

*Acceptance the-
ory of authority.*

The result of this reasoning is what has become commonly known as the *acceptance theory of authority*.[23] Authority, or the right to command, depends upon whether or not the subordinates obey. Naturally, one could reason that it is possible for the executive to bring sanctions, but this will not necessarily ensure acceptance of the orders, for the employee may be willing to accept any fate dealt out by management.

*Zones of indif-
ference are im-
portant.*

The entire acceptance theory of authority would be quite threatening if this were all there was to it. Management might literally be at the mercy of the subordinates. However, Barnard very astutely noted that it was often possible to secure the consent and cooperation of subordinates. First, the four conditions necessary for acceptance are generally present, so the person usually accepts the communication as authoritative. Second, each individual has a "zone of indifference." Orders falling within this zone are accepted without question. The others either fall on the neutral line or are conceived of as clearly unacceptable. The indifference zone tells the story, and it will be either wide or narrow, depending upon the inducements being accorded the individual and the sacrifices he is making on the part of the organization. The effective executive assures that each individual feels he is receiving more from the organization than he is giving. When this occurs, the indifference zone is widened and the subordinates are agreeable to accepting most orders. Third, the refusal to obey on the part of one person will affect the efficiency of the organization and will often prove to be a threat to the other members. When this happens, fellow workers will often bring pressure against the individual to comply. The result is a general stability within the organization.

**Barnard's
Contribution**

Barnard made several important contributions to management theory. First, he presented functions of the executive in analytical and dynamic terms, in contrast to the descriptive writers who had preceded him. Second, he stimulated interest in topics such as communication, motivation, decision making, objectives and organizational relationships. Third, he advanced the work of Fayol, and Mooney and Reiley. These individuals were concerned with management from the standpoint of principles and functions, but Barnard, drawing upon his interest in the psychological and sociological aspects of management, extended these ideas to include the interaction of people in the work force.

SUMMARY

The most significant contributions to early management theory were made by Fayol and Barnard. However, as seen by Urwick's

---

[23]This basic concept was espoused earlier, when Machiavelli wrote about consent of the masses. See Chapter 1.

synthesis, all of the people mentioned in this chapter played a role. Yet before continuing, it is important to place these contributors in proper perspective.

Today, Fayol, Mooney, Reiley and Urwick are referred to as *classical* management theorists because they focused their attention on the functions and principles of management and organization, giving minimum consideration to the human element. Barnard, who examined and wrote about management more from the standpoint of people than from the standpoint of functions and principles, is often referred to as a human relationist or *behaviorist*. Thus, early contributions to management theory came from both classical and behavioral theorists, and the concepts they espoused would serve as the basis for the development of a modern management theory.

Thus far, all emphasis has been on the management of work. Little attention has been given, with the exception of Barnard, to the role of individual and group behavior in the work place. However, this area was being studied by early researchers, and they will be the focus of attention in Chapter 4.

REVIEW AND STUDY QUESTIONS

1. Why is Henri Fayol known as the Father of Modern Management Theory?

2. What did Fayol mean by "Technical ability is the most important quality at the bottom of the industrial ladder and administrative ability at the top"?

3. Identify and describe Fayol's five management functions.

4. What is functional foremanship?

5. What did Fayol mean by "a principle of management"?

6. What contribution did James Mooney and Alan Reiley make to management theory?

7. Even though Lyndall Urwick made no original contribution in terms of input to management theory, he is a management scholar. Do you agree or disagree with this point of view?

8. According to Chester Barnard, what are the three essential executive functions? Explain.

9. What is the acceptance theory of authority? Do you agree with it?

SELECTED REFERENCES

Alford, L. P. *Management's Handbook.* New York: The Ronald Press Company, 1923.

Balderson, C., V. S. Karabasz and R. P. Brecht. *Management of an Enterprise.*

New Jersey: Prentice-Hall, Inc. 1935.

Barnard, C. I. *The Functions of the Executive.* Cambridge, Mass.: Harvard University Press, 1938.

Basset, W. R. *The Organization of Modern Business.* New York: Dodd Mead & Company, 1921.

Blomfield, D. *The Modern Executive.* New York: H. W. Wilson Company, 1924.

Church, A. H. *The Making of an Executive.* New York: D. Appleton and Company, 1923.

Dutton, H. P. *Principles of Organization as Applied to Business.* New York: McGraw-Hill Book Company, 1931.

Fayol, H. *General and Industrial Management.* London: Sir Isaac Pitman & Sons, Ltd., 1949.

Mee, J. F. *Management Thought in a Dynamic Economy.* New York: New York University Press, 1963.

Merrill, C. F., ed. *Classics in Management.* New York: American Management Association, 1960.

Metcalf, H. C., and L. Urwick, eds. *Dynamic Administration. The Collected Papers of Mary Parker Follett.* New York: Harper & Brothers Publishers, 1924.

Mooney, J. D., and A. C. Reiley, *Onward Industry!* New York: Harper & Brothers Publishers, 1931.

Robinson, W. *Fundamentals of Business Organization.* New York: McGraw-Hill Book Company, 1925.

Sheldon, O. *The Philosophy of Management.* London: Sir Isaac Pitman & Sons, Ltd., 1923.

Urwick, L. *The Elements of Administration.* New York: Harper & Brothers Publishers, 1943.

Wren, D. A. *The Evolution of Management Thought.* New York: The Ronald Press, 1973.

CASE: TECHNICIANS AND MANAGERS

One day recently, a management consulting firm in New York City received a phone call from a local industrial machine manufacturer. The company's board of directors had just concluded its quarterly meeting and had decided that something had to be done to improve operations. For the sixth consecutive quarter, profits had declined. Sales were higher than ever, but costs were apparently out of control.

The consultants spent ten weeks examining the firm's operations. Everyone in the company was interviewed, from the chief executive to the janitor. When the team was finished with its analysis, it submitted a 212-page report to the board. One of its key findings was:

Since its inception, the company has had a policy of promoting from within. The prime criterion for these promotions appears to be technical competence. This is as true at the upper levels as at the lower ones. And it is not uncommon to find managers down on the machine floor examining and commenting on technical problems. Unfortunately, this leaves little time for managing. In fact, managerial functions such as planning, organizing and controlling are given almost no attention. What the company needs is an influx of outside management people who will place *less* attention on the technical side of the job and *more* on the management side.

Questions

1. How do these findings fit into Fayol's philosophy of management?

2. How common is it to find managers spending more time on the technical than managerial side of their job? Explain.

3. How can these problems be overcome?

CASE: A CALL FOR FORMAL TRAINING

College enrollments began to drop off in the mid-1970's, and private colleges and universities felt the effects most strongly. In an attempt to minimize the impact on his institution, William Smith, president of a large private university in the East, urged the faculty to do all it could to stimulate enrollments.

In response to the president's request, faculty in the College of Business decided to spend one day a week making scheduled appearances in local high schools to encourage graduating seniors to come to their university. If any of the students expressed interest, the faculty member would take down his or her name, address and area of interest and turn the information over to the president's office. Depending upon the individual's desired major, a faculty member would then call on the student and his parents at home.

One of these students, Richard Makinaw, indicated an interest in majoring in business, specifically management. As a result, Fred Quilting, a professor of management, arranged for an appointment with Richard and his family for the purpose of explaining to them what the College of Business could offer. Richard seemed impressed, but his father did not. Part of the conversation was as follows:

Professor Quilting, I've got a very successful retail store and I want my son to come into the business with me. From what you say, your university could prepare him to take over some of my duties and, someday, run the entire operation himself. However, I'm not so sure that he can learn management from a book. I've been in the retail business for over twenty years, and most of what I've learned about management, I picked up the hard way.

Certainly, Mr. Mackinaw, we can't hope to give Richard all the experience and knowledge you have about management. But we can familiarize him with the basics of management and provide him with some important training.

I don't know. His mother and I are going to have to talk it over. My real concern is whether Richard would be better off joining me in the business right after he graduates from high school or whether he should go on to college and study management formally.

Questions

1. Can management be studied in the classroom?

2. What are the advantages of studying management in college as opposed to learning about it on the job?

3. What recommendation would you make to Mr. Mackinaw? Explain.

CASE: GETTING IT ALL TOGETHER

A group of graduating seniors in a large midwestern business college recently received permission from the president of a local manufacturing firm to make a management analysis of his operations. The analysis was going to serve as the basis for their term paper in Advanced Management, a course required for all graduating seniors, but the results would be reported to the company. Thus, there were benefits for both sides.

The students began by interviewing the top management personnel. Then they turned their attention to departmental operations. Finally, they focused on the company's financial statements.

In their final report to the president, the seniors indicated that they believed the firm's biggest problem was a lack of coordination. In support of this finding, they pointed to the responses they received when they asked the top managers, what do you think next year's sales will be? The answers, in dollars, were as follows:

President	4,500,000
Vice president of Manufacturing	7,000,000
Vice president of Marketing	10,000,000
Vice president of Finance	4,000,000
Vice president of Administration	5,500,000

Sales the previous year had been $4 million. This indicated to the seniors that the top managers were not coordinating their sales forecasts and operating activities. Furthermore, these forecasts were being used as the basis for all departmental operations. As a result, manufacturing was ordering more materials than it should have, based on the budget allocated to it. These expenditures were resulting in excessive increases in inventory. Meanwhile, the sales department was spending far more than it should have. And while expenditures were up, sales were not, further aggravating the inventory situation.

The students summed up their report by saying that the entire firm lacked coordination of operations. If the firm were to remain in the profit column, wrote the seniors, the managers are going to have to "get it all together." Otherwise, losses of up to $175,000 could be expected in the current fiscal year.

Questions

1. How important is coordination to effective management?

2. What do you think brings about lack of coordination? Explain.

3. How can effective coordination be achieved?

4. What recommendations would you make to management? Explain.

CASE: WHO IS IN CHARGE HERE?

Webber Printing, a Midwest job printer, was founded in 1937. For the first twenty years of its existence, the firm prospered slowly. However, in the late 1950's, thanks to a large investment in new machinery and equipment, the company expanded its operations and sales began to increase at an annual rate of 45 per cent. By 1964, Webber Printing had passed the $20 million mark. From then on, sales began to increase at a decreasing rate. Nevertheless, by 1974 the company topped the $100 million mark.

Success, however, had its price. In 1967, despite all attempts by the management to discourage such action, the workers voted to unionize. For years, Charles Webber, president and founder, had prided himself on having a nonunion shop. He had continually paid union scale and attempted to match all fringe benefits being provided by his unionized competitors. The men appreciated his efforts, but, as one of them put it, "After Mr. Webber dies, all of this could change. A union provides us assurance that we won't lose everything we've gotten over the years."

The union brought a new era to management-worker relations. Previously, everything had been done on a rather informal basis. Now the company organized into two armies: the management and the union. Over the next decade, at contract time both sides drove as hard a bargain as they could. However, the union had the upper hand because there was a shortage of qualified personnel in the area and a great demand for the company's printing services. Management capitulated to both salary and fringe benefit requests.

This turn of events angered Bob Handley, manager of one of the company's units. He felt the union was getting too big for its britches, and he refused to take any guff from the workers. He kept a close watch on his people and threatened to fire any of

them who could not do "a fair day's work for a fair day's pay."
In turn, the union complained that Bob was a troublemaker. His
boss, Fred Wandott, called him in for a talk.

Bob, we've been getting some pressure from the union to ask you to loosen up
and quit pushing the men so hard. Now, I know you have only the best interest
of the firm in mind, but I think you'll get more work out of the men if you
don't treat this union thing as a personal vendetta.

Mr. Wandott, I think those guys believe they're running this company. I'm the
manager and they're the subordinates. They're supposed to obey my orders.

I realize that. But remember, you're only effective if they obey you. What good
is a manager whose men refuse to comply with his orders? Now, you're going
to have to ease up and realize that authority is a two-way street. There's the
person who gives the orders and the individual who agrees to obey them.

Questions

1. What does Mr. Wandott mean by authority being a two-way street?

2. Does Bob believe in Barnard's acceptance theory of authority? Does Mr. Wandott?
   Explain.

3. How could Barnard's "zone of indifference" concept be of value to Bob in handling
   this problem? Explain.

CHAPTER 4

THE HUMAN ELEMENT IN THE WORK PLACE: EARLY RESEARCH

GOALS OF THE CHAPTER

In the last two chapters, attention was primarily focused on what can be called the management of work. However, in the first half of the twentieth century, there were also those interested in researching the human element in the work place. The goals of this chapter are to examine the work of two such individuals. First, the research of Hugo Münsterberg, famous for his pioneering work in the field of industrial psychology, will be reviewed. Then, the work of Elton Mayo, who conducted important sociological research, the most famous of which was the Hawthorne studies, will be examined. Throughout the chapter, psychological concepts such as perception and mental skills, and sociological concepts, such as group norms, values and interactions will be discussed. In particular, attention will be focused on:

a. Hugo Münsterberg's popularization of psychology;
b. his attempts to bridge scientific management and industrial efficiency via psychology;
c. his famous trolley experiment;
d. Elton Mayo's mule spinning inquiry;
e. the initial purpose of the Hawthorne experiments;
f. the results of the illumination experiments;
g. the findings obtained from the relay assembly test room experiments;
h. the importance of the massive interviewing program;
i. the significance of the bank wiring room experiments;
j. the norms and sentiments subscribed to by members of the bank wiring room; and
k. the findings and implications of the Hawthorne studies.

Historical Pictures Service, Chicago

Hugo Münsterberg

Hugo Münsterberg *was born in Danzig, Prussia, and educated in some of Europe's best schools, receiving his Ph.D. from Leipzig in 1885, where he studied under Wilhelm Wundt, the Father of Modern Psychology, and his M.D. two years later from Heidelberg. In 1892 he came to Harvard as a visiting professor. Five years later he returned to direct that university's Psychological Laboratory.*[1]

Although Münsterberg initially limited his work to laboratory experiments, he soon began expanding his psychological interests to include widely diverse fields such as law, sociology, medicine and business. He became for his day the world's greatest authority on everything "from sex education to scientific management, from temperance to job training, from Emerson the essayist to Emerson the efficiency engineer, from table tipping to employee testing."[2] *He also popularized psychology by showing how it could be of value to everyone. Much of his work was written not in a scholarly fashion but in a popular style for newspapers and magazines. One result was that he was in great demand as a writer, lecturer and consultant. Businesses flocked to him, anxious to have psychology brought down from its pinnacle and applied to practical problems.*[3]

In December 1916, while lecturing to a class of 60 Radcliffe girls on elementary psychology, he suddenly collapsed and died of a cerebral hemorrhage at the age of 53, cutting short a dynamic and fruitful career. His contributions have been of such great value to business that he is known as the Father of Industrial Psychology.

Scientific Management And Psychology

One of Münsterberg's major objectives was to strengthen the bridge between scientific management and industrial efficiency by complementing the work of Taylor and his associates.[4] Münsterberg noted that the efficiency engineers placed great empha-

[1] *Encyclopaedia Britannica*, 1973 edition, Vol. 15, p. 997.
[2] "Famous Firsts: Measuring Minds for the Job," *Business Week*, January 29, 1966, p. 60.
[3] His value to Harvard was so great that by 1908 he was receiving the highest salary the university had ever paid to anyone. In 1914, with the outbreak of WWI, Münsterberg pleaded Germany's cause. An irate English alumnus offered Harvard $10 million to fire Münsterberg, who in turn promised to resign if half that amount were given. However, the university declined the offer and Münsterberg remained at his post.
[4] Hugo Münsterberg, *Psychology and Industrial Efficiency* (Boston: Houghton Mifflin Company, 1913).

Mental skills are as important as physical skills.

sis upon the physical skills of the worker, but virtually overlooked psychological or mental skills:

Wherever the question of the selection of the fit men after psychological principles is mentioned in the literature of this [scientific management] movement, the language becomes vague, and the same men, who use the newest scientific knowledge whenever physics or mathematics or physiology or chemistry are involved, make hardly any attempts to introduce the results of science when psychology is in question.[5]

The only effort to employ "scientific psychology," in Münsterberg's opinion, was made by Mr. S. E. Thompson, cited in Taylor's *Principles of Scientific Management*.[6] Mr. Thompson owned a bicycle ball bearing factory. In his plant there were 120 girls inspecting ball bearings and picking out the defective ones. Since they worked ten and one half hours a day, it was evident that endurance was a necessary characteristic. However, Mr. Thompson recognized that perception accompanied by quick response action was also important to the job. He therefore had the reaction time of the girls tested and began laying off the slower workers. By the time the experiment was finished, output was the same as before but the number of workers had been reduced from 120 to 35. In addition, the accuracy of the work was increased 67 per cent, the working hours were reduced and the wages of the girls doubled. To Münsterberg, this experiment highlighted what he called the "psycho-technical problem."

We have to analyze definite economic tasks with reference to the mental qualities which are necessary or desirable for them, and we have to find methods by which these mental qualities can be tested. . . .the interests of commerce and industry can be helped only when both sides, the vocational demands and the personal function, are examined with equal scientific thoroughness.[7]

Vocational Testing

Münsterberg's interest in studying the man as well as the job led him into the area of vocational testing. His thesis was that tests should be designed that would help screen out unfit job applicants and workers. His most famous experiment was conducted for the Electric Railway Service.

The Trolley Experiment. In 1912, the American Association for Labor Legislation became concerned over the number of accidents caused by trolleys in various cities. They asked Münsterberg to look into the matter to see if he could devise a solution for reducing these mishaps.

Initially, Münsterberg investigated the most obvious possibilities, namely, that motor men with a high accident rate suffered either from poor vision or slow reaction time to hazardous situ-

---

[5] *Ibid.*, p. 52.
[6] Frederick Winslow Taylor, *The Principles of Scientific Management* (New York: Harper & Brothers Publishers, 1911) pp. 86–97.
[7] Munsterberg, *op. cit.*, p. 57.

ations. Neither of these hypotheses, however, proved to be accurate. Attention was therefore shifted from physical to mental ability.

It was then that Münsterberg defined the real problem. A good trolley driver must be able to observe all the people and objects in front of him, noting those that are moving parallel to his car and those that intend to cross in front of the trolley. Münsterberg decided to see if he could devise a test for identifying those operators who had this ability and those who did not.

The test that emerged from his psychological lab is illustrated in Figure 4–1. It was a series of cards, each divided into half-inch boxes and measuring nine boxes wide and twenty-six boxes long. Down the center of the card ran two heavy lines representing the trolley tracks, on each side of which were four half-inch boxes. In these boxes, in irregular fashion, Münsterberg placed the digits 1, 2, and 3. The "1" represented a man on foot, who could move one box; the "2" stood for a horse, which could move two boxes; the "3" was a car, which could move three boxes. This represented the kind of traffic that the trolley operator could expect to encounter. Of course, not all of it would be moving across the tracks. Münsterberg therefore colored the digits, red indicating traffic moving toward the tracks and black representing traffic moving parallel to the tracks. The cards were then placed in a box with a window. The person being tested could look through the window and see the

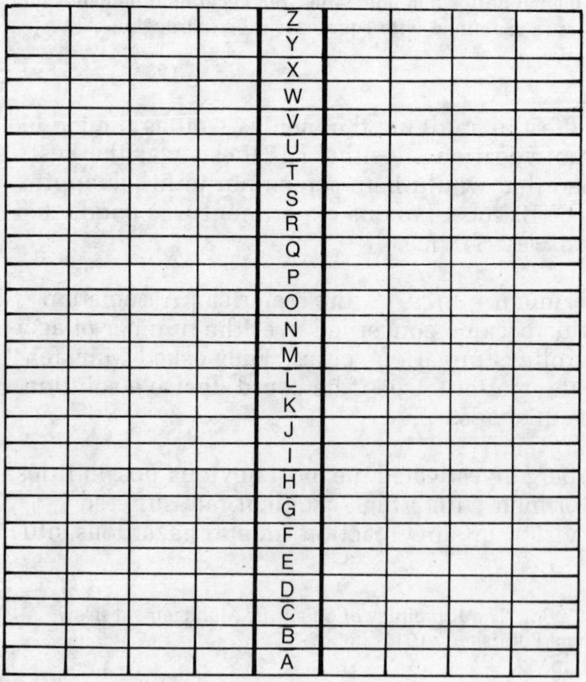

A screening test for trolley operators was designed.

FIGURE 4–1 Münsterberg's Trolley Operator Test With Numbers Omitted. This is a representative card designed the way Münsterberg described it in *Psychology and Industrial Efficiency.* He did not, however, illustrate the manner in which the numbers were arranged on the card.

entire width of the first card as well as five units of its length. By turning a crank on the side of the box he could move from the beginning of the card (Row A) to the end of the card (Row Z). The goal of the test was to move as quickly as possible down the card, noting aloud to the examiner the potential dangers that existed in each of the twenty-six rows. For example, a red "2" located two boxes to the right of center represented a horse that would wind up in front of the trolley. Conversely, a red "3" located two boxes to the right of center stood for a car that would pass over the tracks and not prove troublesome. The big problem, of course, was that of picking out the red numbers and ignoring the black ones. Since the two colors tend to look identical in the distance, the operator had to wait until he moved them closer before making a judgment. The same situation existed on the job. The trolley operator would have trouble judging whether people in the distance intended to cross the tracks or walk parallel to them.

The person taking the test would move through the first card as quickly as possible, telling the test administrator all the dangers he saw. When he finished, the card would be removed and another would pop into view. There were twelve such cards in all, and the man's score was based upon the total time elapsed plus ten seconds for each red number constituting a hazard that went undetected by him.

Ability to concentrate is an important psychological factor.

Münsterberg used this experiment on trolley operators and found that a man's ability to do the job safely and efficiently was related to the score he received on the test. He thus developed a useful instrument for measuring success as a trolley operator. However, he did not stop here, but expanded the concept by developing screening tests for other work groups, from ship's officers to telephone operators. The central objective was always that of identifying whether or not the person was psychologically fit to do the job. Did he have the requisite mental skills? It was Münsterberg's belief that the key to industrial efficiency rested in the worker's ability to concentrate his attention only on elements directly concerned with good job performance. In the case of the trolley operators, an extended field of concentration was necessary if the individual were to identify and avoid possible accidents ahead of him. For other jobs, a narrower field of concentration might be more useful. In either event, psychological testing could be valuable in screening people at *all levels* of an organization.

The results of experimental psychology will have to be introduced systematically into the study of the fitness of the personality from the lowest to the highest technical activity and from the simplest sensory function to the most complex mental achievement.[8]

---

[8]*Ibid.,* p. 96.

Münsterberg's Contributions

Münsterberg made a number of important contributions to management. First, he popularized psychology by showing how it could be of value in many fields, thus heralding the advent of the psychologists into industry. However, it should not be inferred that because his work was popular it was unscientific, for he used his psychological laboratory at Harvard to develop many of the tools he employed in industry. He was a researcher and experimenter as well as a salesman for psychology. Although he may have written for popular consumption, the work he conducted was based on scientific principles and the scientific method.

Second, in addition to studying the psychological traits necessary to do a good job, he concerned himself with the psychological conditions under which the greatest amount of output could be attained. Included in this study were factors such as attention, fatigue, monotony and the impact of social influences.

Third, he addressed himself to securing "the best possible effects," and in so doing, he combined some of the ideas of scientific management with those of psychology. For example, in advertising one wants people to read the ads quickly and accurately (scientific management), remember what was said and take appropriate action (psychology). The importance of effects such as size, color, word choice, typeface and arrangement on the page were investigated. Years later, advertising agencies would be following the same approach in an attempt to evaluate the effectiveness of their own advertising copy. Münsterberg carried this basic concept into the areas of buying, selling and displaying. In each case, he showed how psychology could improve performance. By the time of his death, industrial psychology was well established as one of the important "new" areas of management.

Elton Mayo

Another field in which interest began to grow was that of sociology. One of the earliest and most significant contributors was Elton Mayo, an Australian who taught ethics, philosophy and logic at the Queensland University and later studied medicine in Edinburgh, Scotland. While in Edinburgh, he became a research associate in the study of psychopathology. Then, under a grant from the Laura Spelman Rockefeller Fund, he came to America, joining the faculty of the Wharton School of Finance and Commerce of the University of Pennsylvania. In 1926, he joined the Harvard faculty as an associate professor of industrial research.[9]

[9]Daniel A. Wren, *The Evolution of Management Thought* (New York; The Ronald Press Company, 1972), pp. 277–278.

**MAYO'S
MULE
SPINNING
INQUIRY***

Mayo's most famous early experiment took place in a Philadelphia textile mill in 1923 to 1924. The purpose of the study was to identify the cause of high labor turnover in the mule spinning department. While turnover in the company's other departments was between five and six per cent a year, in the mule spinning department it was up to 250 per cent. Efficiency engineers had experimented with financial incentive schemes, but these had proved fruitless. The president then called in Mayo and his associates. An initial investigation by the researchers revealed that working conditions in this department were basically the same as elsewhere in the mill. However, after talking to the men, the research team realized that certain other conditions were different, especially the fact that the mule spinners had a low opinion of their work. In addition, the job proved to be very solitary in nature, and the men appeared to have no communication with each other.

**Rest
Periods**

*With rest periods,
productivity rose.*

Mayo decided to make some changes in the work pattern to see if this would improve the situation. After securing management's permission, he introduced two ten-minute rest periods in the morning and two more in the afternoon for one of the groups in the department. During these periods the men were encouraged to lie down and, if possible, go to sleep. The results were astounding. Morale improved, labor turnover ended and production, despite the work breaks, remained the same. Soon the entire department was included in the rest-period experiment, and output increased tremendously. Monthly productivity, which had never been above 70 per cent, rose over the next five months to an overall average of 80 per cent, and with it came bonus pay.[10]

Then, suddenly, in response to a great demand for goods, the rest periods were terminated by the supervisor, who felt the company could not afford to lose this time. Output immediately declined, and the workers again became pessimistic and gloomy. Although the work breaks were restored and productivity increased, the men remained melancholy, believing that the rest periods would again be rescinded. However, the company president stepped in and announced that the work pauses would indeed remain. At the same time, the president placed control of these rest periods squarely in the hands of the men; they would determine when to take the breaks. Output reached an all-time high over the next six months, and labor turnover was virtually eliminated.

**Analysis of
The Results**

What led to the high morale, high productivity and virtual elimination of labor turnover? Mayo felt it was the systematic introduction of the rest periods, which not only helped overcome

---

[10]Bonuses were paid on productivity over 75 per cent.
*Mule: a type of spinning machine that makes thread or yarn from fibers; also called "mulejenny."

Psychological factors are important.

physical fatigue but reduced "pessimistic revery."[11] There were thus two factors involved, fatigue and monotony. The first of these is physiological and quite easy to understand. The second is psychological and reflected Mayo's philosophy and training. For some time prior to this textile mill study, he had been writing about the importance of understanding the worker's *psychological* make-up. Everyone, Mayo felt, has mental eccentricities or minor irrationalities. Most people are capable of suppressing them to the degree that they are harmless. They do not lead to, for example, a nervous breakdown. However, Mayo believed that:

What social and industrial research has not sufficiently realised as yet is that these minor irrationalities of the "average normal" person are cumulative in their effect. They may not cause "breakdown" in the individual but they do cause "breakdown" in the industry.[12]

There was, however, more here than Mayo and his associates realized. They had come up with some interesting physiological-psychological conclusions, but time and further research would be necessary before the experiment could be intelligently re-examined and additional, and far more substantial, findings obtained. The Hawthorne studies, which followed shortly thereafter, proved very useful in this regard.

HAWTHORNE STUDIES

The Hawthorne studies (1924–1932) had their roots in the logic of scientific management. The initial purpose of these experiments was to study the effect of illumination on output. The study, sponsored by the National Research Council, was begun in November 1924 at the Hawthorne Works of the Western Electric Company near Cicero, Illinois. Before it was all over, there would be four major phases, the illumination experiments being only the first.

Illumination Experiments

The illumination phase of the Hawthorne studies lasted two and one-half years. During this period, three different experiments were conducted, and as the tests continued, the researchers improved their experimental design. They were, however, unable to ascertain the relationship that existed between illumination and output. In one of the experiments, for example, they divided the workers into two groups. One was designated as the "test group" and worked under variable illumination intensities. The other was used as the "control group" and worked under conditions of constant illumination. In this way, the researchers hoped to measure the impact of variable illumination. However, the results did not turn out as expected. At the end of the experiment the researchers reported that:

---

[11]By revery Mayo meant day-dreaming.
[12]Elton Mayo, "Irrationality and Revery," *Journal of Personnel Research*, March 1923, p. 482.

This test resulted in very appreciable production increases in both groups and of almost identical magnitude. The difference in efficiency of the two groups was so small as to be less than the probable error of the values. Consequently, we were again unable to determine what definite part of the improvement in performance should be ascribed to improved illumination.[13]

No direct relationship between illumination and productivity was found.

On the basis of these illumination experiments, two conclusions were reached. First, lighting was only one factor affecting employee output and it was apparently a minor one at that. Second, attempts to measure the effect of illumination on output were unsuccessful because there were many factors involved that were not controlled and any one of these could have influenced the outcome.

The company, however, did not feel that the experiments had been unsuccessful. On the contrary, they believed that they had gained invaluable experience in the technique of conducting research and were eager to push forward. The result was phase two, the Relay Assembly Test Room experiment. This stage of the program marked the entrance of Elton Mayo and a number of Harvard researchers.

Relay Assembly Test Room

In order to obtain more control over the factors affecting work performance, it was decided to isolate a small group of workers from the regular work force. Five female assemblers and a layout operator were placed in a room. In addition, the researchers put an observer in with them to record everything that happened and to maintain a friendly atmosphere. The girls were told that the experiment was not designed to boost production but merely to study various types of working conditions so that the most suitable environment could be ascertained. They were told to keep working at their regular pace.

For the first four months, some initial work changes were introduced into the room and the overall effect studied. Most of these changes were easily identified by the investigators. For example, in contrast to the regular department, the room was smaller and had better lighting and ventilation. The significance of some changes, however, were not fully grasped at the time. For example, the test room observer took over some of the supervision, but he was very lenient.

The test room observer was chiefly concerned with creating a friendly relation with the operators which would ensure their co-operation. He was anxious to dispel any apprehensions they might have about the test and, in order to do this, he began to converse informally with them each day. Sometimes the topics he brought up pertained to their work, sometimes to personal matters, and occasionally they took the form of a general inquiry as to the attitude of the operators toward the test.[14]

---

[13]F. J. Roethlisberger and William J. Dickson, *Management and the Worker* (Cambridge, Mass.: Harvard University Press, 1949), p. 16.
[14]*Ibid.*, p. 37.

The girls had an improved outlook toward their work.

In addition, the girls were allowed to talk more freely among themselves and, because there were only a small number of them, they formed a much closer relationship than they had had in the regular department.

Once the impact of most of these new changes was noted, the researchers moved the experiment into its second stage. During this period, rest pauses were introduced in order to see what effect they would have on output. The result was an increase in productivity, leading to the initial hypothesis that these pauses reduced fatigue and thereby improved output.

Applying this theory further, the researchers introduced shorter work days and work weeks. Once again, output increased. However, these changes were later terminated, and when original conditions were re-established, output still remained high, indicating that the change in conditions was not the only reason for the increase in output. Some of the investigators hypothesized that the increases were related not to the rest pauses or shorter working hours but to the improved outlook that the girls had toward their work. No one, however, seemed able to answer the question, To what can this improved outlook be related? The researchers, therefore, decided to list the possible causes of these productivity increases. Five hypotheses emerged:

Five hypotheses emerged to explain the improved outlook.

a. the improved material conditions and methods of work introduced in the test room accounted for the increases being witnessed in productivity;
b. the rest pauses and shorter working hours provided relief from cumulative fatigue;
c. the rest pauses did not reduce fatigue as much as they did the monotony of of the work;
d. the increased wages of the test group accounted for the production increases;[15]
e. the changes in the method of supervision brought about the improved attitude and increased output.

After conducting various investigations, the first four hypotheses were rejected. Attention was then focused on the fifth: that changes in the social conditions and in the method of supervision brought about the improved attitude and increased output. In order to gather information on this, management decided to investigate employee attitudes and the factors to which they could be traced. The result was a massive interviewing program that started out simply as a plan for improving supervision, but actually marked the turning point in the research, overshadowing, for a time, all other aspects of the project.

Massive Interviewing Program

In the third phase of the studies, over 20,000 interviews were conducted. The interviewers began by asking employees direct questions about supervision and the work environment in gen-

---

[15]Although the girls had been on a group piece work system in the regular department, the group was very large and the wage incentive was small. In the test room, however, the group was small and the girls were able to earn more money because of their increased effort.

A nondirective interviewing technique was employed.

eral. Although the interviewer made it clear that everything would be kept in strict confidence, the responses to questions were often guarded and stereotyped. The approach was therefore changed from direct to *nondirect* questioning. Now the employee was allowed to choose his own topic. The result was the gathering of a wealth of information about employee attitudes. The researchers realized that the individual's work performance, position and status in the organization were determined not only by the person himself but by the group members as well. His peers had an effect on his performance. In order to study this more systematically, the research entered its fourth and final phase, that of the bank wiring observation room.

Bank Wiring Observation Room

In choosing a department to study, the investigators decided to concentrate on a small group engaged in one particular type of work rather than to encompass many groups with dissimilar jobs. The department chosen for the study was the bank wiring department. In this room there were three types of jobs: wireman, solderman and inspector. The wireman set the pace for the rest by the number of bank terminals he wired. These were then soldered by the solderman and, finally, checked by the inspector. Since it only took one solderman to handle the work of three wiremen, the group consisted of nine wiremen, three solders and two inspectors. For the next six months, the performance of work and the behavior of the group was observed.

The Group's Output.   One finding of this study was that most of the workers were restricting their output. The company norm (or standard) based on time and motion studies called for 7312 connections. The workers, however, completed only 6000 to 6600 connections, depending on the type of equipment being worked on. This informal standard had been formulated by the men, representing what they considered to be a proper day's work. There was no doubt that the men could have met the standard of 7312, but they did not wish to do so. This was made clear both when the observer noted that the men stopped working before quitting time and when most of them frankly told the interviewer that they could easily turn out more work.

Some men restricted their work output.

Why did the men restrict output? One told the interviewer that if they did too much work, the company would raise the expected amount. Another felt they might work themselves out of a job, remarking to the interviewer:

"We've only got so much work to do, you know. Now just suppose a person was doing 6,000 connections a day, say on selectors, that's two whole sets. Now suppose that instead of just loafing around when he gets through he did two more rows on another set. . . . Before long he would have an extra set done. Then where would you be? Somebody could be laid off."[16]

---

[16]Roethlisberger and Dickson, *op. cit.*, p. 419.

Others felt that a slow pace protected the slower workers and preventing them from looking bad and getting bawled out by the management. In addition, it should be noted that management seemed to accept this informal rate as satisfactory, bringing pressure on the men only when they fell below this level.

The Supervisory Situation.   Study of the supervisory situation in the room also provided human behavioral insights, for the manner in which the men treated their superiors differed. The hierarchy of supervisory titles is seen in Figure 4–2.

The workers treated the managers differently.

Most of the employees regarded the group chief as one of themselves. As a result, they thought nothing of disobeying him. The section chief fared a little better, for he was seen as having some authority. Nevertheless, the men often argued with him and did not always obey his orders. The assistant foreman, on the other hand, received much different treatment. The men neither disobeyed him nor argued with his orders. When he was in the room, the workers were on their best behavior. This same pattern existed in the case of the foreman. In fact, when he was present, the men refrained from any activity that was not strictly in accord with the rules. Thus, as one progressed up the organizational hierarchy, the degree of respect, or apprehensiveness, on the part of the men increased.

Group Dynamics.   Another aspect of the group that was closely observed was that of interpersonal relationships. The result was a wealth of information about the informal organization that existed in the room. For example, most of the men engaged in various games, including baseball pools, shooting craps, sharing candy and "binging." The latter, a device used to control individual behavior, consisted of hitting a man as hard as possible on the upper arm. This person was then free to retaliate by striking back with a like blow. Although the overt reason was to see who could hit the hardest, the underlying cause was often one of punishment for those who were accomplishing either too much or too little.

Interpersonal relations were studied.

Another topic of interest concerned the windows in the room. The wiremen were stationed near the windows and it was they

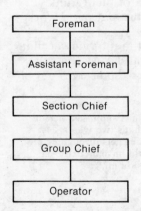

FIGURE 4–2   Partial Hierarchy of the Bank Wiring Observation Room

who opened and closed them. By noting the discussion that accompanied this activity, it was possible for the researchers to draw conclusions about the group's makeup. For example, two of the wiremen (W_5 and W_6)[17] got into a heated controversy over whether one of the windows should be opened or closed. One of the soldermen (S_1) supported the opening of the window and suggested that W_6 hit W_5 if he attempted to close the window. As a result, it remained open, but the two wiremen did not speak to each other for the rest of the morning. Meanwhile, S_1 continued to express his antagonism toward W_5, suggesting that since he did not wish to fight, W_6 should sue him if he tried to close the window again. The group had a lot of fun over this.

Job trading and the helping of one another provided further bases for studying the group's behavior. Some individuals sought help while others gave it, although such action was in direct violation of company rules. This led to interest in the development of friendships and antagonisms. Who liked whom and who disliked whom?

Social Cliques.   By studying the types of games and other interactions of the participants, the investigators were able to divide the men into two groups, or cliques, A and B, as seen in Figure 4–3. Several conclusions were drawn from this finding. First, the men were not integrated on the basis of occupation. Clique A, for example, contained three wiremen, one solderman and one inspector. Second, the location in the room influenced the formation of a clique. The A group was located in the front of the room, the B group in the rear. Third, some of the men were accepted by neither clique. For example, I_3, one of the workers who tended to maintain social distance between himself and the other men, once complained to the Inspection Branch that the workers were goldbricking. The men, in turn, ostracized him. Meanwhile, W_6 was always attempting to dominate clique B. As a result, as seen in Figure 4–3, he was not

The researchers were able to identify social cliques.

---

[17]None of the men in the study were identified by name. Instead, the nine wiremen were identified by the abbreviations W_1 through W_9. Likewise, the three soldermen were represented by S_1, S_2 and S_4, and the two inspectors by I_1 and I_3, respectively.

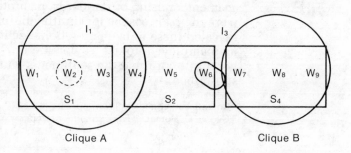

FIGURE 4–3   The Two Cliques in the Bank Wiring Observation Room (From F. J. Roethlisberger and William J. Dickson, *Management and the Worker*, Cambridge, Mass., Harvard University Press, 1939, p. 509. Reprinted with permission.)

entirely accepted by the group. Finally, each clique regarded itself as superior to the other, based on either the things it did or the things it refrained from doing. For example, Clique A did not trade jobs, and did not engage in "binging" as often as did Clique B. Conversely, the members of Clique B did not argue among themselves as often or engage in games of chance, as did Clique A. Each clique had its own code of behavior.

Membership in the Clique.   Each group had certain norms or sentiments to which one had to subscribe if he wished to be accepted as a member. Roethlisberger and Dickson identified these as being:

Norms of behavior were also identified.

1. You should not turn out too much work. If you do, you are a "rate-buster."
2. You should not turn out too little work. If you do, you are a "chiseler."
3. You should not tell a superior anything that will react to the detriment of an associate. If you do, you are a "squealer."
4. You should not attempt to maintain social distance or act officious. If you are an inspector, for example, you should not act like one.[18]

To these, Homans later added:

5. You should not be noisy, self-assertive, and anxious for leadership.[19]

All of these norms were evident in the earlier discussion. The workers set 6000 to 6600 connections as the norm and "binged" those who did more than that amount (numbers one and two above). When I_3 reported the workers to the Inspection Branch, he got himself in trouble with his department (number three). Prior to this time, his attempts to maintain social distance had caused him difficulty with the men (number four). W_6 was not entirely accepted by Clique B because he attempted to dominate them (number five).

The internal goal of the resulting informal organization was to regulate and control the behavior of its members. The external goal was to protect the men from outside interference by management. As long as everyone adhered to the norms developed by the informal organization, the group would be left alone. Thus, behavior was a function of group norms. The men attempted to make the observer and interviewer believe that a fear of things such as working themselves out of a job, management's raising of standards, or protection of slower workers were the real reasons for limiting output. However, analysis revealed these to be mere rationalizations for their behavior. The men employed, to use Taylor's term, "systematic soldiering" because it affirmed the sentiments and norms to which they subscribed.

[18]Roethlisberger and Dickson, *op. cit.*, p. 522.
[19]George C. Homans, *The Human Group* (New York: Harcourt, Brace & World, Inc., 1950), p. 79.

**Findings and
Implications
of Hawthorne**

There is no doubt that the Hawthorne studies constituted the single most important foundation for the behavioral approach to management. The conclusions drawn were many and varied.

Elimination of Mental Revery. In Mayo's opinion, one of the major explanations of the results rested with the elimination of what he earlier called "pessimistic revery." However, based on the findings of the Hawthorne studies, he now realized that rest pauses or changes in the work environment did not, of themselves, overcome this problem. Rather, the key was to be found in the reorganization of the workers. In the case of the textile mill, for example, when the president gave the men control over the rest pauses, he transformed a group of "solitaries" into a well-knit unit by restructuring the social network. Likewise, in the case of Hawthorne, in Mayo's own words:

*The restructuring
of the social net-
work was more
important than
rest periods.*

. . . What the company actually did for the group was to reconstruct entirely its whole industrial situation. . . . The consequence was that there was a period during which the individual workers and the group had to re-adapt themselves to a new industrial milieu, a milieu in which their own self-determination and their social well-being ranked first and work was incidental. . . .

. . . The Western Electric experiment was primarily directed not to the external condition but to the inner organization. By strengthening the "temperamental" inner equilibrium of the workers, the company enabled them to achieve a mental "steady state" which offered a high resistance to a variety of external conditions.[20]

Thus Mayo realized that the results were caused not by scientific management practices (rest periods) but by socio-psychological phenomena (restructuring of social networks).

Hawthorne Effect. A second finding, and probably the most widely cited, is that of the "Hawthorne effect." By this is meant that novelty or interest in a new situation leads, at least initially, to positive results. Applying this concept to the increase in productivity in the relay room, many modern psychologists contend that it was not the changes in the rest pauses that led to increased output but the fact that the girls liked the new situation in which they were considered to be important. The attention lavished on them led them to increase their output. The Hawthorne effect seemed to lead to the decline in revery, but when investigated further, it appears not to have been the only factor involved.

*The novelty of
the situation was
important.*

Supervisory Climate. Luthans[21] points out that not all groups in the study evidenced productivity increases. The girls in the relay assembly test room did more work than ever before, but the men in the bank wiring room restricted their output. Thus,

*The style of
supervision was
another critical
factor.*

[20]Elton Mayo, *The Human Problems of an Industrial Civilization* (New York: The Macmillan Co., 1933), pp. 70–72.
[21]Fred Luthans, *Organizational Behavior* (New York: McGraw-Hill Book Company, 1973), p. 29.

there must be more than a mere Hawthorne effect and the resulting decline in pessimistic revery. In fact, when the girls were asked why they liked working in the test room better than the regular department, they gave the following reasons:

1. the small group
2. the type of supervision
3. earnings
4. novelty of the situation
5. interest in the experiment
6. attention given by officials and investigators[22]

The last three of these reasons represent what might be called Hawthorne effect results; the first three do not.

What, then, accounted for the difference in output between the two rooms? Applying the first three responses of the girls to the relay and bank wiring room, it should be recalled that both were small, cohesive units working on an incentive basis. Thus, the major difference may well have been the *type of supervision*. In the relay room the observer took over some of the supervisory functions, but in a very lenient manner. In the bank wiring room, however, the regular supervisors were used to maintain order and control. The observer was relegated to a minor role, having none of the authority of his relay room counterpart.

This particular finding downplays the "Hawthorne effect," which has probably been overemphasized for far too long. As C. E. Turner, a consultant to the studies, has stated:

We at first thought that the *novelty* of test room conditions might be partly responsible for increased output but the continuing increase in production over a 4-year period suggests that it was not of great importance.[23]

This same basic finding was substantiated by Mayo himself who, in his original analysis of supervision and productivity in the relay room, noted:

. . . getting closer supervision than ever before, the change is in the quality of the supervision. This—the change in quality of supervision—is by no means the whole change, but it is an important part of it.[24]

The Light From Hawthorne.　The illumination experiment at Hawthorne served to "light the way" for the human relations research that was to follow. Mayo and his colleagues from Harvard, as well as representatives of the company who participated in the studies, deserve a great deal of credit. There were times when the results were so baffling that the average researcher

---

[22]C. E. Turner, "Test Room Studies in Employee Effectiveness," *American Journal of Public Health*, June 1933, p. 583.
[23]*Ibid.*
[24]Mayo, *op. cit.*, p. 75.

would have thrown up his hands in disgust and walked away. There were other times, such as in the illumination and relay room experiments, when tests were reconducted because some independent variable had not been considered in the initial design. It was difficult for the investigators, in the early days of the human relations movement, but they persevered and, as a result, two important milestones were reached.

First, important insights into individual and group behavior were uncovered. The researchers had no illusions about the amount of work to be done. There was still much more to do, but a start had been made. Second, attention was focused on the supervisory climate, providing an impetus for later research on leadership style.[25]

SUMMARY

The scientific managers were interested in making changes in the work environment that would result in increased output. The classical management theorists concerned themselves with the study of effective management principles, whereas those with a behavioral interest, such as Barnard, attempted to add a human dimension to this analysis. At the same time, there were others who were conducting formal human behavior research. One of these was Hugo Münsterberg, a psychologist, who provided the impetus for the development of industrial psychology. Another of these individuals was Elton Mayo, a sociologist who conducted studies that provided insights into the norms and values of work groups.

The next chapter will take the material in these last three chapters, scientific management, management theory and the human element in the work place, and examine them in perspective. In this way, the stage will be set for a discussion of modern management theory and practice in Part II.

REVIEW AND STUDY QUESTIONS

1. Why is Hugo Münsterberg known as the Father of Industrial Psychology?

2. In what way can vocational testing be of value to the manager?

3. How did Münsterberg screen out the fit from the unfit trolley operators?

[25]For example, there were the pioneering studies conducted by Ronald Lippett and Ralph K. White under Kurt Lewin at the University of Iowa. One of their most famous articles is Kurt Lewin, Ronald Lippett and Ralph K. White, "Patterns of Aggressive Behavior in Experimentally Created 'Social Climates,'" *The Journal of Social Psychology*, May 1939, pp. 271–276.

4. What were Münsterberg's major contributions to management? Explain.

5. How important were rest pauses in Mayo's mule spinning inquiry? What other factors were significant?

6. Did the Hawthorne researchers find any relationship between illumination and output? Explain.

7. Why did the output of the girls in the relay assembly test room increase? Give your reasoning.

8. Why did the men in the bank wiring room restrict their output? Explain.

9. What were the norms to which the workers in the bank wiring room subscribed? Identify and describe them.

10. Of what significance to management were the Hawthorne studies? Explain.

SELECTED REFERENCES

Drever, J. The Psychology of Industry. London: Methuen & Co., Ltd., 1921.

Edie, L. D. Practical Psychology for Business Executives. New York: H. W. Wilson Company, 1922.

Hartness, J. The Human Factor in Works Management. New York: McGraw-Hill Book Company, 1912.

Hollingworth, H. L., and A. T. Poffenberger. Applied Psychology. New York: D. Appleton and Company, 1918.

The Human Factor in Industrial Preparedness. Chicago: Western Efficiency Society, 1917.

Luthans, F. Organizational Behavior. New York: McGraw-Hill Book Company, 1973.

Münsterberg, H. Business Psychology. Chicago: LaSalle Extension University, 1915.

Münsterberg, H. Psychology and Industrial Efficiency. Boston: Houghton Mifflin Company, 1913.

Münsterberg, M. Hugo Münsterberg, His Life and Work. New York: D. Appleton and Company, 1922.

Myers, C. S. Mind and Work, New York: G. P. Putnam's Sons, 1921.

Roethlisberger, F. J., and W. J. Dickson. Management and the Worker. Cambridge, Mass.: Harvard University Press, 1939.

Rowntree, B. S. The Human Factor in Business. London: Longmans, Green & Co., Ltd., 1921.

CASE: A MATTER OF INTELLIGENCE

In industry today there are all sorts of tests that have been devised for screening job applicants. Some of these are designed to measure general intelligence. The following represent five simple illustrations of the types of questions often found on these tests:

1. Using the letters in the word Minneapolis, write as many four-letter words as you can in the next two minutes.

2. Which of the following words is nearest in meaning to the word gregarious?
   a. lethargic
   b. friendly
   c. rich
   d. amorous
   e. egregious

3. As quickly and accurately as possible, carry out the following arithmetic calculations:

$$799 \atop +842 \qquad\qquad 9007 \atop -6498 \qquad\qquad 429 \times 87 = \text{_____}$$
$$5460 \div 7 = \text{_____}$$

4. Which number should come next in the sequence of the following five numbers?

   10   14   13   17   16

   a. 18
   b. 20
   c. 15
   d. 12
   e. 17

5. Place an asterisk in front of the pair(s) of numbers below that are identical.

   a. 42444. . . .43444
   b. 51752. . . .51752
   c. 481333. . . .418333
   d. 224879. . . .244789
   e. 616616. . . .616166

Questions

1. Of what value to management are general intelligence exams? How can they help a company in the screening process?

2. There are also exams that have been devised to measure motor skills such as reaction time, manual dexterity and control precision. How can these be of value to a business firm?

3. Which of these types of exams, intelligence or motor skills, do you think would be used to screen people for managerial positions? Explain.

CASE: THE FIREFIGHTER

A fire recently broke out on the third floor of a machine shop on Long Island. According to a spokesman for the fire department, workers on the floor had apparently been throwing oily rags in the corner for three or four days and they had not been picked up by the maintenance crew. As a result, when a careless worker flipped a lighted cigarette butt onto the rags, they immediately ignited.

As soon as they saw the blaze, most of the workers on the floor vacated the premises and gathered out in the parking lot. However, it was at least 15 minutes before anyone turned in an alarm. This was done by Pedro Rodriguez, a new employee who was delivering some equipment to one of the work stations when he suddenly saw the blaze. Acting quickly, Pedro pulled the fire alarm and then raced to the wall for a fire extinguisher. When the firemen arrived they found the new employee vigorously fighting the blaze. Thanks to his assistance, the fire was quickly brought under control. The first fireman on the scene told management, "Without that guy's quick thinking, you might have lost the whole building. He managed to confine the fire to one small area until we could get here and put it out." A thankful management gave Pedro a $10-a-week salary increase and a check for $500. Most of the workers, however, did not share the management's point of view. Some of their remarks included:

That guy Rodriguez is an idiot. He could have gotten his tail burned off. And for what? A crummy $500 and a small raise.

My job around here is running a drill press. They don't pay me to fight fires or even to report them. It's not in my job description.

Six months later, Pedro quit the company. When asked why, he said, "I don't like working with these guys. Somehow we just don't get on."

Questions

1. Based on the data in this case, what conclusions can you draw about the norms and values of the workers? Do they have a code of expected behavior? What is it?

2. If you were told that there was a union in this shop, would that help explain the comments made by the workers? Would it be possible to draw any conclusions about worker-management relations? Explain.

3. Why did Pedro quit? Give your reasoning.

CASE: A BIG INFLUENCE

Department Two at Bibly Manufacturing was never noted for its productivity record; not before Mr. Bob Fesser showed up, that is. However, soon after Bob took over as departmental manager things began to turn around. The first noticeable change occurred in efficiency. Previously, Department Two had been operating at 73 per cent of productivity, but within six months of Bob's arrival, this figure rose to 96 per cent. In addition, the number of people who were leaving the department dropped dramatically from 17 per cent to 2 per cent; and the records department showed that Department Two had the lowest tardiness of any unit in the plant.

It was not long before these figures came to the attention of the vice president of manufacturing, Mr. Albert Silverstein. Mr. Silverstein was greatly impressed but, at the same time, apprehensive, for he was something of a cynic. The minute anything extraordinary happened he would want to know "how come?" And this was true not only for poor results but for good results as well. After all, he reasoned, anything that deviates significantly from the norm should be studied, and there is no such thing as a manager who gets good results without costing the company some money. By this Mr. Silverstein meant that many managers try to improve productivity by cracking the whip, and in the long run, this leads to poor morale and high labor turnover. In the case of Bob, however, Mr. Silverstein was even more interested, because he had achieved outstanding results without increasing labor turnover. The vice president decided to call in Bob's boss, Mr. Al Shermann, for a talk.

Al, I've asked you in because I've been looking over the latest productivity reports. I was particularly impressed with Department Two's results. What seems to be going on down there?

Quite frankly, Mr. Silverstein, I'm as surprised as you are. However, ever since we hired Bob Fesser, things have turned around.

Tell me about him. What type of fellow is he?

Well, he certainly is easy to get along with—a very personable guy. In addition, he's really interested in the men. He's been in to see me a number of times about various things such as working conditions and work procedures. Every time, he tells me what a good job the men are doing and how much they rely on him to carry the ball for them. In fact, of all my departmental managers, I think he's the one I'd go to bat for first. And I don't say that just because his productivity record is so good.

This intrigued Mr. Silverstein, but he was still not sure why Bob was doing so well. He therefore called in one of the supervisors from Department One, Pete Wharton, whom Mr. Silverstein had known since school days.

Pete, I'm interested in learning about Bob Fesser over in Department Two. Do you know anything about him?

Sure, he has the best productivity record in the plant.

Can you tell me why?

Well, I can tell you what his people say about him. They like him. It seems that Bob goes to bat for his men. He establishes a link between them and Mr. Shermann. The men feel if they really need something they can rely on him to get it for them, because he'll go to the boss and fight for it. There are other reasons as well, but I think that is the main one.

Questions

1. How important is it for a manager to go to bat for his men? Is this one of the norms the men use in judging their boss?

2. Would Bob have done well as a supervisor in the bank wiring observation room? Explain.

CASE: I'VE GOTTA BE FREE

Don Fallon was one of the star salesmen of a large national life insurance firm. In 1974 he sold well over $1.5 million in life insurance, and for the past ten years he had been the leading salesman in his office. As a result, when the office manager, Ken Richardson, decided to retire, the job was offered to Don. But Don turned it down. When asked why, he gave the following explanation:

What do I want with a job like that? Sure the pay is good and an office manager is guaranteed a salary, so I wouldn't have to worry about whether I'm going to sell $1.5 million in life insurance next year. But, on the positive side, I can probably not only make more money by staying in my current job, but I get a chance to do things my own way. For example, last month my wife and kids and I went off to the mountains for a week. For Christmas, we're all going to visit my parents in Florida for ten days. In addition to all this vacation time, I keep my own office hours. Some days I'm here at 7 a.m., other days I don't come in at all. Now if I were to take the office manager's job, I'd have to give up all this freedom and control over my job and follow a rigid schedule. I'd have to be in here from 8:30 a.m. until 5 p.m. That's not for me. I've got to be free to operate my own way.

Questions

1. How important is it for an individual to have some control over his work schedule?

2. If Don were forced to become the office manager, might he suffer from pessimistic revery? Explain.

3. Are there some jobs in which individuals cannot be allowed to choose their own hours? Give some illustrations. What can management do in these cases to keep morale high?

CHAPTER 5

EARLY MANAGEMENT THOUGHT IN PERSPECTIVE

GOALS OF THE CHAPTER

The scientific managers, early management theorists and human relations researchers all made significant contributions to management, and all were complementary to one another. Taylor and his associates conducted important time and motion study research in the 1880 to 1920 era. Then along came the early theorists in the years between 1915 and 1945, providing important information about the administrative side of management. Finally, from 1924 to 1955, there were the human relations researchers, who added a new level of sophistication to management thought. The goal of this chapter is to place these three groups in perspective, first by examining some of the weaknesses and shortcomings of each, and then by reviewing the positive side of their contributions. In particular, attention will focus on:

a. shortcomings of the scientific managers;
b. the deficiencies of the classical management theorists;
c. inadequacies of the human relations approach; and
d. a review of the positive side of the picture.

SCIENTIFIC MANAGEMENT SHORT-COMINGS

Although the scientific managers made many important contributions to management, much of their work reflects a very limited understanding of the human element in the work place. For example, most of them seriously believed that money was man's *prime* motivation. This belief resulted in the development of various incentive payment plans such as Taylor's differential piece rate; if the employee would work harder, he would earn more money. Such thinking led these traditionalists to view the worker as an "economic man."

Economic Man

The term "economic man" refers to a person who makes decisions that *maximize* his economic objectives. In the case of the worker, he is the individual willing to stay on the job from dawn until dusk in order to take home the greatest paycheck possible. Wage incentive plans are very important to him because they provide this economic opportunity.

Lacking a solid understanding of human behavior, the scientific managers were unable to comprehend why all the employees did not take advantage of any chance to maximize their income. For example, they would have been unable to understand why most of the workers in the bank wiring room were willing to restrict output, unless, of course, it was to protect their jobs. It never occurred to them that some people might be happy to earn a satisfactory amount of money, being "satisficers" rather than "maximizers." Simon has distinguished between these two types as follows:

Economic man selects the best available alternative.

> While economic man maximizes—selects the best alternative from among all those available to him; his cousin, whom we shall call administrative man, satisfices—looks for a course of action that is satisfactory or "good enough." Examples of satisficing criteria that are familiar enough to businessmen, if unfamiliar to most economists, are "share of market," "adequate profit," "fair price."[1]

The Irrationality of Rationalism

Man is a complex being.

A second shortcoming, complementary to the economic man theory, was their view of the worker as a totally rational human being who would weigh all alternative courses of action and then choose the one that would give him the greatest economic return. This thinking, of course, completely ignored any consideration of social factors. Furthermore, Blau notes, "To administer a social organization according to purely technical criteria of rationality is irrational, because it ignores the nonrational aspects of social conduct."[2] The term "complex" would have been much more appropriate than "economic," for there are many things, besides money, that motivate the worker.

The Black Box

The scientific managers could have overcome these problems if they had concerned themselves with what is called the "black box" concept. For example, if a company introduces a new incentive payment plan and productivity increases by 10 per cent, this can be diagrammed in the following way:

[1]Herbert A. Simon, *Administrative Behavior*, 2nd edition (New York: The Free Press, 1966), p. xxv.
[2]Peter M. Blau, *Bureaucracy in Modern Society* (New York: Random House Inc., 1956), p. 58.

FIGURE 5-1   Incentive Payment Plan Results

But *why* is there an increase in productivity? Is it brought about by the opportunity to earn more money? Is it caused by an increase in morale because the workers think management is interested in their well-being? Or is there a third, as yet undetermined, reason? As seen in Figure 5–2, the answer rests in the black box or *transformation process*, which takes place between the input and the output.

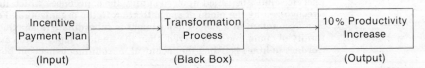

Incentive Payment Plan	→	Transformation Process	→	10% Productivity Increase
(Input)		(Black Box)		(Output)

FIGURE 5–2 The Transformation Process

The scientific managers did not analyze the transformation process.

An understanding of the human element requires an analysis of what goes on in this transformation process. The Hawthorne researchers attempted to study this process, by ascertaining, for example, why output increased in the relay room but did not increase in the bank wiring room. The scientific managers, however, were unconcerned with this line of thinking. They knew that workers produce more while working individually as opposed to working in groups, and they used this information to guide them in organizing their work force. Their basic approach to the management of people was simplistic, and they pursued the matter no further.

CLASSICAL MANAGEMENT DEFICIENCIES

The basic weakness of the classical theorists, especially Fayol, was that their writings on principles of management were often too general to be of much help to the practicing manager, as illustrated by the unity of command principle.

Unity of Command

As will be recalled, the unity of command principle states that everyone should have one, and only one, boss. Gulick, another of the classical theorists, has indicated quite clearly the importance that early management theorists assigned to this principle.

The significance of this principle in the process of co-ordination and organization must not be lost sight of. In building a structure of co-ordination, it is often tempting to set up more than one boss for a man who is doing work which has more than one relationship. Even as great a philosopher of management as Taylor fell into this error in setting up separate foremen to deal with machinery, with materials, with speed, etc., each with the power of giving orders directly to the individual workman. The rigid adherence to the principle of unity of command may have its absurdities; these are, however, unimportant in comparison with the certainty of confusion, inefficiency, and irresponsibility which arise from the violation of the principle.[3]

[3]Luther Gulick, "Notes on the Theory of Organization," as in Luther Gulick and L. Urwick, eds., *Papers on the Science of Administration* (New York: Institute of Public Administration, 1937), p. 9.

However, this principle seems to conflict with another, namely, that of specialization (or division of labor), which states that efficiency will be increased if one task is divided among members of a group. Simon notes:

> ... if unity of command, in Gulick's sense, is observed, the decisions of a person at any point in the administrative hierarchy are subject to influence through only one channel of authority; and if his decisions are of a kind that requires expertise in more than one field of knowledge, then advisory and informational services must be relied upon to supply those premises which lie in a field not recognized by the mode of specialization in the organization. For example, if an accountant in a school department is subordinate to an educator, and if unity of command is observed, then the finance department cannot issue direct orders to him regarding the technical, accounting aspects of his work.[4]

Unity of command is considered too inflexible a principle.

In short, if unity of command were to be as vigorously enforced as Gulick suggested, specialization would be impeded. Realistically, it is necessary to introduce some flexibility into the interpretation of the principle. In so doing, however, other problems arise, for now the principle lacks some of its previous "authority" and may be less useful in solving administrative problems. An analysis of the span of control principle makes this even more clear.

Span of Control

Span of control refers to the number of individuals who report to a given superior. The principle states that a superior can handle only a limited number of subordinates effectively. Credit for its formulation is given to Sir Ian Hamilton, commander of the British forces during the battle of Gallipoli in World War I. Hamilton believed that the "right" span of control was between three and six, the number declining as one moves up the organizational hierarchy. The number varied among classical theorists, but most contended that the span should be no greater than nine.

The span of control principle offers little operative assistance.

Although this is an interesting idea, and its implications for organization will be discussed in a later chapter, it really provides little operative assistance to the manager. For example, in an organization with ten thousand people, if each manager has three subordinates, there will be seven levels in the hierarchy. Conversely, if each manager were to increase his span to ten, the number of levels could be reduced to four and the vertical flow of communication throughout the structure greatly enhanced. But which is best, a span of three or a span of ten? The principle as stated offers little assistance.

The Problem with Principles

The classical theorists who enumerated these lists of principles attempted to make management more of a science and less of an art. Although this was an admirable objective, in the process

---

[1]Simon, *op. cit.*, pp. 23–24.

they built a rigidity into some of the principles, such as unity of command; in the case of others, such as span of control, they employed a superficiality.

Thus, close analysis of classical principles reflects many short-comings. Overly mechanistic and nebulous, they dealt with authority, responsibility and span of control as concepts. However, when managers attempted to apply these ideas to the organizational structure, the outcome was far from satisfactory.

INADEQUACY OF THE HUMAN RELATIONS APPROACH

The Hawthorne studies had a significant impact on management thought. For one thing, they complemented the work of the traditionalists. This is clearly seen in Figure 5–3, in which the contributions from Taylor, Fayol and Mayo are applied to an organization chart. Taylor did the majority of his work at the foreman-worker level; Fayol's contribution came at the administrative management level; the Hawthorne studies cut across the entire spectrum, providing information that was valuable to management at all levels. However, there were a number of problems with the studies and the resulting human relations movement.

The Scientific Method and Hawthorne

One of the major criticisms of the human relations approach is directed at the very heart of the movement: some researchers claim that the Hawthorne studies were *not sufficiently scientific*. These critics contend that the researchers brought preconceived ideas and biases with them that affected their interpretation of the results. There are others who contend that the evidence that

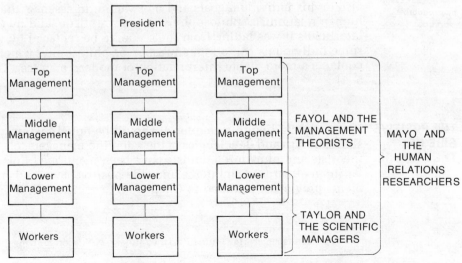

FIGURE 5–3 Contributions to Management Thought

*The research pro-
cedure is criti-
cized.*

supported the conclusions was just plain flimsy. Landsberger, in *Hawthorne Revisited*[5], criticized the studies further, contending that the plant was not really typical, because it was a thoroughly unpleasant place in which to work; the researchers accepted management's objectives, viewing the worker as a mere means for attaining these goals; and the researchers gave inadequate attention to the personal attitudes people brought with them to the job, overlooking the effect of the unions and other extra-plant forces.

The Human Relations Philosophy

Another criticism of the human relations movement is directed at its very philosophy, which Megginson has summarized in the following way:

This philosophy held that the business organization was a social system and that the employees were largely motivated and controlled by the human relationships in that system. Thus, the emphasis changed from an economic view of employees, in which the purpose of their productivity was to maximize the profit of the firm, to one of organizing and manipulating the human relationships among personnel so that employees would receive the greatest personal satisfaction from their working environment.

The basic assumption of the human relations approach was that the goal of human administration should be to provide the workers with job satisfaction. It was believed that employee participation should be obtained in order to produce job satisfaction and to improve employee morale. The assumption behind this belief was that greater job satisfaction would result in greater productivity. These cause and effect relationships — employee participation → job satisfaction, and job satisfaction → increased productivity — were the essence of the human relations philosophy.[6]

*Happy workers
are not necessar-
ily productive
workers.*

However, recent research challenges this concept that "happy workers are productive workers." Actually, job satisfaction is a multi-dimensional variable, impossible to explain in such simplistic terms. Output depends not only on a person's morale but also on his individual goals and motivation. In essence, the human relationists' philosophy was too simplistic, and by the late 1950's it was fading from the scene, to be replaced by what some individuals call a human resources philosophy, which contains a more viable interpretation of modern man (see Table 5-1).

THE POSITIVE SIDE OF THE PICTURE

Before concluding this chapter, it should be noted that only the shortcomings and deficiencies of the scientific managers, classical theorists and human relationists have been mentioned thus far in an attempt to counterbalance the positive accomplishments previously outlined in Chapters 2 to 4. After all, if one is

---

[5]Henry A. Landsberger, *Hawthorne Revisited* (Ithaca, N.Y.: Cornell University Press, 1958).
[6]Leon C. Megginson, *Personnel: A Behavioral Approach to Administration* (Homewood, Ill.: Richard D. Irwin, 1972), p. 7.

TABLE 5-1 Partial Comparison of Human Relations Philosophy
with Human Resources Philosophy

Human Relations	Human Resources
1. People need to be liked, to be respected and to belong.	1. In addition to wanting to be liked, respected and needed, most people want to contribute to the accomplishment of worthwhile objectives.
2. The manager's basic job is to make each employee believe that he is part of the departmental team.	2. The manager's basic job is to create an environment in which subordinates can contribute their full range of talents to the attainment of organizational goals. In so doing, he must attempt to uncover and tap their creative resources.
3. The manager should be willing to explain his plans to his subordinates and discuss any objections they might have. On routine matters, he should encourage participation by them in the planning and decision-making process.	3. The manager should allow participation in important matters as well as routine ones. In fact, the more important the decision, the more vigorously he should attempt to involve his subordinates.
4. Within narrow limits, individuals and groups should be permitted to exercise self-direction and self-control in carrying out plans.	4. The manager should continually try to expand his subordinates' use of self-control and self-direction, especially as they develop and demonstrate increased insight and ability.
5. Involving subordinates in the communication and decision-making process will help them in satisfying their needs for belonging and individual recognition.	5. As the manager makes use of his subordinates' experiences, insights and creative abilities, the overall quality of decision making and performance will improve.
6. High morale and reduced resistance to formal authority may lead to improved performance. They should at least reduce intradepartmental friction and make the manager's job easier.	6. Employee satisfaction is brought about by improved performance and the chance to contribute creatively to this improvement.

Adpated from Raymond E. Miles, "Human Relations or Human Resources?"
Harvard Business Review, July–August 1965, p. 151.

to see these groups in proper perspective, he must examine the weaknesses as well as the strengths.

Yet it would be unfair not to give credit to these three groups for their accomplishments. Certainly they made mistakes, but they were breaking new ground, and many of the facts known to us today remained mysteries to them. Yet they persisted, gathering information that proved useful. The scientific management pioneers helped American industry reach new heights of efficiency. Contributions from the early management theorists have helped train executives in the principles of planning, organizing and controlling. Human relations research provided important insights into human behavior in the work environment. It was noted, for example, that Mayo's early research in the textile mill resulted in some important physiological-psychological findings. By the mid-1940's, as more research was completed, however, he was able to reassess his earlier conclusions and formulate some new theories about the workers. One of these concerned the rabble hypothesis.

Mayo's Philosophy Revisited

The *rabble hypothesis* holds that workers are a disorganized group of individuals, each acting in his own self-interest. Management's goal is to show each worker that this self-interest is best served when he conducts himself in the manner desired by the company. This, of course, was the very approach subscribed to by Taylor.

The rabble hypothesis is invalid.

Mayo concluded that this hypothesis was invalid, because the individual does not operate independently. Rather, his actions are fashioned, at least in part, by the work group; the other members have a collective influence on him. That is one reason why, for example, technology and changing conditions are often viewed negatively by the workers. These conditions disturb the cohesiveness that exists among the members. The result is often a disequilibrium, manifested by complaints about supervision and working conditions. The individual becomes dissatisfied because the group's unity is under attack.

When this occurs, Mayo noted, there are three basic types of responses an individual can make. First, there is the *logical* response, wherein the individual uses discrimination and individual judgment. Second, there is the *nonlogical* response, which is a result not of deliberation, but of social conditioning. It is adequate in handling the situation, but it is a direct result of training according to a social code of behavior. Third, there is the *irrational* response, often employed by groups that face a situation they are unable to handle. They cannot reason their way through the problem, so a logical solution is out of the question. But their social training is inadequate to cope with the problem, so a nonlogical response is ineffective. This leaves only an irrational response, which is precisely the course of action they follow.[7] They have lost their capacity for disciplined cooperation.

An irrational response often occurs when an organization attempts to apply new knowledge to technical practice at too high a speed for general social adjustment. One of the most famous illustrations is found in the research study conducted by Trist and his associates, when they investigated the effects of changing technology on the nationalized coal mines in Great Britain.[8] Prior to World War I, the miners tended to work in small, independent teams. Each team was autonomous, and the individuals identified very strongly with their respective groups. New advances in technology and equipment, however, led to changes in the composition of the work groups. Under the new system, 40 to 50 people were placed in each group and were spread over an area of about 200 yards. This change in the work pattern impeded close interpersonal relationships and group identifications. As a result, productivity suffered. In an effort to rectify the situation, the management restored many of the social and small group relationships. In turn, productivity, morale and attendance improved substantially. Through this type of human relations study, the importance of factors such as group cohesiveness was recognized.

Technology can impede group cohesiveness.

Improved Research Design

Another benefit stemming from the work of these human relations pioneers was improved research design. Some of the early Hawthorne experiments, for example, were redone because the researchers realized they were not controlling some of the causal variables. Their concern with formulating an adequate research procedure has carried over to the present day, as reflected in the high degree of importance currently assigned to the scientific method as a research tool. Although there is no universally accepted method, there is general agreement as to the basic steps involved. They are the following:

Steps in the scientific method.

1. *Identify the problem.* **Precisely what is the objective of the entire investigation?**

2. *Obtain preliminary information.* **Gather as much available data as possible about the problem area. Obtain background information.**

3. *Pose a tentative solution to the problem.* **State a hypothesis, which can be be tested and proved to be either right or wrong, that is most likely to solve the problem.**

4. *Investigate the problem area.* **Using both available data and, if possible, information gathered through experimentation, examine the problem in its entirety.**

---

[7]Elton Mayo, *The Human Problems of An Industrial Civilization* (Cambridge, Mass.: Harvard University Press, 1946), pp. 157–158.
[8]E. L. Trist and K. W. Bamforth, "Some Social and Psychological Consequences of the Longwall Method of Coal-getting," *Human Relations*, February 1951, pp. 3–38.

5. *Classify the information.* **Take all the data that has been gathered and classify it in an order that expedites its use and helps establish a relationship with the hypothesis.**

6. *State a tentative answer to the problem.* **Draw a conclusion regarding the right answer to the problem.**

7. *Test the answer.* **Implement the solution. If it works, the problem is solved. If not, go back to step 3 and continue through the process again.**

The method is highly regarded by researchers. As Kerlinger notes:

> The scientific method has one characteristic that no other method of attaining knowledge has: self-correction. There are built-in checks all along the way to scientific knowledge. These checks are so conceived and used that they control and verify the scientist's activities and conclusions to the end of attaining dependable knowledge outside himself.[9]

The refinement of this procedure has played a key role in modern management.

SUMMARY

In perspective, all three groups, the scientific managers, the classical theorists and the human relationists, had shortcomings. Yet, it must also be realized that they complemented each other, helping to form the basis for modern management theory and practice. The efficiency goals of the scientific managers and classical theorists gave way to the human relations philosophy of treating people well, which in turn has been replaced, as seen in Figure 5–4, by a human resources philosophy of using people well.

With this chapter ends Part I of the book. By now, the reader has been well grounded in the important historical manage-

---

[9]Fred N. Kerlinger, *Foundations of Behavioral Research,* 2nd edition (New York: Holt, Rinehart, and Winston, Inc., 1973), p. 6.

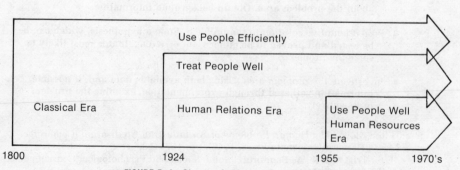

FIGURE 5–4   Changes in Managerial Philosophy

ment information he or she will need. The focus of attention will therefore be shifted to modern management theory and practice, answering questions such as Where is management thought today? What ever happened to the ideas espoused by Taylor? Are the concepts of Fayol still in vogue? What role are the behaviorists currently playing?

REVIEW AND STUDY QUESTIONS

1. What is meant by the term "economic man"?

2. In understanding human behavior, what is meant by the term "irrationality of rationalism"?

3. How is the transformation process useful in understanding human behavior?

4. What is the major argument often raised against classical management principles? Be specific in your answer.

5. Did the Hawthorne researchers use the scientific method? Explain.

6. What is some of the criticism directed toward the Hawthorne studies?

7. Is a happy worker a productive worker? Explain.

8. How does the human relations philosophy differ from the human resources philosophy?

9. What was Mayo's rabble hypothesis? Was it an accurate hypothesis?

10. What is the scientific method? Outline the steps in the process.

SELECTED REFERENCES

Anderson, B. F. *The Psychology Experiment: An Introduction to the Scientific Method*. Belmont, Calif.: Wadsworth Publishing, 1966.

Argyris, C. *Personality and Organization*. New York: Harper & Row, Publishers, 1957.

Dubin, R. *Human Relations in Administration*, 2nd edition. Englewood Cliffs, N.J.: Prentice-Hall, Inc., 1961.

Landsberger, H. A. *Hawthorne Revisited*. Ithaca, N.Y.: State School of Industrial and Labor Relations, Cornell University, 1958.

Mayo, E. *The Human Problems of an Industrial Civilization*. Cambridge, Mass.: Harvard University Press, 1946.

Simon, H. A. *Administrative Behavior*, 2nd edition. New York: The Free Press, 1965.

Shepard, J. M. "On Alex Carey's Radical Criticism of the Hawthorne Studies," *Academy of Management Journal*, March 1971, pp. 23–32.

Roethlisberger, F. J. *Management and Morale*. Cambridge, Mass.: Harvard University Press, 1941.

CASE: MY BOSS DOESN'T UNDERSTAND ME

Today, many workers feel that their superiors do not really understand them. Managers are accused of having very set, and very erroneous, ideas about how to handle their people. These include concepts such as people (a) dislike work; (b) have to be threatened with punishment to get them to attain organizational objectives; (c) lack ambition; (d) dislike responsibility; and (e) want to be told what to do. Does management really operate under these assumptions? Robert Townsend, former president of Avis Rent-a-Car, seems to think so. He summarizes the above five managerial assumptions like this:

1. **Office hours nine to five for everybody except the fattest cats at the top. Just a giant cheap time clock. (Are we buying brains or hours?)**

2. **Unilateral promotions. For more money and a bigger title I'm expected to jump at the chance of moving my family to New York City. I run away from the friends and a life style in Denver that have made me and my family happy and effective. (Organization comes first; individuals must sacrifice themselves to its demands.)**

3. **Hundreds of millions of dollars are spent annually "communicating" with employees. The message always boils down to: "Work hard, obey orders. We'll take care of you." (That message is obsolete by fifty years and wasn't very promising then.)**[1]

Questions

1. Did the scientific managers operate according to the above five managerial assumptions? Explain.

2. What have we learned from the Hawthorne research that shows that these assumptions are wrong? Explain.

3. What can management do to overcome these erroneous assumptions?

CASE: FOR A FEW DOLLARS MORE

A national manufacturing firm recently received a number of large orders for industrial equipment. Realizing that they would be unable to fill the orders unless a dramatic increase in output could be achieved, the company instituted an incentive plan to supplement the current hourly wage. Under this new program, all increases in productivity would result in direct pay increases of similar magnitude. For example:

Old Hourly Salary	Productivity Increase	Productivity Bonus	New Hourly Wage
$3.50	10%	$ .35	$3.85
$3.50	20%	$ .70	$4.20
$3.50	30%	$1.05	$4.55
$3.50	40%	$1.40	$4.90
$3.50	50%	$1.75	$5.25

[1]Robert Townsend, *Up the Organization* (Greenwood, Conn.: Fawcett Publications, Inc., 1971), p. 120.

In addition, the company was willing to apply the same incentive scheme for Saturday work, which paid time and a half, and Sunday work, which paid double time. Top management indicated that it was shooting for a 40 per cent increase in productivity across the board.

Within sixty days, however, it became evident to management that the plan was not working. On average, productivity was up only 17 per cent, and, despite all management efforts to promote weekend work, only 23 per cent of the workers were willing to work on Saturday and 14 per cent on Sunday.

One manager, in giving his opinion of the situation said, "What more do the workers want? Under this new pay scheme they can increase their salaries way above what they would ordinarily earn. However, most of the men I talked to say they're not interested in the extra money. One of them told me he spent the whole weekend working in his garden. Another took his kids fishing for two days. I just don't understand these guys. I guess the Protestant Ethic is dead. These guys would rather loaf than work."

One of the workers, however, gave a different reason for the less-than-expected productivity increases. "Who cares about the extra money?" he asked. "I'm making more than enough now. What am I going to do with an extra $2,000? Better that I stay home and enjoy my family and watch television on Sunday. I'm not going to knock myself out for a few dollars more."

Questions

1. Why is the incentive scheme having so little effect?

2. How would Frederick Taylor interpret the results?

3. What suggestions would you make to the management? Explain, incorporating into your answer the black box concept.

CASE: THE NEW ASSEMBLY TECHNIQUE

A consumer appliance firm recently brought in a consulting team to examine its operations. Everything had been going well, but the firm was interested in finding out if there were any changes the team could recommend that might further increase productivity. After analyzing assembly operations for a few days, the consultants suggested a change in the way a small household appliance was being put together. At present, there were five major parts to the item. These were placed on tables next to each of five female assemblers. Each would assemble their part and pass the appliance to the next person. The last assembler would place the finished product on a cart.

The consultants suggested a new technique. Instead of having each assembler perform one function on the apppliance, why not have each assemble an entire appliance? Of course, this would reduce specialization, but it would increase morale because the assembler would feel that the work was now more meaningful. The idea sounded fine to management and they ordered it implemented. To do this, a change in the work layout was necessary. Each of the assemblers was placed inside a table shaped like a horseshoe. On top of the table were all the parts to be assembled.

For the next six weeks, management watched the productivity from these workers. At the end of this period, output was 67 per cent of what it had been when the assemblers worked as a team. The company therefore decided to have the supervisor ask the workers if they wanted to go back to the old method. All agreed that they did. When asked why, one of the women said, "I just work better in a group." Another remarked, "I miss the old way of assembling these appliances. Sure, I like the feeling I get from putting together an entire product by myself, but not as much as I do being part of our assembly team. We've got a good working relationship, and I'd like to keep things that way."

Questions

1. Specifically, why did output decline under the new assembly method?

2. In your view, what do the women like best about the old assembly method?

3. In light of your above answers, how can technology negatively affect output?

CASE: USE ME WELL

Not long ago, a New York based firm decided to open an office in Paris. Many of the firm's international customers were located in France, and the company felt it could provide better service to these people if it had a representative stationed nearby.

There were a number of people in the company who seemed to have both the desire and the necessary prerequisites to head up the office. One of these was Ben Milton, who had been with the company for ten years and had an excellent working knowledge of the firm's operations. In hopes of being appointed to the foreign office, Ben went in and talked to his superior, Dick Allen. However, Dick tried to discourage him from taking the job. "What do you want to go to Paris for?" he asked. "There's going to be plenty of work over there, and with the currency exchange problems you'd probably wind up making less money than if you just stayed home. Believe me, it's going to be a thankless job. Besides, don't you like it here? Don't we treat you well?" Ben admitted that they did, but he was, nevertheless, interested in the overseas position and said he would appreciate any help Dick could give him.

A few weeks later the decision was announced. A younger man who had been with the firm for five years was given the job. Two weeks later, Dick went on vacation for a month. When he returned, much to his surprise, he found a letter of resignation on his desk. Ben Milton had left the company a week before. One part of his letter read, "I feel that I am not being used to the best of my ability. I have therefore decided to take a position where I can employ my talents to the fullest." Some time later Dick heard that Ben was managing an office in Brussels for one of the company's competitors.

Questions

1. What was Ben looking for in his job that he did not find?

2. Why was Dick surprised to learn that Ben had resigned?

3. What basic error did Dick make in handling Ben's request? How does it relate to the human resources philosophy?

PART II

MODERN MANAGE-MENT THEORY AND PRACTICE

In this part of the book, modern management theory and practice will be examinèd. Part II is divided into five sections, A
through E. The first, which encompasses Chapter 6, will outline the three schools of management thought that are currently
the most popular. Then, having set the stage, the next three
sections, Chapters 7 through 14, will review the basic ideas
and concepts subscribed to by members of these schools.
Finally, the last section, consisting of Chapter 15, will address
itself to the current status and future direction of management
theory. In particular, the issue of synthesizing the three schools
into one will be examined.

The major goals of Part II are to acquaint the reader with modern management theory by providing a framework within which
to analyze the area and to familiarize him with effective management practices. The ideas and concepts in this part of the
book form the foundation of effective management. By the end
of Chapter 15, the reader should have a good understanding
of both how management has developed since the days of the
early Hawthorne research and where it is going. In addition,
he should have gathered together useful information on some
of the most basic and most current management tools and techniques.

The Development of Modern Management Theory

In this section the development of modern management theory will be reviewed. It will be remembered from Part I that there were many people who made contributions to early management thought. Some of these, such as Henri Fayol, attempted to put together a framework within which management could be analyzed. Others, such as Taylor and his associates, emphasized time and motion study. Still others were concerned with the socio-psychological side of the job, as seen in the case of Mayo and his associates. What ever happened to these ideas? The answer is, they are still with us today, although in modified form. In Chapter 6 it will be seen that the concepts of these three groups have contributed to the formation of modern schools of management thought. The goal of Chapter 6 is to provide a framework within which the reader can understand these current developments.

CHAPTER 6

MODERN SCHOOLS OF MANAGEMENT THOUGHT

GOALS OF THE CHAPTER

Since World War II, a great deal of management research has been conducted. The concepts of Taylor, Fayol, Mayo and their associates have been expanded in an attempt to provide increased knowledge about the field of management. The result has been that, at least at the present time, management theory is in the "schools" phase, and any student who approaches the field without a basic understanding of these schools does so at a considerable disadvantage.

These schools represent viewpoints regarding what management is and how it should be studied. Of course, not everyone in management can be placed in a particular school; some defy such simple categorization. Nevertheless, the background and training of management theorists and practitioners is reflected in their beliefs about management and, in most cases, make them candidates for one of the three schools of thought that will be examined in this chapter. The first is the management process school; the second, the quantitative school; the third, the behavioral school.

Today, these three schools represent the most prominent trends in management thought, although they certainly are not universally accepted. For example, authors such as Koontz and O'Donnell list seven schools of thought: (a) management process, (b) empirical, (c) human behavior, (d) social system, (e) decision theory, (f) communications center and (g) mathematical.[1] Others, such as Miner, opt for five: (a) classical, (b) human

---

[1] Harold Koontz and Cyril O'Donnell, *Principles of Management: An Analysis of Managerial Functions*, 5th edition (New York: McGraw-Hill Book Company, 1972), p. 35.

relations, (c) structuralist, (d) behavioral humanist and (e) decision making.[2] Nevertheless, the three that will be discussed in this chapter encompass virtually all the ideas put forth by these other authors and provide a general picture of management theory as it currently exists.

The goals of this chapter are to examine these three schools in depth. Particular attention will be focused on:

a. the basic beliefs and tenets of the management process school;
b. the ideas to which advocates of the quantitative school subscribe;
c. the composition and philosophy of the behavioral school;
d. the weaknesses present in each of the schools; and
e. the possibility of synthesizing the three into a unified composite.

MANAGEMENT PROCESS SCHOOL

The management process, or classical, school traces its ancestry to Fayol. The primary approach used by this school is to identify the managerial functions. It will be remembered that Fayol identified them as planning, organizing, commanding, coordinating and controlling. Proponents of this school view these functions as a process that is carried out by the manager.

During the years immediately following World War II, this school grew and flourished. The major reason for its acceptance can be traced to the basic framework it provides for the systematic study of management. By identifying management functions and then examining each in detail, a student is provided with a wealth of information about the field. Although modern management scientists (quantitative theorists) and behaviorists might take issue with this statement, some of the most prominent books in the field have been based on a process framework. Table 6–1 presents Fayol's management process followed by those of nine other current textbook authors or co-authors. As seen in the table, there is universal agreement regarding the functions of planning, organizing and controlling, whereas there appears to be disagreement about the others. However, many process school advocates place the blame on *semantics*. What one person calls motivating, another includes in his definition of organizing. If the functions were spelled out in detail, everyone would have the same list of subfunctions or activities.

An On-going Framework

Process approach provides a skeletal design.

A major tenet of the process school is that by analyzing management along functional lines, a framework can be constructed into which all new management concepts can be placed. A skeletal design emerges of, for example, planning, organizing and controlling. Any new mathematical or behavioral technique that can improve managerial performance will fall into one of these three functional areas. The result is an enduring

---

[2]John B. Miner, *Management Theory* (New York: The Macmillan Company, 1971), pp. 145–150.

TABLE 6–1   The Management Process As Seen By Various Authors*

Functions \ Authors	Fayol	Albers	Dale	Haimann & Scott	Hicks	Koontz & O'Donnell	Newman, Summer & Warren	Sisk	Terry	Voich & Wren
Planning	X	X	X	X	X	X	X	X	X	X
Creating					X					
Organizing	X	X	X	X	X	X	X	X	X	X
Commanding	X									
Staffing			X	X	X	X				
Motivating					X					
Directing		X	X			X				
Influencing				X						
Actuating									X	

	Communicating	Coordinating	Controlling	Innovating	Representing	Leading
		X	X			
			X	X	X	
			X			X
	X		X			X
			X	X	X	
			X			X
			X			

*Sources:

1. Henri Fayol, General and Industrial Management (London: Sir Isaac Pitman & Sons, Ltd., 1949).
2. Henry H. Albers, Management: The Basic Concepts (New York: John Wiley & Sons, 1972).
3. Ernest Dale, Management: Theory and Practice, 3rd edition, (New York: McGraw-Hill Book Company, 1973).
4. Theo Haimann, and William G. Scott, 2nd edition, Management in the Modern Organization (Boston: Houghton Mifflin Company, 1974).
5. Herbert G. Hicks, The Management of Organizations: A Systems and Human Resources Approach, 2nd edition (New York: McGraw-Hill Book Company, 1972).
6. Harold Koontz, and Cyril O'Donnell, Principles of Management: An Analysis of Managerial Functions, 5th edition (New York: McGraw-Hill Book Company, 1972).
7. William H. Newman, Charles E. Summer, and E. Kirby Warren, The Process of Management: Concepts, Behavior and Practice, 3rd edition (Englewood Cliffs, N.J.: Prentice-Hall, Inc., 1972).
8. Henry L. Sisk, Management and Organization, 2nd edition (Chicago: South-Western Publishing Company, 1973).
9. George Terry, Principles of Management, 6th edition (Homewood, Illinois: Richard D. Irwin, Inc., 1972).
10. Dan Voich, Jr., and Daniel A. Wren, Principles of Management: Resources and Systems (New York: The Ronald Press, 1968).

systematic design. Although this concept is under attack today, there is little doubt that the framework provided by the management process school has been the major reason for its acceptance by students and practitioners alike. As Terry points out, "the management process school offers a broad, easy-to-understand, conceptual framework of management."[3]

Management As a Process

Management is viewed as an interrelated functional process.

Management process proponents see the manager's job as a process of interrelated functions. For example, in the case of planning, organizing and controlling, Figure 6–1 does *not* represent management as a process because the functions follow in sequential order and there is only an indirect relationship between planning and controlling. Everything seems to be rigidly predetermined. Instead, Figure 6–2 is more accurate because it represents management as consisting of many *interrelated* functions, which are neither totally random nor rigidly predetermined. They are, instead, dynamic functions, each one playing an integral role in a larger picture, which consists of the integration of all the functions. The total is seen as being more than the sum of its parts.

Management Principles

Another belief of process school advocates is that management principles can be derived by means of an intellectual analysis of the managerial functions. By dividing the manager's job into its functional components, principles based upon each function can be extracted. For example, there is the *primacy of planning* principle, which states that, at least initially, planning precedes all other managerial functions. A manager must plan before he can organize and control. *Absoluteness of responsibility*, a principle of organizing, states that a manager cannot escape re-

---

[3]George Terry, *Principles of Management*, 6th edition (Homewood, Ill.: Richard D. Irwin, Inc., 1972), p. 89.

FIGURE 6–1   Noninterrelated Management Functions

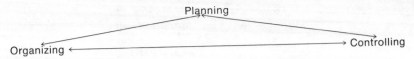

FIGURE 6-2　Interrelated Management Functions

sponsibility for the activities of his subordinates. He may delegate authority to his people, but he cannot delegate all the responsibility. If something goes wrong, he, as well as his subordinate, is responsible. A principle of control is the *exception principle*, which holds that a manager should concern himself with exceptional cases and not routine results. The reasoning is that significant deviations, such as very good or very bad profit performance, merit the manager's time far more than average or expected results.

Principles are used as general guidelines.

These principles are designed to improve organizational efficiency. They must *not*, however, be looked upon as rules, since a rule is supposed to be inflexible. For example, "no smoking" is a rule because it demands a certain kind of action and allows no deviations. Conversely, a principle, as used here, is merely a useful guideline and does not require rigid adherence. Advocates of the management process school, therefore, view principles as *general* guidelines that must remain constant focal points for research. If a particular principle proves invalid or useless, it should be discarded, but it must not be assumed that a principle will be useful at all times or under all conditions, or that a violation constitutes invalidation. Since management is an art as well as a science, the manager remains the final arbiter in choosing and applying these principles.

Universality of Management Functions

Advocates believe that management process is universal.

Process school advocates also believe that basic management functions are performed by all managers, regardless of enterprise, activity or hierarchical level. The manager of a manufacturing plant, the administrator of a hospital and the local chief of police all carry out the same managerial functions. This is also true for their subordinate managers all the way down the hierarchy, although the percentage of time devoted to each function will, of course, vary according to the level. For example, using planning, organizing and controlling as illustrations, low-level managers, who are concerned with detailed and routine types of work, tend to do more controlling and less planning and organizing. However, as one progresses up the organizational chain, the work requires more creativity and administrative ability, resulting in an increase in the amount of time needed for planning and a decrease in that required for controlling (see Figure 6-3).

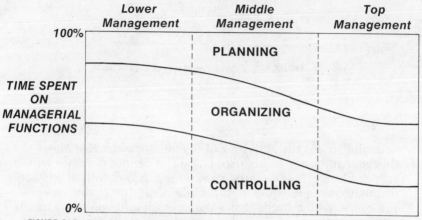

FIGURE 6-3   Functions Performed by Managers at Different Levels of the Hierarchy

**A Philosophy
of
Management**

The process school also stresses the development of a management philosophy. This requires answering questions such as:
Precisely what does a manager do? What kinds of values are
important to management? What values are important to the
workers? The development of a management philosophy results
in the establishment in the manager's mind of relationships
between material things and human beings. Process school
advocates believe that a manager can accomplish this feat more
easily if he follows the management process, because his activities revolve around certain functions, and in carrying them
out, he employs the fundamental beliefs and attitudes to which
he subscribes. The result is a *modus operandi* that links the
management process with the fundamental ideals, basic concepts and essential beliefs of the manager. The outcome is a
philosophy that helps the manager win the support of his subordinates in achieving organizational objectives. It also provides
him with a framework for future action.

*A philosophy of
management
can be devel-
oped.*

The process school has many advantages, the major one undoubtedly being the framework it offers for analyzing the field.
Although viewed by many of its critics as static and too simplistic to be useful, it has been better received by practitioners
and students than any of the other schools.

**QUANTITA-
TIVE SCHOOL**

The quantitative, or management science, school consists of
those theorists who see management as a system of mathematical models and processes. Proponents of this school are greatly
concerned with decision making and, to a large degree, are
modern-day adherents of Taylor's scientific management movement. A great deal of their attention is given to defining objectives and the problems that surround their achievement. This
type of orderly, logical methodology is very helpful in con-

structing the kinds of models needed for solving complex problems. Moreover, the approach has been very effective, as will be seen later in the book, in dealing with inventory, materials and production control problems.

In the post-World War II era, many management scientists appeared on the business scene. Today, they go by various and sundry titles, from management analysts to operations researchers to systems analysts. However, they share a number of common characteristics, namely: (a) the application of scientific analysis to managerial problems; (b) the goal of improving the manager's decision-making ability; (c) a high regard for economic effectiveness criteria; (d) a reliance on mathematical models; and (e) the utilization of electronic computers. For purposes of this discussion, all individuals meeting these criteria shall be collectively placed in the quantitative school. Two topic areas that have been of major interest to these people are optimization and suboptimization.

Management scientists share some common characteristics.

Optimization and Suboptimization

In Chapter 5, it was noted that most managers do not maximize their goals, they satisfice them. The manager does not try to make all the profit he can, but he does strive for a satisfactory level. There are times, however, when profit can be maximized through, for example, the *optimization* of production, i.e., the combining of all the resources in just the right balance. This is a very difficult task, and to attain it an approach called *suboptimization* is often used. In a production setting consisting of materials being ordered, processed and finished, for example, the firm would attempt to suboptimize each of these three components. Terry explains the process in this way:

Suppose our objective is to maximize production profits. To achieve this we optimize production. To this end, we suboptimize input, process, and output. Step number one: input, or raw materials being received, can be suboptimized and will depend upon forecast demand, inventory carrying cost, and order processing cost. Likewise, step number two: process, or materials processed, can be suboptimized independently by adequate consideration to production capacity, machine setup cost, and processing cost for each product. Lastly, number three: suboptimization of output, or products finished, is obtained by considering product demand and transportation cost. Thus by suboptimization of the production components, optimization of production is approached. The result is not a certainty because of inventory costs, but satisfactory results can be determined quite accurately.[4]

Each step in the production process (ordering, processing and finished goods) is affected by suboptimization factors (see Figure 6–4). The firm does not purchase all the raw materials it can; nor does it process or ship the maximum amount possible. Instead, it finds a balance that results in the ideal production level and the maximization of profit.

---

[4]*Ibid.*, p. 73.

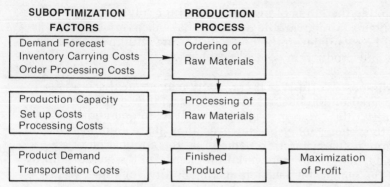

FIGURE 6-4 Optimization of Production and Maximization of Profit

Mathematical Models

Optimization of resources is often achieved with the use of a mathematical model. The model can be a single equation or a series of equations, depending upon the number of factors involved and the complexity of the situation. In the construction of these models, management scientists have found calculus to be one of the most useful branches of mathematics because it allows them to measure the rate of change in a dependent variable in relation to changes in an independent variable. For example, if a company increases the size of its plant and cost per unit declines, the management might be very interested in learning the extent to which the production facilities can be expanded before the cost per unit will begin to increase. If the firm has a mathematical model constructed for this purpose, it merely has to determine at what point the cost per unit change moves from negative to either zero or positive, for at this point costs stop decreasing.

Problem solving via mathematical models is widely employed.

The same basic concept can also be used by, for example, an appliance store manager who wants to know how many different product lines he should carry. Assume that he formulates the following mathematical equation, which, to the best of his knowledge, is accurate:

$$Y = 16\,X - X^2$$

where Y is equal to maximum profit and X is equal to the number of product lines carried. The equation states that maximum profit is equal to sixteen times the number of product lines (16X) minus the number of product lines squared ($-X^2$). By increasing the value of X, the respective values of Y can be attained. For example:

when $X = 0$
$\quad Y = 16 \times 0 - 0^2$
$\quad Y = 0$
when $X = 1$
$\quad Y = 16 \times 1 - 1^2$
$\quad Y = 15$

By constructing the entire table up to the point where Y again equals zero, it is possible to identify the entire range of positive profit values.

X	0	1	2	3	4	5	6	7	8	9	10	11	12	13	14	15	16
Y	0	15	28	39	48	55	60	63	64	63	60	55	48	39	28	15	0

Thus, the number of product lines that should be carried is eight, as this will result in a maximization of profit.

Overview and Contributions

Although highly simplified, the above mathematical model is representative of that employed by the management scientists. In fact, it is common to find adherents of this school relying strongly on mathematical tools and techniques such as linear programming, simulation, Monte Carlo theory, queuing theory and game theory, topics that will be covered in Chapter 11. The quantitative school has gained many supporters in recent years. The increasing use of computers accompanied by the development of more sophisticated mathematical models for use in the solution of business problems has accounted for many of the advances made by this school. In addition, it has played an important role in the development of management thought by encouraging people to approach problem solving in an orderly fashion, looking more carefully at problem inputs and relationships (see Figure 6–5). This school has also promoted the need for goal formulation and the measurement of performance.

BEHAVIORAL SCHOOL

The behavioral school grew out of the efforts of people such as Gantt and Münsterberg, who recognized the importance of the individual in the work place, as well as to others such as Mayo and Barnard. Today, it is common to find individuals in

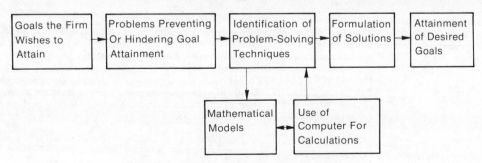

FIGURE 6–5   Problem Solving via a Quantitive Approach

this school with training in the social sciences, including psychology, sociology, anthropology, social psychology and industrial psychology, applying their skills to business problems.

Behavioral school proponents are largely concerned with, as one would expect, human behavior. They contend that because management entails getting things done through people, the effective manager must understand the importance of factors such as needs, drives, motivation, leadership, personality, behavior, work groups and the management of change; they are going to have a direct effect on the manager's ability to manage. Although all members of the behavioral school share this philosophy, some place emphasis on the individual, others on the group. The behavioral school, therefore, consists of two "branches": the human behavior branch and the social system branch.

Human Behavior

Some focus primarily on individual behavior.

Some behaviorists are very interested in interpersonal relations and are oriented toward individual and social psychology. They belong to the *human behavior branch* of the behavioral school.

Their focus is the individual and his motivations as a socio-psychological being. Their emphasis varies from those who see psychology as a necessary part of the manager's job—a tool to help him understand and get the best from people by responding to their needs and motivation—to those who use the psychological behavior of individuals and groups as the core of management.[5]

Members of this branch believe that the individual, not just the work group, must be understood if the manager is to do an effective job.

Social Systems

Others are highly sociological in their approach.

The other branch of the behavioral school, often confused with their human behavior cousins, consists of individuals who see management as a social system or collection of cultural interrelationships. Known collectively as the *social systems branch*, they are highly sociological in nature, viewing human organizations as systems of interdependent groups, primary and secondary alike.

The recognition of organized enterprise as a social organism, subject to all the pressures and conflicts of the cultural environment, has been helpful to both theorist and practicing manager. Among other helpful aspects are the awareness of the institutional foundations of organization authority, the influence of the informal organization, and such social factors as those Wight Bakke has called the "bonds of organization." Likewise. . . Barnard's insights . . .have brought the power of sociological understanding into the realm of management practice.[6]

---

[5]Koontz and O'Donnell, *op. cit.,* p. 38.
[6]*Ibid,* p. 39–40.

Advocates of the social systems branch see the manager as an individual who must interact with and deal with groups. For this reason, they place great emphasis on the need to understand both the formal and the informal organization.

Overview and Contributions

Although the human behavior branch stresses the importance of understanding the individual (psychology) and the social systems branch places prime importance on the knowledge of group behavior (sociology), the two are actually interdependent. The group is made up of individuals, but the whole is actually greater than the sum of its parts. Both psychology and sociology are important to the behaviorists regardless of the priorities assigned to each area.

Although the behavioral school lacks the type of framework used by management process advocates, it certainly does not lack structure. For example, communication, motivation and leadership, a few of the topics with which the school is concerned, are areas of major analysis. However, instead of working from functions to activities and principles as do the management process advocates, the behaviorists work in the opposite direction; they start with human behavior research and build up to topics or functions. Thus, theirs is a much less rigid and more empirically based school of thought. Wortman and Luthans have enumerated several major contributions made to the field of management by these behaviorists including:

Behaviorists are highly empirical in their approach.

(1) *conceptual*, the formulation of abstract concepts and explanations about human behavior in the organization; (2) *methodological*, the empirical testing of these concepts; and (3) *action*, the formulation of managerial policies and decisions based on these concepts and on research on human behavior. These contributions have led to an increasing acceptance by management of the behavioral approach.[7]

TOWARD A UNIFIED THEORY?

Is there really a legitimate basis for these three schools of management thought or should a synthesis be immediately undertaken? Many writers in the field believe a coalescence of the differing viewpoints can be achieved, but one of the key obstacles, in their view, is that of *semantics*; everyone is really saying the same thing, but they are using different words. One group of authors believes that "As is so often true when intelligent men differ in their interpretations of problems, some of the trouble lies in key words."[8]

There is still much disagreement.

Another major barrier is identified as differing *definitions of management*. If the field were clearly defined in terms of fairly specific content, differences between the various schools of

[7]Max S. Wortman, Jr., and Fred Luthans, eds., *Emerging Concepts in Management* (New York: The Macmillan Company, 1969), p. 160.
[8]Koontz and O'Donnell, *op. cit.*, p. 42.

management might be reduced to the point where a synthesis would be possible. Although the idea sounds plausible, the outlook at the present time is not good. One of the reasons is the current lack of research.

> The choice of a school or writer to follow presents a serious dilemma. . . . "I don't know" remains the appropriate answer. When sufficient research has been compiled, the schools will fade of their own accord. That they have not faded is good evidence that the quantity and quality of research to date is insufficient to render judgment.
>
> . . . No amount of argument between conflicting schools. . .is likely to achieve either consensus or truth.[9]

Advocates of each of the three schools believe strongly in their own point of view and resist attempts to be synthesized or integrated. For example, process school spokesmen have been vigorous in their attempts to bring the quantitative and behavioral people into their domain. However, the latter groups view their own contributions to management as much too significant to be relegated to the kind of secondary position being advocated for them by the process people. Nor are they necessarily wrong, for each of the three schools has its weaknesses as well as its strengths, and currently, no one of them possesses the characteristics necessary for a successful and meaningful, integration of management theory.

THE WEAKNESSES OF THE SCHOOLS

The process school, although the most widely accepted, at least for the teaching of basic management, is also subject to the most frequent attack.

Process School Weaknesses

A static approach?

One of the foremost arguments against the school is that it pays only lip service to the human element; actually, management is regarded as a very static and dehumanized process. Although its advocates argue that this is not the case at all, behaviorists in particular remain unswayed.

Are management principles universally applicable?

Many also attack the school's foundation, claiming that management principles are not universally applicable. They see them as being most appropriate in stable production line situations, where unions are not very strong or where unemployment is quite high. However, when used in professional organizations, the principles often require modification, their application being contingent upon the specific situation. This is why Fayol and his associates, who operated under stable production-line situations, were able to use them effectively, whereas modern managers, operating under dynamic conditions, have trouble

---

[9]Miner, *op. cit.*, p. 150.

doing so.[10] In addition, there is a tendency among principle proponents to formulate generalizations as principles even though they have not been empirically validated.

A third argument, along the same lines, centers on the universality of the management process. Do all managers perform the same basic functions? There is considerable controversy on this point. Research has revealed that although similarities exist between various positions within firms, the same is not true between firms. When professional[11] (law firms, research and development (R & D) laboratories, architectural firms, hospitals, universities) and administrative (manufacturing companies, retailing firms, insurance agencies, transportation companies) organizations are compared, studies have shown that the latter tend to be more bureaucratic, placing emphasis on rules, policies, procedures and hierarchical authority. Conversely, in professional organizations, this power and authority tends to shift from the managerial jobs to those of the nonmanaging professions.[12] For example, in hospitals, doctors sometimes have as much freedom to make decisions as do top administrators. Nurses often have more freedom of action or discretion in carrying out their tasks than do certain middle managers. When Bell measured the amount of discretion employed by occupational groups in an eastern hospital in carrying out their work assignments, as seen in Table 6–2, he found that the higher the degree of professional training, the greater the amount of discretion the employees exercised.[13]

Is management process universal?

Results such as these have led Miner to conclude that "when decision-making authority is dispersed. . .some very sizeable changes in managerial functions must occur, relative to administrative organizations.[14] He continues by noting that:

> . . . analysis of professional versus administrative organizations once again leads to the conclusion that managerial functions are not universal. Not only do managerial jobs differ in their mix of functions depending on their level and the particular department involved, but they also differ from organization

---

[10]*Ibid.*, pp. 139–140.

[11]As used here, professional organizations are those which: (a) are recognized by society as having professional status; (b) are encouraged and influenced by a professional association or society; and (c) have a set of specialized techniques supported by a body of theory. For further information on this point, the reader is directed to John B. Miner, *The Management Process: Theory, Research and Practice* (New York: The Macmillan Company, 1973), pp. 58–63.

[12]See Richard H. Hall, "Some Organizational Considerations in the Professional-Organizational Relationship," *Administrative Science Quarterly*, December 1967, pp. 461–478; and Gerald D. Bell, "Predictability of Work Demands and Professionalization as Determinants of Workers' Discretion," *Academy of Management Journal*, March 1966, pp. 20–28.

[13]Bell, *op. cit.*, p. 23.

[14]John B. Miner, *Management Theory, op. cit.*, p. 88.

TABLE 6–2   Occupations and Their Average Discretion Scores in a
            Professional Organization

Occupation	Average Discretion Score
Administrator	5.7
Doctor	5.6
Department head (nursing)	5.2
Department head (others)	5.4
Assistant department head (nursing)	4.9
Assistant department head (others)	5.0
Nurse (staff)	4.5
Dietary supervisor	3.7
Plumber, carpenter (semi-skilled worker)	3.2
Secretary	3.1
Pharmacist	3.0
Laboratory technician	3.0
Orderly	3.0
X-ray technician	2.3
Nurses' aide	2.2
Cook	2.0
Dietary helper	1.4
Housekeeper, launderer, etc.	1.3

Source: Gerald D. Bell, "Predictability of Work Demands and Professionalization as Determinants of Workers' Discretion," *Academy of Management
Journal*, March 1966, p. 23. Reprinted with permission.

to organization. **This interorganizational difference is particularly noticeable
when administrative and professional types are compared.**[15]

**Quantita-
tive School
Weaknesses**

The quantitative school is attacked on the grounds that it fails
to see the complete picture. Is management a system of mathematical models and processes or is this too narrow a view?
Critics opt for the latter, calling management science a tool and
not a school. They note that management is used in physics, engineering, chemistry and medicine, but it has never emerged
as a separate school in these disciplines. Why should it do so

*A tool or a
school?*

in the field of management? There is no doubt that the management sciences have supplied very useful tools for the manager to employ in solving complex problems. Inventory, material
and production control have all been facilitated thanks to these
quantitative contributors. However, what about human behavior? How does one write an equation that solves "people"
problems? Both the process and behavioral schools attack the
quantitative theorists on this point and they appear hard
pressed to refute the argument.

**Behavioral
School
Weaknesses**

The major argument lodged against the behaviorists is that they,
like the management science people, do not see the complete picture. Psychology, sociology and related areas are all

[15]*Ibid.*, p. 93.

important in the study of management, but there is more to the field than just human behavior; some forms of technical knowledge are also needed. The process school provides an important structural framework around which to study human behavior. The quantitative school offers an objective, quantifiable approach to decision making. Without these supplemental elements, the manager cannot adequately apply his knowledge of behavior.

Failure to see the complete picture?

To be an effective manager, one must have more than a mere working knowledge of the human, dynamic model. True, the people in the work place constitute a continually changing social system, and an understanding of man's nonrational behavior is needed to supplement the assumptions of rationality often attributed to workers by their superiors. However, argue the critics, the behavioral school is only one segment, albeit an important one, of the total picture, and in and of itself, incomplete.

A CONCEPTUAL FRAMEWORK

As noted earlier, at the present time there appears a need for further research if the three schools are ever to be synthesized. In addition, it should be realized that there are some who oppose any such action, contending that fundamental and inescapable differences exist among the various schools, making a unified theory of management impossible.

Whether or not the three schools will ever come together is a matter of current debate. However, the student of management is well advised to travel all three roads: process, quantitative and behavioral, for each makes important contributions to the study of management.

SUMMARY

The reader has now been introduced to the three basic schools of management thought that are currently in vogue. Each has some important concepts to contribute to management; each has some important weaknesses that have yet to be surmounted. And the overriding question remains: Can the three be systematically synthesized? This is a matter of current debate, which demands an in-depth examination of each school before an answer is attempted. The next eight chapters will be devoted to this task.

REVIEW AND STUDY QUESTIONS

1. What are the basic beliefs of management process school advocates?

2. How important are management principles to process school advocates?

3. Precisely what is meant by the term "universality of management functions"?

4. What background or training do management scientists have?

5. What is meant by the term optimization? Suboptimization?

6. What are some of the contributions made to management theory by the management scientists?

7. Identify the two major branches of the behavioral school. Describe both.

8. What contributions have the behaviorists made to management?

9. How would you identify the primary weaknesses of the process school? The quantitative school? The behavioral school?

10. Will the three schools of management ever be merged or synthesized? Give your reasoning.

SELECTED REFERENCES

Albers, H. H. *Principles of Management: A Modern Approach,* 4th edition. New York: John Wiley & Sons, Inc., 1974.

Brown, R. V. "Do Managers Find Decision Theory Useful?" *Harvard Business Review,* May–June 1970, pp. 78–89.

Elbing, A. O. *Behavioral Decisions in Organizations.* Glenview, Ill.: Scott, Foresman and Company, 1970.

Fayol, H. *General and Industrial Management,* trans. Constance Starrs. London: Sir Isaac Pitman & Sons, Ltd., 1949.

Kelly, J. *Organizational Behaviour.* Homewood, Ill.: Richard D. Irwin, Inc. and the Dorsey Press, 1969.

Koontz, H., ed. *Toward a Unified Theory of Management,* New York: McGraw-Hill Book Company, 1964.

Koontz, H. "The Management Theory Jungle," *Academy of Management Journal,* December 1961, pp. 174–188.

Koontz, H., and C. O'Donnell. *Principles of Management: An Analysis of Managerial Functions,* 5th edition. New York: McGraw-Hill Book Company, 1972.

Miller, D. W., and M. K. Starr. *The Structure of Human Decisions.* Englewood Cliffs, N.J.: Prentice-Hall, Inc., 1967.

Miner, J. B. *Management Theory.* New York: The Macmillan Co., 1971.

Miner, J. B. *The Management Process: Theory, Research, and Practice.* New York: The Macmillan Company, 1973.

Muse, W. V., "The Universality of Management," *Academy of Management Journal,* June 1967, pp. 179–184.

Richards, M. D., and P. S. Greenlaw. *Management Decision Making.* Homewood, Ill.: Richard D. Irwin, Inc., 1972.

Wadia, M. S. *Management and the Behavioral Sciences.* Boston: Allyn & Bacon, 1968.

Woolf, D. A. "The Management Theory Jungle Revisited," *Advanced Management Journal,* October 1965, pp. 6–15.

Wortman, M. S. Jr., and F. Luthans, eds. *Emerging Concepts in Management.* New York: The Macmillan Company, 1969.

CASE: THE MANAGER'S JOB

In gathering data for his term paper "The Functions of the Manager," Bill Wadsworth, a junior at a large eastern business school, decided to interview five executives, all from different organizations. To each he asked the same question, "In your view, what are the functions of a manager?" Some of the executives explained their answers at great length, others merely listed a lot of managerial functions. In either event, at the end of the interview Bill would review their comments and then tell them how he was going to summarize their answer. All agreed with his summation. The result of his five interviews was the following:

Functions	Manager 1	Manager 2	Manager 3	Manager 4	Manager 5
Planning	X	X	X	X	X
Organizing	X	X	X	X	X
Staffing			X		
Communicating		X			
Coordinating	X				
Motivating	X			X	
Directing			X		
Controlling	X	X	X	X	X

Questions

1. How do you account for the apparent discrepancies in the replies of the managers? Explain.

2. If you were told that one of these managers was from an insurance company and the others were from manufacturing firms, which of the above managers would you conclude to be the insurance man? Give your reasoning.

3. If you were told that one of the above five managers was a hospital administrator, which would you conclude to be the administrator? Give your reasoning.

CASE: THE ADVERTISING BUDGET

The importance of advertising was always something that Jay Hallen, owner of a large retail store, wondered about. In 1973 his store had an advertising budget of over $90,000, an increase of 17 per cent from the previous year, but Jay was really not sure how much of this money was being wisely spent. Nevertheless, he knew advertising was important, so he followed a simple guideline, spending 6 per cent of estimated sales for advertising.

In mid-1973 Jay received an announcement about a one-week management seminar being sponsored by a local university. Realizing that he had some middle-level managers who could profit from this training, he sent two of his up-and-coming people. When they returned, he learned that one of the speakers was a university professor who had talked about the need for constructing mathematical models for decision making purposes. One of the man's major points was that many companies spend more money on advertising than they should. However, unaware of where to draw the line, they continually spend more and more each year. In fact, he noted, a large percentage of firms tend to tie advertising to their sales forecast; i.e., if they estimate sales at $1 million, they spend $100,000; if they project sales at $2 million, they spend $200,000. "Actually," the speaker said, "this is a very simple, and generally erroneous, approach. The only way to really ascertain how much to spend on advertising is to measure previous expenditures and results."

Jay was unsure of exactly what the man meant, but he liked the basic idea, so he called the university and asked the professor if he would consider undertaking a consulting assignment. The professor agreed, and for the next week he examined the company's past sales figures and advertising expenditures and conducted some computer analysis. At the end of that time he concluded that advertising effectiveness could be determined with the following formula:

$$Y = 10 \times - x^2 + 50,000$$
where:
Y = total sales
x = total advertising expenditures/$10,000

Questions

1. Using just the above formula, how much sales income will the store obtain with advertising expenditures (per $10,000) from $10,000 to $110,000?

2. Based on the above answers, how much advertising should this company do? Explain.

3. How useful are management scientists in the field of management? Explain.

CASE: A STATE OF CONFUSION

"Bill," said Jack Tuner, training director at Willowby Insurance, "how would you like to attend a training session in New York City this coming week?"

What's it going to be about?

Since when have you gotten so particular? Usually, when the company intends to send a few people to a training session, you jump at it. I can remember that winter you talked me into sending you to Miami Beach. You were sure interested in going to seminars then.

Yeah, but that was when I only had a little work to do. Now I've got work piled up on my desk and I don't want to run off to just any old training session.

I wouldn't ask you to go to just any training session. Besides, you know that I'm only asking you to repay a favor. Anyway, do you want to go or not?

Tell me what it's going to be about.

It's called "Understanding Today's Worker."

Yeah, well thanks, but I'm not interested.

Why not?

Because the last time you sent me to one of those behavioral seminars I came away more confused than before. Look, a lot of research being conducted in the behavioral sciences is great research, but it has no real applicability. I mean, there is just no way to take it back to the job and use it.

You mean those people never tell you how you can apply it?

Oh no, they do that. The problem is that the way they explain it and the way it really works are two different things. In short, I really think I'm a lot better off just doing things my own way and not messing around with all these new behavioral theories. They just leave me all confused.

Questions

1. Have the behaviorists really made any contribution to management? Explain.

2. How important is it to understand today's worker?

3. What does Bill mean by his statement that behavioral seminars leave him confused? Explain.

CASE: ONE OUT OF THREE

A midwestern insurance company recently had an opening in one of its lower-middle management positions. After evaluating a number of possible candidates, the selection committee narrowed its list to three people.

The first candidate was a newly hired management trainee who had only recently received a master's degree in business from a large eastern university. The man's major area of study at the undergraduate level had been general management, whereas at the postgraduate level he had a concentration in management theory and insurance. Although the company liked the individual's general management background and felt his insurance courses provided him with some of the technical training he would need in supervising company personnel, some of the committee members were afraid that the man's background was too general. "We need someone with a little more background and training in this business," said one of the members.

The second individual being considered for the position was a salesman who, for the past two years, had been the leading salesman in his regional office. He did not want to remain a salesman for the rest of his life, so when he learned that the company was looking for a lower level middle-manager, he immediately applied for the job. On the positive side, the committee liked his track record. "This man has illustrated that he can deliver in the field," said one member. "This has seasoned him for the management ranks. After all, isn't a manager a salesman selling management's point of view to the employees?" On the negative side, however, some of the committee members were afraid that the man might be too interested in personal selling and its behavioral aspects and fail to see "the complete picture." One of them put it this way: "There's more to managing than just getting along with people."

The third person being considered for the job worked in the firm's actuarial department. He did fine technical work, and one committee member who felt this man would be ideal for the job remarked, "The backbone of an insurance company is its actuarial department. This fellow knows the ins and outs of insurance. This technical competence will help him do a good job." There was, however, concern that the man might be too used to working with numbers and not accustomed to managing people. "Technical skill is important," said one member, "but it's no substitute for handling people."

After discussing the three individuals for the better part of an hour, the chairman called for action. "Gentlemen, we have to make a decision on this matter today. Now we have a fair idea of the strong and weak points of each candidate. What do you say we choose one of the three and then adjourn for lunch?" Everyone agreed.

Questions

1. What characteristics of training would you look for in choosing from among the three candidates?

2. Which of the three candidates do you think would be most likely to be a management process advocate? A quantitative school supporter? A behavioral school advocate?

3. Based on your answer to the above question, which of the three would you choose for the job? Why?

The Management Process School

The goal of this section is to examine the tenets of the management process school. It should be noted that the province of this school is determined by the managerial functions placed within its sphere. In this section, three functions will be examined: planning, organizing and controlling. The reason for choosing these and no others is that virtually all management process advocates agree that the three are indeed within the realm of the process framework. Furthermore, many writers and researchers contend that the process school is less empirical and more philosophical than the quantitative or behavioral schools. This second criterion also favors the present choice.

Chapter 7 will be devoted exclusively to the planning process. In particular, attention will be focused on the need for comprehensive and strategic planning. Also, unavoidably crossing over into the behavioral school, the values of management in the planning process will be discussed. In addition, short-run or operational planning will be covered.

In Chapter 8, the organizing process will be reviewed. This chapter will present many of the "nuts-and-bolts ideas" involved in integrating the people with the structure. Some of the more important concepts will include: the various forms of departmentalization available to the manager; organization by committee; types of authority; and the need for understanding the informal organization.

Finally, in Chapter 9, the control function will be examined with prime attention given to the need for effective feedback and evaluation. Some of the topics that will be reviewed include budgeting, break-even analysis, key area control and management audits.

THE PLANNING PROCESS

GOALS OF THE CHAPTER

"If you don't know where you are going, any path will get you there," but when one has a goal, as businesses have, planning is essential. The goal of this chapter is to examine the planning process.

First, comprehensive planning will be discussed, followed by strategic, intermediate and operational planning. Finally, the advantages and limitations of planning will be reviewed. In particular, attention will be focused on:

a. the current trend toward comprehensive planning;
b. the three basic foundations of strategic planning;
c. management values and their effect on the planning process;
d. the manner in which a firm forecasts external environmental conditions;
e. the approach used in forecasting internal environmental conditions;
f. the importance of "developing a niche";
g. the way in which long- and intermediate-range objectives are determined;
h. the importance of operational planning;
i. the value of a planning organization to management; and
j. the advantages and limitations of planning.

COMPREHENSIVE PLANNING

Comprehensive planning incorporates all levels of the organization.

Modern businesses operate in a highly dynamic environment in which change is a constant factor. As a result, it has become more and more necessary for companies to determine their objectives carefully, and then systematically to construct plans for attaining them. This has become a continuous process throughout every organization. Naturally, as seen in Figure 7–1, managers at the upper levels should be greatly concerned with long-range or strategic planning, whereas the attention of those at the lower levels ought to be focused mainly on operational planning. Yet research indicates that some top managers have not been devoting requisite attention to long-range planning. Rather, they tend to spend most of their time worrying about short-

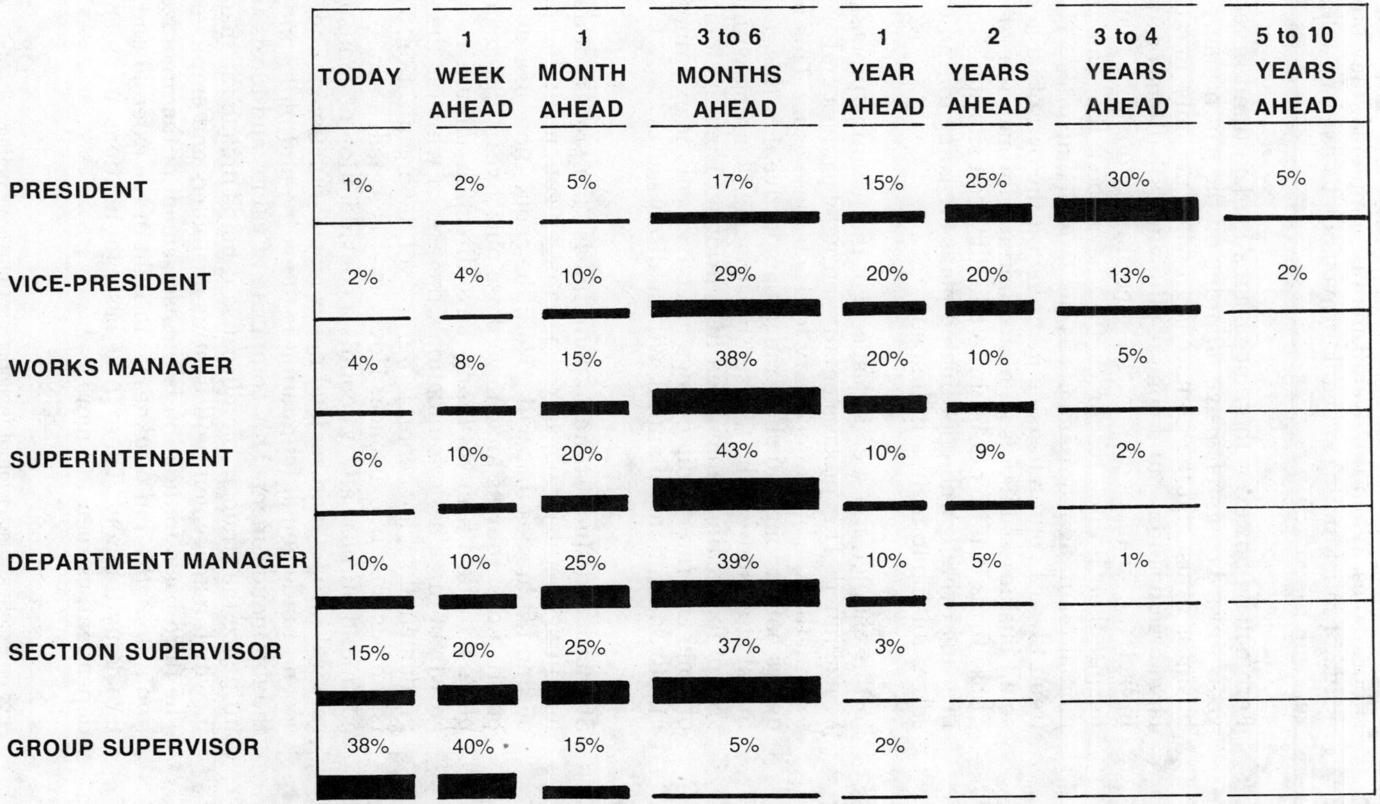

	TODAY	1 WEEK AHEAD	1 MONTH AHEAD	3 to 6 MONTHS AHEAD	1 YEAR AHEAD	2 YEARS AHEAD	3 to 4 YEARS AHEAD	5 to 10 YEARS AHEAD
PRESIDENT	1%	2%	5%	17%	15%	25%	30%	5%
VICE-PRESIDENT	2%	4%	10%	29%	20%	20%	13%	2%
WORKS MANAGER	4%	8%	15%	38%	20%	10%	5%	
SUPERINTENDENT	6%	10%	20%	43%	10%	9%	2%	
DEPARTMENT MANAGER	10%	10%	25%	39%	10%	5%	1%	
SECTION SUPERVISOR	15%	20%	25%	37%	3%			
GROUP SUPERVISOR	38%	40%	15%	5%	2%			

FIGURE 7-1 The Planning Process from a Hierarchical and Time-Span Perspective (From Ralph M. Besse, "Company Planning Must be Planned." Reprinted by special permission from DUN's April, 1957, p. 48. Copyright, 1957, Dun & Bradstreet Publications Corporation.)

run goals and performance results. In fact, it is not uncommon to find some chief operating executives who believe that comprehensive planning is something that can be delegated to their subordinates. When the overall plan is completed, they breathe a sigh of relief, noting, "Thank heavens that's over, now let's get back to work!"

Fortunately, however, there has been a marked trend in recent years toward *comprehensive planning* on the part of many business firms, and the number is growing, not only among large organizations but among medium and small ones as well. In fact, the smaller companies are beginning to realize that, despite their limited resources, they have about the same fundamental planning requirements as the larger companies.[1] This trend toward comprehensive planning on the part of large and small businesses alike is going to continue through the 70's. Those firms that do not begin to take the requisite steps toward insuring overall, well-coordinated plans are going to find themselves unable to maintain the pace.

In this chapter, the specific aspects of the planning process will be examined. This process entails setting objectives and formulating the steps necessary to reach these goals. This requires both a long and short-range perspective. For this reason, initial attention will be focused on strategic planning with the area of forecasting being given high priority. Then the topics of long- and intermediate-range objectives will be examined. Finally, operational planning will be discussed.

STRATEGIC PLANNING

Steiner has defined *strategic planning* as "the process of determining the major objectives of an organization and the policies and strategies that will govern the acquisition, use, and disposition of resources to achieve those objectives."[2] Strategic plans provide a firm with long-range direction and are an outgrowth of three basic foundations, the first of which is the fundamental *socio-economic purpose* of the organization: Why is the business in existence? However it is stated, a socio-economic purpose always entails a consideration of company survival (profits) and societal needs (social functions). The second fundamental foundation is the *value and philosophy of the top management*. This composite of values and ideals will influence the strategic plan because it helps dictate the manner in which management will treat its customers and employees. The third basic foundation is the assessment of the *organization's strengths and weaknesses* in light of the external and internal environment. These three basic foundations are interdependent, as seen in Figure 7–2.

---

[1]For an excellent discussion of this area see George A. Steiner, ed., *Managerial Long Range Planning* (New York: McGraw-Hill Book Company, 1963), p. 17.
[2]George Steiner, *Top Management Planning* (New York: The Macmillan Company, 1969), p. 34.

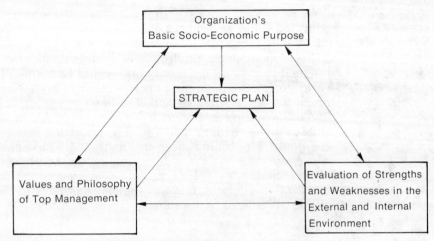

FIGURE 7-2 Basic Foundations of Strategic Plan

Basic Socio-economic Purpose

The basic purpose for existence must be identified.

More and more business firms are beginning to re-evaluate their purpose for existence. For example, years ago, when Henry Ford entered the automobile business, he saw his basic mission as one of providing people with a basic necessity—a form of transportation. People needed cars to get them places and he could provide these vehicles. General Motors broadened this idea, viewing the automobile as a luxury as well as a necessity. As a result, the firm offered the customer more extras and a wider line, albeit at a higher price, and replaced Ford as the number one automobile manufacturer. The nation's railroads have done the same, restating their purpose for existence so that they are no longer in the passenger-carrying business but in the transportation business. Today, almost all their profits are derived from the freight they carry. The movie industry has also redefined its basic mission and is no longer merely in the movie business; it is now in the business of informing as well as entertaining people. Unless an organization can define its socio-economic purpose, and redefine it as conditions change, it will lack a clear understanding of its basic mission and have great difficulty in constructing a strategic plan.

Management Values

In this decade, the area of social responsibility has received a tremendous amount of attention. Equal opportunity, ecology and consumerism have all become focal points for management consideration and action. Why did these issues rise to the fore? Part of the answer rests with external actions such as government legislation. However, even more significant (and generally overlooked) have been the social action programs proposed by businesses themselves. What led to such action? The answer rests in the values and beliefs of the top management.

Every manager in the organization brings a certain set of values to the work place with him, and every generation tends to have

Management values will influence the strategic plan.

differing values. The basic profile of the 1950 manager is different from that of the 1970 executive, and the manager of the 1980's will have still different values. In the late 1960's, General Electric's Business Environment Section conducted a study designed to explore the trends that would be taking place in the world during the upcoming decade. After interviewing educators in the social sciences and studying current writings of over fifty authors, the researchers constructed a profile of significant value systems changes that would be occurring between 1969 and 1980. The profile is seen in Figure 7–3. These changing values are going to have a direct impact on the philosophy of future managers as well as on the environment in which the organization operates. Because the manager lives in society, he will be influenced by its values.

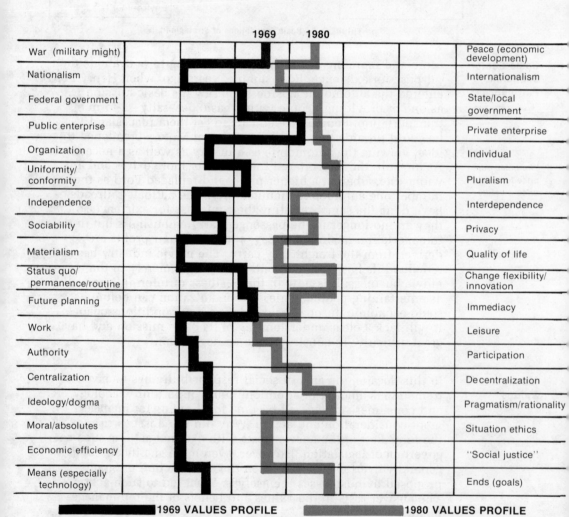

FIGURE 7–3 Profile of Significant Value-System Changes: 1969 to 1980, as Seen by General Electric's Business Environment Section (From Ian Wilson, "How Our Values Are Changing," *The Futurist,* February 1970, p. 9, published by the World Future Society, P.O. Box 30369, Bethesda Branch, Washington, D.C. 20014. Reprinted with permission.)

Evaluation of the Environment An evaluation of the external and internal environment assists the management in identifying organizational strengths and weaknesses. Based on these findings, objectives can be formulated.

External Environmental Forecasting. Forecasting of the external environment can be done in a number of ways, depending on what the management would like to know. One thing, however, is clear. The environment is always changing, and the greater the change, the more important it is for the organization to gather data about it.

One way in which the dynamic environment of the business world can be seen is through a sales comparison made of the twenty largest industrials in the United States in 1960 and 1970. As shown in Table 7–1, only eight of the top ten firms of *Fortune*'s 500 in 1960 had maintained their position in this elite group by 1970, the other two having fallen into the second-ten category. Furthermore, of the second group of ten, only four were still in the top twenty in 1970, the other six having fallen further back. The table illustrates that no firm is ever

TABLE 7–1   Fortune's 20 Largest Industrials in 1960 and 1970
(On Basis of Sales)

Rank in 1960	Rank in 1970
1. General Motors	1. General Motors
2. Standard Oil (N.J.)	2. Standard Oil (N.J.)
3. Ford Motor	3. Ford Motor
4. General Electric	4. General Electric
5. U.S. Steel	5. I.B.M.
6. Socony Mobil Oil	6. Mobil Oil
7. Chrysler	7. Chrysler
8. Texaco	8. International Telephone & Telegraph
9. Gulf Oil	9. Texaco
10. Western Electric	10. Western Electric
11. Swift	11. Gulf Oil
12. Bethlehem Steel	12. U.S. Steel
13. Du Pont (E.I.) de Nemours	13. Westinghouse Electric
14. Standard Oil (Ind.)	14. Standard Oil of California
15. General Dynamics	15. Ling-Temco-Vought
16. Westinghouse Electric	16. Standard Oil (Ind.)
17. Shell Oil	17. Boeing
18. Armour	18. Du Pont (E.I.) de Nemours
19. International Harvester	19. Shell Oil
20. National Dairy Products	20. General Telephone & Electronics

Source: *Fortune*, July 1961 and May 1971.

TABLE 7–2   Change in Selected Firms in Fortune's 500 Between
1960 and 1970 (On Basis of Sales)

Firm	Rank in 1960	Rank in 1970
Spencer Chemical	490	–
Harris Intertype	491	282
Grolier	492	409
American Petrofina	493	377
Gould-National Batteries	494	300
H.H. Robertson	495	410
Harshaw Chemical	496	–
American Forest Products	497	–
Sundstrand	498	353
National Homes	499	477
Maremount	500	401

Source: Fortune, July 1961 and May 1971.

standing still; it must be moving forward or it is falling behind. This is seen more dramatically in the case of the last ten industrials in Fortune's 500 in 1960 as compared with those in 1970 (see Table 7–2). If this dynamism is taking place among the large industrials, the nation's smaller business firms must be undergoing even more dramatic changes because they lack the size and financial strength of their giant counterparts. Thus, their need for forecasting change must be even greater.

Various types of economic forecasts can be used to project developments in the external environment.

1. *Economic Forecasting.*   The most common type of external forecasting is the *economic forecast.* If the economy is in an upswing, many businesses will find their positions improved; sales will rise and, return on investments will increase. Conversely, a downturn will have a dampening effect. Much depends on the current state of the economy as reflected by gross national product (GNP), which is the value of goods and services produced in a year.

A. Extrapolation.   The simplest form of economic forecast is that of *extrapolation.* This is nothing more than a projection of the current trend into the future. If a firm sold $100,000 worth of goods in 1972, $200,000 in 1973 and $300,000 in 1974, they might estimate continual $100,000 growth increments for the rest of the decade. Generally, of course, this is dangerous, because it fails to take into account changing environmental conditions as reflected in economic cycles. However, in certain cases, such as population growth or life expectancy, a long term forecast based on extrapolation can be fairly accurate.

B. Leads and Lags.   The National Bureau of Economic Research has discovered that when the economy turns up or down there are some indicators that seem to precede the change, some that coincide with it and still others that follow. There is thus a lead group, a coincident group and a lag group.

Of greatest importance to forecasters are the lead indicators, for they tend to signal upcoming changes in the economic cycle. In all, there are eight statistics, including business failures, new orders for durable goods, residential building contracts, average weekly hours worked, industrial common stock prices, new incorporations, commercial and industrial building contracts, and the wholesale price index. Some of these (business failures) tend to lead general business trends by as much as nine months while others (new incorporations and the wholesale price index) are only three months ahead. Many forecasters place great stock in these indicators, because they feel they provide the best clues regarding what is likely to happen.

Lag indicators are important in that they follow the economic cycle, making it possible to anticipate changes. The five lag indicators are consumer installment credit, retail store sales, personal income, manufacturers' inventories and bank rates on business loans. If the economy is in an upswing, retail stores can expect a general increase in sales, and if it is in a downturn, they can brace for a decline and begin taking appropriate steps to meet these conditions.

Unfortunately, the lead and lag method is more than a matter of merely plugging various values into a mathematical equation. Qualitative judgements must also be made to determine the impact of the indicator. For example, if the number of residential building contracts increases, orders for durable goods rise and the average number of weekly hours worked goes up, the GNP may start to rise. However, does this indicate that the company should float a new stock issue? Supposedly, the price of industrial stocks will begin to rise, but there is no certainty of this. In short, the lead and lag method helps the forecaster predict the future, but in so doing he is only making an educated guess. There is no guarantee that he is right.

    C. Econometrics.   Another forecasting technique that is being widely employed today is that of *econometrics*. This is a mathematical approach in which the main variables are brought together in a series of equations. GNP can then be forecast based on various assumptions arrived at through these equations. This technique provides the forecaster with a picture of what to expect under, for example, the most optimistic, most likely and most pessimistic conditions.

The results can be further analyzed by applying them to the specific industry and company. For example, if General Motors estimates that there will be between 12 and 14 million automobiles sold (pessimistic and optimistic) and they will capture between 46% and 51% of the market, sales will range from 5.52 to 7.14 million cars inclusive. This data can be used to construct initial income statements, illustrating profit and loss at various levels of sales. It is also possible to estimate production and marketing costs at these levels. Then, if the forecasters like, they can make changes in one area while leaving everything else the same. For example, what impact would a 15% increase in advertising have on industry and company sales? The value of the econometric model rests in the fact that it not only assists the company in forecasting the future, but it also helps them predict results of various changes in strategy.

The impact of government control must be evaluated.

2. *Governmental Action.*   Few companies escape the influence of governmental control. Most businesses face a host of laws designed to prevent monopoly, promote competition and encourage ethical practices. In addition, there is the ever-present concern with monetary action, whereby the federal government can regulate credit through the federal reserve banks and open market operations. This spurs the economy forward or, in the case of run-away inflation, helps put on the brakes. Likewise, via fiscal action the federal government can pump money into the economy or draw it out either through higher taxes or a refusal to spend what has been currently collected. For these reasons, the government will have a direct impact on business strategy.

The effect of government action on aerospace provides a dynamic illustration. During the early 1960's, the federal government pumped billions of dollars into aerospace. The industry boomed as companies were awarded giant contracts and, in turn, subcontracted with smaller firms for some of the necessary hardware. Hundreds of thousands of jobs were created as America raced through Projects Mercury, Gemini and Apollo. Then, once the moon was reached, the enthusiasm died. Public opinion polls showed that people no longer gave space research the high priority it once enjoyed. The war in Vietnam and inflation had become overriding issues, and governmental monetary and fiscal policy began to reflect these concerns. As a result, funds for aerospace were cut, and the stock of these firms plunged as layoffs occurred and cutbacks were made in an attempt to salvage what was left. By the early 1970's, some of the giants of the aerospace industry were only shells of what they had been.

Sales forecasting can be conducted in a number of ways.

3. *Sales Forecasting.*   Businesses forecast the economy in general so as to set the stage for determining their own particular sales forecast. Some use an econometric approach, but not all businesses have the expertise for employing such a sophisticated technique. For them, the questions, how many goods (or services) will we sell, to whom, when, where and how, in light of our economic projections, requires a more down-to-earth sales forecast. In arriving at an answer, the first place to which a firm often turns is its own sales records. A survey of *current sales information* will indicate what products are selling best in which areas and to what kind of customers. Further sales forecast data can often be obtained from the United States Bureau of the Census, the Department of Commerce, local trade associations and the Chamber of Commerce.

Another, and often supplemental, method of gauging sales is the *jury of executive opinion*. In this approach, various executives in the organization are brought together for the purpose of constructing the sales forecast. Sometimes they work independent of each other; other times they form a joint opinion. In both cases, there is an input to the sales forecast based on what these executives believe will take place. Another version entails the review and modification of the forecast by the manager of marketing research. The value of the jury of executive opinion approach is that it allows input from executives who are in a position to make intelligent "guesstimates" about the future.

Another supplemental approach, often called the *grass-roots method*, entails a survey of the sales force. Since these men are in the field on a continuous basis, they should have some general ideas about what will and will not sell. These ideas are obtained by the sales manager, who compiles the results and sends them up the line. Here the composites from salesmen in all the districts and regions are aggregated and sent to central headquarters, where they are compared with the forecast constructed by a staff. Finally, changes are made based on management decisions regarding advertising, product line, price and other such considerations. Then the forecast is reviewed and approved. The major advantage of the grass-roots method is that it obtains sales information from the people who are doing the actual selling.

A third supplemental approach is that of *user expectation*. How does the customer feel about the product? By going out and asking, the firm can obtain valuable information from the basic source, the consumer. Although some customers may say one thing and do another, if the firm obtains a large enough sample, it is possible to negate the impact of such responses.

Internal Environmental Evaluation.   A forecast of external environmental factors provides the organization with important planning information. However, this data must be supplemented with an evaluation of the internal environment, focusing particularly on the question, what are the company's internal strengths and weaknesses? In answering this question, there are two factors with which the manager need concern himself: material resources and personnel competence.

Material resources such as cash, plant and equipment must be evaluated.

1. *Material Resources.*   The plant capacity plus the amount of cash, equipment and inventory a company has on hand are important because they constitute the tools with which a strategic plan can be fashioned. In fact, oftentimes these resources will help dictate a particular type of strategy. For example, a business with a large plant capacity will have a large fixed expense. However, if it can manufacture at capacity, the firm can spread these costs over many items, thereby reducing the cost

per unit. This company will undoubtedly compete vigorously with a low price strategy. Conversely, a small manufacturer will not have so high a fixed expense but he will also have less units among which to spread these costs. As a result, it is impossible for him to meet the big manufacturer head-to-head in a price war. Instead, he will devise a strategy that his competitor cannot or will not effectively combat such as high price coupled with a great degree of personal selling.

A second reason for evaluating material resources is to ascertain the financial strength of the firm. If a company has $1 million in cash and $9 million in other assets, it can often maintain a strategic posture far longer than a firm with only one-tenth of these assets. In turn, this raises the question, how long should a firm remain with a particular strategic plan? The answer is, until it pays off or becomes evident that the results are not going to justify the costs. Unfortunately many firms adopt strategic plans that are not in accord with their material resources and, as a result, find themselves continually revising and modifying their plan. A strategic plan should always be tempered by the material resources available.

The competencies of the personnel must be identified.

    2. Personnel Competence. The personnel in every organization will have a distinctive area of competence; there is something they do extremely well. For example, in a firm such as *The New York Times*, it is the ability with which the personnel can gather information from all over the world and compile it quickly, accurately and in readable form. In contrast, many small papers use their people to gather local news happenings and rely upon AP and UPI sources to provide them with international news. Analogously, the "Big Three" auto manufacturers in America have the personnel needed to mass produce and market cars, whereas Rolls Royce is in the same basic business but concentrates its efforts less on marketing and more on production quality. Because a strategic plan must draw upon the company's strengths, personnel competence is an important consideration.

DEVELOPING A PROPITIOUS NICHE

Based on the external and internal environmental analysis, the philosophy of the management and the socio-economic mission of the organization, long-range objectives can be formulated. Before turning to that topic, however, it should be noted that every strategic plan must be designed so as to develop or take advantage of a particular niche. Every organization must find a thing(s) it does best and build a strategy around this forte or strength. For example, *The New York Times* has a specific market niche, selling its papers to thousands of people every day. It is not, however, the largest selling newspaper in New York City; this position is held by the *New York Daily News.* Anyone who has ever read the two papers knows that the *Daily News* is a picture newspaper written in a very easy to read style. It is much more appealing to the mass market than is *The New York Times*. Yet it would be foolish for *The Times* to copy the style of its competition. To do so would mean abandoning a niche in which its competencies are best employed. The basic mission, philosophy of management and strength of *The Times* are all geared toward its current style of news coverage. This is what is known as *leading from strength*. Every well-formulated plan draws upon the organization's fortes in fashioning the most successful strategy possible.

Surprising as it may seem, many businesses do *not* lead from strength. Instead of utilizing their fortes, they tend to hold back and respond defensively to the environment. In fact, many managers spend an inordinate amount of time trying to straighten out little problem areas instead of boldly taking advantage of their strengths. They do not have a strategic or long-range plan. Most of their time is spent on day-to-day matters. They are like chess players who seize poisoned pawns because the immediate capture of any enemy is given priority over the long-range development of their own pieces.

The firm must build a strategy that capitalizes on its strengths. By identifying a niche in which its competencies can be effectively employed, an organization focuses in on goals. However, in so doing, Drucker notes, the successful manager must never try to cover too much territory. Instead, he must "milk" a propitious niche for all it is worth, according to the following recommended guidelines.

1. Economic results require that managers concentrate their efforts on the smallest number of products, product lines, services, customers, markets, distribution channels, end uses, and so on which will produce the largest amount of revenue. Managers must minimize the attention devoted to products which produce primarily costs, because their value is too small or too splintered.

2. Economic results require also that staff efforts be concentrated on the very few activities that are capable of producing truly significant business results—with as little staff work and staff effort as possible spent on the others.

3. Effective cost control requires a similar concentration of work and efforts on those very few areas where improvement in cost performance will have significant impact on business performance and results—that is, on those areas where a relatively *minor* increase in efficiency will produce a *major* increase in economic effectiveness.

4. Managers must allocate resources, especially *high-grade human resources*, to activities which provide opportunities for high economic results.[3]

These basic ideas are employed by a number of firms, including General Electric, which handles its strategic business plan like an investment portfolio, pruning the losing lines and backing

---

[3]Peter F. Drucker, "Managing for Business Effectiveness," *Harvard Business Review*, May–June, 1963, p. 56.

the successful ones through systematic analysis.[4] Another is the SCM Corporation, which has only recently revised its entire product line by dropping nonprofitable products and concentrating its efforts on squeezing more profit from the remaining lines.

LONG- AND INTERMEDIATE-RANGE OBJECTIVES

From long-range goals, intermediate-range objectives can be formulated.

On the basis of the socio-economic purpose, values of the top managers, and an analysis of the external and internal environment, a business will formulate its long-range objectives. For a manufacturing firm, as seen in Figure 7–4, some of the more common goals will relate to manufacturing, finance and marketing. However, in long-range perspective these goals are often nebulous. It is therefore helpful to reduce them to intermediate-range objectives, thereby increasing the amount of specificity and making the goals more action-oriented. For example, in Figure 7–4 there is a long-range objective of increasing sales by 15% a year. How can this be attained? First, the intermediate-range goals are clearly defined, that is: to win a contract currently up for bid to sell widgets to a large West Coast manufacturer; to increase the size of the plant; and to establish

[4]"GE's Jones Restructures His Top Team," *Business Week*, June 30, 1973, pp. 38–39.

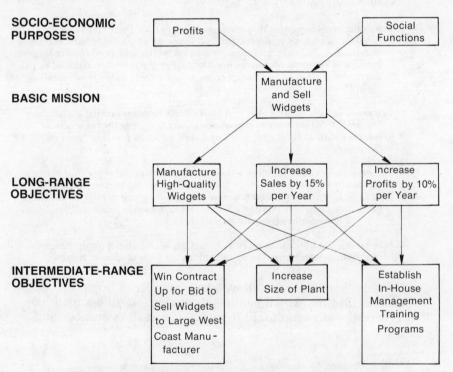

FIGURE 7–4   Interrelationships of Long- and Intermediate-Range Objectives

in-house management training programs. In addition, all the
long-range objectives relate the basic mission of manufacturing
and selling widgets. This mission, in turn, is directly related to
the socio-economic purposes of the organization. The manufacturing and sale of widgets will result in profits as well as the
fulfillment of certain social functions such as the satisfaction
of demand for this particular good. There is thus an *interrelated
hierarchy of objectives,* and the strategic plan assists the firm
in identifying its long-range objectives and formulating the derivative intermediate-range goals.

**OPERATIONAL
PLANNING**

*Operational plan-
ning is action-
oriented.*

The third and final type of planning is *operational* planning.
Operational planning is short-range in contrast to strategic
planning, and most low- and intermediate-level administrators
spend a good deal of their time carrying out these short-range
plans. Figure 7–5 shows the relationship between strategic and
operational planning. Strategic planning can be viewed as the
formulation of long-range objectives whereas operational planning is the implementation of these decisions.

The time-lapse between the formulation stage and the implementation stage may be as great as a decade, although it is most
common to find firms opting for a five-year plan. For example,
one survey of 420 companies revealed the following planning
period distributions:[5]

No corporate plan	16%
Five years only	53%
Ten years only	11%
Five to ten years	8%
Less than five years	6%
More than ten years	6%

Most operational plans are divided into functional areas. In a
manufacturing enterprise setting, for example, they would appear as in Figure 7–6. This plan is much more specific than its
strategic counterpart, with goals and targets spelled out in great

---

[5]Reported in Steiner, *op. cit.,* p. 22.

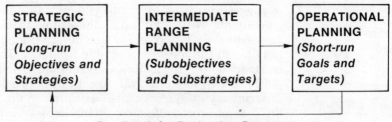

Feedback for Evaluation Purposes
FIGURE 7–5 A Planning Structure.

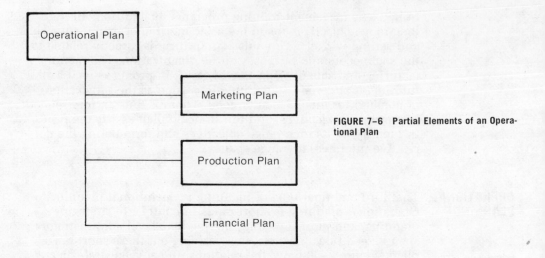

FIGURE 7–6   Partial Elements of an Operational Plan

detail. This is because as the plan comes down the chain of command, the level of abstraction decreases and the degree of specificity increases.

Marketing Plan

Selling current products and developing new ones are important marketing objectives.

Most marketing plans have two main objectives, selling current products and helping develop new ones. The former entails the setting of quotas and market shares for the various product lines. These objectives are translated into operational plans through advertising budgets, the maintenance of a sales force, the assignment of quotas and the determination of product prices. Then, at the end of the given period, i.e., six months or a year, performance will be evaluated and goals or targets revised accordingly.

Concurrently, the marketing plan will entail some consideration of new product development. Every business knows that each product has a limited life cycle (see Figure 7–6). Some goods will maintain their market position for years while others may never really get off the ground, and today's big sellers may have no market demand five years from now. For these reasons, product planning is necessary, the basis of which is generating new product ideas. Sometimes these will come from the research and development lab; other times they may be the result of suggestions from top management, salesmen, customers or consultants. No matter where they come from, however, only approximately two of every one hundred ideas will ever materialize in the form of profitable products. The rest will either be screened out for technical, economic or market test reasons (95%) or will just plain fail to sell, despite all initial signs to the contrary (3%). A recent illustration of the latter is found in the case of Frost 8/80, a dry, white whisky introduced by the Brown-Forman Distillers Corporation. Despite an extensive market research program that pointed to widespread acceptance,

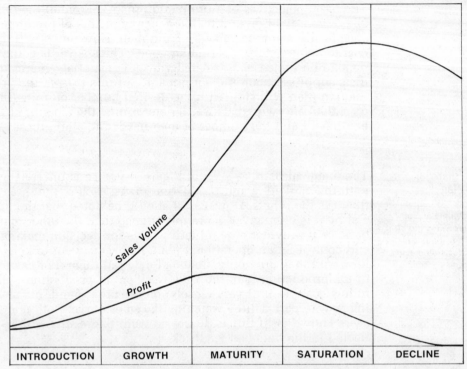

| INTRODUCTION | GROWTH | MATURITY | SATURATION | DECLINE |

FIGURE 7–7 Typical Life Cycle for Goods and Services

production was halted after two years because sales were too low to justify further effort. The company lost a total of approximately $2 million.[6]

Production Plan

The main production objective is to satisfy consumer demand.

The production plan is designed to satisfy consumer demand by turning out the desired amount of goods. Sometimes production capability will be greater than estimated demand; other times it will be necessary for the manufacturing department to go to a second or third shift to meet this demand. Both instances illustrate that marketing and production planning are actually intertwined.

[6]Frederic C. Klein, "An Untimely End: How A New Product Was Brought to Market Only to Flop Miserably," *Wall Street Journal*, January 5, 1973, p. 1.

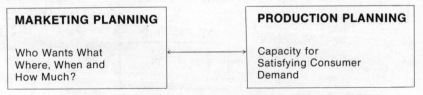

MARKETING PLANNING	PRODUCTION PLANNING
Who Wants What Where, When and How Much?	Capacity for Satisfying Consumer Demand

FIGURE 7–8 Interrelationship of Marketing and Production Planning

The basic objectives of a production plan will entail the purchase, coordination and maintenance of factors of production, specifically machines, material and men. How much will it cost to manufacture a particular good? The answer is going to depend on the costs associated with raw materials, merchandise, supplies, labor and equipment. For this reason, the production plan will start with the desired number of units (the objective) and work backward, determining the amount of equipment and the number of men needed to attain these goals.

Financial Plan

Financial plan provides quantitative basis for decision making and control.

The financial plan, as seen in Figure 7–9, also is interrelated with the marketing and production plans; each of the three influences the others. However, it should be noted that the financial plan is often given more importance than the other plans because it provides a quantitative basis for decision making and control. In an operational plan, managers want to know how well they are doing; financial data tell them. For example, in the production plan the vice president of production will follow cost per unit very closely; on the other hand, his marketing counterpart will be watching the sales curve. Both managers know that if things do not go well, the results will be reflected in the financial feedback.

Harmonizing Functional Plans

Budgets are useful in harmonizing plans.

One way in which a firm will harmonize these three functional plans is through the use of the *budget*. Many managers believe the budget is a control technique, but actually it is a planning tool as well because it provides a basis for action. Expected results can be expressed in numerical terms; cash flows can be projected; man hours to be worked in the current period can be calculated; and units of production can be determined. Furthermore, research shows that when plans are linked to budgets, overall accuracy tends to be greater than when they are not.[7]

Another way in which management harmonizes operational plans is by setting *financial objectives*. For example, what is a

[7]Richard F. Vancil, "The Accuracy of Long-Range Planning," *Harvard Business Review*, September–October 1970, p. 100.

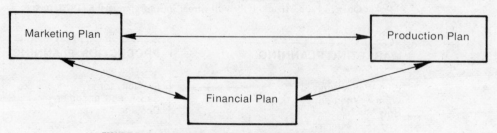

FIGURE 7–9   Interrelationships of Operational Planning Components

fair return on investment? Perhaps the company believes 16 per cent is a desirable goal and establishes this as a target for the year. This determination is going to affect the three functional plans, for, as seen in Figure 7–10, the cost of sales, the cost of production and the cost of capital will all influence the rate of return.

$$ROI = \frac{Sales}{Total\ Investment} \times \frac{Earnings\ as\ a}{Percentage\ of\ Sales}$$

FIGURE 7–10 Return on Investment

Financial ratios are helpful planning tools.

A second financial objective might deal with the maintenance of liquidity such as keeping the *current ratio* (current assets/current liabilities) at 1.5:1 or higher. A firm might choose to make this calculation on a semi-annual basis, taking any necessary corrective action at that point. Table 7–3 provides an illustration of the XYZ Company over an 18 month period, starting with its inception in December 1972. As can be seen, the company is very liquid as of December 31, 1972. The current ratio cannot be computed because the firm has no current liabilities. However, over the next three semi-annual periods, this ratio can be calculated. On June 30, 1973, it is 2.08, showing that the company has twice as much money in current assets as is needed to pay current liabilities. By December 31, the ratio is down to 1.8, and the following June it stands at 1.23. The firm may be in a precarious financial position for two reasons. First, the current ratio is sinking, indicating a rapid decline in the ability to meet current obligations. Second, as seen from a cursory analysis of the comparative financial statements, there has been a rapid increase in inventory, indicating that either the marketing plan is not materializing according to schedule or the production plan is too optimistic. In either event, the firm is building up its inventory too fast.

TABLE 7–3 Comparative Balance Sheet of XYZ Company

For Period Ending December 31, 1972

Assets		
Current Assets		
Cash	$100,000	
Fixed Assets		
Plant and Equipment (Net)	100,000	
Total Assets		$200,000
Liabilities		
Stockholder's Equity		
Capital Stock	$200,000	
Total Liabilities and Stockholder's Equity		$200,000

(*Table 7–3 continued on following page.*)

TABLE 7–3 Comparative Balance Sheet of XYZ Company — Continued

For Period Ending June 30, 1973

Assets

Current Assets
  Cash $ 50,000
  Inventory
      Raw Materials $ 20,000
      Work in Progress   70,000
      Finished Goods   110,000
  Total Inventory   200,000
Total Current Assets $250,000

Fixed Assets
  Plant and Equipment (Net) $120,000
Total Assets $370,000

Liabilities

  Accounts Payable $ 50,000
  Accrued Salaries   35,000
  Taxes Payable   35,000
Total Current Liabilities $120,000

Stockholder's Equity

Capital Stock $200,000
Retained Earnings   50,000 $250,000

Total Liabilities and Stockholder's Equity $370,000

For Period Ending December 31, 1973

Assets

Current Assets
  Cash $ 40,000
  Accounts Receivable   20,000
  Inventory
      Raw Materials $ 30,000
      Work in Progress   90,000
      Finished Goods   130,000
  Total Inventory $250,000
  Prepaid Expenses   5,000
Total Current Assets $315,000

Fixed Assets
    Plant and Equipment (net)   160,000
Total Assets $475,000

Liabilities

    Accounts Payable $ 70,000
    Notes Payable   15,000
    Accrued Salaries   50,000
    Taxes Payable   40,000
Total Current Liabilities $175,000

Stockholder's Equity

    Capital Stock $200,000
    Retained Earnings   100,000
Total Liabilities and Stockholder's Equity $475,000

For Period Ending June 30, 1974

Assets

Current Assets
    Cash $ 20,000
    Accounts Receivable   20,000
    Inventory
        Raw Materials $ 35,000
        Work in Progress   100,000
        Finished Goods   140,000
    Total Inventory $275,000
    Prepaid Expenses   5,000
Total Current Assets $320,000

Fixed Assets
    Plant and Equipment (net) $270,000
Total Assets $590,000

Liabilities

    Accounts Payable $120,000
    Notes Payable   30,000
    Accrued Salaries   60,000
    Taxes Payable   50,000
Total Current Liabilities $260,000

Stockholder's Equity

    Capital Stock $200,000
    Retained Earnings   130,000
Total Liabilities and Stockholder's Equity $590,000

This finding becomes even clearer if the *quick ratio* (current assets-inventory/current liabilities) is computed. Since this calculation compares only the firm's most liquid assets to current liabilities, it is a very strong measure of the company's ability to meet these incoming bills. From June 1973 to December 1974 the ratio has moved from .42 to .37 to .17. The plan of action for the firm is clear. Inventory must be sold and not permitted to build up, and, if possible, long-term debt or equity capital should be considered as a means for improving liquidity. As seen in Figure 7–11, the financial plan is the fulcrum upon which the marketing and production plans are balanced. If one side is out of equilibrium, it will be reflected in the financial data and corrective action will have to be taken.

This concept of balancing the various areas of production is what was previously identified as suboptimization. Rather than attempting to maximize production, for example, the company strikes a balance between what it can produce, sell and finance. With effective planning, suboptimization of these areas can result in greater profits.

USE OF A PLANNING ORGANIZATION

As noted previously, in many firms managers at the lower levels are most concerned with day-to-day problems. They do not have time to construct strategic plans; their interest rests in carrying out operational plans. For this reason, it is common to find departments drawing up their own budgets with supporting justifications for any proposed capital expenditures and forwarding these proposals to top management. Here departmental plans are combined into divisional plans, which in turn are reviewed, modified if necessary and, finally, approved by the top management.

A planning organization can help a firm design a comprehensive plan.

However, the development of a comprehensive plan is never quite so simple as it might initially appear. There is always a tremendous amount of coordination required. For this reason, many firms, especially corporations, have begun developing

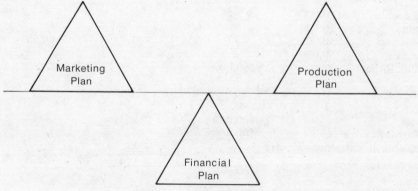

FIGURE 7–11 Functional Plan Fulcrum

PHASE	ACTION	TIME SPAN	TOTAL TIME ELAPSED
I	Establish executive planning committee	6–12 months	6–12 months
II	Select director of planning and provide *ad hoc* staff committee	About 12 months	18–24 months
III	Director develops permanent planning staff at corporate level; division planning committees added	12–36 months	30–60 months
IV	Appoint vice-president of planning and corporate development reporting to president and executive planning committee; select division planning coordinator	12–24 months	42–72 months
V	Specialize corporate development planning, and evaluation functions; provide division planning staffs reporting to division heads but with relationship to corporate development and planning department	12–36 months and beyond	60–108 months

FIGURE 7-12 Time Phases of a Planning Organization (From R. Hal Mason, "Developing A Planning Organization," *Business Horizons*, August 1969, p. 62. Reprinted with permission.)

their own *planning organization*. It often takes from five to eight years before this structure is functioning smoothly (see Figure 7–12), yet there are two important advantages to be gleaned from it. First, some companies lack a complete appreciation for planning at the highest ranks of the organization. A planning organization can surmount this lack of complete commitment. Second, many managers throughout the structure have never really been taught the concept of planning. A planning organization helps overcome this deficiency.

Organizational Metamorphosis

Mason reports that a planning organization often begins at the top management level with the formation of a committee to identify and organize data on the firm and its industry position.[8] In Phase I attention is given to the development of a framework within which long-range planning can take place.

Planning organizations often go through five phases.

Phase II entails the formation of the first formal long-range plan. At best, it is often a rudimentary guide, lacking in both depth and breadth. The plan is constructed by an executive

[8]This five-phase metamorphosis comes from R. Hal Mason, "Developing a Planning Organization," *Business Horizons*, August 1969, pp. 61–69.

planning staff at the upper divisions, which acts as a consultant to the rest of the organization.

In Phase III, which occurs about three years after the plan's inception, the planning organization prepares its first comprehensive five-year plan. This is done through the coordination and integration of the plans prepared by the major operating units. It is a "bottom-up" approach, with the departments within each division or unit drawing up plans and sending them up the line. Thus the division carries out the majority of the total planning effort. During this phase, divisional planning committees will be added to the operating units to assist both the unit and the planning organization. These committees will assess reporting procedures and information generated about products, customers and competitors. For its part, the planning organization will assist the committee in the design of the information and reporting systems.

By the time the committee reaches Phase IV, the annual preparation of a long-range plan will have become routine. Operating divisions have usually become attuned to developing plans that are in harmony with each other. At this stage, it is also common to find organizational planning taking on greater importance and the head of the planning organization appointed to the vice presidential rank, reporting directly to the president.

In Phase V, the final developmental step is reached. Mason describes the phase as follows:

> The activities of planning groups at all levels tend to shift their attention increasingly toward corporate development activities, which include the matching of opportunity to corporate capabilities and the development of those capabilities. The formal development of planning information has become routine in certain ways, and each division is aware of the types of data it must generate for planning purposes. An integrated set of plans is put together within a format, and corporate action is evaluated relative to plan. The machinery for developing plans and updating the corporate plan exists and is functioning. This frees the planning group so that it can devote a growing share of its total resources to searching the environment, evaluating corporate strengths and weaknesses, and identifying opportunities for corporate growth and profit improvement.[9]

This type of organization is being employed by an increasing number of firms that realize that intelligent planning requires a concerted effort on the part of the management.

ADVANTAGES OF PLANNING   A number of important advantages can be obtained by planning. First, it forces a firm to *forecast* the environment. No longer does the management assume a "wait and see" attitude. Instead, the company begins evaluating conditions and formulating its own response. Passivity gives way to activity.

---

[9] *Ibid.*, pp. 68–69.

Second, planning gives the company *direction* in the form of objectives. Once the organization knows what it can and cannot do over the next one to five years, it can begin setting goals. Day-to-day operational thinking gives way to more long-run designs.

Third, planning provides a basis for *teamwork*. Now that the goals are clearly defined, work assignments can be determined and everyone can begin to contribute to the fulfillment of these objectives. This often leads to high morale and also helps develop management talent. The manager can now delegate authority to his subordinates and begin to evaluate performance. Without planning, this would be a haphazard dream; with planning, it is a reality.

Finally, planning helps management learn to *live with ambiguity*. This is especially true in long- and intermediate-range planning. Management must realize that there is virtue in vagueness. To demand clarity in all things leads to a refusal to do anything beyond operational planning.

PLANNING IS NO GUARANTEE
The development of the long-range plan and its integration with short-range plans is very useful. However, there is no guarantee that merely because a firm plans it will be successful. Many things can go wrong, and they always relate back to the premises upon which the plan was formulated.

Sometimes, information coming in from the field is *erroneous*. Salesmen may give strong endorsement to a particular modification of a current product, but the modified good may not sell very well. What potential customers say they are going to do and what they end up doing may be two different things. This is a problem inherent in market research.

A second basic problem is the *economy*. A plan predicated on a rising economy will run into trouble if a downturn is encountered. For example, during the early and mid-sixties, the economy boomed and many organizational planners saw the future as more of the same. After all, it is far easier (and to many, more logical) to extrapolate the present than to answer the question, when will the bloom be off the rose? If a company has increased its sales by 25 per cent a year for the last five years, it is very difficult for them to estimate the following year's increase at 15 per cent. Psychologically, they are taking a 10 per cent cut. For this reason, many firms tend to extrapolate the economy during good times and estimate an upturn or leveling out during poor times. The economy is designed to fit the plan instead of vice versa.

A third problem can be the company's *financial position*. A plan may rely heavily on strong advertising and personal promotion, but if the company is unable to finance this kind of campaign, the plan could fall flat. In fact, a downward spiral may occur with reduced promotional expenses leading to the nonmaterialization of sales, which results in the cutback of any further promotional effort. The publishing industry often faces this problem because of its small profit margin. For example, a textbook will be given an estimated sales price of $10.00 and an annual market potential of 5000 copies. In addition, the advertising budget will be set at $10,000 for the first year and $5000 for the second. However, internal budgetary cuts may re-quire changes in this plan; the price may be raised to $12.50 to help cover home office expenses. Yet such a move may result in a decline in demand down to 3500 copies. Revenue has now dipped from an expected total of $50,000 to an actual total of $43,750. This, in turn, may lead the company to eliminate the follow-up advertising budget. Once the initial plan runs into trouble, everything goes awry because of the host of sequential cause-effect relationships. Every attempt to reestablish an equi-librium leads to further problems.

A fourth common problem is *lack of coordination*. The objec-tives are clear, but the functional departments do not synchron-ize their efforts. Sometimes this is caused by personnel's loss of enthusiasm for their own plan; more commonly, it results when the proposed plan is modified by higher authority. In either event, the human element comes into play and plans are not implemented according to a previously determined sched-ule.

In summary, planning is no panacea for dealing with the future. There are many things that can go wrong. Nevertheless, com-panies that do plan increase their chances for success, and it is for this reason that the planning process is important to management.

SUMMARY   In this chapter, comprehensive planning, consisting of strategic, intermediate and operational plans, has been examined. Prime attention was given to long-run considerations, with note being made that most firms tend to be too short-run oriented. The roles played by the determination of the firm's basic socio-economic mission, values of the top management, and analysis of the organization's strengths and weaknesses in the formula-tion of the strategic plan were examined in detail. The latter, as was seen, requires accurate economic and sales forecasting coupled with a frank and honest evaluation of the company's material resources and personnel competencies. Only in this way can a niche be identified and long-range objectives formu-lated.

Although the long-range plan provides general direction, the intermediate and especially the operational plan are also important because they offer more specific direction. The operational plan often consists of derivative functional plans such as marketing, production and finance plans, designed to attain short-run objectives while harmonizing with the previously determined long-range goals. Such short-range plans provide management with a method for gauging how things are going, serving as a basis from which to adapt or modify current plans and construct future ones.

Of course, no plan can be successfully implemented without a competent organization. There must be some process of bringing the work and the people together. This topic will be the focus of attention in the next chapter.

STUDY AND REVIEW QUESTIONS

1. Why has there been a marked trend toward comprehensive planning on the part of many business firms?

2. What is meant by "strategic planning"?

3. What are the three basic foundations of strategic planning? Describe each.

4. How do management values affect the planning process?

5. How does a firm conduct external environmental forecasting? Be specific.

6. How does a firm evaluate its internal environment?

7. What does "developing a niche" have to do with planning?

8. What is meant by operational planning?

9. How can a planning organization be useful to management?

10. What are some of the advantages of planning? Explain.

11. What are some of the disadvantages of planning? Explain.

12. What are some of the common problems that can cause a plan to go awry? Explain.

SELECTED REFERENCES

Apgar, M. IV. "New Business From New Towns?" *Harvard Business Review*, January–February 1971, pp. 90–109.
Chambers, J. C., S. K. Mullick, and D. A. Goodman. "Catalytic Agent for Effective Planning." *Harvard Business Review*, January–February 1971, pp. 110–119.
Drucker, P. F. "Managing for Business Effectiveness." *Harvard Business Review*, May–June 1963, pp. 53–60.

Drucker, P. F. *Management: Tasks, Responsibilities, Practices.* New York: Harper & Row, Publishers, 1974, Chapters 5–10.

George, G. C., and E. L. Segura. "How to Get a Better Forecast." *Harvard Business Review,* March–April 1971, pp. 99–109.

Gerstner, L. V., Jr. "Can Strategic Planning Pay Off?" *Business Horizons,* December 1972, pp. 5–16.

Gilmore, F. F. "Formulating Strategy in Smaller Companies." *Harvard Business Review,* May–June 1971, pp. 71–81.

Golightly, H. O. "What Makes a Company Successful?" *Business Horizons,* June 1971, pp. 11–18.

Kalman, J. C., and R. M. Cyert. "Strategy: Formulation, Implementation and Monitoring." *Journal of Business,* July 1973, pp. 349–367.

Litschert, R. J. "The Structure of Long-Range Planning Groups." *Academy of Management Journal,* March 1971, pp. 33–43.

McDonald, P. R., and J. O. Eastlack, Jr. "Top Management Involvement With New Products." *Business Horizons,* December 1971, pp. 23–31.

Mason, R. H. "Developing a Planning Organization." *Business Horizons,* August 1969, pp. 61–69.

Most, K. S. "Wanted: A Planning Model for the Firm." *Managerial Planning,* July–August 1973, pp. 1–6.

Smallwood, J. E. "The Product Life Cycle: Key to Strategic Marketing Planning." *MSU Business Topics,* Winter 1973, pp. 29–35.

Steiner, G. A. "Changing Managerial Philosophies." *Business Horizons,* June 1971, pp. 5–10.

Steiner, G. A. *Top Management Planning.* New York: The Macmillan Co., 1969.

Steiner, G. A. "Rise of the Corporate Planner." *Harvard Business Review,* September–October 1970, pp. 133–139.

Thune, S. S., and R. J. House. "Where Long-Range Planning Pays Off." *Business Horizons,* August 1970, pp. 81–87.

Wheelwright, S. S. "Strategic Planning in the Small Business." *Business Horizons,* August 1971, pp. 51–58.

Wilson, I. "How Our Values Are Changing." *The Futurist,* February 1970, pp. 5–9.

CASE: JUST LEAVE US ALONE

The Clayton Corporation was founded by Mr. Bud Clayton in 1956. In the early years the going was rough, but by 1965 things had started to improve, and in the late 60's, while the economy was dipping, Clayton's business was never better. Sales and profits set new highs between 1968 and 1973, as seen by the following company data:

	Sales	Net Profit
1968	$2,600,000	$210,000
1969	2,900,000	245,000
1970	3,300,000	265,000
1971	4,000,000	300,000
1972	4,850,000	325,000
1973	6,000,000	395,000

The firm's record was so outstanding, in fact, that a number of large corporations made offers to buy them. Finally, after careful consideration, the offer from a large eastern conglomerate was accepted. In addition to a very lucrative financial settlement, the conglomerate agreed that Mr. Clayton and his management team would remain at the helm with business continuing as usual. The only major change was that all long-range plans and short-range performance goals (profitability, return on investment, sales, etc.) would have to be cleared with the planning organization at the conglomerate's headquarters so as to insure overall organizational coordination.

Initially everything went smoothly, but by the end of the first year, it was apparent things were not going well at all. Mr. Clayton called a meeting of his top people to see if things could be ironed out. He also persuaded the vice president of corporate planning and his two staff assistants to fly in for the conference. Mr. Clayton sensed bad feelings between his people and the central planning group and believed it was time for both parties to air their gripes. The basic points of view presented by the two groups were as follows:

Clayton Group

Before we were purchased by the eastern conglomerate, we used to run our own show around here. After all, who knows more about how to manufacture and sell our product than us? But now we're asked to coordinate our plans with those of seven other companies. And sometimes our suggested plans apparently don't fit in because they're rejected or modified by the corporate planning department. Well, we're fed up being told how to run our own end of the business. This concept of overall coordinated planning is having a drastic effect on the morale of our management team. Why don't you people just leave us alone?

Corporate Planning Group

We have eight major companies in our conglomerate. The only way we can make these eight work as one is to coordinate their long- and short-range planning. Sure, no one likes to be told the way to do their job. And we don't mean to. But there has to be some harmony if we're to work as one big team. Now we can understand that managers don't like having their plans modified or revised, but this just can't be helped. And until the management of the Clayton Company realizes that they're part of a team, we're going to continue to have this problem. Big companies can't offer the personal touch that small ones can. When you become the member of a conglomerate you have to be willing to give up a little autonomy. Perhaps the Clayton Management should try seeing things from our point of view.

Questions

1. Can a conglomerate operate as "one big team" without running into the kind of problems seen in this case?

2. Is the Clayton management right? Is the central planning organization indifferent to its problems?

3. How can this problem be solved? Present your solution.

4. How has the Clayton Corporation's position been modified in regard to suboptimization?

CASE: A BETTER MOUSETRAP[1]

"If you build a better mousetrap," it is said, "the world will beat a path to your door." But will it really? The Woodstream Company had manufactured traps for catching all kinds of animals from elephants to grizzly bears. One day, the firm decided to design and manufacture a streamlined mousetrap.

A product designer was brought in to design a trap that would be modern enough for people to notice the change. The final product was made of plastic and looked like a sardine can with an arched doorway at floor level through which mice could enter. Any mouse coming through the doorway would trip a spring and be choked to death by a wire which, acting like an upside-down guillotine, would snap up from below.

The company called the new product "Little Champ" and priced it at 25¢, in contrast to the wooden ones, which sold at two for 15¢. Although the price was higher than average, the trap was easier to set, extremely efficient and, perhaps best of all, could be cleaned and reused. It did not have to be thrown out with the mouse.

Looking forward to a booming demand, the company sent the traps out to hardware dealers across the nation. And there they sat on the shelf gathering dust. Despite the changes in the efficiency features, no one wanted them. Why? One individual explained the situation in this way:

"The company tried to develop a space-age mousetrap by researching the sleeping, eating and crawling habits of mice." . . . **"The little woman — who usually has to contend with the dead mouse — all thought nothing of throwing away the old wooden snap-trap, mouse and all. But the new 25-cent trap was a different story — she didn't care for extracting the dead mouse and cleaning the trap."**

Whatever the reason, the venture failed. Mr. Woolworth was unable to generate interest, although he certainly tried. For example, during the New York City garbage strike he wired Governor Rockefeller of New York, offering to ship a million rat traps for $144,000. But the governor was not even interested, and the Woodstream Company finally gave up on the product.

Questions

1. What kind of planning should the Woodstream Company have done before manufacturing these traps?

---

[1]This case is adapted from Stephen J. Fansweet, "Dick Woolworth Builds a Better Mousetrap — and Falls on his Face," *Wall Street Journal*, September 24, 1970, p. 1.

2. Why was the company unable to sell the traps? Do you agree with the above analysis or are there other reasons? Explain.

3. Is there anything the company can now do with the traps or is the venture a total loss?

CASE: MILKING THE COW

Mark Anderson had been president of Anderson Printing for five years, having left a high-paying job as a salesman for a large eastern publishing firm to return to the family business. "We were on the verge of selling out," he told Willy Chishilm, his management consultant. "My dad, who started the business, had died, and the other members of the family didn't want anything to do with it. That was when I began to look into the possibility of taking over the helm and seeing what I could do. Well, I don't have to tell you the story. You've been here for a week now looking over operations and examining our financial statements. You know better than anyone how well we've done over the last four years."

Willy moved his chair closer to the desk and placed some papers on top of it. "Mark, you look just great on paper. I have absolutely no arguments with your technical operations. Some of the new machinery you purchased is going to save you a lot of money in the long-run. And the morale of your staff is sky high. My management team has been talking to your people since Wednesday and there hasn't been one negative comment about anything."

"Surely this isn't your way of telling me that everything is perfect."

"No, it's merely my way of leading up to a plan of action that I would like to recommend to you. In a nutshell, you are just too short-run oriented. You have no real idea of where you are going. You've got a couple of banks that you are supplying with printed material and a lot of walk-in business and that's all."

"Say, don't forget that we have seventeen firms in town that send all their printing orders to us also."

"Okay, them too. However, that's all you've got. You are tied directly into the orders you are getting from these 'captive businesses' and anyone coming in off the streets and that's it."

"So what's so wrong with that? Look at our sales. In 1973 we did over $1 million of business. In 1974 we had sales of $1.25 million. This year we're anticipating $1.5 million, but at the rate we're going it's going to be closer to $1.7. It seems to me we're in great shape."

"Financially speaking, you are. However, have you any idea where Anderson Printing is going to be in 1979? Or how about 1989? What are your long-range plans?"

"Willy, I don't horse around with long-range planning. I don't need it. In this town there are two large banks and they send all their business to us. In addition, there are those other seventeen companies, most of them insurance firms, that need an awful lot of printing done. All I have to do is keep worrying about the next three months. That's my long-range plan, ninety days into the future. As long as I know I have enough financing at the bank and my collections are taking place on time, I have a good cash flow. What else is there to running a successful business?"

"Mark, do you think the banks you print for got to be as large as they are by planning ninety days into the future?"

"No, but then they don't have my situation. This business has a number of companies that rely upon it exclusively for their printing. There is no company in town that can match my price on any job because I've got the best equipment and can offer higher quality and lower prices than any of them. So why do I need to worry about long-range planning? My whole plan consists of keeping the machines in working order and not letting the competition get any technological jumps on me. That's the only way they can beat me out of a job, and it's just not going to happen. In a manner of speaking, I've carved a niche for myself. This niche is a very fat, profitable cow, and my job is to sit here and milk that cow for all it's worth. The last thing on my mind is long-range or, as you call it, strategic planning. Who needs it? When you've got a good thing going, enjoy it. What can long-range planning do for a business like mine?"

Questions

1. What are the advantages of long-range planning? Be specific.

2. What arguments should Willy raise in defense of his long-range planning proposal?

3. Can long-range planning really be of any value to Anderson Printing or is the firm better off remaining with its current short-range planning approach? Explain.

CASE: PRUNING THE PRODUCT LINE[1]

During the late 1960's and early 1970's, things just did not seem to be going well at the SCM Corporation. Fortunately, some of

[1]The data in this case can be found in "SCM Tries a Comeback with Fewer Products," *Business Week*, July 21, 1973, pp. 42–43; and "Shaking Up Crown Zellerbach's Line," *Business Week*, January 5, 1974, p. 52.

its lines were doing well. For example, one of its acquisitions, the Glidden Company, accounted for 25 per cent of all sales and 56 per cent of all earnings in 1972. But overall, operations were sluggish and profits nonexistent. For example, reported *Business Week:*

SCM got off to a fast start in copiers, a business it entered in 1959, with a low-cost, desk-top machine that used a liquid toner and coated paper. . . . But SCM ignored the needs of the marketplace. It was late in introducing console models and then had operating problems with its machines. The company also lacked a consistent marketing approach.

In addition, the company lost money in office machines from 1970 on, and its profits in typewriters, the firm's oldest business, had peaked in 1969.

However, under its current president, Paul Elicker, the company has begun turning around by shaking out its losing lines and stimulating growth in the remainder. For example, Glidden had been strongly oriented toward the construction and household market, which grows at about a 4 per cent annual rate. The division is now expanding into steel and aluminum sheet covering, which grows at a 12 per cent annual rate. In metals, the company is concentrating on such specialty items as new high-strength copper and aluminum-oxide alloy. In paper products, it is placing emphasis on fine rather than commodity-grade papers.

Meanwhile, SCM realized it could not compete effectively in the field of standard-size electric typewriters, and it withdrew from the field. The same was true in the case of mechanical calculators and vacuum cleaners. These cutbacks resulted in write-offs of $24 million over three years and were reflected in bleak financial statements. Yet the firm feels that by dropping nonprofitable lines and trying to squeeze more profits from fewer products, it can obtain greater financial success.

A similar approach to the product line is being undertaken by Crown Zellerbach, the nation's second largest paper manufacturer, in an attempt to deal with the current paper shortage. Instead of offering a wide selection of products, the company is cutting back the number of lines. *Business Week* reports that the firm

. . . now offers newsprint in only one weight and one color: white. A year ago it offered two weights and four colors. The $1-billion San Francisco company has also dropped colored computer tabulating cards and several grades of printing papers, curtailed production of jumbo rolls of unbleached kraft paper, shifted a huge tonnage of unbleached kraft paper to bleached, and cut the varieties, colors, and sizes of all its bags and wrapping papers.

The paper industry, in fact, is spearheading the drive toward product-mix refinement. Demand for all types of paper products now outpaces industry capacity, and high prices abroad are luring many American paper companies from price-controlled markets at home. Now energy shortages threaten the domestic supply even more.

To improve its profit picture, Crown Zellerbach is dropping some product lines and putting more emphasis on others. In one plant, for example, the firm used to turn out 57 grades of industrial specialty paper for 30 customers. Today it manufactures 25 grades for 15 customers.

Is the approach paying off? Crown seems to think so. In the first nine months of 1973 it earned $79 million on sales of $1 billion. Its previous record, in 1968, was $59 million in profits, and that was on a 12-month basis.

Questions

1. How does SCM's strategy reflect Drucker's philosophy of finding a propitious niche? What about Crown Zellerbach? Explain.

2. How could SCM have done a better job in marketing its copier machine? Bring into your discussion the topic of strategic planning.

3. How would you define SCM's current plan of action? What types of acquisitions would you expect it to make in the future?

4. How might the paper and energy shortages have affected Crown Zellerbach's strategic plan? How can a company forecast such events as these and deal with them in the planning process? Be specific in your answer.

CHAPTER 8

THE ORGANIZING PROCESS

GOALS OF THE CHAPTER

Organizing entails the assignment of duties and the coordination of efforts among all organizational personnel so as to ensure maximum efficiency in the attainment of predetermined objectives. The goals of this chapter are to examine the nature, purpose and function of organizing. Attention will be focused on:

a. the most widely used types of departmentalization;
b. the common advantages and disadvantages of committees;
c. span of control and its impact on organizational structure;
d. line, staff and functional authority;
e. common line-staff conflicts;
f. decentralization and delegation of authority; and
g. the informal organization.

FROM STRATEGY TO STRUCTURE

Strategy is a prerequisite for structure.

It has already been noted that the planning process encompasses strategic, intermediate and operational plans. Our model can now be expanded, as seen in Figure 8–1, to include the organization structure, hence the often used phrase "from strategy to structure," which research has shown to be an accurate statement. Chandler, after conducting intensive studies of General Motors, Du Pont, Standard Oil of New Jersey and Sears, Roebuck and Company, proved that strategy is indeed a prerequisite for structure.[1] If an organization does not know where it is going, there is no intelligent basis for organizing human effort and material resources. This chapter will be

---

[1]Alfred D. Chandler, Jr., *Strategy and Structure* (Garden City, New York: Anchor Books, Doubleday & Company, Inc., 1966).

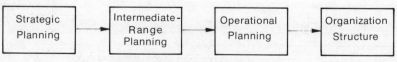

FIGURE 8–1   From Strategy to Structure

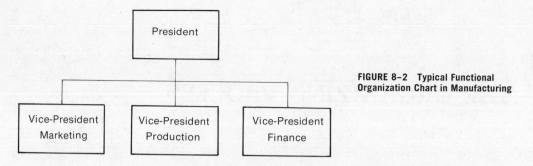

FIGURE 8-2 Typical Functional
Organization Chart in Manufacturing

devoted to the various structures and concepts that can assist the manager in this process.

COMMON FORMS OF DEPARTMENTALIZATION

Perhaps the easiest way to grasp the function of organizing is to examine the mechanics of the process. By dividing the work and the personnel into group activities, departments can be formed for the purpose of specialization. The three most widely used types of departmentalization are functional, product and territorial.

Functional Departmentalization

Functional departmentalization, the most widely used form of departmentalization, occurs when an enterprise organizes itself around the firm's major activities. In a manufacturing enterprise, in which these prime or *organic* functions are marketing, production and finance, a typical functional organization chart would be that shown in Figure 8-2.

Functional departmentalization is the most widely used.

In nonmanufacturing firms these functions differ. For example, in a large bank they often include comptroller, operations, legal and public relations. In an insurance company it would be common to find actuarial, underwriting, agency and claim adjustment. In a public utility organic functions would include accounting, sales, engineering and personnel. These are all illustrations of major functional departments, which, in turn, can have *derivative departments*. For example, expanding Figure 8-2 to include second-level functional departments might result in the following:

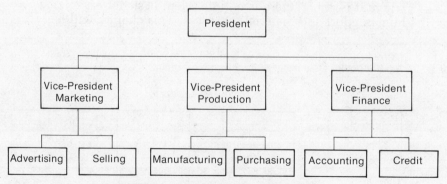

FIGURE 8-3 Derivative Functional Departments

Similar charts could be drawn for all functionally organized enterprises, but the structure need not stop at the second level. There may be third-, fourth- and even fifth-level functional departments, depending on the size of the enterprise.

Perhaps the major reason why functional departmentalization is so widely employed is the emphasis it places on basic activities, providing a basis for specialization. There are, however, drawbacks. This form of departmentalization can create "tunnel vision," whereby functional specialists see nothing but their own area of interest. Also, in some instances, firms will adopt functional departmentalization because they see other companies doing it, even though another form, departmentalization by product, for example, would actually be more beneficial.

Product Departmentalization

Product departmentalization has been increasing in importance, especially among multi-line, large-scale enterprises. General Motors, Ford, Du Pont, RCA and General Electric all employ it. Many firms using this form were originally organized functionally, but as they grew larger, a reorganization along product lines became necessary. A simplified illustration for a manufacturing firm appears in Figure 8–4.

Product departmentalization is employed by many multi-line, large-scale companies.

The organic functions of marketing, production and finance can still be found in the structure, but prime attention is now given to the product lines. All activities related to a particular product are brought together.

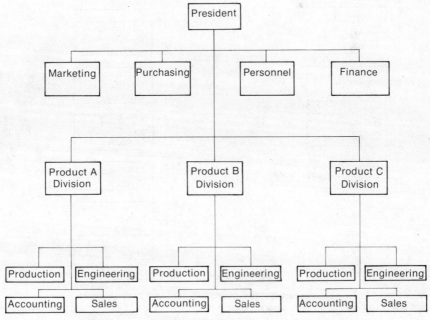

FIGURE 8–4 Product Organization Chart for a Manufacturing Firm

Perhaps the main advantage of this form is its value in facilitating coordination and permitting specialization. This can be especially beneficial if the firm is large. For example, in 1974 General Electric had ten major operating groups, each containing no less than five and, in some cases, as many as ten divisions. The consumer products and industrial groups are shown in Figure 8–5. If the company had opted for functional departmentalization, massive effective coordination would have proved impossible.

This organizational form can also facilitate the measurement and control of operating performance. Since all revenues and costs can be differentiated and assigned to a particular product line, cost centers can be established, high profit areas can be cultivated, and unprofitable product lines can be dropped.

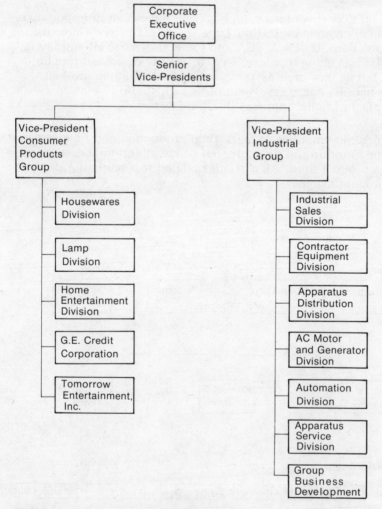

FIGURE 8–5   General Electric Partial Organization Chart Consumer Products Group and Industrial Group (From 1974 Annual Report.)

Product departmentalization also provides an excellent opportunity for training executive personnel. Since the department or division is multi-functional, it often operates like a complete company, providing executives with a wealth of diversified functional experience that is useful in overcoming tunnel vision and seasoning them for the future. This can be very important to a manager who will one day be the chief executive charged with coordinating marketing, finance and production activities. To overemphasize any one of these areas to the detriment of the others can have catastrophic results. A manager who rises through the marketing ranks, for example, may find his sympathies rest with this department and he might favor it in the decision-making process; product departmentalization can minimize this problem.

On the other hand, this form does have potential problem areas. First, the product divisions may try to become too autonomous, thereby presenting top management with a control problem. Second, because of its emphasis on semi-autonomism, product departmentalization works well only in those organizations that have a sufficient number of personnel with general management ability. Third, it is common to find product divisions duplicating some of the facilities found at the top levels of the structure, making it an expensive organizational form.

Territorial Department-alization

When an enterprise is physically dispersed, as in the case of a large-scale organization, it is not uncommon to find *territorial departmentalization*, as seen in Figure 8–6. Contrasting this figure with that of product departmentalization (Figure 8–4) illustrates how similar the two forms really are.

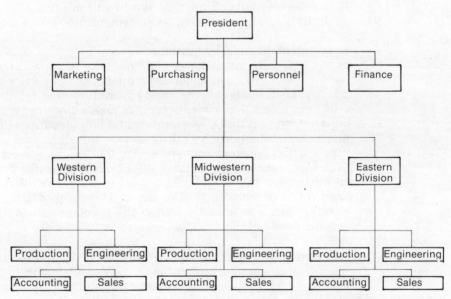

FIGURE 8–6 Territorial Organization Chart for a Manufacturing Firm

Geographically dispersed organizations often employ territorial departmentalization.

The major advantage of a territorial organization is that of local operation. For example, by manufacturing close to the supply of raw materials a firm can produce its product at a lower cost per unit. Furthermore, by setting up a local sales department the personnel can get to know their customers and markets much better.

The disadvantages are the same as those found in product departmentalization. It is often difficult for top management to control operations, and there is a tendency to duplicate services.

Other Types of Departmentalization

Functional, product and geographic are only three types of departmentalization. There are numerous other forms, some of the most common being departmentalization by simple numbers, by time, by customer and by equipment or process.

In addition, there are a number of other forms of departmentalization.

Departmentalization by *simple numbers* is used when the success of the undertaking depends exclusively upon manpower. In community chest drives, for example, each manager is given a number of volunteers and a section of the city to canvass. Success depends to a great extent on the number of people available to ring doorbells. Another illustration is the military, in which portions of the infantry are still organized on the basis of numbers of men. In a business setting, common labor crews are also organized this way.

Departmentalization by *time* is one of the oldest ways of grouping activities. It often consists of, for example, dividing the work force into three shifts: day, swing and graveyard. Police departments all over the world still use this approach, as do industrial firms facing great demand for their goods.

Departmentalization by *customer* is used by organizations such as meat packers, retail stores and container manufacturers. The meat packer will have major departments such as dairy and poultry, beef, lamb and veal, and by-products; the retail store will have major departments such as men's clothing, women's apparel and children's wear; the container company will have major departments such as drug and chemical; closure and plastics; and beverage industries. Another example is educational institutions, which often offer both regular (day) courses and extension (night and off-campus) courses, catering to the needs of different groups of students. This form of departmentalization helps organizations meet the special and widely varying needs of their customers.

Equipment or process departmentalization is often used in manufacturing organizations, as in the establishment of an electronic data processing department. Similarly, in many plants it is common to find lathe presses or automatic screw machines arranged in one locale. The basic value of this organizational form is the economic advantages brought about by such groupings. By placing these machines together, greater efficiency can be obtained.

All the basic departmentalization patterns examined thus far represent common organizational forms. It should be noted, however, that every enterprise will employ its own particular variation. Most will have some form of *hybrid* design; that is, for example, a *basically* functional organization chart with traces of product, equipment, process, customer and/or territorial departmentalization. The chart is seldom what could be called *purely* functional or product or territorial.

COMMITTEE ORGANIZATIONS   Another common organizational form is that of the *committee.* Research indicates that committees are being increasingly employed in business. In general, there are two types. The most common is that appointed for a particular purpose (*ad hoc*). After analyzing a problem situation or conducting some research, the committee gives its recommendations and disbands. The other type is often known as the *standing committee,* many of which are also advisory. If, however, they have the authority to order their recommendations implemented, they are called *plural executives.* The most common illustration of a plural executive is the board of directors, although in a large corporation it is not uncommon to find high-level policy committees such as the executive committee or finance committee also serving in such a capacity.

Another common organization form is the committee.

Advantages of Committees   Committees have some very important advantages to offer. Three of the most commonly cited are group deliberation, motivation and coordination.

Group Deliberation.   A committee has more knowledge, experience and judgment than any one individual alone. In short, two heads are better than one. When an organization focuses the attention of a committee on a particular problem, the result is often a solution superior to that which could be obtained from any one member working independently.

Motivation.   Research has shown that when subordinates are permitted participation in the decision-making process, enthusiasm for accepting and implementing the recommendations often increases. The personnel support the program because they had a hand in fashioning it. Committees can provide the basis for such action.

Coordination.   Committees are also useful in coordinating plans and transmitting information. In the implementation of a major program, for example, many departments may be involved, and a committee can help each see where it fits in the overall plan. It can also obtain agreement on what each is going to do and when, thereby coordinating overall efforts.

Disadvantages of Committees

Despite all their advantages, committees have become the butt of many jokes, such as "a camel is a horse designed by a committee," because the drawbacks to using this organizational design often outweigh the returns. Three of the most commonly cited disadvantages are waste of time, compromise, and lack of individual action.

Waste of Time.   The adage "time is money" can be well applied to committees. Many of them are far too large and spend an excessive amount of time discussing trivial matters. On the issue of size, Parkinson has noted that there is an ever constant pressure to increase the number of people on a committee if for no other reason than to include more individuals with specialized knowledge.[2]

On the issue of time spent on trivial matters, he notes that complex issues often confound people and, because they are unwilling to admit their ignorance of the subject matter, lead them to adopt a policy of silence. The result is the dispatching of crucial decisions, such as allocating $10 million for an atomic reactor, within a matter of minutes. However, on simple issues, understandable to all, such as the construction of a $2350 bicycle shed for use by the clerical staff, committee members come alive. Comprehending both the issue and expense (and realizing they were lax in their participation in the atomic reactor topic), they spring into action with newfound vigor.[3] Parkinson attributes this phenomenon to the *law of triviality*, which states that "the time spent on any item of the agenda will be in inverse proportion to the sum involved."[4]
If this is true, many committees may indeed not be worth the cost.

Compromise.   Committees always pose the danger of compromise. After haggling over an issue for an extended period of time, the group may decide to mediate the matter. No one gets what he is after, but the ultimate decision is one everybody can live with. Unfortunately, the result is often a mediocre decision, representing the least common denominator.

Lack of Individual Action.   There are some things that individuals do better than committees. For example, one very famous American Management Association report found that although committees were considered very useful in handling jurisdictional questions such as interdepartmental disputes, many executives regarded them as ineffective in carrying out

---

[2]C. Northcote Parkinson, *Parkinson's Law* (Boston: Houghton Mifflin Company, 1957), Chapter 3.
[3]*Ibid.*
[4]*Ibid.*, p. 24.

functions such as decision making, organizing, executing and leadership.[5]

Instead, individual action was preferred. Thus, there are times when committees do not perform so well as the individual manager.

Using Committees Effectively

Five important guidelines for using committees effectively.

In light of the above drawbacks, there are several important guidelines to follow if committees are to be effectively employed. First, the objective of the group must be clearly stated. Second, participants must be carefully chosen, providing the expertise needed to attain the objective. Third, the size must be manageable, allowing for discussion and healthy disagreement without becoming too unwieldy in the process. Fourth, an agenda indicating the topics for discussion and analysis must be sent out beforehand so everyone will be prepared to begin immediately. Fifth, the chairman must be able to encourage participation while keeping the group headed toward the objective. Although these guidelines do not ensure success, they have been found to improve committee performance markedly because of their value in overcoming common pitfalls.

SPAN OF CONTROL

Another important organizing concept is *span of control,* which refers to the number of people reporting to a given superior. Many of the classical theorists believed the ideal span to be between three and six. Although this number is open to dispute, the span will certainly have a great deal of influence on the organizational design. For example, taking two companies with approximately the same number of personnel, Figure 8–7 illustrates how the structure would appear if a

------

[5]Ernest Dale, *Planning and Developing the Company Organization Structure,* Research Report No. 20 (New York: American Management Association, 1952), p. 92.

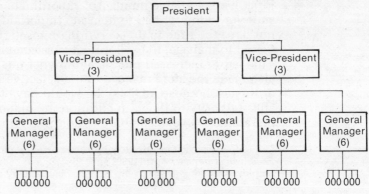

FIGURE 8–7   Narrow Span of Control

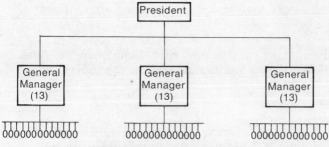

FIGURE 8-8   Wide Span of Control

narrow span of control were employed, while Figure 8–8 shows a company with a wide span of control.

A narrow span of control requires the organization to have more levels in the hierarchy. Thus, the structure looks very much like a pyramid. Conversely, the organization with the wide span of control has fewer levels and a very rectangular shape; it is not very deep, but very wide. The former organization chart is known as a tall structure and the latter as a flat structure.

Flat and Tall Structures

Classical bureaucratic structures are typically very tall, characterized by narrow spans that allow the manager to exercise *tight control.* Having only a few subordinates, it is possible for him to be aware of everything his people are doing.

The most famous departure from the narrow span was made by Sears, Roebuck and Company and is often attributed to James C. Worthy, a management consultant and former vice president of the company.[6] After experimenting with both conventional and flat structures, Sears concluded that, on the basis of sales volume, profit, morale, and management competence, the flat design was superior. Several factors accounted for the results. First, having a large number of subordinate managers, the superior found he had to delegate important decisions; he did not have the time to do everything himself. In turn, by being forced to manage, the subordinates became better at their jobs. This led to increased morale and higher quality performance. It also made the store manager more selective in choosing subordinates, because he knew he would have to delegate considerable authority to them. In addition, by reducing the number of hierarchical levels, communication was improved. Such a struc-

[6]James C. Worthy, "Organizational Structure and Employee Morale," *American Sociological Review*, April 1950, pp. 169–179; and "Factors Influencing Employee Morale," *Harvard Business Review*, January 1950, pp. 61–73.

There are bene-
fits to both flat
and tall struc-
tures.

ture helped overcome what Drucker, one of the best known and
most highly regarded authorities on management today, calls
the major malorganization symptom. He states it this way:

> The most common and most serious symptom of malorganization is multiplica-
> tion of the number of management levels. A basic rule of organization is to
> build the *least possible* number of management levels and forge the shortest
> possible chain of command.[7]

This does not mean, however, that flat structures are always
superior. Carzo and Yanouzas, for example, have conducted
research that showed that groups operating under a basically
tall structure had significantly better results than those operating
under a flat structure.[8] Other researchers have reached similar
conclusions. Thus, there are arguments to be made for each
side, indicating that the "right" span is a function of the situation; the manager, the subordinates and the work itself must
be considered. Perhaps House and Miner have summarized this
entire area best:

> The implications for the span of control seem to be that (1) under most circum-
> stances the optimal span is likely to be in the range 5 through 10; (2) the larger
> spans, say 8 through 10, are most often appropriate at the highest policy-
> making levels of an organization, where greater resources for diversified
> problem-solving appear to be needed (although diversified problem-solving
> without larger spans may well be possible); (3) the breadth of effective
> spans of first line supervisors is contingent on the technology of the organiza-
> tion; and (4) in prescribing the span of control for specific situations
> consideration must be given to a host of local factors such as the desirability
> of high group cohesiveness, the performance demands of the task, the
> degree of stress in the environment, task interdependencies, the need for
> member satisfaction, and the leadership skills available to the organization.[9]

In summary, the correct span of management will vary from
case to case.

AUTHORITY-
RESPONSIBILITY
RELATIONSHIPS

Concurrent with the formation of an organization structure is
the need for assigning specific duties to the personnel. Often
companies will construct *position descriptions,* outlining the
functions each individual is to perform, his authority and
responsibility, and his organizational relationships, *i.e.,* to
whom does he report, with whom will he be interacting and
to whom must he be responsible?

Sources of
Authority

It has already been noted that authority is "the right to
command." The *formal theory of authority,* which supports
the organizational hierarchy, contends that authority comes

---

[7]Peter F. Drucker, Management: *Tasks, Responsibilities, Practices* (New York:
Harper & Row, Publishers, 1974), p. 546.
[8]Rocco Carzo, Jr., and John N. Yanouzas, "Effects of Flat and Tall Organization
Structure," *Administrative Science Quarterly,* June 1969, pp. 178–191.
[9]Robert J. House and John B. Miner, "Merging Management and Behavioral
Theory: The Interaction Between Span of Control and Group Size," *Administrative Science Quarterly,* September 1969, pp. 461–462.

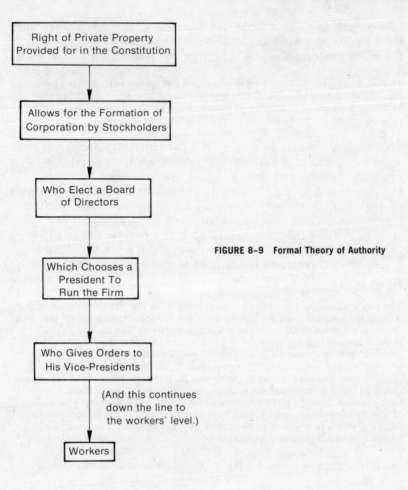

FIGURE 8-9   Formal Theory of Authority

from the top, as seen in Figure 8-9. Barnard, however, argued that authority actually comes from the bottom, because no one has authority unless subordinates accept his directives, *i.e.*, the famous *acceptance theory of authority*.

There are several other theories of authority. One is the *authority of the situation*. For example, if oily rags thrown into the corner of a machine shop suddenly start a fire and an alert machinist calls the fire department, he is exercising authority of the situation. Although his authority is situational in nature, there is no doubt that he has the right to command. Crisis situations or those calling for instant action often impel those present to assume authority, whether or not it has been formally delegated to them.

Another theory of authority is known as the *authority of knowledge*. The person who knows the most about the situation may find himself in charge of the operation. For example, the President of the United States is on his way to Paris for a summit conference. Twenty minutes out of Dulles International the plane encounters engine trouble. The pilot tells the President they are turning back. Although the Commander in Chief has the authority to countermand this order, he does not, because he realizes the pilot knows far more about how to handle the situation than he does. Superior knowledge gives the pilot his authority.

It is evident that there is more than one source of authority. And the acceptance theory, in particular, illustrates that the concept is dynamic, pointing the way to consideration of such topics as power and the role of the informal organization. First, however, we must consider the three major types of authority, namely, *line authority, staff authority* and *functional authority.* Each is an essential part of the basic framework of an organization structure, and although, like the forms of departmentalization just examined, they are always modified in practice, they are, and will continue to be, of central importance to the understanding of the organizing process.

There are three major types of authority.

TYPES OF AUTHORITY

Line authority is direct authority.

Line Authority. Line authority, the most fundamental type of authority, is often referred to as *direct authority* because it encompasses the right to give orders and have decisions implemented. All superiors have line authority over their subordinates. The military provides a classic illustration. The general has line authority over the colonel, who has line authority over the major and so on down the hierarchy. Analogously, the president of a company, as seen in Figure 8–10, has line authority over the vice presidents. In turn, the vice president of production can give direct orders to his subordinates, the heads of manufacturing and purchasing, and they, in turn, have direct authority over their respective subordinates. Line authority results in a chain of command, often called the *scalar chain,* which runs from the top to the

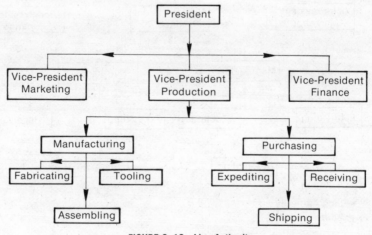

FIGURE 8–10 Line Authority

bottom of the organization and establishes an authority-responsibility relationship throughout.

Staff Authority.   Staff authority is auxiliary authority. Its scope is limited in that it does not provide the right to command. Rather, the nature of the staff relationship is *supportive*. Individuals with staff authority assist, advise, recommend and facilitate organizational activities. As an organization grows in size, executives face increasingly complex problems. Line authority alone is inadequate, and as a result, staff relationships are created.

Staff authority is auxiliary authority.

One of the most common examples of staff authority is the subordinate manager who provides auxiliary services for his superior in the form of recommendations or advice. Another example is the appointment of an assistant to the President, whose job is to counsel the chief executive. A third illustration is the lawyer who is charged with providing legal advice to the president.

Line-Staff Problems

Many firms have found, to their dismay, that although staff authority can be advantageous, it can also lead to authority conflicts between the line and staff executives. One of the major causes rests in the attitudes of the two groups. For example, it is common to find that the line executive is the older fellow who came up the hard way. If he has a college degree, many of the hours may have been earned through correspondence

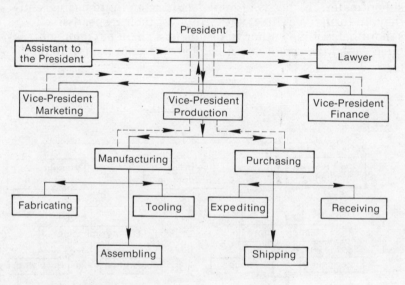

——► Line Authority
--- ► Staff Authority

FIGURE 8–11   Line-Staff Organization

study or night classes. Conversely, his staff counterpart is often a younger executive, perhaps with a master's degree in market research, who has many "bright ideas" about how to improve sales. The line executive sees the young man as lacking in practical experience. The staff executive sees the older man as unwilling to try new ideas.

A second problem arises from the fact that the line executive has ultimate responsibility for the decisions he makes. If he accepts the staff recommendation and the results are poor, he cannot pass the buck. This makes him wary of staff advice. Conversely, staff people see hesitancy or refusal on the part of the line as indecisiveness and inability to recognize substantive recommendations. They feel the line should accept their expertise outright instead of having to be sold on the recommendations through diplomatic persuasion.

Some of the other common reasons for line-staff conflicts are brought about by the following attitudes and philosophies:

Line	Staff
1. Highly action-oriented.	1. Concerned with studying a problem in depth before making recommendations.
2. Highly intuitive in contrast to being analytical.	2. Highly analytical in contrast to being intuitive.
3. Often shortsighted.	3. Often too long-range-oriented.
4. Often ask the wrong kinds of questions.	4. Have answers and therefore spend their time looking for questions.
5. Want simple, easy-to-use solutions.	5. Complicate the situation by providing esoteric data.
6. Accustomed to examining some of the available alternatives and choosing one of them.	6. Interested in examining all of the possible alternatives, weighing them, analyzing them and then choosing the "best" one regardless of time or cost restraints.
7. Highly protective of the organization.	7. Highly critical of the organization.

Various causes of line-staff conflicts.

When these attitudes and philosophies are present, the organization will find it is not achieving maximum benefit from the staff people. However, it is not necessary for these conditions to exist. There are various approaches that can be used to improve line-staff relations.

Improving Line-Staff Relations

There are a number of steps for improving line-staff relations.

One of the most effective ways to facilitate line-staff cooperation is to get everyone to understand the nature of their authority relationships. If the line people realize that they are responsible for making operating decisions and staff people are there to assist them, the former may obtain a greater appreciation of the latter. Likewise, staff people must understand that theirs is only an auxiliary function; they must *sell* their ideas to line people. They cannot order implementation of their recommendations; they must persuade the line manager to adopt them.

A second approach is to encourage the line to *listen* to the staff. As seen in Chapter 1, the Catholic Church has used the concept of compulsory staff service for centuries, requiring the solicitation of staff advice. Although such a mandatory approach can have serious drawbacks in a business setting, a line manager should at least be encouraged to listen to his staff. Many line executives have found that their proposals and plans are more readily accepted if they consult with the staff people before submitting them. Such an approach ensures a united front when top management asks the staff how they feel about the proposal.

A third method is that of keeping *staff specialists informed* on matters that fall within their province. No assistants can help a line manager who fails to tell them the kind of information he will need or the types of decisions confronting him. When this is done, however, it paves the way for effective staff work.

Another useful method is that of *completed staff work.* This involves studying the problem and presenting a solution or recommendation in such a way that the line executive can either approve or disapprove the action. All details are worked out by the staff prior to presentation. Although the approach can involve a tremendous amount of time on the part of the staff people, it saves the line manager from being subjected to continual meetings and discussions on the matter. The entire project is assumed by the staff specialists, and the line man is not bothered with details until the entire issue is finally presented to him. This technique not only provides a basis for justifying the existence of staff, but also gives them an opportunity to sell their ideas to the line.

Functional authority is the right to give orders in a department other than one's own.

Functional Authority.   As an organization grows in size, specialization increases. In addition to the use of line and staff authority, many firms also employ functional authority, which can be defined as *authority in a department other than one's own.* This authority is delegated to an individual or department concerning a specified policy, practice or process being carried out by individuals in other units, and it can be exercised by managers in both line and staff departments.[10] For example, in a product departmentalization structure, certain line managers (see Figure 8–12) may have functional authority over the product division managers. In such a case, the vice president of finance may be able to require the divisions to keep particular kinds of accounting records while the vice president of marketing may be able to request weekly sales data be sent to him in tabular form. In a manner of speaking, the vice presidents have a slice of line authority in the divisions. It should be noted, however, that this is *limited* authority based on expertise and designed to improve organizational efficiency. For this reason, it is common to find functional authority limited to telling people *how* they are to do something and *when* it should be done; it seldom involves where, what, or who, for this would seriously undermine the divisional manager's own line authority. Furthermore, the president will virtually always tell the division heads that he is going to delegate functional authority to the vice presidents of marketing, engineering, production and finance, and get their opinions. In this way, there is a minimum of power grabbing.

Functional authority can also be delegated to staff specialists. For example, the president may have many auxiliary personnel, including a public relations director and legal counsel. In a pure staff situation, each offers him advice in their area of expertise. However, the president may find it more efficient to delegate functional authority to these people. Rather than

---

[10]Line departments carry out activities directly related to the accomplishment of the firm's major objectives, whereas staff departments carry out activities that are indirectly related to these objectives.

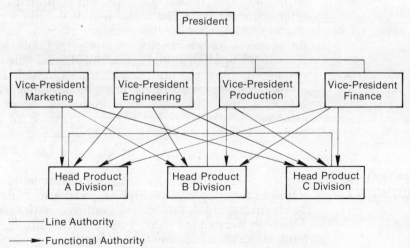

FIGURE 8-12   Line Departments with Functional Authority

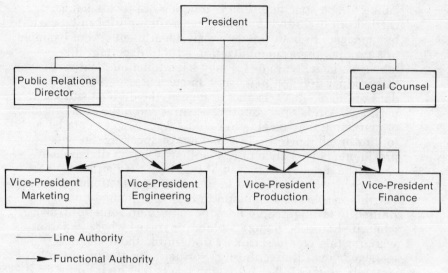

FIGURE 8-13   Staff Departments With Functional Authority

having everything cleared through him, the president allows them to issue their own directives in their area of expertise to the line managers. This situation is illustrated in Figure 8–13. A pure staff relationship no longer exists.

Functional authority can undermine a manager's authority.

Problems with Functional Authority.   The major problem in employing functional authority is the danger of undermining the integrity of managerial positions. For this reason, it is important to indicate precisely who has functional authority and in what matters. Unfortunately, many organizations do not. As a result managers take wide latitude in their interpretation of the types of matters falling within their functional authority domain, and confusion ensues. In theory, this authority is supposed to be limited authority, but in practice the reverse is often more accurate. Defining functional authority in writing is one way of reducing this problem. Another way is to limit the scope of such authority, whenever possible, so that it does not extend more than one hierarchical level below that of the manager holding the functional authority. Such a rule prevents a top executive from undermining other managers in the structure by giving orders directly to their subordinates. In summary, although functional authority has advantages for the organization, it should be employed with prudence.

DECENTRALIZATION OF AUTHORITY   For some time now, many firms, especially large ones, have followed a policy of decentralizing authority. The term "decentralizing" should not be confused with that of delegating. Although the two are closely related, *decentralization* is much more encompassing in nature, reflecting a philosophy on the part of management regarding which decisions to send down the line and which to maintain near the top for purposes of organizational control. All organizations are characterized by some degree of decentralization, absolute centralization being virtually impossible. For this reason, decentralization must be viewed as a relative and not as an absolute concept. Dale has noted that the decentralization is greater:

Decentralization is a relative concept.

1. The greater the number of decisions made lower down the management hierarchy.

2. The more important the decisions made lower down the management hierarchy. For example, the greater the sum of capital expenditure that can be approved by the plant manager without consulting anyone else, the greater the degree of decentralization in this field.

3. The more functions affected by decisions made at lower levels. Thus companies which permit only operational decisions to be made at separate branch plants are less decentralized than those which also permit financial and personnel decisions at branch plants.

4. The less checking required on the decision. Decentralization is greatest when no check at all must be made; less when superiors have to be informed of the decision after it has been made; still less if superiors have to be consulted before the decision is made. The fewer people to be consulted, and the lower they are on the management hierarchy, the greater the degree of decentralization.[11]

Determinants of Decentralization

The degree of decentralization is dependent upon a number of factors.

Many factors will influence decentralization of authority. Most are beyond control of the individual manager, hence the previous statement discerning between this term and delegation, in which the manager decides which duties to assign to a subordinate. The following represent some of the most important determinants of the degree of decentralization.

Cost Factors.   As a rule of thumb, the greater the cost involved, the more likely it is that the decision will be made at the upper levels. It is not uncommon to find a firm with a policy permitting all expenditures of $500 or less to be approved by an operating department while all others have to be decided on by a centralized purchasing or finance committee. In this way, top management is able to control major expenditures, for example, for capital equipment. Many organizations, including General Motors, employ highly centralized controls in the financial area.

Uniform Policy.   A desire for uniform policies is another cause for centralization of authority. Standardization of quality, price, credit and delivery can be beneficial because it ensures that everyone will be treated alike. Similarly, standardization of financial and accounting records makes it easier to compare the performance of various units and analyze their overall efficiency. When the firm wants everything done in a particular way, centralization of policy is desirable.

---

[11]Dale, *op. cit.*, p. 107.

Company Size. As a firm gets larger, it is impossible to maintain the old degree of centralization; top management cannot continue to hold such a tight grip on the reins. It is common to find such firms reorganizing and assigning more authority to the various departments and operating units. In this way, the company reduces the expenses that often accompany growth. The units operate on a more autonomous basis, the top management concerning itself with tasks such as planning, financing, evaluating and controlling the overall operations of the firm. Day-to-day activities are handled at the lower levels.

Philosophy of Top Management. Many firms are highly centralized, whereas others are highly decentralized because of the character and philosophy of the top management, which has a great deal of influence on the degree of decentralization. Henry Ford's firm was highly centralized because that was the way he wanted it; Ford decided matters for the entire company. Conversely, General Motors has been highly decentralized for years because in 1920 A.P. Sloan was able to get his reorganization plan accepted by the board of directors. In essence, it called for decentralization of operating authority to the divisions while maintaining centralized control at the top levels. Dale has described the two principles on which the recommendations rested as:

1. The responsibility attached to the chief executive of each operation shall in no way be limited. Each such organization headed by its chief executive shall be complete in every necessary function and enabled to exercise its full initiative in a logical development. (Decentralization of operations.)

2. Certain central organization functions are absolutely essential to the logical development and proper coordination of the Corporation's activities. (Centralized staff services to advise the line of specialized phases of the work, and central measurement of results to check the exercise of delegated responsibility.)[12]

Philosophy of Subordinate Managers. The philosophy of subordinate managers will affect decentralization in that it can either encourage or discourage such a policy. If subordinates want decentralization, top management may feel there is little to be gained by maintaining all important decision making at the upper levels. The desire by the subordinates for independence and the willingness to assume increased responsibility may convince them to become more decentralized. Conversely, if there is a shortage of managerial manpower, leaving the current group of subordinates with an excessive amount of work, the subordinates may encourage top management to maintain a more centralized approach.

Functional Area. Some functional areas of enterprise will be more decentralized than others. For example, in a manufactur-

---

[12]Ernest Dale, *The Great Organizers* (New York: McGraw–Hill Book Company, 1960), p. 87.

ing firm, production will often be highly decentralized. As the size of the facilities increases, authority will be decentralized so that it rests at the operating level. After all, who knows more about production operations than the people carrying them out? Sales also will often be decentralized for this same reason. Of course, in the case of budgets and controls there will still be a great deal of centralization, as there will be in the areas in which overall control is necessary such as pricing, advertising and market research. Finance will be highly centralized in order to provide top management with an opportunity to maintain control over the entire organization. Although decisions on small expenditures may be made at the lower levels, those having a serious effect on the company's profit or financial stability will be made at the top.

THE ART OF DELEGATION

Delegation is a process the manager uses in distributing work to his subordinates. The process encompasses three basic steps: the assigning of duties to the subordinates; the granting of authority to carry out these duties; and the creation of an obligation whereby the subordinate assumes responsibility to the superior to complete the task satisfactorily.[13]

Delegation, like decentralization, is often a matter of personal preference on the part of the manager. However, while some will delegate so much work to their subordinates that they will virtually abdicate their role as manager, it is far more common to find the reverse occurring. Many managers tend to hang on to everything, refusing to allow their subordinates to try their hand at anything. This unwillingness to let go is based on the assumption that the manager can do the job better than the subordinate, so why bother to delegate? Unfortunately, this attitude is often self-defeating, because it leads subordinates to the conclusion that they are not trusted by their superior. It also results in a failure to develop effective management talent. After all, how can a junior executive ever be expected to fill his boss's shoes if he never gets the opportunity to do so?

Steps to improved delegation.

These deficiencies can be overcome if the manager is willing to follow certain key steps. First, he must agree to try delegating authority and do so in explicit terms. The subordinates must know exactly what they are to do and what kinds of results are going to be expected. Second, careful matching of the man with the job must be undertaken. Third, if there is a problem, the manager should have some form of "open-door" policy, whereby the subordinate can obtain assistance. Fourth, broad, not narrow, controls should be established so that the manager knows if things are going well; prime attention should be paid

---

[13]William H. Newman, Charles E. Summer, and E. Kirby Warren, *The Process of Management: Concepts, Behavior, and Practice,* 3rd edition (Englewood Cliffs, N.J.: Prentice-Hall, 1972), p. 42.

to significant deviations while minor problems are overlooked, at least initially. In this way, the manager controls the situation without giving the impression that he is trying to monitor everything. After all, the subordinate should be expected to make some mistakes, regardless of his capabilities. Fifth, when the job is done, the manager should praise the subordinate's performance in the areas in which good results were obtained and express a willingness to work with him in improving the other areas. This can best be done by delegating more tasks to the subordinate, indicating that he still has the manager's trust and confidence.

THE INFORMAL ORGANIZATION Attention has thus far been focused exclusively on the formal organization as designed and implemented by management. No organization, however, actually operates in this manner. The individuals in the structure tend to remake it, changing things to meet their own needs. Although it is true that functional design theorists contend that an organization should initially be developed without regard for the human element, it is not long before this ideal structure gives way to a more practical one. Bakke termed this a *fusion process*, stating that:

> When an individual and an organization come together in such a way that the individual is a participant in, and a member of, the organization and the two are mutually dependent on each other, both are reconstructed in the process. The organization to some degree remakes the individual and the individual to some degree remakes the organization.[14]

Consideration of this informal structure introduces a more dynamic view of the organization than is available from a mere analysis of the formal design. Although this topic will be covered in greater depth in Chapter 12, it is helpful at this point to regard the informal organization as a structure that is superimposed on the formal one.

The informal organization is not shown on the organization chart. The organization chart cannot show all the formal relationships that exist in the organization. To attempt to depict, for example, functional authority would lead to a mass of lines running all over the page. Likewise, it is virtually impossible to draw the informal organization. Not only are the relationships varied, but they are continually changing. Formal lines are sometimes abandoned in the name of expediency and managers turn to unofficial channels in order to get things done. For example, the head of a production unit has a personal friend in the purchasing department whom he calls whenever it appears that some ordered raw materials will not arrive on time. His friend checks on the shipment and expedites it. A foreman on the assembly line has outstanding rapport with the union.

---

[14]E. Wight Bakke, *The Fusion Process* (New Haven: Labor and Management Center, Yale University, 1953), pp. 12–13.

When the labor contract comes up for re-negotiation, the industrial relations department calls in the foreman and asks him what to include in the new contract. The foreman is not a member of this department but he has an unofficial input into the contract. A production supervisor has a knack for developing new methods. As a result, he ends up with *de facto* jurisdiction over the methods department, even though this department is part of engineering.

Power and Authority

Informal relationships supplement formal authority. Realistically speaking, *real authority* consists of formal authority delegated by one's superior (authority of the position) and personal power. Upon what does personal power depend? Numerous factors can be cited.

Sources of informal power.

Association with the right groups is helpful. The manager who belongs to the same country club as the company president may strike up a social friendship with the top executive. Once other members of the organization learn this, the manager may find individuals, including his immediate superior, much more willing to comply with his requests. The same is often true of the shop steward in a powerful union. The foreman may feel there is far more to be gained by keeping this man happy than by making demands on him. The last thing the foreman wants is a union-management rift, and the shop steward may be useful to him in preventing it.

Experience and *drive* are still other power factors. People who know their job and do it well find others willing to cooperate and assist them; interdepartmental doors are open to them. In addition, their superiors tend to rely on them and back them up if they run into a roadblock. No manager can afford to have productive subordinates stymied. Research shows that socio-psychological factors such as drive, decisiveness and determination not only are positively viewed by others but often establish a credibility about the man as someone who can be relied on. As a result, real power increases.

Education can also be helpful; some companies view it as a major criterion for promotion. When one group of researchers conducted a massive computer analysis of some 3202 individuals employed in the marketing department of a major petroleum corporation, they found education to be one of the most important variables in the promotion process.[15] In addition, their research revealed that not all the promotables were ranked very high on job performance, indicating that there is more than one route to securing power.[16]

---

[15]James W. Walker, Fred Luthans, and Richard M. Hodgetts, "Who Really Are the Promotables?" *Personnel Journal*, February 1970, pp. 123–127.
[16]Fred Luthans, James W. Walker, and Richard M. Hodgetts, "Evidence on the Validity of Management Education," *Academy of Management Journal*, December 1969, pp. 451–457.

Other power factors include *religion, politics, race* and *national origin.* In some firms, especially at the upper levels, a Republican WASP may have more power than a Democratic Catholic because the people at the top belong to the former category. On the other hand, in Boston this same person may be at a decided disadvantage. Likewise, despite legislation to the contrary, race and national origin are still bases for the establishment of power relationships.

Formal and Informal Organizational Relationships

The informal organization is an inevitable product of human social processes. Unfortunately, too many organizations view it as a destructive element that must be weeded out. Actually, the informal organization has some very important advantages to offer. Primarily, it is a source of satisfaction for the members, often bringing about much higher morale than would otherwise be the case. This was clearly seen in the bank wiring room of the Hawthorne plant.

The informal organization can be very helpful to the company.

Early writings in the field pictured the informal organization as disruptive, the role of management being one of manipulating the group into accepting formal goals. Today, it is evident that such manipulation is seldom necessary. Oftentimes the goals of the formal and informal organizations are mutually reinforcing. Of course, this is not always true, but until management is certain that the informal organization is in conflict with the formal, all attempts should be made to nurture the relationship. It does management no good to try to form a clear-cut distinction between the two. Actually, they are interrelated parts of a complex system. Management's job must be that of creating an organizational climate in which the goals and expectations of both groups can be attained.

SUMMARY

In this chapter, the nature, purpose and function of organizing were examined. It was noted that organizing covers a very broad area and offers many alternatives to the manager. There are numerous forms of departmentalization available; wide or narrow spans of control can be employed; and various types of authority can be delegated. Attention was particularly focused on problem areas, such as line-staff conflicts, by way of illustrating that organizing is certainly no mechanical function. There is a great deal of judgment involved in effectively coordinating all elements in the structure. This challenge was made even clearer with the introduction of the informal organization and the concept of personal power, for they bring a type of dynamism into the formal structure.

Although the organizing process brings the people and the work together, management still needs a basis for comparing the plan and the results. This activity, commonly referred to as the controlling process, will be the subject of the next chapter.

REVIEW AND STUDY QUESTIONS

1. What is meant by "from strategy to structure"? Explain by including a discussion of the planning process in your answer.

2. What are the most widely used forms of departmentalization? List them.

3. How does functional departmentalization differ from product departmentalization? How does it differ from territorial departmentalization? What are the advantages associated with each?

4. What are the common advantages and disadvantages of committees?

5. How does a tall structure differ from a flat one?

6. What impact does the span of control have on the structure?

7. What is meant by the term "authority"? Where does authority come from?

8. What is line authority? Staff authority? Functional authority? Explain by using an illustration of each.

9. What are some common line-staff conflicts? What gives rise to them? How can they be prevented or overcome?

10. How does decentralization differ from delegation? Give an illustration of each.

11. What are some of the factors that influence the degree of delegation that will take place in an organization? Differentiate between those that encourage it and those that discourage it.

12. What are some of the key steps to improving a manager's ability to delegate authority?

13. How does the formal organization differ from the informal? What role does personal power play? Explain in your own words.

14. Are the objectives of the formal and informal organization always in conflict? Defend your answer.

SELECTED REFERENCES

"Ampex Switches Back to Centralization." *Business Week*, June 16, 1973, pp. 70–72.

Belasco, J. A., and J. A. Alutto. "Line Staff Conflicts: Some Empirical Insights." *Academy of Management Journal*, December 1969, pp. 469–477.

Blankenship, L. V., and R. E. Miles. "Organizational Structure and Managerial Decision Behavior." *Administrative Science Quarterly*, June 1968, pp. 106–120.

Chandler, A. D., Jr. *Strategy and Structure*. Garden City, New York: Anchor Books, Doubleday & Company, 1966.

Child, J. "Predicting and Understanding Organization Structure." *Administrative Science Quarterly*, June 1973, pp. 168–185.

Clark, P. A. *Organizational Design: Theory and Practice*. London: Tavistock Publishing, 1972.

Curcuru, E. H., and J. H. Healey. "The Multiple Roles of the Manager." *Business Horizons*, August 1972, pp. 15–24.

Dale, E. *Planning and Developing the Company Organization Structure.* Research Report No. 20, New York: American Management Association, 1952.

Dale, E. *The Great Organizers*, New York: McGraw-Hill Book Co., 1960.

Drucker, P. F. *Management: Tasks, Responsibilities, Practices.* New York: Harper & Row Publishers, 1974, Chapters 41–48.

Ford, C. F. "Structuring the Organization for Fast Decision-Making." *Human Resource Management*, Summer 1973, pp. 2–12.

"GE's Jones Restructures His Top Team." *Business Week*, June 30, 1973, pp. 38–39.

Golembiewsi, R. T. "Personality and Organization Structure: Staff Models and Behavioral Patterns." *Academy of Management Journal*, September 1966, pp. 217–232.

Hellreigel, D., and J. W. Slocum, Jr. "Integrating Systems Concepts and Organizational Strategy." *Business Horizons*, April 1972, pp. 71–78.

House, R. J., and J. B. Miner. "Merging Management and Behavioral Theory: The Interaction Between Span of Control and Group Size." *Administrative Science Quarterly*, September 1969, pp. 451–464.

Jones, H. R., Jr. "A Study of Organization Performance for Experimental Structures of Two, Three, and Four Levels." *Academy of Management Journal*, September 1969, pp. 351–365.

Logan, H. H. "Line and Staff: An Obsolete Concept?" *Personnel*, January–February 1966, pp. 26–33.

Maier, N.R.F., and J.A. Thurber. "Problems in Delegation." *Personnel Psychology*, Summer 1969, pp. 131–139.

Parkinson, C. N. *Parkinson's Law.* Boston: Houghton Mifflin, 1957.

CASE: I DID IT MY WAY

Whenever one spoke of Shayling Inc., one was speaking of Mr. Peter Shayling, founder, owner, president and chairman of the board. Shayling, Inc., was one of the largest television retail and repair stores in the city, with gross sales of over $3 million. Mr. Shayling delighted in telling customers how he had started out in a small shop on the outskirts of town and gradually increased the size of his business to where he could afford to move into his current, modern midtown facilities.

When the store was very small, Mr. Shayling and his wife did everything, including keeping the books. The only outside assistance they had was an accountant who came in every three months to balance the ledgers and compute the taxes. Gradually, as volume increased, Mr. Shayling began hiring help. First, he brought in a television repairman; then he hired a salesman. By mid-1974 there were fifteen people working for him, nine in the repair and delivery shop, six on the sales floor.

Although things appeared to be going well, Mr. Shayling, however, admitted to his wife that he was disturbed by the large turnover of salesmen; on an average, he was losing one a month. He was also losing an average of one repairman every other month. About this time he received a call from a group of master's students in a nearby college of business who were taking an upper division management course that required them to analyze a local concern. They wanted to know if Mr. Shayling would let them write their paper on his company. Although initially skeptical, he was impressed by the fact that the team would put together a list of recommendations that would be turned over to him, so he agreed. "It's like getting free consulting," he told his wife.

Six weeks later, the team sent him a copy of their paper. The analysis and recommendations were of great interest to Mr. Shayling. He felt the team had done an admirable job, and he intended to implement many of their suggested changes. However, there was one part of the paper with which he disagreed. It read as follows:

The high salesman turnover can be directly attributed to the owner's failure to delegate authority. No salesman is ever able to introduce a product to a customer or close a sale without Mr. Shayling getting into the act; he is everywhere. The result is a decline in morale brought about by the fact that the owner seems to lack faith in his own personnel. An analogous situation exists in the repair shop, although not to the same degree. In summary, Mr. Shayling should spend more time managing and less time looking over people's shoulders.

In defense of his actions, Mr. Shayling noted to his wife that the students undoubtedly lacked an understanding of the television repair business. "You've got to be on top of everything all the time," he said. "And far from getting in the way, I am really quite helpful to the salesmen. After all, who knows more about how to sell than me? I built this store from nothing and I did it my way. And there's no substitute for success. In fact, far from changing this habit, I think the salesmen would do an even better job if I spent more time helping them out."

Questions

1. Is failure to delegate a cause of poor morale? Explain.

2. How is Mr. Shayling's action typical of many owner-managers? Explain.

3. How can Mr. Shayling overcome his problem? Be specific in your recommendations.

4. Could the report have been worded differently so as to sell Mr. Shayling the recommendation? Explain.

CASE: A NEW SWITCH

Fun-For-All is a national manufacturing firm that produces and sells toys and games. Prior to 1968, the company specialized in children's toys, but in the late sixties adult games began to gain acceptance and Fun-For-All followed suit. The basic feature of the adult games is that they have no single, correct strategy and, as a result, they require a great deal of thought on the part of the participant. For example, Monopoly, from Parker Brothers, has a basic strategy that often depends upon chance rather than skill. If the player is wise, he buys as much land as he can and starts putting houses, and eventually hotels, on his property. However, true adult games such as chess are much more complex. There is no one right way to win a chess match; it all depends upon what one's opponent does and upon one's own skill.

In 1972, two months prior to the famous Fischer-Spaasky match in Iceland, Fun-For-All accurately predicted that the young American would win and began manufacturing an inexpensive ($19.95) wood-carved chess set. As the match progressed, the number of Americans who became interested in chess increased dramatically. By the end of the world championship match, thanks to timing and a strong advertising program, the firm had sold four times the number of sets it had initially forecast.

In 1974, because of growing sales, the management of Fun-For-All was considering a reorganization. At the time the firm was organized along functional lines (see Figure 8–14). However, the president thought the company might be wiser to change to product departmentalization, and some of the people in marketing also seemed to think that it would be a good idea. The production department, however, felt there was more to be gained from functional rather than product departmentalization. The finance people seemed indifferent about the matter, but indicated they would make an analysis of the two structures if the president desired.

The president's reorganization plan was to set up three product divisions: boy's toys, girl's toys and adult games. The first two divisions accounted for over 75 per cent of the firm's sales, but the latter was growing rapidly and would, according

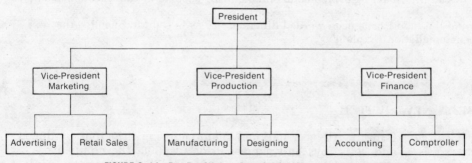

FIGURE 8–14   Fun-For-All, Inc. Organization Chart, September, 1974

to marketing estimates, account for over 50 per cent of all sales by 1978.

Questions

1. Draw the proposed reorganization chart. Be as complete as possible.

2. What are the advantages of product departmentalization over functional departmentalization?

3. What recommendations would you make to the president before deciding to switch from functional to production departmentalization? Explain.

CASE: A MATTER OF OPINION

Abraham Liefeld had been a production manager for over thirty years, and there was virtually nothing he did not know about production. Mr. Liefeld's new assistant, Barney Shackler, had great admiration for him. Barney felt he had learned more about how to handle workers and obtain increased output in his first four weeks on the job than in his four years of undergraduate business school.

During this initial period, Barney tried to keep his eyes and ears open; he was determined to learn as much about the job as possible. For example, he knew that Jack Charlton, another production manager, was a good friend of Mr. Liefeld's, and if Mr. Charlton ever called Mr. Liefeld for a favor and he was not in, Barney should take care of it himself or see that it was done immediately. Gradually, he also began to learn the names and positions of other people with whom the production department came in contact on a rather regular basis. One of these was Fred Ackerman from personnel who often visited Mr. Liefeld. Barney knew Mr. Liefeld was interested in hiring some production supervisors and he had asked Mr. Ackerman to take out some ads and to keep scouring the local colleges and universities when he went out recruiting.

About six months after Barney had started, he knew his way around pretty well. At least he thought he did, until he inadvertently walked into Mr. Liefeld's office to find his boss and Mr. Ackerman in a shouting match. When they saw him their tempers immediately cooled. Barney backed out the door. A few minutes later he noticed Mr. Ackerman leaving and he went back in.

I'm sorry, Mr. Liefeld. I didn't realize you had anyone in here with you.

That's okay, Barney. Come on in. I think it's about time you realized that not everyone around here agrees with everyone else all of the time.

But what conflict can you be having with Mr. Ackerman? Isn't he in personnel?

Yes, but he screens all incoming people. Remember those tests you took as part of your application process?

Sure.

Well, they're designed to find out something about your management potential. At least that's what Ackerman says. Supposedly, eight out of ten people who do well on them become good supervisory managers and the other two do not. Mr. Ackerman wants us to use that test as a screening device.

And you don't want to?

Let's put it this way. I want to see a man face-to-face and talk with him. I know what to look for in a good supervisor; I don't need any test to tell me how a man can handle himself. There's a young fellow who did poorly on the exam but I want to hire him. Mr. Ackerman disagrees.

Can he force you to use the test as a screening device?

No. His entire job is to evaluate the applicants and give me his recommendations. I decide who to hire in this department. That guy's getting a little too big for his britches. He's supposed to be advising me and he winds up giving me orders. Imagine, telling me that that young fellow I interviewed last week did poorly on the exam and I should forget about hiring him. Well, until the president decides that Ackerman has more savvy about how to run this department than I do, I'm going to make all the hiring decisions.

Questions

1. What kind of authority does Mr. Ackerman have? How do you know?

2. What kind of line-staff conflict is represented here? Explain.

3. How can these problems be prevented in the future? Be specific in your answer.

CASE: HOSPITAL BUSINESS

Equipped with a newly earned bachelor's degree in business administration from a large eastern university, Greg Ritter set out to nail down a career in the business world. However, when interviews with several local and national firms proved fruitless, he decided to investigate job openings in a nearby hospital.

It had never occurred to Greg that hospitals had need for people with his qualifications—he had thought of them in terms of highly specialized technical experts such as open-heart surgeons, intensive-care nurses and medical technologists. When he learned from the hospital's Director of Personnel that the hospital was strongly oriented toward management—even to the extent of maintaining its own Management Development Department—he began to feel as if there were opportunities in the hospital field for breaking into the management ranks.

As Mr. Biggs, Director of Personnel, outlined the position opening in the Management Development Department, Greg listened
with growing enthusiasm. Sensing his interest, Mr. Biggs
immediately arranged an interview with Arlene Kimball,
Director of the Management Development Department.

Arlene escorted Greg into her office, one wall of which was
lined with shelves of books on management, behavioral
psychology and training. Arlene explained to Greg that her
department was responsible for assisting administrators,
directors, managers, department heads and supervisors—all of

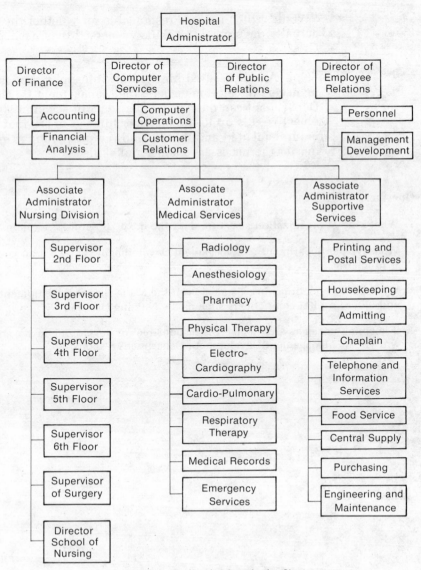

FIGURE 8-15   Hospital Organization Chart

whom were considered members of the hospital's management team—in acquiring or improving managerial skills. In forecasting the services that her department would need to provide over the next few years in order to carry out that mission, Arlene found that she would need to add to her staff a person with a business administration background who could serve as an internal consultant to managers. This was the position that she now offered Greg. "As a management development consultant, you would work with, for example, nursing supervisors and help them diagnose their managerial knowledge, attitude and skill needs within the overall context of the management needs of the hospital. With them you would then prepare a planned approach for meeting those needs."

"Would I then become responsible for whether the managers actually developed the skills we agreed they needed?" asked Greg.

"No," Arlene assured him. "Our philosophy here is that managers develop managers; the Management Development Department can only assist managers in accomplishing that objective. It's up to the manager himself to see that the plan is implemented and that he and the people reporting to him master the necessary managerial skills."

Questions

1. What kind of organization structure does the hospital employ? Explain.

2. What type of department is Management Development? On what do you base your answer?

3. What kind of relationship exists between the Management Development Department and other hospital components such as the Nursing Division? Explain.

4. If hospital managers are themselves responsible for developing managers, for what is the Management Development Department responsible?

CHAPTER 9

THE CONTROLLING PROCESS

GOALS OF THE CHAPTER

If an organization attains its objectives, more ambitious ones can be formulated. If it falls short of these goals, a revised plan is in order. In either case, an evaluation must be conducted, and this is where the controlling process comes in.

The goals of this chapter are to examine the nature and process of control with prime focus on traditional, specialized and overall control techniques. In particular, major attention will be devoted to:

a. the three basic steps in the controlling process;
b. the importance of feedback;
c. the requirements of an effective control system;
d. the value of budgeting in the control process;
e. break-even point analysis and its importance for the manager;
f. the benefits associated with information design;
g. PERT as a control technique;
h. the usefulness of milestone budgeting and program budgeting;
i. the value of overall control methods such as return in investment and key area control; and
j. the benefits that can be derived from external, internal and management audits.

THE BASIC CONTROLLING PROCESS

As Fayol noted, "The control of an undertaking consists of seeing that everything is being carried out in accordance with the plan which has been adopted, the orders which have been given, and the principles which have been laid down. Its object is to point out mistakes in order that they may be rectified and prevented from occurring again."[1]

The three basic steps in this controlling process are the establishment of standards, the comparison of performance

[1]Henri Fayol, *Industrial and General Administration* (Translated from the French edition by J.A. Coubrough, Geneva: International Management Institute, 1929), p. 77.

against these standards, and the correction of deviations that have occurred. The latter two, of course, can only be attained through the establishment of effective feedback. This section will examine these three basic steps and the role of feedback in the controlling process.

Establishing Standards

Standards provide a basis against which performance can be measured. These standards are often a result of the goals the organization formulates during its planning phase. Sometimes they are very specific, being expressed in terms of costs, revenues, products or man-hours worked. Other times they are more qualitative in nature such as a desire to maintain high morale among the employees or to design a public relations program for gaining community goodwill.

Comparing Performance With Standards

Ideally, management should design a control system that permits it to identify major problems before they occur. For example, research shows that an individual's attitude toward the job declines before his productivity goes down. If management could identify this lead factor, it could begin taking steps to prevent the impending decline in output. However, since this is often more idealistic than practical, the next best step is to identify such deviations as early as possible. Most competent managers do so through use of the exception principle, which holds that attention should be focused on especially good or especially bad situations. In this way, the manager avoids spreading himself too thin by trying to control every deviation.

Some standards are not easily measured.

The major problem most managers encounter is *how* to measure actual performance. Some standards are easily measurable, whereas others require custom-made appraisals. Still others seem to defy any form of accurate evaluation. For example, how does one really measure worker motivation, since motivation is an intervening variable? It is an internal, psychological process that is not directly observable and can only be judged by drawing inferences about a person. If one appears interested in his work he is motivated, and vice versa. Yet this appraisal may well be inaccurate. Another common performance measurement dilemma occurs when a firm tries to evaluate a top-level manager such as the vice president of finance. Whatever criteria are used, they are often vague in nature. Management has found that as the work becomes less technical, standards are often difficult to develop and appraisals exceedingly hard to make. For this reason, in recent years there has been a trend toward evaluating personnel almost exclusively on objective bases. If the standard is not measurable, it is not employed. This approach is useful in that it greatly reduces subjective, biased evaluations while providing direction for the subordinates who now know the bases on which their performance will be judged.

Correcting Deviations

The correction of deviations should begin with an investigation of why the error occurred. Sometimes a planning premise may have been wrong. Sales may have been lower than anticipated because of an overly optimistic forecast. Or a strike in the plant may have caused unexpected delays in production. The cause of the deviation will help determine the appropriate action. The key point to be noted here is that some problems are no one's fault. From time to time even the best market forecasts will be wrong. An example of this was illustrated in Chapter 7 in the case of Frost 8/80, the dry white whisky that, despite an extensive market research program, failed to achieve wide-spread acceptance. And in the case of a union strike, the walkout may be more a function of union demands than of management offers. For example, the company may be able to give a maximum offer of 15 per cent in salary and 4.2 per cent in fringe benefits over a two-year period. If the union refuses to settle for anything less than 20 per cent and 5.7 per cent respectively, a strike may be inevitable. In short, not all deviations are directly attributable to any one individual, and if management continually tries to assess blame for every error, employee attitudes toward work may suffer.

After the cause is identified, problem-solving measures can be enacted.

Of course, there are times when a manager will make an error in judgment or a worker will handle an order improperly. When this occurs, corrective action may require the replacement of the individual or the assignment of additional training. However, the action can only be determined after the specific causes of the deviation have been evaluated.

Establishing Effective Feedback

An ideal control system provides timely *feedback* that can be used to monitor and correct deviations. A basic illustration is provided by the human body. If something happens that causes the body to leave its "normal" state, basic control mechanisms will attempt to reestablish the status quo. This self-regulating or control property is known as *homeostasis*. For example, if a person cuts his finger, the body will begin working to coagulate the blood and close the wound. The feedback mechanism in the human system can perform phenomenal feats if conditions are not too severe, i.e., one suffers a massive heart attack or is hit by a Mack truck.

This same basic concept of feedback is present in the thermostat system of a home. The desired temperature is determined by setting an indicator, and this is communicated to the system that controls the furnace. If a family desires 68°F, the heating unit will maintain the temperature at this level, turning on and off as necessary.

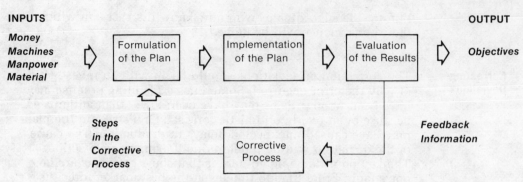

FIGURE 9-1 Simple Feedback Process

An organization also requires a feedback system. With the information provided by such a system, the company can monitor activities by identifying those that are not in accord with plans and taking the necessary corrective action. The establishment of such a system results in the type of process depicted in Figure 9-1.

It should be noted, however, that organizational control systems differ from those found in the human body and the home thermostat in that the latter are often automatic and employ, at least in the short-run, only data from within the system. Organizational control, on the other hand, is seldom automatic. Usually, by the time feedback results are evaluated, other errors have occurred, and the organization is involved in a game of "catch-up." In addition, organizational control employs data from outside the system. This occurs in the corrective process when the manager decides how to handle deviations, thereby introducing new decisions or inputs into the process. For this reason, mechanical control systems are often known as *closed-loop* systems, whereas organizational control systems are often called *open-loop* systems. Naturally, the latter must be viewed on a spectrum. If most organizational decisions are handled via established policies or procedures, the system is more automatic than one requiring the manager to formulate his own action. Nevertheless, even with feedback, organizational control presents a challenge to the manager.

Organizations must develop effective feedback control systems.

REQUIRE-MENTS FOR AN EFFECTIVE CONTROL SYSTEM

The process of control is not an automatic phenomenon. If the organization wants an effective control system, it has to tailor one to its own specifications. In addition to the two previously mentioned requirements, namely, that controls be objective and the manager employ the exception principle, the following are some other prerequisites for an effective control system.

Provide Useful, Understandable Information

Control systems will differ from organization to organization and from manager to manager. Information that is valuable to one man may be useless to another. The key question each must ask is, what information do I need to control the activities within my jurisdiction? This approach is valuable for two reasons. First, it forces the manager to decide what he needs to know and in what form. This is known as information design and results in useful, understandable data. Second, it provides a basis for screening out reports and information that he may be receiving which are of no value to him in the control process.

Timeliness

Controls should report deviations quickly. In addition, a well-designed system should be capable of identifying potential problem areas before they manifest themselves. For example, forecasting a cash flow for the next ninety days based on optimistic, most likely and pessimistic conditions can provide management with a short-run financial picture. If it appears likely that the company will run out of cash, i.e., only under the most optimistic conditions will it remain in the black, there is still time to negotiate a loan with a local bank. In this way, controls become lead rather than lag factors.

Flexibility

Most plans will deviate from expectations and some will be outright failures. Unless a control system is flexible, it will be unable to maintain control of operations during these periods. The value of flexible control can be readily seen in the use of budgets that are increased or contracted based on the volume of business (flexible budgets). These techniques help management control operations regardless of economic conditions.

Economical

A control system must be worth the expense. However, it is often difficult to determine when the marginal costs associated with the system equal the marginal revenues obtained from it. Naturally, a small company cannot afford to install the expensive systems employed by a large corporation, but what about a minor expenditure such as a time clock? If a firm puts one in, will tardiness be reduced? Will work output increase? The answer to the first question may be "yes" while the answer to the second may be "no." People might show up on time and not leave early for home, but that does not mean they will do more work. They may just sit around waiting to clock out at 5 p.m. On the other hand, productivity may rise, and although a large firm may be able to absorb low productivity, a small one may not, so the system might prove useful to the latter. In either event, if a firm decides to put in the time clock, it must be willing to compare results both before and after the installation. Only in this way can it be sure that the control mechanism was economical. This guideline also applies to revenues and expenses associated with control systems that are much more difficult to evaluate. For example, what is the cost-benefit ratio attached to a new monthly progress report that must be submitted by all unit managers? This may be difficult to answer, requiring a highly subjective estimate. Nevertheless, some attempt must be made to do so.

Lead to Corrective Action

An effective control system must lead to corrective action; merely uncovering deviations from plans is not enough. The system must also disclose where the problem areas are and who is responsible for them. From here management can evaluate the situation and decide upon the appropriate action. Figure 9–2 provides an illustration of the controlling process in action.

TRADITIONAL CONTROL TECHNIQUES

There is a large number of control techniques that can be employed by management. Some of the more traditional ones include budgeting, break-even point analysis and personal observation.

Budgeting

When budgets were mentioned earlier in the book (Chapter 7), it was noted that organizations often use them to harmonize functional plans. As such, the budget is a type of plan specifying anticipated results in numerical terms. However, it is also a control device that provides a basis for feedback, evaluation and follow-up.

Comprehensive Budgeting. Many organizations use comprehensive budgeting when all phases of operations are covered by budgets. This often begins with the submission of budget proposals by subordinate managers. After discussion with the superiors, the proposals are adjusted, if necessary, and then
A "from-the-bottom-up" approach is used.
forwarded to higher management. The result is a bottom-up approach, which ensures consideration of the needs and desires of, and participation by, lower management. However, the process does not stop here. At the top of the organization there is often a budget committee, which reviews the entire program. In a manufacturing firm, for example, this committee may consist of the president and the vice presidents of finance, marketing and production, who have line authority to make whatever final budget revisions are necessary. In other cases, the committee may be staffed by lower ranking personnel who have advisory authority only. In either case, the result is an integration of the individual budgets into a comprehensive one and the paring away of excessive requests. Thus, although everyone has an input into the budget, the top management maintains the authority to make necessary adjustments. This is very important once one realizes that some departments will request 130 per cent of what they need and hope to be cut back no more than 20 per cent. Of

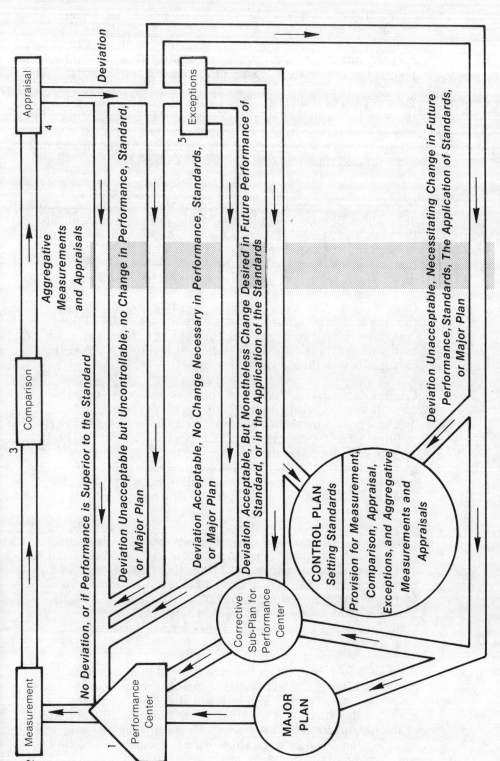

FIGURE 9-2 Controlling Process in Action (From Dale A. Henning, *Non-financial Controls in Smaller Enterprises,* University of Washington Bureau of Business Research, Seattle, 1964, p. 22. Reprinted with permission.)

course, the challenge is knowing where to cut. An overall 30 per cent reduction in budget requests is harmful to those units that are not padding their estimates and helpful to those that are. For this reason, management must impress on its people the importance of submitting reasonable budgets.

There are five basic types of budgets.

Basic Types of Budgets. There are various kinds of budgets that can be employed by an organization. In essence, they can be classified into five basic types: revenue and expense budgets; cash budgets; capital expenditure budgets; production, material and time budgets; and balance sheet budgets.

Revenue and Expense Budgets. This is the most common form of business budget. Encompassed within the revenue side are the sales and "other" incomes the firm expects to obtain during the period. The expense budget, on the other hand, contains the costs associated with ensuring these revenues such as direct labor, materials, administrative overhead and rent.

Cash Budgets. The cash budget is simply a forecast of cash receipts and expenditures. The ability to meet bills as they come due is vital to a firm's existence, but to have too much cash sitting idle is foolish. Cash budgeting attempts to strike a balance between these two extremes.

Capital Expenditure Budgets. Capital expenditures usually constitute a long-run commitment. Investments in plant, machinery and inventory are often tied up for extended periods of time. Since capital recovery takes so long, a firm must be very careful not to tie up too much of its money in these assets. However, a failure to maintain modern, efficient facilities can reflect a penny-wise dollar-foolish philosophy. Thus the company must carefully tie this budget into its strategic plan.

Production, Material and Time Budgets. Some budgets are expressed in physical rather than monetary terms because it is easier to control operations on this basis. Material and production output, for example, are often budgeted in terms of units. Manpower is expressed in terms of man-days or labor-hours. Eventually, of course, these are translated into monetary quantities, but for control purposes physical terms are employed.

Balance Sheet Budgets. A balance sheet budget forecasts the assets, liabilities and net worth of the organization at the end of the particular period and indicates the effect of the budgeted plans on these items. It provides an estimated financial picture of the organization for the period. This allows management to compare the latest balance sheet with the expected one for purposes of analyzing projected changes. It also provides a basis for comparing the actual financial statement at the end of the period with the anticipated one in evaluating the overall accuracy of the budget.

Avoiding Inflexibility in Budgeting.   Budgets are useful planning and control tools, but they can prove cumbersome if overbudgeting occurs. Spelling out all expenses in detail deprives the manager of freedom of action. It can also lead to assigning higher priorities to the budget than to organizational objectives.

Various forms of flexible budgets are being used.

In order to avoid such inflexibility, there has been increasing interest given to the *variable expense budget*. This budget is used to complement the original one. With it, expenses and allowances are computed for different levels of activity. Then, after the budget period is over, calculations are made regarding what the expenses for each unit *should* have been. If activity was as expected, departments should be within their budgets. If, however, volume was much higher than expected there will be many who overspent. The company will then, based on a predetermined formula, compute what the expenses should have been and adjust departmental budgets accordingly. The variable budget, however, is not a substitute for a comprehensive budgetary program; rather, it is a supplement to it.

Some companies use a variation of the variable budget known as the *supplemental monthly budget*. Under this approach, a minimum operational budget is determined. Then, prior to the beginning of each month, a supplemental budget is drawn up that provides the units with additional funds based on volume expectations for the period. This approach differs from the variable budget in that adjustments are made before the period begins rather than after it is over.

Another version of the flexible budget is the *alternative budget*. Under this approach, the company establishes budgets for various levels of operations: high, medium and low. Then, at the beginning of the particular period, managers are told under which budget they will be operating.

Approaches such as these all indicate the need for flexibility in the budgeting process; and as sources of information feedback, they can provide a very useful function to the manager. However, one must be careful not to become too reliant on them. Budgets must be regarded only as tools for attaining organizational control.

Break-Even Point

Another common control technique is break-even analysis. At the end of any given period of operation, an organization hopes to make a profit. To do this, total revenue must be greater than total costs. For purposes of analysis, costs can be divided into

two categories: fixed costs and variable costs. Fixed costs are
those that will remain constant (at least in the short-run) regardless of operations. Examples include property insurance,
property taxes, depreciation and administrative salaries.
Variable costs are those that will change in relation to output.
In a manufacturing enterprise, labor salaries and cost of
materials are typical examples.

*Break-even
point occurs
when total fixed
and variable ex-
penses are cov-
ered.*

In computing the break-even point (BEP), three cost-revenue
components are of major importance to the manager: total fixed
cost, selling price per unit and variable cost per unit. By
subtracting the variable cost associated with the unit from its
selling price, a margin-above-cost is obtained. This margin can
then be applied to the total fixed cost with the BEP occurring
when the total of these margins equals total fixed cost. In
simple mathematical terms:

$$BEP = \frac{TFC}{P - VC}$$

where: TFC = total fixed cost
        P   = price per unit
        VC = variable cost per unit

Consider the following example. Company A has conducted
market research on a new product and determined that at $10
each it can sell 25,000 units. The firm's total fixed costs are
$120,000 and its variable cost per unit is $4. Given this
information, will the venture be profitable? The answer is
going to depend on the BEP. Applying the relevant data to the
formula results in the following:

$$BEP = \frac{\$120,000}{\$10 - 4}$$

$$= \frac{\$120,000}{6}$$

$$= 20,000 \text{ units}$$

The firm's BEP is 20,000 units. Figure 9–3 illustrates this
solution graphically. Since sales are projected at 25,000 units,
the venture should prove profitable. However, if market research
showed a demand of anything less than 20,000 units, the
company could not break even on the project.

BEP analysis is a useful control device because it emphasizes
the marginal concept. In addition, it helps establish initial
guidelines for control; i.e., fixed costs should remain at
$120,000, variable cost per unit should be $4, and profits should
occur after 20,000 units are sold. If costs or expected sales
change, the management has a basis for evaluating the impact
and taking the necessary corrective action.

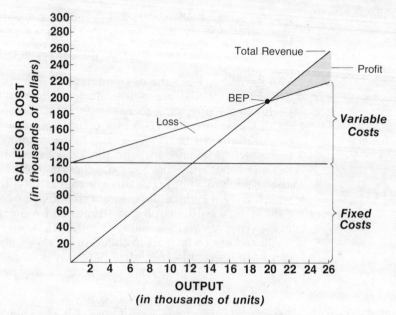

FIGURE 9–3   Break-Even Point Computation

Personal Observation	Another common control technique is personal observation. Although it is employed in virtually every organization, it is especially common in small and medium-sized firms. Non-profit organizations that are under little pressure to show results on a time-cost basis also make wide use of it.
A firsthand view can be useful.	

Although personal observation alone is an incomplete form of control, it is an excellent supplement to budgets and break-even analysis. There are many things that a manager cannot discover from reporting forms that he can obtain with a casual stroll through the work place. There is no substitute for a firsthand view of operations, and personal observation provides just this.

SPECIALIZED CONTROL TECHNIQUES	In addition to traditional control techniques, management has developed many specialized tools to improve the quality of control. Space does not allow a discussion of all of them, but three will be examined: information design, time-event analyses and program budgeting.

Information Design	Information design is critical to an organization, especially in light of modern computers that can provide a wealth of data on virtually any area the manager would like to examine. Without some system for filtering out relevant from irrelevant information, an individual can find himself swamped with reports and numbers, most of which are meaningless to him. As Koontz and O'Donnell have pointed out:
The manager receives only pertinent data.	

Managers who have experienced the impact of better and faster data processing are justly concerned with the danger of information indigestion. Their

appetites for figures whetted, the data originators and processors are turning
out material at an almost frightening rate. Managers are complaining of being
buried under reports, projections and forecasts which they either do not have
time to read or cannot understand, or which do not fill their particular needs.[2]

The result has been the development of specialized organizational systems and procedures designed to provide information
useful to the operating manager; and this data can be presented
in whatever form is needed for control purposes. In some large
corporations, all the manager has to do is determine what he
needs, when he needs it, and the format in which he would like
it. Oftentimes these are periodic reports that he will automatically receive. A spin-off of this concept is seen in corporations
which have a service department that keeps executives up to
date by forwarding copies of articles and reports, appearing
in newspapers and journals, on topics that the managers have
indicated are of interest to them. In this way, the individual
can keep up on his specialized area without personally having
to spend a lot of time searching journals for useful information.

**Time-Event
Analyses**

Some of the most successful approaches to control have been
attained through techniques that permit the manager to see
how all the segments of the project interrelate; evaluate overall
progress; and identify and take early corrective action on
problem areas. One of the earliest techniques, still in use, is
the chart developed by Henry Gantt. The principles contained
in it have served as the basis for both Program Evaluation and
Review Technique (PERT) and milestone scheduling, which
will be examined later in this section.

*The Gantt chart
is a control tech-
nique that is
easy to read and
understand.*

Gantt Chart. The Gantt chart has proved to be a useful planning and control technique. The basic concept involves the
graphic depiction of work progress over a period of time. An
illustration is provided in Figure 9–4.

An examination of the figure reveals that there are three orders
being filled, and each requires certain operations to be performed. For the week illustrated in the chart, Order 1 is
scheduled for manufacturing on Monday and Tuesday,
assembling on Wednesday, painting on Thursday and testing
on Friday. Order 2 is scheduled for manufacturing on Monday,
Tuesday and Wednesday, assembling on Thursday and painting
on Friday. Order 3 is scheduled for manufacturing on Monday
and Tuesday, assembling on Wednesday and Thursday and
painting on Friday. The solid vertical lines indicate the time
required for each operation; the dotted horizontal lines denote
progress; and the "V" after Thursday indicates that the chart
reflects the situation as of the close of business on that day.

---

[2]Harold Koontz and Cyril O'Donnell, *Principles of Management: An Analysis
of Managerial Functions,* 5th edition (New York: McGraw-Hill Book Company,
1972), p. 611.

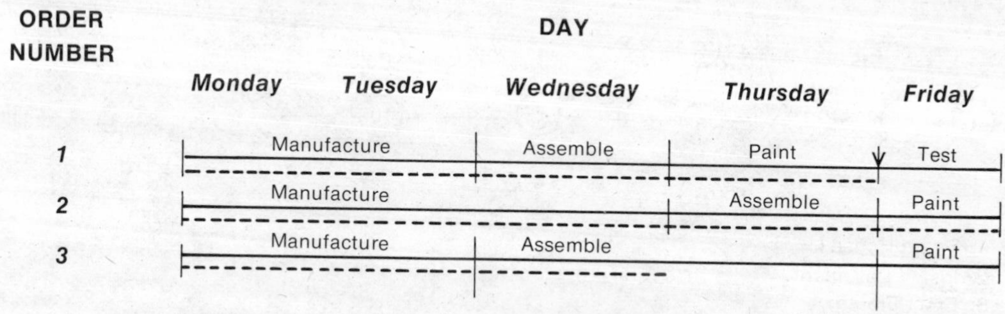

ORDER NUMBER	DAY				
	Monday	Tuesday	Wednesday	Thursday	Friday
1	Manufacture		Assemble	Paint	Test
2	Manufacture			Assemble	Paint
3	Manufacture		Assemble		Paint

FIGURE 9–4 Simplified Gantt Chart

Based on this information, it is evident that Order 1 is on time, Order 2 is a day ahead and Order 3 is a day behind. With this information, the manager is in a position to control the situation by, for example, transferring those working on Order 2 to Order 3 and making up the lost day. This concept of identifying the work to be done and plotting it on a time axis has provided the foundation for PERT.

Program Evaluation and Review Technique. PERT was developed by the Special Projects Office of the United States Navy and applied to the planning and control of the Polaris Weapon System in 1958. The technique has proved very useful in managing complex projects.

PERT Network. PERT employs what is called a time-event network. In building the network, events and activities are first identified. An *event* is a point in time when an activity is begun or finished and is generally represented in the network by a circle. An *activity* is an operation required to accomplish a particular goal and is represented in the network by an arrow. Figure 9–5 illustrates a simple PERT network that might be used to construct a house. The events are numbered for purposes of identification. Of course, an actual PERT network would not be used for such a simple project, but the basic concept is the same. It should be noted that the network not only identifies all the events but also establishes a relationship between them. For example, in Figure 9–5 event 3 cannot be completed before event 2 and event 8 must be finished before going on to event 10.

Relationships between the events are determined.

Expected time can be calculated.

Once the network is constructed, attention is focused on time estimates. Quite often the people responsible for each activity assist in determining optimistic, most likely and pessimistic time estimates for accomplishing their respective activities. These estimates are then used to compute the *expected time* for each activity. The equation for this is:

$$t_E = \frac{t_o + 4t_m + t_p}{6}$$

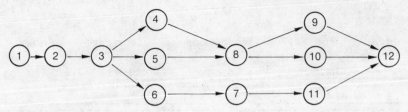

1. Begin House
2. Install Basement
3. Erect Frame
4. Put in Floors
5. Put on Roof
6. Put Brick Around Bottom of House
7. Finish Upper Outside Part of House
8. Wire Inside
9. Install Electric Heating Unit
10. Install Electric Kitchen Appliances
11. Put in Doors and Cabinets
12. Complete House

FIGURE 9-5   Simple PERT Network

where:

$$t_E = \text{expected time}$$
$$t_o = \text{optimistic time}$$
$$t_m = \text{most likely time}$$
$$t_p = \text{pessimistic time}$$

Figure 9–6 illustrates a PERT network with the three estimates for each activity and the expected time, expressed in weeks, directly below in parentheses. For example, the expected time between events 1 and 2 is:

$$t_E = \frac{8 + 4(10) + 12}{6}$$

$$t_E = 10 \text{ weeks}$$

The critical path is the longest path.

For control purposes, it is now possible to determine the *critical path*, which is that sequence of activities and events that is longer than any other. In Figure 9–6 there are only five possible paths through the network. Along with their expected times, they are:

Path	Expected Times	Total
1 – 2 – 3 – 6 – 11 – 14	10.0 + 5.0 + 6.0 + 13.8 + 12.0	46.8
1 – 2 – 3 – 7 – 11 – 14	10.0 + 5.0 + 5.2 + 14.8 + 12.0	47.0
1 – 2 – 4 – 8 – 12 – 14	10.0 + 2.0 + 15.0 + 8.0 + 6.0	41.0
1 – 2 – 4 – 9 – 12 – 14	10.0 + 2.0 + 10.3 + 7.0 + 6.0	35.3
1 – 2 – 5 – 10 – 13 – 14	10.0 + 2.2 + 18.0 + 10.0 + 4.0	44.2

Path 1 – 2 – 3 – 7 – 11 – 14 is the critical path, since it is longer than any other.

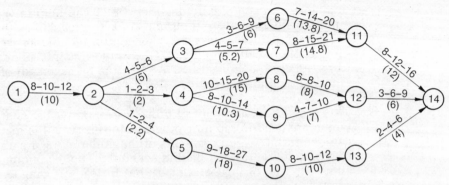

FIGURE 9-6   PERT Network With Time

The final component that must be considered is slack. *Slack* is the time difference between scheduled completion and each of the paths. If, for example, the project in Figure 9–6 had to be completed within 52 weeks, all the paths would have slack. On the other hand, if the completion date was 40 weeks, four of the paths would have negative slack. In this case, they would have to be shortened if the schedule was to be met. There are a number of ways of doing this. Hopeman lists these as follows:

1. The expected time for particular activities may be reduced, if possible.

2. Men, machines, materials, and money can be transferred from slack paths to the critical path or near-critical paths.

3. Some activities may be eliminated from the project.

4. Additional men, machines, materials, and money may be allocated to the critical path or near-critical paths.

5. Some of the activities which are normally sequential may be done in parallel.[3]

Strengths and Limitations.   Perhaps the major advantage of PERT is that it forces managers to plan. In addition, because of the times assigned to each activity, it provides a basis for identifying critical areas and correcting or monitoring them. On the other hand, PERT is only practical for nonrecurring undertakings, and it must be possible to assign times to the events despite the fact that the entire project is new to the company. In addition, some managers have bemoaned PERT's emphasis on time without consideration to cost. As a result, in recent years there has been the development of PERT/COST, in which costs are applied to activities in the network.

A useful technique for less complex projects.   **Milestone Scheduling.**   Although PERT is useful for sophisticated projects, it is often abandoned as the undertaking comes

---

[3]Richard J. Hopeman, *Production: Concepts Analysis Control*, 2nd edition (Columbus, Ohio: Charles E. Merrill Publishing Company, 1971), p. 388.

to a close and complexity declines. PERT can help integrate and simultaneously analyze thousands of activities, but as the project winds down, less complex control techniques can be more economically employed. One of these is milestone scheduling, an approach used by NASA in the management of the Apollo Program.[4]

This scheduling and control procedure employs bar charts, which are used to monitor progress. In this way, the manager can determine which segments of the undertaking are ahead of schedule, on time or behind schedule. The technique is very similar to that of the Gantt chart, but instead of being used exclusively for production activities, it can be employed for virtually any undertaking.

In Figure 9–7, there are three milestones. The first was begun in January, is scheduled for completion at the end of August, and is on time. The second was begun in March, is scheduled for completion in October, and is currently a month ahead of expectations. The third was begun in April, is scheduled for completion in December, and is currently running a month behind expectations. Milestone scheduling allows the manager to see a program in its simpler parts, thereby providing more effective control than sophisticated techniques.

Program Planning Budgeting System

One of the latest control techniques, employed primarily in governmental and institutional organizations, is the programming-planning-budgeting system (PPBS). Developed at the Rand Corporation, the concept was introduced into the Defense Department in 1961 by Robert McNamara. In 1965, President Johnson directed the principal agencies of the federal government to take steps to implement it.

In essence, PPBS requires that a program proposal be presented in package form, outlining the desired goals and the steps that

[4]*Program Scheduling and Review Handbook* (Washington, D.C.: National Aeronautics and Space Administration, NHB2330.1, October 1965).

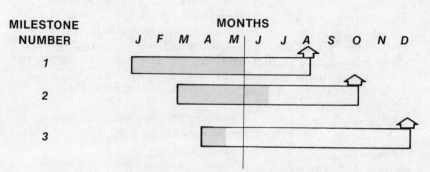

FIGURE 9–7 Simplified Milestone Schedule

will be taken to attain them. Secretary McNamara, for example, required that all proposals explain: (1) the contribution they would make toward accomplishing Defense Department objectives; (2) all pertinent costs that were part of the proposed program; (3) future implications in terms of cost and projected benefits; and (4) the analysis that was employed in evaluating alternative approaches for attaining the same goals. The logic behind the last criterion was, in the Secretary's view, that such analysis would improve Pentagon decision making by ensuring the maximization of scarce resources.

The value of PPBS.

The major value of PPBS is that it ties the budget to the objective and not to some time schedule. In so doing, prime attention is focused on the cost-benefit ratio. As a result, budgeting becomes not just a control technique but a planning and control tool as well.

PPBS, or program budgeting as it is often called, has worked well in the Defense Department. It also has great value for all public agencies in which the focus is often on the budget as a control technique and not as an integrated management tool for allocating resources. Usually in these agencies, allocations are made on a line or item-of-expenditure basis because it is easier to maintain accounting and fiscal control of expenditures. Yet this hampers management's flexibility and often leads to inefficiency. A program budgeting system can often be more useful. Williams, in analyzing the value of such a system to a state-run, out-patient psychiatric clinic, concluded that on an item-of-expenditure basis, mental health programs could not

The technique has promise for business.

be evaluated on a rational, economic basis. As a result, citizens, were receiving less efficient and effective treatment.[5] If this is true for a small state clinic, it is probably more true for larger state and federal agencies; and the application need not stop here. The emphasis PPBS gives to integrated planning and control and the use of cost-benefit analysis indicates that the technique has value for business as well.

CONTROLLING OVERALL PERFORMANCE

Most of the techniques discussed thus far are useful in controlling specific activities, but they do not measure overall performance. In this section, some of the tools used for evaluating total accomplishments will be examined, including profit and loss, return on investment, key area control and auditing.

Profit and Loss

Perhaps the most commonly employed overall control is the income statement, which shows all revenues and expenses for the particular period of operation and provides a basis for comparing actual and expected results. Of course, primary concern is going to be given to whether or not the firm finished in the black, but it is also possible to ascertain where the firm

---

[5]Ronald W. Williams, "An Application of a Planning-Programming-Budgeting System to an Out-Patient Psychiatric Clinic." (Master's thesis, University of Nebraska, Lincoln, 1969).

TABLE 9–1 Income Statement for Three Competitive Corporations
December 31, 1974

	Corporation A	Corporation B	Corporation C
Net sales	$18,000,000	$27,000,000	$30,000,000
Cost of sales			
Cost of goods sold	$13,140,000	$19,980,000	$22,200,000
Selling and administrative expenses	1,260,000	3,240,000	1,500,000
Depreciation	900,000	4,320,000	1,800,000
	15,300,000	27,540,000	25,500,000
Profit from operations	$ 2,700,000	$ (540,000)	$4,500,000
Other income	180,000	540,000	300,000
Total income	$ 2,880,000	0.	4,800,000
Interest expense	360,000	810,000	600,000
Profit before taxes	2,520,000	(810,000)	4,200,000
Taxes	1,260,000		2,100,000
Net profit	$1,260,000	($810,000)	$2,100,000

went wrong during the period, thereby establishing a basis for corrective action. Table 9–1 illustrates income statements for three competitive corporations: A, B and C. A cursory analysis reveals that A and C were profitable, whereas B was not.

One way of obtaining a closer examination of this financial data is to break down all items from the income statement into percentages of net sales. If this is done, Table 9–2 results.

It can now be seen that Corporation B's problem rests with excessive selling and administrative expenses and high depreciation. All other expenditures are in line with the competition. In the case of the first expense, costs are getting out of hand and the firm has to start cracking down on both selling and administrative expenditures. In the case of the second, the firm's depreciation policy is causing high write-offs and resulting in a bleak financial picture. However, it should be noted that a company may do this deliberately, preferring to depreciate machinery and equipment rapidly even though *Analysis of finan-* it has a negative effect on profits. The firm is more interested *cial statements* in recovering its investment than worrying about the profit *can provide the* picture. The lesson to be learned here is that financial figures *basis for effec-* can be juggled. A low depreciation rate will make the profits *tive control.* look high, whereas a high depreciation rate will make them look low. In short, management can manipulate its earnings.[6] Thus, in evaluating operations the manager must identify those costs that are not being properly controlled and concentrate attention on correcting the situation. In the above case, it is selling and administrative expenses that merit this emphasis.

[6]For an excellent discussion of this area see Abraham J. Briloff, *Unaccountable Accounting* (New York: Harper & Row, Publishers, 1972).

TABLE 9–2 Expense Expressed As Percentage of Sales

	Corporation A	Corporation B	Corporation C
Net Sales	100.0	100.0	100.0
Cost of Sales			
Cost of goods sold	73.0	74.0	74.0
Selling and administrative expenses	7.0	12.0	5.0
Depreciation	5.0	16.0	6.0
Profit from operations	15.0	(2.0)	15.0
Other income	1.0	2.0	1.0
Total income	16.0	0.0	16.0
Interest expense	2.0	3.0	2.0
Profit before taxes	14.0		14.0
Taxes	7.0		7.0
Net Profit	7.0	(3.0)	7.0

Return on Investment.   One of the most widely used control techniques is that of return on investment (ROI), which measures how well a firm is performing with the assets at its command. The method for computing ROI is presented in Figure 9–8.

ROI measures a firm's ability to manage its assets.

The reason why ROI is favorably viewed by so many companies is that it answers the question, how well are we doing with what we have? After all, a firm with $4 million in profits is far ahead of one with $10,000 in profits. However, if the former company has a total investment of $10 billion but the latter has one of only $10,000, the smaller firm is doing far better than the larger in terms of overall performance. According to the ROI approach, profits are relative and efficiency is of major importance.

The ROI concept need not be restricted to overall company results. It can be brought down to the divisional product level by way of measuring how well each division is doing. By comparing results with expectations, problem areas can be pinpointed for control purposes. The important thing to remember about ROI is that a good return will vary by industry, and results can only be judged in comparison with the competition. Also, exclusive reliance on this technique can lead to preoccupation with financial factors.[7] For this reason,

---

[7]For example, for years Du Pont would not approve a new product program yielding less than a 20% ROI. As a result, they passed up xerography and the Land (Polaroid) camera. See "Lighting a Fire Under the Sleeping Giant," *Business Week*, September 12, 1970, pp. 40–41.

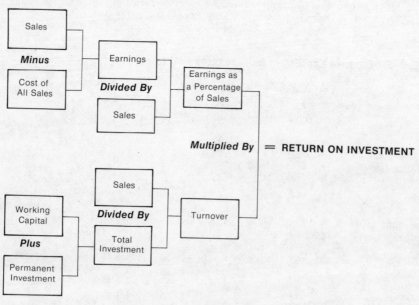

FIGURE 9–8   Computation of Return on Investment

it is advantageous to supplement profit and/or ROI with other overall control techniques such as key area control.

Key Area Control

General Electric provides a good illustration of a firm employing key area control. For two decades now, the company has measured results in eight areas: profitability, market position, productivity, product leadership, personnel development, employee attitudes, public responsibility and integration of short- and long-range goals. The firm has not been able to develop the desired measurements for all of these areas, but by concentrating attention on them it has been possible to obtain an appraisal of overall performance.

It is interesting to note that GE prefers to use profitability rather than ROI. In recent years, some financial experts have supported this approach, concluding that regardless of the firm's efficiency, the final criterion of success is always profit. In any event, only one of the eight key areas relates directly to profit. The remainder are related to environmental factors (political, economic and social) vital to overall control, as the following descriptions illustrate.

Profitability. **Total profits after all expenses, including cost of capital, are deducted.**

Market Position. **Share of the market is one of the key criteria here. In addition, the company attempts to measure customer satisfaction and to discover what the consumer wants but is not getting.**

Productivity. **Goods and services produced and sold are compared with the necessary inputs to arrive at some measure of productivity.**

Product Leadership. **Includes market position, innovation and the ability to take advantage of new ideas in producing successful new products.**

Key control areas used by General Electric.

Personnel Development. **The key criterion employed here is whether or not people are available when needed. Is there an adequate supply of manpower for meeting new and complex assignments in addition to filling vacancies?**

Employee Attitudes. **Absenteeism, labor turnover and safety records are some of the criteria employed to evaluate attitudes. Another is the use of employee surveys.**

Public Responsibility. **Attention in this area is focused on many groups, including employees, customers and the local community. In each case, indices have been developed to evaluate how well the company is doing.**

Integration of Short- and Long-Range Goals. **By encouraging formulation of long-range planning, the company ensures that short-run goals reflect these long-range objectives.**

The GE approach is only one of many that can be employed for key area control. However, it highlights the importance of determining major criteria and monitoring performance in accord with the results obtained. No organization can maintain control of every aspect of operation. Instead, it must identify those that provide a basic picture of how well things are going and abide by the feedback obtained. Some organizations also rely upon various forms of auditing to help perform this function.

Auditing

When one hears the word audit, he may immediately think of a public accounting firm. However, there are three basic types of audits useful for overall control: external audits, internal audits and management audits.

External Audit.   An external audit is conducted by outside accounting personnel and entails the examination and evaluation of the firm's financial transactions and accounts. This audit is generally performed by a certified public accounting firm, which expresses an opinion of the company's financial statements regarding their fairness, consistency and conformity with the accepted principles of accounting. Usually this audit entails a detailed verification of all important balance sheet items with a view toward ascertaining whether the major assets, liability and capital accounts are being accurately reported. The CPA firm does not delve into non-financial areas such as evaluating plans, policies and procedures. However, when one realizes that the auditors will only certify accounts that are in order, it is evident that they provide an indirect control over all operations.

Internal Audit.   An internal audit is conducted by the organization's own staff specialists. In essence, the auditing team examines and evaluates the firm's operations, determining where things have gone well and where corrective action is needed. Generally, much of their work is restricted to the

Internal audits are conducted by company personnel.

financial area, but this need not be the case. They can also be useful in evaluating non-quantitative areas. When this occurs, the internal audit goes further than its external counterpart and approaches what is commonly known as the management audit.

Management Audit.   A management audit picks up where a financial audit leaves off. Sometimes this is conducted by the firm itself and is known as a *self-audit,* an approach first advocated by McKinsey back in the 1930's.[8]

Some management audits are carried out by the firm itself.

The purpose of the self-audit is to examine the company's position on a periodic basis, i.e., every two, three or five years. By studying the market trends, technological changes and political and social factors affecting the industry, the company can construct a forecast of the external environment.

[8]Billy E. Goetz, *Management Planning and Control* (New York: McGraw-Hill Book Company, 1949), p. 167.

Next, attention is turned to the firm itself. How well has it maintained its industry position? What is the competitive outlook? How do the customers feel about the firm's products? Answers to these questions help relate the company to its industry.

On the basis of the results, the firm can examine overall objectives and policies. From here, attention can be focused on programs, procedures, personnel, management and financial positions. As the self-audit continues, attention moves from the macro- to the micro-level so that eventually all segments and activities of the company are analyzed. The problem with the self-audit, however, is that many firms do not find time to conduct one. Furthermore for those who do, there are some very real dangers associated with using the company's own personnel, including bias and lack of competence.

Others are conducted by outside organizations.

One way of overcoming this problem is to employ an *external management audit* such as that conducted by the American Institute of Management. Founded a number of years ago by Jackson Martindell, the institute uses a list of 301 questions to rate companies in the area of fiscal policies, health of earnings, fairness to stockholders, research and development, sales vigor, economic function, directors, corporate structure, executive ability and production efficiency.[9] Each of the ten areas is assigned a point value, with 3,500 of the 10,000 possible points allotted to managerial elements. To obtain a rating of "excellent," the company must receive 7,500 points.

Yet this is only one technique for conducting a management audit. Many others are available from the approach recommended by Greenwood[10] for evaluating the overall firm to the one employed by the Defense Department in evaluating companies bidding on major defense contracts. It now appears that the future will see even greater interest in this area, for in the last decade management consulting and accounting audit firms have found management audits to be an attractive area for expansion. After all, it is but a small step from their current activities to management auditing. Perhaps the future will see even the development of a certified management audit analogous to the current independent certified accounting audit.

SUMMARY   In this chapter the controlling process has been examined. The three basic steps in this process are the establishment of

[9]Jackson Martindell, *The Scientific Appraisal of Management* (New York: Harper & Brothers, 1950) and *The Appraisal of Management* (New York: Harper & Brothers, 1962).
[10]W. T. Greenwood, *A Management Audit System*, revised edition (Carbondale, Ill.: School of Business, Southern Illinois University, 1967).

standards, the comparison of performance with these standards, and correction of deviations. The key to the entire process rests on effective feedback.

In attaining this feedback, various control techniques are available to the manager. Some of the more traditional include budgeting, break-even point analysis and personal observation. Some of the more specialized entail information design, time-event analyses such as PERT and milestone scheduling, and PPBS. These are not, however, designed to control overall performance. To do this, the manager must turn to other techniques such as profit and loss, return on investment, key area control and auditing.

**REVIEW AND
STUDY
QUESTIONS**

1. What are the three basic steps in the controlling process? Describe each in your own words.

2. Why is feedback so important for effective control?

3. What are the requirements for an effective control system? List and explain some of them in your own words.

4. Of what value is budgeting in the controlling process? Does it lead to inflexibility? Explain.

5. How can the break-even point assist the manager in controlling operations? Explain, incorporating the following terms into your discussion: unit price, total fixed cost, and variable cost per unit.

6. What is meant by the term information design? How is it of value to the manager?

7. Why is PERT a useful control technique? Explain in your own words, incorporating into your discussion the following terms: events, activities, expected time, and the critical path.

8. Why is return on investment so widely used as an overall control technique? Is it better than a profit and loss approach? Explain.

9. What is meant by key area control? What are some of the areas used by General Electric in controlling its operations? Explain in your own words.

10. How useful are external audits in the control process? Internal audits? Management audits? Which is best, and why?

**SELECTED
REFERENCES**

"A Better Basis for Better Decisions." *Business Week*, September 9, 1972, pp. 137, 139.
Anthony, R. N. "What Should 'Cost' Mean?" *Harvard Business Review*, May–June 1970, pp. 121–131.

Buchele, R. B. "How to Evaluate a Firm." *California Management Review*, Fall 1962, pp. 5–17.

Burton, J. C. "Management Auditing." *The Journal of Accountancy*, May 1968. pp. 41–46.

Drucker, P. F. *Management: Tasks, Responsibilities, Practices.* New York: Harper & Row, Publishers, 1974, Chapter 39.

Gibbons, C. C. "The Psychology of Budgeting." *Business Horizons*, June 1972, pp. 47–58.

Koontz, H., and R. W. Bradspies. "Managing Through Feedforward Control." *Business Horizons*, June 1972, pp. 25–36.

Macleod, R. K. "Program Budgeting Works in Nonprofit Institutions." *Harvard Business Review*, September-October 1971, pp. 46–56.

Martin, R. "Resident Experts: Many Companies Decide Management Consulting Can Be Done By Insiders." *Wall Street Journal*, May 2, 1973, pp. 1, 10.

Martindell, J. *The Appraisal of Management.* New York: Harper & Row, Publishers, 1962.

Mautz, R. K., and F. L. Neumann. "The Effective Corporate Audit Committee." *Harvard Business Review*, November–December 1970, pp. 57–65.

Michaels, E. G., III. "Quick Profit Improvements by Reducing Costs." *Business Horizons*, December 1970, pp. 87–94.

Mockler, R. J. "The Corporate Control Job: Breaking the Mold." *Business Horizons*, December 1970, pp. 73–77.

Schoderbek, P. P. "A Study of the Applications of PERT." *Academy of Management Journal*, September 1965, pp. 199–210.

Schonberger, R. J. "Custom-Tailored PERT/CPM Systems." *Business Horizons*, December 1972, pp. 64–66.

Tannenbaum, A. S. *Control in Organizations.* New York: McGraw-Hill Book Company, 1968.

Weston, J. F. "ROI Planning and Control." *Business Horizons*, August 1972, pp. 35–42.

CASE: SAFETY MARGINS

George Wayland had been with the company for only a couple of months, but already he could tell that the job was to his liking. One of the things he enjoyed most was the increased responsibility. For example, he had been told to make up a departmental budget for the next fiscal year. After pouring over past budgetary requests and talking to his subordinates, he submitted his proposal. The next step in the process was to meet with his superior and defend the requests, and the proposal would then be sent up the line. George had been told by his subordinates that top management seldom cut back any requests. The key hurdle was getting one's superior to approve the recommended budget.

As a result, George spent most of the morning preparing himself for this meeting. He felt that everything in his request was essential, but he wanted to be able to defend each item. The meeting, however, did not quite go according to expectations.

George, I've examined your budget request and would like to talk to you about a few items. For example, under administrative expenses you estimate $47,612.

Yes sir. I can show you the worksheet I used if you'd like.

Oh, that's not necessary. The only reason why the figure caught my eye was that it was such an odd amount. Look, let's round it off to $50,000.

Okay.

And there are a few other budget estimates I see here that are also in need of rounding, so I'll just change them also.

How much of an estimate does that make it?

It's exactly $210,000.

Well, that's a little bit higher than what I need. Are you sure it's okay?

Sure, don't worry about it. You can never tell when something is going to cost just a little bit more than you initially thought.

It's all right with me if it's all right with you.

Fine. And, oh, by the way, how did you arrive at these other estimates?

Well, I worked back from what I thought my department would be doing this fiscal year to how much it would cost to get this work done. There's a manual that was sent around to me, and I took my basic format from it.

That certainly is one way to get a handle on it, George. But let me suggest that you be sure to add some safety margins to each of your requests.

Safety margins?

Sure, you know. A little something extra just in case things go wrong. Besides, you never know when management is going to cut around here, and it always pays to have asked for a little more than you need when that happens. Do you know what I mean?

I think so.

Fine, well here's your budget back. Add in 10 per cent across the board and send it back in to me. I'll forward it from here.

Questions

1. Is George's superior right or wrong in suggesting that he change his budget requests? Explain.

2. How common do you think this kind of action is?

3. What are the dangers in overestimating budget requests? Be specific.

4. Why do you think this conversation occurred? Explain.

CASE: EFFICIENCY VS. PROFITABILITY

Fred Forsythe was a product division manager at Darby Inc., a large midwestern manufacturing firm. In the late 1950's, the

Darby management decided to abandon its profitability control guideline and begin evaluating product divisions on the basis of return on investment. In this way, it was felt, overall efficiency could be measured.

The idea was fine with Fred, and for the next decade his division's ROI rose from 12.3 per cent to 15.7 percent. However, during the late 60's, the division began to encounter vigorous competition, and although the market for their product increased, Fred found himself spending more and more money on advertising and personal selling to maintain market share. The result was an eventual decline in ROI to 13.7 per cent by 1974. This in turn prompted comments from the top management, and Fred found himself being called into his boss's office.

Fred, the board of directors has been reviewing product division ROI's, and your's is the only one that has declined. Quite frankly, they're concerned.

Well, I am too, but if they think you can improve ROI in such a competitive industry, they're crazy. That's why we've been spending all that money on advertising and personal selling. I'd like to know one company that's making a greater ROI than we are. Or one competitive division that can match mine. There are none.

I'm sure that's true. But the question is, what are you going to do to improve your division's ROI?

I'd like to pose a different question. Why is the board evaluating my division on ROI? Don't they know when you get as large as we are, in as competitive an industry as this, that ROI slips? Why don't they evaluate me on profitability? My profits are up over last year, but I can't hold my ROI performance at an all-time high.

Do you want to write them a letter outlining your proposal?

No, but I do think it's time people stopped overrating ROI as a control technique.

Questions

1. What are the advantages of using ROI as an overall control technique? What are the disadvantages?

2. Should the board switch back from ROI to profits? Give your reasoning.

3. What action would you recommend for Fred? Explain.

CASE: A POSSIBLE COMPROMISE

When Paul Richman founded his company in 1949, he never dreamed that sales would pass the $25 million mark by 1974.

Nevertheless, that was exactly what happened. Not that it was easy; many times the company ran into problems that seemed virtually insurmountable. And it took a lot of hard work and some luck to finally see the light at the end of the tunnel.

One of the groups to whom Mr. Richman was most grateful was his public accounting firm. When he first hired them to audit his books in 1952, he thought they would merely certify that all major accounts were in order. However, he found that they went further, offering him some suggestions on how he could manage his money a little more wisely. Over the years, Mr. Richman came to rely on this advice and found, more often than not, that the auditors were right.

In late 1974, the auditing firm approached Mr. Richman with another suggestion. They recommended that he hire them to carry out a management audit of his entire company. For a couple of years, the auditing firm had been conducting these management evaluations for other firms. They estimated, based on this experience, that the cost of the audit would be more than paid for within a few months, thanks to the cost saving recommendations that would be forthcoming. Mr. Richman thought it was a good idea, but his internal auditor counseled him against such action. "Certified public accountants should refrain from entering this area," he said. "To do otherwise can endanger their objectivity. After all, you would not want your books certified by me because I am the internal auditor. If there were a discrepancy somewhere I could easily overlook it and tell you that everything was in fine shape. You need an external check to be sure that I am keeping accurate and honest books. In the same way, if you use your external auditors to conduct a management review, there is pressure on them to audit future financial returns in such a way as to be favorable to you. After all, if you follow their advice, it should be reflected in your financial position. This in turn can affect their objectivity. If you want a management audit, let's bring in the American Institute of Management people, but let's stay away from using our external auditors for this function."

Questions

1. What are the advantages to be gained from a management audit? Explain.

2. How realistic is the internal auditor's advice? Give your reasoning.

3. What would you recommend Mr. Richman do if he is determined to have a management audit conducted? Explain.

CASE: THE DEAN'S DILEMMA

Things had certainly changed at State University. When Dean Williams had first come to the College of Business in 1969, it seemed that life was much simpler. However, as inflation spiraled upward, the taxpayers of the state gave every indication that they were through pouring money into the university. As a result, the administration announced that there would have to be a tightening up everywhere. Departmental lines would be cut and hiring determined on a need basis. And if this were not enough, legislators began raising the question of faculty evaluations. How do we know we are getting our money's worth, they asked, if there is no evaluation process?

In response to the question, the university administration announced that it was going to look into the matter. Thereupon, each dean was asked to poll his college and decide what form of evaluation process they felt was fair for judging performance. In the College of Business, two camps sprang up. The first wanted to evaluate teaching as the first prerequisite, with community affairs and research as secondary. The other group wanted to place research as primary and teaching and community affairs as secondary. The positions could be summarized as follows:

TEACHING IS PRIMARY

Position for: **The university has been established by the people of this state to perform a specific service; namely, the dissemination of knowledge to the students. And this is the primary basis on which teachers should be evaluated. This process should take two paths: evaluations by the students in the classroom and evaluation by the departmental chairman based on classroom observation.**

Position against: **Teaching is certainly important, but there is no way to judge truly effective performance. The students are going to be biased in their opinion, those receiving the highest grades being more positive in their comments about the instructors than those receiving the lowest grades. Thus the system encourages an easy grading policy. In addition, the chairman is incapable of judging all his people because he is not an expert in every area. For example, how can a management chairman, with an emphasis in organizational behavior, judge a colleague teaching mathematical decision making? Teaching is valuable, but because it cannot be quantified, it should be discarded as a basis for evaluation.**

RESEARCH IS PRIMARY

Position for: **The only objective criterion available for judging teaching ability is research. A professor who conducts research is going to be better prepared than one who does not. In addition, the instructor has a responsibility to not only teach but to enhance the reputation of the university as well, and this can be done most effectively through research. In short, "publish or perish" is the only way to improve the quality of education, and it should be the basis for all evaluations.**

Position against: To engage in a policy of publish or perish is to get into the numbers game. In addition, how is one to evaluate the contribution of each article? And in the case of books, is not remuneration in the form of royalties sufficient? Why should people be promoted or receive high evaluation when all they are doing is enhancing their own financial positions? Research is important, but it must not be allowed to occupy a primary position.

Questions

1. How should faculty performance be evaluated? Explain.

2. In light of your answer to the above question, what kinds of measuring tools should a dean employ to ensure that his faculty is doing a good job? Explain in detail.

THE QUANTITATIVE SCHOOL

The goal of this section is to familiarize the reader with some of the basic ideas and concepts of the quantitative, or management science, school. As with the other two schools, there is no universal agreement regarding its domain. There can be argument on all but the most quantitative subjects within this section simply by raising the question, does the material fit into one of the other schools? A good example is the topic of decision making. The process and behavioral schools would both claim that this area is within their domain. With this contention there is no argument, for decision making knows no bounds; it is an integral part of every manager's job. However, it will be discussed within this section because it offers an excellent opportunity to examine the entire area of modern quantitative decision making and is therefore of major importance to an understanding of the management sciences.

In Chapter 10 the decision-making process will be examined, and it will be noted that this process is certainly no mechanical function. There are personal values involved in choosing from among alternatives, and to picture management scientists simply as cold, calculating mathematicians is erroneous. In Chapter 11 this concept of choosing from among alternatives will be extended through an examination of some of the important tools and techniques of operations research that are currently being employed by the modern manager.

CHAPTER 10

FUNDAMENTALS OF DECISION MAKING

GOALS OF THE CHAPTER

The goals of this chapter are to examine the fundamentals of decision making. First, the steps in the process will be reviewed, followed by an analysis of the impact of personal values on the decision-making process. Next, the types of decisions and the conditions under which they are made, i.e., certainty, risk and uncertainty, will be scrutinized. Finally, two of the more common decision-making techniques, marginal and financial analysis, will be reviewed in detail. Particular attention will be focused on:

a. the steps in the decision-making process;
b. rationality and decision making;
c. value orientation and its effect on decision making;
d. a classification system for analyzing all decisions, including organizational and personal decisions, basic and routine decisions, and programmed and nonprogrammed decisions;
e. the three basic conditions under which decisions are made;
f. the role of objective and subjective probability;
g. the benefits of marginal analysis; and
h. the values of financial analysis.

DECISION-MAKING PROCESS

Decision making involves choosing from among alternatives.

Decision making is commonly defined as *choosing from among alternatives*. Simon has identified the process as: searching the environment for conditions calling for a decision; inventing, developing and analyzing the available courses of action; and choosing one of the particular courses of action.[1] However, this three-step process, consisting of intelligence, design and choice activities, is only one of many decision-making methods.

---

[1]Herbert A. Simon, *The New Science of Management Decision* (New York: Harper & Row, Publishers, Inc., 1960), p. 2.

A second and more detailed method is the following:

1. Identify the problem.
2. Diagnose the situation.
3. Collect and analyze data relevant to the issue.
4. Ascertain solutions that may be used in solving the problem.
5. Analyze these alternative solutions.
6. Select the approach that appears most likely to solve the problem.
7. Implement it.

Regardless of the specific process employed by the manager, some formal diagnosis must be conducted, alternative solutions formulated and analyzed, and a decision made regarding the approach to take. This is as true in the development of strategic, intermediate and operational plans as it is in solving simple job problems.

One of the primary characteristics of this entire process is its dynamism, the steps being implemented within a time framework. The past is the time dimension in which the problem is identified and diagnosed. The present is the point at which the alternatives are formulated and a choice made regarding the plan of action. The future is the time period during which the decision will be implemented and an evaluation made regarding the outcome.

RATIONALITY AND THE MEANS-END HIERARCHY

There are degrees of rationality in decision making.

In Chapter 5, when Mayo's rabble hypothesis was examined, it was noted that not all decisions made by the workers are rational. Some are non-rational, others are irrational. The same is true at the managerial level. In addition, there are *degrees* of rationality. A man lost in the desert may wander in circles. Although this may be the wrong solution to the problem, is it not rational? After all, virtually everyone caught in this dilemma does it. This raises the question, precisely what is meant by the term *rational*? Some people assign the term to actions that attain a given end. In this case, the man in the desert is not acting rationally because his actions are not leading him out of his dilemma. Other individuals feel that rational refers to choosing the best alternative of those available. In this case, the man may be acting rationally because of the alternatives facing him. He may conclude that no one knows he is lost, so he cannot rely on a search party's finding him. His only salvation rests in saving himself, by, for example, finding the nearest oasis. The only way to do this is to start walking and hope to locate one before too long.

Some decision theorists believe that rational decisions will be forthcoming if appropriate means for reaching desired goals are chosen. However, it is often difficult to separate means from ends, for every end is really just a means to another end. This is what is known as the *means-ends hierarchy*. When the man in the desert finds the oasis, he will remain there, using it as his base of operations (means) until he can establish contact with the outside world and have help sent to him (end). The plane that takes him out (means) will allow him to return to his old way of life (end).

It is difficult to separate means from ends.

In summary, rationality, as viewed within the decision-making framework, is a relative term, dependent upon the situation and the individuals involved. An objectively rational *organizational* decision designed to ensure the company a profitable year may be welcomed by the employees until they learn that it calls for the elimination of all Christmas bonuses; then it is seen as a non-rational or irrational decision. Likewise, *personally* rational decisions such as the establishment of 30-minute coffee breaks to eliminate excessive fatigue may be favorably viewed by the workers but seen by the management as disastrous to overall company efficiency. One reason, then, for this imprecision in decision making is the personal values of the people involved.

PERSONAL VALUES AND DECISION MAKING

A manager's personal values will influence his decision making.

Every manager has a certain set of values he brings to the work place. In Chapter 6, the General Electric changing-value profile for 1969–1980 was presented. These values can be further broken down and applied to managers on an individual basis. Spranger has identified six such values: economic, theoretical, political, religious, aesthestic and social. The description of each is presented in Figure 10–1. When Guth and Tagiuri employed this classification scheme with high-level United States executives attending the Advanced Management Program of the Harvard Business School Seminar, they obtained the following average profile:[2]

Value	Score
Economic	45
Theoretical	44
Political	44
Religious	39
Aesthetic	35
Social	33
	240

The scores represent the importance of the values as seen by the average manager in the study.

The economic, theoretical and political scores seem justifiably high, for the top manager must be interested in efficiency and profit (economic), possess conceptual skills required for endeavors such as long-range planning (theoretical), and be able to get along with people and convince them to work together

---

[2]William D. Guth and Renato Tagiuri, "Personal Values and Corporate Strategy," *Harvard Business Review*, September–October, 1965, p. 126. The questionnaire was designed to yield 240 points distributed over the six values.

1. The *theoretical* man is primarily interested in the discovery of truth, in the systematic ordering of his knowledge. In pursuing this goal he typically takes a "cognitive" approach, looking for identities and differences, with relative disregard for the beauty or utility of objects, seeking only to observe and to reason. His interests are empirical, critical, and rational. He is an intellectual. Scientists or philosophers are often of this type (but they are not the only ones).

2. The *economic* man is primarily oriented toward what is useful. He is interested in the practical affairs of the business world; in the production, marketing, and consumption of goods; in the use of economic resources; and in the accumulation of tangible wealth. He is thoroughly "practical" and fits well the stereotype of the American businessman.

3. The *aesthetic* man finds his chief interest in the artistic aspects of life, although he need not be a creative artist. He values form and harmony. He views experience in terms of grace, symmetry, or harmony. Each single event is savored for its own sake.

4. The essential value for the *social* man is love of people—the altruistic or philanthropic aspect of love. The social man values people as ends, and tends to be kind, sympathetic, unselfish. He finds those who have strong theoretical, economic, and aesthetic orientations rather cold. Unlike the political type, the social man regards love as the most important component of human relationships. In its purest form the social orientation is selfless and approaches the religious attitude.

5. The *political* man is characteristically oriented toward power, not necessarily in politics, but in whatever area he functions. Most leaders have a high power orientation. Competition plays a large role in all life, and many writers have regarded power as the most universal motive. For some men, this motive is uppermost, driving them to seek personal power, influence, and recognition.

6. The *religious* man is one "whose mental structure is permanently directed to the creation of the highest and absolutely satisfying value experience." The dominant value for him is unity. He seeks to relate himself to the universe in a meaningful way and has a mystical orientation.

FIGURE 10-1   Spranger's Value Orientations (From William D. Guth and Renato Tagiuri, "Personal Values and Corporate Strategy," *Harvard Business Review,* September–October, 1965, pp. 125–126. Reprinted with permission.)

as a team (political). However, the researchers also found that the profiles varied considerably in regard to religious, aesthetic and social values, indicating that one must not be too hasty in trying to construct a stereotype of the "typical" executive.

The personal values of each manager can have a significant effect on the decision-making process. This is one reason why social action programs, for example, internally generated and heavily funded by the company itself, have been undertaken by many business firms in recent years.[3] Managers are just more

[3]See, for example, Fred Luthans and Richard M. Hodgetts, "Government and Business: Partners in Social Action," *Labor Law Journal,* December 1969, pp. 763–770.

oriented toward social responsibility than they were a decade ago. However, this must not be construed to mean that the firm is going to expend all its energies on such programs. In fact, when researchers in one study asked businessmen whose companies were *known* to have social action programs to rank their responsibilities to society, the stockholders, the management and the workers, they received the results shown in Figure 10–2.

Businessmen were interested in fulfilling their social responsibility but were not going to put such programs ahead of their obligations to the stockholders. Again, personal values play an important role in the decision-making process.

TYPES OF DECISIONS

Managers make many decisions, and in order to obtain a clear understanding of the decision-making process, a classification system is useful. Three such systems are available, each based on different types of decisions. They are: organizational and personal decisions, basic and routine decisions, and programmed and nonprogrammed decisions.

Organizational and Personal Decisions

Organizational decisions can be delegated to others.

Organizational decisions are those the executive makes in his official role as a manager. The adoption of strategies, the setting of objectives and the approval of plans constitute only a few of these. Such decisions are often delegated to others, requiring the support of many people throughout the organization if they are to be properly implemented.

Personal decisions are not delegated.

Personal decisions are related to the manager as an individual, not as a member of the organization. Such decisions are not delegated to others because their implementation does not require the support of organizational personnel. Deciding to retire, taking a job offer from a competitive firm or slipping out and spending the afternoon on the golf course are all personal decisions.

Although it is possible to distinguish between organizational

INTEREST GROUPS	WEIGHTED AVERAGE*
Stockholder	237
Society	195
Employees	170
Management	125

FIGURE 10–2   Relative Ranking of Corporate Responsibility (From Fred Luthans and Richard M. Hodgetts, "Government and Business: Partners in Social Action," *Labor Law Journal*, December 1969, p. 764.) *The weighted average was determined by assigning four points for a first place ranking on down to one point for a fourth place ranking. The maximum point value possible was 264.

and personal decisions according to definition, in practice it is not. For example, when a company president who believes in equal opportunity for all decides to make a concerted effort to hire the hard-core unemployed, a personal decision is translated into an organizational one. Many decisions made by managers have both organizational and personal elements in them.

Basic and Routine Decisions

Basic decisions can have major effects on the organization.

A second approach is to classify decisions into basic and routine categories. *Basic decisions* can be viewed as much more important than routine ones. They involve long-range commitments, large expenditures of funds and such a degree of importance that a serious mistake might well jeopardize the well-being of the company. Selection of a product line, the choice of a new plant site or a decision to integrate vertically by purchasing sources of raw materials to complement the current production facilities are all basic decisions.

Routine decisions have only a minor impact on the firm.

Routine decisions are often repetitive in nature, having only a minor impact on the firm. For this reason, most organizations have formulated a host of procedures to guide the manager in handling these matters. Since some individuals in the organization spend most of their time making routine decisions, these guidelines are very useful to them.

Procedures are guides to action and usually consist of a list of chronological steps entailed in attaining some objective.

At this point it may be helpful to define what is meant by procedures and policies. *Procedures* are guides to action. Often referred to as types of plans, they relate the chronological steps entailed in attaining some objective. Sometimes procedures are drawn up for use in a particular department. In a retail store, for example, there may be five steps involved in allowing a person to return faulty merchandise, from ascertaining that the goods were not damaged by the buyer to getting an "O.K." from the department manager. Other times, procedures are organizational in nature such as if there is a discrepancy in a paycheck, the employee must tell the payroll department, have his pay recalculated and, if there was an error, return the incorrect check for a revised one. Procedures are very useful in helping individuals with routine decisions because they break down the process into steps.

Policies are guides to both thinking and action.

Policies, often confused with procedures, are also types of plans, but they are guides to *thinking* as well as to action. As a result, they do not tell a manager how to do something; they merely channel his decision making along a particular line by delimiting his span of consideration. For example, a department may have a policy of hiring only those with a college education. However, how does one define a college education? If the manager is willing to accept one year of job experience and three years of formal college as the equivalent of a four-year diploma, it is evident that there is more than mere action involved; thinking is needed to determine the equivalency line. The manager knows he will accept no one without a college degree or its equivalent (action) and can confine his energies to evaluating the latter cases (thinking). In this case, a policy is helpful to the manager because it limits the number of people eligible for a job in his department. At the organizational level, policies are also useful. For example, a firm may have a policy of setting up new plants in cities with a population of at least 100,000. This is a guide to action because it limits the number of eligible cities. It is a guide to thinking because now the executive must decide in which particular city to build the new plant. Policies play an important role in handling basic decisions.

Programmed and Nonprogrammed Decisions

Programmed decisions are routine; unprogrammed decisions are novel and unstructured.

Simon, borrowing from computer technology, has proposed the classification of decisions into the areas of *programmed* and *nonprogrammed*. These two types can be viewed on a continuum, programmed being at one end and nonprogrammed at the other. Programmed decisions correspond roughly to the routine decisions, with procedures playing a key role. Non-programmed decisions are similar to the category of basic decisions, being highly novel, important and unstructured in nature. Policies play an important role in making these decisions. The value of viewing decision making in this manner is that it permits a clearer understanding of the methods that accompany each type. Figure 10–3 presents Simon's traditional and modern decision-making scheme.

DECISION-MAKING CONDITIONS

There are three possible conditions under which decisions can be made: certainty, risk and uncertainty.

Certainty

Certainty is present when the manager knows the outcome of each alternative.

Certainty is present when the manager knows exactly what will happen. Although conditions of certainty exist in but a small percentage of decisions made by the manager, they are present. For example, $1,000 invested in a government note for one year at six per cent will return $60 in interest. Although it can be argued that there is a degree of risk in everything including government notes, for all practical purposes this investment can be labeled as "a sure thing."

Likewise, the allocation of resources to various product lines often constitutes decision making under conditions of certainty. The manager knows his resources and the amount of time it will take to process them into finished goods. If there are two or three processes available to him, he can conduct a cost-contribution study to determine which is most profitable (if profit is his decision guideline) or which will produce the good most quickly (if speed is of the essence). In dealing with

DECISION-MAKING TECHNIQUES

TYPES OF DECISIONS	Traditional	Modern
Programmed: Routine, repetitive decisions Organization develops specific processes for handling them	1. Habit 2. Clerical routine: Standard operating procedures 3. Organization structure: Common expectations A system of subgoals Well-defined informational channels	1. Operations Research: Mathematical analysis Models Computer simulation 2. Electronic data processing
Nonprogrammed: One-shot, ill-structured, novel, policy decisions Handled by general problem-solving processes	1. Judgment, intuition, and creativity 2. Rules of thumb 3. Selection and training of executives	Heuristic problem-solving techniques applied to: (a) training human decision makers (b) constructing heuristic computer programs

FIGURE 10-3　Traditional and Modern Techniques of Decision Making (From Herbert A. Simon, *The Shape of Automation*, Harper and Row, Publishers, Inc., New York, 1965, p. 62.)

fixed quantities such as raw materials and machines, the manager is often making decisions under certainty, his prime goal being that of determining the objective he wishes to obtain. Once this is accomplished, he can simply evaluate his alternatives and choose the best one.

Risk

Risk is present if the manager has only partial information for evaluating the outcome of each alternative.

Most of the manager's decisions are made under *risk* conditions; that is, some information is available but it is insufficient to answer all questions about the outcome. One method often used to assist the decision maker is that of probability estimates.

Probability Estimates.   Although the manager may not know with a high degree of certainty the outcome of each decision, he may be able to estimate some level of probability for each of the possible alternatives. Such estimates are often based on experience. The manager draws on past occurrences in determining the likelihood of particular events. Naturally, no situation is ever identical to a previous one, but it may be sufficiently similar to justify using experience as a guide. Probability assignments permit a determination of the expected values of all events. For example, consider the case of the firm with four available strategies: A, B, C and D. Each has a conditional value, which is the profit that will be returned to the firm if it is implemented and proves successful; a probability, which is a likelihood of success; and an expected value, which is the result of the conditional value multiplied by the probability. These data can be arranged as in Figure 10–4.

The figure illustrates that the manager should opt for strategy D because it promises the greatest expected value. Although it has the lowest conditional value of all four, the probability of success is far higher.

Objective and Subjective Probabilities

If a probability can be determined on the basis of past experience, it is known as an *objective probability*. What is the probability of obtaining a head in the toss of a fair coin? It is 0.5. Over the long-run, there will be just as many heads as

AVAILABLE STRATEGIES	CONDITIONAL VALUE	SUCCESS PROBABILITY	EXPECTED VALUE
A	$1,000,000	0.05	$50,000
B	800,000	0.10	80,000
C	750,000	0.20	150,000
D	400,000	0.65	260,000

FIGURE 10–4   Expected Values for Strategies A–D

Objective probability can be assigned on the basis of past experience.

tails. Likewise, many companies are able, on the basis of past experience, to assign objective probabilities to events such as predicting success on a particular psychological test. If a person ranks in the top 20 per cent, his success as a manager may be 0.8, indicating that eight out of every ten in this category have done well as managers.

Subjective probability is often assigned on the basis of "gut feel."

Sometimes, however, it is not possible to determine a suitable objective probability estimate. The manager may not feel he has sufficient information to determine whether the success probability is 0.5 or 0.8. In this case, he must make a subjective estimate, employing what is commonly called "gut feel."

Although not so precise as an objective probability, *subjective probability* is nevertheless better than just completely ignoring the probabilities of occurrence associated with the various alternatives. It also provides a basis for sharpening one's judgment in the case of future subjective probability assignments.

Risk Preference. The assignment of probabilities is never so simple as it might appear. The decision maker who finalizes the assignment is the ultimate arbiter, and different managers will assign varying estimates to identical alternatives for various reasons.

> . . . it can hardly be denied that the same top managers who make a decision involving risks of millions of dollars . . . in a given program with a chance of success of, say, 75 percent, would not be likely to do that with their own personal fortune, at least unless it were very large. Moreover, the same manager willing to opt for a 75 percent risk in one case might not do so in another. Furthermore, a top executive may go for a large advertising program where the chances of success are 70 percent, but might not decide in favor of an investment in plant and equipment unless the probabilities for success were higher. In other words, attitudes toward risk vary with events, as well as with people and position.

Some managers are risk takers; others are risk averters.

While we do not know much about attitudes toward risk, we do know that some people are risk averters in some situations and gamblers in others, and that some people have by nature a high aversion to risk and others a low one.[4]

The risk preference of the manager will play a key role in determining his probability assignments. Figure 10–5 presents the preference curves of high-, average- and low-risk takers. The **S**-curve illustrates the risk preferences of people in their personal lives. When the stakes are low, most individuals tend to be more willing to gamble than when they are high. For example, the author has asked businessmen if they would be willing to accept an outright gift of $5 or would prefer to take a chance on winning $15 or nothing against the correct call

---

[4]Harold Koontz and Cyril O'Donnell, *Principles of Management: An Analysis of Managerial Functions,* 5th edition (New York: McGraw-Hill Book Company, 1972), p. 198.

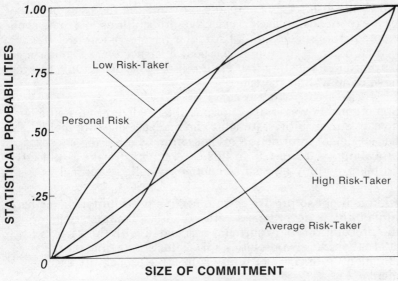

FIGURE 10–5 Risk Preference Curves

of the flip of a fair coin. Most businessmen opt for the latter
alternative, being willing to gamble for $15 or nothing.
Conversely, when the stakes are raised to $50,000 and $150,000
respectively, most managers choose the $50,000 sum certain.
Actually they are wrong, for the expected value of the $150,000
is $75,000 ($150,000 × 0.5) since the odds are fifty-fifty that
they will call the flip of the coin correctly. However, the
managers prefer the guaranteed $50,000.

Uncertainty

*Probability esti-
mates should be
developed even
if the manager
feels he is mak-
ing a decision
under uncer-
tainty.*

Uncertainty decisions are those for which the manager feels
he cannot develop probability estimates because he has no
way of gauging the likelihood of the various alternatives. It
is very difficult to say precisely when this occurs. Many
individuals contend that experience and the ability to general-
ize from similar situations make uncertainty impossible; the
manager can always assign some probability estimates to a
decision matter. Yet there are times when the executive may
feel he is indeed dealing with uncertainty. Nevertheless,
research shows that he is wise to construct conditional values
for each alternative under each state of nature. For example,
an airplane manufacturer is considering the production of a
giant helicopter for the military and there are three basic design
versions under serious consideration: A, B and C. The former
is the most sophisticated and expensive of the three, while
the latter is the least sophisticated and least expensive of the
group. The two basic states of nature are seen as being either
a generation of peace or continual fighting of brush fire wars.
Furthermore, the manufacturer assigns the following conditional
values to the respective strategies and states of nature:

| | STATES OF NATURE | |
STRATEGIES	Generation of Peace	Continual Brush Fire Wars
Helicopter A	−$250,000	$5,000,000
Helicopter B	1,000,000	1,000,000
Helicopter C	4,500,000	500,000

FIGURE 10-6   Conditional Values Associated With Manufacturing Giant Helicopter

If peace prevails, the military will buy the least expensive helicopter, but if brush fire wars continue, they will purchase the most expensive.

Equal probability can be applied to all events.

What decision should the manager make? If there is no reason for believing that one event is more likely to occur than any other, the manager can employ what is called the *Laplace criterion*, which applies equal probabilities to all states of nature. If this approach is followed, the firm should manufacture helicopter C, because it offers an expected value of $2,500,000 ($4,500,000 × 0.5 + $500,000 × 0.5), which is greater than that from any of the other strategies as seen in Figure 10-7.

A pessimistic approach can be used.

A second approach is the use of the pessimism criterion, or the *maximin* as it is often called, which holds that the manager should ascertain the worst conditions for each strategy, which, as seen in Figure 10-6, are − $250,000, $1,000,000 and $500,000 for A, B, and C respectively. Then the one that offers the best payoff under these conditions should be implemented. This would call for the manufacture of helicopter B. By using this approach, the manager maximizes his minimum gain, hence the term maximin.

An optimistic approach can be taken.

A third approach is the use of the optimism criterion, commonly called *maximax*. Since the manager is unsure of the outcome, it is just as rational to be optimistic as pessimistic. He should

| | STATES OF NATURE | |
STRATEGIES	Generation of Peace	Continual Brush Fire Wars
Helicopter A	−$125,000	$2,500,000
Helicopter B	$500,000	$ 500,000
Helicopter C	$2,250,000	$ 250,000

FIGURE 10-7   Expected Values for Manufacturing Giant Helicopter Using Laplace Criterion (Equal Probability)

| STRATEGY | CONDITIONAL VALUES | | WEIGHTED VALUES | | SUM OF WEIGHTED VALUES |
	Best Condition	Worst Condition	Best Condition	Worst Condition	
Helicopter A	$5,000,000	−$250,000	$4,000,000	−$ 50,000	$3,950,000
Helicopter B	1,000,000	1,000,000	800,000	200,000	1,000,000
Helicopter C	4,500,000	500,000	3,600,000	100,000	3,700,000

FIGURE 10-8   Application of Optimism Criteria to Conditional Values for Helicopter Manufacture (0.8 Optimism and 0.2 Pessimism)

therefore look on the bright side of things and assign a probability of, for example, 0.8 to the likelihood of the most favorable outcomes of each strategy and 0.2 to the least favorable outcomes of each. Then these best and worst conditional values associated with these three strategies can be multipled by their respective probabilities to obtain weighted values as seen in Figure 10-8. Finally, these values can be added. In this instance, helicopter A is the best choice. Using this approach, the manager maximizes his maximum gain.

Dealing with decisions under uncertainty is no easy task. In the three approaches used here, a different strategy emerged as most favorable each time. The assumptions the manager makes regarding conditional values and probability estimates and the methods he employs in evaluating the alternatives will all influence the outcome.

DECISION-MAKING TECHNIQUES

Thus far attention has been mainly focused on the environment in which the manager makes decisions, i.e., certainty, risk and uncertainty. However, it is also useful to examine some of the specific techniques that have proved valuable in the decision-making process, two of which are marginal analysis and financial analysis.

Marginal Analysis

For years, marginal analysis has been of interest to economists. Samuelson has explained the essence of the concept by the following description:

The "marginal-product" of a productive factor is the extra product or output added by one extra unit of that factor, while other factors are being held constant. Labor's marginal-product is the extra output you get when you add one unit of labor, holding all other inputs constant. Similarly, land's marginal-product is the change in total product resulting from one additional unit of land with all other inputs held constant. . . .[5]

---

[5]Paul Samuelson, *Economics*, 9th edition (New York: McGraw-Hill Book Company, 1973), pp. 537–538.

The manager can use the concept to answer questions such as how much more output will result if one more worker is hired? The answer, often called marginal physical product, provides a basis for determining whether or not one new man will bring about profitable additional output.

By adding one worker, output may be increased.

Marginal Physical Product. Consider the case of the new shipping manager who has five men loading five trucks. After pondering the matter, the manager hires five new men so there are now two people loading each truck. The result, as seen in Figure 10–9, is that the total number of boxes loaded per day rises from 800 to 2000. The two men working as a team are able to do more than they could if working independently. By hiring a third man for each team, the daily total rises to 2900.

Continuing on, as seen in the figure, the total mounts to 4000 and then drops off to 3700 when the number of workers per truck reaches seven. Why? Various causes can be cited. On the physical side, there may be just too many people involved and they are getting in each other's way. On the behavioral side, the seven men may be doing more horseplaying than when there were only six, or they may have agreed informally to hold down output. In either event, it is evident that seven workers per team are too many.

If the manager's decision must rest solely on output, six is the ideal team size. However, it should be noted that there is a diminishing marginal physical product after the second man is hired. The contributions from the third through the sixth increase the total but reduce the *average* from one thousand boxes when there are two workers to 967, 875, 780 and 667 respectively as the next four men are added. This rise in the total output with the accompanying decline in the marginal physical product is seen in Figures 10–10 and 10–11 respectively.

NUMBER OF WORKERS PER TRUCK	TOTAL BOXES LOADED	MARGINAL PHYSICAL PRODUCT
0	0	800
1	800	1,200
2	2,000	900
3	2,900	600
4	3,500	400
5	3,900	100
6	4,000	(300)
7	3,700	

FIGURE 10–9 Units of Marginal Physical Product

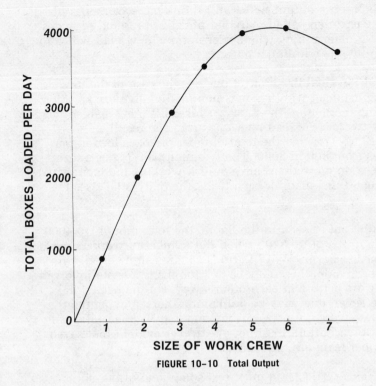

FIGURE 10-10   Total Output

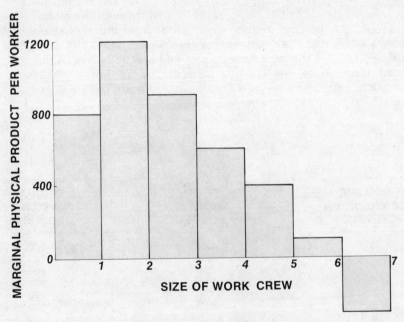

FIGURE 10-11   Bar graph of Physical Product

NUMBER OF WORKERS	SALARY COST PER DAY	PER CENT PROFIT PER BOX BEFORE LOADING SALARIES	BOXES LOADED	TOTAL PROFIT BEFORE LOADING SALARIES	TOTAL PROFIT
1	$20	.05	800	$ 40.00	$20.00
2	40	.05	2,000	100.00	60.00
3	60	.05	2,900	145.00	85.00
4	80	.05	3,500	175.00	95.00
5	100	.05	3,900	195.00	95.00
6	120	.05	4,000	200.00	80.00
7	140	.05	3,700	185.00	45.00

FIGURE 10-12   Profit per Truck

Profit Consideration

However, profit is of more importance than mere physical output.

The decline in marginal output will limit the size of the work crew. More realistically, however, the manager will refine his decision further with a consideration of profit. How much money will the company make at each work crew size? Figure 10-12 shows total profits under the premise that there is a five-cent profit for every box loaded if all costs except work crew salaries are considered. It is evident from the data that the company stands to make $95 a day if the work crew has either four or five men. Any other size will result in a decline in this profit. In summary, the manager must consider profit as well as productivity in making his decision.

Earlier it was noted that most managers are satisficers (administrative men) and not maximizers (economic men). However, in some cases, especially production, the manager will often be far closer to the end of the spectrum represented by economic man than to that represented by administrative man. For example, consider the case of the aerospace firm that is pondering the acceptance of a subcontract to build communication satellite systems. The major contractor wants eight of them built and would like to know if the company is willing to undertake the contract. The purchase price of each system will be $18,000. In order to determine the profitability of the venture, the firm must first construct its cost and revenue data as seen in Figure 10-13. The information reveals that if the company manufactures all eight systems, it will lose $26,000. The ideal production is six, for at this point the firm will net $32,000. This is also seen in Figure 10-14 in which the data is presented graphically. The profit point at which the distance between total revenue and total cost is greatest is that corresponding to six units. The company should therefore refuse the contract.

Marginal revenue and marginal cost must be computed.

The solution can be verified further if the *marginal revenue* and *marginal cost* data in Figure 10-13 are examined. For every unit manufactured, the company obtains marginal revenue of $18,000. However, it also has an accompanying marginal cost associated with the production. A close scrutinization of this

NUMBER MANUFACTURED	TOTAL REVENUE	TOTAL COST	TOTAL PROFIT	MARGINAL REVENUE	MARGINAL COST
1	$ 18,000	$ 30,000	($12,000)	$18,000	$30,000
2	36,000	35,000	1,000	18,000	5,000
3	54,000	40,000	14,000	18,000	5,000
4	72,000	50,000	22,000	18,000	10,000
5	90,000	60,000	30,000	18,000	10,000
6	108,000	76,000	32,000	18,000	16,000
7	126,000	110,000	16,000	18,000	34,000
8	144,000	170,000	(26,000)	18,000	60,000

FIGURE 10-13   Costs and Revenues Associated With Manufacture of Communications Systems

marginal revenue (MR) and marginal cost (MC) data shows that at six units the firm will increase overall profit by $2,000 ($18,000 − $16,000). At seven units, overall profits will decline by $16,000 because the marginal revenue is $18,000 but the marginal cost associated with this unit is $34,000. The company should therefore agree to manufacture no more than six units. The profit maximization rule is to manufacture to the point where MC equals MR or, if they do not equalize, the last point where MR is larger than MC (as occurred in this case). Such an

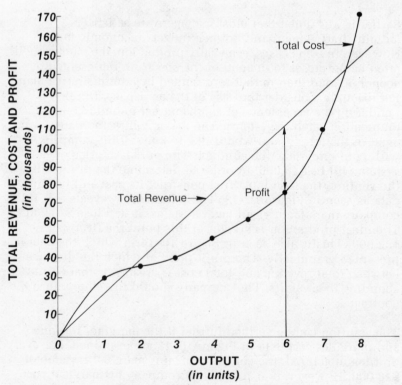

FIGURE 10-14   Maximum Profit Determination

analysis can prove a useful decision-making technique for the manager because it not only helps identify the maximum profit point but also prevents him from undertaking unprofitable ventures.

Financial Analysis

Although marginal analysis is useful to the manager, it is a specialized technique that considers situations one at a time. As such, it is not a particularly helpful long-range guide to action. To provide a dynamic view of the future, many managers have turned to financial analytical techniques, which can be used for functions such as estimating the profitability of an investment, calculating the payback period and/or analyzing discounted cash inflows and outflows.

After-tax profitability is one guideline.

Consider the situation of the manager who is evaluating the purchase of two machines, A and B, on one basis only, *after-tax profitability*. Which machine will provide the most net profit for the firm? Machine A costs $150,000 and has an estimated useful life of five years. Machine B costs $200,000 and also has a five-year useful life. As seen in Figure 10–15, when depreciation and taxes are deducted, Machine A will return $55,000 in net

MACHINE A

Year	Added Income Before Taxes	Depreciation	Taxable Income	After-Tax Income (assuming 50 percent tax rate)
1	$30,000	$30,000	$ 0	$ 0
2	50,000	30,000	20,000	10,000
3	60,000	30,000	30,000	15,000
4	80,000	30,000	50,000	25,000
5	40,000	30,000	10,000	5,000
			$110,000	$55,000

MACHINE B

Year	Added Income Before Taxes	Depreciation	Taxable Income	After-Tax Income (assuming 50 percent tax rate)
1	$ 40,000	$40,000	$ 0	$ 0
2	60,000	40,000	20,000	10,000
3	80,000	40,000	40,000	20,000
4	100,000	40,000	60,000	30,000
5	40,000	40,000	0	0
			$120,000	$60,000

Notes:

1. Investment for Machine A is $150,000; Machine B, $200,000.
2. Both machines have an estimated life of 5 years.
3. Depreciation is on a straight-line basis.

FIGURE 10–15   Evaluating an Investment on the Basis of Net Profit

income, whereas Machine B will net the firm $60,000. Therefore, on the basis of after-tax profitability, Machine B will be the manager's choice.

It should be noted, however, that although the B alternative is more profitable, it also entails an added investment of $50,000. This raises the question, has the manager made a wise choice by allowing net profit to be his guide? After all, should the company not expect to obtain more profit from the larger investment? Sometimes a manager is on sound ground when opting for the alternative returning the greatest net profit; other times, however, he may forego his consideration of profit *Payback period* and concentrate on the *payback period*, that is, how long it will *is another.* take the company to recover its investment. Figure 10–16 presents the cumulative cash recovery period. Estimating weekly recovery as 1/52 of the annual total, it will require approximately 3 years, 33 weeks to recover the $150,000 invested for Machine A and 3 years and 37 weeks to recover the $200,000 invested for Machine B. On the basis of the payback period, the manager would opt for Machine A.

A third approach, and even more useful than the previous two, *Discounted cash* is that of a *discounted dollar analysis* of cash inflows and *flow is a third.* outflows. The manager could evaluate the two alternative investments by determining the initial costs and the expected returns for the next five years. However, to make the analysis realistic, he might choose to discount the future inflows of funds by some discount rate such as ten per cent. The purpose of the discounted cash flow approach is to make all dollars equal by stating them in terms of current dollars. How much are these

MACHINE A

Year	After-tax Income	Depreciation	Annual Cash Recovery	Cumulative Cash Recovery
1	$ 0	$30,000	$30,000	$ 30,000
2	10,000	30,000	40,000	70,000
3	15,000	30,000	45,000	115,000
4	25,000	30,000	55,000	170,000
5	5,000	30,000	35,000	205,000

MACHINE B

Year	After-tax Income	Depreciation	Annual Cash Recovery	Cumulative Cash Recovery
1	$ 0	$40,000	$40,000	$ 40,000
2	10,000	40,000	50,000	90,000
3	20,000	40,000	60,000	150,000
4	30,000	40,000	70,000	220,000
5	0	40,000	40,000	260,000

FIGURE 10–16   Evaluating an Investment on the Basis of Payback Period

MACHINE A

Year	Outflows of Cash	Inflows of Cash	Discount Factor	Discounted Dollars
0	$150,000	$ 0	1.000	$150,000
1	0	30,000	0.909	27,270
2	0	40,000	0.826	33,040
3	0	45,000	0.751	33,795
4	0	55,000	0.683	37,565
5	0	35,000	0.621	21,735
Scrap Value (20%)		30,000	0.621	18,630
				$172,035

MACHINE B

Year	Outflows of Cash	Inflows of Cash	Discount Factor	Discounted Dollars
0	$200,000	$ 0	1.000	$200,000
1	0	40,000	0.909	36,360
2	0	50,000	0.826	41,300
3	0	60,000	0.751	45,060
4	0	70,000	0.683	47,810
5	0	40,000	0.621	24,840
Scrap Value (20%)		40,000	0.621	24,840
				$220,210

FIGURE 10-17 Discounted Cash Flows for Machines A and B

future inflows worth in terms of today's dollars? The longer the manager has to wait for the inflows, the less they are worth in current dollars. This is seen in Figure 10–17, in which the inflows of cash are discounted at a ten per cent rate. In addition, a scrap value of twenty per cent has been estimated for the two machines at the end of their useful life. The results show that Machine A, in terms of current dollars, will return $172,035, whereas Machine B will return $220,210. Since the cost of capital has already been considered in the discount rate, the B alternative is most desirable.

SUMMARY   In this chapter the decision-making process has been examined. Decision making is more than a list of steps; there is a great deal of subjective as well as objective evaluation taking place in the process. For example, the personal values of the top manager will play a significant role in the assignment of risk and uncertainty probabilities. In fact, decision making may well be 75 per cent subjective, 25 per cent objective.

Nevertheless, the manager must be as rational as possible, employing all techniques and guidelines available to him in choosing from among the various alternatives. These include following procedures and policies as well as the implementation of common tools such as marginal analysis and financial analysis. Yet these represent only a few of the techniques that are available to the modern manager, and in the next chapter we will examine many others that are also commonly employed.

REVIEW AND STUDY QUESTIONS

1. What is meant by the term decision making?

2. What are the steps in the decision-making process? Explain each.

3. What is meant by the term rationality? Are all decisions rational ones? Defend your answer.

4. How does value orientation affect the decision-making process? Give an illustration.

5. What are meant by organizational and personal decisions? Basic and routine decisions? Programmed and nonprogrammed decisions? Give an illustration of each.

6. How does a procedure differ from a policy?

7. What are the three basic conditions under which decisions are made? Explain each.

8. What roles do objective and subjective probability play in the decision-making process?

9. How does risk preference affect the decision-making process?

10. Of what benefit is marginal analysis to the manager in the decision-making process? Give an illustration.

11. Of what value is financial analysis to the manager in the decision-making process? Give an illustration.

SELECTED REFERENCES

Drucker, P. F. *Management: Tasks, Responsibilities, Practices.* New York: Harper & Row, Publishers, Inc., 1974, Chapter 37.

Greiner, L. E., D. P. Leitch, and L. B. Barnes. "Putting Judgment Back into Decisions." *Harvard Business Review*, March–April 1970, pp. 59–66.

Guth, W. D., and R. Tagiuri. "Personal Values and Corporate Strategy." *Harvard Business Review*, September–October 1965, pp. 123–132.

Ives, B. D. "Decision Theory and the Practicing Manager." *Business Horizons*, June 1973, pp. 38–40.

Kaufmann, F. "Decision Making—Eastern and Western Style." *Business Horizons*, December 1970, pp. 81–86.

Marks, B. A. 'Decision Under Uncertainty: A Poet's View." *Business Horizons*, December 1971, pp. 67–72.

Richards, M. D., and P. S. Greenlaw, *Management Decision Making.* Homewood, Ill.: Richard D. Irwin Inc., 1972.

Shell, R. L., and D. F. Stelzer, "Systems Analysis: Aid to Decision Making." *Business Horizons*, December 1971, pp. 67–72.

Sihler, W. W. "Framework for Financial Decisions." *Harvard Business Review,*
    March–April 1971, pp. 123–135.
Simon, H. *The New Science of Management Decision.* New York: Harper & Row,
    Publishers, Inc., 1960.
Williams, L. K. "Some Correlates of Risk Taking." *Personnel Psychology,*
    Autumn 1965, pp. 297–310.

CASE: I'LL BE HOME FOR CHRISTMAS

The Whelson Company's finance committee had been in
session for over seven hours. The question at issue was, should
the firm invest $100,000 in new machinery or should the money
be used to increase the size of the advertising budget? Most of
the time had been spent examining the feasibility of buying the
new machines. It was estimated that the company stood to earn
an average of $40,000 a year before taxes for the next five years
if it opted for the machines. At this point, the chairman took
control of the meeting.

Chairman: Well, gentlemen, you've all heard from the head of manufacturing.
What do you think?

Joe: I think we should purchase the recommended machinery.

Bob: Well, I don't. We've been here seven hours and we really haven't even
looked at the proposal to ferret this $100,000 into the advertising campaign.
Now I have a computer printout and an accompanying report here based on
some econometric forecasting done by a joint planning and marketing
department group that shows that an increase of $100,000 in our advertising
would result in gross sales of over $1,000,000 over the next three years. That
means $280,000 gross profit, gentlemen. I don't see how we can afford to pass
it up.

Joe: How were those estimates arrived at?

Bob: Well, it's a pretty mathematical approach but you're certainly welcome to
look at the report and the printout.

Joe: No thanks, I don't understand mathematics that well. Besides, those are
only estimates and I'm not so sure those quantitative boys really know what
they're talking about.

Bob: Well, let's look at some of their reasoning.

Chairman: Bob, we all appreciate your concern but we've been here since nine
o'clock this morning and we've worked right through the lunch hour. Now
tomorrow is Christmas Eve and I think a lot of us want to spend the holidays
with our families. I'd like to wrap this up within the next hour.

Bob: Mr. Chairman, we can't possibly analyze the advertising alternative in
that time period. Couldn't we stay late this evening or come back on the
twenty-sixth and wrap it all up?

Joe: Bob, we stand to make a good profit from an investment of $100,000 in
new machinery. I really don't see any reason for prolonging the meeting to
analyze the other alternative. The one we've been discussing is sure good
enough for me.

With that the group took a vote and decided to recommend the purchase of the new machinery.

Questions

1. Why did the committee reject Bob's proposal? Give your reasoning.

2. At the time of their decision, which of the following values was of greatest importance to the executives: economic, theoretical, political, religious, aesthetic or social? Explain.

3. What does this case illustrate about the impact of personal values on the decision-making process?

CASE: ONE, TWO OR THREE

George Redin had fought the proposed increase in plant facilities. "It's a poor idea," he told the board of directors, "because there just isn't enough demand to sustain this increased supply. Four major firms have entered our industry in the last year and three more are knocking on the door; they know a profitable venture when they see one. The days of high prices and high profits are over. We are in for at least a decade of severe competition. Instead of increasing our capacity, we ought to be considering a new industry in which we can invest funds and maybe make a 15 per cent return on investment. Right now we have all our eggs in one basket and we are jeopardizing them by increasing our commitment with a 25 per cent increase in plant."

The board listened attentively but outvoted the president. Plant expansion was ordered and would be completed within eighteen months. George decided that the only way to salvage the company was to find some way of increasing demand for the product. After ten months of investigation and research, the president and his top executives agreed that there were three basic strategies available. First, they could increase the amount of advertising from $300,000 to $400,000. This would result in total sales of $30,000,000. Second, they could lower the price of the product by 20 per cent. Market research data indicated that this would lead to sales of $60,000,000. Finally, they could opt for a strong research and development program. If $1 million was invested in R & D, sales for the upcoming year would be $25 million. In terms of success probability, the executives estimated that the first of these strategies had a 60 per cent chance of succeeding, the second had a 20 per cent chance, whereas the third had a 70 per cent success probability. In addition, the tax rate associated with each of the three was 48, 50 and 46 per cent respectively.

Questions

1. Is this a case of decision making under certainty, risk or uncertainty? Explain.

2. What are the expected values associated with each of the three strategies? Show all your calculations. In light of your work, which of the three strategies should the management choose?

3. Will the net profit margin before taxes associated with each of the three strategies have any bearing on the final decision? Explain why or why not.

CASE: THE PROFITABLE PEN

Jack Price, president of Wilten Manufacturing, and his staff of planning advisors had spent the morning discussing the manufacture of a new felt pen. The process for the pen had been discovered in their R & D lab. The company's plan was to blanket the New York City area with an advertising campaign announcing the new product. Although the pen would be priced higher than that of the competition, its estimated life was four times that of the average felt pen currently on the market.

Using market research and all the information they could obtain about the success of competitive firms, the following demand schedule and total cost figures were compiled for the first year of operations:

Price	Felt Pens Demanded	Total Cost
$1.20	Virtually zero	$ 80,000
1.10	100,000	90,000
1.00	115,000	100,000
.90	130,000	105,000
.80	140,000	115,000
.70	150,000	130,000
.60	155,000	145,000
.50	160,000	170,000

Realizing that this was probably the most accurate information they would be able to obtain, the president and his advisors decided to push ahead with the production and sale of the new pen if the figures indicated the venture would be profitable. Then, if they were successful in the New York City area, they would expand their market to the national level. However, if the current data indicated that the product could not be successfully marketed because of lack of demand and/or excessive costs, they would sell the process to one of their competitors. The president saw little problem with this latter alternative, since the company had applied for a patent on the process and company attorneys indicated that there would be no trouble getting one. Initial estimates placed the value of the felt pen process at $60,000.

Questions

1. Based on the data in the case, can the pen be manufactured and marketed successfully? Explain in detail.

2. Would the firm be better off marketing the pen or selling the process? Show your calculations.

CASE: THE CAR DEALER'S DILEMMA

A local car dealer has been making an estimate of the number of cars he will sell with each of three strategies under two different states of nature. His data reveals the following:

Strategies	States of Nature	
	Average Growth of GNP	Dynamic Growth of GNP
Low Price	1,300 cars	1,400 cars
Increased Advertising	1,200 cars	1,600 cars
Improved Service	1,250 cars	1,500 cars

Questions

1. Using the Laplace criterion, which applies equal probability to all states of nature, which of the above three strategies should the dealer implement? Give your reasoning.

2. If the dealer uses the maximin approach, which of the above three strategies should he implement? Explain.

3. If the dealer employs a maximax criterion and assigns a 0.8 probability to dynamic growth and a 0.2 probability to average growth, which of the above alternatives should he implement? Explain.

CHAPTER 11

MODERN QUANTITATIVE DECISION-MAKING TOOLS AND PROCESSES

GOALS OF THE CHAPTER

Mathematical decision making has been receiving increased emphasis in recent years. The goal of this chapter is to examine some of the mathematical tools and processes currently being employed by managers. Before doing so, however, it should be noted that a quantitative approach has both advantages and disadvantages. On the positive side, for example, it is possible to screen out many of the subjective processes that often cause a decision to go awry. Also, in solving complex problems, faster and more accurate solutions can sometimes be obtained by use of a mathematical approach. On the other hand, quantitative tools cannot guarantee effective decision making; they have numerous limitations. For example, if the mathematical expression or model does not properly represent reality, the answer will be wrong. If, for example, a manager estimates that Decision A will produce either $1 million or nothing and has a success probability of 10 per cent, whereas Decision B will produce either $200,000 or nothing and has a success probability of 90 per cent, he would be wise to choose Decision B. The former has an expected payoff of only $100,000 [($1 million) (.10) + ($0) (.90)], but the latter has an expected pay-off of $180,000 [($200,000) (.90) + ($0) (.10)].

However, what if the manager is wrong in his estimates and Decision A's probability for success is really .90 while that of Decision B is only .10? Then, because of erroneous probability assignments, the manager has made a serious mistake. Decision A's expected payoff of $900,000 [($1 million) (.90) + ($0) (.10)] will be much larger than that of Decision B's $20,000 [($200,000) (.10) + ($0) (.90)]. Second, sometimes the costs associated with a quantitative solution do not justify the returns; i.e., a mathemathical approach may be much more expensive than a nonmathematical one. Third, many times it is difficult to quantify all the necessary variables associated with a problem. In such cases, a quantitative approach may not be possible.

Nevertheless, many managers are finding mathematical tools and techniques very helpful in the decision-making process. These tools, for the most part, fall under the heading of *operations research* (OR) and this chapter will examine some of them. In certain cases, a mathematical explanation will be made, whereas in others, because of time and space limitations, only a qualitative description will be given. In particular, attention will be focused on:

a. the definition of operations research;
b. the importance of the economic order quantity formula in solving inventory control problems;
c. the value of linear programming in the decision-making process;
d. game theory and its role in providing the manager with important insights into the elements of competition;
e. queuing theory as a technique for balancing waiting lines and service;
f. the Monte Carlo method and its value in simulating the effects of various decisions;
g. decision trees and their role in helping the manager examine the long-run as well as short-run effects of his decisions; and
h. heuristic programming, a highly intuitive and subjective OR technique.

OPERATIONS RESEARCH   The application of quantitative methods to decision making began in earnest during World War II. The approach has been termed *operations research* or *management science.* Simon tersely summed up its history when he wrote:

Operations research is a movement that, emerging out of the military needs of World War II, has brought the decision-making problems of management within the range of interests of large numbers of natural scientists and, particularly, of mathematicians and statisticians. The operations researchers soon joined forces with mathematical economists who had come into the same area—to the mutual benefit of both groups. And by now there has been widespread fraternization between these exponents of the "new" scientific management and . . . industrial engineering. No meaningful line can be drawn any more to demarcate operations research from scientific management or scientific management from management science.[1]

Since it is so difficult to identify specifically the domain of operations research, there has been considerable confusion over the use of the term. Some attach it to any new mathematical

[1]Herbert A. Simon, *The New Science of Management Decision* (New York: Harper & Row, Publishers, Inc., 1960), p. 15.

approach to decision making. Others (e.g., mathematicians, physicists, engineers) claim there must be an interdisciplinary approach involved. Still others contend that the process or technique must be sophisticated before it falls under the heading of OR. In an attempt to make the area understandable, Koontz and O'Donnell have identified the essential methods of OR as applied to decision making as follows:

The essential methods of OR.

1. An emphasis on models that symbolize the relationship among the variables that are involved.
2. An emphasis on goals and the development of techniques for measuring effectiveness.
3. The incorporation of at least the most important variables into the model.
4. The design of a mathematical model.
5. The quantification of all variables to the greatest degree possible.
6. The supplementation of quantifiable data with the use of probability.[2]

Using these basic essentials, a number of problem solving tools and techniques have been developed, including inventory control, linear programming, game theory, queuing theory and Monte Carlo simulation, which will be examined in this chapter.

INVENTORY CONTROL

One common problem faced by managers is that of maintaining adequate inventories. On the one hand no one wants to have too many units available because there are costs associated with carrying these goods. On the other hand, a store that runs out of inventory risks losing a customer's business in the future. In resolving this dilemma, it is necessary for the manager to analyze costs and formulate some assumptions about supply and demand.

There are two types of costs that merit the manager's consideration. The first are *clerical and administrative costs,* which are expenses associated with ordering inventory. Every time an order for more goods is placed, some time and effort is expended. Naturally, if a firm wished to reduce these particular costs to their lowest possible level, they could place one order covering all the goods they would need for the entire year. However, this is unrealistic in light of the second type of costs, popularly known as *carrying costs.* Carrying costs refer to the amount of money invested in the inventory, as well as other sundry expenses covering storage space, taxes and obsolesence. The greater the inventory the firm carries, the greater these expenses are going to be.

---

[2]Adapted from Harold Koontz and Cyril O'Donnell, *Principles of Management: An Analysis of Managerial Functions,* 5th edition (New York: McGraw-Hill Book Company, 1972), pp. 183–184.

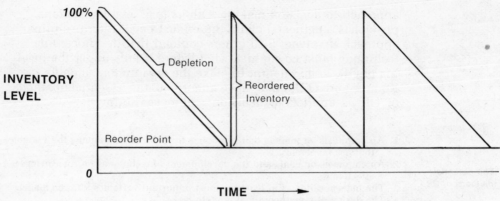

FIGURE 11–1   Constant Depletion Rate

Solving the Problem

Assumptions made in determining optimal inventory size.

One way for the manager to solve his inventory problem is to make certain assumptions regarding future demand for his goods from which he can attempt a solution. Three of the most common assumptions made in determining optimal inventory size are: demand is known with certainty; the lead time necessary for reordering goods is also known with certainty; and the inventory will be depleted at a constant rate. This last assumption can be diagrammed as in Figure 11–1.

Naturally, these three assumptions are not realistic, but they do provide a basis from which the manager can make a decision. Now he has to decide if he wishes to use what can be labeled a trial-and-error approach, or if he wants to employ an OR tool known as the economic order quantity (EOQ) formula.

In order to illustrate the importance of the EOQ formula, the following problem will be solved using both approaches. Mr. Smith is the manager of an appliance department for a large eastern discount store. He has estimated the annual demand for blenders for the upcoming year to be 5000. He has calculated the order costs (clerical and administrative) as $100 per order, and carrying costs have been broken down into component parts as follows: (a) value of a blender is $20; (b) insurance, taxes and other expenses are five per cent per year; and (c) average inventory carried at any one time is equal to total inventory divided by 2. It should be noted that carrying costs consist of the value of the inventory tied up at any one time and the costs associated with these particular goods.

In the first instance, if Mr. Smith takes the above data and constructs the total costs associated with each of a number of reorder levels the following will result:

TABLE 11-1   Trial-And-Error Approach

Number of Orders Placed	Size of Each Order	Order Cost	Carrying Cost (Inventory /2 × $20 × 0.05)	Total Cost
1	5000	$100	$2500.00	$2600.00
2	2500	200	1250.00	1450.00
3	1667	300	833.50	1133.50
6	833	600	416.50	1016.50
10	500	1000	250.00	1250.00
20	250	2000	125.00	2125.00

Based on the above data, the manager would be best off by placing six orders of 833 blenders each throughout the year. However, two points should be noted. First, Mr. Smith does not know that six is the ideal number of times to reorder. He merely knows that of the above alternatives, six is the best. However, what about the other reorder possibilities, namely, 4, 5, 7, 8, 9 and 11 to 19? Second, many inventory problems are much too sophisticated to be solved by such a simple approach. For this reason, the aforementioned EOQ formula is often employed. The formula is:

$$EOQ = \sqrt{\frac{2DA}{vr}}$$

where:

The economic order quantity formula.

D = expected annual demand
A = administrative costs per order
v = value per item
r = estimate for taxes, insurance and other expenses

When the data is placed in the formula, it appears as follows:

$$EOQ = \sqrt{\frac{2(5000)\,(\$100)}{(\$20) \times (0.05)}}$$

$$EOQ = \sqrt{\frac{\$1,000,000}{\$1.00}}$$

$$EOQ = \sqrt{1,000,000}$$

$$EOQ = 1000$$

This means that the manager's best decision would be to reorder in quantities of 1000. This will require the placement of five orders throughout the year, an alternative not pursued by Mr. Smith. The answer can be further verified through hand calculation. Five orders will result in total order costs of $500. The carrying costs will equal 1000 ÷ 2 × ($20 × 0.05), or $500 more. Thus, by ordering five times a year and not six, the manager can improve his total cost by $16.50 ($1016.50 − $1000).

This EOQ formula is used by many firms in solving their inventory control problems. However, it is only one of many mathematical techniques that have been developed to help the manager make decisions. Another is linear programming.

LINEAR PROGRAM-MING

One of the most widely used techniques of operations research is that of linear programming. It has been described as:

What is linear programming?

. . . a technique for specifying how to use limited resources or capacities of a business to obtain a particular objective, such as least cost, highest margin, or least time, when those resources have alternative uses. It is a technique that systematizes for certain conditions the process of selecting the most desirable course of action from a number of available courses of action, thereby giving management information for making a more effective decision about the resources under its control.[3]

Characteristics of linear program-ming problems.

All linear programming problems must have two basic characteristics. First, two or more activities must be competing for limited resources. Second, all relationships in the problem must be linear. If these two conditions exist, the technique can be employed. One of the easiest ways to grasp the fundamentals of the approach is to use it in solving a particular problem. Following is a simple illustration of an allocation problem, using one of the most common linear programming approaches, the graphic method.

The Graphic Method

Company A wishes to maximize its profit by manufacturing two products: Model A and Model B. There is a wholesaler who has signed a contract promising to take all the goods the company can manufacture over the next 30 days off its hands at a predetermined price. The basic question, therefore, is how many units of each to manufacture. Analysis reveals the following information:

TABLE 11–2   Company A's Resources

Mathematical expression of the constraints.

| | Hours Required Per Unit | | | | |
Product	Manufacturing	Painting	Assembly	Test	Profit Per Unit
Model A	15.0	1.0	3.0	3.0	$400
Model B	10.0	1.0	2.0	–	$300
Hours Available During Next 30 Days	21,000	1,200	3,000	2,400	

[3]Robert O. Ferguson and Lauren F. Sargent, *Linear Programming* (New York: McGraw-Hill Book Company, 1958), p. 3.

How many Model A and Model B units should be manufactured? Merely by looking at the data it is virtually impossible to say. However, certain conclusions can be drawn in regard to constraints. For example, no more than 21,000 hours of manufacturing time are available to produce the two models. The constraint can be written in this way:

$$15A + 10B \leq 21{,}000 \text{ hours}$$

Likewise, the other three constraints (painting, assembly and test) can be expressed as follows:

$$1A + 1B \leq 1200 \text{ hours}$$
$$3A + 2B \leq 3000 \text{ hours}$$
$$3A \leq 2400 \text{ hours}$$

In addition, maximization of the profit objective can be expressed by the statement:

$$\text{Profit maximization} = \$400A + \$300B$$

subject, of course, to the initial four constraints and the fact that A and B cannot be negative, i.e., there is no such thing as negative production and so $A \geq 0$ and $B \geq 0$.

Having identified the constraints and the profit maximization function, the maximum number of units that can be manufactured can now be determined. That is:

$$15A + 10B \leq 21{,}000 \text{ hours}$$
$$\text{if:} \quad B = 0$$
$$\text{then:} \quad 15A \leq 21{,}000$$
$$A \leq 1400$$

Conversely:

$$\text{if:} \quad A = 0$$
$$\text{then:} \quad 10B \leq 21{,}000$$
$$B \leq 2100$$

Thus, if only one model is produced, the greatest number of Model A and Model B units that can be manufactured is 1400 and 2100 respectively. This can be graphed as shown in Figure 11–2.

The maximum number of units of A and B respectively that can be painted is:

$$1A + 1B \leq 1200 \text{ hours}$$
$$\text{if:} \quad B = 0$$
$$\text{then:} \quad 1A \leq 1200$$
$$A \leq 1200$$

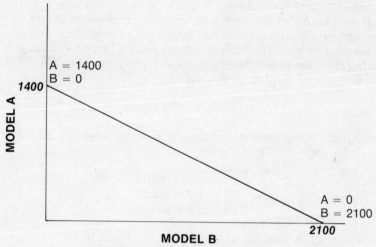

FIGURE 11-2 Manufacturing Constraints

Conversely:

$$\text{if:} \quad A = 0$$
$$\text{then:} \quad 1B \leq 1200$$
$$B \leq 1200$$

This can be graphed as shown in Figure 11-3.

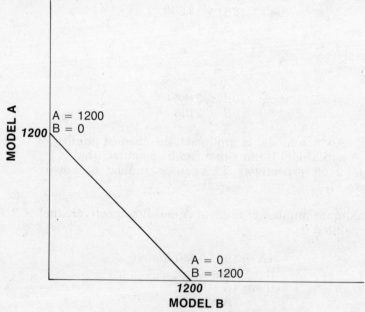

FIGURE 11-3 Painting Constraints

In terms of the assembly constraint, the number of Model A and Model B units that can be assembled can be determined as follows:

$$3A + 2B = 3000$$
$$\text{if:} \quad B = 0$$
$$\text{then:} \ 3A = 3000$$
$$A = 1000$$

Conversely:

$$\text{if:} \quad A = 0$$
$$\text{then:} \ 2B \leq 3000$$
$$B \leq 1500$$

This can be graphed as shown in Figure 11–4.

Finally, although Model B requires no testing, the number of Model A units that can be tested can be determined as follows:

$$3A \leq 2400$$
$$A \leq 800$$

This can be graphed as shown in Figure 11–5.

All four graphs can then be consolidated as seen in Figure 11–6. The area that is shaded represents the *feasibility area;* that is, any combination of Model A and Model B can be

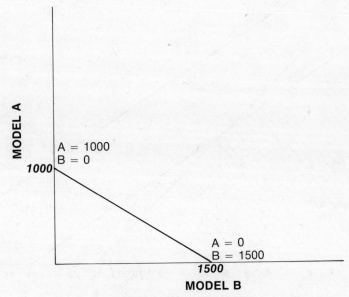

FIGURE 11–4 Assembly Constraints

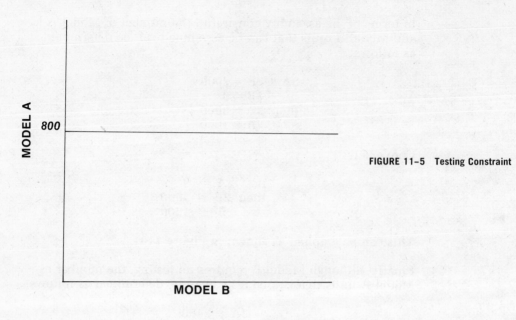

FIGURE 11–5   Testing Constraint

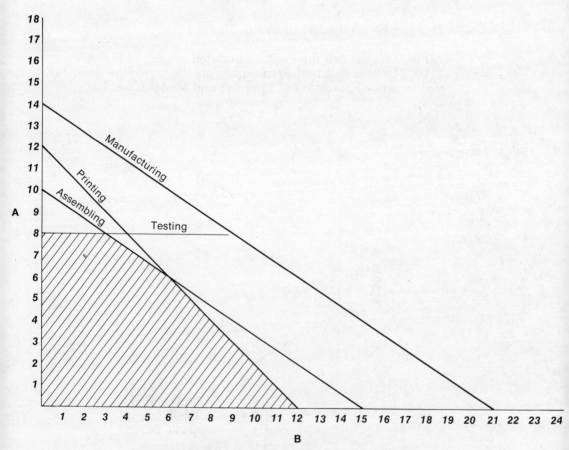

FIGURE 11–6   Feasibility Area (in hundreds of units)

*The feasibility
area represents
all possible
production com-
binations.*

produced as long as it falls within this area. Everything outside
of the area is infeasible because those particular combinations
will require more manufacturing, painting, assembling and/or
testing hours than are available.

The next question is, what combination of those that are feasible should be manufactured? It has already been ascertained
that:

$$\text{Profit maximization} = \$400A + \$300B$$

Therefore, for every three units of A or four units of B sold, the
profit will be identical, namely, $1200. The ratio of A to B will
be 3:4. If this ratio is maintained, starting as close to the origin
as possible and gradually working outward, all combinations of
feasible production can eventually be analyzed. Figure 11–7

*Computation of
the isoprofit line.*

shows this "isoprofit line" for $1200. If this line is continued
on out to its furthest point from the origin, it will either come
to rest on one of the lines forming the feasibility boundary
area or it will "nick" one of the four points labeled A, B, C
and D respectively in the figure. The slope of the isoprofit line
shows that it will probably touch one of the four points before
continuing out into the infeasible area, and this is precisely that
happens. The isoprofit line will touch point C, and it is here
that profit is maximized at 600 units of Model A and 600 units

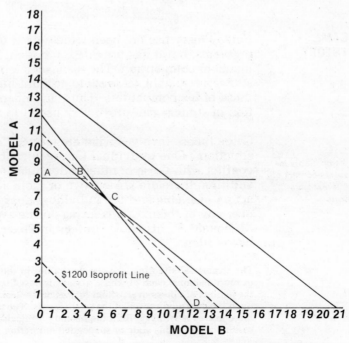

FIGURE 11–7 $1200 Isoprofit line (in hundreds of units)

of Model B. This can be verified by examining all four points—
A, B, C and D.

Point A: $400 (800) + $300 (\quad 0 \quad) = $320,000
Point B: $400 (800) + $300 (\quad 300) = $410,000
Point C: $400 (600) + $300 (\quad 600) = $420,000
Point D: $400 (\quad 0 \quad) + $300 (1200) = $360,000

No other combination will result in as much profit as that
obtained at point C. If the reader wishes, he can test this statement, as long as he remembers to keep in mind the constraints
that are present, e.g., one unit of A cannot be traded for one
unit of B because it takes more time to manufacture a unit of
A than to manufacture a unit of B.

*Limitations of
linear program-
ming.*

Linear programming can be used in the solution of many kinds
of allocation decision problems, but its application is certainly
limited. For example, to be employed effectively, the decision
problem must be formulated in quantitative terms. In many
instances, the costs associated with gathering this data outweigh
the savings obtained from the use of the technique. Likewise,
many allocation problems do not lend themselves to this
approach because the relationship between the variables is not
linear, although approximate solutions are sometimes possible.
Finally, unless all variables are known with certainty, i.e., the
model is deterministic, it is sometimes impossible to use the
technique. Nevertheless, the approach has many advantages and
its application in the area of business decision making is
increasing.

GAME THEORY

Game theory has not been widely used in solving business
problems, but it has provided important insights into the elements of competition. The manager's job is to choose the best
strategy available, taking into account his own actions and
those of his competitors. Thus, an understanding and appreciation of strategy can prove very useful to him.

*Game theory in-
volves conflict of
interest situa-
tions.*

Game theory involves what are termed "conflict of interest"
situations. One individual (or organization) has goals that
conflict with those of other individuals (or organizations). In
addition, there are always two or more alternative courses of
action available and the individual does not have full control
over any of them. Commenting on the aspect of conflict,
McDonald, in his book *Strategy in Poker, Business and War*,
has written;

The strategical situation in game theory lies in the interaction between two
or more persons, each of whose actions is based on an expectation concerning
the actions of others over whom he has no control. The outcome is dependent
upon the personal moves of the participants. The policy followed in making
these moves is strategy. Both the military strategist and the business man act
continuously in this state of suspended animation. And regardless of the

amount of information given them—short of the ideal of perfect information—they generally act in the final analysis on hunch; that is, they gamble without being able to calculate the risk.[4]

**Saddle
Point
Zero-Sum
Games**

*In a zero-sum
game, one party's
gain is the other
party's loss.*

Most analysis conducted in the area of game theory has involved two-party *zero-sum* games. This means that there are two competitors and that one person's loss is the other person's gain. This concept can be seen more clearly if a payoff matrix is constructed, showing what each party stands to win or lose. Before doing so, however, it should be noted that a basic assumption of game theory is that no one side is any smarter than the other, so the payoffs in the matrix are known by *both* sides. The question is, in light of these payoffs, what should each side do?

For example, consider the case of the two managers in the seventh game of the World Series. It is the bottom of the ninth, and the home team is behind 1 to 0. There are two outs, but the pitcher has just walked a man to load the bases. The two managers now face crucial decisions. The man whose team is in the field intends to bring in a new pitcher. However, he is uncertain of whether to call on his ace left-hand reliefer or his ace right-hand reliefer. The home team manager is debating whether to send his regular hitter, who is the pitcher, to bat or to bring out a pinch hitter. In terms of payoffs, both men conclude the following number of runs will result under the various conditions:

		TEAM IN FIELD	
		Star Left-Hand Reliefer	*Star Right-Hand Reliefer*
TEAM AT BAT	*Regular Hitter*	0	1
	Pinch Hitter	1	2

FIGURE 11–8   A Payoff Matrix

If the manager sends the pitcher up to bat, he will bring in a run against the right-hander but will be a third out against the left-hander. On the other hand, if a pinch hitter is put in, the home team will score one run off the left-hander and two off the right-hander. In light of this information, what should each manager do?

---

[4]John McDonald, *Strategy in Poker, Business and War* (New York: W. W. North & Company, Inc., 1950), p. 16.

The matrix shows that the home team manager has nothing to lose and everything to gain by using a pinch hitter. He will secure at least a tie and might win the game right here. The other manager stands to lose the game if he brings in his right-hand reliefer, but he might secure a tie and another chance at victory in extra innings if he brings on his left-hand reliefer. If this logic is correct, the pinch hitter should face the left-hand reliefer.

Using the concepts of minimax and maximin, a saddle point or ideal strategy can be determined.

The logic can be verified by employing two of the most useful ideas to be developed in game theory. These are the concepts of minimax and maximin. *Minimax* involves minimizing the maximum loss, whereas *maximin* involves maximizing the minimum gain. Both of these concepts can be applied to the above payoff matrix to determine if there is a "saddle point" or ideal strategy. This is done by first determining the smallest number in each row (Row Minima) and then ascertaining the largest number in each column (Column Maxima). They are shown in Figure 11–9.

Then, if the largest number in Row Minima equals the smallest number in Column Maxima, there is a *saddle point*. In the matrix in Figure 11–9, this occurs when the pinch hitter faces the star left-hand reliefer. Thus, the logic previously arrived at was correct.

This game theory concept can also be applied in a business setting. Consider, for example, two companies Y and Z, with the following four alternative strategies:

A = lower price
B = improve product quality
C = increase advertising
D = hire more salesmen

The payoff matrix for these respective strategies, in terms of gains and losses for Company Y, is seen in Figure 11–10.

TEAM IN FIELD

		Star Left-Hand Reliefer	Star Right-Hand Reliefer	ROW MINIMA
	Regular Hitter	0	1	0
TEAM AT BAT	Pinch Hitter	1	2	1
COLUMN MAXIMA		1	2	

FIGURE 11–9   Minimax and Maximin Concepts

COMPANY Z STRATEGIES

		C	D
COMPANY Y **STRATEGIES**	**A**	$3 Million	$3 Million
	B	−$4 Million	+$5 Million

A 2 × 2 matrix illustration.

FIGURE 11–10   Company Y Payoff Matrix

In light of this, which strategy is most desirable to Company Y? The answer would appear to be strategy A, for the company stands to gain $3 million, regardless. By following this strategy, they are minimizing their maximum loss and maximizing their minimum gain. Conversely, strategy C appears to be most desirable to Company Z, for they stand to lose no more than $3 million and might gain $4 million. It thus appears that there is a saddle point at A,C. In order to test this, once again the numbers in Row Minima and Column Maxima must be ascertained. When this is done, the following matrix results:

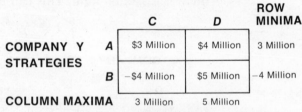

COMPANY Z STRATEGIES

		C	D	ROW MINIMA
COMPANY Y **STRATEGIES**	**A**	$3 Million	$4 Million	3 Million
	B	−$4 Million	$5 Million	−4 Million
COLUMN MAXIMA		3 Million	5 Million	

FIGURE 11–11   Determining if a Saddle Point Exists

Computation of the saddle point.

Since the largest number in Row Minima is equal to the smallest number in Column Maxima, there is a saddle point or ideal strategy. This occurs at point A,C. Thus, once again, it was possible to identify the ideal strategy by means of a visual analysis.

The basic concept of game theory can be expanded into even larger matrices. For example, consider the effect of the following six strategies:

Company Y
A = lower price
B = improve product quality
C = increase advertising

Company Z
D = open more distribution centers
E = provide easier credit terms
F = hire more salesmen

When these six strategies are placed in a matrix, the following
payoffs, from the standpoint of Company Y, result:

COMPANY Z STRATEGIES

		D	E	F
COMPANY Y STRATEGIES	**A**	$2 Million	$6 Million	$12 Million
	B	$14 Million	$8 Million	$10 Million
	C	−$4 Million	$4 Million	−$6 Million

A 3 × 3 matrix illustration.

FIGURE 11–12   Company Y Payoff Matrix

The payoffs show that strategy B is most favorable to Company
Y, whereas strategy E is most favorable to Company Z. However, this matrix is a little more difficult to analyze than the
previous one, so it is desirable first to ascertain whether or not
there is a saddle point. This can be done as follows:

COMPANY Z STRATEGIES

		D	E	F	ROW MINIMA
COMPANY Y STRATEGIES	**A**	$2 Million	$6 Million	$12 Million	2 Million
	B	$14 Million	$8 Million	$10 Million	8 Million
	C	−$4 Million	$4 Million	−$6 Million	−6 Million
COLUMN MAXIMA		14 Million	8 Million	12 Million	

FIGURE 11–13   Saddle Point Calculation

Computation of the saddle point.

There is a saddle point, the ideal strategy being B,E. Thus
Company Y should initiate strategy B and Company Z should
opt for strategy E. Remember, it pays neither side to opt for
any other strategy if there is a saddle point. For example,
according to the above matrix, if Company Y maintains strategy
B, Company Z stands to lose much more than $8 million if
it switches to either strategy D or F. Likewise, if Company Y
changes to strategy A or C while Company Z stays with strategy
E, Company Y will not gain so much as before.

Non-Zero-Sum Mixed Strategy Games

The prior illustrations have all been examples of zero-sum games, but in a realistic business setting zero-sum conditions rarely occur. Consider, for example, that profit per unit is $1, demand is 1000 units and total profit in the market is $1000. Firms A and B both wish to obtain profits of $750 but, based on current information, this is impossible; the combined profits of the two cannot exceed $1000. Thus, only the firm capturing 75 per cent of the market will succeed. On the other hand, if the demand were to increase from 1000 to 2000 units, both companies could capture equal shares of the market and more than attain their respective goals. Because there are increases in demand, most businesses do not face the conditions characteristic of zero-sum games when dealing with sales volume. Most decisions are not made at the direct expense of the competition. They are thus *non-zero-sum* in nature.

Most situations are non-zero-sum in nature.

Likewise, most strategy situations do not have saddle points. For example, consider the following matrix, a slight adaption of Figure 11–13, with its accompanying Row Minima and Column Maxima calculations:

		COMPANY Z STRATEGIES			ROW MINIMA
		D	**E**	**F**	
COMPANY Y STRATEGIES	**A**	$2 Million	$14 Million	$10 Million	2 Million
	B	$8 Million	$6 Million	$12 Million	6 Million
	C	−$4 Million	$16 Million	−$6 Million	−6 Million
COLUMN MAXIMA		8 Million	16 Million	12 Million	

FIGURE 11–14   Mixed Strategy

In most strategy situations there is not a saddle point.

There is no saddle point, for the maxima of Row Minima is $6 million, whereas the minima of Column Maxima is $8 million. When there is no saddle point, it becomes necessary to design a *mixed* strategy. For example, if Company Y chose strategy B, Company Z would go to strategy E, choosing to lose $6 million. However, if Y knew what Z was going to do, it would opt for strategy C, thereby increasing its payoff from $6 million to $16 million. In turn, if Company Z knew this, it would choose strategy D, thereby gaining $4 million; and so it goes, each company second guessing the other. The only way to take advantage of the situation would be to determine some combination or mixed strategy. The method of calculating this will not be discussed here, but it should be noted that this mixed approach is far more realistic than that of the ideal or saddle-point strategy. If one firm found itself in an unfavorable saddle-point situation, it would alter its strategies drastically, thereby upsetting the old payoff matrix and establishing one more favorable to itself. Also, this examination of game theory has dealt with only two competitive sides. In a business setting. however, a firm is generally competing against many companies. Nevertheless, the concept of game theory has proved very useful in understanding the elements of competition. Its basic ideas have been experimentally expanded into bargaining and negotiating interactions and, for almost two decades now, have been employed in general management simulation games to train managers in strategy formulation and implementation.[5]

QUEUING THEORY

Queuing theory helps the manager balance waiting lines and service.

Another OR technique is that of queuing theory, often called *waiting-line theory*, which employs a mathematical technique for balancing waiting lines and service. These lines will occur whenever there is an irregular demand, and the manager must decide how to handle the situation. If the lines become too long and the waiting time proves excessive, customers will go elsewhere with their business. Conversely, if there is too much service, customers will be very happy but the costs will outrun the revenues. If, for example, one goes grocery shopping on Saturday morning, every cash register may be manned and the average waiting time may be fifteen minutes. Since these conditions exist all over town, the manager must be concerned only with keeping the registers manned. However, what should he do during slack periods such as Tuesday morning? If he assigns only two people to the registers, he may have a sudden influx of customers waiting in long lines. On the other hand, if he keeps all the registers manned, and there are only a few customers, most of the help will just be standing around doing nothing.

Naturally, the supermarket manager presents a very simple illustration because it takes little effort to move people from the stockroom to the cash register and back. As long as there is a sufficient number of employees on hand, they can be transferred around the store and waiting lines are not a serious problem. However, the same basic concept can be applied to a business firm faced with, for example, a problem of plant layout. How many loading docks and fork trucks will be needed to keep waiting time on the part of the company's delivery trucks at an acceptable level? If there are too many docks and fork trucks, there will be no waiting time for loading and unloading, but the expense associated with building the facilities will be quite great. Conversely, if there are too few docks and fork trucks, there will be a great deal of waiting time. Queuing theory can help provide an answer to this problem by means of mathematical equations. Sometimes, however, when arrival and service rates are not controllable, it becomes difficult to evaluate alternatives by means of equations alone. When this occurs, a Monte Carlo approach can often prove useful.

---

[5]For example, see Richard M. Hodgetts, *Top Management Simulation* (Braintree, Mass.: D. H. Mark Publishing, 1970).

MONTE CARLO TECHNIQUE

The Monte Carlo technique uses a simulation approach for the purpose of creating an artificial environment and then evaluating the effect of decisions within these surroundings. A simple illustration of a simulation is found in the case of aerodynamic testing conducted on model airplanes in a wind tunnel. By simulating the effect of air currents and gale winds on the craft, engineers can evaluate the proposed design and construction.

The Monte Carlo technique allows the manager to simulate various conditions and determine the best answer from the results.

Monte Carlo is another type of simulation that attempts, via a random number generator or table, to simulate a particular environment and the effect of various decisions made within this artificial setting. An example can be found in the case of the plant manager who wants to determine the optimum number of trucks he should have in his delivery fleet. If there are too many, capital investment in the trucks coupled with excessive idle time will prove too high. The optimum number can be determined by using the Monte Carlo technique. First, the number of shipments arriving at the loading dock must be determined; next, the time it takes to make deliveries must be ascertained. Then the expenses of owning and operating the fleet have to be computed. Finally, the costs associated with being unable to make all deliveries on time must be calculated. Employing this basic information plus some other supplemental data and the use of random numbers, it is possible to simulate results based on different fleet sizes. This can be continued until the manager finds the optimum number of trucks. However, the technique is not restricted merely to ascertaining fleet sizes. It has been successfully used in many diverse activities from simulating machine breakdowns to determining arrivals and departures at airports.

DECISION TREES

Another OR tool is the decision tree. Many managers weigh alternatives based on their immediate or short-run results, but a decision-tree format permits a more dynamic approach because it makes some elements explicit that are generally implicit in other analyses. A decision tree is a graphic method that the manager can employ in: identifying the alternative courses of action available to him in solving a problem; assigning probability estimates to events associated with these alternatives; and calculating the payoffs corresponding to each act-event combination. For example, the ABC Printing Company is considering the purchase of two new offset presses. The total cost is $200,000. However, certain individuals in the firm believe the company should spend $25,000 for repairs on the old presses and forego the purchase of this new machinery. After calculating the possible demand the company can expect over the next five years with the new and old presses and the accompanying probabilities, the decision tree in Figure 11–15 was constructed. As can be seen, the gain in net expected payoff

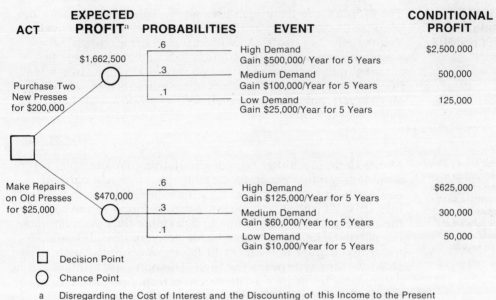

FIGURE 11-15   Decision Tree—Expected Payoff from New Versus Old Machinery

from purchasing the two new presses is $692,500 ($1,162,500 — $470,000).

This net gain in expected payoffs is computed by first determining the amount of money (conditional profit) that can be earned in each event. For example, if the company purchases new presses and there is high demand, the gain will be $500,000 annually for five years. The conditional profit is therefore $2,500,000. Then, multiplying this amount by the probability of the event's occurring (0.6) yields $1,500,000. If the probabilities of medium and low demand are multiplied by their respective conditional profits, the results are $150,000 and $12,500. The sum of three numbers ($1,500,000, $150,000 and $12,500) constitutes the expected profit of $1,662,500 in Figure 11-15. The same procedure can be used in arriving at an expected profit of $470,000 for the decision to make adjustments on the old presses rather than purchasing two new ones.

Decision trees permit the manager to weigh alternatives based on their long-run results.

In the final analysis, the decision tree does not provide any definitive answer. However, it does allow the manager to weigh benefits against costs by assigning probabilities to specific events and then ascertaining the respective payoffs. The decision maker starts at the left side of the tree and extends its branches out to the right. Then, having ascertained the various payoffs, he can roll back the tree from the right side, determining the optimal sequence of decisions as he goes. This is clearly seen in Figure 11-15. Because of the many possibilities that can be evaluated, the decision tree is finding increased favor among managers.

HEURISTIC PROGRAM-MING

Not all operations research approaches rely upon sophisticated mathematics. *Heuristic programming*, generally called heuristic problem solving, is on the opposite end of the spectrum from the rigorous methodology used by some of the OR techniques already examined. Some problems are too large or too complex to be solved by a computer. Others are too unstructured, making a quantitative approach out of the question. In cases such as these, heuristic programming is often employed.

Heuristic programming employs rules of thumb and the use of trial and error.

Heuristic means "serving to discover." Such an approach to problem solving is subjective as well as objective in nature, relying upon experience, judgment, intuition and the advice of associates. Two of the most common heuristic approaches to problem solving are rules of thumb and trial and error.

Many times problems are nothing more than brain twisters that serve to make the manager think. Consider the following example. An epidemic has broken out in a city. All of the twelve local hospitals have called the nearby pharmaceutical manufacturer and asked to have a particular serum delivered immediately. It generally takes three weeks to manufacture this serum, but the pharmaceutical company just happens to have a quantity of it on hand. The serum is placed in vials, wrapped in twelve individual packages and rushed to the shipping dock. By this time, the crisis in the city has become so great that if each hospital does not have its alloted serum within the hour, patients will begin dying. Just as the manager of the shipping dock rushes the packages to the waiting delivery truck, he receives a call from the man who wrapped the packages. One of them is missing a 5-ounce vial of serum. The man is sending the vial down immediately, but in the interim, the manager's job is to ascertain which hospital has been shorted on its serum. The man has only two minutes in which to determine this, and the only tool he has immediately available is a balance scale. How can the manager isolate the package that is missing the vial of serum? Before reading the next paragraph, the reader may wish to formulate his own solution.

There are a number of ways to solve the problem. One is to place six packages on each side of the scale. The side with the light package will not go down so far. Thus, the manager has reduced the number of possibilities to six. Then, by placing these on the scale, three to a side, he can reduce the number of possibilities to three. Now the problem becomes difficult. There is time for only one more weighing. How should it be done? The answer is that if the manager puts one package on each side of the scale and one side drops, he has his answer. Conversely, if both sides balance, the light package must be the one remaining in his hand.[6]

---

[6]Adapted from Paul J. Gordon, "Heuristic Problem Solving: You Can Do It." *Business Horizons*, Spring 1962, pp. 43–53.

These kinds of problems do not warrant sophisticated techniques, and they are far more common than those requiring linear programming and Monte Carlo simulation. Resource allocation, inventory control, plant layout and job shop scheduling are all problems that can sometimes be solved through heuristic programming.

SUMMARY

In this chapter some of the modern quantitative decision-making tools and processes have been examined. Most of these fall under the heading of operations research and vary in complexity and mathematical rigor, yet all are valuable to the manager in the decision-making process.

The economic order quantity formula helps the decision maker decide at what point and in what quantities inventory should be replenished. Linear programming has even more uses from determining price-volume relationships to effectively utilizing the organization's resources. The example used in this chapter illustrated how the technique could be employed to allocate scarce resources while simultaneously maximizing profit. The third technique to be discussed, game theory, is useful in providing the manager with important insights into the elements of competition. Sometimes this competition is best represented as a zero-sum game with a saddle point, but more often it is typified by a non-zero-sum game without a saddle point, in which case, it is necessary to use a mixed strategy in solving the problem. A fourth quantitative technique is queuing or waiting line theory, which employs mathematical equations in balancing waiting lines and service. When it becomes difficult to evaluate alternatives by means of equations alone, many managers turn to the Monte Carlo technique, which uses a simulation approach and provides the decision maker with an opportunity to evaluate the effect of numerous decisions within this simulated environment. Then, based on the results, the manager is in a position to choose the one that best attains the objective.

Still another OR tool, and one that has been receiving increased attention in recent years, is the decision tree. This technique, which is less mathematical than those already mentioned, helps the manager weigh alternatives based on immediate and long-run results by encouraging him to: (a) identify the available courses of action; (b) assign probability estimates to the events associated with these alternatives; and (c) calculate the payoffs corresponding to each act-event combination. The last technique to be examined, heuristic programming, is the least mathematical of all, yet it is used far more often by the manager in his every-day decision making, as evidenced by rules of thumb and the use of trial and error, than any other OR tool.

**REVIEW AND
STUDY
QUESTIONS**

1. What is meant by the term operations research?

2. What are the variables involved in the economic order quantity formula? Of what value is the formula to the manager? Explain.

3. In your own words, define linear programming. What are its advantages to the manager in the decision-making process? What are its drawbacks?

4. What is the graphic technique?

5. Of what value is game theory to the manager?

6. In game theory, what is meant by the term zero-sum game? Non-zero-sum game? Saddle point?

7. Most decisions made by the manager are non-zero-sum in nature. Explain this statement.

8. What is meant by a mixed strategy?

9. What is meant by queuing theory?

10. Of what value is the Monte Carlo method to the manager in decision making? Explain.

11. How do decision trees help the manager in making long-run decisions? Short-run decisions?

12. What is heuristic programming?

13. Many of the daily problems faced by managers are solved by means of heuristic programming. Explain this statement.

**SELECTED
REFERENCES**

Brown, R. V. "Do Managers Find Decision Theory Useful?" *Harvard Business Review*, May–June 1970, pp. 78–79.

Churchman, C. W., R. L. Ackoff, and E. L. Arnoff. *Introduction to Operations Research*. New York: John Wiley & Sons, 1957.

Ferguson, R. O., and L. F. Sargent. *Linear Programming*. New York: McGraw-Hill Book Company, 1968.

McDonald, J. *Strategy in Poker, Business and War*. New York: W. W. North & Company, 1950.

Magee, J. F. "Decision Trees for Decision Making." *Harvard Business Review*, July–August 1964, pp. 126–138.

Malcolm, D. G. "On the Need for Improvement in Implementation of O.R." *Management Science*, February 1965, B48–58.

Paranka, S. "Competitive Bidding Strategy." *Business Horizons*, June 1971, pp. 39–43.

Pollay, R. "The Structure of Executive Decisions and Decision Times." *Administrative Science Quarterly,* December 1970, pp. 459–471.

Richards, M. D., and P. S. Greenlaw. *Management Decision Making.* Homewood, Ill.: Richard D. Irwin, Inc., 1972.

Simon, H. A. *The New Science of Management Decision.* New York: Harper & Row, Publishers, Inc., 1960.

Vandell, R. F. "Management Evolution in the Quantitative World." *Harvard Business Review,* January–February 1970, pp. 83–92.

Virts, J. R., and R. W. Garrett. "Weighing Risk in Capacity Expansion." *Harvard Business Review,* May–June 1970, pp. 132–140.

CASE: AN ECONOMIC APPROACH

Mr. Ed Sharp, local manager of a radio and television retail store, used to reorder merchandise on the basis of "gut feel." As he explained to one of his friends, "I don't know *exactly* when to reorder merchandise, I just use my best judgment." However, one day Paul Sharp, his nephew and a student in the Business College at State University, dropped by the store for a visit. When Paul learned of his uncle's unscientific approach to reordering inventory he was shocked. "You should take a more refined approach to things, Uncle Ed," he said. There are lots of decision-making tools and techniques you could use. For example, there is the economic order quantity formula, which could pinpoint how many units you should order at any one time."

The uncle was impressed and decided to try his nephew's suggestion. Together the two men chose one of the most popular items in the store, a small AM-FM radio. After examining past sales records, they were able to obtain the following information: (a) the expected annual demand for the radio was 750 units; (b) the administrative costs associated with placing an order were $20; (c) the value of each radio was $30; and (d) the estimate for taxes, insurance and other expenses was 10 per cent.

Questions

1. Using a trial-and-error approach, construct a table showing the size of each order, the order cost associated with this size, the carrying cost and the total cost if the uncle reorders inventory 1, 2, 3, 4, 5, 10 and 20 times per year.

2. Using the EOQ formula in this chapter, determine the most economic reorder quantity.

3. How much money can the uncle save the store if he uses the EOQ formula rather than trial and error, assuming that he now reorders five times a year? Explain.

CASE: A LITTLE OF THIS AND A LITTLE OF THAT

The Willowby Corporation had lost quite a bit of money in the previous year. As a result, its president, Fred Wilson, was determined to maximize profits as quickly as possible and show good first-quarter results. In attempting to carry out this objective, Harvey Landau, production manager at Willowby, found himself confronted with a resource allocation problem. The company was manufacturing two kinds of industrial machines: Type A and Type B. After examining the resources available to him, Harvey determined that he could solve the problem by means of the graphic method of linear programming. An analysis of the situation revealed that the following combinations and constraints for the two products were present:

Constraints	Type A	Type B
Assembly Time	120 machines	240 machines
Available Paint	150 machines	150 machines
Special Casing for Type A	100 machines	——
Special Casing for Type B	——	120 machines
Engines	180 machines	180 machines

After plotting these constraints on a graph, he determined that there were five points within the feasibility area, permitting the following combinations of Type A and Type B to be manufactured:

1. 100 A and   0 B
2. 100 A and   40 B
3. 90 A and   60 B
4. 30 A and 120 B
5.   0 A and 120 B

In addition, each unit of A would result in a $300-profit to the firm and each unit of B would bring in $200 in profit.

Questions

1. Verify the accuracy of the above five points by drawing a graphic representation of the constraints.

2. Which of the above five alternatives is most profitable to the firm? Show your work.

3. What other types of problems could Harvey solve by means of the graphic method? Give an illustration.

CASE: HALF AND HALF

A group of high school seniors were touring the facilities of a large bakery not long ago. Although the students were impressed with the mechanization of the operations, they were more interested in finding out how the firm decided how much bread or how many cakes to bake. When the tour was over, the students were taken to the cafeteria for coffee and pasteries and asked if they had any questions. One of the seniors asked, "How do you know how many and what types of, for example, cookies to bake?" The tour guide smiled. "I'll tell you what," he said, "let me call one of our staff specialists in here and have him give you an answer to that." A few minutes later the man showed up with a portable blackboard and some papers containing production statistics.

I understand you're interested in finding out how we go about deciding how much of everything to bake. Actually, we use a mathematical approach whenever we can. There's a lot less guesswork in the business than there was twenty years ago. Let me explain, using baked cookies as an illustration.

Earlier in the day we took an inventory to seen how much cookie mix, icing, labor and oven space we had available for making both sugar and iced cookies, the only kinds we bake. Our calculations showed that we had enough cookie mix to bake, in dozens, either 2000 sugar or 1200 iced cookies. In addition, we had enough labor time to bake 1500 sugar or 1000 iced cookies, enough icing for 800 iced cookies and enough oven space for 1200 sugar or iced cookies. Let me write those numbers on the blackboard for you along with the profit per dozen, which is 15¢ in the case of sugar cookies and 20¢ in the case of iced cookies.

The speaker then turned around and put the following data on the blackboard:

	Sugar Cookies	Iced Cookies
Cookie Mix	1200-dozen	1200-dozen
Labor	1500-dozen	1000-dozen
Icing	———	800-dozen
Oven Space	1200-dozen	1200-dozen
Profit	15¢ per dozen	20¢ per dozen

Now, given this information coupled with the fact that we know we can sell everything we make, how many of each type should we bake?

The students looked at the numbers but were confused. One individual pointed out that the firm could bake no more than 1200-dozen sugar and 800 dozen iced cookies, but no one seemed to know how to calculate the best combination of the two. After pondering the problem for five minutes, everyone admitted defeat. "Don't feel too bad," said the speaker." "Just by looking at the data it is impossible to say. However, by using a mathematical technique we can prove that the best combination to bake is 600-dozen sugar and 600-dozen iced. At this point profit is maximized.

The students were impressed. On the way out of the building one of them remarked, "I never realized baking was such a science. At my house it is still an art."

Questions

1. How much profit will the firm make if it bakes 600-dozen sugar and 600-dozen iced cookies? Show your calculations.

2. How is this company suboptimizing its resources? Optimizing its production? Maximizing its profit?

3. How important are mathematical tools and techniques to the modern manager?

CASE: THE BIG PAYOFF

Bill Hammer, science editor of a large publishing house, is about ready to release a new basic biology textbook. He is very interested in obtaining a large share of the basic biology text market. Although there are many competitors, there is one in particular who is also coming out with a new biology book. Therefore, Bill must formulate his strategy very carefully. For this reason, instead of just designing his own plan of action, he has decided to ask himself, what is the opposition going to do? He has come up with six basic strategies. The first three are those he intends to implement, the second three are those that he has heard will be employed by the competition. They are:

Bill's Strategy

A. Price the book lower than any other on the market
B. Provide 10,000 complementary copies to university professors
C. Hire more salesmen to call on university professors and explain the strongpoints of the text

Opposition's Strategy

D. Give large quantity discounts to the bookstores
E. Increase the advertising budget substantially
F. Print the text on extremely high quality paper so as to enhance its aesthetic value

In addition, Bill has concluded, after giving the matter a great deal of thought, that the following payoff matrix represents the outcomes that will occur given each of the above strategies.

OPPOSITION

		D	E	F
	A	6	4	9
BILL	B	9	3	2
	C	7	1	5

Questions

1. After determining the numbers in Row Minima and Column Maxima, is there a saddle point? If so, what is your advice to Bill regarding strategy? If not, of what value is the above information to Bill?

2. If the competition is aware of the above payoff matrix and concludes it to be an accurate representation of reality, what will they do? Explain, bringing the concept of mixed strategy into your discussion.

THE BEHAVIORAL SCHOOL

The goal of this section is to familiarize the reader with some of the basic ideas and concepts of the behavioral school. Of course, to put all behavioral concepts into this school is erroneous, for the management process and management science people also value the importance of human behavior at work. Nevertheless, much of the latest, and most interesting, research conducted in management has been done by behaviorists, and it is important not to underrate their contribution to management theory.

In Chapter 12 the communication process will be examined with major attention given to both interpersonal and organizational communication. Unless the manager can communicate with his people, he has no basis for either motivating or leading them. In particular, this chapter will focus on the communication process; some of the common barriers to effective communication; steps for overcoming these barriers; and the need to establish understanding between superiors and subordinates.

Then, in Chapter 13, the subject of motivation will be examined. Initial attention will be placed on the importance of understanding why people act as they do. In addition, some of the basic assumptions managers have about their employees will be reviewed. Then, current research findings designed to help the manager understand workers in general and individuals in particular will be presented.

Finally, in Chapter 14, the area of leadership effectiveness will be examined. How does a manager prevail on his subordinates to devote their efforts to attaining organizational goals? In way of answering this question, one-, two- and three-dimensional leadership models will be reviewed. Emphasis will also be placed on the importance of contingency leadership styles.

CHAPTER 12

INTERPERSONAL AND ORGANIZATIONAL COMMUNICATION

GOALS OF THE CHAPTER If management entails getting things done through people, communication is the essence of it, for without effective communication no one would know what they were supposed to be doing. Nor would there be any basis for answering questions, solving problems, obtaining feedback or measuring results. The goal of this chapter is to examine interpersonal and organizational communication, with special emphasis on the following areas:

a. the communication process;
b. steps entailed in implementing effective communication;
c. common barriers to effective communication, including perception, language, logic, abstraction, status and resistance to change;
d. formal and informal channels;
e. written and oral communication; and
f. techniques that can be used to improve managerial communication.

INTERPERSONAL COMMUNICATION One of the most important forms of communication is interpersonal communication, which entails the transmission of *meaning* from one person to another.

Communication Process In the communication process, the sender constructs his message and passes it to the receiver. This individual interprets the message and takes action, hopefully, in a manner satisfactory to the sender.[1]

---

[1]For an excellent discussion of this topic see David K. Berlo, *The Process of Communication* (New York: Holt, Rinehart & Winston, Inc., 1960).

Many models have been developed to explain the communication process. One of these, formulated by Raymond Ross and presented in Figure 12–1, illustrates the process in complete yet easy-to-understand terms. The basic ideas contained in the figure will be developed throughout this chapter.

Steps in the Communication Process.   The important thing to note is that effective communication requires *both* information and understanding. Unfortunately, too many managers overlook the importance of understanding and subscribe to what is known as the *conveyor theory of communication.* Communication is seen as a conveyor that carries messages from one person to another. No real consideration is given to whether the receiver understands or accepts the communiqué. This type of communication is ineffective. Effective communication consists of four steps: attention, understanding, acceptance and action.

Many managers use the conveyor theory of communication.

Attention entails getting the receiver to listen to what is being communicated. Quite often this requires overcoming message competition, which occurs when the receiver has other things on his mind. For example, the listener may have three pressing problems out on the assembly line. In this case, the manager who is communicating with him faces message competition because he must get the man to put aside these problems and listen to him for the moment. If the attention of the receiver is not secured, the communication process can go no further.

Attention involves getting the receiver to listen.

Understanding means that the receiver grasps the essentials of the message. Many managers find that their attempts to communicate break down at this stage because the receiver does not really know what he is supposed to do. Some executives try to surmount this problem by asking the subordinate *if* he understands the message. Unfortunately, such attempts are generally useless because all the pressure is on the person to say "yes." Instead, the manager should ask the subordinate *what* he understands. By having the individual repeat the message in his own words, it becomes clear whether or not accurate understanding has been achieved.

Understanding means that the receiver comprehends the message.

Acceptance implies a willingness on the part of the receiver to comply with the message. As noted earlier in the discussion of the acceptance theory of authority, feelings and attitudes of subordinates often dictate whether or not something will get done. In this phase of the process it is sometimes necessary for the manager to sell the subordinate on the idea. For example, employees in a particular company may have a habit of taking turns clocking in their fellow workers. Management, upon learning of this, may order the supervisors to halt the practice. However, the lower level managers may be opposed to enforcing the directive, believing it will lead to a confrontation with the men. The department manager may have to point out

Acceptance requires a willingness to comply.

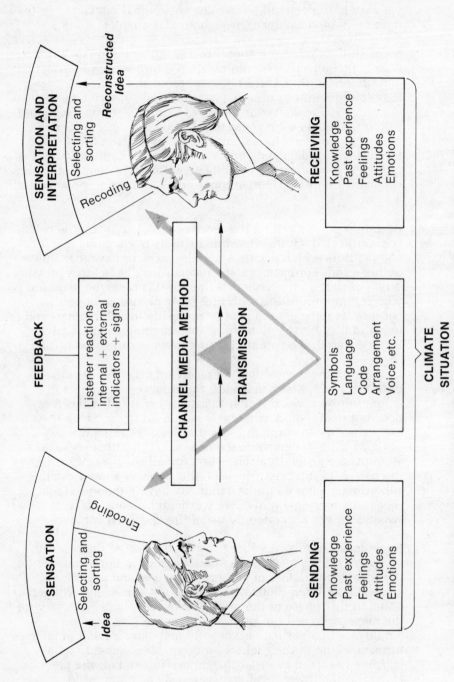

FIGURE 12-1 The Communication Process (From Raymond S. Ross, *Speech Communication: Fundamentals and Practice* © 1965. Reprinted with permission of Prentice-Hall, Inc., Englewood Cliffs, N.J.)

that the practice is in violation of company rules. In addition, some of the men may be arriving late because they know they are being clocked in on time. Once the supervisors realize that management is asking for no more than an equitable solution, they may prove more willing to go along with the directive.

Action entails implementation of the communiqué.

The *action* phase entails implementation of the communication. The challenge facing the manager in this stage is seeing that things are done in the agreed upon manner. Sometimes unforeseen delays will occur; other times expediency will require a change in the initial agreement. Unless the manager allows himself time to check on the progress, communication may falter at this point. For example, a manager calls in his expediter and asks him to check on a particular order and see that it is sent out by the end of the day. The expediter traces the order, finds it, has it filled, packaged, stamped and sent down to the mail room by 4 p.m. However, unless the manager checks, it may occur to no one that the last mail pickup is at 3:30 p.m., and the order will sit in the mail room until the next day. By making himself available for assistance and ensuring that proper action is taken on directives, the manager helps the communiqué reach this fourth and final phase.

Since the manager spends approximately 70 per cent of his time receiving and transmitting information, it is vital that he be able to communicate effectively. This calls for a knowledge and understanding of the four steps in the communication process.

COMMON BARRIERS TO EFFECTIVE COMMUNICATION

There are numerous barriers to effective communication. Some managers may be inadequate; some subordinates may be unreceptive. More commonly, however, both groups are competent in their jobs and are trying to communicate with each other. Why then does communication break down? One barrier has already been examined, namely, message competition. Some of the others include perception, language, status and resistance to change.

Perception

Perception can be defined as a person's view of reality.

The overriding cause of most communication problems is perception, which can be defined as a person's view of reality. Since no two people have had the same training and experiences in life, no two see things *exactly* alike. The sender's meaning and the receiver's interpretation are not always identical, but it is not necessary that they be so; it is sufficient if the receiver understands the essence of what is being transmitted. In short, from the sender's point of view, the receiver's comprehension must be satisfactory. To some managers this means that subordinates should be "in the ball park," while to others it means "doing it the way I would have done it."

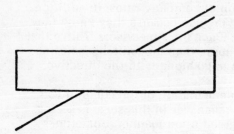

FIGURE 12-2 Using just your eyes, if the line at the bottom of this diagram were drawn through it and emerged at the top, which of these answers would be correct? (a) it would run right into the shorter, lower line at the top; (b) it would run right between the two lines; (c) it would run right into the longer, upper line at the top.

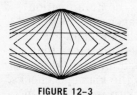

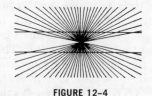

In which of these two diagrams do the two horizontal lines bend in at the ends? In which of the two do the lines bend out at the ends?

FIGURE 12-3   FIGURE 12-4

Sensory and Normative Reality. The differences in perception can be attributed to the differences in one's conception of reality. *Sensory reality* is physical reality. A chair, a horse and a car all represent physical reality. When managers and subordinates communicate about physical reality there are few communication problems. Both individuals know what is meant by a chair, a horse and a car. The meanings are clear. However, there are times when meanings are not definitive and the receiver of the message may have a different interpretation of the communiqué. This is known as *normative* or interpretive reality. Whenever two individuals discuss matters of personal opinion, for example, there is a good chance of communication breakdown.

Sensory reality is physical reality.

Normative reality is interpretive reality.

Sensory and normative reality can be placed on a continuum such as:

Sensory _____ Normative
Reality   Reality

FIGURE 12-5 What do you see here?

As one moves from sensory to normative reality, interpretations become increasingly relative. There is no longer any one right answer but rather a lot of right answers. Figures 12–2 to 12–6 illustrate this idea graphically. Before reading on, look at the five figures and answer the question accompanying each.

FIGURE 12–6   What do you see here?

Each of the first three figures has one right answer. In the first, as can be verified by placing a piece of paper along the lower line, alternative "a" is correct. In the next two, neither of the lines running across the diagrams bend in or out; they are all parallel. However, the background design makes it appear as if the first is bending out (Figure 12–3) and the second is bending in (Figure 12–4).

The next figure (Figure 12–5) has three common answers. Most people see a bird or a duck with a big beak looking to the left. The second most common response is a body of water surrounded by land with an island in the middle; in the center of the island is a small lake. The "spots" north and south of the island are clouds. The third most frequent response is that it is a picture of rabbit looking to the right, the bird's beak becoming the rabbit's ears. The author has found that most older (50 years or more) people opt for the lake and the island interpretation. Younger people (20 to 50) see a bird or a duck. Grammar and high school students tend to agree overwhelmingly that it is a rabbit. Naturally, any of these three could be right because the picture is purposefully designed to have more than one possible interpretation.

The final figure (Figure 12–6) receives many different interpretations. Some people see a mask; others believe it is an elephant; still others claim it is burned toast. Another common answer is that it is part of a dock, the ruffles in the upper part representing the rope used in tying up a boat. Still another interpretation is a silhouette of a woman with her hands over her head. Once again, there is no one right answer. Whatever the person sees is what is there. The point to be extracted from this is that some of the messages sent by the manager to the subordinate are similar to these last two figures. What the manager believes he said and what the subordinate interprets may be two different things. Too often superiors think their messages fall within the realm of sensory reality; they are crystal clear. Actually, the messages are interpretive and fall within the realm of normative reality. Figure 12–7 illustrates the different interpretations that are possible from one, supposedly "crystal clear," message.

Language, Logic and Abstraction

Aristotelian laws of logic.

Managers use language as the method of representing their ideas. As such, it is the basis for most communications. Of course, the astute manager gears his communique to the level of his audience through careful word selection and sentence construction. In addition, he employs certain laws of logic such as those advocated by Aristotle. First is the *law of identity*—a house is a house. Second is the *law of the excluded middle*—the object is either a house or it is not a house. Third is the *law of noncontradiction*—something cannot be a house and not a house at the same time. These simple laws of logic relate to communication because they help the manager construct and convey his message in a manner that is understandable. They reduce confusion.

Although these laws are helpful, the manager still faces the problem associated with *abstraction*. Any time something is left out of the message, abstraction occurs. Yet, if the manager allowed for no abstraction, he would be spending all his time spelling out his communiqués in detail. This is, of course, impossible. He must assume that if he takes care in formulating his message, the subordinates will interpret it the way he wants them to. Yet this is not always the case, as seen when the subject of inference is examined.

An inference is an assumption made by a listener.

Inference. An inference is an assumption made by the listener that may or may not be accurate. Any time a message requires interpretation of the facts, inference enters the picture. The speaker implies and the listener infers. For example, many restaurants have a policy of establishing waiting lists when all their tables are filled. Yet, unknown to many customers, sometimes preferred clientele are moved to the front of the list and seated almost immediately. Professional people such as clergymen and doctors often qualify. Whenever faced with such a waiting list, a colleague of the author makes it a habit not only to use the title "Dr." in front of his name but also asks that he be paged immediately should he receive a call from

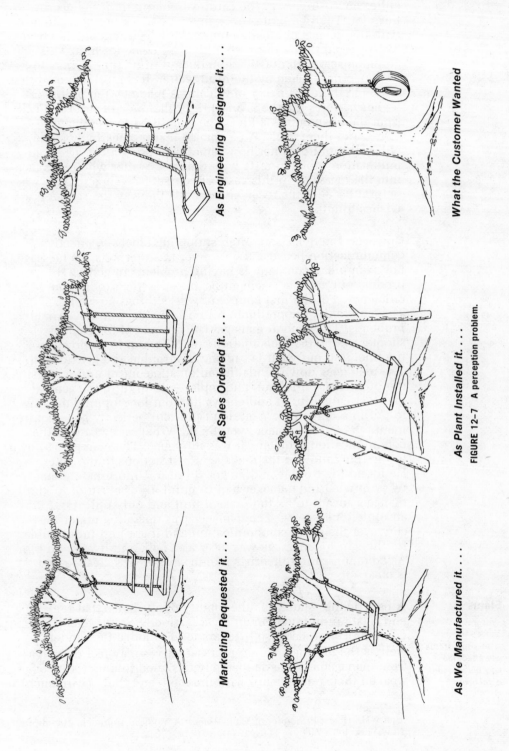

As Engineering Designed it. . . .

What the Customer Wanted

As Sales Ordered it. . . .

As Plant Installed it. . . .

FIGURE 12-7   A perception problem.

Marketing Requested it. . . .

As We Manufactured it. . . .

either neurosurgery or the cardiovascular unit at the nearby hospital. Then he writes his name on a piece of paper along with his license number so the parking lot attendant can bring his car around in a hurry should a call come for him. This gimmick serves to drastically reduce waiting time thanks to the inferences made by the head waiter. It should be noted that although there are many implications made by the professor, he never *states* that he is an M.D. or that he *will* receive a call from the hospital. As a Ph.D., he is entitled to use the term "Dr.", and there is always a chance that the nearby hospital will call him no matter how remote the possibility. The communication problem rests with the head waiter who reads facts into the message. In this case, of course, inference proves helpful because the receiver responds the way the sender wishes him to.

However, inferences are often stumbling blocks to effective communication because the receiver misinterprets the message. For example, a company is having problems in getting its product out and management begins stressing production efficiency. For the first couple of weeks things go well. The, suddenly, the production line again starts to have some problems. The general manager calls in one of his trouble shooters, explains the situation and tells him to go down to the line, find out what is causing the trouble and get rid of it. The man goes down, finds the automatic control unit is causing the problems, pulls it off and replaces it. In turn, the general manager calls him in and chews him out for stopping the line to put in a new unit. "You don't pull out perfectly good equipment," he tells the man, "you fix it." What really caused the communication problem? It was inference. The man going down to the line followed the manager's instructions to the letter. He found the trouble and he got rid of it. Unfortunately that was not what the manager had in mind. By "get rid of it" the manager meant to fix the present unit and only pull it out if absolutely necessary. The manager was operating under the conveyer theory of communication and it got him into trouble. He thought his message was clear as a bell, and it was—to him. As communication theorists like to say "what's clear to you is clear—to you."

Status

A person's status will affect the way his message is received.

Albers defines status as "the totality of attributes that rank and relate individuals in an organization."[2] Status affects communication because listeners tend to judge the sender as well as the message. Union representatives may feel directives from management are deliberately designed to undermine or weaken their relationship with the men, and they regard such

---

[2]Henry H. Albers, *Principles of Management: A Modern Approach*, 4th edition (New York: John Wiley & Sons, 1974), p. 172.

communiqués as troublesome. On the other hand, complaints from the men are seen as accurate descriptions of problems and firm bases from which to file charges against management. The union representatives and the membership may have high regard for each other but hold the management in low esteem.

Conversely, management often discounts complaints made against its people as "union rhetoric." However, very few managers regard communiqués from higher echelons as anything but authoritative. Furthermore, the higher in the hierarchy the message originates, the more likely it is to be accepted, because such executives have a great deal of status among the other managers. In short, if a person has status with the listener, he is regarded as accurate or credible. If he does not, the message is discounted accordingly.

Resistance to Change

Basically, people resist change. And the greater the proposed change, the stronger the resistance. For this reason, one of the principles of communication states that the greater the change, the farther in advance notice must be given. A company planning to change work procedures may find it necessary to announce the upcoming changes four weeks prior to their enactment. The same firm planning to move the company plant from Brooklyn to Staten Island may find it necessary to announce the move 18 months beforehand.

Change is inevitable, but so is resistance. There are various techniques people employ in coping with change. For example, consider the case of the company that announces its intentions of hiring the hard-core unemployed. How do the personnel cope with this policy change? One way is *avoidance*, in which they pretend no policy changes have been announced; they simply ignore the directive. A second common approach is *rejection*. "Oh, I know what they said, but that's just talk to improve our community image." The third, and most common, is *distortion*, in which the receiver interprets the message to suit himself. Those opposing the policy say the company will bring in one or two token employees, but that is all. Those favoring the policy claim that virtually all new hiring will be of the hard-core unemployed.

People cope with change in various ways, including avoidance, rejection and distortion.

The manager's job is to overcome resistance to change. One way of accomplishing this is to explain how these new ideas can be beneficial to the subordinates as well as to the management. The difficulty of the task is clearly seen in Table 12–1. Research shows that although superiors believe they communicate information about impending changes, subordinates do not agree. Furthermore, careful scrutinization of the table indicates that this communication breakdown increases as one moves down the hierarchy. The problem is severe between the top staff and foremen, but it is even more severe between the foremen and the workers.

TABLE 12-1   Do Superiors Tell Subordinates in Advance About Change?

	Top Staff Say About Themselves	Foremen Say About Top Staff	Foremen Say About Themselves	Men Say About Foremen
Always	70%	27%	40%	22%
Nearly Always	30	36	52	25
More Often than Not		18	2	13
Occasionally		15	5	28
Seldom		4	1	12

Source: Adapted from Rensis Likert, *New Patterns of Management* (New York: McGraw-Hill Book Company, 1961), p. 52.

COMMUNICATION CHANNELS   There are two types of communication channels available to the manager, formal and informal. Each can be useful in carrying information to and receiving feedback from other parts of the hierarchy.

Formal Channels   Formal channels are those established by the organization's structure. An organization chart, as seen in Figure 12–8, provides a simple illustration of what is meant by the expres-

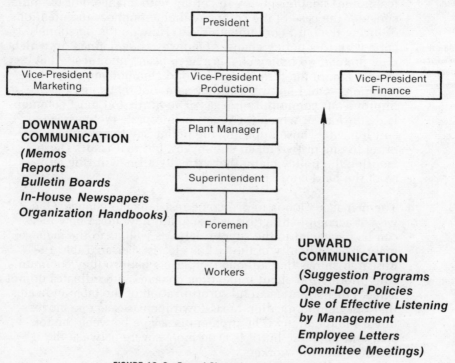

FIGURE 12-8   Formal Channels of Communication

sion "going through channels." This is true whether the communication is going down the chain or coming up. The following discussion examines these channels, with major attention devoted to downward and upward communication and the problems associated with each.

Five basic purposes of downward communication.

Downward Communication.   Downward communication is used to convey directives from superior to subordinate. The classical theorists placed prime attention on this form of communication and today many organizations continue to do so. Katz and Kahn have identified the five basic purposes of such communication as being: to give specific job instructions; to bring about understanding of the work and its relationship to other organizational tasks; to provide information about procedures and practices; to provide subordinates with feedback on their performance; and to provide a sense of mission by indoctrinating the workers as to organizational goals.[3]
A downward orientation also helps link the levels of the hierarchy by coordinating activities between them.

Drawbacks associated with downward orientation.

There are, however, drawbacks associated with such an orientation. First, it tends to promote an authoritative atmosphere, which can be detrimental to morale. Second, it places a heavy burden on subordinates because much of the information coming down the organizational hierarchy will be expanded, affecting an increasing number of personnel. Third, because of distortion, misinterpretation or ignorance, information is often lost as it comes down the line. For example, Nichols, studying communication efficiency in 100 business and industrial firms, recorded the following loss of information between six hierarchical levels.

---

[3]Daniel Katz and Robert L. Kahn, *The Social Psychology of Organizations* (New York: John Wiley & Sons, 1966), p. 239.

Level	Percentage of Information Received[4]
Board	100
Vice Presidents	63
General Supervisors	56
Plant Managers	40
General Foremen	30
Workers	20

---

[4]Ralph G. Nichols, "Listening is Good Business," *Management of Personnel Quarterly*, Winter 1962, p. 4.

This communication problem is brought on by the *number of links* in the chain. The greater the number of people involved, the more likely that information loss will occur. One way of overcoming these problems is to supplement downward orientation with an upward emphasis.

Upward communication channels carry information from subordinates to superiors.

Upward Communication.   The upward communication channel provides subordinates a route for conveying information to their superiors. However, research indicates that it does not receive adequate attention from management. For example, Likert has reported that when he and his colleagues at the Institute for Social Research asked managers to think of the most important and difficult communication problem they had faced during the previous six months, approximately 80 per cent said it dealt with downward communication. Only 10 per cent indicated that it involved upward communication.[5]

In achieving accurate feedback from their subordinates, many managers rely upon techniques such as suggestion boxes and "open door" policies. However, as seen in Table 12–2, research data shows that these approaches are often ineffective.

In many firms, upward communication is poor.

Subordinates do not feel so free to discuss their views as their superiors believe. Furthermore, upward communication is so poor in many firms that studies have consistently revealed managers as incapable of placing themselves in their subordinates' shoes and accurately responding to the question, what do the workers want from their jobs? Table 12–3 clearly illustrates this, showing that upward organizational channels need to receive a great deal more attention from the manager.

At present, Figure 12–9 seems to represent accurately the frequency and intensity of superior-subordinate communication.

---

[5]Rensis Likert, *New Patterns of Management* (New York: McGraw-Hill Book Company, 1961), p. 46.

TABLE 12–2   How Free Do Subordinates Feel to Discuss Important Job Matters With their Superior?

	Top Staff Say About Foremen	Foremen Say About Themselves	Foremen Say About the Men	Men Say About Themselves
Very Free	90%	67%	85%	51%
Fairly Free	10	23	15	29
Not Very Free		10		14
Not Free at All				6

Source: Adapted from Rensis Likert, *New Patterns of Management*, (New York: McGraw-Hill Book Company, 1961), p. 47.

TABLE 12-3 What Do Workers Want From Their Jobs?

	Responses, as Ranked by:	
	Supervisors	Workers
Good Wages	1	5
Job Security	2	4
Promotion and Growth With Company	3	7
Good Working Conditions	4	9
Interesting Work	5	6
Management Loyalty to Workers	6	8
Tactful Disciplining	7	10
Full Appreciation for Work Done	8	1
Sympathetic Understanding of Personal Problems	9	3
Feeling "In" on Things	10	2

Reported in Paul Hersey and Kenneth H. Blanchard, *Management of Organizational Behavior*, 2nd edition (Englewood Cliffs, N.J.: Prentice-Hill, 1972), p. 39.

Lateral communication occurs between people on the same level of the hierarchy.

Lateral and Diagonal Communication.   Lateral or horizontal communication takes place between departments or people on the same level of the hierarchy. Such an interchange of information often serves to coordinate activities. For example, at the upper levels of a manufacturing firm the vice presidents of marketing, production and finance will coordinate their efforts in arriving at an integrated master plan. Lateral communication also occurs between line and staff departments for the purpose of transmitting technical information necessary to carry out some particular function. As seen earlier, Fayol recommended the use of lateral communication in his famous gangplank theory.

Diagonal communication occurs between people not on the same level of the hierarchy.

Diagonal communication involves the flow of information between departments or individuals that are not on the same level of the hierarchy. This often occurs in the case of line and staff departments, in which the staff has functional authority. It is also common to find diagonal communication between line departments, again in which one of them has functional authority.

INFORMAL CHANNELS

Since formal communication channels represent only a portion of those channels that exist within the structure, much of the communication taking place is informal in nature; it is not

FIGURE 12-9 Frequency and Intensity of Upward and Downward Communication

DOWNWARD COMMUNICATION

UPWARD COMMUNICATION

The "grapevine" carries the connotation of inaccurate information.

planned by superiors. The term most often used to identify these informal channels is "the grapevine."

The Grapevine.   The grapevine can be a source of factual data, although the term carries the connotation of inaccurate information. One reason for this is that anyone can start a rumor or a half-truth circulating through the organization. Since the channel is informal in nature, it is virtually impossible to determine its precise source and thereby authenticate or refute its validity. Nevertheless, the grapevine is very useful in *supplementing* formal channels. Often it is not only a source of factual information but also provides members an outlet for their imagination and apprehensions as well. For example, a male supervisor, realizing that he may be beaten out for the upcoming promotion by his female counterpart who has a better production record, may start a rumor that management is putting emphasis on female promotions. This story can be beneficial to the supervisor for two reasons. One, it may cause management to bend over backwards in giving him the promotion, showing that it is not going to promote women on the basis of sex alone. Two, if he does not get the promotion, he can claim blatant discrimination and save face among his peers. It is therefore quite easy to see the importance of informal communication channels to organizational members, although it should be noted that the manager must not allow the grapevine to serve as a substitute for formal channels.

The cluster chain is characterized by selective communication.

Cluster Chains.   Everyone in an organization can participate in the grapevine either by initiating or passing on information given to them by others. For this reason, the channel is very similar to its formal counterpart, carrying messages in four directions: up, down, horizontally and diagonally. However, since this channel is strictly verbal in nature, it can be formed and disbanded very quickly. This spontaneity prevents it from having permanent membership.

Nevertheless, there is a logical pattern to informal channels of communication. There are certain individuals to whom messages will be deliberately passed and there are others who will be deliberately by-passed. This is often known as the *cluster chain* channel and is characterized by *selective* communication. For example, George, vice president of finance, has just been called into the president's office where he was informed that the "old man" has decided to announce his retirement at the upcoming Christmas party. Several individuals, including George, have been in the running for some time. The president has determined that George will get the job, but he wishes this to remain a secret until the Christmas party in four weeks. When George leaves the office he is elated. He wants to tell someone the news, but on whom can he rely? Finally, he thinks of his best friend Tom. He tells him, and Tom keeps his secret. George has been highly selective in his informal communication.

There are also times when individuals want to get news around quickly but they want it to appear to be a secret. For example, Frank has decided to quit his job if he cannot get a 15 per cent raise, even though he knows the average for the firm is going to be 9 per cent. Rather than call his boss directly, he decides to go through the informal chain, telling the boss's secretary "in secret." It is not long before his superior comes by to visit with him about his upcoming raise.

Other informal communication channels.

The cluster chain is not the only type of chain used in informal communications. Davis has noted that there are three others, as seen in Figure 12–10. There is the *single strand*, in which information is passed through a long line of recipients, for example, from A to Z. There is the *gossip chain*, in which one person tells everyone else, thereby serving as the prime source of information. Finally, there is the *probability chain*, in which information is passed on randomly. The cluster chain, however, is the most predominant, indicating that people are selective in choosing their informal communication channel links.

The Manager and Informal Channels.   In Chapter 8 it was noted that the manager must attempt to use the informal organization to help him attain organizational objectives. The same is true regarding informal channels of communication. One of the greatest advantages of the grapevine is the rapidity with which it can disseminate information. Another is its potential for supplementing formal channels. A third is the predictable pattern of informal communication, which Davis has noted as being: (1) people talk most when the news is recent; (2) people talk about things that affect their work; (3) people talk about people they know; (4) people working near

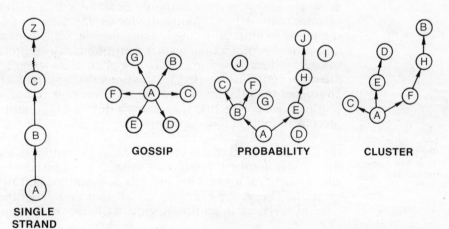

FIGURE 12–10   Informal Communication Channels (Adapted from Keith Davis, "Management Communication and the Grapevine," *Harvard Business Review*, September–October 1953, p. 45.)

each other are likely to be on the same grapevine; and (5) people who contact each other in the chain of procedure, tend to be on the same grapevine.[6]

Although the informal organization is not controlled by the manager, it can be employed in helping him communicate management's point of view. Of course, success will depend to a great degree on the compatibility of the formal with the informal organization. Nevertheless, management must recognize that informal communication networks are an inevitable part of the organization and should endeavor to use them in attaining formal objectives.

COMMUNICATION MEDIA

Media transmission can take the form of words, pictures or actions. *Words* are the most commonly used, as evidenced by both oral and written communication. It is therefore essential for the manager to employ them effectively. *Pictures* are useful as visual aids. The fact that businesses employ them in posters, charts and blueprints is clear evidence of their value. *Action* is an important communication medium, as noted by the adage "actions speak louder than words." A grimace, a handshake, a wink, and even silence, have meaning; people will attach significance to them.

Written Communication

Written communication can take a myriad of forms. Some of the more common are memos, reports, posters, bulletin-board items, in-house newspapers and organization handbooks. There are a number of advantages to be gleaned from written com-

Advantages to written communication.

munications. One of these is the relative permanence of the communiqué, which provides a record of what was transmitted. Another is the value associated with rereading and studying the message should it initially be unclear. Moreover, written messages are often more carefully constructed than oral ones because there is less opportunity for explanation. In addition, if a message must go through many people, written communication provides protection against continuous reinterpretation. In fact, written communications are often used when a directive contains detailed instructions that are too lengthy to be trusted to oral communication. Still another reason favoring written messages is that they carry a degree of formality not present in their verbal counterparts.

Drawbacks to written communication.

On the other hand, there are drawbacks to written communication. For example, it is difficult to keep some forms of written communication up to date, i.e., job descriptions and policy manuals. Things are changing so fast that these are often in need of revision. In addition, some written communiqués are

---

[6]Keith Davis, "Communication Within Management," *Personnel* (November 1954), p. 217.

so lengthy that superiors refuse to read them. An example is seen in the case of reports coming up the line. It is not uncommon for the subordinate to submit a long report and then spend ten minutes briefing his superior on the content. The man does not have time to wade through the paper, so he has the subordinate condense it for him verbally.

Oral Com-munication

Most executives regard oral communication as superior to written since it not only saves time but also provides a basis for achieving better understanding. Some of the more common forms are face-to-face verbal orders, telephones, public address systems, speeches and meetings.

Face-to-face communication is the most effective.

Of these, face-to-face communication is the most effective mode. As with other forms of oral communication, it gives each party an opportunity to respond directly to the other. Disagreement, dissension, fear, tension and anger can often be eliminated by solving the problem on the spot. This give-and-take provides each participant a basis for clarifying his own position and getting a firsthand view of that held by others. In addition, face-to-face communication provides the sender an opportunity to note body language such as gestures and facial responses, thereby obtaining more complete feedback than is available in any other form of oral communication. How a person says something is often as important as what he says.

Limitations among large groups.

Unfortunately, effective face-to-face communication cannot occur among large groups. In communicating with them, the manager must rely on such modes of communication as meetings, speeches and public addresses. A good understanding can often be achieved with these methods, but there is little opportunity for immediate feedback. If someone does not understand the logic behind a particular statement, he must wait until later. Although the manager, if he is able to see the group, can recapitulate or reword part of the message if he feels he is not conveying his ideas properly, he will usually do this only if he feels the majority is confused. If it seems that almost everyone understands, he may well continue, leaving the one or two confused listeners to work out the meaning for themselves. There is also the case in which the manager speaks from a company prepared text, a combination of written and oral communication. Many firms require the manager to stay with the text, thereby limiting his freedom and preventing him from clarifying points he feels are nebulous to the audience.

In summary, there are advantages and disadvantages to both written and oral communication. The manager must be aware of the problems and pitfalls that prevent a message from being properly interpreted by the receiver. Then, by carefully planning his communiqué, he can surmount or sidestep these problems.

**TOWARD
EFFECTIVE
COMMUNICATION**

There are numerous techniques available for improving communication. Some of these help the manager convey his message; others are designed to provide him with *feedback*. Yet all are important because the manager needs to know whether the receiver understands, accepts and is willing to take the required action. He must also know how successful the receiver is in carrying out the directive. Following are some of the most useful techniques for obtaining effective communication.

**Developing
Sensitivity**

The foremost way for the manager to improve communication is to be *sensitive* to the needs and feelings of his subordinates. Although most superiors think they are, research shows they are neither as perceptive nor as sensitive as they believe. The data in Tables 12–1 and 12–2 have illustrated this. If managers were made aware of these findings, it would be a start toward sensitizing them.

*Two-way com-
munication is
important.*

A second useful approach is that of *two-way communication*. By allowing subordinates to speak openly and freely, the manager can assure himself of a more accurate upward flow of information. However, since most do not like to hear unfavorable reports, subordinates tend to screen their comments. Some executives will try to overcome such resistance by telling their people that they want accurate reporting; bad news as well as good is to be communicated. If managers really mean this, upward communication can become a reality. However, if they become flustered and angry, subordinates will again begin paring their reports and removing all unfavorable information. The further up the hierarchy this occurs, the greater the danger to the organization. For example, failure to encourage feedback was one of Hitler's greatest failings as an administrator. As Langer has noted in his secret wartime report, released only recently, Hitler burst into rage whenever bad news was conveyed to him.

It must not be supposed, however, that these rages occur only when he is crossed on major issues. On the contrary, very insignificant matters might call out this reaction. In general they are brought on whenever anyone contradicts him, when there is unpleasant news about which he might feel responsible, when there is any skepticism concerning his judgment, or when a situation arises in which his infallibility might be challenged or belittled. . . . among his staff there is a tacit understanding: "For God's sake don't excite the Fuehrer–which means do not tell him bad news–do not mention things which are not as he conceives them to be."[7]

Such an attitude discourages the free flow of ideas and impedes any development of sensitivity to the feelings of others.

---

[7]Walter C. Langer, *The Mind of Adolf Hitler* (New York: Basic Books, Inc., Publishers, 1972), p. 76.

Employing Understandable, Repetitive Language

Understandable, repetitive language will improve communication.

Technical terminology and multi-syllable words may be impressive, but they can also be troublesome to the listener. The manager should try to use language that is *understandable*. A foreman talking to production line workers must deliver his communiqué appropriately; so too, of course, must the executive making a report to the board of directors. Effective communication will differ according to the receiver, but it must always be understandable. One way of accomplishing this is to use *repetitive language*. Sometimes a message will not be fully grasped the first time and a rephrasing or recapitulation is in order. Another beneficial guideline is to convey information gradually, building the essence of the message as one goes along. This is especially helpful in conveying technical or sophisticated data.

Protecting Credibility

One criterion for managerial effectiveness is credibility, or believability. When the manager communicates with his subordinates, they listen to and obey him because he has demonstrated through his competence, drive, character and past performance that he is worthy of their trust. However, the astute manager knows that he must not only gain credibility, but he must protect it as well. Every time he communicates an order or issues a directive, there is a chance that his credibility may be damaged. One way of illustrating the problem and a method for successfully coping with it is through the use of what is called *balance theory*.

Relevant relationships in balance theory.

As an example, consider the following situation. A manager has just told his subordinate that the company has decided to introduce new work procedures. In this instance there are three relevant relationships: (a) the attitude of the receiver toward the sender; (b) the attitude of the receiver toward the new changes; and (c) the receiver's perception of the sender's own attitude toward the changes. Based on the receiver's perception, either a balanced or unbalanced triad will result. If the receiver has a positive attitude toward both the changes and the sender and he believes the latter also favors the new work procedures, there is a balanced triad, as seen in Figure

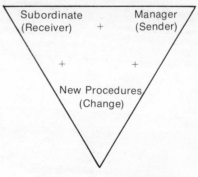

FIGURE 12-11 Balanced Triad

12–11. However, what if the situation is unbalanced because the receiver does not like the new procedures? That is:

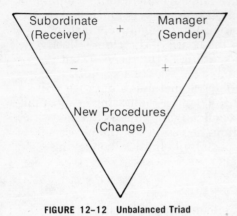

FIGURE 12-12   Unbalanced Triad

How can balance be restored? There are a number of ways, but the important thing to realize is that in the triad there must be all pluses or two minuses and a plus if it is to be balanced.[8]

Thus the manager has three options: (a) he can tell the subordinate that he opposes the new procedures (Figure 12–13); (b) he can allow the subordinate to develop a negative attitude toward him (Figure 12–14); or (c) he can persuade the subordinate to accept the new changes (Figure 12–15).

[8]For an excellent discussion of the balance theory and refinement of this statement about pluses and minuses, see Robert Noel Widgery, "Using Balance Theory in Developing Persuasive Strategies," General Motors Institute, February 1972, pp. 1–10.

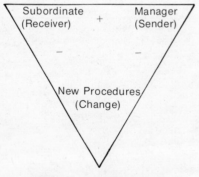

FIGURE 12-13   Balanced Triad

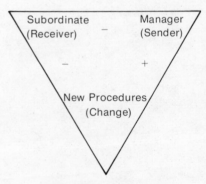

FIGURE 12-14   Balanced Triad

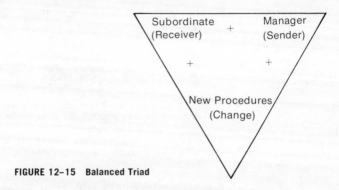

FIGURE 12-15   Balanced Triad

Since the manager's job is to communicate and support directives coming down the line, it is vital that he choose alternative (c). This will not only establish balance and protect the manager's credibility with his own subordinates, but it will also prevent alternative (a) from occurring. One way an effective manager will do this is by empathizing with the subordinate and demonstrating to him that he believes and is positively oriented toward many of the same values and ideals held by the subordinate, i.e., good working conditions, a challenging job, a chance for advancement and recognition. In this way, the manager ensures that the subordinate will continue to rely upon and trust him. Then, having protected his credibility, the manager can direct his attention toward showing the subordinate how the new work procedures will be beneficial to him in attaining these values and ideals. In turn, this will lead the subordinate to alter his perception and view the work changes positively. The result is a balanced triad. By employing balance theory, the effective manager is able to assess communication situations, determine when his credibility is threatened and take necessary steps to protect it.

Establishing balance and protecting credibility.

Avoiding Bad Listening Habits

Approximately 70 per cent of the manager's day is spent communicating. One researcher, in breaking down the sub-functions of communication, has estimated that 9 per cent is spent in writing, 16 per cent in reading, 30 per cent in speaking and 45 per cent in listening.[9] Yet research shows that managers are not good listeners. Nichols has estimated that when people listen to a ten-minute talk, they operate at only 25 per cent efficiency. This is unfortunate, because of all the sources of information a manager has by which he can come to know and accurately evaluate the personalities of the people in his department, listening to the individual employee is one of the most important.

Becoming a more effective listener requires an understanding

---

[9]Ralph G. Nichols, "Listening, What Price Inefficiency?" *Office Executive*, April, 1959, pp. 15–22.

of the ten most common bad habits of listening. Nichols has defined them as follows:

1. *Calling the subject uninteresting.* **Instead of tuning in first and seeing if the speaker has something worthwhile to say, the listener assumes from the start that the topic will be boring.**

2. *Tuning the speaker out because of his delivery.* **The listener allows delivery to take precedence over content.**

3. *Getting overstimulated.* **The minute the listener hears something with which he disagrees he stops listening and starts fuming, thereby missing the rest of the message.**

4. *Concentrating only on facts, to the exclusion of principles or generalizations.* **Facts do not always present the whole picture. Principles and generalizations are often necessary to put everything in its proper perspective.**

Ten most common bad habits of listening.

5. *Trying to outline everything.* **Some speakers are less well organized than others, and until the individual gets into his presentation, it can be difficult to follow him via an outline. He may actually be very unorganized. A good listener must be flexible in his note taking.**

6. *Faking attentiveness.*

7. *Allowing distractions to creep in.*

8. *Tuning out difficult or technical presentations.* **This often occurs when managers are listening to financial or quantitatively oriented reports.**

9. *Letting emotional words disrupt the listening process.* **Any time a word evokes emotion, there is a good chance that the listener will be thrown out of tune with the speaker.**

10. *Wasting thought power.* **Most people speak at the rate of 125 words per minute. However, the brain is capable of handling almost five times that number. If the speaker goes on for more than a few minutes, it presents a temptation to the listener to wander mentally, returning only periodically to check in and see where the speaker is.**[10]

Managers who make a concerted effort to avoid these common pitfalls find that they can improve their level of efficiency far above the 25 per cent average.

Employing the Commandments of Good Communication

Although many guidelines have been put forth to improve communication, one of the most extensive compilations is that constructed by the American Management Association. Often known as the ten commandments of good communication, they are the following:

1. *Clarify ideas before communicating.* **By systematically thinking through the message and considering who will be receiving and/or affected by it, the manager overcomes one of the basic pitfalls of communication — failure to properly plan the communiqué. The more systematically a message is analyzed, the more clearly it can be communicated.**

---

[10]Adapted from *ibid.*

2. *Examine the true purpose of communication.* **The manager has to ask himself what he** *really* **wants to accomplish with his message. Once this objective is determined, the communiqué can be properly designed.**

3. *Take the entire environment, physical and human, into consideration.* **Questions such as, what is said, to whom and when, will all affect the success of the communication. The physical setting, the social climate, and past communication practices should all be examined in adapting the message to the environment.**

4. *When valuable, obtain advice from others in planning communiqués.* **Consulting with others can be a useful method for obtaining additional insights regarding how to handle the communication. In addition, those who help formulate it usually give it active support.**

Ten command-ments of good communication.

5. *Be aware of the overtones as well as the basic content of the message.* **The listener will be affected by not only what is said but also how it is said. Voice tone, facial expression and choice of language all influence the listener's reaction to the communiqué.**

6. *When possible, convey useful information.* **People remember things that are beneficial to them. If the manager wants subordinates to retain the message, he should phrase it so that it takes into consideration** *their* **interests and needs as well as the company's.**

7. *Follow up on communication.* **The manager must solicit feedback in ascertaining whether the subordinate understands the communiqué, is willing to comply with it and then takes the appropriate action.**

8. *Communicate with the future, as well as the present, in mind.* **Most communications are designed to meet the demands of the current situation. However, they should be in accord with the long-range goals as well. For example, communiqués designed to improve performance or morale are valuable in handling present problems. Yet they also serve a useful future purpose by promoting long-run organizational efficiency.**

9. *Support words with deeds.* **When managers contradict themselves by saying one thing and doing another, they undermine their own directives. For example, the executive who issues a notice reminding everyone that they are to be in the building by 8:30 a.m. while he continues to show up at 9:15 a.m. should not expect anyone to take his notice seriously. Subordinates are always cognizant of such managerial behavior and quickly discount such directives.**

10. *Be a good listener.* **By concentrating on the speaker's explicit and implicit meanings, the manager can obtain a much better understanding of what is being said.**[11]

SUMMARY

In this chapter interpersonal and organizational communication have been examined. It was noted that the communication process entails four steps: attention, understanding, acceptance and action. In implementing the process there are two basic kinds of channels, formal and informal. The astute manager uses both to his advantage, keeping in mind that there tends to

---

[11]Adapted from American Management Association, "Ten Commandments of Good Communication," as reported in Max D. Richards and William A. Nielander, *Readings in Management* (Cincinnatti, Ohio: South-Western Publishing, 1958), pp. 141–143.

be an overemphasis on downward communication and an underemphasis on upward. This is unfortunate, for without some form of upward communication there is a distinct lack of feedback. Yet many managers overlook the need for this feedback, tending to follow the old conveyer theory of communication. They send their subordinate a message and he is expected to act accordingly. However, communication does not work that way. People do not always interpret messages in the same way. There are many reasons for this, and all constitute barriers to effective communication. Some of the more important are perception, language, abstraction, inference, status and resistance to change. In order to overcome these barriers, steps must be taken to establish lines of feedback. Some of the more effective techniques are sensitivity, understandable repetitive language, credibility, the avoidance of bad listening habits and a general adherence to the commandments of good communication. Although these ideas might appear obvious to many, it is really quite difficult to adhere to them in practice.[12]

In Chapter 13 motivation will be examined. What motivates people? The answer will differ from person to person, but one thing is certain: if the manager cannot communicate with his people and get the feedback necessary to understand and empathize with their points of view, he has little basis for formulating an intelligent approach to motivating them. Communication helps him establish the basis for this activity.

REVIEW AND STUDY QUESTIONS

1. What is meant by "the communication process"? Explain.

2. What is the conveyer theory of communication?

3. What are the four steps for implementing effective communication? Describe them.

4. What are some of the common barriers to effective communications?

5. What is meant by the term perception? Give an illustration.

6. What is meant by the term inference? Give an illustration.

7. Why do people resist change? Is it really inevitable?

8. What is meant by "going through channels"?

9. What is meant by "informal communication channels"?

---

[12]For an excellent follow-up to the ideas contained in this chapter, the reader is directed to Stewart L. Tubbs and Sylvia Moss, *Human Communication: An Interpersonal Perspective*, (New York: Random House, 1974).

10. What are the advantages of using written communication? Oral communication?

11. How can a manager promote sensitivity? Be complete in your answer.

12. How is balance theory useful to the manager in protecting his credibility? Explain.

13. What are some of the most common bad listening habits?

14. How can a manager obtain feedback for effective communication?

SELECTED REFERENCES

Athanassiades, J. C. "The Distortion of Upward Communication in Hierarchical Organizations." *Academy of Management Journal,* June 1973, pp. 207–226.

Berlo, D. D. *The Process of Communication.* New York: Holt, Rinehart and Winston, Inc., 1960.

Boyd, B. B., and J. M. Jensen. "Perceptions of the First-Line Supervisor's Authority: A Study in Superior-Subordinate Communication." *Academy of Management Journal,* September 1972, pp. 331–342.

Davis, K. *Human Behavior At Work,* 4th edition. New York: McGraw-Hill Book Company, 1972, Chapters 20 and 21.

Dewhirst, H. D., "Influence of Perceived Information-Sharing Norms on Communication Channel Utilization." *Academy of Managment Journal,* September 1971, pp. 305–315.

Foltz, R. G. "Communication: Not An Art, A Necessity." *Personnel,* May–June 1972, pp. 60–64.

Hall, J. "Communication Revisited." *California Management Review,* Spring 1973, pp. 56–67.

Luthans, F. *Organizational Behavior,* New York: McGraw-Hill Book Company, 1973, Chapter 11.

Nichols, R. G. "Listening is Good Business." *Management of Personnel Quarterly,* Winter 1962, pp. 2–9.

Sigband, N. B., *Communication for Management,* Glenview, Ill.: Scott, Foresman and Company, 1969.

Tubbs, S. L., and S. Moss, *Human Communication: An Interpersonal Perspective.* New York: Random House, 1974.

Wickesberg, A. K. "Communications Networks in the Business Organization Structure." *Academy of Management Journal,* September 1968, pp. 253–262.

CASE: GOOD WORK IS EXPECTED

A large eastern pharmaceutical company brought in an outside management consulting firm to analyze its operations. After five weeks, the consultants made their report to management. One of the areas they had investigated was communication between superiors and subordinates. To its dismay, management learned that there were numerous discrepancies between what superiors said they did and what their subordinates said their superiors did. For example, when the consultants conducted a confidential questionnaire survey with 20 percent of the managers and workers, they received the following responses to the question, do you tell your subordinates when they do a good job?

TABLE 12–4 Do You Tell Your Subordinates When They Do a Good Job?

	Top Management Says of Itself	Middle Management Says of Top Management	Middle Management Says of Itself	Lower-Level Management Says of Middle Management	Lower-Level Management Says of Itself	Workers Say of Lower-Level Management
Always	93	82	95	63	98	39
Often	7	14	5	15	2	23
Sometimes		4		12		18
Seldom				6		11
Never				4		9

Management was quite distraught with the findings. As a result, at its next board of directors meeting the chairman proposed that the firm bring back the consultants to advise and counsel them on how they could deal with this problem. The resolution was passed unanimously.

When the middle and lower level managers learned of the action, they expressed surprise. One of them noted, "Just because the data indicates poor communication is no need to get excited. After all, the men say lots of things that aren't accurate." A fellow colleague explained, "Look, I expect subordinates to do a good job. I only tell them when they are doing a poor one. If I praise them every time they did something right, they'd all have swelled heads. My approach is to say nothing."

Questions

1. What does the data in Table 12–4 show? Explain your findings.

2. What do you think of the comments from the two managers? Are they valid?

3. What types of recommendations would you expect from the consultants? Explain.

CASE: A BIG PRODUCTION NUMBER

General O'Hallan's new aide, Captain Marchant, was determined to make a good impression on the "old man." The previous aide had been with the General for six years, and the Captain knew it was going to be tough filling his shoes. Nevertheless, the Captain felt he could do it if he just addressed himself as carefully to the minor matters as he did to the major ones. Generals are impressed, he believed, by an aide's ability to handle nit-picking items with dispatch.

For the first couple of weeks things went smoothly. Although the General gave no indication that he was overly impressed with Captain Marchant's abilities, neither did he seem displeased.

Saturday afternoon was the General's only chance to play golf, and without fail he and the rest of his foursome teed off at 1 p.m. sharp. By 4:30 p.m. they were in the clubhouse having a drink. As they sat there, the General, who had had a rather disappointing round, bemoaned his luck.

If I wasn't in the rough, I was in a trap. The only good thing about this after-

noon is this drink. Golly, they sure know how to make them the way I like
them. This has got to be the best officer's club in the country.

It was then that he asked his aide,

Say, Captain, how many officers, on the average, do you think use these
facilities?

I don't know, sir, but I'd estimate somewhere around 400 a day.

Although the conversation ended there, the Captain filed the
question in the back of his mind. By noon on Monday he had
an answer. He entered the General's office and placed a four-
page computer printout on the desk.

Sir, in reference to your question on Saturday regarding the number of men
who use the officer's club, I asked the accounting department if they'd send
over a printout on last year's statistics. It appears that, on the average, 423
officers use the club on a daily basis. There also are figures here for liquor
consumed, food served and revenue taken in.

The General thanked Captain Marchant and sat down to look
over the printout. The aide was certain he had "scored points"
with his boss. However, at home that evening the General
expressed a different point of view to his wife.

You know dear, I don't think Captain Marchant is going to work out. Last
Saturday I expressed interest in the number of men who use the officer's
club and this morning he brought me in a computer printout with a host of
statistics on it regarding club operations. I figure it must have taken six men
in accounting most of the morning to get that data. That's a real waste
of time as far as I'm concerned. Actually, I just asked him a rhetorical question; I didn't expect him to engage a group of men to find an answer. I just
don't understand him. You ask him a simple question and he turns it into
a big production number.

Questions

1. What are the communication problems presented in this case? Explain.

2. What recommendations would you make to Captain Marchant? Explain.

CASE: A TWO-WAY EXPERIMENT

One day, in way of emphasizing the importance of communication, Mr. Fontane, director of in-house training of a large
western retail chain, decided to conduct an experiment during
his upcoming session with a group of middle managers. When
they were all in the room and settled in their seats, he began
by asking the value of two-way communication. All agreed it
was of prime importance for effective management. He then
asked them how they went about establishing feedback from
subordinates. Although some of the men contributed ideas,

it was evident that the group was unsettled by the question. Finally, one of the managers, Mr. Clauson, spoke up. "Mr. Fontane, two-way communication is great if you have a problem, but most of us really believe we can achieve our goals with successful downward communication. We really don't have trouble getting our meanings across to the workers."

By the hum in the room, Mr. Fontane realized that the rest of the managers basically agreed. "Do you mean to tell me that you are all such good communicators that your subordinates know exactly what you are talking about without asking questions?"

"Well, I'm not saying we're perfect," said Mr. Clauson, "but speaking personally, I can make myself understood if I really have to. When I make the concerted effort, there is no real need for questions. And I'm not kidding or bragging. I've worked at it a long time and I'm just that good."

With that Mr. Fontane asked Mr. Clauson to come to the front of the room and read the piece of paper sitting on the podium. "Gentlemen, while Mr. Clauson is looking at the piece of paper I have left on the podium, I would like the rest of you to get ready to draw. Mr. Clauson is going to describe some diagrams to you. You will note that he is going to tell you how to draw these diagrams. However, you are not to ask any questions, make any noise or provide him with any kind of feedback indicating whether or not you are able to follow the logic of his directives. Just do exactly what he tells you to."

The diagrams that Mr. Clauson was asked to describe to the group are presented in Figure 12–16. The instructions that accompanied the diagrams told him not to use any geometric terms. Instead, he was to get the other people in the room to draw these figures by merely using lines, dots and geographic directions. In addition, he was to keep his head down throughout the experiment so he would be unable to see the group.

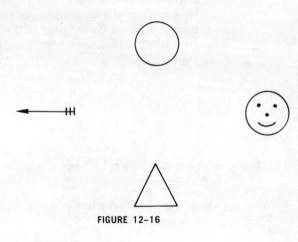

FIGURE 12–16

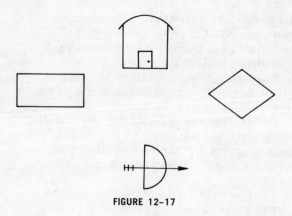

FIGURE 12-17

Mr. Clauson began. By the time he finished it was evident to Mr. Fontane that many of the men were unable to follow some of the directions. "All right, let's play show and tell," he said. "How many of you feel you got all four diagrams right?" Four of the twenty-four men raised their hands. Then Mr. Fontane held up the diagrams for all to see. It turned out that everyone had at least one of them right, but no one had all four correct. In fact, only seven of the men had three right.

Mr. Fontane then ran the experiment again, using the diagrams in Figure 12-17. This time he permitted Mr. Clauson to look out on the group and answer any questions they had. In addition, if he felt that he had lost the men at any point, he could go back and repeat the directions. At the end of this experiment everyone in the room had at least two of the diagrams right and twelve of the men had all of them correct. "Well, Mr. Clauson," said Mr. Fontane, "you seem to have improved markedly over your first performance."

"I know," he replied, "but I never really realized how much can be lost if you don't allow people to ask questions. In fact, I was even more surprised regarding how much feedback I was getting just by looking at their faces and their body movements. I guess your point is that there is a tremendous increase in understanding between one- and two-way communication, right?"

Questions

1. Is there really any correlation between this experiment and two-way communication on the job? Explain.

2. What are some of the most effective ways to promote two-way communication? Explain.

CASE: SPEED AND COMPREHENSION

One of the greatest communication problems is that of getting people to increase their reading speed and comprehension. Take out a clean piece of paper before continuing on with this case. Then read the following assignment. Each of the twenty-four items requests you to execute a prescribed activity.

The items vary in complexity, but you should be able to cope easily with them all, as this not an intelligence test. The exercise is designed to measure only how well you read and carry out instructions with accuracy. You have three minutes in which to complete the exercise. So, be sure to time yourself and remain within this constraint. Enter all your answers on the clean piece of paper.

Read everything before doing anything.

1. Write your name in the upper right corner of the clean piece of paper.
2. Multiply 23 by 68 and place the result under your name.
3. Draw a square on the reverse side of the paper.
4. Draw a circle inside the square.
5. Draw a diamond inside the circle.
6. Write the month and date in the upper left corner.
7. Multiply the square root of 9 by the square of 16.
8. Subtract 1462 from 2221 and place the result in the lower left corner.
9. Underline your answer to question #2.
10. If a farmer has 17 pigs, and all but 12 die, how many pigs are left alive?
11. Add 14,421 to 27,969 and place the result in the lower right corner.
12. Now substract 14,421 from 27,969 and place the answer under the result for #13.
13. Square the number seven and put your answer immediately below.
14. Compute the square root of 169 and add this to the answer you worked out in number 13.
15. Write down the name of the sixteenth President of the U.S.
16. Write Gerald Ford's middle name on the bottom of the page.
17. If Dr. Joyce Brothers married comedian Dickie Smothers, what would her new name be?
18. Which space project was the one that got America to the moon: Gemini, Apollo or Mercury?
19. Who won the last National League Pennant?
20. Who won the last American League Pennant?
21. Who won the first Super Bowl?
22. Take a number from 1 to 10. Add 10. Subtract 5. Multiply by 7. Square the number. What is your answer?

23. Write down the year you graduated from grammar school as a four digit number; that is, for example, 1970. Add to this your present age. Then write down how long you have been out of grammar school. Finally, write down the year you were born. Add all four numbers together.

24. Carry out the instructions in item #1 only and ignore all the rest.

Questions

1. What is the purpose of this exercise? What does it relate about communication problems?

2. How can these problems be overcome? Explain.

CHAPTER 13

MODERN MOTIVATION THEORY

GOALS OF THE CHAPTER

One of the greatest challenges facing the manager is that of motivating his workers. In this chapter, modern motivation theory will be examined. The major part of the chapter will deal with what are called *substantive* or content theories. These are concerned with *what* it is within the individual or environment that stimulates or sustains behavior; i.e., what are the specific things that motivate people? The last part of the chapter will examine three *process* or mechanical theories, which are concerned with explaining *how* behavior is initiated, directed, sustained and halted.

The goals of this chapter are to acquaint the reader with modern motivation theory and to indicate its relevance to management. In particular, attention will be focused on:

a. the relationship between needs and behavior;
b. man's need hierarchy;
c. management's assumptions of how workers should be managed;
d. the incongruity between the formal organization and the mature personality;
e. the value of money, status, working conditions, increased responsibility and challenging work in motivating people; and
f. new process theories of motivation, which stress concentration on the individual to be motivated rather than the way to motivate people in general.

NEEDS AND BEHAVIOR

Motivation is an internal, psychological process.

If the manager is to be successful in getting the workers to attain organizational objectives, he must understand at least the fundamentals of motivation. However, this is not an easy job, for motivation is an *intervening variable*. It is an internal, psychological process; that is, the manager cannot see motivation, he can only assume its presence (or absence) based on observance of worker behavior. If the workers are busy at their

311

tasks, the manager may well infer that they are motivated. If they are standing around talking, he may conclude that they are not.

One way of examining motivation is through a need-satisfaction approach.

This is only a superficial approach and fails to answer the key question, why do people behave as they do? Although there are various answers, one approach is a *need-satisfaction* explanation. Everyone has needs that require satisfaction. In turn, these needs will cause the person to undertake some form of *goal-oriented behavior*, which, hopefully, will satisfy the need. For example, hunger pains may lead a person to go into a nearby cafe and order (and eat) dinner. Using just this information, it is possible to design the following simple diagram of motivation.

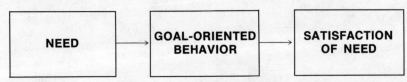

FIGURE 13-1 Simple Motivation Process

Of course, every individual has many needs, but it is the need with the greatest strength that will tend to dictate current behavior.

Once the need has been satisfied, it will decline in importance and another need will become dominant. This "need" theory of motivation has been explained in detail by Abraham Maslow.

MASLOW'S NEED HIERARCHY

According to Maslow, man is a wanting being; there is always some need he wants to satisfy. Once this is accomplished, that particular need no longer motivates him and he turns to another, again seeking satisfaction. These needs can be represented in hierarchical form, with those at the lower levels requiring *basic* satisfaction before the individual can move on to the next level. Figure 13-2 illustrates Maslow's need hierarchy of physiological, safety, social, esteem and self-actualization needs. However, before discussing these, it should be noted that Maslow *never* contended that a need must be satisfied 100 per cent before the next level becomes important. As he has explained:

In actual fact, most members of our society who are normal are partially satisfied in all their basic needs and partially unsatisfied in all their basic needs at the same time. A more realistic description of the hierarchy would be in terms of decreasing percentages of satisfaction as we go up the hierarchy of prepotency. For instance, if I may assign arbitrary figures. . . it is as if the average citizen is satisfied perhaps 85 per cent in his physiological needs, 70 per cent in his safety needs, 50 per cent in his love needs, 40 per cent in his self-esteem needs, and 10 per cent in his self-actualization needs.[1]

[1]Abraham H. Maslow, "A Theory of Human Motivation," *Psychological Review,* July, 1943, pp. 388–389.

FIGURE 13-2 Maslow's Hierarchy of Needs

Self-Actualization Needs

Esteem Needs

Social Needs

Safety Needs

Physiological Needs

Physiological Needs

The most basic needs are physiological.

At the base of the hierarchy are *physiological* needs, which are necessary to sustain life. These include food, water, clothing and shelter. An individual who lacks the basic necessities in life will probably be motivated primarily by physiological needs. As Maslow noted, "A person who is lacking food, safety, love, and esteem would most probably hunger for food more strongly than for anything else."[2] When this is so, Figure 13-3 accurately depicts the need hierarchy.

Research indicates that satisfaction of these needs is usually associated with money — not money itself, of course, but what it can buy. Although one could look at Figure 13-2 and argue that other needs could also be satisfied with money, it seems clear that the value of this factor diminishes as one goes up the hierarchy. Self-respect, for example, cannot be bought.

[2]Abraham H. Maslow, *Motivation and Personality,* 2nd edition (New York: Harper & Row, Publishers, 1954), p. 37.

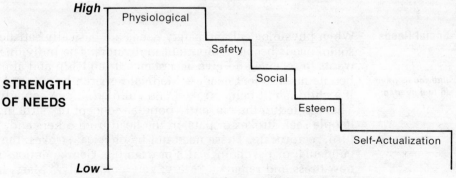

FIGURE 13-3 Need Hierarchy Showing Physiological Needs Dominant

Safety Needs

Then comes safety, which can take many forms.

When physiological needs are basically fulfilled, *safety* needs begin to manifest themselves. One of the most common of these is protection from physical dangers such as fire or accident. In an industrial setting, signs such as "No smoking in this area" and "Beyond this point safety glasses must be worn" provide illustrations of how management attempts to satisfy this need.

A second safety need is economic security. Fringe benefits such as accident, health and life insurance programs help to fulfill this need.

A third common safety need is a preference for an orderly, predictable environment. This may be difficult for one to understand until he realizes that people often feel threatened by work changes or are afraid to voice their opinion on a particular matter for fear of losing their job. When these things happen, safety needs are clearly evident.

Research indicates that there are some individuals who place great emphasis on the safety need. One such group is those whose parents were heavily security-minded. Their parents, often having suffered economic crises, regard themselves as incapable of influencing the environment and they pass this strong security orientation on to their children. The offspring, in turn, seek secure, non-threatening positions in, for example, major corporations or federal bureaucracies, where they can carve out a protected niche for themselves.

Another common cause for the security-minded employee is the overprotective parent. Continually sheltering their child from disappointment by constantly giving him his way, they paint an unrealistic view of the world. Once the young person goes out and suffers a setback, he is thrown for a loss and is unable to cope with the accompanying frustration, tension and anxiety. His subconscious security motives developed through interaction with his parents have not prepared him for this new experience. Safety needs become important to him and he seeks a noncompetitive, sheltered environment.

Social Needs

Individuals need to feel needed.

When physiological and safety needs are basically satisfied, *social* needs become important motivators. The individual wants to receive and give acceptance, friendship and affection. People need to feel needed. Medical research has proved that if a child is not held, stroked and cuddled, it can actually die. This has led to the currently popular concept of "stroking." People seek strokes or pats on the head from others and, in turn, reciprocate. These need not be physical strokes; they can be mental or psychological. For example, George notices Mary's new dress and remarks, "Mary, you look lovely." Mary, in turn, replies, "Thank you, George. You always know how to make a person feel good." Both people pat each other on the head by saying something nice. People need this interaction. When it is refused them, they actually suffer. This accounts for the use by prisons of solitary confinement for maximum punishment. It deprives a person of the fulfillment of his social needs, and there is no more serious way to inflict punishment than psychologically. In a manner of speaking, the prisoner is prevented from giving and receiving strokes.

The concept of stroking explains why Schachter has found that people who have similar beliefs tend to group together.[3] They share a common bond and can reinforce each other's feeling and convictions through stroking. This is especially true when things are not going well, for misery does love company.

Esteem Needs

When physiological, safety and social needs are basically satisfied, *esteem* becomes the dominant need. This need is twofold: the person must feel he is important and he must receive recognition from others that supports these feelings. Recognition is invaluable, for without it the person may conclude he is greatly overrating himself. When those around him, however, make it clear that he is indeed important, feelings of self-esteem, self-confidence, prestige and power are all produced. Of course, satisfaction of the need rests with the person himself. If he believes he is overrated by his peers, nothing they do will be beneficial in convincing him of their sincerity. He may continually feel inferior. However, if he has confidence in himself, respect and support from those around him will serve to justify his confidence.

Feelings of self-esteem and self-confidence are important.

Research shows that as the United States moves toward becoming a middle-class society, esteem-related needs such as prestige are more evident; people want to keep up with the Joneses and be viewed as important. This was clearly indicated in Packard's book *The Status Seekers*.[4] Joining the right country club, obtaining a reputation as a hard worker or earning an advanced degree are some ways of securing this prestige. For example, many teachers who hold a Ph.D. like to be called "Doctor" rather than "Professor" or "Sir" because of the prestige the title carries.

Power is another esteem-related need. The power drive actually begins at childhood when the baby realizes that crying influences his parents' behavior. Adler contends that this ability to manipulate others is inherently pleasurable to the

[3]Stanley Schachter, *The Psychology of Affiliation* (Stanford, Calif.: Stanford University Press, 1959).
[4]Vance Packard, *The Status Seekers* (New York: David McKay Company, Inc., 1959).

child.[5] Of course, during these early years the infant needs this power, because he is helpless without his parents and must have some method for ensuring their assistance. Later in life, when he can fend for himself, this motive of power changes to one of winning respect and recognition from others. When this esteem need is basically satisfied, the self-actualization need becomes important.

Self-Actualization Need

The realization of one's full potential is also important.

Maslow defined *self-actualization* as the "desire to become more and more what one idiosyncratically is, to become everything that one is capable of becoming."[6] The individual attempts to realize his full potential at this level of the hierarchy. He is interested in self-fulfillment, self-development and creativity in the broadest sense of the word.

Of all five needs, the least is known about self-actualization. This is because people satisfy the need in so many different ways that it is difficult to pin down and identify it. However, as Hersey and Blanchard note, competence and achievement are closely related motives, and extensive research has been conducted on them.[7]

Competence provides people with a form of control over their environment.

White has concluded that human beings desire *competence* because it gives them a form of control over their environment.[8] As they mature, people learn their limitations and capabilities from experience, and they work within these confines. For example, it is rare to find an intelligent adult seriously overrating his abilities. He basically knows what he can do and he remains within these parameters, choosing an objective that is attainable such as job mastery. The man pits himself against the work as a goal that is challenging but not beyond attainment. This competence desire is related to the self-actualization need identified by Maslow.

Some individuals have a high need to achieve.

Another such related need is *achievement*. Some individuals will accomplish more than others because their need to achieve is greater. McClelland and his associates at Harvard have been studying this need for over 25 years.[9] They have found that high-achievers are neither low nor high risk-takers. Rather, they set moderately difficult but potentially achievable goals

---

[5]Alfred Adler, *Social Interest* (London: Faber & Faber Ltd., 1938).
[6]Maslow, *op. cit.*, p. 46.
[7]Paul Hersey and Kenneth H. Blanchard, *Management of Organizational Behavior*, 2nd edition (Englewood Cliffs, N.J.: Prentice-Hall, 1972), p. 34.
[8]Robert W. White, "Motivation Reconsidered: The Concept of Competence," *Psychological Review*, September 1959, pp. 297–333.
[9]David C. McClelland et al., *The Achievement Motive* (New York: Appleton Century Crofts, Inc., 1953); and David C. McClelland, *The Achieving Society* (Princeton, N.J.: D. Van Nostrand Company, Inc., 1961).

for themselves. They like a challenge, but they want some influence over the outcome. They are aggressive realists. In addition, they are motivated more by the accomplishment of a particular objective than by the rewards associated with it. Money, for example, is merely used as a means of measuring or assessing progress. High-achievers also have a strong desire for feedback on how well they are doing. They want to know the score.

The Individual and the Hierarchy

Hierarchical levels are not clear-cut.

Maslow's theory has general application for the manager, but several points merit specific attention. First, the hierarchy must not be viewed as a rigid structure. Levels are *not* clear-cut and tend to overlap. When the intensity of one need is on the decline, the next one may be on the rise as seen in Figure 13–4. When, for instance, the safety need passes the peak of the physiological need, it assumes the dominant role and holds it until the social need rises above it.

Some people may remain at certain levels of the hierarchy.

Second, some individuals may remain primarily at the lower levels of the hierarchy, continually concerned with physiological and safety needs. This often occurs among people in underdeveloped countries. Conversely, others may spend a great deal of their time at the upper levels of the hierarchy. If middle-class parents have the best chance of producing high-achievers and the United States is a middle-class society, it follows that Americans probably spend a good deal of their time trying to satisfy social, esteem and self-actualization needs.

Lack of empirical evidence.

Third, the specific order of needs suggested by Maslow may not apply to everyone; there is certainly no empirical support that it does. For example, for some people esteem needs may be more basic than safety needs.

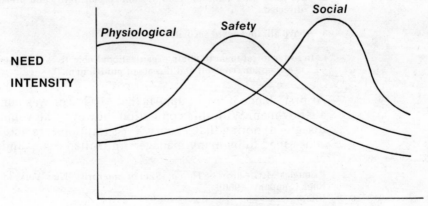

FIGURE 13-4 Changing Needs

People respond differently to identical needs.

Fourth, the same type of behavior from two different people does not necessarily represent the same need. One person may speak in a cocky manner because he is certain of his subject and feels there is no one more qualified to speak on this topic than he. Another person may use the exact same approach to hide his feelings of insecurity. The former may be fullfilling either esteem or self-actualization needs while the latter is fulfilling the safety need.

Maslow's concept is useful for indicating that individuals have needs. However, in order to motivate workers the manager must know which need(s) requires satisfaction. Whatever approach the manager takes, it will be based on his *assumptions* about the worker and his need-satisfactions.

McGREGOR'S ASSUMPTIONS

The late Douglas McGregor provided some important insights into the area of managerial assumptions in his book *The Human Side of Enterprise.*[10] It was McGregor's thesis that "the theoretical assumptions management holds about controlling its human resources determine the whole character of the enterprise. They determine also the quality of its successive generations of management."[11] By this he meant that every management has a philosophy or set of assumptions it uses in handling its workers. In essence, McGregor divided these assumptions into two groups: Theory X assumptions and Theory Y assumptions. Theory X assumptions may be placed on one end of a continuum and Theory Y assumptions on the other.

Theory X Assumptions

McGregor found Theory X assumptions implicit in much of the literature about organization and in many of the current management practices.

These assumptions are:

Theory X assumptions.

1. **People inherently dislike work and, when possible, will avoid it.**

2. **They have little ambition, tend to shun responsibility and prefer to be directed.**

3. **Above all, they want security.**

4. **In order to get them to attain organizational objectives it is necessary to use coercion, control, and threats of punishment.** [12]

At first glance it might appear that McGregor was constructing a straw man. With this contention, however, he vehemently disagreed, noting that Theory X assumptions are actually subscribed to by many managers in United States industry.

---

[10]Douglas McGregor, *The Human Side of Enterprise* (New York: McGraw-Hill Book Company, 1960).
[11]*Ibid*, pp. vi–vii.
[12]*Ibid.*, pp. 33–34.

Furthermore, he noted, "the principles of organization which comprise the bulk of the literature of management *could only have been derived from assumptions such as those of Theory X.* Other beliefs about human nature would have led inevitably to quite different organizational principles."[13]

The result of these assumptions, according to McGregor, is that many managers are giving prime consideration to the satisfactions of physiological and safety needs. However, it is quite easy to see that these needs cannot be satisfied while one is on the job. Money, for example, which can purchase food, clothing and shelter, can only be spent when the worker goes home. Likewise, safety needs as reflected in fringe benefits such as vacations, profit-sharing plans and health and medical coverage yield satisfaction only outside of one's place of work.

Prime emphasis is placed on satisfying low-level needs.

Nevertheless, many managers seem to feel these low-level physiological need satisfiers are of major importance. Why is this so? In the case of money, one answer is found in the simple fact that managers can manipulate this variable rather easily, so they rely upon it as a motivation tool, giving or withholding financial rewards in an effort to stimulate production. Another reason is the attitude of many managers:

> . . .most. . .are highly achievement-oriented; in the psychologist's terms, they are "high in n Ach." We know that such men attach special significance to money rewards. They are strong believers in steeply increasing financial rewards for greater accomplishment. Because they themselves are particularly interested in some concrete measure that will sensitively reflect how well they have done, it is easy and natural for them to mistake this idea for a related one—namely, that the more money you offer someone the harder he will work.[14]

However, as noted earlier, once the employee's physiological and safety needs are taken care of, his attention is focused on higher-level needs, and this is where the problem begins. Management has made no provision for satisfying these needs, so they offer the workers more physiological and safety rewards. If the workers balk at this, management brings out the threat of punishment, which is in accord with the fourth Theory X tenet above. The use of punishment seems to be a logical method of solving the issue; either the workers do the job or management will get tough. However, the problem rests on the fact that management mistakes causes for effects, the result being a self-fulfilling prophecy. Believing punishment is a necessary tool for effective management, the company introduces it the minute the workers start offering resistance, noting "See, it's just like we said. You have to get tough with these people if you want any performance." Yet it is management's fault that the workers are discontent in the first place.

---

[13]*Ibid.*, p. 35.
[14]David C. McClelland, "Money as a Motivator: Some Research Insights." In David R. Hampton, Charles E. Summer and Ross A. Webber, *Organizational Behavior and the Practice of Management*, (Glenview, Ill.: Scott, Foresman and Company, 1973), p. 641.

"What we're really looking for is a not-too-bright young man with no ambition and who is content to stay on the bottom and not louse things up."
(Courtesy of Dick Lucas)

A "carrot and stick" approach is used.

Why do many managers have trouble motivating their workers? The answer rests on the fact that they hold erroneous assumptions about the nature of man. Management believes they should treat their people like children, providing low-level need-satisfaction rewards if the work is done well and withholding these benefits if the work is done badly. This concept of motivation is known as the "carrot and stick" theory. It may be useful in getting a donkey to pull a cart, but it seldom works effectively in motivating human beings. A more realistic set of assumptions are those contained in Theory Y.

Theory X is not new.

An Age Old Phenomenon.   Before examining Theory Y, however, it should be realized that the basic assumptions of Theory X have been in existence for years. The reader may remember that the philosophy of the early business managers was very similar to that of modern Theory X advocates. Knowles and Saxburg have identified the assumptions employed by these early managers as:

1. The employee is a "constant" in the production equation. The implication here is that man has a fixed nature.

2. The employee is an inert adjunct of the machine, prone to inefficiency and waste unless properly programmed.

3. The employee is by nature lazy; only managers honor the "hard work" creed of the Protestant Ethic.

4. The employee's main concern is self-interest. At work, this is always expressed in economic values.

5. Given appropriate expression, these values will make man fiercely competitive among his peers as an accumulator of financial rewards.

6. Man (at least the working man) must therefore be tightly controlled and externally motivated in order to overcome his natural desire to avoid work unless the material gains available to him are worth his effort.[15]

Theory X, then, is certainly not a new phenomenon; it has been in existence for years. The only notable change is that management has been able to reduce economic hardship and improve working conditions among the employees since the time of Taylor and his associates. This has all been done, however, without any change in their *fundamental* theory of management.

Theory Y

Human behavior research has provided the basis for formulating assumptions for a new theory of management, which McGregor called Theory Y. Its assumptions are:

1. **Work is a natural phenomenon and if the conditions are favorable people will not only accept responsibility, they will seek it.**

2. **If people are committed to organizational objectives they will exercise self-direction and self-control.**

Theory Y assumptions.

3. **Commitment is a function of the rewards associated with goal attainment.**

4. **The capacity for creativity in solving organizational problems is widely distributed in the population and the intellectual potentialities of the average human being are only partially utilized.[16]**

In contrast to Theory X, Theory Y presents a dynamic view of man. The individual is seen as having growth and development potential; and the problem of motivation is now placed directly in the lap of management. Since the worker has potential, management must decide how to tap it. No longer can management hide behind the old Theory X assumptions. Management must reevaluate its thinking and begin focusing attention on ways of allowing the workers to attain their upper-level needs.

Theory Y may be unreasonably idealistic.

Theory Y Criticism.   Many individuals think of Theory X as many outmoded assumptions and of Theory Y as a modern, superior view of the worker; but Theory Y also has its critics. For example, some point out that Theory Y is unreasonably idealistic. After all, not everyone is self-directed and self-controlled; many workers seem to like security and shun responsibility. As Fromm has noted, people want freedom, but only within defined limits.[17] Strauss supports this finding,

---

[15]Henry P. Knowles and Borje O. Saxburg, "Human Relations and the Nature of Man," *Harvard Business Review*, March–April 1967, p. 32.
[16]McGregor, *op. cit.*, pp. 47–48.
[17]Erich Fromm, *The Sane Society* (New York: Holt, Rinehart & Winston, Inc., 1955), p. 318.

pointing out that individuals who will accept complete freedom in certain areas will demand restrictions in many others.[18] Maslow also echoes this sentiment, stating that gratification of basic needs is important, but unrestricted indulgence can lead to irresponsibility, psychopathic personality and inability to bear stress.[19]

Need satisfaction may not occur on the job.

A second criticism is that Theory Y advocates tend to believe that the primary place of need satisfaction is on the job. However, many workers satisfy their needs off the job. This is particularly apparent in light of the trend toward a shorter work week; people are seeking satisfaction during their leisure time. Theory Y may thus overemphasize the importance of satisfying higher-level needs in the work place.

The individual and organization are not always in conflict.

A third common criticism involves whether or not there is a personality-organization conflict in large-scale mass-production industries. Critics contend that Theory Y assumes that concepts such as work simplification and standardization have reduced job satisfaction. However, this may be only one cause of organization conflict and may be greatly overemphasized by Theory Y advocates.

Which of the two theories is correct? The answer is going to depend on the situation and will always represent some combination of the two. One thing appears certain, however. Most managers tend to underrate the workers, subscribing more heavily to Theory X than to Theory Y. This has been made very clear by Chris Argyris.

ARGYRIS' IMMATURITY-MATURITY THEORY

Argyris, while at Yale University, made a study of industrial organizations to determine the effect of management practices on individual behavior and personal growth within the organization.[20] According to him, seven changes take place in an individual as he moves from infancy (immaturity) to adulthood (maturity). First, the passive state of the infant gives way to the increasingly active state of the adult. Second, the child is highly dependent but becomes relatively independent as he matures. Third, an infant is capable of behaving in only a few ways whereas an adult can behave in many ways. Fourth, a child tends to have casual, shallow interests; an adult develops

Seven stages of maturity development.

---

[18]George Strauss, "Some Notes on Power-Equalization." In Harold J. Leavitt, ed., *The Social Science of Organizations* (Englewood Cliffs, N.J.: Prentice-Hall, 1963), p. 50.
[19]A. H. Maslow, *Toward a Psychology of Being* (Princeton, N.J.: D. Van Nostrand Company Inc., 1962), pp. 153–154.
[20]Chris Argyris, *Personality and Organization* (New York: Harper & Brothers, Publishers, Inc., 1957); *Interpersonal Competence and Organizational Effectiveness* (Homewood, Ill.: The Dorsey Press, 1962); *Integrating the Individual and the Organization* (New York: John Wiley & Sons, Inc., 1964).

deep, strong interests. Fifth, a child's time perspective is very short, encompassing only the present; an adult's is longer, encompassing the past and future as well as the present. Sixth, an infant is subordinate to everyone whereas an adult is equal or superior to others. Seventh, children lack an awareness of "self" whereas adults are aware of and able to control "self." These seven stages can be viewed as being on a continuum:

Immaturity ——————————— Maturity

Organizations keep people in an immature state.

Argyris contends that most organizations keep their people in a state of immaturity. Position descriptions, work assignments and task specialization lead to routine, unchallenging jobs. They also minimize the amount of control workers have over their environment. This, in turn, encourages them to be passive, dependent and submissive. Keeping people in this state is one of the formal organization's goals. The management likes to control everything, the workers being viewed as small cogs in a big machine. Of course, this type of thinking is incompatible with the development of a mature personality. The result is a formal organization incongruous with the mature individual. Argyris' findings re-echo McGregor's Theory X assumptions, indicating that management's view of the worker may be the major stumbling block in the motivation process. Unaware of what *really* motivates people, management is unable to come up with a viable theory of motivation. One individual who has attempted to shed light on this problem by extending Maslow's hierarchical concept and applying it to the job is Frederick Herzberg.

HERZBERG'S TWO-FACTOR THEORY OF MOTIVATION

In the late 1950's, Herzberg and his associates at the Psychological Service of Pittsburgh conducted extensive interviews with two hundred engineers and accountants from 11 industries in the Pittsburgh area.[21]

The individuals were asked to relate the elements of their job that made them happy or unhappy. An analysis of the findings revealed that when people were dissatisfied, these bad feelings were generally associated with the *environment* in which they were working. When people felt good about their jobs, this was generally associated with the *work itself.* Herzberg labeled the factors that prevent dissatisfaction *hygiene factors* and those that bring about satisfaction *motivators.*

Hygiene Factors

The factors that prevent dissatisfaction are called hygiene factors because their effect on worker satisfaction resembles the

---

[21]Frederick Herzberg, Bernard Mausner and Barbara Bloch Snyderman, *The Motivation to Work,* 2nd edition (New York: John Wiley & Sons, Inc., 1959).

effect of physical hygiene on the body. Consider, for example, an individual who slips on an icy path and suffers superficial hand cuts. At home he washes his hand and puts iodine on the wound. Two weeks later the hand is back to its original state. The iodine did not make the hand any better than it was previous to the injury, but it prevented further deterioration such as gangrene and helped the hand return to its original state.

This is what hygiene does. It takes a negative condition (cut hand) and brings it back to its original position (uncut hand). Conversely, if hygiene is denied, things can go from bad to worse. For example, an individual in excellent health will not become any healthier by eating food but if he does not eat, he will eventually become sick and die. Likewise, breathing will not make a person any healthier but failure to breathe will kill him. Hygiene will not improve health beyond one's original state, but it prevents deterioration by returning the person to his original state, which can be called condition zero.

Hygiene factors prevent dissatis-faction.

Herzberg found that on the job there are many hygiene factors. These include money, supervision, status, personal life, security, working conditions, policies and administration and interpersonal relations (see Table 13–1). These factors do not motivate people, they merely prevent dissatisfaction. They produce no growth in worker output, but they do prevent loss in performance caused by work restriction. They maintain motivation at zero-level, preventing a negative type of motivation from occurring. This is why they are often referred to as maintenance factors.

Motivators

Motivators have a positive effect on job satisfac-tion.

Herzberg found that factors relating to the job itself can have a *positive effect* on job satisfaction and result in increased output. He called these motivators or satisfiers and identified them as the work itself, recognition, advancement, the possibility of growth, responsibility and achievement.

TABLE 13–1   Hygiene and Motivators

Hygiene Factors (Environment)	**Motivators** (Work Itself)
Money	Work Itself
Supervision	Recognition
Status	Advancement
Security	Possibility of Growth
Working Conditions	Responsibility
Policies and Administration	Achievement
Interpersonal Relations	

Motivation-Hygiene Under Attack

Criticism of Herzberg's theory.

Herzberg's two-factor theory presents some interesting ideas, but the reader should also be aware of what the critics say. First, the original study, consisting of accountants and engineers, is attacked as being unrepresentative of the work force in general. Second, although Herzberg has cited replication of the results of his study among groups such as manufacturing supervisors, hospital maintenance personnel, nurses, military officers and professional women,[22] other researchers have uncovered different results.[23] In some cases, hygiene or maintenance factors, such as wages or job security, were found to be viewed as motivators among blue-collar workers. In addition, what one person might call a motivator, another person in the same department might term a hygiene factor. In one study conducted among both managerial and professional workers, Schwab, DeVitt and Cummings found that Herzberg's hygiene factors were as useful in motivating employees as were his motivators.[24] Third, Vroom contends that Herzberg's findings are debatable because his two-factor conclusion was only one of many that could have been drawn from the research.[25] He argues that people are more likely to assign satisfaction to their own achievements and attribute dissatisfaction to company policies. Thus, the findings are interpretive at best.

The criticism indicates that the two-factor theory is certainly not universally accepted and more research is probably needed before definitive conclusions about it can be drawn. As Myers noted, "motivation-maintenance theory, like any theory of management, is at the mercy of its practitioners and will remain intact and find effective utilization only to the extent that it serves as a mechanism for harnassing constructive motives."[26] Nevertheless, Herzberg's theory of job satisfaction has helped extend and apply Maslow's need hierarchy to work motivation.

---

[22]Frederick Herzberg, *Work and the Nature of Man* (Cleveland, Ohio: The World Publishing Company, 1966).

[23]See Marvin D. Dunnette, John P. Campbell and Milton D. Hakel, "Factors Contributing to Job Satisfaction and Job Dissatisfaction in Six Occupational Groups," *Organizational Behavior and Human Performance*, May 1967, pp. 143–174; Charles L. Hulin and Patricia A. Smith, "An Empirical Investigation of Two Implications of the Two-Factor Theory of Job Satisfaction," *Journal of Applied Psychology*, October 1967, pp. 396–402; Carl A. Lindsay, Edmond Marks and Leon Gorlow, "The Herzberg Theory: A Critique and Reformulation," *Journal of Applied Psychology*, August 1967, pp. 330–339; John R. Hinrichs and Louis A. Mischkind, "Empirical and Theoretical Limitations of the Two-Factor Hypothesis of Job Satisfaction," *Journal of Applied Psychology*, April 1967, pp. 191–200.

[24]Donald P. Schwab, H. William DeVitt and Larry L. Cummings, "A Test of the Adequacy of the Two-factor Theory as a Predictor of Self-Report Performance Effects," *Personnel Psychology*, Summer 1971, pp. 293–303.

[25]Victor H. Vroom, *Work and Motivation* (New York: John Wiley & Sons, Inc., 1964), pp. 128–129.

[26]M. Scott Myers, "Who Are Your Motivated Workers?" *Harvard Business Review*, January–February 1964, p. 88.

The Need Hierarchy and Motivation-Hygiene

Herzberg's framework is compatible with Maslow's need hierarchy. Maslow's lower-level needs are analogous to Herzberg's hygiene factors, and his upper-level needs correspond to Herzberg's motivators. The comparison between the two is seen in Figure 13–5. As the figure indicates, Herzberg's hygiene factors encompass Maslow's physiological, safety, social and, to some degree, esteem needs. The reason for placing status in the hygiene category and advancement and recognition in the motivator group is that status is not always a reflection of personal achievement or earned recognition. For example, an individual could achieve status through family ties such as inheritance or marriage. Conversely, advancement and recognition are more often reflections of personal achievement.

However, it must be realized that Maslow and Herzberg both tend to oversimplify the motivational process. Although Herzberg makes an interesting extension of Maslow's theory, neither of their models provides an adequate link between *individual* need satisfaction and the achievement of organizational objectives. Nor do either of their theories really handle the problem of individual differences in motivation. For this one must turn to *process* or *mechanical* theories.

Before doing this, however, two key concepts of modern moti-

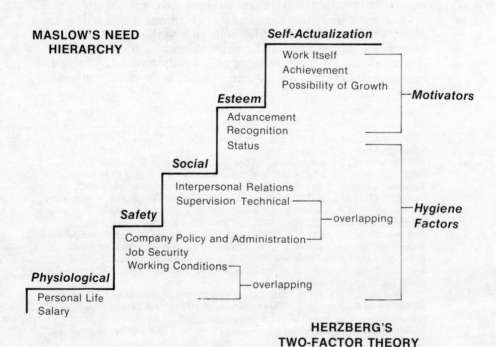

FIGURE 13–5 Comparison of Maslow and Herzberg Models (See also Keith Davis, *Human Behavior at Work*, New York, McGraw-Hill Book Company, 1972, p. 59.)

vation theory will be examined: expectancy theory and learned behavior.

EXPECTANCY THEORY AND LEARNED BEHAVIOR

Some of the most important modern process theories rely on what is called *expectancy theory*. In relating this concept to motivation:

> . . .expectancy theory predicts that an individual will generally be a high performer when he: (1) sees a high probability that his efforts will lead to high performance, (2) sees a high probability that high performance will lead to outcomes, and (3) views these outcomes to be, on balance, positively attractive to himself.[27]

Need-depriva-tion and expect-ancy theory approach are related.

In comparing Maslow's concept of needs with this idea of expectancy, it becomes evident that there are two ways of studying motivational intensity. One can examine need deficiencies, as in the case of Maslow's hierarchy, in which people, because of some perceived deficiency, are pushed toward engaging in a particular form of behavior, or one can examine motivation from the viewpoint of the goals the individual is seeking to attain, in which case motivation is seen as a force pulling the person toward the desired objective. Furthermore, in the case of need deprivation, the emphasis is on internal deficiencies; in the case of expectancy, the focus is on external goals that help alleviate these deficiencies. In essence, although the two ideas are different, they are related. However, today motivation researchers tend to favor the expectancy theory approach. Two of these individuals, Lyman Porter and Edward Lawler, cite the following reasons for choosing this approach:

> Basically, the terminology and concepts involved seem to us to be more applicable to consideration of the complexities of human motivation and behavior, and, therefore, more applicable to understanding the attitudes and performance of managers in organizations. The emphasis in expectancy theory on rationality and expectations seems to us to describe best the kinds of conditions that influence managerial performance. . . .

> Expectancy theory also greatly facilitates the incorporation of motives like status, achievement, and power into a theory of attitudes and performance. There is a considerable amount of evidence that the central motives for most managers are those for *achievement, self-actualization, power and status, and income and advancement.*[28]

In addition, it should be noted that studies employing expectancy theory have been conducted in both private and public organizations among employees ranging from production-line operators to managerial personnel and have proved very successful in providing insights into this area of motivation.

---

[27]L. L. Cummings and Donald P. Schwab, *Performance in Organizations: Determinants and Appraisal* (Glenview, Ill.: Scott, Foresman and Company, 1973), p. 31.

[28]Lyman W. Porter and Edward E. Lawler III, *Managerial Attitudes and Performance* (Homewood, Ill.: Richard D. Irwin, Inc. and the Dorsey Press, 1968), pp. 12–13.

If individuals are indeed motivated by expectations, they must have established some relationship between present action and future reward; i.e., if I work hard, I will be promoted. How is this causal relationship formulated? The answer is found in *learned behavior*. Through either direct or indirect experience, individuals learn to establish cause-effect relationships, which dictate how a person will respond in a given situation.

Reinforcement is one of the key factors in learned behavior.

One of the key factors in learned behavior is *reinforcement*. If an individual does something right and the manager wants to reinforce this behavior, he must respond in a way which the subordinate finds satisfying such as giving the person a pat on the back or a raise. This response will help establish a causal relationship and it is likely that the individual will repeat the behavior in the future. Conversely, if the manager wants to extinguish a given behavior, he can turn to punishment or negative reinforcement such as bawling someone out or demoting him.[29]

When the concept of expectancy theory is combined with that of learned behavior, one has the basis for understanding some of the most important modern motivation theories. One of these is Victor Vroom's expectancy-valence theory.

VROOM'S THEORY

At the present time, Victor Vroom's motivation theory, despite its complexity, is viewed with great favor. His basic concept can be expressed in the following way:[30]

$$\text{Motivation} = \Sigma \text{ Valence} \times \text{Expectancy}$$

Motivation is equal to the summation of valence times expectancy. In order to understand Vroom's theory, three concepts must be grasped: instrumentality, valence and expectancy.

Instrumentality is the relationship an individual perceives between a first- and second-level outcome.

An individual's motivation is a result of the actual or perceived rewards available to him for accomplishing some goal. For example, the company wants Roger to be productive. But what is in it for Roger? This will, of course, depend upon his perception of available rewards, but suppose for a moment that he believes there is a direct correlation between productivity and promotion i.e., promotion depends on productivity. Then, given this assumption, there are two outcomes under discussion. There is the "first-level outcome," which is productivity, and there is the "second-level outcome," which is promotion.

---

[29]See, for example, Fred Luthans and Robert Kreitner, "The Role of Punishment in Organizational Behavior Modification (O.B. Mod.)," *Public Personnel Management*, May–June 1973, pp. 156–161.
[30]Vroom, *op. cit.*, Chapter 2.

This introduces the first of Vroom's three concepts, namely, instrumentality. *Instrumentality* is the relationship perceived by an individual between a first-level outcome and a second-level outcome.

Valence is a person's prefer-ence for a partic-ular outcome.

Next, one has to consider Roger's *valence* or preference for the first-level outcome (productivity), and to make it more meaningful, three variations of productivity will be used: high, average and low. What is Roger's valence for high produc-tivity? This will depend on his desire for promotion. If it is very high, his valence will be positive. If he is indifferent to promotion, it will be zero. If he does not want a promotion, it will be negative. The same logic can be used in determining his valence for average and low productivity. Thus, valence and instrumentality can be brought together in the following way:

Valence or preference $\longrightarrow$ Instrumentality $\longrightarrow$ Second-level
for first-level   *(Perceived relationships*   outcome
outcome   *between first- and second-*   *(Promotion)*
(Productivity)   *level outcomes)*

In a manner of speaking, one must work backward in grasping Vroom's theory, from instrumentality to valence, for an individual's preference for a first-level outcome is dictated by the extent to which he believes this will lead to the attainment of a second-level outcome.

Expectancy is the probability that a specific action will yield a particular first-level out-come.

Vroom's third concept, *expectancy*, is the probability that a specific action will be followed by a particular first-level outcome. For example, what is the probability that if Roger works hard he can attain high productivity? This objective probability will range from zero (no chance) to one (certainty). If Roger is convinced that with hard work he can attain high productivity, his expectancy will be equal to one. These three concepts, instrumentality, valence and expectancy, are incorporated in Figure 13–6.

Motivation is thus equal to the algebraic sum of the products of the valences of all first-level outcomes (the person's preference for each of the first-level outcomes) times the strength of the expectancy that the action will be followed by the attainment of these outcomes (the probability of attaining the respective first-level outcome). This formula helps the manager understand what motivates the *individual* worker.

Of course, Vroom's theory is a difficult one to grasp and usually requires rereading. Nevertheless, current researchers have higher

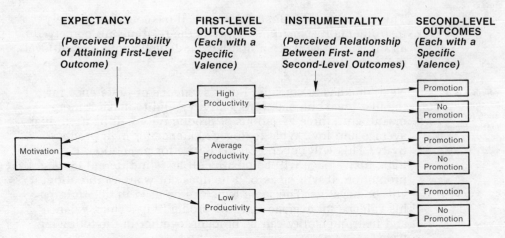

FIGURE 13–6   An Example of Vroom's Expectancy-Valence Model

regard for it than for most of the other motivation theories.
As Hunt and Hill note:

> More work must be done before we can make any statements concerning the
> overall validity of Vroom's model. But the vigor of his formulation, the
> relative ease of making the concepts operational, and the model's emphasis
> on individual differences show considerable promise. We are also encouraged
> by the results of relatively sophisticated studies testing the theory. We believe
> it is time for those interested in organizational behavior to take a more
> thoroughly scientific look at this very complex subject of industrial motiva-
> tion, and Vroom's model seems a big step in that direction.[31]

**PORTER
AND
LAWLER'S
MODEL**

Another modern process theory is that proposed by Lyman
Porter and Edward Lawler.[32] Porter and Lawler's model, also
based on the expectancy theory of motivation, implies that
individuals are motivated by future expectations based on
previously learned experiences. In essence, their model contains
a number of key variables, including effort, performance, reward
and satisfaction. Figure 13–7 illustrates the relationship among
these variables.

It is important to note that Porter and Lawler use a semi-wavy
line between performance and intrinsic rewards to indicate that
a direct relationship exists between performance and these
rewards *if* the job has been designed in such a way that when
the person has performed well he can reward himself with,
for example, an internally generated payoff such as a feeling of
accomplishment. The wavy line between performance and
extrinsic rewards in the figure is used to indicate that such

---

[31]J. G. Hunt and J. W. Hill, "The New Look in Motivation Theory for Organizational Research," *Human Organization*, Summer 1969, p. 108.
[32]Porter and Lawler, *op. cit.*

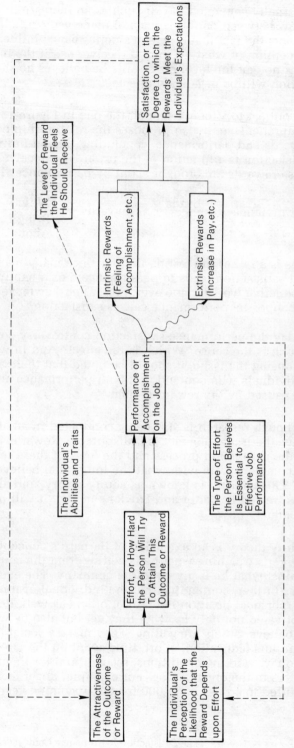

FIGURE 13–7 Porter and Lawler's Motivation Model (Adapted from Lyman W. Porter and Edward E. Lawler III, *Managerial Attitudes and Performance,* Homewood, Ill., Richard D. Irwin, Inc., 1968, p. 165.)

rewards are often not directly related to performance; e.g., an externally generated payoff such as an increase in pay. The arrow between performance and perceived equitable rewards depicts the fact that a person's performance influences his perception of what he should receive, i.e., if the individual does not get the level of rewards he believes he should, satisfaction will be negatively affected.

In contrast to Vroom's model, the one in Figure 13–7 is more comprehensive. It also proposes the relationship between rewards and performance, concluding that an individual's satisfaction is a function of the rewards he receives. In turn, these rewards are brought about by performance. Thus:

$$\text{Performance} \xrightarrow[\text{To}]{\text{Leads}} \text{Rewards} \xrightarrow[\substack{\text{Bring}\\\text{About}}]{\text{Which}} \text{Satisfaction}$$

This is a rather interesting finding since many managers feel that satisfaction leads to performance; i.e., a happy worker is a productive worker. However, Porter and Lawler report just the opposite; performance causes satisfaction.

The perform-ance-satisfaction controversy still rages.

Today the performance-satisfaction controversy continues. Which is the cause? Which is the effect? And in way of confusing the issue, it should be noted that there are some individuals who contend that both performance and satisfaction are caused by the reward system.[33]

Although research is still being conducted in an attempt to resolve the issue, one fact is indisputable. Rewards are important in the motivation process and the level of these rewards must be commensurate with what the individual believes they should be. This concept is known as equity theory, and although it was treated in Porter and Lawler's model, it will be considered separately now.

EQUITY OR SOCIAL COMPARISON THEORY

Equity theory is an extension of Barnard's concept about the worker's weighing what he is getting from the company against what he is giving to the company. The equity theory goes further, contending that the individual evaluates not only his personal position but that of others as well. People are motivated not only by what they get but also by what they see, or believe, others are getting. They make a social comparison of inputs (education, effort, time spent on the job) and rewards (money, working conditions, recognition) for themselves and others in the organization. For example, Roger feels that he is entitled to a raise of $1,000 for the upcoming year. His superior

People compare their rewards with those re-ceived by others.

---

[33]Charles N. Greene, "The Satisfaction-Performance Controversy," *Business Horizons*, October 1972, pp. 31–41.

calls him and tells him he is going to get $1,750. Roger is elated. However, later in the day he discovers that George, his archrival, has received $2,300. Now Roger is angry, because he feels he is giving as much to the company as George but is receiving less. Initially he was happy with the "extra" $750 but now he is not, because social comparison has shown that George is getting a bigger reward than he. Figure 13-8 shows how this social comparison works.

When people feel they are not being properly treated, tension results. In relieving this tension, there are a number of alternatives available. For example, Roger may quit his job. Or he may go to his boss and demand more money, thereby establishing equality with George. Or he may stop comparing himself with George because he cannot hope to keep up, and go find a different rival. Or he may do less work. However, the most likely alternative is that he will change his perception of George's input-reward ratio. For example, "George has three kids and I only have one, so my $1,700 will go a lot further than his $2,300."

It is also interesting to note that some of the literature shows that when a person feels he is overpaid, at least initially, he tends to do more work. In this way he justifies the higher salary. However, over time he will usually reevaluate his skills and position, concluding that he is indeed worth the higher salary. Output will then drop back to its former level. This accounts for the belief of some researchers that money is a short-run motivator at best, and only one tool among many that the manager can use in the motivation process. As McClelland has pointed out, money:

> . . .is a treacherous tool because it is deceptively concrete, tempting many managers to neglect variables in the work situation and climate that really affect productivity. In the near future, there will be less and less excuse for neglecting these variables, as the behavioral sciences begin to define them and explain to management how they can be manipulated just as one might change a financial compensation plan.[34]

SUMMARY In this chapter modern motivation theory has been examined. First, the relationship between needs and behavior was shown

[34]McClelland, op. cit., p. 649.

Roger		George

FIGURE 13-8 Social Comparison   *Compared with*

INPUTS		INPUTS
REWARDS		REWARDS

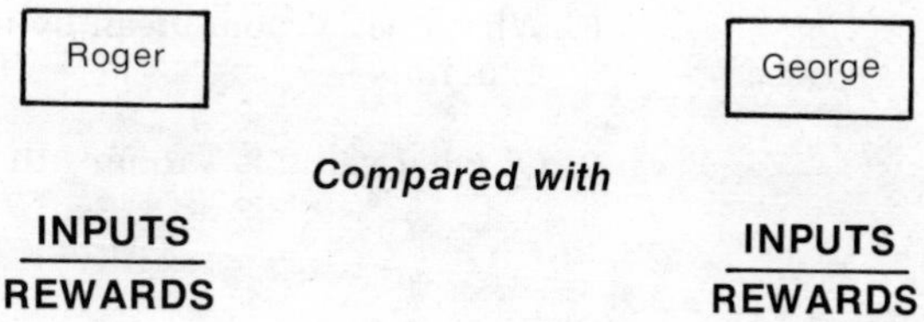

through the use of Maslow's hierarchy. These ideas were then refined and applied to the work place through Herzberg's model.

Both theories provide important *general* insights into workers' behavior because they stress the importance of examining the *causes* of human activity and help answer the question, *what* specific things motivate people?

However, the manager must also be concerned with explaining *how* behavior is initiated, directed, sustained or halted. To do this he must understand process or mechanical theories. In this chapter three of these theories were examined: Vroom's expectancy-valence theory, Porter and Lawler's motivation model and equity or social comparison theory. All three place great emphasis on *individual* motivation.

In the past few years, increased attention has been given to these process theories because of their value in applying general motivation theory to specific situations. Yet, whatever approach the manager uses, one question must remain foremost—what will motivate the worker(s) to attain organizational objectives? Once this is answered, the manager is in a position to examine the area of leadership. Now that he knows what will motivate his people, he can focus his attention on leading them. This will be the subject of the next chapter.

REVIEW AND STUDY QUESTIONS

1. What is the relationship between needs and behavior?

2. What are the five needs in Maslow's hierarchy? What relevance do they have to the study of motivation?

3. What are the assumptions of Theory X? Theory Y?

4. What is Argyris' immaturity-maturity theory? Do you agree or disagree with his findings?

5. What does Herzberg mean by hygiene factors? Identify some of them.

6. What does Herzberg mean by motivators? Identify some of them.

7. What relationship do Herzberg and Maslow's theories bear to one another in general and specifically to motivation? Explain.

8. What does Vroom mean by instrumentality? Valence? Expectancy? Explain.

9. Of what value is Vroom's theory to the practicing manager?

10. How does Porter and Lawler's model expand the ideas presented by Vroom?

11. Of what value is the Porter-Lawler model to the practicing manager?

12. What is meant by equity or social comparison theory? Give an illustration. What is its relevance to motivation theory?

13. In your own words, what are the steps to effective motivation? What should every manager know about the process?

SELECTED REFERENCES

Annas, J. W. "Profiles of Motivation." *Personnel Journal*, March 1973, pp. 205–208.

Behling, O., and F. A. Starke. "The Postulates of Expectancy Theory." *Academy of Management Journal*, September 1973, pp. 373–388.

Bockman, V. M., "The Herzberg Controversy." *Personnel Psychology*, Summer 1971, pp. 155–189.

Charles, A. W. "Theory Y Compensation." *Personnel Journal*, January 1973, pp. 12–18, 26.

Davis, K. *Human Behavior At Work*, 4th edition. New York: McGraw-Hill Book Company, 1972, Chapter 3.

Dunnette, M. D., J. P. Campbell, and M. D. Hakel, "Factors Contributing to Job Satisfaction and Job Dissatisfaction in Six Occupational Groups." *Organizational Behavior and Human Performance*, May 1967, pp. 143–174.

Eckerman, A. C., "A New Look at Need Theory." *Training and Development Journal*, November 1968, pp. 18–22.

Gellerman, S. W., *Management by Motivation*. New York: American Management Association, 1968.

Greene, C. N. "The Satisfaction-Performance Controversy." *Business Horizons*, October 1972, pp. 31–41.

Herzberg, F., B. Mausner, and B. B. Snyderman. *The Motivation to Work*. New York: John Wiley & Sons, Inc., 1959.

Herzberg, F. *Work and the Nature of Man*. Cleveland: The World Publishing Company, 1966.

Hulin, C. L. and P. A. Smith. "An Empirical Investigation of Two Implications of the Two-Factor Theory of Job Satisfaction." *Journal of Applied Psychology*, October 1967, pp. 396–402.

Lindsay, C. A., E. Marks, and L. Gorlow. "The Herzberg Theory: A Critique and Reformulation." *Journal of Applied Psychology*, August 1967, pp. 330–339.

Maslow, A. H., *Motivation and Personality*. New York: Harper & Row Publishers, Inc., 1954.

Maslow, A. H. *Eupsychian Management*. Homewood, Ill.: Richard D. Irwin, Inc., and The Dorsey Press, 1965.

O'Reilly, A. P., "The Supervisor and His Subordinate's Self-Actualization." *Personnel Psychology*, Spring 1973, pp. 81–85.

Porter, L. W., and E. E. Lawler III. *Managerial Attitudes and Performance*. Homewood, Ill.: Richard D. Irwin, Inc., 1968.

Roberts, K. H., G. A. Walter, and R. E. Miles, "A Factor Analytic Study of Job Satisfaction Items Designed to Measure Maslow Need Categories." *Personnel Psychology*, Summer 1971, pp. 205–220.

Vroom, V. H. *Work and Motivation*. New York: John Wiley & Sons, Inc., 1964.

Waters, L. K., and D. Roach. "A Factor Analysis of Need-Fulfillment Items Designed to Measure Maslow Need Categories." *Personnel Psychology*, Summer 1973, pp. 185–190.

CASE: TAKE THE MONEY AND RUN[1]

If the family breadwinner is fired or laid off, the economic effects can be severe. If the individual happens to be an executive making $30,000 to $40,000 a year, the results can be catastrophic. After all, where can a person go to find another job paying that salary? Pearl Meyer, vice president for research at Handy Associates, Inc., a New York management consultant and executive-search concern, has reported that during the 1960's it took the average executive from two months (during most of the decade) to six months (during the 1969–1970 recession) to find a new job.

Many executives are concerned over the possible loss of their employment, whether for failure to perform or merely because of personnel reductions throughout the company. As a result, they have begun requesting "termination agreements." These are promises by the firm to pay the individual a certain sum of money, such as a full year's salary, should they terminate his services. According to Mrs. Meyer, by December 1972, 99 of 100 executives at the top level, one-quarter of those at the $50,000 level and ten per cent of those at the $30,000 rung were asking for and getting such agreements. Of course, the situation was the final determinant of whether or not the firm would consent to such terms. If the company wanted a person from the outside or felt it vital to retain an individual's services within the company, they would give such an agreement. However, the terms differ from executive to executive. Some people, upon separation, get three-month's salary, others get six, others twelve. One executive on the West Coast received an agreement for his $90,000 annual salary plus continued use of the office, secretarial services and the company car. Although these agreements are very expensive for the company, many firms seem to like them better than the usual contract agreements under which the firm can be required to pay out far more money.

Companies also figure the (termination) agreements will spare them some of the costly woes full employment contracts sometimes bring. Last March, when Najeeb E. Halaby resigned under pressure as chairman of Pan American World Airways, his traditional employment contract still had . . . two years to run—at $127,000 a year. So until December next year, Pan Am will be paying Mr. Halaby $27,000 a year more than it currently pays William T. Seawell, the new chairman. Under a typical termination agreement, of course, Mr. Halaby's benefits would have expired in a year or less.

---

[1]The data in this case can be found in Roger Ricklefs, "More Executives Ask—And Get—Pay Pledges Should They Be Fired," *Wall Street Journal*, December 11, 1972, pp. 1, 19.

But at least Pan Am avoided the troubles of National General Corp. After more than a decade in court, the diversified Los Angeles concern is still appealing a suit brought by its former president, John Bertero, an executive who resigned under pressure in 1959. So far, California juries have awarded nearly $2 million to Mr. Bertero. He claims the company illegally cut off his benefits under an employment contract. The company contends, among other things, that the contract itself wasn't valid.

Questions

1. Are termination agreements hygiene factors or motivators? Explain.

2. Do such agreements have any long-run value for the firm?

3. Will the use of such agreements increase or decrease throughout this decade? Give your reasoning.

CASE: THE GREAT ESCAPE[1]

In late 1972, it was evident that the United Auto Workers intended to place major emphasis on leisure time during the next contract negotiation. The *Wall Street Journal* reported that:

. . .most union leaders currently favor some system that would shorten the work-year through longer vacation periods. One plan being seriously considered would credit workers for hours worked, allowing them to build up a bank of points, rewarded with a paid week off. While this plan would require the auto companies to have more workers, the vacations could be staggered over the year and thus avoid big fluctuations in manpower.

A president of one of the locals pointed out that times were changing and people were no longer willing to spend as much time in the work place. The days of "industrial prostitution" were over. People wanted to be home with their families.

Another group was pushing for major improvements in the retirement plan the UAW had secured in 1970. This plan permitted workers with 30 years on the job to retire at 56 with a $500-a-month pension. The newly recommended plan called for "thirty and out" with a $650-a-month pension, cost of living escalator clause and no minimum-age restrictions. Regardless of the contract terms, one fact appeared clear. Most union leaders favored some form of a system that would shorten the work year through longer vacation periods.

[1]The data in this case can be found in Lawrence O'Donnell and Walter Mossberg, "UAW Will Emphasize Escape From the 'Job' in 1973 Contract Talks," *Wall Street Journal*, December 8, 1972, pp. 1, 25.

Auto executives, meanwhile, viewed plans for a shorter work week very coolly. They felt the costs to the company through heavy overtime in peak periods and the expense associated with unused facilities would be exhorbitant. Sidney McKenna, director of industrial relations for Ford Motor Company remarked, "I don't know how to operate this business if everyone wants to say when, where and if he will work. . . . There is very little evidence—in fact, none that I'm aware of—to suggest that a reduction in working time will increase employee satisfaction while at work."

Questions

1. What types of needs will increased leisure satisfy? Explain.

2. If, as according to Theory Y, work is a natural phenomenon, won't the workers become bored with all this free time?

3. Evaluate Mr. McKenna's last statement. Do you agree or disagree? Explain.

CASE: JOIN US

In 1919 the United States Navy's recruiting poster urged young Americans to join up. Some of the specific rewards listed on the poster included travel, trade instruction and pay. A half-century later, in 1972, the poster was quite different. For one thing, the major heading read "Join the Navy and Find Your Place in the World." On the poster were nine pictures. Two of them showed Navy men on vacation in Pompeii and Venice. The remaining seven pictures were of men on the job, most of whom were working with some form of sophisticated electronic equipment.

The text accompanying the advertisement pointed out that the "new Navy still gives young men (and women, too!) a chance to see the world." It then went on to mention job opportunities in computer technology, electronics, welding and aviation mechanics, which provide useful careers in as well as outside of the service. Attention was also called to the fact that besides providing housing, clothing, food and health care, monthly salaries started at $288. In addition, there was a "join-now report-six-months-later" plan. Meanwhile, for new three-year enlistees, the Navy guaranteed them their choice of East or West Coast duty. The ad closed by urging the reader to "be someone special in THE NEW NAVY."

Questions

1. How does the 1919 poster differ from its 1972 counterpart in terms of motivating enlistments?

2. To which of Maslow's needs does the recent poster appeal?

3. From Herzberg's point of view, is the Navy trying to satisfy hygiene or motivation factors or both? Explain.

4. How would Vroom's motivation model help explain why individuals join the Navy? Explain, incorporating into your discussion the concepts of expectancy, instrumentality and valence.

CASE: A NEW DEAL[1]

In late 1972, Gene Cafiero, a group vice president at the Chrysler Corporation, recommended a large-scale program for increasing worker morale and bolstering quality and productivity. The program entailed less bossing and more managing.

One of the ways of implementing the program was to allow workers in the trim department at the Dodge plant in Hamtrack, Michigan, to take a day off, without penalty, merely by clearing it beforehand with their foreman. The program was known as "planned attendance" and it resulted in a decrease in absenteeism and an increase in work quality. As a result, the company was thinking of expanding the program to include the rest of the plant.

In another case, workers in a Detroit parts plant were asked to reevaluate the entire manufacturing operation. The outcome was the rearrangement of one department and the assignment of some men to other jobs in the plant where they were more needed.

In a third instance, two small-parts departments in a Detroit plant were allowed to work without a foreman, and in another plant workers and a foreman designed a new engine and followed it through its break-in period without higher supervision. In both cases, Chrysler reported tremendous success.

Mr. Cafiero saw the new approach as vital to the future of the company. He expressed a belief that management had to stop bossing and start managing. In his view, running plants on

[1]The data in this case can be found in Walter Mossberg, "A Day's Work," *Wall Street Journal*, December 7, 1972, pp. 1, 26.

fear would just not work any longer. Rather, he felt, management must "let responsibility extend down to its lowest practical level and give authority to go along with that responsibility." His attitude about the dignity of man, he felt, dated back to his boyhood days in Brooklyn. His parents had taught him that everyone was good. In 1946, after receiving a degree in psychology from Dartmouth, he entered industry, joining the Chrysler Corporation in 1953 when the firm he was working with was acquired by the automaker. After advanced study in industrial management at M.I.T. under an A.P. Sloan fellowship, he received a Master's degree and returned to Chrysler as a plant manager. Since then he has attained a reputation for understanding the workers while maintaining an image as a cold, tough trouble-shooter.

The United Auto Workers voiced opposition to Mr. Cafiero's program, claiming they were not aimed at solving serious problems but papering over them. Such issues, the union believed, should be negotiated and not treated internally by management. Furthermore, contended UAW vice president Douglas Fraser in a letter to Chrysler's industrial relations director, "If Mr. Cafiero's unilateral experiments have produced any kind of 'revolution' or meaningful change. . .it is undoubtedly the most secret and well-hidden revolution ever to occur in the Chrysler plants. We have a feeling it is also a secret to the workers who are allegedly involved." Management disagreed, pointing out that the annual turnover rate had declined from 47 per cent in 1969 to 17 per cent in 1972. During this same period absenteeism fell from 7.8 per cent to 5.6 per cent.

Questions

1. Is Mr. Cafiero a Theory X or Theory Y manager? Explain.

2. How do you account for the union opposition? Give the positive and negative sides, bringing into your discussion the concept of expectancy theory.

3. Is the program successful in motivating people? What is your reasoning?

4. How would Porter and Lawler explain the apparent increase in worker motivation? Explain.

CHAPTER 14

LEADERSHIP EFFECTIVENESS

GOALS OF THE CHAPTER

What differentiates the effective leader from the ineffective leader? Perhaps the answer rests on the very definition of management, namely, getting things done through people. In any event, there are some managers who are successful at their jobs and others who are not. The goals of this chapter are to investigate the nature of leadership and to examine many current behavioral theories of leadership. The central theme will be leadership *effectiveness*. In particular, attention will be focused on:

a. the relevance of trait theory to the study of leadership;
b. situational theory and why it is so well accepted today;
c. the use of continuum models in understanding leadership;
d. the value of two dimensional models in understanding leadership;
e. three dimensional leadership models and their dynamic nature;
f. the currently popular contingency theory of leadership;
g. the life cycle theory of leadership and its relevance for the modern manager; and
h. the importance of developing an adaptive leadership style.

THE NATURE OF LEADER-SHIP

Definitions of leadership.

Leadership, as McFarland notes, is an "elusive" concept.[1] It has been described in many different ways. Koontz and O'Donnell call it "the art of inducing subordinates to accomplish their assignments with zeal and confidence."[2] Haimann and Scott see it as a "process by which people are directed, guided, and influenced in choosing and achieving

---

[1]Dalton E. McFarland, *Management: Principles and Practices*, 4th edition (New York: The Macmillan Company, 1974), p. 484.
[2]Harold Koontz and Cyril O'Donnell, *Principles of Management: An Analysis of Managerial Functions*, 5th edition (New York: McGraw-Hill Book Company, 1972), p. 557.

goals."[3] Davis defines it as "the ability to persuade others to seek defined objectives enthusiastically."[4] In way of synthesizing current views, it is accurate to say that most writers in the field of management feel leadership is a process of *influencing* people to direct their efforts toward the achievement of some particular goal(s). As such, leadership is a part of management. Of course, the manager must do more than merely lead, but if he fails to influence people to accomplish assigned goals, he fails as a manager.

Every organization needs leaders, but what is it that distinguishes these individuals from others? For years, many people have sought to answer this question by turning to all sorts of quackery. The analysis of handwriting (graphology), the study of skull shapes (phrenology) and the investigation of the position of the stars and other celestial elements upon human affairs (astrology) have all been employed. However, the two most scientific approaches that have been used are trait theory and situational theory.

Trait Theory

Trait theory examines successful leadership from the standpoint of the individual's personal characteristics; that is, what is it about a person that makes him a good leader? In 1940, Charles Byrd examined twenty lists of traits that were attributed to leaders in various surveys but discovered none of the items appearing on all lists.[5] Later in the decade, Jenkins, after reviewing a wide spectrum of studies encompassing such diverse groups as children, and business, professional and military personnel, categorically stated that, "No single trait or group of characteristics has been isolated which sets off the leader from the members of his group."[6] This undoubtedly accounts for the decline in the importance of trait theory. Clear-cut results have just not been forthcoming, the reason being that the method fails to consider the entire leadership environment. Traits are important, but they are only one part of the picture. The members of the work group and the situation itself (task, technology, goals, structure) are also major variables, for leadership is a function of the *leader*, the *follower* and the *situation*, i.e., $L = f(1, f, s)$.

Clear-cut findings have not been obtained.

Yet, despite its failures, one must not be too hasty in discarding trait theory, for it has made some contributions toward clarifying the nature of leadership. For example, studies show that

---

[3]Theo Haimann and William G. Scott, *Management in the Modern Organization* (Boston: Houghton Mifflin Company, 1974), p. 349.
[4]Keith Davis, *Human Behavior at Work*, 4th edition (New York: McGraw-Hill Book Company, 1972), p. 100.
[5]Charles Byrd, *Social Psychology* (New York: Appleton-Century-Crofts, 1940), p. 378.
[6]William O. Jenkins, "A Review of Leadership Studies with Particular Reference to Military Problems," *Psychological Bulletin*, January 1947, pp. 74–75.

there are four traits that appear to be related to successful leadership. Davis identifies these as:

Traits of success-ful leaders.

Intelligence. **Leaders generally are slightly more intelligent than the average of their followers.**

Social maturity and breadth. **Leaders are emotionally mature, capable of handling extreme situations. They are also able to socialize well with others and have a reasonable self-assurance and self-respect.**

Inner motivation and achievement drives. **Leaders have a strong drive to accomplish things.**

Human relations attitudes. **Leaders know they rely on people to get the work done; they therefore try to develop social understanding. They are employee-oriented.**[7]

Yet trait theory tends to be more descriptive than analytical. As such, its value in predicting success has been, at best, very limited.

Situational Theory

Situational theory is perhaps more commonly accepted than is trait theory. These dimensions are finite in number and vary according to the leader's personality, the requirements of the task, the expectations, needs and attitudes of the followers, and the environment in which all are operating.

Situational theory research began in the 1940's, and the efforts are still continuing today. In general, it appears that some leadership styles are more effective than others, depending on the situation. For example, Filley and House, after conducting a review of the literature, found that the following factors tend to have an impact on leadership effectiveness:

1. the history of the organization;

2. the age of the previous incumbent in the leader's position;

3. the age of the leader and his previous experience;

4. the community in which the organization operates;

5. the particular work requirements of the group;

Factors influencing leadership effectiveness.

6. the psychological climate of the group being led;

7. the kind of job the leader holds;

8. the size of the group led;

9. the degree to which group-member cooperation is required;

10. the cultural expectations of subordinates;

---

[7]Davis, *op. cit.,* pp. 103–104. For further information on this area see Fred E. Fiedler and Martin M. Chemers, *Leadership and Effective Management* (Glenview, Ill.: Scott, Foresman and Company, 1974), pp. 22–28; 31–34.

11. group-member personalities; and

12. the time required and allowed for decision making.[8]

Unfortunately, these studies all tend to focus on widely differing variables. Although they are not contradictory, neither are they supportive of one another. Nevertheless, they do illustrate that certain types of leadership behavior are effective in certain kinds of situations.

(By permission of John Hart and Field Enterprises, Inc.)

Leadership Behavior

Having discussed the nature of leadership, attention will now be focused on the various types of *leadership behavior*; that is, how does a leader act with his group?

A Leadership Continuum

The most common approach is to view leadership behavior on a continuum, such as illustrated in Figure 14–1. As one

---

[8]Alan C. Filley and Robert J. House, *Managerial Process and Organizational Behavior* (Glenview, Ill.: Scott, Foresman and Company, 1969), p. 409. See also Fiedler and Chemers, *op. cit.* pp. 28–31.

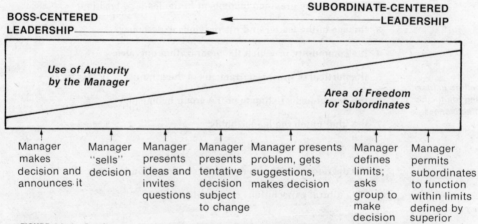

FIGURE 14–1 Continuum of Leadership Behavior (From Robert Tannenbaum and Warren H. Schmidt, "How to Choose a Leadership Pattern," *Harvard Business Review*, May-June 1973, p. 164. Reprinted with permission.)

moves from the left to the right, the manager exercises less authority and the subordinates have greater areas of freedom.

Leadership characteristics.

The manager who stays on the left side of the continuum is known as an *authoritarian leader*. He is an individual who tends to: determine all policy; maintain close control of the subordinates; and tell people only what he feels they need to know to get the work done. Conversely, the manager on the right side of the continuum is known as a *democractic leader*. He tends to allow his people to have a say in what goes on; use less control; and encourage feedback from his subordinates. The types of behavior represented on the continuum illustrate that the manager has various options available to him. Figure 14–1 also indicates that there are two types of leadership style. One emphasizes the work to be done (boss-centered leader) and the other gives attention to the people who are doing this work (employee-centered leader). This basic idea has been developed in greater depth by various researchers such as Rensis Likert.

Likert's Management Systems

The basic concept presented in Figure 14–1 has been expanded through the work of Rensis Likert and his associates at the Institute for Social Research at the University of Michigan. After conducting leadership research in literally hundreds of organizations, Likert has discovered four basic styles, which can be depicted on a continuum from System 1 to System 4 as follows:

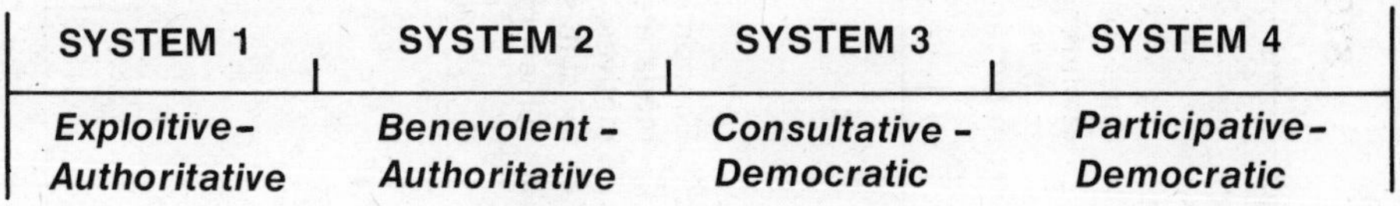

SYSTEM 1	SYSTEM 2	SYSTEM 3	SYSTEM 4
Exploitive–Authoritative	*Benevolent –Authoritative*	*Consultative –Democratic*	*Participative–Democratic*

FIGURE 14–2 Likert's Systems

Four basic systems of leadership.

System 1. Management has little confidence in the subordinates as seen by the fact that they are seldom involved in the decision-making process. Management makes most decisions and passes them down the line, employing threats and coercion when necessary to get things done. Superiors and subordinates deal with each other in an atmosphere of distrust. If an informal organization develops, it generally opposes the goals of the formal organization.

System 2. Management acts in a condescending manner toward the subordinates. Although there is some decision making at the lower levels, it occurs within a prescribed framework. Rewards and some actual punishment are used to motivate the workers. In superior-subordinate interaction, the management acts condescending and the subordinates appear cautious and fearful. Although an informal organization usually develops, it does not always oppose the goals of the formal organization.

System 3. Management has quite a bit of confidence and trust in the subordinates. Although major important decisions are made at the top, subordinates make specific decisions at the lower levels. Two-way communication is in evidence, and there is some confidence and trust between superiors and subordinates. If an informal organization develops, it will either support or offer only slight resistance to the goals of the formal organization.

ORGANIZATIONAL VARIABLE	SYSTEM 1	SYSTEM 2	SYSTEM 3	SYSTEM 4
Leadership Processes Used				
Extent to Which Superiors Have Confidence and Trust in Subordinates	Have no confidence and trust in subordinates	Have condescending confidence and trust, such as master has in servant	Substantial but not complete confidence and trust; still wish to keep control of decisions	Complete confidence and trust in all matters
Character of Motivational Forces				
Underlying Motives Tapped	Physical security, economic needs, and some use of the desire for status	Economic needs and moderate use of ego motives, e.g., desire for status, affiliation and achievement	Economic needs and considerable use of ego and other major motives, e.g., desire for new experiences	Full use of economic, ego, and other major motives such as motivational forces arising from group goals
Character of Communication Process				
Amount of Interaction and Communication Aimed at Achieving Organization's Objectives	Very little	Little	Quite a bit	Much with both individuals and groups

FIGURE 14-3   Likert's Instrument for Measuring Management Systems (Adapted from Rensis Likert, *The Human Organization*, New York, McGraw-Hill Book Company, 1967.)

(Figure 14-3 continued on opposite page.)

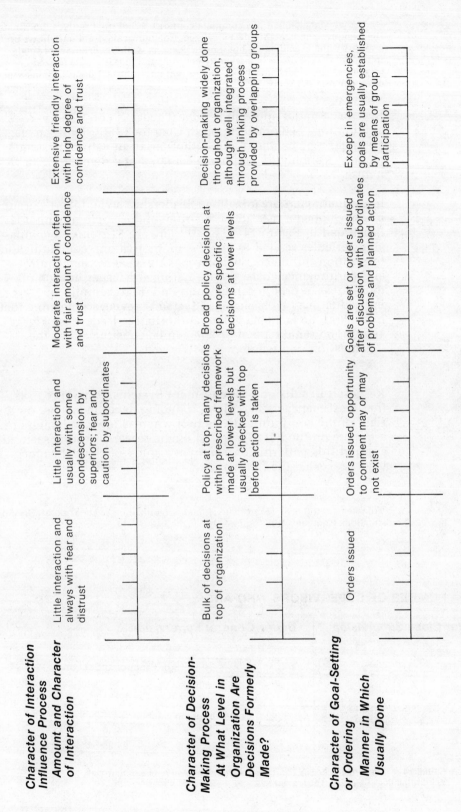

Character of Interaction Influence Process

Amount and Character of Interaction

Little interaction and always with fear and distrust	Little interaction and usually with some condescension by superiors; fear and caution by subordinates	Moderate interaction, often with fair amount of confidence and trust	Extensive friendly interaction with high degree of confidence and trust

Character of Decision-Making Process

At What Level in Organization Are Decisions Formerly Made?

Bulk of decisions at top of organization	Policy at top, many decisions within prescribed framework made at lower levels but usually checked with top before action is taken	Broad policy decisions at top. more specific decisions at lower levels	Decision-making widely done throughout organization, although well integrated through linking process provided by overlapping groups

Character of Goal-Setting or Ordering

Manner in Which Usually Done

Orders issued	Orders issued, opportunity to comment may or may not exist	Goals are set or orders issued after discussion with subordinates of problems and planned action	Except in emergencies, goals are usually established by means of group participation

System 4. **Management has complete confidence and trust in the subordinates. Decision making is highly decentralized. Communication not only flows up and down the organization but among peers as well. Superior-subordinate interaction takes place in a friendly environment and is characterized by mutual confidence and trust. The formal and informal organizations are often one and the same.**[9]

Systems 1 and 4 approximate the Theory X and Theory Y assumptions elaborated upon in Chapter 13. System 1 managers are highly job-centered and authoritarian in nature; System 4 managers are highly employee-centered and democratic in nature.

In evaluating an organization's leadership style, Likert's group has developed a measuring instrument, a sample of which is illustrated in Figure 14–3. In all there are 51 items, encompassing variables related to leadership, motivation, communication, interaction-influence, decision making, goal setting, control and performance goals. By evaluating a manager in each of these areas, a profile can be compiled. For example, an individual may be basically a System 2 manager, meaning that, in general, he is a benevolent-authoritative leader (see Figure 14–2). The same type of profile can be constructed for the organization as a whole.

Research Results and Management Systems.   Likert reports that most managers feel high-producing departments are on the right of the continuum (System 4) whereas low-producing ones are more on the left (System 1). Some research results seem to support this pattern. For example, a study of clerical supervisors revealed the following:

---

[9]Adapted from Rensis Likert, *The Human Organization* (New York: McGraw-Hill Book Company, 1967), pp. 4–10.

NUMBER OF SUPERVISORS WHO ARE:

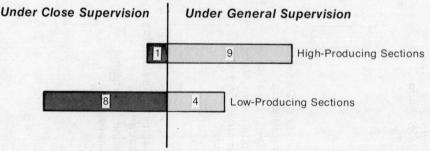

FIGURE 14–4   (Reported in Rensis Likert, *New Patterns of Management,* New York, McGraw-Hill Book Company, 1961, p. 9.)

Those section heads who were closely supervised tended to have lower producing units than those who were under general supervision.

Another study, of railroad maintenance-of-way crews, provided the results in Figure 14–5:

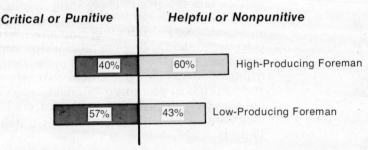

FOREMAN'S REACTION TO A POOR JOB

(in the opinion of the men)

Critical or Punitive   *Helpful or Nonpunitive*

40%   60%   High-Producing Foreman

57%   43%   Low-Producing Foreman

FIGURE 14–5 (Reported in Rensis, Likert, *New Patterns of Management,* McGraw-Hill Book Company, New York, 1961, p. 11.)

Foremen who ignored mistakes or tried to use them as educational experiences in showing their men how to do the job correctly had higher producing sections than their critical-punitive counterparts.

When workers in a service operation were asked how free they felt to set their own pace, the general pattern of responses was similar to that of the previous two studies (see Figure 14–6).

Likert has found that "Supervisors with the best records of performance focus their primary attention on the human aspects of their subordinates' problems and on endeavoring to

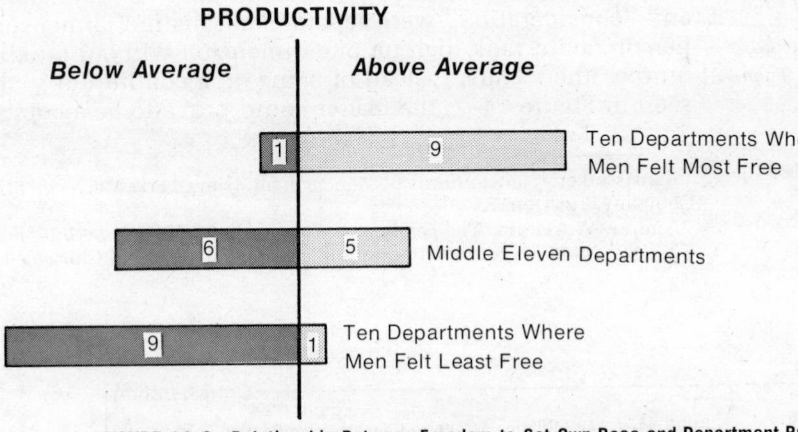

PRODUCTIVITY

Below Average   *Above Average*

1   9   Ten Departments Where Men Felt Most Free

6   5   Middle Eleven Departments

9   1   Ten Departments Where Men Felt Least Free

FIGURE 14–6 Relationship Between Freedom to Set Own Pace and Department Productivity (Reported in Rensis Likert, *New Patterns of Management*, New York, McGraw-Hill Book Company, 1961, p. 8.)

build effective work groups with high performance goals."[10] In short, they are the employee-centered managers.

Two-dimensional Leadership An extension of this leadership continuum is found in two-dimensional leadership models as reflected in the work of Ohio State University researchers and Blake and Mouton's managerial grid.

Ohio State Leadership Research. In 1945, the Bureau of Business Research at Ohio State University began an extensive inquiry into the area of leadership. Eventually, they narrowed down leader behavior into two dimensions: *initiating structure* and *consideration*. Initiating structure referred to "the leader's behavior in delineating the relationship between himself and members of the work-group and endeavoring to establish well-defined patterns of organization, channels of communication, and methods of procedure." Consideration referred to "behavior indicative of friendship, mutual trust, respect, and warmth in the relationship between the leader and the members of his staff."[11]

In gathering information about the behavior of leaders, the researchers developed the now-famous Leader Behavior Description Questionnaire (LBDQ). The LBDQ contains items relating to both "initiating structure" and "consideration" and is designed to describe *how* a leader carries out his activities. Items related to "initiating structure," for example, encompass areas such as the rules and regulations the leader asks his people to follow; the degree to which he tells his followers what is expected of them; and the assignment of members to particular tasks. Items relating to "consideration" deal with topics such as the amount of time the leader finds to listen to group members; his willingness to undertake changes; and whether or not he is friendly and approachable.

"Initiating structure" and "consideration" are separate dimensions. From their work, the researchers found that "initiating structure" and "consideration" were separate and distinct dimensions. A person could rank high on one dimension without ranking low on the other. Thus, instead of being on a continuum such as seen in Figure 14–7, the leader could prove to be a combination

---

[10]Rensis Likert, *New Patterns of Management*, (New York: McGraw-Hill Book Company, 1961), p. 7.
[11]Andrew W. Halpin, *The Leadership Behavior of School Superintendents* (Chicago: Midwest Administration Center, The University of Chicago, 1959), p. 4.

Initiating
Structure ———————————————————————————— Consideration

FIGURE 14–7 An Initiating Structure-Consideration Continuum.

of both dimensions. On the basis of these findings, the researchers were able to develop the following leadership quadrants:

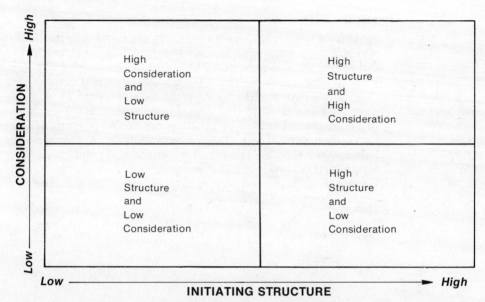

FIGURE 14-8   Ohio State Leadership Quadrants

A leader who is high on "structure" but low on "consideration" is greatly interested in the work side of the job such as planning activities and communicating information necessary to get the tasks done on time. Conversely, a leader who is high on "consideration" but low on "structure" tends to encourage superior-subordinate cooperation and works within an atmosphere of mutual respect and trust. The leader who is high on both dimensions is interested in both the work and the people sides of the job. Which of the three is best? The answer is going to vary. In some situations the individual who is high on structure is superior; other times the manager who is high on consideration is most effective; still other times the leader who is high on both dimensions does the best job.

The quadrant approach to examining leadership behavior is more realistic than a continuum because it permits *simultaneous* consideration of two factors. This undoubtedly accounts for why those who used to view leadership on a continuum are now modifying their views.

Managerial Grid.   Another two-dimensional approach is the managerial grid developed by Robert R. Blake and Jane S. Mouton. After undertaking research of their own, they rejected the Ohio State four-quadrant paradigm and developed their own now-famous grid.[12] Along the vertical axis they placed the term "concern for people" and along the horizontal axis the term "concern for production." In addition, on each axis they placed a scale, ranging from 1 to 9, for measuring *degrees* of concern.

Five basic leadership styles.

As can be seen in Figure 14–9, there are five basic leadership styles. The person who is a 1,1 manager has little concern for either people or production; the term "impoverished" can be used to describe him. The 1,9 manager has great concern for people but little concern for production; the term "country club" is often used to describe this person. The 9,1 manager has a great concern for production but little concern for people; he is often known as a "task" manager. The 5,5 manager has a balance between his concern for people and production although it is certainly not a maximum concern; he is commonly known as a "middle-of-the-road" manager. The 9,9 manager

[12]Robert R. Blake, Jane Srygley Mouton and Benjamin Fruchter, "A Factor Analysis of Training Group Behavior." *Journal of Social Psychology,* October 1962, pp. 121–130.

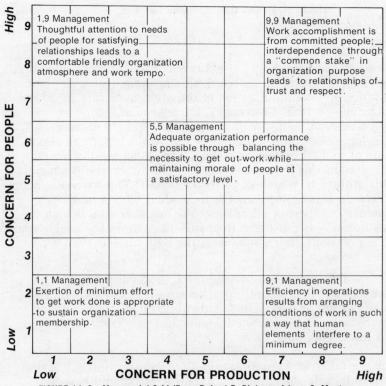

FIGURE 14–9   Managerial Grid (From Robert R. Blake and Jane S. Mouton, "Managerial Facades" *Advanced Management Journal,* July 1966, p. 31. Reprinted with permission.)

demonstrates maximum interest for people and production; the term given to this person is "team" manager.

Unlike much of the research done on leadership, the managerial grid has proven to be a useful tool for developing effective managers. Many companies have found such training helpful to their people in terms of redirecting their orientation and getting, for example, a 1,9 manager more interested in the production side of the job or a 9,1 manager more interested in the people side of the job.

Six Phase Program. In attaining these objectives, Blake and Mouton use a six-phase program. The two initial phases involve management development and the last four help the manager work toward more complex goals of organization development. Briefly outlined, these are:

An implementation program.

Phase 1: Laboratory-Seminar Training. **Conducted by line managers who have already taken the seminar, the purpose of this phase is to introduce the managerial grid concept. During this period managers analyze and assess their own leadership style.**

Phase 2: Team Development. **The concepts from Phase 1 are transferred to the job situation, and each work group or department decides its own 9,9 ground rules and relationships.**

Phase 3: Intergroup Development. **Focus is placed on building 9,9 ground rules and norms between groups in the work unit. Tensions between the groups are identified and examined in way of eliminating them.**

Phase 4: Organizational Goal Setting. **Attention is now focused on overall organizational goals. In addition, the identification of broad problems e.g., cost control, over-all profit improvement and union-management relations, requiring commitments from all levels, is undertaken.**

Phase 5: Goal Attainment. **The goals and problems identified in Phase 4 are studied in greater depth and appropriate actions formulated and implemented.**

Phase 6: Stabilization. **Changes brought about during the first five phases are evaluated and reinforced to prevent any pressure toward "slipping back."**[13]

Which of the managerial grid styles is best? This will depend on the situation. Based on their seminars, Blake and Mouton report that 99.5 per cent of the participants say that a 9,9 style is the soundest way to manage. Furthermore, after taking a reading two to three years after the grid has been used in a company, they have found many managers still holding to their 9,9 position. The second most popular style is 9,1 and the third is 5,5. In short, the most effective style will depend on the situation. Some writers have contended that the grid concept assuming a 9,9 style is best. Actually, it is managers themselves who speak so highly of the 9,9 approach. Blake and Mouton recommend using the style that works best. This "situational

---

[13]Robert R. Blake, Jane S. Mouton, Louis B. Barnes and Larry E. Greiner, "Breakthrough in Organization Development," *Harvard Business Review* November–December, 1964, pp. 137–138.

approach" to leadership also permeates the work of Fred
Fiedler.

**Fiedler's
Contingency
Model**

After years of empirical research, Fiedler has developed what is
commonly called a *contingency model of leadership effectiveness.*[14]

The essence of Fiedler's research is that *any* leadership style
can be effective, depending on the situation. The manager
must therefore be an *adaptive* individual. Employing Blake
and Mouton's terminology, sometimes the leader should be a
9,9 manager, other times a 5,5 and still other times a 1,1
manager. According to Fiedler, three major situational variables
will determine the leader's effectiveness.

1. *Leader-member relations*—**refers to how well the leader is accepted by his
subordinates.**

*The major situa-
tional variables.*

2. *Task structure*—**refers to the degree to which subordinates' jobs are routine
and spelled out in contrast to being vague and undefined.**

3. *Position power*—**refers to the formal authority provided for in the position
the leader occupies.**

Employing these three dimensions, eight combinations or
conditions are possible as seen in Table 14–1.

Which leadership style is most effective? The answer will again
depend on the situation. For example, as seen in Condition I
in Table 14–1, when leader-member relations are good, tasks
are structured and position power is strong, the leader will
be most effective if he is task-oriented. However, as seen in

---

[14]Fred E. Fiedler, *A Theory of Leadership Effectiveness* (New York: McGraw-
Hill Book Company, 1967).

TABLE 14–1   Fiedler's Findings on Leadership Style and Performance

Major Situational Variables

Condition	Leader-Member Relations	Task Structure	Position Power	Effective Leadership Style
I	Good	Structured	Strong	Task-Oriented
II	Good	Structured	Weak	Task-Oriented
III	Good	Unstructured	Strong	Task-Oriented
IV	Good	Unstructured	Weak	Human Relations
V	Moderately Poor	Structured	Strong	Human Relations
VI	Moderately Poor	Structured	Weak	No Data
VII	Moderately Poor	Unstructured	Strong	No Relationship
VIII	Moderately Poor	Unstructured	Weak	Task-Oriented

Condition IV, if leader-member relations are good but the task is unstructured and position power is weak, the employee-oriented leader will be the most effective.

An initial examination of Table 14–1 may leave the reader puzzled. However, a careful scrutinization will reveal that Condition I is the most favorable for the leader; everything is to his advantage. Conversely, Condition VIII is least favorable. Leader-member relations are moderately poor, the task is unstructured and the individual's position power is weak. As one moves from the first to the eighth condition, the situation changes from very favorable to moderately favorable to moderately unfavorable to very unfavorable. In addition, effective leadership style changes from task-oriented (Conditions I to III) to employee-oriented (Conditions IV and V) and then back to task-oriented (Condition VIII). Thus, if the situation is very favorable or very unfavorable, task-oriented leadership style is most effective. If the situation is moderately favorable or unfavorable, human-relations leadership style is most effective.

The importance of Fiedler's model.

Fiedler's model is important for three reasons. First, it places prime emphasis on *effectiveness*. Second, it illustrates that no one leadership style is best; the manager must *adapt* to the situation. Third, it encourages management to *match* the leader with the situation. If the situation is very favorable or very unfavorable, appoint a task-oriented manager; otherwise, use an employee-centered man. Although these findings may appear to conflict with those of, for example, Likert, they actually do not. After all, most situations are going to be of intermediate favorableness or unfavorableness, requiring an employee-centered manager. This is why Likert found such good results occurring among groups with employee-centered leaders (systems 3 and 4). The challenge for management is that of recognizing that effective leadership is contingent upon the three variables described by Fiedler, i.e., leader-member relations, task structure and position power.

Three-dimensional Leadership

In recent years, William Reddin has combined Blake and Mouton's managerial grid with Fiedler's contingency leadership style theory into a 3-D theory of management.[15] In essence, Reddin employs the same basic grid as Blake and Mouton but changes "concern for production" to TO or *task orientation* and "concern for people" to RO or *relationships orientation*. Figure 14–10 depicts the four basic styles of his 3-D theory.

The *separated* style is the one with low task orientation and low relationships orientation; it is separated from both TO and RO. The *dedicated* style describes managerial behavior with a

---

[15]William J. Reddin, *Managerial Effectiveness* (New York: McGraw-Hill Book Company, 1970).

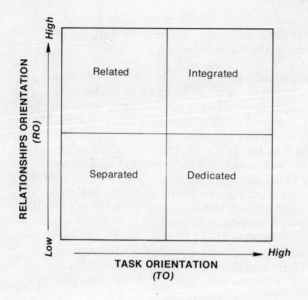

FIGURE 14–10 Reddin's Basic 3-D Management Styles

high task orientation but low relationships orientation; it is behavior that is dedicated to the job. Conversely, the *related* style describes managerial behavior with high relationships orientation but low task orientation; it is behavior that is related to subordinates. The *integrated* style has high task and relationships orientation. It describes managerial behavior, which combines TO and RO.

Reddin has done more than merely redescribe the Blake-Mouton grid in his own words. He has also introduced a third element that turns this two-dimensional grid into a three-dimensional one. It is *effectiveness*, which he defines as "the extent to which a manager achieves the output requirements of his position."[16] Reddin's theory not only goes one step beyond the Blake-Mouton grid, but also reiterates Fiedler's main theme, namely, effectiveness depends on the situation. Some leadership styles are appropriate to a given situation, others are not. Some are more effective, some are less effective. Figure 14–11 depicting Reddin's 3–D model should make this clear.

Effectiveness is important.

The grid in the center, illustrating the four combinations of RO and TO, represents the basic styles. If the manager's behavior is appropriate to the situation, he will be more effective and his style can be found on the back grid in the figure. For example, if his behavior is high relationships-oriented and high task-oriented, the manager will be adopting the style Reddin calls "executive." Conversely, if the behavior is less effective, the manager's style will be found on the front grid, namely, "compromiser."

---

[16]*Ibid.*, p. 3.

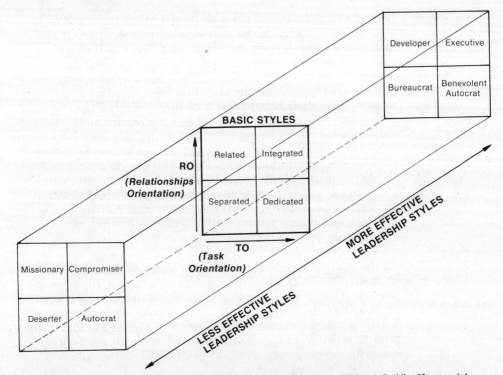

FIGURE 14–11   Reddin's 3-D Leader Effectiveness Model (Adapted from William J. Reddin, *Managerial Effectiveness*, McGraw-Hill Book Company, New York, 1970, p. 230.)

Effectiveness is a matter of degree.

The specific titles given to these four more effective and four less effective styles are not important. Rather, there are two main points to be extracted from this three-dimensional theory. First, every manager will employ some combination of TO and RO in dealing with the situation. This behavior will be either appropriate (more effective) or inappropriate (less effective). Second, one must not view effectiveness as an either-or condition. Rather, it is a continuum, ranging from very effective to very ineffective. Effectiveness is a matter of degree, and the style that was effective in one situation may not be effective in another.

It can now be seen why the 3-D theory is so useful. First, it brings together the concepts of task and relationship orientation, which are proven dimensions of leadership. Second, it stresses that effective leadership behavior depends on the situation. Third, it encourages leaders to be aware of the fact that no one style is always right and as with a night club entertainer constantly facing a new audience, an adaptive style is important.

Life Cycle Theory of Leadership

In recent years, Reddin's 3-D leader effectiveness model has been used as the basis for formulating a *life cycle theory of leadership*. This theory was developed at the Center for

Leadership Research at Ohio University.[17] Its basic theme is that as the maturity of the followers increases, appropriate leadership behavior requires *varying degrees* of task and relationship orientation. The following four stage illustration should make this more clear. When a boy is very young, his parents will initiate all the structure from dressing him to feeding him; their behavior is basically task-oriented. As he gets older, the parents will also begin increasing their relationship behavior by showing trust and respect for him. Now there is a high task and a high relationship orientation. As the boy begins moving into high school and college, however, he starts accepting responsibility for his own behavior. At this point his parents will begin employing low task and high relationship behavior. Finally, when the young man marries and starts his own family, his parents will exercise a minimum of task and relationship orientation with him.

How mature is the worker?

As the individual progresses from a state of immaturity to maturity, he requires different kinds of behavior from his parents. This is also true in a work situation. If the management allows the employee to mature, changing leadership behavior will be needed. This is seen in Figure 14–12. People tend to move from quadrant 1 to quadrant 4, depending on their maturity development. As Hersey and Blanchard note:

> **Life Cycle Theory of Leadership postulates that when working with people of below average maturity, a high task style (quadrant 1) has the best probability of success; whereas in dealing with people of average maturity, the style of quadrants 2 and 3 appear to be most appropriate; and quadrant 4 has the highest probability of success with people of above average maturity.[18]**

[17]The theory was first published by Paul Hersey and Kenneth H. Blanchard, "Life Cycle Theory of Leadership," *Training and Development Journal*, May, 1969, pp. 26–34.
[18]Paul Hersey and Kenneth H. Blanchard, *Management of Organizational Behavior*, 2nd edition (Englewood Cliffs, N.J.: Prentice-Hall, 1972), p. 143.

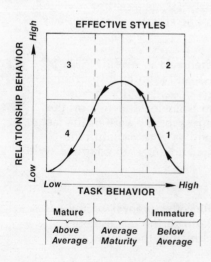

FIGURE 14–12 Life Cycle Theory of Leadership (Adapted from Paul Hersey and Kenneth H. Blanchard, *Management of Organizational Behavior*, 2nd edition, Englewood Cliffs, N.J., Prentice-Hall, 1972, p. 142.)

The life cycle theory complements Blake and Mouton's managerial grid as well as Fiedler's contingency and Reddin's three-dimensional models because it encourages the leader to evaluate his subordinates in determining an effective style.

THE ADAPTIVE LEADER

The personal behavior theories examined in this chapter illustrate there is no such thing as "one best leadership style." The effective manager must be an adaptive individual. Some people contend that an employee-centered manager is more effective than a job-centered manager. Likert's research certainly seems to indicate that this is a valid statement, as does the research of other writers. Davis, for example, notes that "Speaking very generally and recognizing many exceptions, high positive, participative, and employee-centered styles are considered desirable."[19]

No one style of leadership is best.

However, arguments can be made either way. For example, after reviewing a half-dozen experimental studies related to supervisory leadership, Sales found that, in terms of productivity, no one style was consistently superior. Of six studies he reviewed, for which objective production data were available, one reported democratic supervision to be more effective, one reported authoritarian supervision to be more effective and the other four noted no differences of consequence between the two styles.[20] Thus, because there is so much variation, careful consideration of the concepts contained in the Blake-Mouton grid, Fiedler's contingency theory, Reddin's 3-D theory and Hersey and Blanchard's life cycle theory of leadership will continue to be of great value to the practicing manager. The leader must evaluate each situation on its own merits.

The major problem most managers face is that of sizing up the situation. If a system 4 style was always best, the leader would have no trouble determining effective behavior; the challenge would be one of implementing the style properly. However, the issue is never this easy. Furthermore, since effective behavior in one situation may be ineffective in another, as noted by Reddin, the challenge becomes even greater. In short, leadership research has provided a wealth of information about effective behavior and the latest findings all point to the need for a flexible, adaptive style.

SUMMARY

In this chapter leadership has been defined as the process of influencing people to direct their efforts to the attainment of

[19]Davis, *op. cit.*, p. 116.
[20]Stephen M. Sales, "Supervisory Style and Productivity: Review and Theory," *Personnel Psychology*, Autumn 1966, pp. 275–286.

some particular goal(s). What makes an individual an effective leader? Some people feel the answer rests with personal traits and, to some degree, they are right. However, today situation theory is more commonly accepted, that is, some leadership styles are more effective than others, depending on the situation.

One way of studying leadership is by placing the elements of leadership on a continuum. Likert's research, for example, shows that an employee-centered manager is more effective than a job-centered manager. In recent years however, scholars and practitioners alike have found a two-dimensional model more realistic since it sidesteps an either-or approach and allows consideration of two factors. The Ohio State leadership research and the Blake-Mouton grid are illustrations of this two-dimensional approach.

Currently, however, the most widely accepted approach is probably that of Fiedler's contingency model, which places prime emphasis on three major situational variables: leader-member relations, task structure and position power. Fiedler's model is important because it stresses effectiveness, illustrates that no one leadership style is best, and encourages management to match the leader with the situation.

In recent years, Reddin has combined Blake and Mouton's managerial grid with Fiedler's contingency model in arriving at a three-dimensional theory of leadership. Meanwhile, at the Center for Leadership Research at Ohio University, a life cycle theory of leadership has been formulated. Both of these developments have extended knowledge in the area, and both have continued to emphasize the importance of the adaptive leader who can rise to the demands of the situation. In short, the emphasis today is on a flexible style that achieves results.

REVIEW AND STUDY QUESTIONS

1. Of what relevance is trait theory to the study of leadership?

2. Why is situational theory so well accepted today? Explain, incorporating the word "adaptive" into your discussion.

3. What does Likert mean by systems 1, 2, 3 and 4? Which is the best? Why?

4. How do two-dimensional leadership models differ from leader continuum theories? Which is more accurate? Why?

5. What is the managerial grid? What leadership dimensions does it measure?

6. What leadership style is most effective according to managerial grid advocates? Is this right or wrong? Explain.

7. What is the theme of Fiedler's contingency model of leadership effectiveness?

8. What are the three major situational variables in Fiedler's model? Explain.

9. How does Reddin's three-dimensional leadership theory supplement Fiedler's work?

10. How can the life cycle theory of leadership be of value to the manager?

11. What is meant by the "adaptive leader"? Explain.

SELECTED REFERENCES

Blake, R. R., and J. S. Mouton, "Managerial Facades." *Advanced Management Journal*, July 1966, pp. 30–37.

Byron, G. F. "An Investigation of the Relationships among Supervisory Attitudes, Behaviors, and Outputs: An Examination of McGregor's Theory Y." *Personnel Psychology*, Spring 1973, pp. 95–105.

Chaney, F. B., and K. S. Teel. "Participative Management—A Practical Experience." *Personnel*, November–December 1972, pp. 8–19.

Davis, K. *Human Behavior at Work*, 4th edition. New York: McGraw-Hill Book Company, 1972, Chapters 6–10.

Evans, M. G. "Leadership and Motivation: A Core Concept." *Academy of Management Journal*, March 1970, pp. 91–102.

Fiedler, F. E. *A Theory of Leadership Effectiveness*. New York: McGraw-Hill Book Company, 1967.

Fiedler, F. E., and M. M. Chemers. *Leadership and Effective Management*. Glenview, Ill.: Scott, Foresman and Company, 1974.

Filley, A. C., and R. J. House. *Managerial Process and Organizational Behavior*. Glenview, Ill.: Scott, Foresman and Company, 1969.

Heller, F. A. "Leadership, Decision Making and Contingency Theory." *Industrial Relations*, May 1973, pp. 183–199.

Hersey, P., and K. H. Blanchard. *Management of Organizational Behavior*, 2nd edition. Englewood Cliffs, New Jersey: Prentice-Hall, 1972.

Hersey, P., and K. H. Blanchard. "Life Cycle Theory of Leadership." *Training and Development Journal*, May 1969, pp. 26–34.

Likert, R. *The Human Organization*. New York: McGraw-Hill Book Company, 1967.

Likert, R. *New Patterns of Management*. New York: McGraw-Hill Book Company, 1961.

Reddin, W. J. *Managerial Effectiveness*. New York: McGraw-Hill Book Company, 1970.

Tannenbaum, R., and W. H. Schmidt. "How to Choose a Leadership Pattern," *Harvard Business Review*, May–June 1973, pp. 162–175; 178–180.

Tosi, H. L. "The Effect of the Interaction of Leader Behavior and Subordinate Authoritarianism." *Personnel Psychology*, Autumn 1973, pp. 339–350.

Yukl, G. "Toward A Behavioral Theory of Leadership." *Organizational Behavior and Human Performance*, July 1971, pp. 414–440.

CASE: A MATTER OF STYLE

Whisk Insurance, a medium-sized insurance company located in New England, had been taking steps to improve the effectiveness of its management. As a result, it contracted with a private consulting company for some management training. Some of the sessions involved familiarization with and use of the managerial-grid technique. The managers were asked to rate themselves, and their subordinates were also given an opportunity to comment on the leadership ability of their superiors. Chuck Hansen, one of the seminar participants, had been rated as a 7,7 manager by his people. Burt Edems, another participant, had been rated as a 1,9.

When this phase was complete, the trainers took these basic styles and tried to explain why a 9,9 style was the most desirable by stressing the importance of placing maximum emphasis on both the production and the people side of the job. However, both Chuck and Burt disagreed, and both used the same reasoning. Each had excellent efficiency ratings and had been told that they would be promoted within the next six months. Their argument was that their current style was effective. Why should they worry about becoming 9,9 managers? Their 7,7 and 1,9 styles were apparently good enough. They referred to the 9,9 concept as "pie in the sky."

Questions

1. Is the 9,9 concept "pie in the sky" or does it have value? Explain.

2. What answer would you give to both Chuck and Burt if you were the trainer?

3. Is the trainer right or wrong? Explain.

CASE: OLD HABITS

George Chila was known around the company as a "tough cookie." If one had to rate him in terms of Systems 1 to 4, he was definitely a System-1 man. However, he was also a good manager. He seemed to get his work out on time, his men appeared to have respect for him, and he showed promise as a manager. George's superior, Frank Dunbar, decided to send him to a week-long training program entitled "Developing An Effective Leadership Style." Mr. Dunbar believed the training would help improve George's style.

During the program, George was introduced to many different concepts, from Likert's four systems to the Blake-Mouton grid, from Reddin's three-dimensional theory to Fiedler's contingency

model. When it was all over George returned to work and began
to practice much of what he had learned. If employee-
centered managers are often more effective than job-centered
managers, maybe I should try to change my style, he reasoned.
In line with this thinking George took two steps. First, he
called a meeting of the men to discuss work assignments and
get their opinion of things. Second, he told them that from that
point on there was going to be less checking on their work.
He was going to employ loose control and rely on them to do
their jobs right.

For the next three months things went along smoothly. At
first the workers were puzzled by George's sudden change in
style. However, after they realized that he really intended to
be more "employee-oriented" than before, they increased their
output and began to establish lines of communication with
him. George liked the new approach and so did the men.
However, as the end of the year approached, the usual stress
on increased productivity began to manifest itself. First, there
was a memo from top management which was passed out to all
the supervisors. Then Mr. Dunbar called George in to tell him
to keep things going at as fast a clip as possible. Slowly, but
surely, the pressure began to build up. Overtime work was
assigned to the men, and the company went to Saturday and
Sunday shifts. George found himself working a 12-hour day,
six-day week.

With the increased pressure, George started making more and
more decisions without consulting the men. He assigned jobs
as he saw fit and spent more time than usual out on the line
checking up on things. By the middle of October, it was evident
that he had reverted back to his old style. This continued until
the beginning of the year when things were finally back to
normal. During the first week of January he called the men
together.

Listen, Mr. Dunbar has just talked to me and he says we did a real good
job during that end-of-the-year rush. Now that we're back on an even keel,
let's start talking about job assignments and how we're going to handle things
for the next three months. I'd like to show you what Mr. Dunbar wants us to
do and perhaps some of you have ideas on how we can handle these things.

It was then that one of the men spoke up.

Hey, George, before we get into that let me ask you a question. Why didn't
you ask us to help you draw up some work plans during that big end-of-the-
year push?

Well, I don't know. I guess I was just too busy getting things done to think
about it. You know how it is when you get pushed. You find yourself going
back to your old way of doing things. Well, if you find me doing that again,
let me know.

The men promised to do so.

Questions

1. According to his new style, in which would you place George: system 1, 2, 3 or 4? Explain.

2. Why were the men skeptical when George switched from being a work-oriented manager to an employee-oriented manager?

3. How can one keep from slipping back to his old leadership style? Explain.

CASE: THE FAST GUN

Hank Sidney has been president of his company for seven years, and initially things had gone very well. Sales increased an average of 17 per cent a year, and return on investment during this period had never been lower than 15.3 per cent. However, slowly but surely other firms began to realize the kind of profits that could be attained in the industry and they began moving in. As they did, competition increased and the big profit margins began to shrink. Prices dropped as each company tried to capture and retain large market shares. Within a few years, Hank's firm was barely able to keep its head above water. It was then that the board of directors decided that Hank had to go.

This was not an easy choice for the directors to make. Everyone liked Hank. He was a pleasant, easy going, friendly individual. The management respected him and the workers seemed to hold him in the highest regard. Nevertheless, the board felt that the president was unable to turn the company around, and they would have to get someone who could.

The eventual choice was Fred Whitney, a general manager who worked for one of the company's competitors. Fred told the board that he would take the job only if he were allowed to do things his way. In turn, he promised results. The board agreed.

Within six months of his appointment, Fred had fired over half of the old management team and one-third of the workers. In addition, he refused to hire any new personnel. If someone quit or was fired, the others were required to pick up his work. When asked about this, Fred gave the following explanation:

When I came in here the company was going broke. There were too many people in management positions who were doing nothing. I got rid of them. The workers were having a field day. The average guy was putting in a five-hour day. Well, I changed all that by tightening things up. Now everyone around here has to pull his own weight. There's no room for fat when a company is in trouble, so I got rid of it.

It was difficult to argue with Fred in light of the fact that his leadership style seemed to get results. For example, within 18 months of the time he took over, the company had as large a share of the market as ever and return on investment had risen to over 16 per cent.

Some of the directors, however, felt that Fred's style was too rough. They believed that the company was going to get in trouble if it thought a system-1, task-oriented manager could continue to achieve such results in the long-run. These directors acknowledged the fact that Fred had been very successful thus far, but they wondered if there would not be a backlash. Doesn't the task-centered manager run the risk of driving off his best workers and irreparably damaging morale? they asked. One of the directors compared Fred with a fast gun in the old west. "You know," he said, "a fast gun would be brought in to save the town. But once he had done his job the mayor would have to get rid of him because he was bad for the town's reputation. I think Fred falls into this category." The chairman of the board disagreed. "We were elected by the stockholders to protect their interests. When we brought in Fred we told him he could do things his way. Besides, we have to evaluate a man's leadership style by how effective it is. And Fred sure has been effective." On this point no one had anything to say.

Questions

1. Why was Hank ineffective in turning the company around?

2. How do you account for such results? After all, isn't an employee-centered leader superior to a task-centered leader?

3. Do you think Fred should be replaced or retained? Explain.

CASE: CONTINGENCY CHAOS

Harvey Kendehl, a university administrator of a large eastern state-wide system, had just returned from a week-long training program on leadership styles and techniques. Before going back to his office, he dropped in to visit his superior, Dr. Henry Adams, Ed.D., for a few minutes.

Well, Harvey, how did you like that seminar?

Oh, fine, Dr. Adams, just fine.

I sent you there, Harvey, because I feel you have real potential as a manager. I attended that seminar last year and thought it was great. You know, money

for higher education is going to run out. We have to be more efficient with our resources and this means placing a greater stress on effective management. Now tell me, what did you learn?

Well, to be quite frank, Dr. Adams, I'm not really sure.

What do you mean?

Well, we spent an awful lot of time looking at various leadership theories. You know, Likert's management systems, Blake and Mouton's managerial grid, Fiedler's contingency model and Reddin's three-dimensional theory. Stuff like that.

It sounds like you picked up a great deal of knowledge. What seems to be the problem?

It gets back to implementation, Dr. Adams. I find I'm confused about how to apply this stuff.

In what way?

Well, the trainers seemed to believe that Fiedler's contingency model has a great deal of value for effective leadership. But this contingency idea is what throws me. I mean, if effectiveness depends on the situation, then the manager has to size up each one on its own merits. But I think there must be an easier way. For example, they never really proved to me that a system-4 manager was not better than a system-1 manager. Therefore, why not be a system-4 individual and worry about the exceptions to the rule when they crop up? Why spend so much time worrying about each individual situation? Why not develop an effective style and then deal with the exceptions when they manifest themselves?

That certainly is the way most managers do it. But isn't that approach too general? After all, you're not dealing with the individual situation; you're just playing the odds and assuming that your basic style will help you through any situation.

Sure, but at least I have a basic style to get me through most situations. I think if you try to be too much of a "contingent" manager, you'll never be able to develop any one style effectively. I'd rather try to be a system-4 manager than subscribe to Fiedler's contingency theory, which to me leads to an overly flexible and chaotic style.

Questions

1. Evaluate Harvey's comments. What do you think?

2. What response should Dr. Adams make? Be explicit in your answer, bringing into your discussion Fiedler's contingency model and Reddin's 3-D theory.

The Future of Management Theory

The goal of this final section of Part II, which consists entirely of Chapter 15, is to examine modern management theory in terms of where it is now and where it appears to be headed. Primary consideration will be given to the systems school and the situational (or contingency) school of thought, since both appear to hold an important place in the future of management theory.

The beginning of Chapter 15 is devoted to a discussion of the emerging systems school of thought. This is followed by an examination of both general systems theory and applied systems concepts. Next, attention is focused on the general applicability of the systems approach for the practicing manager. Primary consideration is given to viewing the organization as an open system. Then, the three levels of management in the hierarchy are examined in systems terms. Finally, a review of the current status and future development of management theory will be undertaken.

CHAPTER 15

MANAGEMENT THEORY: CURRENT STATUS AND FUTURE DIRECTION

Sections B to D of Part II have presented the current major schools of management thought. The question now is, where does management theory go from here? The answer is, no one knows for sure. However, two major lines of thinking are currently popular. The first contends that the three schools will merge into a systems school. One group of authors has summarized the position in this way:

Although the process, behavioral, and quantitative approaches have been widely adopted, a growing group of practitioners and academicians have felt that another approach which would encompass most, if not all, of these necessary segmental approaches was necessary. They felt that a systems approach would encompass the subsystems emanating from each of the other approaches.[1]

If this is true, the future development of modern management theory can be represented by the following illustration:

---

[1]Max S. Wortman and Fred Luthans, ed., *Emerging Concepts in Management* (New York: The Macmillan Company, 1969), p. 329.

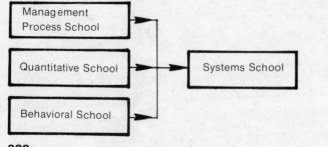

FIGURE 15-1 The Future Direction of Management Theory: One View

There seems to be more support, however, for the second point of view, which holds that there is already a systems school of thought in existence and that the trend is now toward a situational or contingency theory of management. This thinking is represented by the following illustration:

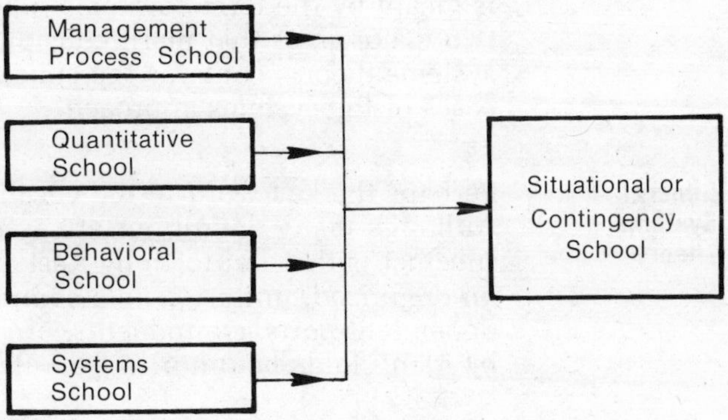

FIGURE 15-2 The Future Direction of Management Theory: A Second View

```
┌──────────────┐
│ Management   │──┐
│ Process School│  │
└──────────────┘  │
┌──────────────┐  │          ┌──────────────┐
│ Quantitative │──┤          │ Situational or│
│ School       │  ├─────────▶│ Contingency   │
└──────────────┘  │          │ School        │
┌──────────────┐  │          └──────────────┘
│ Behavioral   │──┤
│ School       │  │
└──────────────┘  │
┌──────────────┐  │
│ Systems      │──┘
│ School       │
└──────────────┘
```

If one keeps in mind that Figures 15–1 and 15–2 represent only two major points of view, and many scholars and practitioners have their own ideas, it should be evident that there is currently much disagreement about the future direction of management theory.

One thing, however, does appear clear. Any examination of the current status and future direction of management theory must consider the subject of *systems*. Questions such as: What is a system? How is the concept of value to management theory? Is there a systems school of thought? all merit consideration. The goals of this chapter are to deal with these questions and, in the process, offer some general guidance about the direction management theory will take in the next decade. Attention will first be focused on what some people call the "systems school," and on the questions, what is the basic philosophy of this school and why has it not been discussed previously? Then the general area of systems, as applied to organizations, will be examined. Finally, management theory in the future will be discussed. Specific consideration will be given to:

a. the systems school of management;
b. the organization as an open system;
c. the importance of adaptive and maintenance mechanisms in ensuring organization survival;
d. entropy and its effect on open and closed systems;
e. the organization as a contrived system;
f. totally adaptive organization systems;
g. the three levels of managerial systems;
h. the types of managers who function at each of these three managerial levels;
i. the importance of viewing the organization and its personnel from a systems point of view; and
j. management theory in the future.

THE SYSTEMS SCHOOL

The systems school is considered by some to be a new school of management thought that emerged sometime in the 1960's. Although this is open to question, there are many computer and systems analyst people who believe that systems theory has now developed to the stage where the formation of a systems school is justified. Whether or not they are right, it is useful for the student of management to have a general idea of what is meant by the term "systems school." In essence, there are two major areas that merit consideration. The first, general systems theory, contains the conceptual and philosophical bases of the systems approach.

General Systems Theory

Perhaps the key word in the vocabulary of this school is *system*. Although many definitions are available, one of the most succinct is that put forth by Kast and Rosenzweig. A system is *an organized, unitary whole composed of two or more inter-dependent parts, components, or subsystems and delineated by identifiable boundaries from its environmental suprasystem.*[2]

Many systems management concepts originated with general systems theory.

Systems school advocates see all variables in the environment as mutually dependent and interactive. However, before examining the importance of the systems concept to management, some attention should be focused on what is called *general systems theory*. Systems theorists believe that many of the concepts of systems management originated with general systems theory. In addition, an examination of this topic provides a basis for analyzing other important management related areas, including: the movement of individuals into and out of the system; the interaction of individuals with their environment; the interaction of individuals with each other; and the general growth and stability problems of systems.[3]

Systems Levels.   Perhaps the most famous article written on systems theory is "Systems Theory—The Skeleton of Science"[4] by Kenneth Boulding. In this article Boulding put forth a classification of the nine hierarchical levels in the universe.

He described them as follows:

1. The first level can be called the level of *frameworks* and represents a static structure. Examples include geography and the anatomy of the universe.

2. The next level could be referred to as the level of *clockworks* and is characterized by a simple, dynamic system with predetermined, necessary motions. The solar system is an illustration.

3. Next is the level of the control mechanism or cybernetic system, nicknamed the *thermostat* level. The homeostasis model, so important in physiology, is an illustration.

[2]Fremont E. Kast and James E. Rosenzweig, *Organization and Management*, 2nd edition (New York: McGraw–Hill Book Company, 1974), p. 101.
[3]Kenneth E. Boulding, "General Systems Theory—The Skeleton of Science," *Management Science*, April 1956, pp. 200–202.
[4]*Ibid.*, pp. 197–208.

4. Then comes the open system of the self-maintaining structure, which can be called the level of the *cell*. At this level, life and reproduction enter the scheme.

Boulding's system classification scheme.

5. The fifth level is the *genetic-societal level*. This is typified by the plant, which dominates the empirical world of the botanist.

6. Next comes the *animal* kingdom. It is characterized by teleological behavior, increased mobility and self-awareness.

7. Then comes the *human* level. In addition to possessing nearly all the characteristics of animal systems, the individual is also capable of employing language and symbols.

8. The eighth level is that of *social organizations*. At this level, concern is given to the content and meaning of messages, the nature and dimension of value systems, the transcription of images into historical records, the subtle symbolizations of art, music and poetry, and the complex gamut of human emotions.

9. The final level of the structure is *transcendental systems*. These are the ultimates, the absolutes and the inescapable unknowables, which exhibit systematic structure and relationship.[5]

A cursory review of these levels indicates that the first three are concerned with physical or mechanical systems. As such, they have basic value for people in the physical sciences such as astronomy and physics. The next three levels deal with biological systems. They are thus of interest to biologists, botanists and zoologists. The last three are concerned with human and social systems and are of importance to the arts, humanities and, in a more specialized way, modern management.

This classification scheme is important in understanding the systems school because it contains the basic theme of the systems approach: all phenomena, whether in the universe at large or in a business organization, are related in some way.

A second contribution of the article is the emphasis it places on *integration*. One of Boulding's major contentions is that specific disciplines are too narrow in their focus, whereas a general approach lacks substantive content.

Somewhere however between the specific that has no meaning and the general that has no content there must be. . .an optimum degree of generality. It is the contention of the General Systems Theorists that this optimum degree of generality in theory is not always reached by the particular sciences.[6]

Integration of knowledge from many fields is encouraged.

In order to overcome this deficiency, Boulding recommends an integration of knowledge from many fields. "Because, in a sense, each level incorporates all those below it, much valuable information and insights can be obtained by applying low-level systems to high-level subject matter."[7]

---

[5] *Ibid.*, pp. 202–205.
[6] *Ibid.*, pp. 197–198.
[7] *Ibid.*, p. 207.

The thinking of these systems theorists, however, is not confined to such an esoteric area as general systems theory. They have also put forth some concepts that have practical application.

Applied Concepts

Management decision models.

When arguing for a systems school, proponents like to point to useful management tools and techniques that apply the systems concept. Some of these ideas, such as operations research, simulation, PERT and the critical path method, are directly related to *management decision models*.

Another set of tools and techniques can be placed under the heading of the *systems approach*. These are tools that help the manager choose a course of action by analyzing objectives and comparing costs, risks and payoffs associated with the alternate strategies. By employing a big picture or systems approach, the manager can evaluate the interrelationships of all factors under consideration. One such approach, discussed in Chapter 9, is PPBS. Others are systems engineering, which will be examined later in this chapter, and adaptive organization structures, which will be discussed in Chapters 17 and 18.

Systems approach.

Information systems.

A third set of systems tools and techniques are in the category of *information systems*. These are systems that are designed to provide the manager with data and knowledge useful in carrying out his job such as computers, information theory and control systems.

These three main types of tools and techniques all provide illustrations of how the systems concept has proved useful to business. They are classified in Figure 15–3.

A School or A Subsystem?

Is there a systems school of management?

Based on the information so far, it appears that the systems ideas may well be sufficiently different from those of the process, quantitative and behavioral approaches to justify a fourth school. Critics, however, argue that the systems concept is already being used by the three major schools. For example, many of the ideas in Figure 15–3 have already been examined in the last eight chapters. In addition, process advocates argue that management theory consists of planning, organizing and controlling processes; each is thus an interrelated subsystem of the overall management system. Behaviorists claim that for years they have been viewing the organization as a group of interrelated formal and informal systems. Quantitative school proponents feel that the systems school is really a part of their own; certainly that was the way it was presented in Chapter 6. Systems analysts, computer programmers, and so on, were all placed in the quantitative school, and there is a good reason for this. As one researcher has noted:

Starting in about 1970, the quantitative approach turned away from emphasis on narrow operations research techniques toward a broader perspective of

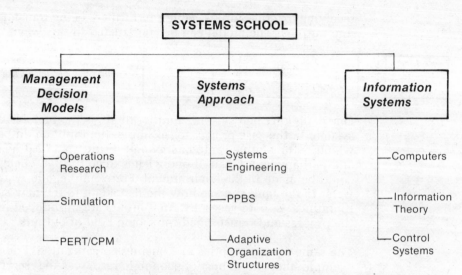

FIGURE 15–3   A Classification of the Systems School (Adapted from Richard J. Schonberger, "A Taxonomy of Systems Management," *Nebraska Journal of Economics and Business*, Spring 1973, p. 36.)

management science. The management science approach incorporates quantitative decision techniques and model building as in the OR approach, but it also incorporates computerized information systems and operations management. This latter emphasis in the quantitative approach marked the return toward a more broadly based management theory.[8]

Is the systems approach, then, sufficiently different to justify a new school or is it really a subsystem of one or more of the current approaches? Whatever the answer, it does appear that by the 1980's there will indeed be a fourth school of management thought. For the purposes of this text, however, the school will be viewed as still in its formative stage and will be considered in the quantitative area.

Systems concept has general value for management.

Yet the systems *concept* itself is too important to be dropped without further elaboration. It contains many useful ideas with which the student of management should be familiar. One of these is that of viewing the organization as an open system.

THE ORGANIZATION AS AN OPEN SYSTEM

Open system constantly interacts with its external environment.

When the planning process was discussed in Chapter 7, the areas of environmental analysis and forecasting were examined. Likewise, in Chapter 8, when the organizing process was reviewed, common forms of departmentalization were examined. However, when these processes are analyzed from a systems approach, the organization is seen as operating in an *open system*, constantly interacting with its external environment. These open systems are characterized by *flexible equilibrium* as depicted in Figure 15–4. They are continually

[8]Fred Luthans, "The Contingency Theory of Management," *Business Horizons*, June 1973, p. 68.

receiving external inputs, which in turn are being transformed into outputs. The model can be constructed in this way:

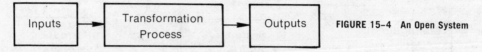

FIGURE 15–4   An Open System

One common open system, familiar to all, is the biological system. In the case of fish, for example, the input could be food, which is transformed into energy and results in a healthy, and perhaps larger, fish. If one wishes to go further, changes could be made in the environment. For example, add warm water to the tank and see how the fish adapt to the new surroundings. In both cases, external inputs are introduced into the process and transformed into some kind of outputs.

The same process applies to a business organization. For example, there are a host of economic resources that serve as inputs such as men, money, machines, material and information. In systems theory thinking, these can be combined in some fashion (organization process) for the purpose of attaining certain output, as seen in Figure 15–5:

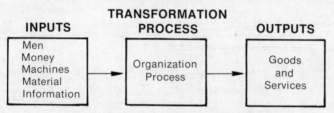

FIGURE 15–5   The Organization as an Open System

This basic model can be made more sophisticated by breaking down the organization process into some preliminary design such as marketing, production and finance departments as in Figure 15–6. In this illustration, the relationships between each of the departments and (a) the external environment, (b) the other two departments and (c) the organization at large become clearer.

FIGURE 15–6   A More Refined Design of an Open System

Adaptive and Maintenance Mechanisms

Two other important systems concepts useful in analyzing open systems are adaptive and maintenance structures. In an open system, the organization must be able to adapt. At the same time, however, it must maintain a relative state of balance.

There are thus two mechanisms in operation. The first, *adaptivity*, encourages response to the external and internal environments. The second, *maintenance*, attempts to stop the system from changing so rapidly that it is thrown out of balance. These two forces may sometimes be in conflict, but both are vital to an organization's survival.

Adaptive forces lead to change.

Adaptive forces lead to change and keep the organization viable. On the other hand, they can create tension and stress. For example, consider the case of a business firm that wishes to hire a junior accountant. The company needs the man to help handle the increase in accounts that has occurred over the last year. It turns out, however, that the starting salary for such an individual is higher than that of some lower-level managers who have been with the firm for three years. The company must hire the man if it is to keep up, but to do so may create anxiety among some of the established personnel. Although this may be a natural reaction, it illustrates the problems associated with adapting to environmental conditions.

Maintenance forces are conservative influences.

Maintenance forces are conservative influences that work to prevent disequilibrium. The problem is that they may stunt an organization's growth by encouraging timidity when boldness is needed. In addition, excessive attention to maintenance factors can result in a break down of the open system. In Figure 15–6 this could begin to happen if the firm decided not to hire the new man. By choosing to maintain present conditions, the company is failing to adapt to its external environment. If it continues to ignore developments in the external arena by concentrating all of its attention on maintaining intracompany equilibrium, the firm will become a closed system. When this occurs, the business faces the danger of entropy.

Entropy and Contrived Adaptivity

Closed systems are characterized by entropy.

One of the characteristics of a closed system is entropy. This is a term that originated in thermodynamics and applies to all physical systems. It refers to the tendency of a closed system to move toward a chaotic, random or inert state. Webster defines *entropy* as "the ultimate state reached in the degradation of the matter and energy of the universe."[9] All closed physical systems are subject to this force of entropy. Over a period of time the force increases and, ultimately, the system stops. Since it is a closed network with no external inputs, there is really no hope for survival. Eventually, entropy will take its toll.

In open biological and social systems, however, entropy can be arrested and may even be transformed into negative entropy. This is brought about through external inputs. Biological

---

[9]*Webster's Third New International Dictionary*, volume 1 (Chicago: Encyclopedia Britannica, Inc., 1966), p. 759.

systems, at least in the short-run, provide a good illustration. Drawing upon the resources in their surroundings, organisms are able to survive for a period of time. For most humans, food, clothing and shelter are the basic resources. As one ages, increased attention is given to medicine. Eventually, however, death occurs, for even biological systems are subject to deterioration.

Social systems are contrived.

Social systems, however, are another matter; they are not mechanical or biological, they are *contrived*. Human beings establish them for a particular purpose and although the individuals may die, others can take their place and keep the system alive. As Katz and Kahn note:

> Social structures are essentially contrived systems. They are made of men and are imperfect systems. They can come apart at the seams overnight, but they can also outlast by centuries the biological organisms which originally created them. The cement which holds them together is essentially psychological rather than biological. Social systems are anchored in the attitudes, perceptions, beliefs, motivations, habits, and expectations of human beings.[10]

In order for the social system to continue, however, there must be the proper balance between maintenance and adaptive forces.

> If the system is to survive, *maintenance substructures* must be elaborated to hold the walls of the social maze in place. Even these would not suffice to insure organizational survival, however. The organization exists in a changing and demanding environment, and it must adapt constantly to the changing environmental demands. *Adaptive structures* develop in organizations to generate appropriate responses to external conditions.[11]

These systems concepts of flexible equilibrium, adaptive mechanisms, maintenance mechanisms, entropy and contrived adaptivity are all useful in understanding the truly dynamic nature of the modern organization. It is important to realize, however, that an effective organization can also employ these concepts in maintaining a viable, adaptive, on-going organization system.

TOTALLY ADAPTIVE ORGANIZATION SYSTEMS

Adaptive organizations can survive indefinitely.

The organization is a man-made system, capable of indefinite survival if the proper balance between maintenance and adaptive forces can be attained. Figure 15–7 provides an illustration of a totally adaptive business organization system. The figure shows how marketing and production activities can be carried on in the attainment of organizational goals. The finance department and the rest of the enterprise are represented in the boxes entitled "Current State of the Organization," indicating that the decisions made by both marketing and production are going to depend on conditions in the remainder of the

---

[10]Daniel Katz and Robert L. Kahn, *The Social Psychology of Organizations* (New York: John Wiley & Sons, Inc., 1966), p. 33.
[11]*Ibid.*, p. 39.

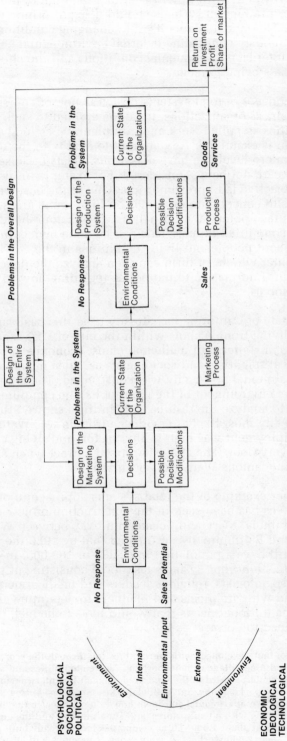

FIGURE 15-7 A Totally Adaptive Organization System (Adapted from Stanley D. Young, "Organization Total System," *Proceedings of the 4th Annual Midwest Management Conference*, Carbondale, Illinois, 1966.)

organization. There is also a control process built into the model which, in turn, will lead to a redesign of the marketing and/or production systems should disequilibrium manifest itself. The model adapts itself to changing conditions by continuously contrasting external environmental conditions with internal environmental conditions and the effect of both on the goals being pursued.

Total systems design has great promise.

The concept of total systems design is not, of course, restricted to business organizations. It can be applied to such diverse activities as police work and city planning as long as the *total* system is examined. Any attempt to deal with the organization on a micro-level can have disastrous effects because all input factors are not being considered. For example, in police work the objective is to prevent crime. One of the best ways to do this is to concentrate resources on high-crime areas and thereby discourage potential criminals as well as apprehend those who have committed crimes. This can be done by feeding information about people and living conditions in the city into a computer which, in turn, can then analyze the data and provide relevant information to the police regarding how to organize their forces.

The state of California has already used this basic approach in identifying trouble spots within the city of Los Angeles. Employing a team of mathematicians, economists, physicists, political scientists and sociologists as "idea men," a mathematical model of the city was constructed. Then, after simulating the environment of the metropolis, the computer was called upon to analyze the results. The findings showed that the area of the city most likely to evidence trouble was Watts. Unemployment was high in this sector, and living conditions were very poor. The analysis proved correct when shortly thereafter the famous Watts riots occurred.

Another example of the total systems approach to organizing resources has been seen in the construction of new cities such as Columbia, Maryland, located midway between Washington D.C. and Baltimore. It is estimated that by 1980 the 14,000-acre city will have a population in excess of 100,000. In constructing the site, an *ad hoc* systems task force consisting of psychologists, sociologists, religious leaders and medical personnel worked with architects and planners to determine all the social and institutional needs that would have to be met. One writer described the project as follows:

The plan that developed, with constant testing through the economic model, comprised nine village or neighborhood-type communities and a downtown business center; a third of the land area was left for interweaving natural woodlands, parks, paths, and artificial lakes. Since last spring, close to 500 homes, garden apartments, and town houses have risen in the first of the villages, along with a bank, stores, and supermarket, and the population now stands at about 1,000. Three companies have already built plants that will employ some 2,500 workers. A wide range of incomes will be accomodated, with homes ranging from $13,000 to $15,000 and upward and rentals from $100. The economic model is revised quarterly to keep it responsive to the market and to control finances and the pace of development, which proceeds steadily on critical-path scheduling to keep the multitude of parallel projects going on simultaneously in phase to meet the end objectives.[12]

It should now be apparent that systems concepts are very useful in both understanding and relating an organization to its environment. However, the general concept can also be applied within the firm in the examination of managerial systems.

MANAGERIAL SYSTEMS

Having viewed the organization as an open, adaptive system, attention will now be focused on *managerial systems*. Parsons has suggested three managerial levels in the hierarchy of complex organizations: technical, organizational[13] and institutional.

The *technical* level is concerned with the actual production and distribution of products and services. This not only entails turning out physical output but also includes the areas that support this activity, i.e., research and development, operations research and accounting.

The *organizational* level coordinates and integrates work performance at the technical level. It is concerned with obtaining the continued flow of inputs into the system; maintaining the necessary markets for the outputs from the system; determining the nature of technical tasks; ascertaining the scale of operations; and establishing operating policies.

The *institutional* level is concerned with relating the activities of the organization to the environmental system. As Parson notes:

. . .not only does. . .an organization. . .have to operate in a social environment which imposes the conditions governing the processes of disposal and procurement, it is also part of a wider social system which is the source of the "meaning," legitimation, or higher level support which makes the implementation of the organization's goals possible. Essentially, this means that just as a technical organization (at a sufficiently high level of the division of labor) is controlled and "serviced" by a managerial organization, so, in turn, is the managerial organization controlled by the "institutional" structure and agencies of the community.[14]

The managerial system spans all three levels by organizing the people, directing the technical work and relating the organization to its environment. However, before examining the role

---

[12]Lawrence Lessing, "Systems Engineering Invades the City," *Fortune*, January 1968, p. 220.
[13]Parsons called the second level "the management level," but since there are managers at all three levels, the middle one will be referred to here as the "organizational level."
[14]Talcott Parsons, *Structure and Process in Modern Societies* (New York: The Free Press, 1960), pp. 63–64.

of the manager in this overall system, a closer view of these three levels is in order. First, it is possible to illustrate them as a composite system, as in Figure 15–8:

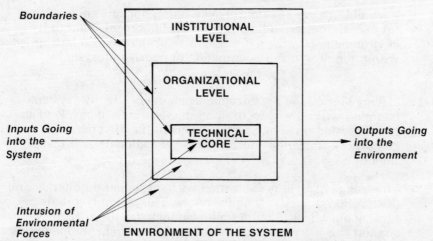

FIGURE 15–8   The Organization as a Composite System (Adapted from Thomas A. Petit, "A Behavioral Theory of Management," *Academy of Management Journal,* December 1967, p. 346.)

Technical level is highly closed system-oriented.

The technical level or core is concerned with turning out a product or service at a profit. In order to do this, it often attempts to set up a boundary between itself and the external environment, thereby forming a closed system. The reasoning is that if the environment is too dynamic, people will never get anything done; they will be continually responding to external influences. Modern technology provides an illustration of the intruding environmental force and its effect at this level. For example, many times a company will find that the product it is manufacturing is obsolete even before it leaves the assembly line. However, at some point in time the design must be frozen and production begun. The technical core is subject to external influences, but it does attempt to minimize them.

Institutional level is very open system-oriented.

Conversely, at the institutional level there is a great degree of uncertainty over environmental conditions, and the organization is unable to set up major boundaries. As a result, management at this level is by nature a very open system, and primary attention is devoted to innovation or adaptation.

Organizational level coordinates other two levels.

The organizational level operates between these two extremes. It coordinates the technical and institutional levels; tries to straighten out irregularities and disturbances occurring in both; and serves as an all-around mediator. In a manner of speaking, it is a buffer between the maintenance forces (technical level) and the adaptive forces (institutional level). Petit has described the three levels in this way:

> The technical level has a boundary that does not seal it off entirely from the firm's environment but does have a high degree of closure. The organizational level has less closure and consequently is more susceptible to the intrusion of external elements. The institutional level has a highly permeable boundary and therefore is strongly affected by uncontrollable and unpredictable elements in the environment.[15]

The three levels are interrelated, constituting subsystems in this overall organizational structure. Each level has individual characteristics, but for effective performance there must be coordination among them. At the same time, however, it is possible to examine the specific requirements of each organizational level in order to classify the managers who work there.

Types of Managers

In the past, most managers were classified by organizational level (executive, middle manager, first line supervisor) or function (sales manager, production manager, financial manager). Today, however, managers are being classified according to many criteria, including the work itself, time horizon and decision-making strategy.

Technical Managers.   Because technical managers are concerned with producing goods and services as economically as possible, they tend to have an engineering point of view. They are also pragmatic, quick to adopt what will work for them and discard what will not. They like problems with concrete solutions such as what criteria to employ when investing in fixed equipment or the optimal relation that should exist between production and inventory levels. They work best when confronted with quantitative (as opposed to qualitative) issues. They also tend to have a very short-run time horizon, being most interested in the operational aspects of the job.

Technical managers have engineering viewpoints.

Institutional Managers.   Institutional managers face the challenge of coping with uncertainty brought on by uncontrollable and unpredictable environmental elements. For them, major concern rests with ensuring the organization's survival. This is done in two ways. First, institutional managers are continually surveying the environment, noting both opportunities and threats. Second, based on the findings they develop cooperative and competitive strategies for dealing with these elements, thereby reducing uncertainty. In order to conduct this surveillance and construct a viable strategy, they need to have a long-run time perspective. They tend to be philosophical in viewpoint, capable of translating qualitative environmental changes into quantitative estimates of their impact on the

Institutional managers have philosophical viewpoints.

---

[15]Thomas A. Petit, "A Behavioral Theory of Management," *Academy of Management Journal*, December 1967, p. 346.

organization. This requires wisdom, experience and good judgment in the formulation of strategy.

Organizational Managers.   As already noted, the organizational managers coordinate the efforts of the technical and institutional levels. In order to do this, the organizational manager needs to be something of a politician, capable of adopting a short- or long-run perspective, depending on the situation, and able to achieve a compromise between the technical and institutional managers.

Organizational managers are mediators.

> Organizational managers use the decision-making strategy of compromise. The best interests of the firm are not served by following either the computational [techical manager] or judgmental [institutional manager] strategies exclusively. The organizational managers attempt to influence the balance between the two according to the nature of the problems facing the firm. Since these problems may be either immediate or in the future, organizational managers have both a short-run and a long-run time horizon.
>
> The viewpoint of the organizational manager is basically political. He must always be concerned with what is possible rather than ideal in mediating between technical and institutional managers.[16]

Figure 15–9 shows the differences among these three types of managers.

THE SYSTEMS POINT OF VIEW   The systems point of view suggests that management is continually facing a dynamic environment consisting of forces that are not within its total control. Of course, some organiza-

---

[16] *Ibid.*, p. 348.

TYPE OF MANAGER	TASK	POINT OF VIEW	TECHNIQUE	TIME PERSPECTIVE	DECISION-MAKING STRATEGY
Technical	Technical Rationality	Engineering	Quantitative	Short-run	Computational
Organizational	Coordination	Political	Mediation	Both Short- and Long-run	Compromise
Institutional	Deal with Uncertainty and Relate the Organization to its Environment	Philosophical and Conceptual	Environmental Survey; Strategy Formulation	Long-run	Subjective and Judgmental

FIGURE 15–9   Characteristics of Managers in the Managerial System (Adapted from Thomas A. Petit, "A Behavioral Theory of Management," *Academy of Management Journal,* December 1967, p. 349.)

tions have attempted to overcome this problem. The giant trusts of the early 1900's and the major conglomerates of the current day both represent attempts by powerful organizations to obtain major control over their environment. For the most part, however, the organization and the environment still constitute *interacting* forces.

The same pattern exists within the organization itself. Managers in all departments and at all levels are *interdependent*. Job descriptions and work assignments, for example, represent only general guidelines regarding what the managers are supposed to be doing. In actuality, as Sayles notes:

> . . . systems concept emphasizes that managerial assignments do not have these neat, clearly defined boundaries; rather, the modern manager is placed in a network of mutually dependent relationships. . . . The one enduring objective is the effort to build and maintain a predictable, reciprocating system of relationships, the behavioral patterns of which stay within reasonable physical limits. But this is seeking a moving equilibrium, since the parameters of the system (the division of labor and the controls) are evolving and changing. Thus the manager endeavors to introduce regularity in a world that will never allow him to achieve the ideal. . . .Only managers who can deal with uncertainty, with ambiguity, and with battles that are never won but only fought well can hope to succeed.[17]

Organizing is a dynamic process.

This appears to be a very radical change from the organizing process that was discussed in Chapter 8 in very clear, rigid and easy-to-grasp terms. Now it seems that the process is becoming topsy-turvy. It must be remembered, however, that with this modern-systems view the element of dynamism takes on new dimensions and the heretofore simple concepts of planning, organizing and controlling are viewed from a much more realistic perspective.

Having covered the important aspects of systems theory and their relevance for understanding modern management, it is now time to return to the initial question posed at the beginning of the chapter: what will be the future development of management theory?

MANAGEMENT THEORY IN THE FUTURE

Systems and contingency schools are emerging.

At this point in time, no author can definitively state what will happen in the development of management theory by 1980. However, it appears likely that the three major schools of thought will see the addition of a fourth member. At the same time, there is a great deal being done to synthesize many of the ideas of these schools via a situational or contingency theory of management. This theory contends that there is no approach appropriate to all situations. Effective organization structure, motivation process and leadership style are all determined by

---

[17]Leonard Sayles, *Managerial Behavior* (New York: McGraw–Hill Book Company, 1964), pp. 258–259.

the situation. One of the leading proponents of this belief is Luthans, who writes:

> The beginning of a path called contingency or sometimes situational is just starting to emerge . . . by 1980 this path may be the one that leads management out of the existing jungle of theories. The pressure leading to a contingency theory has largely come from people who are actually practicing management.[18]

The systems concepts and the emergence of a situational or contingency theory are developing simultaneously and both are having a major effect on the current status of modern management theory. However, except for the systems material in this chapter and a handful of concepts already discussed earlier, (PPBS, OR, control systems) a great deal of attention has not yet been given to the very latest systems developments in the field. This will be the goal of Part III, in which other important systems concepts will be explained and some major contingency theory ideas will be developed.

SUMMARY

In this chapter the so-called systems school of management has been examined. First, attention was focused on general systems theory because of the importance assigned to it by system school advocates. Then the applied concepts of the systems approach, presented from its advocates' point of view, were reviewed. Finally, the question of whether the systems approach is a new school or a subsystem of a current one was examined. Although it is difficult to deny the existence of a systems body of knowledge, it appears that the systems school is still in its formative stages and has not yet completed its break with the quantitative school.

Attention was then focused on the general value of understanding the systems concept. First, the organization as an open, adaptive system was examined. Since business organizations are contrived systems, they can survive the onset of entropy and, unlike their biological counterparts, exist indefinitely. Of course, this will depend on how well they are managed. On the one hand, they must be responsive to change (adaptive mechanisms); on the other hand, they must not change so quickly that they are seriously thrown out of equilibrium (maintenance mechanisms). Finding the right balance is one of the keys to indefinite survival.

Next the systems concept was used to examine managerial systems. In a complex organization, there are three levels in the managerial system: technical, organizational and institutional. The technical level is concerned with producing the

---

[18]Luthans, *op. cit.*, pp. 69–70.

goods or services. The organizational level coordinates and integrates the technical and institutional level. The institutional level relates the activities of the organization to the environmental system. Within this system there are three types of managers, one for each of the levels. The technical manager is a "nuts and bolts" kind of individual; the organization manager is a political-mediator type of person; and the institutional manager is a conceptual-philosophical type of decision maker. Yet, although there are different levels and interests within the structure, all three must combine their talents and energies in the attainment of overall organizational objectives.

In order to do this, the manager must plan, organize and control. He must also make decisions and employ the latest quantitative methods where applicable; and he must understand and utilize the abilities of his subordinates through effective communication, motivation and leadership. In short, the management process, quantitative and behavioral schools are all important to the modern manager, and today he is drawing upon the concepts of all three in carrying out his duties. The systems approach encourages this.

The last section of the chapter examined management theory in the future. Whether or not the systems approach is worthy of being considered a school of management thought, it is making progress in that direction. At the same time, however, a situational or contingency theory of management seems to be emerging which encourages the manager to use the concepts of whatever school is necessary in attaining his desired goals. As might be expected, some of the biggest supporters of the contingency approach are practicing managers.

These two concepts, systems and situational management, have only been introduced in this chapter. However, they will be further explained in the upcoming section of the book in which new developments in the field are reviewed. Chapter 16 will concentrate on two of these systems concepts, namely, management information systems and the computer.

REVIEW AND STUDY QUESTIONS

1. Of what value is general systems theory to the systems school of management? Explain.

2. What is meant by an open system?

3. What impact does entropy have on a system?

4. In what way is a business organization a contrived system?

5. What are maintenance mechanisms? What are adaptive mechanisms? How do they affect the organization structure?

6. What is meant by a totally adaptive organization?

7. What are the three managerial levels in the hierarchy of complex organizations? Describe each.

8. How do the tasks and viewpoints of the managers of these three hierarchical levels differ? Explain.

9. Of what value is the systems approach to the practicing manager?

10. Will there ever be a systems school of management? Explain.

11. What is meant by the situational or contingency theory of management? How useful is it to the practicing manager?

SELECTED REFERENCES

Boulding, K. "General Systems Theory—The Skeleton of Science." *Management Science*, April 1956, pp. 197–208.

Cleland, D. I., and W. R. King. *Management: A Systems Approach*. New York: McGraw-Hill Book Company, 1972.

Johnson, R., F. E. Kast, and J. E. Rosenzweig. *The Theory and Management of Systems*, 3rd edition. New York: McGraw-Hill Book Company, 1973.

Kast, F. E., and J. E. Rosenzweig. *Organization and Management*, 2nd edition. New York: McGraw-Hill Book Company, 1974.

Kast, F. E., and J. E. Rosenzweig. "General Systems Theory: Applications for Organization and Management." *Academy of Management Journal*, December 1972, pp. 447–465.

Luthans, F. "The Contingency Theory of Management." *Business Horizons*, June 1973, pp. 67–72.

Parsons, T. *Structure and Processes in Modern Societies*. New York: The Free Press, 1960.

Petit, T. A. "A Behavioral Theory of Management." *Academy of Management Journal*, December 1967, pp. 341–350.

Phillips, D. C. "The Methodological Basis of Systems Theory." *Academy of Management Journal*, December 1972, pp. 469–477.

Seiler, J. A. *Systems Analysis in Organizational Behavior*, Homewood, Ill.: Richard D. Irwin, Inc., 1967.

Tersine, R. J. "Systems Theory in Modern Organizations," *Managerial Planning*, November–December 1973, pp. 32–40.

Von Bertalanffy, L. "The History and Status of General Systems Theory." *Academy of Management Journal*, December 1972, pp. 407–426.

Wortman, M. S., Jr., and F. Luthans, ed. *Emerging Concepts in Management*, New York: The Macmillan Company, 1969.

Young, Stanley D. *Management: A Systems Analysis*. Glenview, Ill.: Scott, Foresman and Company, 1966.

CASE: A GREAT BIG SECRET

Jackson & Jackson, a large west coast manufacturer, instituted an in-house supervisory training program under its new president, William Hopkinson. During the initial phase, 10 per cent of the managers received training related to both the technical and human relations sides of their jobs. Some critics of the program suggested that the training be suspended at this point since it was really of little value to the supervisors. An analysis of the results, however, showed that every manager participating in this initial training phase had been able to attain an increase in his unit's output. The training therefore continued.

Over the next twelve months all the remaining supervisors were put through the program. During this period productivity increased 27 per cent over the previous year. In commenting on the value of the program, the vice president of manufacturing said that he had noticed a number of the supervisors entering the plant earlier than usual in the morning and some staying past the closing whistle.

The results led proponents of the program to call it an unqualified success, but its opponents disagreed. Their arguments took two lines of attack. First, they pointed out that not all supervisors had been able to attain productivity increases. If the training was beneficial, this should have occurred. Second, they argued that the surge in output would be short-lived. One of them put it this way:

What we have here is the old "Hawthorne effect." The supervisors are all excited about being part of this new program, but it won't last long. The training is now complete and the novelty is already beginning to wear thin. Everyone will soon be returning to their old way of doing things. That's the problem with training programs. The initial results are fantastic, but they soon drop off.

Furthermore, there's the old cause-effect identification problem. Look at it this way. We have a new input—the training program. We have a new output— 27 per cent increase in productivity. However, what *causes* this increase? Is it really the training program or is it something else? What takes place in the transformation process or the black box? Quite frankly, no one knows, so why attribute it to the training program? Maybe these productivity increases would have occurred in any event. Who knows? It's really all a great big secret.

Questions

1. What is taking place in the transformation process that is causing the 27 per cent productivity increase? Explain, employing the systems concept in your answer.

2. Why does the individual in this case refer to the productivity increase as a "great big secret"?

CASE: INPUT–OUTPUT

The union at MacKelvey Incorporated had been negotiating a new contract with management for over three months, and with only thirty days left, there was still no agreement. The management was willing to give a 3.4 per cent increase in salary and a 3 per cent increase in fringe benefits; the union was asking for 5.2 and 3.9 per cent respectively. However, Mr. Paul Aherne, vice president of industrial relations who had been heading the negotiations all along, reported to the president, George Neffen, that he felt an agreement might be near:

Mr. Neffen, I think the union would settle for a 4.1 per cent salary raise and a 3.3 per cent increase in fringe benefits. We've done quite a bit of negotiating over the past ten weeks and I'm sure I know their mind.

Actually, Paul, the board of directors had hoped that the 3.4 and 3 per cent proposals would lead to a contract.

I see little chance of that, Mr. Neffen. If we maintain our present position we'll either have to hope that the union is willing to work without a contract or face the very real possibility of a strike.

Actually, neither of those alternatives are going to be viewed very favorably by the board, Paul. On the other hand, we certainly don't want to negotiate a contract any higher than we have to.

Mr. Neffen, let me be frank. I think we're almost there now. However, if we force the union to work without a contract or, heaven forbid, strike, we're going to damage one of our most important assets — union-management harmony. We have to think of the men as inputs in the process of management. If we do something to that input we stand the chance of seriously endangering the output, namely, our products and services. I think we should promote the current good will that exists between us.

Questions

1. If you regard the men as an input and the goods and services as an output, how would you describe the transformation process in this case?

2. How does this union contract negotiation fit into a discussion of the systems approach to management?

3. Do you think the company would be wise to follow the advice from the vice president of industrial relations? Explain.

CASE: MODIFICATIONS, MODIFICATIONS

George Chilvers was plenty angry. For the past twelve months he had been in charge of designing a new jet fighter for the United States Navy. After countless days of revising the initial design and incorporating extensive changes, his group was prepared to submit their design for approval. However, just as they were about to do this, George received a call from his boss asking him to come up to the office immediately. The gist of their conversation was as follows:

George, I've called you in because before you submit your plan I want you to know that there's a lot of pressure on us to present the most sophisticated design possible. In addition, if there are any major flaws that result in eventual cost overruns, we're really going to catch it. Congress is fed up with paying for contractor mistakes.

Mr. Adkinson, we've designed this craft five times now—I don't think there's a thing we haven't changed for the better at one time or another. I think it will be the finest plane the Navy has ever had.

I'm glad to hear that, George, because the president has really sold the big brass on this one.

Well, believe me, when we submit our design later in the week they'll be impressed.

Actually, George, we want you to wait a month before doing that. We still have a little time before the drawings are due and the president has asked me to have you go over the material once more.

What for?

To see if you can't improve it a little bit. Surely there's something new you can add here and there.

Mr. Adkinson, if you gave me a year I could design an aircraft that's twice as good as this one but I think there's a point beyond which it's not practical to go. We have a contract and a design that more than fulfills those require-ments. At some point you have to quit making changes, freeze the plan and get on with the production. If we keep delaying we'll never get to the manufacturing stage.

I understand that, George, but the president wants to be sure that the design is as good as possible. So for the next month I want you and your team to review and make any minor modifications on the material which will improve the overall design.

Questions

1. How would you classify George? Is he a technical, organizational or institutional manager? Explain.

2. Is Mr. Adkinson a technical, organizational or institutional manager? Explain. How about the president? Explain.

3. How does George's viewpoint as a manager differ from his superior's? Be specific.

CASE: A SYSTEMS VIEW

Alan Bashion, general manager of a major food chain, met with his people once a month. He liked to look on these meetings as a chance to communicate new ideas and exchange information on any problems that had cropped up in the recent month. During one of these meetings he brought up the topic of a systems approach to management. He had recently done some reading on the subject and felt it could be applied to the management of his own stores.

You know, another thing I want all of you to start doing is to think of your department as a system. This is a new idea in management but its a real good one.

One of the managers asked Mr. Bashion what he meant by a "system."

A system is a host of interrelated items. Each has an effect on and can be influenced by the others. It's like the human body. An attack on any one part can influence the other parts because the body is a system. An organization is the same. If any one part of it has trouble, this can affect the other parts. You people will have to do some reading on this topic. I'll have the secretary send all of you some references on the subject.

With this the meeting broke up and the managers began filing out. Some of them went across the street for lunch. During the meal the following conversation took place:

You know, I'd still like to know how the organization is like a system. That part evaded me completely.

Don't feel bad, I doubt whether anyone understood what he was talking about.

I wonder if he knew.

Well, in any event, if he sends us that material we can read it and find out what it is all about. Sometimes I think Mr. Bashion throws out new ideas before he really understands them himself.

Questions

1. What is meant by the systems approach to management?

2. Does Mr. Bashion really understand the systems concept? Explain.

3. What should a person know if he is truly to understand the systems approach?

PART III

RECENT DEVELOPMENTS IN MANAGEMENT

The goal of Part III is to examine recent developments that are taking place in the field of management. Some of these are direct extensions of work done by quantitative or behavioral people, but primarily they are integrative in nature, and not confined to any one of the schools exclusively. In addition, some of the areas, such as social responsibility and international management, do not fit into any particular framework and thus are best discussed in this part of the book.

In Chapter 16 the topic of systems management, initially introduced in Chapter 15, will be extended. First, management information systems and their role in the organization will be examined. Both the mechanical and human dimensions of MIS will come under scrutiny. Then the role and impact of the computer will be reviewed, with particular attention given to its effect on organization structure and company personnel.

The computer is not the only technological breakthrough to affect business, and in Chapter 17 other technological advances will be examined from the standpoint of the opportunities they offer and the challenges they present to management. In addition to technological forecasting, primary attention will be given to the impact of technology on both the personnel and the structure.

Then, in Chapter 18, modern organization structures will be examined. Because of increasing technology and change, business is finding that the old line-staff organizations are no longer sufficient; they are too rigid and inflexible. For this reason, many companies are turning to project, matrix and free-form organization designs to help them meet the challenge and threat of change.

Yet the focus of recent developments is not on organization design exclusively. Management is also interested in ways to motivate and lead their personnel, and some of the tools and techniques for doing so were reviewed in Chapters 13 and 14. In Chapter 19 still others will be examined, including human resources accounting, job enrichment, management by objectives, sensitivity training, transactional analysis and organizational behavior modification.

Next, in Chapter 20, the focus will be shifted from the internal to the external arena with social responsibility as the subject of attention. The modern business firm realizes that it must be responsive to the needs of not only its customers and workers but also the public at large. In this chapter the areas of equal opportunity, ecology and consumerism will be discussed, with major consideration given to the challenges they present to business.

Continuing this external focus, Chapter 21 will examine the challenges and opportunities that face those firms that decide to expand their operations into the international arena. In particular, attention will be devoted to evaluating the possible advantages and disadvantages associated with going overseas, the various issues in organizing, staffing and controlling such an undertaking, and the role of the multinational American corporation in the international economic arena.

Finally, in Chapter 22, management in the future will be examined. First, a concise review of past events will be undertaken. Then future developments on the horizon, heretofore undiscussed, will be examined, including the trend toward corporate democracy, the scramble for young executive talent and the continual trend toward professionalism.

CHAPTER 16

MANAGEMENT INFORMATION SYSTEMS AND THE ROLE OF THE COMPUTER

GOALS OF THE CHAPTER

As noted in Chapter 15, the modern organization consists of a host of interrelated departments and units. In administering them, management depends upon various sources of information, both external and internal to the firm. For this reason, in recent years many companies have developed management information systems. The initial goal of this chapter is to examine the function and design of such systems.

The second goal of the chapter is to study the role and impact of the computer in the organization. Many firms have computerized their information systems. However, the function of the computer is not restricted to this use; other benefits are also available, and these will be reviewed, as will the drawbacks associated with these machines. Finally, the impact of the computer on employment, organization structure and the computer personnel themselves will be studied. In particular, attention will be focused on:

a. the design of a management information system;
b. the importance of including MIS determinants and key success variables in the design;
c. the value of using a "from the top down" approach;
d. the dysfunctional behavior which can accompany the introduction of a management information system;
e. the fundamental elements of a computer;
f. the general uses to which the computer can be put by management;
g. how "what if" questions can be answered via computerized simulation;
h. drawbacks to the use of the computer; and
i. the impact of the computer on the organization and its personnel.

MANAGEMENT INFORMATION SYSTEMS

As emphasized in preceding chapters, the manager has many functions. He is a strategist who must formulate objectives; he is a disseminator of information who must communicate these goals to other organizational members; and he is a company spokesmen who must provide information to outsiders. As such, he can be thought of as a nerve center responsible for obtaining external and internal information and passing it on to various groups. This information processing system can be depicted in the following way:

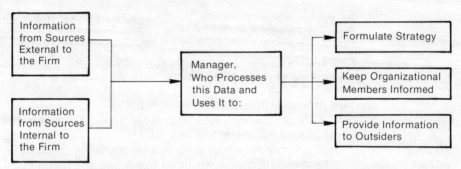

FIGURE 16-1   Manager as an Information Processor (Adapted from Henry Mintzberg, "The Myths of MIS," *California Management Review*, Fall 1972, p. 93.)

Perhaps the major problem the manager faces is that of receiving more information than he really needs. To deal with this problem, in recent years many firms have developed their own *management information system* (MIS). Kennevan defines MIS as

> . . .an organized method of providing past, present and projection information relating to internal operations and external intelligence. It supports the planning, control and operational functions of an organization by furnishing uniform information in the proper time-frame to assist the decision-making process.[1]

Designing an MIS

Management information systems have one primary goal: providing the manager with the necessary data for making intelligent decisions. Since, as noted in Chapter 15, there are three basic levels in the organization, each with different interests and viewpoints, it is evident that much of this decision-making information will have to be tailor-made to meet the needs of the respective level. The way in which this can be done becomes more clear when one recognizes that there are two basic inputs necessary in any effective MIS. The first can be called *major MIS determinants*. These are factors that play a role in structuring the type of information management will be receiving. According to Zani, these are opportunities and risks, company strategy, company structure, management and

Major MIS determinants.

[1]Walter J. Kennevan, "Mis Universe," *Data Management*, September 1970, p. 63.

decision-making processes, available technology, and available information sources.[2]

The roles of these determinants will become more evident in the next section when an MIS blueprint is examined.

The second input consists of *key success variables*. These are factors and tasks that determine success or failure. They will differ, of course, from company to company and from industry to industry.

For a consumer goods company manufacturing nondifferentiated products, the key success areas might be product promotion and understanding customer responses to product, marketing, and competitive changes.

For a manufacturer of commodity products, manufacturing and distribution cost control and efficiency might be the major determinants of success.[3]

The Blueprint Itself.   The well-designed management information system blueprint brings together these MIS determinants and key success variables, and well it should, for all these factors are interrelated. For example, the general business environment (opportunities and risks) and the company resources (men, money, machines, material and information) help establish overall strategy. In turn, this strategy serves as a basis for development of the organization structure. All four of these factors are related to the organization's key success variables. This interrelationship is schematically illustrated in Figure 16–2.

Blueprint brings key success variables together.

As seen in Chapter 15, the organization is structured to include three levels of managers, all of whom will be needing information vital for decision making. Those at the institutional level will be greatly interested in major developments in the external and internal arenas that will have an impact on the organization's strategic plan. Managers at the organizational level will need information that will help them coordinate the activities of institutional and technical levels. Individuals at the technical level will require data related to the production of goods and services. In designing the information-decision system for each level, primary attention must be focused on the relevance of the data to decision making. Stoller and Van Horn describe the design method as follows:

In essence, the approach consists of (1) defining the operating and planning decisions that are required to manage the organization, (2) exploring the types of policies available for making each decision, (3) determining the data requirements implied by each decision policy, and (4) developing preferred processing techniques for the desired data set.[4]

---

[2]William M. Zani, "Blueprint for MIS," *Harvard Business Review*, November–December 1970, p. 96.
[3]*Ibid.*, p. 98.
[4]David S. Stoller and Richard L. Van Horn, *Design of a Management Information System* (Santa Monica, Calif.: The Rand Corporation, p–1362, November 22, 1958), p. 2.

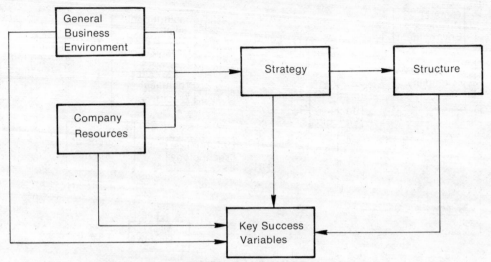

FIGURE 16–2   A Partial MIS Blueprint (Adapted from William M. Zani, "Blueprint for MIS," *Harvard Business Review*, November–December 1970, pp. 96–97.)

Decision-making information will differ by level.

The information required at the top levels will be very general in nature, forming the basis for strategic planning decisions. These include setting objectives, designing the organization structure and choosing new product lines. At the intermediate (organizational) level the data will need to be somewhat more specific. It will include information useful for activities such as formulating budgets, planning working capital, and measuring, appraising and improving management performance. At the lower (technical) level the data will have to be very specific and might even be programmed through the use of mathematical models and techniques. It will include information on things such as production scheduling, inventory control and the measurement, appraisal and improvement of worker efficiency.

Working with these information requirements, the organization will develop an overall MIS design, which will remain in operation for as long as it is useful. However, with new sources of information developing all the time, new information requirements springing up among the managers and information technology continually changing, the system will have to be revamped periodically. Nevertheless, employing just the information in this section, it is possible to extend Figure 16–2 and develop a total MIS blueprint as seen in Figure 16–3.

It should be noted that the design not only gives primary emphasis to MIS determinants and key success variables but also is structured with the needs of management in mind. It follows a "from the top down" philosophy. This is important, for as Zani notes:

If the design of management information systems begins on a high conceptual level and on a high managerial level as well, a company can avoid the

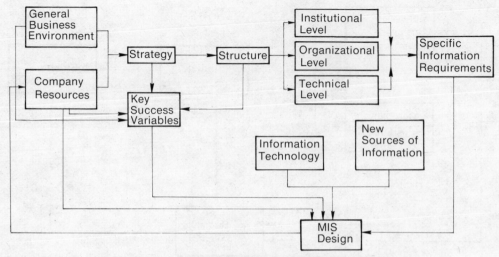

FIGURE 16–3   Total MIS Blueprint

unfortunate "bottom up" design phenomenon of recent history and begin to
develop the real, and very great, potential of MIS as a tool for modern
management.[5]

In recent years many firms have begun employing management
information systems. The benefits an MIS offers make it a very
valuable management tool, but no discussion of MIS would be
complete without some consideration of its impact on organizational personnel.

MIS and the
Impact
of Change

Whenever change is introduced into an organization, there is a
chance that it will result in dysfunctional behavior. Quite
simply, change tends to frighten people, and the greater the
change the more likely the personnel will resist or employ
defense mechanisms of one form or another.

How is the introduction of a new MIS received by organizational
personnel? Often it is seen as a more efficient information tool
and is welcomed. However, because of the changes it brings, it
is sometimes viewed by employees as a threat and can result
in the development of frustration or anxiety. The response, of
course, will depend on the situation. What one must realize is
that like all other changes introduced into the system, MIS
may cause behavioral problems. The first part of this section
will review some of these problems by illustrating that an MIS
is more than a mechanical process; there are also human
dimensions to be considered in its implementation.

[5]Zani, *op. cit.*, p. 100.

MIS can cause dysfunctional behavior.

Factors Causing Dysfunctional Behavior.   Recent research indicates that when an MIS is introduced into the organization there are five major factors that can cause dysfunctional behavior.[6]

First, the introduction of an MIS often results in the redefinition of departmental boundaries. Some people are going to be transferred to other departments; others are going to stay in their present unit but will be given new or expanded duties. In either case, these changes, even though they may bring about greater operating efficiency, can cause employee resistance because they upset the status quo in the formal organization structure.

Second, there may be an accompanying effect on the informal structure. "An organization tends to develop a system of values, ethical codes, taboos, special working relations. . . . The impact of a new system on the informal structure can be as serious in terms of creating behavioral disturbances as the impact on the formal structure."[7]

Third, some people, especially older ones with many years of company service, often see the development as threatening. They believe the new system will replace them.

Fourth, in many organizations change is introduced without proper consideration of the opinions, fears or anxieties of the personnel. When this happens, the management information system faces trouble from the very start.

Fifth, and closely related to the above factor, is the method of introducing change. McGregor has noted that, "A fair amount of research has pointed up the fact that resistance to change is a reaction primarily to certain methods of instituting change rather than an inherent human characteristic."[8] Of course, these are not the only types of dysfunctional behavior. They are, however, the most common and can result in a host of frustration reactions.

Common frustra-tion reactions include aggres-sion, projection and avoidance.

Frustration Reactions.   When one or more of the above factors are present, the personnel may encounter frustration. This frustration can manifest itself in many ways. The three general patterns most often associated with the introduction of a new management information system are aggression, projection and avoidance. In way of bringing all of this together, consider the case of a company that installs a new MIS and, in the

---

[6]G. W. Dickson and John K. Simmons, "The Behavioral Side of MIS," *Business Horizons*, August 1970, pp. 59–71.
[7]*Ibid.*, p. 61.
[8]Douglas McGregor, "The Scanlon Plan Through a Psychologist's Eyes," in C. A. Walker ed., *Technology, Industry and Man* (New York: McGraw–Hill Book Company, 1968), p. 124.

process, redefines departmental boundaries and breaks up an informal organization. How do the members of the informal group respond to the situation? Using a needs-satisfaction approach, Figure 16–4 provides an illustration.

Aggression is an attack (physical or nonphysical) against the object believed to be causing the problem. Sometimes this takes the form of sabotage. More commonly it occurs when people try to "beat the system." The following is an example:

The setting was an information system in a complex organization designed to collect man-hours in different work stations on a daily basis. Workers were frequently rotating from one work station to another during the day, and were supposed to clock in and out each time they moved from one station to another. During the course of an interview, one worker indicated that there had been some "ganging up" on an unpopular foreman. Workers would not punch out of a particular area when leaving for another work station or would punch in at the unpopular foreman's area and then work in a different area.[9]

Projection occurs when people blame something (or someone) for their own shortcomings. For example, the manager is incompetent, but he claims that with the new MIS he is not receiving sufficient information for making effective decisions.

Avoidance takes place when people withdraw from a situation because it is too frustrating for them. This can occur in regard to a management information system when, for example, the

----

[9]Dickson and Simmons, *op. cit.*, p. 62.

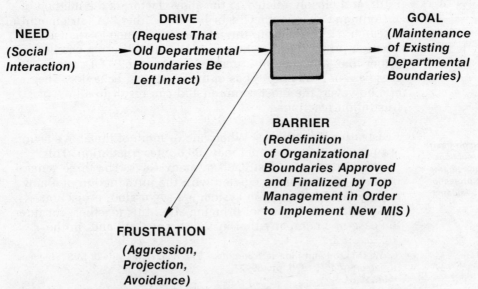

FIGURE 16–4 Frustration Created by New MIS (Format adapted from Fred Luthans, *Organizational Behavior*, New York, McGraw-Hill Book Company, 1973, p. 463.)

manager finds he can receive the same information in less time from a different source, so he ignores the MIS output.

The Organization and MIS. Thus far the negative aspects of MIS on the organization have been examined in general terms. In order to make a more specific analysis, however, it is necessary to consider the impact of MIS on four distinct subgroups in the hierarchy. These are: (1) operating personnel, (2) operating management, (3) technical staff and (4) top management.[10] Each will respond differently to a new MIS.

The *operating personnel* consists of two basic groups, non-clerical and clerical. The nonclerical people perform functions such as filling out forms or entering prepunched cards in a source recorder. When an organization computerizes and/or brings in a new MIS, these people often feel threatened. Although some turn to minor sabotage such as "forgetting" to do certain things or making deliberate mistakes, most employ projection. The system is blamed for everything that goes wrong in the office.

Organization subgroups respond differently.

Clerical workers are concerned principally with processing input and converting them into outputs, and they are considered part of the information system itself. Changes in their work patterns may entail, for example, moving them from a manual to an electronic data processing (EDP) system. Although some people may be displaced, most are maintained on greatly upgraded jobs which require more education and formal training. Initially, however, these workers react negatively because they believe they are going to be replaced. Like their nonclerical counterparts, they adopt a projection type of behavior and start blaming the new system for any mistakes that occur.

Operating management consists of all management personnel from first line supervisors up to and including middle management. These individuals receive much of the output from information systems. However, these systems also tend to centralize decision making and increase control of higher-level managers over their subordinates. As a result, when these operating managers fight the system, they do so by providing inadequate support to it and by failing to use the decision-making information provided by it. In so doing, they employ aggression, avoidance and projection.

The *technical staff*, consisting of programmers and systems designers, is most involved with the MIS. For this reason, it exhibits none of the common dysfunctional behavior patterns. On the other hand, the technical staff does not get along well with the operating management people. There seems to be

---

[10]*Ibid.*, pp. 63–67.

a natural clash between the system designers (technical staff) and the system users (operating managers).

Top management is little affected by new management information systems. Recent research, for example, shows that many top executives just do not get involved in designing the corporate MIS. Some may attend short computer courses in order to obtain background information on the area, and many pay lip service to the value of MIS in effective decision-making systems. Most executives, however, are unconcerned with the area. The reasons for resistance (by work group) are explained in greater depth in Table 16–1.

Before continuing on, it should be noted that this section has examined the behavioral effects of MIS with primary emphasis on some of the dysfunctional aspects. However, this does not have to be the situation. Many of these frustration reactions can be prevented if management: (a) works closely with the affected units, training them to understand and accept the new system by pointing out the benefits to the company, while ensuring that any displaced personnel will be given jobs elsewhere in the organization; (b) designs the system with cogent inputs from all affected groups so that information from the MIS is both timely and useful; and (c) attains top management support from the very beginning. There are many advantages to be gained from a management information system and a firm can obtain them if it is aware of the potential problems and pitfalls associated with the establishment of such a system.

TABLE 16–1 Causes for Resistance to MIS (by working groups)

	Operating (nonclerical)	Operating (clerical)	Operating Management	Top Management
Threats to economic security		X	X	
Threats to status or power		X	X*	
Increased job complexity	X		X	X
Uncertainty or unfamiliarity	X	X	X	X
Changed interpersonal relations or work patterns		X*	X	
Changed superior-subordinate relationships		X*	X	
Increased rigidity or time pressure	X	X	X	
Role ambiguity		X	X*	X
Feelings of insecurity		X	X*	X*

X = The reason is possibly the cause of resistance to MIS development.
X* = The reason has a strong possibility of being the cause of resistance.

Source: G. W. Dickson and John K. Simmons, "The Behavioral Side of MIS," *Business Horizons*, August 1970, p. 68. Reprinted with permission.

THE ROLE AND IMPACT OF COMPUTERS

The past three decades have seen the entry of automation into business enterprises. Webster defines *automation* as "the technique of making an apparatus (as a calculating machine), a process (as of manufacturing) or a system (as of bookkeeping) operate automatically."[11] In broad terms, there have been four main areas of automation development: (1) automatic machinery; (2) integrated materials handling and processing equipment; (3) control mechanisms; and (4) electronic computers and data-processing machines.[12] The fourth category, in particular computers, will be the center of focus here because of the role they are playing and the impact they are having on business.

Modern Computers

Computers are of two types: analog and digital.

Modern computers are of two general types: *analog* and *digital*. The analog computer is a measuring machine used principally by engineers in solving job-related problems. The digital computer is a counting machine that, by electrical impulses, can perform arithmetic calculations at a speed far in excess of human capacity and for this reason is of great value to business firms.

The basic concept of the digital computer dates back hundreds of years. However, Charles Babbage, the English mathematician and mechanician, is regarded as the originator of the modern automatic computer. In 1834, he conceived the principle of the analytical engine, which was similar to the modern day computer in that it would handle a large number of variables that could be fed into the machine on punched cards.

Computer power has increased dramatically.

Today, of course, with the advent of the electronic computer, Babbage's concept has been developed in far greater depth than he ever imagined. For example, McFarland reports that between 1955 and 1970 computer speeds increased by a factor of 1,000 to 1, computation costs went down on the order of 400 to 1, and memory capacity increased by 1,000 to 1.[13] In addition, there has been the introduction of "time sharing," whereby a number of people can use the computer at the same time and encounter no delay in receiving results; the machine can process all their programs simultaneously. How has all this been possible? The answer rests on the great technological advances that have occurred in the computer field. For example, by 1973 one writer was describing these changes in the following way:

Digital computers are now in their third generation—whenever new computers that embody substantial technological or state-of-the-art improvements are

---

[11]*Webster's Third New International Dictionary*, volume 1 (Chicago: Encyclopedia Britannica, 1968), p. 148.

[12]Dalton E. McFarland, *Management: Principles and Practices*, 4th edition (New York: The Macmillan Company, 1974), p. 96.

[13]Dalton E. McFarland, *Management: Principles and Practices*, 3rd edition (New York: The Macmillan Company, 1969), p. 323.

introduced, a new generation is said to have been born. The first generation utilized vacuum tubes and magnetic drums (and sometimes magnetic cores) as memory units. The second employed solid state devices and used a drum or magnetic cores for the memory, but later examples of this generation used disks for the storage of data. The third generation is characterized by miniaturized circuitry, so small that as many as 50,000 transistors and diodes will fit in a thimble. [14]

Today, a fourth generation of computers is arriving on the scene. These machines have even smaller circuitry, larger storage capacity, greater complexity and the ability to perform with one machine tasks that were previously carried out by two or more computers.

The fundamental elements of the computer have remained the same.

Despite the development of new features, the fundamental elements of a computer have remained basically the same: input, processing and output. First, the data is fed into the computer. This generally takes the form of punched cards, magnetic tape or some kind of printed document. Then the material is processed, with the computer coordinating material, making computations on data or working out logical decisions. Finally, the material is translated into output. This often takes the form of printed material, punched cards or a picture displayed on a screen. Since the computer can perform these operations in a fraction of the time it would take to complete them manually, it has become an important management tool. However, it is necessary to realize that a computer will only do what it is programmed to do.

Computer Programming

The computer program provides the machine with the step-by-step directions it is to follow. This program is usually fed into the computer on punched cards or, if it is going to be used over and over again, stored on tape or disk and called into action by the operator. Generally these programs are written in computer language. Two of the more common are FORTRAN (FORmula TRANslation), which is designed for scientific work, and COBOL (Common Business Oriented Language), which is used for business programs.

If the program is to be executed properly, it is often useful first to construct a flow chart of the operation. This chart can then be translated into computer language. Figure 16–4 illustrates the flow diagram used by an investor who is pondering the purchase of a new stock. The individual has certain prerequisites which all new stocks must meet. First, they must be listed on the New York Stock Exchange. Second, their price/earnings ratio must be under ten. Third, the current price must not be within 80 per cent of its annual high. If these three conditions are met and there are sufficient funds available in his bank or brokerage accounts, he will buy the stock. If not,

---

[14]Ernest Dale, *Management: Theory and Practice* 3rd edition (New York: McGraw-Hill Book Company, 1973), p. 649.

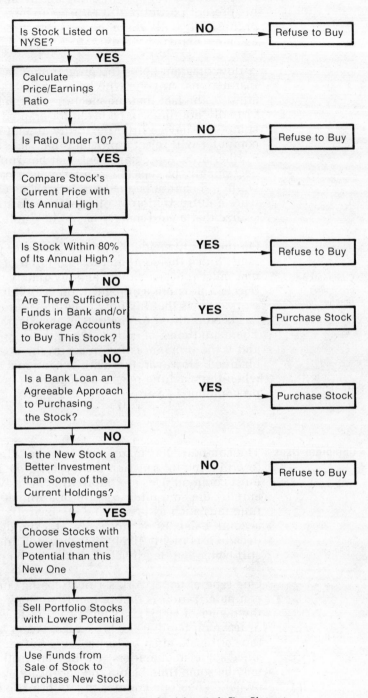

FIGURE 16-5   Stock Investor's Flow Diagram

he will evaluate the wisdom of taking a bank loan to buy the stock. Otherwise, he will compare the new stock with those in his present portfolio. If it appears to be a better buy than any of those currently there, he will sell these issues and purchase as many shares of the new stock as he can with the proceeds.

A flow diagram helps the programmer see the logic of his instructions. Anyone who has ever done any programming can attest to the fact that the machine operates like a moron; virtually nothing can be taken for granted (although the latest computers have a little flexibility along these lines). The computer will reject a program that lacks explicit instructions. Furthermore, a program deck that has run countless times will occasionally be rejected as erroneous because one of the cards is worn and cannot be read properly. This can result in hours of work and frustration as one searches for the error only to realize that a card merely has to be duplicated.

Computer pro-
gramming
teaches logic.

On the positive side, however, computer programming teaches logic. Since the computer has no mind of its own, the programmer must proceed slowly and accurately. When the machine rejects a program as illogical, the individual, despite all his work, knows that his flow diagram is erroneous; something has been omitted or one part of the diagram is nonsensical. There are times, of course, when the computer will miss a card, and if the program is fed in again, the desired output will be obtained. However, these are exceptional cases. Generally, when the machine rejects a program, it is almost always the programmer's error.

Computer Uses The computer has many uses from handling routine paperwork to providing information for top-level decision making. The most common uses are the routine ones. Most companies employ the computer to perform arithmetic and bookkeeping functions such as processing the payroll, computing customer account balances or processing stockholder lists. During this decade it is highly likely that much of this routine paperwork still being handled by clerks will also be computerized.

One type of paperwork seriously being considered for computerization is that of handling stock certificates. Today, the owner of stock is issued a certificate which he can keep or leave on hand at the brokerage. When he sells the security, the certificate must be turned over to the new buyer. However, since some stockholders will buy and sell in the same day, it may be some time before the certificate ever gets to its rightful owner. When one couples this information with the fact that the corporation needs to know the name and address of all stockholders of record for dividend and voting purposes, it is easy to see how this entire area has become a mass of paperwork. Eliminating the use of certificates and putting all this information on a computer could result in far more accurate record keeping.

One of the widest uses of the computer is for *inventory control.* In retail stores, for example, it is common to find small coded tickets attached to all merchandise. When the items are sold, the tickets are torn off and sent to a central locale where the

Inventory control. data is either placed on punched cards or read directly into the computer. In this way, the number of units on hand can be determined on a day-to-day basis and more inventory can be ordered at the appropriate time. Recently, some firms have automated their operations even further, and, via machines on the sales floor, can report transactions directly to the computer for inventory purposes.

Another major application of the computer is in making *airline reservations.* This is an illustration of what is known as "real time." The computer is relating what is going on as it is

Airline reserva- happening. In the case of reservations, the airline clerk feeds
tions. the information into a central computer via a console. The computer in turn scans its memory, reports whether there are any seats available on the desired flight, and automatically sends back a confirmation while simultaneously reducing the number of available seats.

Another approach that is gaining in popularity is that of the *data bank.* Information on some area is fed into the computer memory, thereby creating a bank of data. In this way, individuals with questions on this subject can obtain ready answers. Airlines use this concept in regard to scheduled flights and departure times. For example, a man in San Francisco has business in Chicago on Friday. He then wants to go on to

Data banks. New York. What is the earliest flight he can catch after 6 P.M. on Friday that will take him to Kennedy International? The agent in San Francisco will probably not know since he seldom handles Chicago to New York requests, but the airline will have this standard information in the computer so he can readily get it for the passenger. Some insurance companies use the data bank as a depository for all insurance policies. Agents seeking answers to policyholder questions can obtain, through telecommunications, up-to-date responses. Other firms feed personnel information into the data bank, including statistics such as salaries, work experience, educational background and performance appraisals. In this way, they can obtain an immediate profile of an individual being considered for promotion or a list of personnel with a particular skill or training.[15]

---

[15]See, for example, James W. Walker, Fred Luthans, and Richard M. Hodgetts, "Who Really Are the Promotables?" *Personnel Journal,* February 1970, pp. 123–127.

Automatic bank tellers.

Another computer application that is gaining acceptance is the *automatic bank teller*. Today, in certain parts of the country, an individual can obtain money from a bank-teller machine after hours or on weekends by means of a special credit card. By placing this card in the machine, which is hooked up to a computer, and entering through a keyboard his personal identification code number and the amount he wishes to withdraw, the customer will automatically receive a packet of money and a coded receipt.[16] Furthermore, if the supply of funds allocated to the automatic teller begins to run low because of excessive withdrawals, the computer will alert a bank manager who can come down and make more money available. In addition, the computer-run machine is capable of receiving deposits, transferring funds from checking to savings (and vice versa) and accepting time-credit loan payments.

Simulation. In recent years, computers have also been employed to handle "what if" questions. By simulating a situation, the manager can plug in different decisions and evaluate the outcome of each.

If, say, the manager enters the price, the expected volume, and certain budgetary decisions, the computer will provide a pro forma profit and loss statement for that item. The judgment of the manager is used to suggest alternatives for consideration. The power of the computer is used to carry out the manager's understanding of the quantitative relationships between inputs and outputs—e.g., prices, volumes, and annual profits. The judgment of the manager is . . . called on to determine if the answer is acceptable or if further trials should be made to secure data or judgments which may produce a more acceptable output.[17]

The key to the successful use of the computer in this instance is determined by how well the company has been able to simulate actual conditions. If the model is accurate, the information being fed back to the manager is reliable; if not, the data upon which he is basing his decision is worthless.

Computer simulations.

A number of firms have been moving toward the use of computer simulation in helping their managers make decisions. In addition to the effect of price on quantity, other typical "what if" questions include:

If a proposed new item of equipment is purchased or leased, what will be the effects on profits and cash flow of alternative financing methods?

If a wage increase is granted, what will be the effect on production rates, use of overtime, risk of seasonal inventory, and so on, for a production program?[18]

---

[16]Currently, in most places, withdrawals are limited to a maximum of $150 a day.

[17]Curtis H. Jones, "At Last: Real Computer Power for Decision Makers," *Harvard Business Review*, September–October 1970, p. 79.

[18]James B. Boulden and Elwood S. Buffa, "Corporate Models: On-Line, Real-Time Systems," *Harvard Business Review*, July–August 1970, p. 67.

The questions, along with the assumptions made by the simulation designer and/or manager are fed into the computer and evaluated according to the probability of their occurrence. The answer is then printed out in whatever form is desired, e.g., rate of return, cost analysis, balance sheet, income statement. Figure 16-6 provides a general illustration.

In addition, some firms have developed models that help them make decisions when some particular problem develops. Consider the following:

> At 9:32 A.M., a blowout! A blast furnace breaks down in the steel plant. Cold iron will have to be heated to produce the molten iron normally supplied to the refining process from this furnace. Processing time will be almost doubled, reducing the shop's production capacity by 60%. The cost per ton of steel will certainly rise sharply as a result of the increased processing time. But how much will it rise?

> Using a remote time-shared computer terminal in his office, a manager at Inland Steel Company defines the new conditions resulting from the equipment failure and enters them in a set of models which simulate the steelmaking process and the costs involved. At 11:26 A.M.—less than two hours later, the same morning—he estimates the new cost figures and prepares a revised corporate profit projection . . . . the computer has vastly enhanced his decision-making capability.[19]

Thus, the computer has proved to be a valuable tool for management decision making. However, there are some very important drawbacks which also merit consideration.

---

[19]*Ibid.*, p. 65.

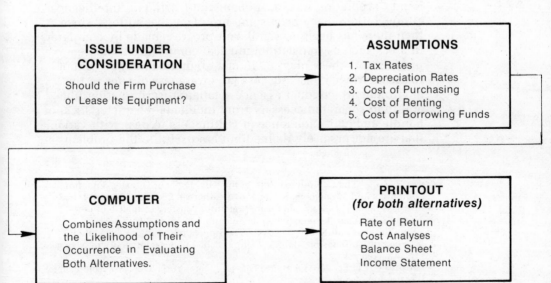

FIGURE 16-6   Simulation of a Purchase Vs. Lease Strategy

Drawbacks to Computers

Expensive play toys.

The most common argument raised against computers is that they are expensive investments that are never fully utilized. However, many managers, determined to have the latest, most sophisticated equipment, allow themselves to be sold more hardware than they really need. Zipf points out that, "We have seen over the past 12 years some incredible blunders. Twinkling lights, spinning tapes, and pastel cabinets seem to have a mesmerizing effect on some managers. In a pell-mell rush to be among the first to play with a new toy, enormous sums have been wasted."[20]

Overrating computer information.

Second, managers have a habit of overrating computer results, failing to remember that the output is only as valid as the input. Luthans and Koester, for example, conducted an experiment in which they determined that individuals with no computer training are more willing to abide by information presented in computer printout form than in noncomputer printout form and vice versa. In short, people who lack a computer background are often awed by computer results and assign to them a validity and reliability that is not actually justified.[21]

Overrating computer capability.

Third, managers tend to overrate the capabilities of the computer. In reality, the limitations of the machine are quite severe, but many decision makers see these machines as characterized by HAL, the on-board computer in *2001: A Space Odyssey*.[22] Highly sophisticated, HAL is capable of phenomenal feats. In fact, he can virtually think like a human. Unfortunately, there is an error in his program but, being humanlike, he fights for survival and kills most of the crew before he is finally deprogrammed and rendered harmless. In reality, HAL is still very much of a concept. As Dreyfus noted in his now-famous Rand Corporation memo, *Alchemy and Artificial Intelligence*, although there have been some promising beginnings, since then there has been no significant progress made by computers in areas such as translation, musical composition, theorem proving and chess playing. In fact, digital computers cannot replicate fringe consciousness (an awareness of cues in the environment), conduct essence-accident discrimination (the ability to separate necessary from incidental characteristics) or handle ambiguity tolerance (a willingness to deal with variables that are not precisely defined but are useful to the problems at

---

[20]A. R. Zipf, "The Computer's Role in the 'Dividends or Disaster' Equation," *Computers and Management*, The 1967 Leatherbee Lectures (Boston: Harvard Business School, 1967) as found in "Retaining Mastery of the Computer," *Harvard Business Review*, September–October 1968, p. 70.

[21]Fred Luthans and Robert Koester, "The Impact of Computer Generated Information on Decision Making," Unpublished paper (University of Nebraska, Lincoln, Nebraska).

[22]Arthur C. Clarke, *2001: A Space Odyssey* (New York: The New American Library, Inc., 1968).

hand).[23] Although these attributes are essential to decision making, they continue to remain outside the realm of current computer capability.

In fact, many of the promises made about the computer, outside the sphere of computational work, have just not materialized. Jones reports that, with the possible exception of logistics, the current trend is actually away from, not toward, computerized management decision making. Companies such as Western Electric, Hughes Aircraft and Fairfield Manufacturing have all, to varying degrees, followed this retrenchment approach, shifting all or part of the decision-making functions from the computer to man. Of course, other companies are moving in the opposite direction, but the point is that the computer is only a management *tool* and not a replacement for the human decision maker, especially at the upper levels of the hierarchy. Brady has made the following observation along these lines:

> . . . there is one area where I do not anticipate that the computer will become much of a factor. That area is the setting of corporate goals and objectives. Even given tremendous advances in computer and systems technology, and even given the full understanding and appreciation by top and middle managers of the capabilities and usefulness of the computer, I am convinced that managerial judgment will always play the dominant role in the making of major strategic decisions.[24]

As long as the manager is aware of what the computer cannot do, he is in a good position to evaluate its use to him in the decision-making process.

Impact of the Computer

When it became evident that the computer was gaining widespread acceptance in industry, all sorts of predictions were made about its impact on the organization. Some people said the computer would cause mass unemployment. Others forecast changes in the organization structure itself. Still others predicted a takeover of top management by computer experts. Now that a sufficient period of time has transpired, these predictions can be reviewed and evaluated.

Mass-Unemployment Issue.   Research shows that there actually has been little unemployment among clerical workers because of computerization. In fact, one researcher has reported that "Computers have not resulted in widespread clerical unemployment so far because industry's paperwork load has grown so fast; in many cases computerization has merely permitted companies to keep up with the growing burden without prohibitive expense."[25]

Computerization has caused little unemployment.

---

[23]Jones, *op. cit.*, p. 78.
[24]Rodney H. Brady, "Computers In Top-Level Decision Making," *Harvard Business Review*, July–August 1967, p. 76.
[25]Ernest Dale, *Organization*, (New York: American Management Association, 1967), p. 275.

The same is true at the management level. Work is growing
fast enough to offset most computerized trends toward
unemployment. For example, Lee has reported that in research
conducted in a manufacturing company and a utility, the
number of management personnel actually increased slightly in
the affected departments.[26] In another survey, Vergin found "no
cases of middle managers either being eliminated or suffering
financial downgrading because of the shift of duties to the
computer. . . ."[27] The computer seems to have brought about
very little unemployment.

Organization Structure.   A large number of predictions have
also been made about the effect of computers on the
organization structure. In the late 1950's, Leavitt and Whisler
predicted that middle-management jobs would become highly
structured, programmers and R&D people would move upward
into the top management group and large industrial organizations would recentralize.[28] During the late 1960's, however,
Dearden predicted that the computer would have no impact on
the organization of top and divisional management and
limited impact on the other levels.[29]

*Computerization
has had a limited
impact on organi-
zation structure.*

Which of these predictions is correct? Current research findings
tend to substantiate much of Dearden's claims. For example,
Hofer studied an independent division of a large multi-product
corporation with sales over $200 million and a small company
with sales of around $8 million. After examining all changes in
the formal structure over a 12-year period, he concluded that
there were "no instances in which the computer had caused
changes in structure at either the general management level or
at the top functional level in those components whose
principal tasks did not involve the processing of substantial
amounts of quantitative data."[30] The only major changes he
found occurred at the operational level where these great
amounts of quantitative data were processed. Here, new jobs
were created and old ones modified or eliminated.

Why were there not more changes? The answer very simply was
that the computer did not affect the tasks that these other

---

[26]*The Impact of Electronic Data Processing Upon the Patterns of Business
Organization and Administration* (School of Business, State University of
New York, Albany, 1965), pp. 27–31. Cited in Dale, *Management: Theory and
Practice*, p. 668.
[27]Roger C. Vergin, "Computer Induced Organization Changes," *MSU Business
Topics*, Summer 1967, pp. 64–65.
[28]Harold J. Leavitt and Thomas L. Whisler, "Management in the 1980's"
Harvard Business Review, November–December 1958, pp. 41–42.
[29]John Dearden, "Computers: No Impact on Divisional Control," *Harvard
Business Review*, January–February 1967, p. 104.
[30]Charles W. Hofer, "Emerging EDP Pattern" *Harvard Business Review*, March–
April 1970, p. 17.

organizational personnel were performing. Furthermore, managers in the firm being studied indicated that they felt this would continue to be the case in the future. For example, a sales manager noted:

> There is not much potential for changes in structure in the sales section due to the computer. The way we organize depends on our sales volume, the size and location of our customers, the number and nature of our channels of distribution, the number and diversity of our product lines, and so on, and these factors are not affected by the computer.[31]

An engineering manager echoed these basic sentiments.

> I do not expect major changes in the organizational structure of the engineering section in the near future due to the increased use of the computer, although I do feel that the computer will increase the productivity of our present personnel.

> The reason for this is the fact that in the engineering section organizational structure is based on the physical characteristics of the products we produce, the nature of the production process, and the level of new product development and cost reduction activities rather than on the ways we process data.[32]

In summarizing his findings, Hofer predicted that by the mid-1970's the computer would have no significant effect on any of the major characteristics of the formal structure. He further postulated that at the operational level the magnitude of change would be less than that which has occurred to date.[33]

Computer Personnel in the Organization. When computers were first introduced into the organization, they were assigned to the accounting and financial departments because these areas seemed to have the greatest need for them. However, by the late 1960's the department responsible for the EDP function was changing. In a sample investigation encompassing 40 per cent of *Fortune's* top 500 industrials, Schoderbek and Babcock found a growing number of firms setting up separate EDP departments to administer this function. They reported that:

> Although 69.7 percent of the companies responding indicated that the original position of EDP was within the accounting department, at the present time only 45.0 percent have continued with this arrangement. A separate and independent electronic data processing function has been established in 49.5 percent of the firms. . . .[34]

The reason for this change was the increased importance of the EDP function as a company-wide service of value to all departments, not just one or two as was previously the case.

---

[31]*Ibid.*, p. 22.
[32]*Ibid.*, p. 22.
[33]*Ibid.*, p. 169.
[34]Peter P. Schoderbek and James D. Babcock, "The Proper Placement of Computers," *Business Horizons*, October 1969, p. 39.

*EDP departments
are being moved
up the hierarchy.*

In addition, the researchers reported that the EDP function has been moved up in the managerial hierarchy. In 1960 Dale found that most EDP managers were in middle management.[35] However, Schoderbek and Babcock discovered that the majority of these departments (53.7 per cent) were located at the upper level of the hierarchy. Furthermore, although three-quarters of them originally reported to a financial officer, at the time of this study only half were under his jurisdiction. Instead, many firms were having the EDP department report to the vice president. Efficiency seemed to be the main reason.

> . . . the higher the level of the computer location the more successful EDP appears to be. Of the 31 installations reporting to vice-presidents, 25 have experienced no significant problems. On the other hand, 45 of the 55 departments reporting to the financial executive encountered organizational problems. In general, EDP activity appears to be most efficient when placed at a high level in the organization.[36]

Recent research also indicates that EDP people are working more closely with top management than previously. However, there is no empirical evidence supporting the contention that computer people are taking over management decision making. Currently, their major problem appears to be one of getting management to listen to them and to utilize their services.

SUMMARY

In this chapter two topics have been examined: management information systems and the computer. Although many information systems are computerized, this is not universally true. Nevertheless, the two areas have one common characteristic: they help interrelate the departments and units of the organization into a harmonious system.

The primary goal of any MIS is to provide decision-making information to the manager. For this reason, a well-designed system must be planned with the needs of management in mind and must follow a "from the top down" philosophy. In addition, the system must discriminate by organization level, providing the right kinds of information to each. For example, top management will need general information from which they can formulate strategic plans. Middle management will need more specific data for drawing up budgets and measuring and appraising managerial performance. Lower-level management will need very specific data for use in areas such as production scheduling and inventory control.

The introduction of a management information system can bring about dysfunctional behavior such as aggression,

---

[35]Ernest Dale, *The Decision-Making Process in the Commercial Use of High-Speed Computers* (Ithaca, Graduate School of Business and Public Administration, Cornell University, 1964), p. 20.
[36]Schoderbek and Babcock *op. cit.*, p. 42.

projection and avoidance. In order to overcome these problems, management must be willing to adopt a participative decision-making approach that introduces the new system, relates its advantages to the personnel and assures that if any people are replaced because of it, employment will be secured for them elsewhere.

The modern computer is often employed as part of an MIS, providing necessary information to managers throughout the hierarchy. In addition to performing bookkeeping and arithmetic functions, it is also being used, for example, for inventory control and airline reservations. Another one of its latest applications is answering "what if" questions through simulation.

Despite their great value, computers have some important drawbacks of which management must be aware. First, many companies tend to buy a more complex computer than they need. Second, many managers place too much faith in computer printout results. Third, many managers tend to overrate the capabilities of the computer. There are a large number of things man still does much better than any machine and qualitative decision making is one of them.

What impact have computers had on the organization and its personnel? First, despite fears to the contrary, there has been little unemployment. Work has grown so fast in many industries that computers have merely allowed the company to keep up. Second, the computer has had virtually no effect on organization structure at either the general management level or the top functional level in those components whose principal tasks did not involve the processing of substantial amounts of quantitative data. Third, recent years have seen a trend toward taking the EDP function out of the accounting and financial departments and putting it in a separate department. In addition, EDP is now reporting further up the hierarchy than ever before. Nevertheless, it appears unlikely that the computer people are going to usurp the decision-making function at the top levels.

Although this chapter examined the computer in some depth, this machine is only one of the new technological advances affecting business; there are many others that also merit consideration. They will be discussed in chapter 17, which is devoted to the area of technology and organization.

REVIEW AND STUDY QUESTIONS

1. What is a management information system? Explain.

2. Exactly what is the primary objective in the design of an effective MIS?

3. What role should MIS determinants and key success variables play in an MIS design?

4. What are the three common dysfunctional forms of behavior often associated with the introduction of a new management information system? Explain each.

5. According to recent research, how do the operating personnel tend to oppose the introduction of an MIS? The operating management? The technical staff? The top management?

6. How does the modern computer differ from its 1950 counterpart? What new technological changes have occurred? What new ones can be expected in the next decade?

7. Why is the computer program so important to the processing of computerized data?

8. What are four common uses of the computer? Explain.

9. How is the computer being employed in answering "what if" questions? Give an illustration.

10. What are the basic drawbacks to the use of computers?

11. What impact has the computer had on employment at the clerical level? Management level?

12. Specifically, what effect has computerization had on organization structure? Explain.

13. What changes have occurred in the past decade in regard to the place of EDP personnel in the organization?

SELECTED REFERENCES

Baker, J. D. "Rational Computerization." *Business Horizons,* April 1972, pp. 36–40.

Boulden, J. B., and E. S. Buffa, "Corporate Models: On-Line, Real-Time Systems," *Harvard Business Review,* July–August 1970, pp. 65–83.

Clarke, A. C. *2001: A Space Odyssey,* New York: The New American Library, Inc., 1968.

Dearden, J. "Computers: No Impact on Divisional Control." *Harvard Business Review,* January–February 1967, pp. 99–104.

Derman, I. H. "Do You MIS'Understand?" *Business Horizons,* October 1972, pp. 55–64.

Dickson, G. W., and J. K. Simmons. "The Behavioral Side of MIS." *Business Horizons,* August 1970, pp. 59–71.

Ernst, M. L. "Computers, Business, and Society." *Management Review,* November 1970, pp. 4–12.

Field, G. A. "Behavioral Aspects of the Computer." *MSU Business Topics,* Autumn 1970, pp. 27–33.

Hartman, R. I. "Some Managerial Implications of the Cybernation Revolution." *Personnel Journal,* January 1969, pp. 42–47.

Hay, L. E. "What *Is* An Information System?" *Business Horizons,* February 1971, pp. 65–72.

Hofer, C. W. "Emerging EDP Pattern." *Harvard Business Review,* March–April 1970, pp. 16–31, 169–171.

Jones, C. H. "At Last: Real Computer Power for Decision Makers." *Harvard Business Review*, September–October 1970, pp. 75–89.

King, W. R. "The Intelligent MIS — A Management Helper." *Business Horizons*, October 1973, pp. 5–12.

Lloyd, J. H. "Establishing a Computer-Based MIS for the Small Business." *Managerial Planning*, July–August 1973, pp. 14–16, 23.

McLean, E. R. "How Effective is Your Data Processing Organization?" *California Management Review*, Fall 1973, pp. 95–100.

"Minicomputers That Run the Factory." *Business Week*, December 8, 1973, pp. 68–76.

Mintzberg, H. "The Myths of MIS." *California Management Review*, Fall 1972, pp. 92–97.

Schoderbek, P. P., and J. D. Babcock. "The Proper Placement of Computers." *Business Horizons*, October 1969, pp. 35–42.

Swart, J. C., and R. A. Baldwin. "EDP Effects on Clerical Workers." *Academy of Management Journal*, December 1971, pp. 497–512.

Zani, W. M. "Blueprint for MIS." *Harvard Business Review*, November–December 1970, pp. 95–100.

CASE: WE TOLD YOU SO

A large eastern insurance company recently brought in one of the nation's major computer firms to see if something could be done about the mass of paperwork confronting their lower-level personnel. After analyzing the needs of the company, the firm recommended the purchase of a giant computer. Their proposal was based on a cost-saving estimate of $3 million spread over the expected life of the machine (ten years).

After a series of top-level conferences, management decided to make the purchase. This information was then passed on to the lower-level managers, who, with the help of their own people and some of the staff from the systems department, started revising job assignments. Most of the routine, paper-processing tasks were to be reassigned to the computer. The rest of the work was to be handled by the regular clerical personnel. The problem, however, was that under this plan over 60 per cent of the work was to be allocated to the computer. As a result, the staff was concerned about its continued employment.

Management tried to allay these fears by categorically stating that all efforts would be made to find work in other departments for any displaced persons. In making good on this promise, within the first month the firm transferred 30 per cent of the personnel to other units. However, this merely served to increase anxiety among the remaining members. As one of them said, "You mark my words. There just aren't enough jobs in the company to absorb everyone. So it's just a matter of time before the company announces that it will be laying off some of us." The statement seemed to reflect the sentiments of the other members because at just about this time the management noticed a decline in cooperation from these people. Both the managers and the systems engineers who were revising the work schedules found many of the workers unwilling to answer questions about their work assignments or providing only minimal information. In fact, one manager described the workers as "downright hostile." Another said, "They think they're going to be fired, so they're doing everything they can to screw us up."

As a result, it took three weeks longer than anticipated to get everything straightened out and transferred to the computer. Meanwhile, what about the personnel? Well, true to their fears, 20 per cent of the original department was laid off.

Questions

1. Although it was not explicitly stated in the case, what kinds of dysfunctional behavior might the workers have initiated? Explain.

2. How could management have overcome this problem in the first place?

3. Was management honest with the employees or did it lie to them about the effect of computerization on their job? Defend your answer.

CASE: THE OLD WAYS ARE BEST

When the Randler Corporation brought in an outside management consulting firm, it asked them to examine company operations from top to bottom. Return on investment had not been over 6 per cent in three years, and the top management felt something had to be done. The company was relying on the consultants to tell them what this should be.

Six weeks later, the consultants submitted their list of recommendations. One of these called for the design of a new management information system. "Managers, at the present time, are relying too heavily on an outdated and ineffective reporting system," read part of the report. "This system should be scrapped and a new one designed from the top down, with major emphasis given to providing up-to-date, relevant data useful for decision making."

The idea sounded fine to the top staff and they ordered the EDP (electronic data processing) department to design a new MIS. After talking to people at all levels of the hierarchy and evaluating the current reporting system, the EDP people submitted their proposal. The plan looked fine on paper, and the corporate president ordered it implemented.

Over the next twelve months, however, the company's return on investment failed to reflect any great changes in efficiency. As before, ROI stood below 6 per cent. When top management decided to find out why, one of the areas they examined was the new MIS. In essence, they discovered that managers at all levels of the organization were still relying on their old reporting systems. Virtually no one was using any of the data being provided by the new system. When one of the managers was asked why he was not utilizing the new system, he replied, "Why should I? I have my own reporting system and it tells me all I need to know. If you ask me, this whole new MIS design was a just a waste of money."

Questions

1. What kinds of information should a manager receive from a well-designed information system? Explain, incorporating "key success variables" into your answer.

2. What error did the company make in this case?

3. What recommendations are now in order? Explain.

CASE: WHAT IF?[1]

In October, 1969, Inland Steel bought a simulation program from On-Line Decisions, Inc., a computer software firm in Berkeley, California. With this model the steelmaker was able to simulate its annual profit and profit plan and make a five-year profit projection. In describing the usefulness of the program, Inland's comptroller explained, "You can test the effect of changing several variables at once. Calculating the effect of a change in scrap prices, for example, used to take as long as 12 manweeks. Now we can do it in minutes." In addition, the company was using the model to assist in top-level decision making in areas such as market research, budgeting, product profitability, cash flow, works accounting, facilities planning, corporate planning and financial staff support.

In describing the model, James Boulden, president of On-Line and a developer of the simulation, said:

The model works best for manufacturing companies. . . . It's not well suited for use by a distribution organization with a huge inventory because of the large data storage costs . . . use of the broad based simulator wouldn't be

[1]The data in this case can be found in "Pass the Simulation," *Industry Week,* March 23, 1970, pp. 47–48.

economical. . . . "The model is also better for a large volume or process type
company rather than a job shop, but we could do it. It's also much better for
planning purposes than process control. Clients typically work on annual,
monthy, or even weekly projections. We want to get this down to daily use."

Commenting on its success in developing and selling these
models, Mr. Boulden explained that the company currently
had twenty clients, ranging in size from $500 million to $2
billion in sales. He predicted that "by the end of this year,
one out of ten of the top 500 manufacturing companies will
be our customers."

Questions

1. How valuable can these simulation models be in providing information for managerial decision making?

2. What are the drawbacks to this approach? Explain.

3. Do you think the future will see more or less of these computer simulation models?
   Why?

CASE: JUST AROUND THE CORNER

Electronic banking promises to be one of the major revolutions
in the field of finance in this century; evidence of its progress
is everywhere. Much of it is tied into the newly developed
electronic funds transfer system (EFTS), whereby individuals
using telephones or credit cards with magnetic stripes or
optically encoded sections can transfer money, for example,
from their own checking account to that of the retail store
from which they are buying merchandise. As one illustration,
the Seattle First National Bank has devised a system to allow
customers with touch-tone telephones to pay their bills by
phone. Time magazine explains it this way:

The "In-Touch" system is made possible because the bank subsidiary's
computer can interpret touch telephone tones as commands—something
that cannot be done with rotary-dial telephones. By pressing a combination of
numbers, the customer can transfer funds from his account to the accounts
of cooperating businesses with which the customer deals.

The system is somewhat complicated. Using his home or office phone, the
customer must first punch a seven-digit number to get access to the computer,
then enter his personal identification number, then another code number for
the bill-payment service, then a fourth code number for the company to receive
the payment, then a fifth number to indicate the amount of the transaction (all
numbers are kept secret between the bank and the telephone users). A com-
puter-simulated "voice" confirms each step of the transaction over the phone,

so that a customer runs no great risk of paying somebody else's bill by punching the wrong numbers.[1]

Yet this is only one of many illustrations of what is going on in the field. *Business Week* reports still others, including:

In Wilmington, Del., consumers carrying a plastic WSFS "money card" get a 2% discount if they charge purchases at participating merchants. The card authorizes immediate transfer of funds from the customer's Wilmington Savings Fund Society account to the merchant's bank account.

In Columbus, Ohio, after a nine-month test in suburban Upper Arlington, City National Bank & Trust Co. is forging ahead with plans to install 125 terminals in 60 major stores and supermarkets in the Columbus area that will permit "paperless" payments by customers with credit cards. Cleveland Trust Co., Ohio's largest bank, plans to tie in to test "cashless/checkless" transactions in Cleveland.

In Atlanta and San Francisco, automated clearing houses are distributing company payrolls electronically and automatically crediting employees' bank accounts. Banks are urging customers to use single multi-payment checks to pay many bills at once. The Atlanta Payments Project has further plans to set up a regional electronic payments system that will extend electronic cashless, checkless transactions to the retail sales level.[2]

These developments have led one bank executive to conclude that ". . . by 1977, 5 % of the metropolitan areas of the country will have EFTS in place and by 1983, that will grow to 35 % of the metropolitan areas."[3] The cashless-checkless society appears to be just around the corner.

---

[1]"Dial-a-Payment," *Time*, July 9, 1973, p. 59.
[2]"The Quickened Pace of Electronic Banking," *Business Week*, September 15, 1973, p. 116.
[3]*Ibid.*

Questions

1. Would these accomplishments have been possible without the use of the computer? Explain.

2. Is the computer really helpful to banking? After all, by making transactions easier, is it not encouraging individuals to spend more money than they would ordinarily?

3. What other areas will computers revolutionize during the decade of 1975–1985? Explain.

CHAPTER 17

TECHNOLOGY, MANAGEMENT AND THE ORGANIZATION

GOALS OF THE CHAPTER Much of man's progress can be accounted for by technological advances. Discoveries in the areas of agriculture, transportation and communication, for example, have all allowed man to live a more leisurely life, while breakthroughs in the medical arena are providing him a greater amount of time in which to enjoy these new things. Technology is also having its impact on business.

The first goal of this chapter is to examine some modern technological advances, such as communication technology and power production, that are providing both opportunities and challenges to modern business. The second objective is to explore the area of technological forecasting with particular attention devoted to nontechnical factors and their role in such a forecast. The final goal is to examine the impact of technology on both the organization's personnel and its structure. In particular, attention will be focused on:

a. the various stages of technological growth from the time prior to the Industrial Revolution to the modern day;
b. some of the modern technological advances that can be expected in the next three decades in the areas of communication technology and power production;
c. the two basic types of technological forecasts;
d. the problems involved in evaluating the impact of technical and non-technical factors on such a forecast;
e. the effect of technology on organizational personnel; and
f. the impact of technology on the organizational structure.

TECHNOLOGY: AN HISTORICAL PERSPECTIVE

Technology consists of knowledge and technique.

Stages of Technology.

Technology consists of two important ingredients: *knowledge and technique*. Man's ability to apply an idea (knowledge) in a particular way (technique) has been the basis for much of his progress. A cursory review of the stages of technology from the time just prior to the Industrial Revolution to the current day will make this clear.

First there was the era of *handicraft technology*, typified by craftsmen who made things with their hands. Cobblering, tailoring, and carpentering are all examples. The domestic and putting-out systems were also part of this stage. The eighteenth century, however, saw an end to most of this handicraft technology.

In its place came *mechanized technology*, characterized by power-driven machinery. This was the beginning of the factory system, and for the next two hundred years mankind remained in this era, prospering from a host of inventions from the flying shuttle to the steam engine to the cotton gin.

The next stage was that of *mechanistic technology*, which began around the turn of this century. This stage was characterized by the assembly line, such as that used by Ford to build his Model T, and standardized, interchangeable parts, such as those employed by Whitney a full century earlier in the production of muskets and clocks.[1]

Since then, the assembly line has been developed to the stage where machines are now linked together and integrated in such a fashion that they are performing many functions automatically. These developments represent *automated technology* or, as some people have contended, the second industrial revolution.

At the current time, a fifth stage, *cybernated technology*, is beginning. Cybernetics refers to automatic control, and today, with cybernated technology, machines are running and controlling other machines, thereby freeing man for other tasks.

Naturally, it is impossible to say where one stage of technology ended and another began because the time periods have actually overlapped. Currently, for example, some business firms are in the automated technology stage whereas others are in the cybernated technology stage. Nevertheless, the entire area presents tremendous opportunities and challenges to management. A closer look at modern technological advances will make this more clear.

---

[1]Alex Groner et al., *American Business and Industry* (New York: American Heritage Publishing Co., Inc., 1972), pp. 63–64.

'But we don't know enough about it. Does it have side effects?
Is it physically or psychologically addictive? Can it cause mutant
genes?. . .' (Reprinted from the (Toledo) Blade with permission.)

MODERN TECHNOLOGICAL ADVANCES: OPPORTUNITIES AND CHALLENGES

Ninety per cent of all the scientists who ever lived are still alive today, and half of all the knowledge acquired by man in his history has been gathered within the last decade. Applying this knowledge to practical uses has led to many innovations. In addition, not only are the number of these inventions and techniques increasing but also the amount of time between their discovery and application is decreasing, as illustrated in Table 17–1.

Wolfbein reports that some of the more important areas in which technological advances are having the greatest impact include agriculture, improved machinery and materials handling, advances in transportation, communication technology and power production. Space prohibits a discussion of all of these, but attention will be focused on the last two by highlighting the opportunities and challenges that technology holds in store for business.

Communication Technology: An Opportunity

What does the future hold for the businessman in regard to communication technology? Some of the things he has been promised include the ability to:

1. talk face-to-face with associates regardless of distance;

The future promises great progress in communication technology.

2. participate in nationwide (and worldwide) meetings without leaving his office building;

3. perform a large amount of executive functions from his home;

4. have access to unlimited computer resources; and

5. own and operate private telecommunications facilities.[2]

Some of this new communication technology will be used for conveying person-to-person information via voice or video-telephone. The rest will be employed for carrying data to and from, or between, computers. Carne has noted that:

Projections of future telecommunications growth show that the domestic network will almost double in size by the mid-1980's. By this period, we will have over 200 million telephones, including 3 million videotelephones. Some 250,000 computers will have been installed; 200,000 of these computers will be connected to approximately 10 million terminals.

Furthermore, nearly 60% of the United States will be connected to cable systems that provide limited return capabilities. Overhead, a few (perhaps 4) privately owned satellites will provide long-haul connections between important traffic centers in the 50 states. On the ground, several (perhaps 10) companies will compete with existing carriers to provide specialized services.[3]

---

[2] E. Bryan Carne, "Telecommunications: Its Impact on Business," *Harvard Business Review*, July–August 1972, p. 125.
[3] *Ibid.*, p. 131.

TABLE 17-1   From Discovery to Application

Innovation	Year of Discovery	Year of Application
Electric motor	1821	1886
Vacuum tube	1882	1915
Radio broadcasting	1887	1922
X-ray tubes	1895	1913
Nuclear reactor	1932	1942
Radar	1935	1940
Atomic bomb	1938	1945
Transistor	1948	1951
Solar battery	1953	1955
Stereospecific rubbers and plastics	1955	1958

Source: Seymour Wolfbein, "The Pace of Technological Change and the Factors Affecting It," *Manpower Implications of Automation*, Papers presented by U.S. Department of Labor at the O.E.C.D. North American Regional Conference on Manpower Implications of Automation (Washington, D.C., December 8–10, 1964), p. 19.

Thus, communication technology will help the businessman convey information, store data and utilize the power of the computer as never before. However, not all of this new technology will make life easier; some of it will merely stop things from getting worse. The area of power production provides an illustration.

Power Production: A Challenge

The United States is currently facing an energy shortage. What is causing the problem? There are numerous answers, but the following provide some relevant data on the crisis as of the early 1970's.

1. Americans use twice as much electric power per capita as Britain and six times as much as the world average.

America's use of resources for power.

2. Americans produce 1.7 billion tons of fossil fuel every year but use 1.9 billion tons (30% of the world's consumption).

3. The U.S. consumes 15 million barrels of oil a day (30% of the world's consumption).

4. The U.S. uses over 22 trillion cubic feet of natural gas every year (49% of the world's consumption).

5. Americans burn over 530 million tons of coal a year (known reserves stand at 2 trillion tons).[4]

Various approaches for rectifying the situation are currently under study. Some individuals have suggested raising the price of energy, but research shows that people are more influenced by the cost of the equipment or appliance than the price of the energy it consumes. Rather, the answer appears to rest with improved technology.

Efficient Use of Energy.   One method being given serious consideration is that of using energy more efficiently. For example, although modern auto engines are designed to create less environmental pollution, they also get fewer miles to the gallon and thus use more fuel. A reverse of this trend would help

Energy conservation is now under way.

alleviate the energy crisis. So too would *improved building insulation,* which could cut down on heat loss. Currently, "Building standards required for Federal Housing Administration insurance have been raised to levels that reduce heat loss by 40%."[5] Such insulation could also result in fuel savings for air conditioning. Netschert reports that, "A further opportunity for air-conditioning savings lies in a method now being investigated under a National Science Foundation grant—namely, to store the "cold" overnight and thus to reduce the load on the air-conditioning equipment during the day."[6]

---

[4]"Energy Crisis: Are We Running Out?" *Time,* June 12 1972, pp. 49–50.
[5]Bruce C. Netschert, "Energy vs. Environment," *Harvard Business Review,* January–February 1973, p. 138.
[6]*Ibid.*

Another area under study is *electricity generation and trans-mission.* Even the most modern plants operate at only 40 per cent of efficiency. New approaches are therefore being examined. One is magnetohydrodynamics (MHD), which is:

> . . . a method of generating electricity directly, with no moving parts, from the flow of a plasma through a magnetic field. MHD, with possible efficiency levels of 50% to 60%, carries with it the additional attractive advantage of totally eliminating fly ash and sulfur and nitrogen oxides. Moreover, if an MHD unit is operated in conjunction with a gas turbine (rather than steam), there is no need for cooling water.[7]

The *fast-breeder reactor,* which has been called the best hope for meeting the nation's growing demand for clean energy, is also currently being studied. This machine can produce slightly more fuel than it uses, thereby extending fuel supplies indefinitely.[8] The Atomic Energy Commission intends to have a $500 million demonstration plant in operation by 1980.

Alternative Power Sources.   Scientists are also seeking alternative power sources such as the *earth's heat.* For example, the Pacific Gas & Electric Company has the nation's only geothermal

Alternative power sources are being sought.

plant. Using drilled wells and natural vents in the earth's surface, engineers capture sulfurous, superheated steam and use it to drive the utility's turbine engines. Along these same lines, the Los Alamos National Laboratory is trying to exploit the dry, hot (600°F) granite underneath most of the earth. By sinking two 15,000-foot wells beneath the surface and pumping cold water down one, scientists hope to get hot steam to flow up the other. If successful, this dry-rock system, could provide all the electricity the United States will need for the next thirty centuries.

And the ideas go on and on. Some scientists are working on a *fusion process.* "The ideal solution is to reproduce the sun's own process of joining atomic nuclei to produce clean, safe energy. The process, which also powered the hydrogen bomb . . . could fill the world's electricity needs for millions of years."[9] Others are seeking to collect *sunshine* and transform it into power. Still others are investigating possibilities such as harnessing the ocean's tides, combining animal manure and carbon dioxide under heat and pressure to produce oil, and burning garbage as a low-grade fuel.

Can the United States meet the current energy challenge? If its past record is any indication, the answer is undoubtedly "yes."

---

[7]*Ibid.*
[8]For the engineering or physics-minded reader, the process has been described as follows: "The original fuel (fissionable uranium 235, or plutonium) is surrounded by a "blanket" of nonfissionable uranium 238, which absorbs neutrons from the chain reaction in the core. These neutrons transmute the U-238 in the blanket into plutonium, which can fuel another breeder." *Time, op. cit.,* p. 52.
[9]*Ibid.,* p. 55.

As one analyst has noted, ". . . of 50 major industrial innovations of the twentieth century, 32 were initiated wholly or partly
in the United States and 38 were brought wholly or partly
to final commercial application in this country."[10] Thus, the
United States has great potential for solving technological
problems. The major question for the manager, however, is
how will these new developments affect my company? The
answer can be found through technological forecasting.

TECHNOLOGICAL
FORECASTING

Today, more than ever before, management needs to evaluate
and assess the impact of technology on organizational strategy
and survival. This requires an examination of the firm's
operations with a view toward answering questions such as:

1. is the company operating in a technologically sensitive environment?

2. is the firm a leader or a follower in its operational environment?

3. are operations sufficiently large to justify technological forecasting
   activities?

4. how much of a commitment will have to be made in terms of people,
   budget and facilities?

5. does management want occasional, informal technological forecasts or
   periodic, formal ones?[11]

Types of
Technological
Forecasting

If management decides to undertake technological forecasting,
there are two fundamental approaches: exploratory and
normative.

Exploratory
forecasting
projects the
future according
to logical tech-
nological prog-
ress.

Exploratory forecasting begins with the current knowledge and
predicts the future based on logical technological progress. As
such, it is a rather passive process. Forecasters using this
method tend to assume that current technological progress will
continue at the same rate and that this advance will not be
affected by external conditions. Then, later, they can speculate
on how the forecast might be affected by the nontechnical
environment.

Electronics development provides an illustration of how this
method could be used. Immediately after World War II,
transistors were expensive and qualitatively unpredictable.
Since then, however, their price has declined, their quality has
improved, and their application has become widespread. If a
business firm had decided to conduct an exploratory forecast
right after World War II, it would have been possible to predict
these events.

---

[10]Harvey Brooks, "What's Happening to the U.S. Lead in Technology?" *Harvard
Business Review*, May–June 1972, p. 113.
[11]Adapted from Daniel D. Roman, "Technological Forecasting in the Decision
Process," *Academy of Management*, June 1970, p. 136.

Industrial firms, in particular, have found great value in this type of forecasting because it is not very difficult to do. In turn, the results can help the company in its search for clues as to market entry, potential competition and ease of expansion into related product areas.

Normative forecasting begins with an identification of some future technological objective such as the development of a

Normative forecasting works from the future back to the present.

space shuttle by 1991 and works back to the present, identifying the obstacles that will have to be surmounted along the way. Attention is devoted not only to technical factors but to nontechnical factors as well. For example, when will the technical know-how for a space shuttle be available, and how will this time estimate be affected by governmental allocations, i.e., will the government put a lot of money into the project and develop it quickly or will it take a longer time because of reluctance or lack of enthusiasm on Washington's part? In contrast to exploratory forecasting, normative forecasting is a much more dynamic process.

The Delphi Technique

Whichever of the two methods are used, technological forecasting presents a challenge. Fortunately, there are many techniques available to the forecaster. These range in nature from highly intuitive to ultra-sophisticated and include such catchword approaches as morphological analysis, scenario writing and envelope forecasting.[12]

Currently, however, the most popular technological forecasting approach, developed by the Rand Corporation, is the Delphi technique. At present, between fifty and one hundred major corporations are using it. In essence, the approach pools the opinions of experts and calls for:

1. a prediction of important events in the area in question, from each expert in a group, in the form of brief statements;

2. a clarification of these statements by the investigator; and

3. the successive, individual requestioning of each of the experts, combined with feedback supplied from the other experts *via* the investigator.[13]

In the first round of questioning each expert might be asked to list, for example, the developments he believes will occur in his field within the next twenty years that will have a significant effect on the company. He may also be asked to comment on the desirability, feasibility and timing of these developments. Figure 17–1 provides an illustration of the format that might be used.

---

[12]For descriptions of these see John P. Dory and Robert J. Lord, "Does TF Really Work?" *Harvard Business Review*, November–December 1970, p. 20.
[13]"The Basic Delphi Method," *Harvard Business Review*, May–June 1969, p. 81.

DESIRABILITY			FEASIBILITY			TIMING (YEAR BY WHICH PROBABLE EVENT WILL HAVE OCCURRED)		
High	*Average*	*Low*	*High*	*Likely*	*Unlikely*	*10% Probability*	*50% Probability*	*90% Probability*

FIGURE 17-1 Delphi Technique, Round One

1. List all anticipated technical events that will have a significant impact on the firm over the next twenty years.

2. Evaluate each in regard to desirability, feasibility, and timing.

Delphi allows the participants to revise their estimates.

Then, in round two, each expert receives from the investigator a composite of the predictions made by the others, and he is given the opportunity to modify his original estimates. This is usually followed by still further rounds, often a total of five. The result is generally a consensus among the participants regarding the most significant events that will affect the company (events A, E, H and I), the likelihood of their eventual development (90 per cent, 70 per cent, 60 per cent and 40 per cent) and the time period in which they can be expected to occur (1982, 1985, 1987 and 1990). Table 17–2 illustrates the results of some Delphi forecasts.

Despite its apparent lack of scientific rigor, Delphi has proved very successful. In fact, the Rand Corporation has validated the technique through controlled experimentation. However, its use has not been confined exclusively to technological forecasting. It has also been successfully employed, for example,

TABLE 17–2   Examples of Delphi Forecasts

Description of Event	Year Selected by Respondents as Date of Probable Occurrence		
	25%	50%	75%
There will be a single national building code.	1975	1977	1980
Polymers will be created by molecular tailoring, with service temperature ranges in excess of 1,000°F.	1971	1976	2000
SST aircraft will be in regular service over land areas.	1980	1982	1985
Hydrocarbon/air fuel cell will be commercially available.	1974	1983	1990
A source of transplant organs for humans will be developed through selective breeding of animals that are tissue compatible.	1990	2015	2015

Source: First two examples from "McGraw-Hill Survey of Technological Breakthroughs and Widespread Applications of Significant Technical Developments," Department of Economics, McGraw-Hill Book Company, Inc., 1968; third example from "Delphi Studies as an Aid to Corporate Planning," Industrial Management Center, Austin, Texas, 1970; fourth from James R. Bright, ed., *Technological Forecasting for Industry and Government*, particularly, "The Delphi Method—an Illustration"; last example, T. J. Gordon and Robert H. Ament, "Forecasts of Some Technological and Scientific Developments and Their Societal Consequences," Report No. 6, The Institute for the Future, in Alan R. Fusfeld and Richard N. Foster, "The Delphi Technique: Survey and Comment," *Business Horizons*, June 1971, p. 65.

to help participants formulate responses to questions whose answers are already known. For example, how many votes were cast for Lincoln in 1860, or how many oil wells were there in Texas in 1960? In most cases, after a few rounds of questioning, the consensus has moved close to the actual answer. It can thus be seen why Delphi is so popular.

Technical and Nontechnical Factors

Technical factors such as chance occurrence can undermine a forecast.

The major problem confronting the forecaster is that of evaluating technical and nontechnical factors. In the technical area, for example, a pharmaceutical company might estimate that there will be chemical control of hereditary defects through molecular engineering by 1990. However, what if by *chance occurrence* someone stumbles onto a discovery and makes a major breakthrough in this field in 1983? How can one forecast such developments?

Nontechnical factors such as lack of public acceptance can also undermine a forecast.

Meanwhile, on the nontechnical side, there is the problem of lack of *public acceptance*. The American supersonic transport (SST) is an illustration. In 1963, when the United States learned that the British and French were going to combine their efforts to build an SST, the Concorde, President Kennedy urged the Congress to allocate funds for a feasibility study. By 1970, the plane was already in the mock-up stage, but by this time the entire project had become a political issue. The Nixon Administration stood squarely behind the development and production of the craft, but the public apparently did not, as reflected in the vote of the Congress. One reason was undoubtedly research, such as that conducted by a Ph.D. candidate at Columbia University, which showed that the government and the contractors stood to lose large sums of money if the plane was built. People were just not going to pay the extra money to get, for example, from New York to London a few hours earlier.[14] Nontechnical factors (lack of demand for the aircraft, lack of profit for all parties involved) proved to be more important than the technical ones.[15]

The forecaster must thus evaluate technical progress and nontechnical constraints. These two concepts can be brought together as seen in Figure 17–2, which illustrates the process of technical innovation. Since the forecast must incorporate changes in the social, political and economic environment as well as in the technical environment, it is evident that formal

[14]For an in-depth review of this area see Richard M. Hodgetts, "The Rise and Fall of the SST," Intercollegiate Case Clearing House, Harvard University, Soldier's Field, Boston, Mass.

[15]The reader might be interested to know that the Concorde is apparently proving to be a financial dilemma. By 1973 Air Canada, Pan Am, TWA and United had all cancelled their options to buy the plane. And although the world's airlines still held options for 42 of these craft, there were firm orders for only nine and letters of intent for but two more. See "The Bleak Arithmetic of the Concorde," *Business Week*, February 10, 1973, p. 29.

forecasting techniques are incomplete. The manager must also employ an informal scanning process, asking the question, is there anything else that we have not yet considered that might affect our forecast? Sometimes the answer is so obvious that it is overlooked. Consider the following case of a technology manager in a large company:

> Several years ago he initiated a technological forecasting effort on a one-shot basis, using a morphological technique with some Delphi inputs. Over 100 fields of technology were selected for study, with the objective of identifying broad areas of expertise where the company should develop or maintain a capability in the future. After an extensive forecasting procedure, 12 areas of potential importance were selected and recommended to the planning committee. Yet, as the manager of technology later noted, even after this rigorous search, one of the most significant areas—environmental control—was not identified.[16]

TECHNOLOGY AND THE PERSONNEL

The technological forecast will have an impact on the organization's goals since the goals will be reflections of the forecast. However, the impact of technology extends beyond this, affecting the human dimensions as well.

Technology, Tension and Effectiveness

Bringing people and technology together can cause tension. There is, for example, a relationship between effectiveness and tension, as illustrated in Figure 17–3. Up to a point (B), some degree of pressure, accountability, responsibility, pride and obligation are necessary. However, if tension is increased

---

[16]Dory and Lord, *op. cit.*, p. 22.

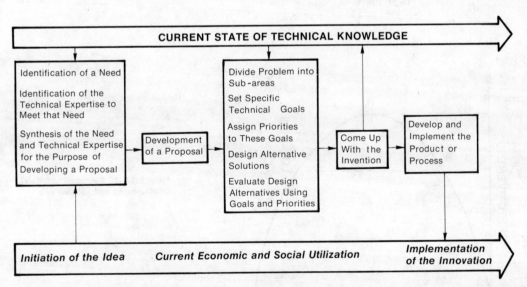

FIGURE 17–2 Process of Technical Knowledge (Adapted from James M. Utterback, "The Process of Technological Innovation Within the Firm," *Academy of Management Journal,* March 1971, p. 78.)

beyond this point (to C, for example), effectiveness can decline. [17]

Technology can cause tension and impair personnel effectiveness.

The same is true in the case of technological capability and effectiveness, as seen in Figure 17–4. To the left of Point E there is insufficient technological capability for getting the job done, whereas to the right of this point there is too much.

Figures 17–3 and 17–4 can be brought together and overlapped in three-dimensional style. As Boettinger notes:

> . . . if a brilliant technologist makes optimal provision of tools (Point E) to an inept manager who operates at Points A or C, he has wasted his time. If an ideal manager, carrying his people to Point B, has been furnished the wrong processes of equipment (points D or F), his people cannot catch rivals who have skilled technologists looking after their interests.
>
> One can compensate for bad technology, to some extent, with greater leadership, and for poor leadership with superb technology. But peak performance can never be achieved without peaks in *both* domains—the human and the technical. [18]

The challenge is thus one of introducing neither too much nor too little tension or technology, and this is not an easy task.

Effect on the People

At the worker level, for example, technology can affect the social relationships that exist among the men by bringing about changes in elements such as the size and composition of the

---

[17]The data in this section can be found in Henry M. Boettinger, "Technology in the Manager's Future," *Harvard Business Review*, November-December 1970, pp. 4–14, 165.
[18]*Ibid.*, p. 14.

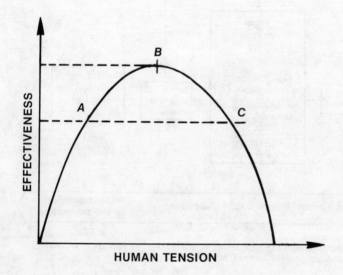

FIGURE 17–3 Relationship Between Effectiveness and Tension

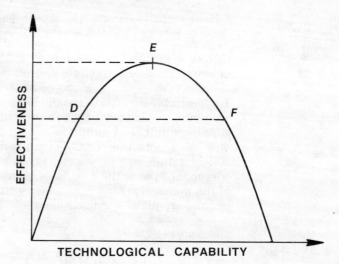

FIGURE 17-4 Relationship Between Effectiveness and Technological Capability

work group or the frequency of contact with the other workers. This was seen in Chapter 5 when Trist's longwall coal-getting study was discussed. It will be remembered that the miners initially worked in small, independent, cohesive groups. However, new advances in technology and equipment led to changes in the composition of these work groups. The result was a decline in productivity. Only when the management restored many of the social and small group relationships did output again increase.[19] Technological advance may also lead to the abolition of jobs or the reduction of tasks to simplistic levels. All these changes brought about by technology will affect the psycho-social system.

Technology can affect the psychosocial system.

In order to prevent too great an upheaval, it is necessary for management to consider the human as well as the technical needs of the organization. One of the most important studies in this area was conducted by Mann and his associates at the Institute for Social Research.[20] After analyzing the effect on the personnel of a changeover to electronic data processing equipment in a major utility over a five-year period they found:

One of the most pressing problems during this period was the maintenance of a high level of group morale and individual job satisfaction. Every attempt was made to arrive at solutions that would be satisfactory to each individual. While the general policy of reassignment served as guidelines, many unique solutions had to be invented in individual cases. The old problem remained of

[19]E. L. Trist and K. W. Bamforth, "Some Social and Psychological Consequences of the Longwall Method of Coal-getting," *Human Relations*, February 1951, pp. 3–38.
[20]Floyd C. Mann and Lawrence K. Williams, "Observations on the Dynamics of a Change to Electronic Data-Processing Equipment," *Administrative Science Quarterly*, September 1960, pp. 217–256.

devising a solution that would meet the employee's personal needs, the company objectives, and still be perceived as appropriate publicly.[21]

Unless the impact of technology on the worker is considered, organizational effectiveness and efficiency will suffer.

Technology also affects the managerial staff. Today, managers are more specialized than ever before, as seen through the ever-growing number of public relations, operations researchers and other staff personnel in the organization. Whereas primary consideration was previously given to breaking jobs into their component parts, the emphasis today is on integrating the work of the managers. This is especially true in industries in which technology plays a major role.

[21]Ibid., pp. 244–245.

TABLE 17-3   A Comparison of Some of the Key Dimensions of Mechanistic and Organic Organization Structures

Systems and Their Key Dimensions	Characteristics of Organization Systems	
	Closed/Stable/ Mechanistic	Open/Adaptive/ Organic
Environmental Suprasystem		
General nature	Peaceful	Turbulent
Predictability	High certainty	High uncertainty
Technology	Stable	Dynamic
Degree of environmental influence on organization	Low	High
Overall Organizational System		
Emphasis of organization	On performance	On problem solving
Predictability of actions	Relatively certain	Relatively uncertain
Decision-making process	Programmable	Nonprogrammable
Goals and Values		
Overall values	Efficiency, predictability, security, risk averting	Effectiveness, adaptability, responsiveness, risk taking
Involvement in setting objectives	Primarily from the top down	Wide participation, including people from the bottom as well as from the top
Technical System		
Knowledge	Highly specialized	Highly generalized
Time perspective	Short-term	Long-term
Interdependency of tasks	Low	High

(Table 17–3 continued on opposite page.)

Burns and Stalker, for example, undertook a study of a number of British and Scottish firms. These companies were operating in stable technologies and environments, but they were trying to move into the electronics field, which is characterized by rapidly changing technology.[22] The researchers found that in making this transition, these companies underwent significant changes in their management systems. Initially they were *mechanistic*, characterized by formal job descriptions and a rigid organization structure. Everyone knew what they were doing and to whom they reported. In the new environment, however, an *organic* managerial system developed. (See Table 17–3 for a comparison of some of the key dimensions of

Technology can also lead to the replacement of mechanistic structures by organic ones.

[22]Tom Burns and G. M. Stalker, *The Management of Innovation* (London: Tavistock Publications, 1961).

TABLE 17–3   A Comparison of Some of the Key Dimensions of Mechanistic and Organic Organizations Structures — Continued

Systems and Their Key Dimensions	Characteristics of Organization Systems	
	Closed/Stable/ Mechanistic	Open/Adaptive/ Organic
Structural System		
Procedures and rules	Many, often formal and written	Few, often informal and unwritten
Levels of the hierarchy	Many	Few
Source of authority	Position in organization	Knowledge of individual
Responsibility	Attached to position	Assumed by individual
Psycho-social System		
Interpersonal relationships	Formal	Informal
Personal involvement	Low	High
Motivation factors	Emphasis on low-level needs (Theory X)	Emphasis on upper-level needs (Theory Y)
Leadership Style	Autocratic	Democratic
Managerial System		
Content of communications	Decisions and instructions	Advice and information
Control process	Impersonal use of devices such as rules and regulations	Interpersonal contacts, persuasion and suggestions
Means of resolving conflict	Superior uses the "book" in handling the matter	Group resolves issue with situational ethics

Adapted from Fremont E. Kast and James E. Rosenzweig, *Contingency Views of Organization and Management* (Chicago: Science Research Associates, Inc., 1973), pp. 315–318.

mechanistic and organic organization structures.) Management had to adapt to changing conditions and the old, mechanistic structure gave way to a more flexible one. Managers found themselves interacting more with each other and placing greater emphasis on lateral than vertical communication. In order to survive in this new dynamic environment, the managers began to restructure the old line-staff relationships and devise more modern, flexible ones. Technology thus affects not only the people but the structure itself.

TECHNOLOGY AND STRUCTURE

One of the most significant studies evaluating the impact of technology on structure was conducted by Joan Woodward.[23] Her research, encompassing 100 firms in a London suburb, sought to determine how structural variables affected economic success. She found the answer by analyzing the types of technology the firms were employing. There were three types in all:

1. *Mass and large batch production.* **This type of technology is used for mass-production items. Automobiles and television sets are illustrations.**

2. *Continuous process production.* **This type of technology is employed in producing continuous-flow production items. The manufacture of chemicals or the processing of oils are illustrations.**

3. *Unit and small batch production.* **This type of technology is used for "one-of-a-kind" products or those built to customer specifications. Lunar modules and locomotives are illustrations.**

The appropriateness of the organizational structure, she found, was dependent on the type of technology the firm used. If the company employed mass-production techniques, a mechanistic structure seemed to work best. Conversely, if the firm used continuous-process or unit production, in which technology plays a more significant role, an organic structure seemed to work best. These findings are illustrated in Table 17–4.

In addition, Woodward found that the organic structures tended to be more human relations oriented than the mechanistic ones.

---

[23]Joan Woodward, *Industrial Organization: Theory and Practice* (London: Oxford University Press, 1965).

TABLE 17–4   Woodward's Research Findings

Mechanistic	Organic
Mass production	Continuous process Unit production

Follow-Up Research

Since Woodward's initial study, other researchers have also attempted to evaluate the importance of technology on the organization. Perhaps the most widely known of these is that by Zwerman who, using 55 firms from the Minneapolis area, replicated Woodward's research in the United States.[24] In essence, he corroborated her basic findings,[25] concluding that the "type of production technology was most closely and consistently related to variations in the organizational characteristics of the firms. . . ."[26]

Numerous research studies have been conducted on the effect of technology on structure.

In a related study, Lawrence and Lorsch[27] posed the question, what form of management is best under which conditions? Employing a sample of ten industrial organizations, they grouped them by degree of marked and technological change. The six in the plastics industry were categorized as operating in a highly dynamic environment; the two in the consumer foods industry were seen as being in an environment with an "intermediate" degree of change; the two in the standardized container industry were identified as being in a relatively stable environment. The researchers found that to be successful, those in the dynamic environment needed a flexible structure, whereas those in the stable environment were most effective with a mechanistic management system, and those in the intermediate environment needed to operate somewhere between the two extremes.

Meyer, studying the impact of automation on the formal structure, investigated 254 state and local government departments of finance.[28] He found that automation creates interdependency in the organization, and nonhierarchical (organic) structures are better able to deal with the situation than are rigid, hierarchical (mechanical) ones.

Although other research can be cited to further substantiate these findings,[29] the general pattern is already clear: technology has a definite impact on organizational structure (see Table 17–5). It is thus possible to extend Chandler's thesis of "from

---

[24]William L. Zwerman, *New Perspectives on Organization Theory* (Westport, Conn.: Greenwood Publishing Corporation, 1970).

[25]Because of a lack of firms in continuous-process operations, however, he was unable to make any inferences about this particular group.

[26]Zwerman, *op. cit.*, p. 148.

[27]Paul R. Lawrence and Jay W. Lorsch, *Organization and Environment* (Boston: Harvard Graduate School of Business Administration, 1967).

[28]Marshall W. Meyer, "Automation and Bureaucratic Structure," *American Journal of Sociology*, November 1968, pp. 256–264.

[29]For example, see Edward Harvey, "Technology and the Structure of Organizations," *American Sociological Review*, April 1968, pp. 247–259.

TABLE 17-5   Research Findings Relating Technology and Organization Structure

Researcher	Organization Structure		
	Mechanistic	Intermediate	Organic
Woodward	Mass production		Continuous process Unit production
Zwerman	Mass production		Unit production
Lawrence and Lorsch	Stable environment	Intermediate degree of stability	Dynamic environment
Meyer	Low degree of interdependency		High degree of interdependency

Adapted from Robert T. Keller, "A Look at the Sociotechnical System," *California Management Review*, Fall 1972, p. 89.

strategy to structure"[30] by incorporating the technological factor in Figure 17–5:

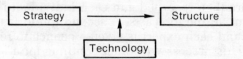

FIGURE 17–5 Impact of Technology on Structure

One final point merits attention. Technology is not the *only* factor affecting structure, nor is it always the most critical. (In fact, Hickson found it to be of significant importance only for small organizations.[31]) Where it does play a role, it is the effect on such variables as the span of control and manager-manager and manager-subordinate relationships that is important. As Woodward has noted:

Among the organizational characteristics showing a direct relationship with technical advance were: the length of the line of command; the span of control of the chief executive; the percentage of total turnover allocated to the payment of wages and salaries; and the ratios of managers to total personnel, of clerical and administrative staff to manual workers, of direct to indirect labour, and of graduate to non-graduate supervision in production departments.[32]

SUMMARY

This chapter has examined technology and its impact on the business firm. Many changes have occurred in the modern world because of technological advances. However, the major question for the businessman is, what impact will technology have on the company? One way of answering this query is through technological forecasting.

There are two types of technological forecasts: exploratory and normative. An *exploratory* forecast is one that starts with the current state of knowledge and predicts the future based on logical technological progress. Forecasters who use this method tend to play down the nontechnical environment. A *normative* forecast is one that identifies a particular technological objective and estimates at what point in the future it will be attained. Instead of working from the present to the future, however, the forecaster works backward, from the time he believes the breakthrough will occur to the present. In addition, the normative forecaster gives high consideration to the nontechnical environment.

[30]Alfred D. Chandler, Jr., *Strategy and Structure* (Garden City, New York: Anchor Books, Doubleday & Company, Inc., 1966).
[31]David J. Hickson, D. S. Pugh and Diana C. Pheysey, "Operations Technology and Organization Structure: An Empirical Reappraisal," *Administrative Science Quarterly*, September 1969, pp. 378–397.
[32]Woodward, *op. cit.*, p. 51.

In conducting a technological forecast, many techniques are available from morphological analysis to scenario writing to envelope forecasting. The most popular method at present is the Delphi technique, which pools the opinions of experts, each predicting when a particular future event will occur. These estimates are then recorded and each individual is given a composite of all the forecasts. A second round is then conducted and each expert is given a chance to revise his estimates. This process will often continue for a total of five rounds and generally results in a consensus of opinion among the experts. Although Delphi may appear to lack scientific rigor, the Rand Corporation has validated the approach through controlled experimentation.

Regardless of the technique employed, these forecasts must evaluate both technical and nontechnical factors. On the technical side there is not only the rate of progress to be considered but also the likelihood of a major accidental breakthrough that will throw all forecasts awry. On the non-technical side there is the issue of public acceptance.

Many companies are well aware of the impact of technology on strategy and profit. However, technological advances also affect the organizational personnel from the workers right up to the managers. At the worker level, technology affects social relationships as well as job content. At the managerial level, it encourages greater integration of effort.

Technology also affects the organization structure by causing changes in factors such as the length of the line of command, the span of control of the chief executive and the ratio of managers to total personnel. In addition, mechanistic designs tend to give way to organic ones. This has been seen in the research of Woodward, Zwerman, Lawrence and Lorsch, and Meyer, to name but a few.

What do these new organic structures look like? How do they work? When, specifically, are they used? These questions will be answered in Chapter 18, in which modern organization structures are examined.

REVIEW AND STUDY QUESTIONS

1. Technology consists of two important ingredients: knowledge and technique. Explain this statement.

2. In your own words, briefly outline the changes that have occurred as mankind progressed from handicraft technology to cybernated technology.

3. Why is the amount of time between the discovery of inventions and their application decreasing?

4. What are some of the changes that can be expected during the next decade in the area of communication technology? How will these affect the manager?

5. Why is the United States facing an energy crisis? What are some of the technological approaches being considered? Explain.

6. How does a manager conduct an exploratory technological forecast? A normative technological forecast?

7. How can a manager use the Delphi technique in making a technological forecast? Explain by discussing the steps in the process.

8. Why are nontechnological factors so important in a technological forecast?

9. What impact can technology have on workers? On managers?

10. What is a mechanistic organization structure? Give an example.

11. What is an organic organization structure? Give an example.

12. Based on recent research, what effect does technology have on organization structure? Include in your answer the research conducted by Joan Woodward.

SELECTED REFERENCES

"A Laser System That Spots Product Defects." *Business Week,* June 2, 1973, pp. 80, 82, 84.

Boettinger, H. M. "Technology in the Manager's Future." *Harvard Business Review,* November–December 1970, pp. 4–14, 165.

Brooks, H. "Whats Happening to the U.S. Lead in Technology?" *Harvard Business Review,* May–June 1972, pp. 110–118.

Burns, T., and G. M. Stalker. *The Management of Innovation.* London: Tavistock Publications, 1961.

Carne, E. B. "Telecommunications: Its Impact on Business." *Harvard Business Review,* July–August 1972, pp. 125–132.

Dory, J. P., and R. J. Lord. "Does TF Really Work?" *Harvard Business Review,* November–December 1970, pp. 16–28, 168.

Hickson, D. J., D. S. Pugh, and D. C. Pheysey. "Operations Technology and Organization Structure: An Empirical Reappraisal." *Administrative Science Quarterly,* September 1969, pp. 378–397.

Hunt, R. G. "Technology and Organization." *Academy of Management Journal,* September 1970, pp. 235–252.

Lawrence, P. R., and J. W. Lorsch. *Organization and Environment.* Boston: Harvard Graduate School of Business Administration, 1967.

Mesthene, E. G. *Technological Change,* Cambridge, Mass: Harvard University Press, 1970.

Netschert, B. C. "Energy vs. Environment," *Harvard Business Review,* January–February 1973, pp. 24–28, 133.

North, H. Q., and D. L. Pyke. "'Probes' of the Technological Future." *Harvard Business Review,* May–June 1969, pp. 68–82.

Rezler, J. *Automation and Industrial Labor.* New York: Random House Inc., 1969.

Roman, D. D. "Technological Forecasting in The Decision Process." *Academy of Management Journal,* June 1970, pp. 127–138.

Swager, W. L. "Technological Forecasting In Planning. *Business Horizons,* February 1973, pp. 37–44.

Utterback, J. M. "The Process of Technological Innovation Within the Firm."
   Academy of Management Journal, March 1971, pp. 75–88.
Woodward, J. *Industrial Organization: Theory and Practice*. London: Oxford
   University Press, 1965.
Zwerman, W. L. *New Perspectives on Organization Theory*. Westport, Conn.:
   Greenwood Publishing Corporation, 1970.

CASE: FASTER THAN A SPEEDING BULLET[1]

Technology is increasing at a tremendously rapid rate. In the
field of transportation, for example, the fastest means of travel
available to man in 6000 B.C. was the camel caravan, which
averaged around eight miles per hour. By 1600 B.C., when the
chariot was invented, the maximum speed rose to twenty miles
per hour. It was not until the 1880's, with the help of the advanced steam engine, that man was able to reach speeds of
100 miles per hour. It had taken a million years to attain this
goal, but now the pace picked up. Within the next sixty years,
thanks to the invention of the airplane, man was moving at
400 miles per hour. Twenty years later that speed had
doubled. And in the 1960's, rocket planes were approaching
speeds of 4000 miles per hour, and astronauts and cosmonauts
were circling the earth in space capsules at 18,000 miles per
hour. If progress in the field of transportation during the last
generation were plotted on a graph, the line would run off the
page.

The same general acceleration can be seen in many areas,
because the amount of time between a product's invention and
its fruition is decreasing. For example, it was 2000 years from
the time when Appollonius of Perga discovered conic sections
until they were applied to engineering problems. In more
recent time, the same pattern exists. In 1836, using technology
over twenty years old, a machine capable of mowing, threshing,
tying straw into sheaves and pouring grain into sacks was
invented. It was not until the 1930's, however, that such a
product was actually marketed. Likewise, the first typewriter
patent was issued in 1714, but over 150 years passed before
these machines became commercially available. And it was a
full century between the time Nicholas Appert discovered how
to can food and the time when canning became important in
the food industry.

In the twentieth century this gap has decreased dramatically.
Robert Young of the Stanford Research Institute has found that
for a group of appliances introduced before 1920, including
the refrigerator, the vacuum cleaner and the electric range, it
took approximately 34 years between introduction and peak

---

[1]The data in this case can be found in Alvin Toffler, *Future Shock* (New York:
Bantam Books, Inc., 1971).

production. For a group introduced between 1939 to 1969, including television, the electric frying pan and the washer-dryer combination, however, the time span was only eight years. In Young's words "The post-war group demonstrated vividly the rapidly accelerating nature of the modern cycle."

When one examines the above facts, it becomes evident that technology, fueled by ever-increasing scientific knowledge, is bringing about fantastic changes at an ever-increasing rate. With it, however, comes the possibility that man will be unable to cope with these new conditions; it is too much, too fast. This has led Toffler to conclude:

> Our first and most pressing need, therefore, before we can begin to gently build a humane future, is to halt the runaway acceleration that is subjecting multitudes to the threat of future shock while, at the very same moment, intensifying all the problems they must deal with—war, ecological incursions, racism, the obscene contrast between rich and poor, the revolt of the young, and the rise of a potentially deadly mass irrationalism.

Questions

1. How can man learn to live in such a technologically accelerative environment?

2. Is business facing a situation similar to that described in this case? Explain.

3. What changes can be expected in business organization structures because of technology?

4. What impact will technology have on the organization's personnel? Explain.

CASE: THE NEXT BEST THING TO BEING THERE[1]

By late 1971, companies in the communication industry were reporting that many different types of telephone gadgets and "extras" could be purchased, thanks to modern technology. For example, some firms were having taped music installed on the "hold" line so callers could listen to music while waiting to be connected with their party. Other available services or hardware included:

1. automatic switchboards which were rigged to give a "beep" on the busy line. Then, if the person being called did not put the party on hold and answer the call, the switchboard would automatically ring a nearby phone.

---

[1]The data in this case can be found in "The Revolution in the Phone Business," *Business Week*, November 6, 1971, pp. 66–69, 72–74.

2. small plugless or cordless PABX's which were much easier to manage, thereby freeing the receptionist for other tasks.

3. priority overrides so that executives who needed to could break into busy lines.

But companies in the industry were doing more than just designing new telephone gadgetry. Many were also interested in building communication satellites.

Lofted into stationary orbit 22,000 mi. above the equator, a communications satellite acts as a single microwave relay station. But instead of having a limited range, it can bounce anything, from television pictures to telegraph channels, from Hawaii to Maine and any points in between at equal cost.

The cost benefits are significant, compared to ground-based systems. For a minimum investment of about $46 million, a satellite system can blanket the whole continent with long-distance communication links. In the U.S., which is already wired with cable and microwave from coast to coast, satellite communications will provide economical, extra capacity.

Some of the firms which had applications pending before the Federal Communication Commission included AT&T, Fairchild Hiller, RCA, Western Union, Comsat and Hughes Aircraft. The payback period on these communication satellites was expected to be around three to four years.

Questions

1. How important is improved telephone service for business?

2. Do you think these new technological advances will mean higher costs? Explain.

3. What further new developments affecting business do you think there will be by the 1980's? Explain.

CASE: 1985: AN EARLY LOOK[1]

What do the 1980's hold in store for business? In an attempt to answer this question, four large corporations, Lever Brothers, Monsanto, Scott Paper and Du Pont, have given financial backing to an undertaking called Project Aware, a unique attempt to predict the economic, technological and social environment these firms will face during the decades of the 1980's. Using the Delphi technique, the Institute for the Future, which is conducting the analysis, released its first results in August 1973. Some of the predictions were the following:

---

[1]The data in this case can be found in "A Think Tank That Helps Companies Plan," *Business Week*, August 25, 1973, pp. 70–71.

1. Quality of life—In all likelihood it will decline. Although economic standards will rise, expectations of citizen's will outrun the nation's ability to fulfill them.

2. Energy crisis—Will probably be resolved by such market forces as rising prices and the development of new energy sources.

3. Worker discontent—Changes in manufacturing methods and the use of job enrichment could increase productivity by as much as 50 per cent but worker discontent will increase throughout the decade.

4. Business procedures—Will probably not change much although after about 1985 the costs of computer entry, storage and access will fall beneath the cost of paper files.

In addition to the above, the Institute for the Future predicted the probability of the following events occurring by 1985:

Event	Percent Probability
Many chemical pesticides phased out	95
National health insurance enacted	90
Spending on environmental quality exceeds 6% of GNP	90
Insect hormones widely used as pesticides	80
Community review of factory locations	80
Substantial understanding of baldness and skin wrinkling	40
A modest (3%) value-added tax passed	40
Wide use of computers in elementary schools	25
Development of cold vaccines	20
Autos banned in central areas of at least seven cities	20
Breeder reactors banned for safety reasons	20

Are such predictions useful to companies in formulating long-range plans? *Business Week* reports that a number of businesses are incorporating Delphi methods into their corporate planning. Of course, the results of such predictions may be inaccurate, but as one manager put it, "a Delphi study tells you what ballpark you're playing in."

Questions

1. What did the above manager mean by his statement about Delphi telling you "what ballpark you're playing in"?

2. What kinds of questions can the Delphi technique answer that would be of value to business?

3. If, as reported in this case, worker discontent will increase in the 1980's what impact do you see this having on organization structures? Explain, incorporating into your discussion the concepts of mechanistic and organic organization designs.

CASE: MORE ORDER, NOT LESS

When Nebbing Incorporated started business in 1947, its three founders stated the firm's basic mission as one of "inventing and manufacturing sophisticated telecommunication equipment." Over the next 25 years the company prospered, thanks to the high degree of technical expertise possessed by the owners and the staff they hired. In 1973, however, the three men decided that they had had enough. They wished to retire and spend the rest of their years in leisure. They therefore sold Nebbing to a large national conglomerate for $40 million. This was the conglomerate's first venture into the communication industry; its initial success had come in manufacturing. Nevertheless, the board of directors liked Nebbing's profitability picture and felt that the company would be making an excellent acquisition.

Soon after the takeover, the Nebbing personnel were told that there would be no radical changes; it was to be "business as usual." The only change the conglomerate intended to institute was that of reorganizing the structure; the new owners wanted to install a line-staff organization. When asked about this, the president of the firm said, "We feel Nebbing is too disorganized. We want to create more formal lines of communication and authority-responsibility relationships. This way everyone will know what he is supposed to be doing and to whom he should report. At present, this is not the case."

Within six months after the reorganization, however, Nebbing's financial statements indicated that something was wrong. Instead of obtaining high profitability, the newly acquired company was reporting its first loss in years. The president and his advisors were unable to explain why. One of the board members put it this way. "We tried to straighten out the firm's chaotic nature by introducing some order into the structure. But instead of becoming more profitable, they're now losing money. The president has talked it over with us and decided to call in a management consulting firm. Perhaps we need more of a formalized structure than we initially thought. In any event, something has to be done."

Questions

1. Why is the new organization structure not working? Explain.

2. What do you think of the president's comment about Nebbing being too disorganized?

3. What recommendations would you make to this firm? Explain, bringing into your discussion the topics of mechanistic and organic structures.

CHAPTER 18

MODERN ORGANIZATION STRUCTURES

GOALS OF THE CHAPTER One of the greatest challenges facing the modern manager is that of coping with change. Some of this change is brought on by conditions in the external environment and some of it is internally generated. In either case, the organization must be capable of meeting the demands of the situation. One way in which this is being done is through the use of modern organization structures. Business firms are finding that with these new adaptive, flexible designs they are better able to interact with their external environment. At the same time, these structures encourage the use of modern motivation and leadership techniques. Theory X assumptions are replaced by Theory Y assumptions, and fixed ideas about leadership give way to a contingency approach. The goal of this chapter is to examine some of the modern organization structures being used by today's manager. Particular attention will be focused on:

a. the decline of bureaucratic structures;
b. the project organization and its value in handling "one-of-a-kind" undertakings;
c. the matrix structure and its ability to blend project and functional organizations together via a hybrid design;
d. the free-form organization with its highly unstructured nature; and
e. the new trend toward contingency organization design.

THE DECLINE OF BUREAUCRATIC STRUCTURES In the extreme, there are two types of organization designs: bureaucratic and adaptive. If placed on a continuum, they would appear as in Figure 18–1.

Bureaucratic
Structures ——————————————— Adaptive
Structures

FIGURE 18–1 An Organization Structure Continuum

The bureaucracy is a highly structured organization. In its *ideal* form, this structure has five main characteristics. Max Weber, the German sociologist who made one of the earliest and best known studies of this organizational design, identified these characteristics as:

1. a clear-cut division of labor resulting in a host of specialized experts in each position;

Characteristics of an ideal bureaucracy.

2. a hierarchy of offices, with each lower one being controlled and supervised by a higher one;

3. a consistent system of abstract rules and standards which assures uniformity in the performance of all duties and the coordination of various tasks;

4. a spirit of formalistic impersonality in which officials carry out the duties of their office; and

5. employment based on technical qualifications and protected from arbitrary dismissal.[1]

Of course, no organization employs the bureaucracy in its ideal form; however, many use some version of it. The problem with these organization structures is that, to a large degree, they are proving to be unworkable. Quite simply, they lack the ability to cope with the stress, change and tension brought on by today's complex environment. One reason is that they are too closed-systems oriented. A second reason is that they attempt to regiment their personnel with detailed rules and procedures.

In their place are evolving modern structures capable of dealing with a dynamic environment and a complex employee. To a large degree, these new structures incorporate much of the latest thinking contained in earlier chapters, especially those related to communication, motivation, leadership and the systems concept (Chapters 12 to 15). Furthermore, as McFarland points out, these new structures "are not merely variations or improvements in the bureaucratic model; they represent extensive departures from the underlying assumptions, theories, structures, and aims of the bureaucratic model."[2] One of these new designs is known as the project organization.

THE PROJECT ORGANIZATION   The use of the project organization has increased throughout the last decade. It is currently being employed in numerous and diverse undertakings from building dams, weapon systems and spacecraft to conducting research and development, choosing distribution center sites and redesigning bank credit-card

---

[1]Peter M. Blau, *Bureaucracy in Modern Society* (New York: Random House Inc., 1956), pp. 28–33.
[2]Dalton E. McFarland, *Management: Principles and Practices*, 4th edition (New York: The Macmillan Company, 1974), p. 154.

systems. Although the project organization can take various forms, there is one overriding characteristic which distinguishes it from the usual line and staff departments: once the project has been completed, the organization is phased out. This is made clear by its very definition. Project management is "the gathering of the best available talent to accomplish a specific and complex undertaking within time, cost and/or quality parameters, followed by the disbanding of the team upon completion of the undertaking."[3] In a manner of speaking, the project manager and his personnel work themselves out of a job. The group members then go on to another project, are given jobs elsewhere in the organization or, in some cases, are phased out entirely.

The major advantage of the project form of organization is that it allows a project manager and his team to concentrate their attention on one specific undertaking. The manager makes sure that his project does not get lost in the shuffle of organizational activities, because he is there to look after it. As Cleland and King point out, "The project managers act as focal points for their project activities. . . ."[4]

Although the structure has many advantages, its application is limited. For example, one writer has recommended the following criteria for the use of a project structure: (1) definable in terms of a specific goal; (2) somewhat unique and unfamiliar to the existing organization; (3) complex with respect to interdependence of activities necessary to accomplishment; (4) critical with respect to possible gain or loss; and (5) temporary with respect to duration of need.[5]

Criteria for using a project structure.

Planning The Project

Once it has been determined that a project organization will be used, the objectives must be set, the personnel obtained, the structure formulated, and a control system designed for obtaining feedback. Although the organization will be more fluid than its conventional line-staff counterpart, there will still be the assignment of authority and responsibility. The structure will therefore be formalized to some degree. A project manager will be appointed to oversee the undertaking and personnel will be assigned to him. Some of them will remain through the duration of the project while others may be involved for only a short period of time. The duties of the project personnel are thus going to vary with the objectives and the organizational structure. In the development and production of a ballistic

[3]Richard M. Hodgetts, "An Interindustry Analysis of Certain Aspects of Project Management" (Ph.D. diss., University of Oklahoma, 1968), p. 7.
[4]David I. Cleland and William R. King, *Systems Analysis and Project Management* (New York: McGraw–Hill Book Company, 1968), p. 164.
[5]John M. Stewart, "Making Project Management Work," *Business Horizons,* Fall 1965, pp. 54–68.

missile, for example, many people would be assigned to support the project. Collectively, they would have responsibility for the following activities:

1. ascertaining the overall organizational strategic plan;
2. determining both the technical specifications of the missile and the desires of the customers, i.e., the federal government;
3. building, testing and evaluating the prototype;
4. establishing reliability, maintainability and supportability requirements of the project;
5. determining supply sources for the project items that must be purchased;
6. negotiating and managing all contracts associated with the project;
7. developing and maintaining all schedules designed to produce the missile on time;
8. seeing that technical manuals and reports required for the project are drawn up and distributed;
9. planning, installing, operating and maintaining the completed project;
10. providing supportability for the missile after it is produced, i.e., spare parts, support equipment and trained personnel;
11. continually monitoring all costs associated with the project;
12. establishing product design and performance characteristics;
13. providing the most up to date technology within time and cost parameters; and
14. identifying and developing the personnel skills that will be required in using the product.[6]

Designing The Project Structure

Once the objectives have been ascertained, the project structure can be designed, which may take numerous forms from simple to very complex. In the simple structure, seen in Figure 18–2, the project manager is put in charge of an undertaking and given direct authority over the team members. The project manager has all the resources he needs for getting the job done, and the departments under his control are exact duplicates of the permanent functional organization. This type of design is often referred to as a *pure* or *aggregate project structure*. However, since it is also one of the most expensive ways to organize a project because of its duplication of facilities, its use is generally reserved for very large undertakings. More common is the structure in which a project manager occupies the role of advisor to the general manager, who in turn administers the entire project within a functional organization hierarchy (see Figure 18–3). A third variation, and most common of all, is the matrix structure.

Pure project structure is reserved for large undertakings.

THE MATRIX STRUCTURE

A *matrix structure* is a hybrid form of organization containing characteristics of both project and functional structures. Nevertheless, it is common to find the terms "matrix organization" and "project organization" used interchangeably, although there are very distinct differences between the two. The major difference is that in contrast to the project organization, personnel in the matrix structure are only *loaned* to the project manager for the undertaking. There is thus a dual

Matrix structure is functional and project organization hybrid.

[6]Adapted from Cleland and King, *op. cit.*, pp. 169–170.

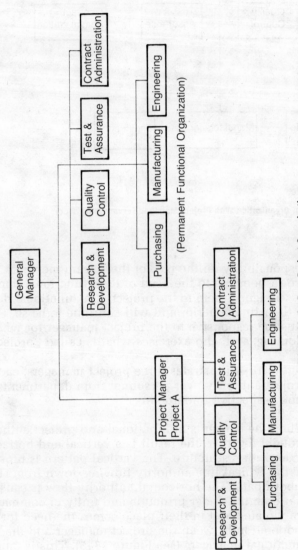

FIGURE 18–2 Pure Project Organization

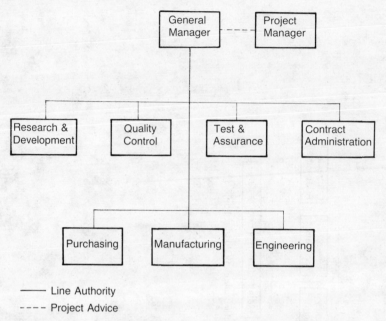

── Line Authority
---- Project Advice

FIGURE 18–3   Functional Organization With Project Manager Serving in Advisory Capacity

responsibility on the part of these team members. First, they are responsible to the head of their functional department who has assigned them to the project. The functional department head is their line superior and will continue to be so. Second, they must be responsive to the project manager for whom they are working, and who exercises what is called "project" authority.

Figure 18–4 illustrates three project managers, each with project authority over personnel from departments supporting their respective undertakings.

When the concepts of functional and project authority are brought together, the result is a vertical and horizontal organization structure. The vertical pattern is brought about by the typical line authority flowing down from superior to subordinate. The horizontal authority flow is caused by the fact that both the scalar principle and unity of command principle are violated and in their place comes the need for close cooperation between the project manager and the respective functional managers (see Figure 18–5). This is more clearly seen if the concept of project authority is examined in detail.

Projects authority flows horizontally.

Project Authority

Project authority has been identified and placed in perspective by one researcher who has written:

One major problem has been cited consistently in studies made of the project [matrix] organization: while the functional managers have line or direct

Project authority defined.

authority over their subordinates, the project managers must work through the respective functional managers, who supply the team personnel, in running their projects. The project managers have an "authority-gap" because they do not possess authority to reward or promote their personnel. They lack complete authority over the team and thus possess what is called "project authority." Because their responsibility outweighs their authority, the project managers must find ways of increasing their authority and thus minimizing their "authority-gap."[7]

This lack of complete authority means that the project manager cannot rely exclusively upon conventional line authority. Instead, he must work with the functional managers, convincing them that they should support his project by giving him the priorities he will need to finish the undertaking within the assigned time, cost and quality parameters. This calls for a horizontal relationship, one manager coordinating his activities with another. Legal authority such as the hierarchical flow, position descriptions and policy documents are of little value to most project managers. Instead, they must rely upon "reality" authority such as negotiation with their peers, the building of alliances with the functional managers and the effective use of the informal organization. (See Table 18–1, which compares the functional and project organizations in detail.)

Reality authority replaces legal authority.

In investigating leadership techniques used by project managers to supplement their project authority and overcome their "authority-gap," the author discovered a general pattern. All

[7]Richard M. Hodgetts, "Leadership Techniques in the Project Organization," *Academy of Management Journal*, June 1968, p. 211.

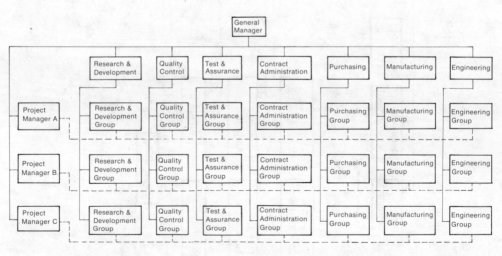

—— Line Authority

––– Project Authority

FIGURE 18–4 Matrix Organization

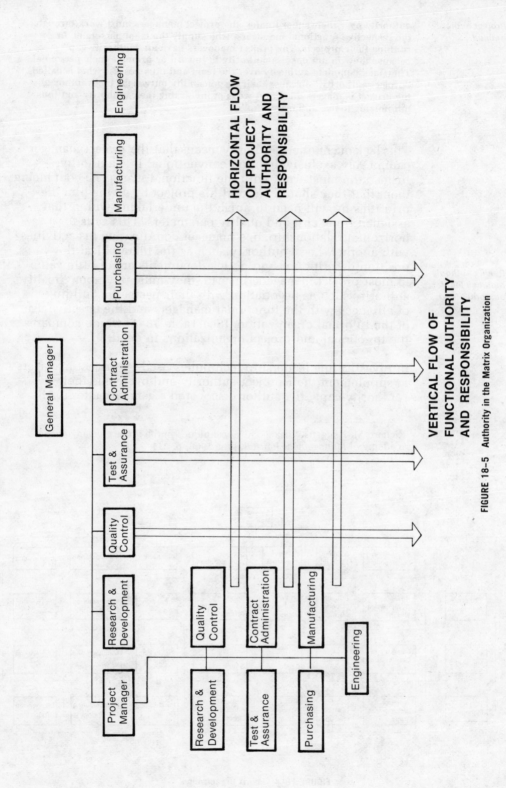

FIGURE 18–5   Authority in the Matrix Organization

TABLE 18–1 Comparison of the Functional and the Project Viewpoints

Phenomena	Project Viewpoint	Functional Viewpoint
Line-staff organizational dichotomy	Vestiges of the hierarchical model remain, but line functions are placed in a support position. A web of authority and responsibility relationships exists.	Line functions have direct responsibility for accomplishing the objectives: line commands, staff advises.
Scalar principle	Elements of the vertical chain exist, but prime emphasis is placed on horizontal and diagonal work flow. Important business is conducted as the legitimacy of the task requires.	The chain of authority relationships is from superior to subordinate throughout the organization. Central, crucial, and important business is conducted up and down the vertical hierarchy.
Superior-subordinate relationship	Peer to peer, manager to technical expert, associate to associate relationships are used to conduct much of the salient business.	This is the most important relationship; if kept healthy, success will follow. All important business is conducted through a pyramiding structure of superiors-subordinates.
Organizational objectives	Management of a project becomes a joint venture of many relatively independent organizations. Thus, the objective becomes multilateral.	Organizational objectives are sought by the parent unit (an assembly of suborganizations) working within its environment. The objective is unilateral.
Unity of direction	The project manager manages across functional and organizational lines to accomplish a common interorganizational objective.	The general manager acts as the head for a group of activities having the same plan.
Parity of authority and responsibility	Considerable opportunity exists for the project manager's responsibility to exceed his authority. Support people are often responsible to other managers (functional) for pay, performance reports, promotions, and so forth.	Consistent with functional management; the integrity of the superior-subordinate relationship is maintained through functional authority and advisory staff services.
Time duration	The project (and hence the organization) is finite in duration	Tends to perpetuate itself to provide continuing facilitative support.

Source: David I. Cleland, "Understanding Project Authority," *Business Horizons*, Spring 1967, p. 66. Reprinted with permission.

project managers in the study indicated that personality and/or persuasive ability were important. In addition, some of them relied upon negotiation, competence and/or reciprocal favors. The use of these approaches illustrates the importance that project managers assign to reality authority.

Of course, the specific project manager's need for these techniques is going to vary. On those projects where he is given little formal authority, the horizontal relationships will be of great importance. Conversely, in those cases where a great deal of authority has been delegated to him, the structure is less a matrix organization and more a pure project organization. Research shows that smaller projects (those with less dollar size) tend to be more common than do larger ones, and their project managers tend to have less formal authority than do those who are overseeing larger undertakings.[8] This means that they have to rely more on a human relations than on a formal authority approach. For example, in 41 of the firms he surveyed, the author found that there was a continuum ranging from small project organizations to large ones. As one progresses across the continuum, project authority declines in importance and formal authority replaces it. Informal leadership techniques such as negotiation, personality, and/or persuasive ability, competence and reciprocal favors are not so useful to the manager of a large project as they are to the manager of a small project. One project manager, involved in a multibillion dollar undertaking explained this phenomenon in the following way:

. . . it would appear to be vital . . . that the organizational environment, into which the project manager is placed, be such that he need not depend entirely on negotiating ability, a dynamic personality, etc., to perform his most important job. For this reason the organization of a project, in a manner to give the project manager the control he needs over the area of budgeting, planning, and scheduling becomes a basic consideration. The organization must be so designed that the project manager indeed does control the people assigned to the project, in the sense they are responsible to him. Thus, the organization gives the project manager his authority so he can divide more of his time to obtaining the schedule, cost, and technical performance goals of the project.[9]

Thus the project manager's challenge is often related to the amount of formal authority delegated to him.

Advantages of Matrix Organizations

Although the manager of a matrix organization faces many challenges, there are also numerous advantages to employing such a structure. Cleland and King identify these as being:

1. The project is emphasized by designating one individual as the focal point for all matters pertaining to it.

2. Utilization of manpower can be flexible because a reservoir of specialists is maintained in functional organizations.

---

[8]*Ibid.*, pp. 211–219.
[9]*Ibid.*, p. 218.

3. Specialized knowledge is available to all programs on an equal basis; knowledge and experience can be transferred from one project to another.

Benefits associated with using a matrix structure.

4. Project people have a functional home when they are no longer needed on a given project.

5. Responsiveness to project needs and customer desires is generally faster because lines of communication are established and decision points are *centralized*.

6. Management consistency between projects can be maintained through the deliberate conflict operating in the project-functional environment.

7. A better balance between time, cost and performance can be obtained through the built-in checks and balances (the deliberate conflict) and the continuous negotiations carried on between the project and the functional organizations.[10]

Both the matrix and project organizations represent modern structures for effective organizing. Another such design that is being employed by more and more firms is the free-form or organic organization structure.

FREE-FORM ORGANIZATIONS

The *free-form organization structure* has proved very useful in large-scale organizations, which suffer most severely from the negative effects of bureaucratization. In essence, this structure can take any form, but the objective is always the same: the design must assist the executive in managing change. For this reason, firms using a free-form structure tend to play down the organizational hierarchy with its emphasis on departmentalization and job descriptions. Instead, all attempts are made to free the men from petty controls. In fact, some individuals have even suggested doing away with the traditional worker-boss relationship.

Free-form structure discourages petty controls.

With rigid bureaucratic rules discarded, the manager is given the freedom he needs to get the job done right. Many times the only controls top management employs are those related to profits or the allocation of scarce resources. In turn, it is common to find managers in these free-form organizations handling their subordinates in the same way. Reliance on consensus plays a major role and two-way communication is encouraged. The organization operates more as a team than as a department with a structured superior-subordinate relationship. Many of the theories of McGregor, Likert and Argyris are put into practice.

Synergism and Strategic Planning

Another common characteristic of free-form structures is their emphasis on getting all departments, units and subsidiaries to work together. Although some organization forms such as the

---

[10]Cleland and King, *op. cit.*, p. 172.

*Cooperative
action is attained
via strategic
planning.*

holding company will have many separate unrelated, semi-autonomous firms operating under one banner, free-form companies tend to have fewer such holdings, and they try to blend them together in harmonious fashion. As a result of this cooperative action, or synergism, the total effect is greater than the sum of the individual parts working independently. This is accomplished to a great degree at the top level of the organization.

The central management will draw up a strategic plan designed to obtain the greatest synergistic effect from its units. Resources are then allocated on the basis of this potential synergism. Although the units are encouraged to plan, the final decision on all strategic plans is made by top management. In this way, the master plan for each division can be revised in light of *overall* enterprise commitments and objectives.

*Emphasis is given
to decentralized
operation with
centralized
control.*

The main synergistic ingredient is centralized control with decentralized operation. There is also a strong emphasis on organizing along the lines of profit centers. In addition, managers are urged to take risks and operate their unit more from a human-behavior standpoint than ever before. Perhaps this is the reason why firms using free-form structures tend to stress the need for young, dynamic managers unshackled by Theory X assumptions. It also accounts for why free-form organizations are most widely used by firms whose operations are "highly adaptive to products or services on the frontier of public use (e.g., air pollution devices) and those meeting an essential and high demand industrial, consumer, or military need (e.g., electronic devices, lenses and frames, space-age hardware)."[11] Still another characteristic of these structures is their use of computerized performance evaluations, which are used to determine if a division or department is contributing to overall profitability. If not, it is likely that the unit will be pruned from the organization.

Fortune magazine recorded in 1967 that of 46 true conglomerates, 12 were free-form. The magazine further stated that the most successful of the conglomerates seemed to be "newer" companies that had roots in high technology and fewer commitments to the past.[12] These are the same characteristics possessed by free-form structures.

Free-Form Organizations in Action

*Polaroid uses
sun-satellite
systems.*

Numerous firms have employed free-form structures. One of these is the Polaroid Corporation, which uses it within the formal organizational pattern. Company managers have dubbed it a "sun-satellite system."

---

[11]John H. Pascucci, "The Emergence of Free-form Management," *Personnel Administration*, September–October 1968, pp. 37–38.
[12]Thomas O'Hanlon, "The Odd News About Conglomerates," *Fortune*, June 15, 1967, pp. 177.

Every individual in the overall structure . . . plays two roles. On the primary job assigned to him, he is literally the sun of his own solar system. He is the expert. He is the boss. He is *it*. In this role, he is surrounded by satellites. These satellites serve him. They feed him ideas, back him up, listen to him when he needs listening to, do chores and perform feats for him.[13]

Polaroid's management contends that there are a number of advantages to this free-form structure. First, the individual is secure as a "sun" in his own system. He therefore feels no risk in freely helping out others. Second, in handling new or difficult tasks, it is possible to form task groups quickly. Naturally, the structure requires rapid communication and calls for a considerable degree of self-discipline on the part of all. However, these are, as indicated earlier, prerequisites for the effective use of any free-form structure.

Another company using this structure is the International Minerals & Chemical Corporation (IMC), which has done pioneering work in the industrial marketing of chemicals, fertilizers and food additives. In the mid-sixties, IMC established a new function, organization planning, and brought in a former consultant to direct the activity. A specialist in free-form management, his job became one of suggesting change.

IMC employs "cross-hatching."

Soon thereafter the firm started using a concept called "cross-hatching." Teams literally flowed in and out of the organizational structure in much the same way as Polaroid's sun satellites were superimposed on the formal structure. Managers began talking more and more in terms of team work. The director of organization planning pointed out in reference to the new structure that the unity of command concept was inaccurate and that "a man has as many bosses as there are demands upon him, as in life."[14] In short, the structure was designed to fit the job and not vice versa.

A third firm that has turned to the free-form structure is the Insurance Company of North America. In an industry that saw companies increase their fields of specialization from fire to property, casuality and life insurance, structures mushroomed haphazardly. Corporations consisted of many small companies

INA reorganized, using a free-form structure.

with no overall direction. It was commonplace to find managerial duplication, organizational overlap and inefficiency throughout the structure. INA faced a similar situation. Underwriting was fragmented by major line of insurance. Field service and production activities serving primary customers contained areas of overlapping activities. Leadership was divided. Policy holder services were handled by separate management so that functions such as audit, inspection and claims were all going their separate ways. To straighten out the situation, INA reorganized, using a free-form structure. The

[13]Jack B. Weiner, "The New Art of Free-Form Management," *Dun's Review and Modern Industry,* December 1964, p. 32.
[14]*Ibid.,* p. 54.

old authoritarian concept of management based on strict
obedience was scrapped in order to tap the full potential
of each individual. The result, in the president's own words,
was that, "Each member of management joins with all the
others in an united effort to achieve the objectives sought. And
each member of management reaches up to share with his
superior or superiors their responsibilities and their objectives."[15]

In addition to Polaroid, IMC and INA, other organizations that
employ free-form structures include IBM, Litton Industries,
American Standard, Xerox and Textron. Textron, for example,
following the free-form concept of evaluating performance and
pruning away unprofitable units, has gotten rid of its textiles
mills while adding metal products, precision machines, and
other consumer and industrial products to its manufacturing
lines. Free-form structures, however, are not without their
drawbacks or challenges.

**The Challenges
of Free-Form
Structures**

*Management
principles are
de-emphasized.*

The major challenge of the free-form structure is that it discards
or de-emphasizes management principles such as unity of
command and the scalar chain. In their place comes a form of
situational management in which individuals are encouraged
to interact and work with other members of the organization.
Operating within the profit-center concept, they are encouraged
to carry out their strategic plans in an environment designed to
meet change. Although technology may have a severe impact
on their work, their organizational structure is designed to take
advantage of these changes. For the dynamic, mature manager
the new environment is a welcome relief; for the average
manager it is a nightmare. Tension, anxiety and fear creep in.
The lack of rigidity disrupts the average individual's orientation,
and many managers are unable to adapt to the new system.

*Structures help
manage change.*

Second, free-form structures are designed to manage change.
This is why they are found in firms operating in highly
technical industries. All organizations, however, do not operate
in this kind of environment. Thus, the structure can have
limited value for some firms.

*Free-form design
encourages
excellence.*

Third, free-form structures encourage excellence. The managers
are placed on their own and allowed to use the approach they
feel works best in attaining the objective.

But if free-form management can bestow such benefits, why don't more
companies adopt it? Perhaps the major reason is that time-worn management
methods and structures are also protective devices for assigning responsibility
for failure. The point is sharply emphasized by Robert H. Schaffer....
"The easiest place to camouflage failures in obtaining goals," insists Schaffer,
"is the well-fractioned organization where, as any veteran can testify, stalled

---

[15]*Ibid.*, p. 56.

performance almost always is attributable to 'the system,' to other departments or to forces that lie outside the control of any department."[16]

The use of free-form structures appears to be increasing for various reasons. First, managers are demanding more flexible organizations to meet the changes and challenges of the seventies. Second, managers are more competent than ever before so they can effectively utilize these new organizational structures. Third, technological increases during the decade are going to put pressure on companies to modernize their organizational designs. Fourth, the bureaucratic super-structures will no longer do the job; too much dependence on organization charts and job descriptions merely stunts the growth of the enterprise. For many, free-form structures will prove to be the answer.

CONTINGENCY ORGANIZATION DESIGN

The right organization structure will depend on the situation.

The key word currently characterizing organization design is *contingency*. Earlier, Fiedler's research was examined and it was noted that the *right* leadership style will depend on the situation. The same is true of organization structure. Today, the development of structures in which there is minimum attention given to the formal division of duties is resulting in increasingly flexible designs. Mechanistic structures are, in many cases, being replaced by organic ones. Of course, each company will have to evaluate its own situation, but, as Lorsch and Lawrence note, there does seem to be a distinct trend toward contingency organization design.

> During the past few years there has been evident a new trend in the study of organizational phenomena. Underlying this new approach is the idea that the internal functioning of organizations must be consistent with the demands of the organization task, technology, or external environment, and the needs of its members if the organization is to be effective. Rather than searching for the panacea of the one best way to organize under all conditions, investigators have more and more tended to examine the functioning of organizations in relation to the needs of their particular members and the external pressures facing them. Basically, this approach seems to be leading to the development of a "contingency" theory of organization with the appropriate internal states and processes of the organization contingent upon external requirements and member needs.[17]

Influencing Forces

Shetty and Carlisle re-echo these sentiments about contingency design, noting that the *best* organization structure will vary according to situation. In essence, it is going to be a function of forces in the managers, the subordinates, the task and the environment.[18] *Forces in the managers* are readily evident. If a superior feels his people are basically lazy, he will design a structure to reflect these views and will refuse to delegate

---

[16] *Ibid.*
[17] Jay W. Lorsch and Paul R. Lawrence, *Studies in Organization Design* (Homewood, Ill: Richard D. Irwin and The Dorsey Press, 1970), p. 1.
[18] Y. K. Shetty and Howard M. Carlisle, "A Contingency Model of Organization Design," *California Management Review*, Fall 1972, pp. 38–45.

*Forces in the
managers, sub-
ordinates, task
and environment
will all help
determine the
best structure.*

much authority. Conversely, if he is a Theory Y manager, he
will be more prone to use a design that facilitates decentralization and delegation of authority. *Forces in the subordinates*
are things such as a desire for autonomy and an opportunity
to participate in decision making. If these factors are present,
they will have an impact on the structure. *Forces in the task*
often reflect themselves in technology. "Technology may
determine the extent to which the job may be programmed,
that is, employee behaviors may be precisely specified. The
kind of organization required in a low task structure is not the
same as that required in a high task structure."[19] *Forces in
the environment* include the availability of resources, nature
of the competition, predictability of demand and the type of
products or services being provided by the company.

These four interacting factors influence the type of organizational
design that will evolve, as seen in Figure 18–6. By employing
this framework, a company can identify the conditions
enhancing or impeding a particular structure. Sometimes it
needs a more flexible design, other times a more structured
one.

**The organization appropriate in one market-technology environment may be
irrelevant or even dysfunctional in another environment. A firm producing
a standardized product sold in a stable market may require a pattern of
organization altogether different from a company manufacturing a highly
technical product for a more dynamic market. There is no one pattern of
organization style that is universally appropriate.[20]**

**A Matter
of "Fit"**

In essence, then, management must look for the right "fit"
among the personnel, the organization characteristics and the
task requirement. Morse and Lorsch recently illustrated this
when they made an analysis of four business firms, two highly
effective and two less effective. One of the highly effective
firms was an Akron container manufacturing plant in which
formal relationships were highly structured, rules were specific

---

[19]*Ibid.*, p. 42.
[20]*Ibid.*, p. 44.

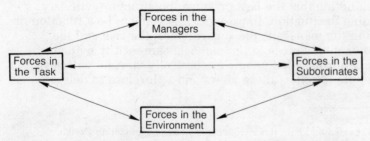

FIGURE 18–6   Forces Affecting Organization Structure (Adapted from Y. K. Shetty
and Howard M. Carlisle, "A Contingency Model of Organization Design," *California
Management Review*, Fall 1972, p. 44.)

TABLE 18–2 Differences in "Climate" Characteristics in High-Performing Organizations

Characteristics	Akron	Stockton
1. Structural orientation	Perceptions of tightly controlled behavior and a high degree of structure	Perceptions of a low degree of structure
2. Distribution of influence	Perceptions of low total influence, concentrated at upper levels in the organization	Perceptions of high total influence, more evenly spread out among all levels
3. Character of superior-subordinate relations	Low freedom vis-à-vis superiors to choose and handle jobs, directive type of supervision	High freedom vis-à-vis superiors to choose and handle projects, participatory type of supervision
4. Character of colleague relations	Perceptions of many similarities among colleagues, high degree of coordination of colleague effort	Perceptions of many differences among colleagues, relatively low degree of coordination of colleague effort
5. Time orientation	Short-term	Long-term
6. Goal orientation	Manufacturing	Scientific
7. Top executive's "managerial style"	More concerned with task than people	More concerned with people than task

Source: John J. Morse and Jay W. Lorsch, "Beyond Theory Y." *Harvard Business Review*, May–June 1970, p. 66. Reprinted with permission.

A people-organization-task fit is important.

and comprehensive and the time orientation was short-term. The other was a Stockton research lab where formal relations were less well defined, rules were minimal and flexible and the time orientation was long-term (see Table 18–2). Both firms, despite these differences, were successful because their structures brought the task and the people together in the right way. Conversely, in the two less effective plants they studied, the researchers found that the formal and informal organizational characteristics did not fit the task requirements nearly so well as in their successful counterparts. It is thus important that there be a correct task-organization-people fit.

In arguing for an approach which emphasizes the fit among task, organization, and people, we are putting to rest the question of which organizational approach—the classical or the participative—is best. In its place we are raising a new question: What organizational approach is most appropriate given the task and the people involved?

For many enterprises, given the new needs of younger employees for more autonomy, and the rapid rates of social and technological change, it may well be that the more participative approach is the most appropriate. But there will still be many situations in which the more controlled and formalized organization is desirable. Such an organization need not be coercive or punitive. If it makes sense to the individuals involved, given their needs and their jobs, they will find it rewarding and motivating.[21]

SUMMARY

In this chapter it was noted that the use of bureaucratic structures is beginning to decline. One reason is that the inherent assumptions upon which these designs are based are unrealistic. The organization cannot function as a highly closed system, and mechanical rules and regulations have limited value in motivating and leading modern man.

In overcoming these bureaucratic deficiencies, many firms are turning to adaptive organization structures. These new designs are based on a number of assumptions. One is that the organization is an open system operating in a dynamic environment. A second is that Theory Y assumptions represent the modern employee more accurately than do Theory X assumptions. Modern organization structures employ these ideas in bringing together the personnel, the task and the environment. In this chapter a number of these modern designs have been examined.

The first of these to be discussed was the project organization. It was noted that this form entails "the gathering of the best available talent to accomplish a specific and complex undertaking within time, cost and/or quality parameters, followed by the disbanding of the team upon completion of the undertaking." The project organization has been widely employed in numerous and diverse ways from building dams and weapon systems to conducting research and development and designing bank credit-card systems. The major advantage of this organization form is that it allows the project manager and his team to concentrate their attention on one specific undertaking.

The matrix structure is a hybrid form of organization, containing characteristics of both the project and functional structures. In a matrix design personnel are only loaned to the project manager. There is thus a dual responsibility on the part of team members. They are responsible to the line manager who loaned them to the project and the project manager for whom they are working. The result is a vertical and horizontal flow of authority. Since the project manager has only "project" authority, he must rely on human-relations techniques such as negotiation, personality and/or persuasive ability, competence and reciprocal favors.

---

[21]John J. Morse and Jay W. Lorsch, "Beyond Theory Y," *Harvard Business Review*, May–June 1970, p. 68.

Another modern organization design is the free-form or organic structure. This design can take any shape, but it always has the characteristic of playing down rigid bureaucratic rules and an emphasis on self-regulation. A number of conglomerates have adopted this organization form, including Polaroid, International Minerals & Chemical Corporation, Insurance Company of North America, IBM, Litton Industries, American Standard, Xerox and Textron. Perhaps the greatest advantage of a free-form structure is its value to the manager in coping with change.

What kind of structure is best? There is no right answer to this question; it depends on the situation. This is why the area of contingency organization design is currently so important. Some firms need a mechanistic structure, others work better with an organic one. The answer will depend on the forces in the managers, the subordinates, the task and the environment.

An effective structure brings the people and the work together in a harmonious fashion. This chapter has examined some of the new designs being used to attain this goal. Chapter 19 will review some of the latest techniques being employed to manage the organization's most important asset — its people.

REVIEW AND STUDY QUESTIONS

1. What are the characteristics of an ideal bureaucracy?

2. Why is the bureaucratic form of organization declining today?

3. What is a project organization?

4. When can a project organization be used effectively? Explain.

5. A matrix structure is a hybrid form of organization, containing characteristics of both project and functional structures. Explain this statement.

6. What is "project" authority?

7. How is the free-form organization useful to large-scale organizations?

8. How do free-form organizations employ synergy in their strategic planning?

9. What is meant by "contingency organization design"?

10. Shetty and Carlisle have noted that the best organization structure is going to be a function of four forces. Identify and explain all four.

11. What do Morse and Lorsch mean by the need for a task-organization-people fit? Explain.

SELECTED REFERENCES

Butler, A. G., Jr. "Project Management: A Study in Organizational Conflict." *Academy of Management Journal*, March 1973, pp. 84–101.

Child, J. "Predicting and Understanding Organization Structure." *Administrative Science Quarterly*, June 1973, pp. 168–185.

Cleland, D. I. "Understanding Project Authority." *Business Horizons*, Spring 1967, pp. 63–70.

Cleland, D. I., and W. R. King. *Systems Analysis and Project Management.* New York: McGraw-Hill Book Company, 1968.

Dale, E. *Management: Theory and Practice.* 3rd edition. New York: McGraw-Hill Book Company, 1973, Chapter 8.

Haire, M., ed. *Modern Organization Theory.* New York: John Wiley & Sons, Inc., 1959.

Hodgetts, R. M. "Leadership Techniques in the Project Organization." *Academy of Management Journal*, June 1968, pp. 211–219.

Kast, F. E., and J. E. Rosenzweig. *Contingency Views of Organization and Management.* Chicago: Science Research Associates, Inc., 1973.

Kast, F. E., and J. E. Rosenzweig. *Organization and Management: A Systems Approach*, 2nd edition. New York: McGraw-Hill Book Company, 1974, Chapter 9.

Likert, R. *The Human Organization.* New York: McGraw-Hill Book Company, 1967.

McFarland, D. E. *Management: Principles and Practices.* 4th edition, New York: The Macmillan Company, 1974, pp. 154–172.

Mockler, R. J. "Situational Theory of Management." *Harvard Business Review*, May–June 1971, pp. 146–155.

Morse, J. J., and J. W. Lorsch. "Beyond Theory Y." *Harvard Business Review*, May–June 1970, pp. 61–68.

Reimann, B. C. "On the Dimensions of Bureaucratic Structure: An Empirical Reappraisal." *Administrative Science Quarterly*, December 1973, pp. 462–476.

Shetty, Y. K., and H. M. Carlisle. "A Contingency Model of Organization Design." *California Management Review*, Fall 1972, pp. 38–45.

Ways, M. "Tomorrow's Management: A More Adventuresome Life in a Free-Form Corporation." *Fortune*, July 1, 1966, pp. 84–87+.

Wilemon, D. L., and J. P. Cicero. "The Project Manager: Anomalies and Ambiguities." *Academy of Management Journal*, September 1970, pp. 269–282.

Young, S. *Management: A Systems Analysis.* Glenview, Ill.: Scott, Foresman and Company, 1966.

CASE: NEW TIMES, NEW STRUCTURES

Bureaucratic structures employ calculable rules and operate with little, if any, regard for people. Although there is precision and speed in much of what they do, there is also strict subordination of the individual interest to that of the organization. In summarizing some of the current criticisms of bureaucracies, Warren Bennis has compiled the following list of deficiencies:

1. **Bureaucracy does not adequately allow for personal growth and the development of mature personalities.**

2. **It develops conformity and "group think."**

3. **It does not take into account the "informal organization" and the emergent and unanticipated problems.**

4. Its systems of control and authority are hopelessly outdated.

5. It has no adequate juridical process.

6. It does not possess adequate means for resolving differences and conflicts between ranks, and most particularly, between functional groups.

7. Communication (and innovative ideas) are thwarted or distorted due to hierarchical divisions.

8. The full human resources of bureaucracy are not being utilized due to mistrust, fear of reprisals, etc.

9. It cannot assimilate the influx of new technology or scientists entering the organization.

10. It modifies personality structure so that people become and reflect the dull, gray, conditioned "organization man."[1]

These problems are reason enough for business firms to begin thinking about designing more humanistic structures. A further impetus is being provided by our changing environment. Kast and Rosenzweig, for example, have listed the following changes as some that will be affecting organizations during the current decade:

1. Organizations will be operating in a continually changing environment.

2. The size and complexity of organizations is going to increase.

3. Organizations are going to have major problems in gathering and using knowledge; as a result, intellectual activities are going to be heavily stressed.

4. Greater emphasis is going to be placed on suggestion and persuasion and less on coercion and the use of authoritarian power.

5. Participants at all levels of the organization are going to have influence on company matters, not just the people at the top.

6. New methods for attaining interorganizational coordination will be developed to deal with problem interfaces with other organizations.

7. Computerized information decision systems will have an increasing impact on organizations.

8. The number and influence of scientists and professionals in the organization will increase.

9. There will be a decline in the number of independent professionals in the organization and an increase in the number of salaried professionals.

10. The goals of complex organizations will expand and emphasis will be given to satisficing a number of them rather than maximizing any one in particular.[2]

[1]Warren Bennis, "Beyond Bureaucracy," Trans–Action, July–August 1965, p. 32.
[2]Adapted from Fremont E. Kast and James E. Rosenzweig, Organization and Management: A Systems Approach, 2nd edition (New York: McGraw–Hill Book Company, 1974), pp. 617–618.

As a result, in many firms there will be a movement away from the mechanistic-bureaucratic structure and toward a flexible organic system.

Questions

1. Do you think that organizations are beginning to move toward more flexible-organic systems? Explain.

2. In addition to the reasons cited in the case, why else might business firms be abandoning their old bureaucratic structures?

3. In what industries would you expect to find organic structures widely used? In what industries would you expect to find firms staying with a basically mechanistic-bureaucratic structure? Explain.

CASE: THE GLORIFIED COORDINATOR

Bill Lesikar, a graduate student at State University, was writing a paper on modern organization structures. As part of his research he interviewed project, matrix, and free-form organization managers in ten major corporations throughout the city. One of the managers worked in a consumer products firm. He explained his job as follows:

I'm responsible for developing a consumer product. In order to get the job done, I've been assigned people from the various functional departments: research, design, manufacturing and test. Of course, these people will stay within their own departments, but when I need them, they will work for me.

Most of last week was spent figuring out when I'd have to have these people. I'm going to need the research and design personnel starting next week. Then, when they're finished with the product, I'll have it manufactured and tested. This will come in about two months. The reason I know the schedule so well is that this week I have to go around to the functional managers and ask them to assign me people for the project. They'll want to see the time schedule and then they'll figure out who they can let me have. Of course, these people will continue to report to their functional boss, but they'll be working on my project. Nevertheless, I suppose you'd be right if you called me a glorified project coordinator or expediter. After all, my only goal is to get everyone together and make sure the product is manufactured on time. Then, it will be tested in various sections of the country and if it catches on, the company will set up a new product department to handle it. Meanwhile, I'll go on to another project.

Questions

1. What kind of authority does the project manager have over the project personnel in this case?

2. Is this a project, matrix, or free-form organization? Give your reasoning.

CASE: FLY ME TO THE MOON

In his second State of the Union address to the Congress in May 1961, President Kennedy stated, "I believe that this nation should commit itself to achieving the goal, before this decade is out, of landing a man on the moon and returning him safely to earth." The race to the moon was on!

The United States undertook three distinct projects in all: Mercury, Gemini and Apollo. Mercury's primary objective included investigating man's capabilities in the space environment and developing manned space flight technology. Gemini's primary goals entailed subjecting two men and supporting equipment to long duration flights, effecting rendezvous and docking maneuvers with other orbiting vehicles, and perfecting methods of re-entry and landing. Apollo's primary goal, quite simply, was to put two men on the moon, allow them to carry out limited exploration and then return them safely to earth.

To achieve this primary goal, the United States needed a spacecraft to get the astronauts into and out of the moon's orbit and a lunar excursion module (LEM) to take them down to the moon's surface and return them to the spacecraft. In order to build these two pieces of equipment, the National Aeronautics and Space Administration (NASA) solicited contracts. The award for the spacecraft was made to North American Aviation while Grumman Aircraft received the LEM contract. In addition, NASA set up a project organization, known as the Apollo Spacecraft Program Office (ASPO), to monitor the contractors and see that the hardware was built on time and within cost and quality parameters. As the contractors built the spacecraft and the LEM, ASPO personnel would check to see that everything was going according to schedule. If there was a problem, for example, and the contractor wanted to change the design of the hardware, it had to be cleared through ASPO. In short, the Apollo program people were charged with seeing that the contractor did the job right. Although ASPO headquarters were located in Houston, the personnel were continually flying out to see the contractors and having reports sent to them so they could ascertain the progress that was being made.

Questions

1. What kind of authority did the ASPO have over the contractors? Explain.

2. Is the ASPO a project, matrix, or free-form organization? Give your reasoning.

CASE: A TEAM APPROACH[1]

There are many approaches to organizing the work force. One of these, currently being explored by General Electric, is that of worker teams. *Business Week* described the process as follows:

The idea is to identify a task and then assign a group of 5 to 15 people to handle it. The key is to give the group as much responsibility as possible. [Herbert] Meyer [a GE personnel research executive] cites a group of welders in a fabricating plant where the team approach was tried. The welders were given responsibility for scheduling and planning their work load. They determined, for example, how much time it would take to meet specifications on any items requiring special welding techniques, a job formerly done by a methods-and-standards engineer.

The 12 welders were experienced enough to decide which one of them would do a specific job and the time it would take, Meyer says. "The responsibility meant the men had a bigger say in how they did their jobs, and we found that they all became more committed to the work as team members," says Meyer. Methods engineers are now freed to work on new product models while the welders decide how the daily work is going to be done. The efficiency and quality of work, Meyer adds, has improved significantly, because the team has a real stake in the outcome.

Questions

1. How would you describe this type of organization structure? Explain.

2. What are the critical factors that account for its success? Explain.

---

[1]The data in this case can be found in "Management Itself Holds the Key," *Business Week*, September 9, 1972, pp. 143, 146.

CHAPTER 19

THE MANAGEMENT OF HUMAN ASSETS: TOOLS AND TECHNIQUES

GOALS OF THE CHAPTER

Many company presidents claim that their most important asset is their people. Whether they believe it or not, the statement is an accurate one. The goal of this chapter is to examine some of the latest tools and techniques being used in managing the organization's human assets. In the first major section of this chapter the area will be approached from an accounting-investment standpoint. The remainder of the chapter is focused on modern behavioral tools and techniques useful in managing people. In particular, emphasis will be placed on:

a. the importance of discerning between manipulation and motivation;
b. the value of viewing human assets as a company investment;
c. the need for evaluating human assets on a periodic basis;
d. the reasons why management by objectives is so popular in American industry today;
e. the manner in which job enrichment is being used to motivate personnel;
f. the value of sensitivity training for the modern manager;
g. the benefits of transactional analysis in understanding and communicating with subordinates; and
h. the potential of behavior modification in helping organizations manage their human assets.

THE GREAT JACKASS FALLACY

Many chief executives seem to realize that they are not as effective as they could be in handling their people. Some of them, for example, when recently asked to describe the effect they have on their subordinates, replied:

I believe that a real business leader is incapable of generating a climate where people can grow.

473

Hell, none of us would work for people like ourselves!

A real executive under any one of us would leave because he couldn't stand it.

We couldn't work for dominant characters such as ourselves. We are leaders.[1]

Workers know the difference between motivation and manipulation.

On the other hand, most companies realize that they must take steps to combat the above problems. It is important to note, however, that some managers will adopt the newest approaches for handling their personnel but still fail, because under the guise of motivating their people, they actually attempt to manipulate them. This is what Levinson calls the "great jackass fallacy."[2] Workers know the difference between motivation and manipulation; they are not fooled. As a result, the best technique or tool in the world is useless in the hands of an insincere manager. The ultimate success of the methods discussed in this chapter rest solely with management.

HUMAN RESOURCES ACCOUNTING

The company balance sheet reflects the firm's physical assets such as cash, accounts receivable, inventory and plant. However, it does not account for either the productive capability of the workers or the good will of the customers. In the case of the personnel, for example, there are many variables that can make one firm superior to another, including:

1. Level of intelligence and aptitudes
2. Level of training
3. Level of performance goals and motivation to achieve organizational success
4. Quality of leadership
5. Capacity to use differences for purposes of innovation and improvement, rather than allowing differences to develop into bitter, irreconcilable, interpersonal conflict
6. Quality of communicating upward, downward and laterally
7. Quality of decision making
8. Capacity to achieve cooperative teamwork versus competitive striving for personal success at the expense of the organization
9. Quality of the control processes of the organization and the levels of felt responsibility which exist
10. Capacity to achieve effective coordination
11. Capacity to use experience and measurements to guide decisions, improve operations, and introduce innovations.[3]

Nowhere on the balance sheet are these factors accounted for. In an attempt to overcome this deficiency, an area known as *human resources accounting* has developed. The method has taken two paths: viewing the acquisition and development of personnel as an investment, and obtaining a regular evaluation of these assets by measuring what are called "causal" and

---

[1]Chris Agyris, "The CEO's Behavior: Key to Organizational Development," *Harvard Business Review*, March–April, 1973, p. 57.
[2]Harry Levinson, "Asinine Attitudes Toward Motivation," *Harvard Business Review*, January–February 1973, pp. 70–76.
[3]Rensis Likert, *The Human Organization* (New York: McGraw-Hill Book Company, 1967), p. 148.

"intervening" variables. The following discussion will examine both of these approaches.

Personnel as an Investment

If a company is to be successful, it needs to hire and maintain competent personnel. How much are these people worth to the firm? This is a question human resources accounting attempts to answer. As Likert points out, this term

> ... refers to activity devoted to attaching dollar estimates to the value of a firm's human organization and its customer goodwill. If able, well-trained personnel leave the firm, the human organization is worth less; if they join it, the firm's human assets are increased. If bickering, distrust, and irreconcilable conflict become greater, the human enterprise is worth less; if the capacity to use differences constructively and engage in cooperative teamwork improves, the human organization is a more valuable asset.[4]

A dollar-investment approach is used.

One way for the company to decide how much its human assets are worth would be to determine the amount of money it took to hire, train and retain these people. Offsetting this figure will be factors such as retirement, transfers, separations and obsolescence (or failure to keep up) on the part of the personnel. If one wished to include the customer in this analysis, the cost of maintaining good will could be written in and loss of customer orders (ill will) deducted.

This approach is, of course, very subjective. After all, how does one really decide the costs associated with the retention or loss of personnel? No definitive answer will be presented here, because the entire area is still in the developmental stages. It should be noted, however, that some companies are actually trying to reflect human resources in their financial statements.[5] If human resources accounting continues to grow at its current pace, other firms will undoubtedly be doing the same.

Periodic Evaluation of Human Resources

A second suggested approach is periodic evaluation of the state of the company's human resources. One way of doing this, in the opinion of some human resource accounting people, is to use Likert's four management systems which were discussed in Chapter 14. By determining whether a company is operating under Systems 1, 2, 3 or 4, they believe it is possible to draw conclusions about how the human resources are being managed. Their primary thesis is that the current state of a company's human resources will be reflected in future performance. If today's workers are operating under a System-3 or System-4 manager, future performance should be high. If they are working under a System-1 or System-2 manager, future performance will be lower.

---

[4]*Ibid.*, pp. 148–149.
[5]William C. Pyle "Monitoring Human Resources—On Line," *Michigan Business Review*, July 1970, pp. 19–32; and D. M. C. Jones, "Accounting for Human Assets," *Management Decision*, Summer 1973, pp. 183–194.

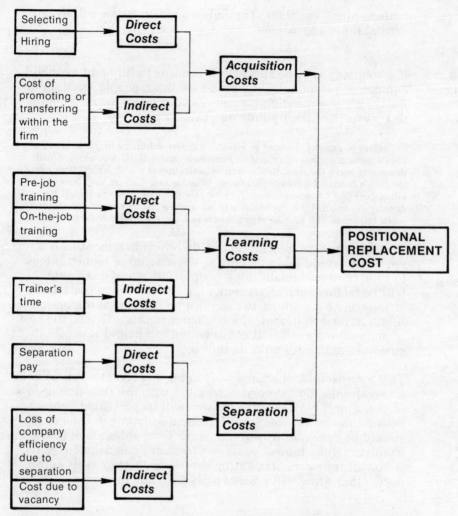

FIGURE 19–1 Determining Human Resource Replacement Costs (Adapted from Eric G. Flamholtz, "Human Resource Accounting: Measuring Positional Replacement Costs," *Human Resource Management*, Spring 1973, p. 11.)

When Likert's management systems are used to measure the current state of the human resources, questions such as those presented earlier in Figure 14–3 are employed. Based on the responses, the researchers attempt to put together a profile of the system under which the company is operating. In addition, three types of variables are examined. These are:

1. *Causal* (or independent) *variables,* which determine the results the company is going to achieve. Management decisions, business strategies and leadership behavior are all illustrations.
2. *Intervening variables,* which reflect the internal state of the organization. Loyalty, attitude and motivation are all illustrations.
3. *End-result* (or dependent) *variables,* which reflect the organization's achievements. Earnings, productivity and costs are all illustrations.

According to human resources people, a company's earnings, productivity and costs (end-result variables) are a result of causal variables such as business strategies and leadership behavior. However, one must do more than merely analyze cause-effect relationships. It is also necessary to examine the transformation process or *intervening variables*. For example, why does a particular leadership behavior result in higher earnings? The answer may well be found in factors such as loyalty, attitude and motivation.

Intervening variables are important.

This particular concept has important implications for management because it indicates that a change in leadership style (causal variable) will result in change in factors such as costs or earnings (end-result variables) only if there is change in factors such as loyalty, attitude, motivation, and so on (intervening variables). This particular idea is often used by human resources accounting people to illustrate what they call the *liquidation of human assets*. In essence, they believe that a company that wishes to increase its current earnings can do so if it moves toward System 1. Figure 19–2 provides an illustration.

Changes in Leadership Style.   As seen in Figure 19–2, by changing its strategy and leadership behavior (causal variables) the company's short-run financial position (end-result variable) improves. Of course, this lasts for only a few years and then

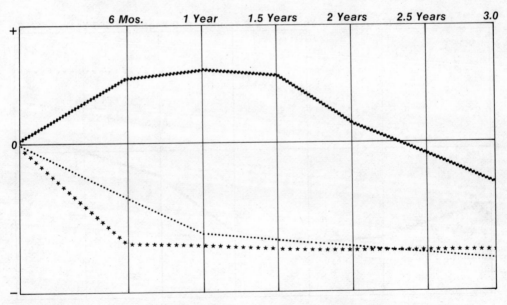

FIGURE 19–2   Moving Toward System I (Courtesy of Dr. Tony Hain, General Motors Institute.)

deteriorates. However, one point to be noted from Figure 19–2 is that as the firm moves toward System 1, leadership behavior declines; managers become increasingly autocratic and start applying pressure in an attempt to improve earnings. This behavior is followed by a decline in employee attitudes and motivation. During this same period, it is also common to find some of the best workers leaving the firm. The company is thus liquidating its human resources. In a manner of speaking, it is analogous to selling machinery and equipment at a discount. On the positive side, however, the financial picture (earnings) improves and, in the above illustration, remains there for two years before finally dropping below the initial level of zero.

The same basic concepts are used by human resources people to explain what happens when a company moves toward System 4, illustrated in Figure 19–3. First the leadership behavior (causal variable) is changed. This is followed by improvement in attitudes (intervening variable) and then improvement in earnings (end-result variable).

If the management moves toward System 1, it can milk or liquidate its human assets and achieve short-run increases in earnings. However, after a given time period the intervening variables will come into play and these earnings will decline. Thus, in the short-run, when a critical financial situation develops, it may be advisable to change to System 1, but this approach cannot be maintained indefinitely.

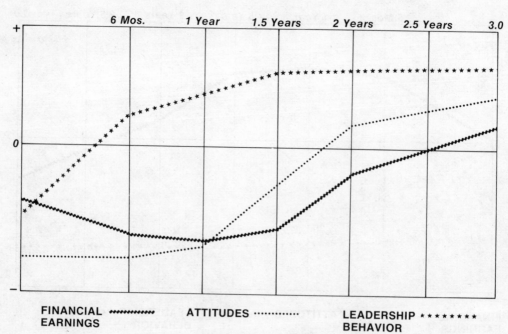

FIGURE 19–3 Moving Toward System 4 (Courtesy of Dr. Tony Hain, General Motors Institute.)

Conversely, moving toward System 4 may not result in any increases in earnings for quite a while. As Likert points out, *"Changes in the causal variables toward System 4 apparently require an appreciable period of time before the impact of the change is fully manifest in corresponding improvement in the end-result variables."*[6] This entails a good deal of faith on the part of the management, for they must be willing to continue moving toward System 4. In the long-run, however, earnings will improve.

Human resources researchers thus believe that the firm's current financial position may not reflect the true status of the causal and intervening variables, for these are lead factors. However, changes in these variables will be reflected in *future* financial statements, and this is why they are so important.

Causal and intervening variables are lead factors.

The measurements of the causal and intervening variables should be obtained for the corporation as a whole and for each profit center or unit in the company. . . . By using appropriate statistical procedures, relationships can be computed among the causal, intervening, and such end-result variables as costs and earnings. . . . These estimates of probable subsequent productivity, costs, and earnings will reveal the earning power of the human organization *at the time* the causal and intervening variables were measured, even though the level of estimated subsequent earnings may not be achieved until much later. These estimates . . . provide the basis for attaching to any profit center, unit, or total corporation a statement of the present value of its human organization.[7]

The *future* of the firm depends on its ability to manage its human assets *today*.

Before ending this discussion, one point must be noted. Figures 19–1 and 19–2 represent only a general pattern of results as postulated by human resources researchers. As Koontz and O'Donnell note, "To date, only a few experiments have been undertaken to measure the investment costs and losses in human resources. While it is believed that present 'value' of human resources . . . can be reasonably well approached through the use of the Likert measurements, there is still little evidence that this has been done with an acceptable degree of creditability."[8]

Today research in human resources accounting continues, but it is only one technique useful in managing human assets. Another is job enrichment.

JOB ENRICHMENT

In late 1972, a government-sponsored study reported what many Americans had long suspected—a high percentage of the

---

[6]Likert, *op. cit.*, pp. 80–81.
[7]*Ibid.*, p. 150.
[8]Harold Koontz and Cyril O'Donnell, *Principles of Management: An Analysis of Managerial Functions*, 5th edition (New York: McGraw-Hill Book Company, 1972) p. 652.

work force dislikes their jobs. This discontent, present among both blue- and white-collar workers, is causing major social, as well as economic, problems. In particular, the government task force found that workers disliked being at the mercy of a system that they could neither communicate with nor influence. These findings have been echoed by many, including Walton, who reports that the roots of worker alienation can be found in the conflict that exists between employee expectations and organization conditions. Some of these include the following:

Worker expectations and employee conditions are in conflict.

1. Employees want the opportunity for challenge and personal growth but the organization gives them simplified work assignments.

2. The workers want to be treated as equals and have something to say about what goes on, but the organization employs a hierarchical approach with status differentials and chains of command.

3. Employee commitment to the organization is heavily influenced by such factors as interest in the work itself and the human dignity afforded by management but the organization continues to emphasize hygiene factors.[9]

In an attempt to overcome these problems and increase employee motivation, some firms are adopting an approach known as *job enrichment*.

Meaningful Work

Job enrichment is an extension of job enlargement.

Job enrichment is an extension of job enlargement, but instead of just giving the person more work, management provides the opportunity for increased recognition, advancement, growth and responsibility. The technique is a direct extension of Herzberg's two factor theory of motivation and has been highly popularized by M. Scott Myers, formerly of Texas Instruments (TI), and Robert N. Ford of the American Telephone and Telegraph Company (AT&T).

Enrichment of the job can take many forms. Myers has encouraged making "every employee a manager" in the sense that they help plan their own work and control the pace and quality of output.[10] Within this framework, the individual knows the deadlines he must meet and the standards he must maintain. In some cases he is even given the authority to check the quality of the output. In short, management relies on him to get the job done right. No one looks over his shoulder; he is on his own. Myers has described one of these situations as follows:

Assemblers on a radar assembly line are given information on customer contract commitments in terms of price, quality specifications, delivery

---

[9]Richard E. Walton, "How to Counter Alienation in the Plant," *Harvard Business Review*, November–December 1972, pp. 71–72.
[10]M. Scott Myers, *Every Employee a Manager: More Meaningful Work Through Job Enrichment* (New York: McGraw-Hill Book Company, 1970).

schedules, and company data on material and personnel costs, breakeven performance, and potential profit margins. Assemblers and engineers work together in methods and design improvements. Assemblers inspect, adjust and repair their own work, help test completed units, and receive copies of customer inspection reports.[11]

Positive results have been obtained.

At AT&T, Ford has reported that after job enrichment was installed in the Shareholder Relations Department there was a 27 per cent reduction in the termination rate and, over a twelve-month period, an estimated cost saving of $558,000.[12] Other firms are introducing the approach on their assembly line. For example Motorola has workers who put together and test an entire unit by themselves.[13] Volvo, Saab,[14] and Cadillac[15] are using job enrichment in building their cars. The two Swedish auto makers are having parts brought to the car and installed by groups of semi-autonomous workers, and Cadillac has abandoned some of its small assembly lines in favor of each worker building one complete part.

Job enrichment can be a very useful technique in overcoming some of the previously mentioned causes of worker alienation because it shifts the emphasis from the traditional management style to a more modern one (see Table 19–1). The key, of course, rests with structuring the job correctly.[16] As Ford points out, "When the work is right, employee attitudes are right. That is the job enrichment strategy—get the work right."[17]

Job Enrichment Under Attack

Not everyone, however, has found that job enrichment pays off. Although individuals such as Herzberg, Myers and Ford[18] sing its praises, others have raised doubts about the technique.[19]

---

[11]M. Scott Myers, "Every Employee a Manager," *California Management Review*, Spring 1968, p. 10.

[12]Robert Janson, "Job Enrichment: Challenge of the 70's," *Training and Development Journal*, June 1970, p. 7.

[13]"Motorola Creates a More Demanding Job," *Business Week*, September 4, 1971, p. 32.

[14]"Swedes Will End Assembly Lines," *The New York Times*, December 28, 1971, p. 15.

[15]"G.M.: The Price of Being 'Responsible'," *Fortune*, January 1972, p. 172.

[16]Richard C. Grote, "Implementing Job Enrichment," *California Management Review*, Fall 1972, pp. 16–21.

[17]Robert N. Ford, "Job Enrichment Lessons from AT&T," *Harvard Business Review*, January–February 1973, pp. 106.

[18]William J. Paul, Jr., Keith B. Robertson, and Frederick Herzberg, "Job Enrichment Pays Off," *Harvard Business Review*, March–April 1969, pp. 61–78; M. Scott Myers, "Overcoming Union Opposition to Job Enrichment," *Harvard Business Review*, May–June 1971, pp. 37–49; Robert N. Ford, *Motivation Through the Work Itself*, (New York: American Management Association, 1969).

[19]For an excellent summary of these criticisms see William E. Reif and Fred Luthans, "Does Job Enrichment Really Pay Off?" *California Management Review*, Fall 1972, pp. 30–37.

TABLE 19–1　Characteristics of Traditional and Modern Management Styles

Traditional Style	Modern Style
1. Management dictates the goals and standards to the subordinates.	1. Management and the sub-ordinates participate in setting goals and standards.
2. The manager checks worker performance and evaluates it as either an achievement or a failure.	2. The manager encourages the subordinates to check their own performance and counsels them on how to capitalize on their mistakes.
3. The manager works out all the shortcuts and does all the innovating.	3. The manager encourages his subordinates to develop their own new methods and induces them to innovate.
4. The manager is basically a Theory X individual.	4. The manager is basically a Theory Y individual.

Adapted from William J. Roche and Neil L. MacKinnon, "Motivating People with Meaningful Work," *Harvard Business Review*, May–June 1970, p. 100.

Kilbridge, for example, discovered that assembly-line workers in a television plant did not necessarily regard the repetitive work as either frustrating or dissatisfying.[20] In another study, Reif and Schoderbek found that some workers actually liked routine jobs because it gave them time to daydream or socialize without impairing their productivity.[21]

It is not necessary to seek out new companies using the technique if one wishes to uncover shortcomings of job enrichment. Findings at TI and AT&T illustrate that many of the early promises just have not materialized. Fein, for example, has assessed TI's program as follows:

Texas Instruments' management was probably more dedicated to job enrichment than any other company in the world. They earnestly backed their managing philosophies with millions of dollars of efforts. After 15 years of unrelenting diligence, management announced in its 1968 report to the stockholders its program for "increasing human effectiveness," with the objective: "Our goal is to have approximately 10,000 TI men and women involved in team improvement efforts by the end of 1968 or 1969." Since TI employed 60,000, the program envisioned involving only 16 percent of its work force. The total involved was actually closer to 10 percent.[22]

---

[20] M. D. Kilbridge, "Do Workers Prefer Larger Jobs?" *Personnel*, September–October 1960, pp. 45–48.

[21] William E. Reif and Peter P. Schoderbek "Job Enlargement: Antidote to Apathy," *Management of Personnel Quarterly*, Spring 1966, pp. 16–23.

[22] Mitchell Fein, "Approaches to Motivation" (Hillsdale, N.J., 1970), p. 20.

In the case of AT&T, Ford himself has reported that "Of the nineteen studies, nine were rated 'outstandingly successful,' one was a complete 'flop,' and the remaining nine were 'moderately successful'."[23] One reason for such cases may well be, as found by a recent study, that firms using job enrichment "seem to have a limited understanding of the concept, are unsure of how or where to apply it, and have only a vague notion of what to expect from it or how to evaluate it."[24]

Job enrichment has short- comings.

In short, job enrichment has not been an overwhelming success. Why not? Reif and Luthans have proposed three reasons: some workers do not find satisfaction in the work place, so job enrichment has no value for them; some workers prefer boring or unpleasant jobs with good social interaction to enriched jobs that reduce the opportunity for such interaction; and some workers react to the technique with feelings of inadequacy and fears of failure.[25] This is not to say that job enrichment is worthless; there are many benefits to be gained from it. On the other hand, it must not be viewed as an organizational panacea for managing human assets. There are benefits and drawbacks, and management must be aware of both.

MANAGEMENT BY OBJECTIVES

Another approach that has gained in popularity is *management by objectives* (MBO), which, like job enrichment, gives the subordinate a voice in what goes on. MBO was first advocated by Drucker,[26] but it has been made famous by Odiorne, who describes it as:

> . . . a process whereby the superior and subordinate managers of an organiza- tion jointly identify its common goals, define each individual's major areas of responsibility in terms of the results expected of him, and use these measures as guides for operating the unit and assessing the contribution of each of its members.[27]

The MBO process.

In essence, the process entails a meeting between superior and subordinate for the purpose of setting goals for the latter that are in line with overall company objectives. The two individuals jointly establish: (a) what the subordinate will do; (b) by what period of time; and (c) how performance will be evaluated. Finally, when the allotted time period is over, they meet again to review the results and set further goals.

One of the greatest benefits of MBO is the participation it allows the subordinate in the goal-setting process. In addition, the clear statement of what is to be done and how performance

---

[23]Ford, *Motivation Through the Work Itself, op. cit.,* p. 188.
[24]Fred Luthans and William E. Reif, "Job Enrichment: Long on Theory, Short on Practice," *Organizational Dynamics,* Winter 1974, p. 33.
[25]Reif and Luthans, "Does Job Enrichment Really Pay Off?" *op. cit.,* p. 36.
[26]Peter F. Drucker, *The Practice of Management* (New York: Harper & Brothers, Publishers, 1954).
[27]George S. Odiorne, *Management by Objectives* (New York: Pitman Publishing Corporation, 1965), pp. 55–56.

will be measured is useful in reducing ambiguity and employee anxiety. Finally, there is the fact that MBO can be used by virtually any organization, public or private.[28]

Yet, despite all its advantages, MBO can be a complete flop if it is not implemented properly. One of the key factors in implementation is top management support. Research shows that the most successful implementations are those in which the top-level managers explain, coordinate and guide the program.

In addition, there are many errors that managers make when they sit down with their subordinates to identify and define what they are to do. Kleber has identified some of these as:

1. **Setting goals that are too easy to attain.**

2. **Setting goals that are actually unattainable.**

Common MBO errors.
3. **Setting goals which conflict with company policies.**

4. **Holding the subordinate accountable for something beyond his control.**

5. **Failing to get a commitment from the subordinate as to the agreed upon goals.[29]**

If management is aware of these problems, MBO has a much better chance of being implemented successfully.

Perhaps the greatest potential of this technique is that it provides the basis for effective decision making, communication and control through its emphasis on participative decision making and two-way communication. To date there is little empirical research to validate the effectiveness of MBO as an overall management system, but the technique is widely used and holds a great deal of promise for the future.

SENSITIVITY TRAINING

One of the reasons why many managers handle their workers ineffectively is that they simply do not understand them. Since the late 1940's a technique known as *sensitivity training* has gained wide acceptance in business organizations as a method for overcoming this deficiency.

The general approach used in this training is that of group discussion. With a leader who is skilled in the technique, the group decides what it wants to talk about or do. Since everything is so unstructured, many of the participants feel frustrated. As Davis notes:

Basically, sensitivity training is small-group interaction under stress in an unstructured encounter group which requires people to become sensitive to

---

[28]See, for example, Rodney H. Brady, "MBO Goes to Work in the Public Sector," *Harvard Business Review*, March–April 1973, pp. 65–74.
[29]Thomas P. Kleber, "Forty Common Goal-Setting Errors," *Human Resource Management*, Fall 1972, pp. 10–13.

one another's feelings in order to develop reasonable group activity. . . .

In this environment they are encouraged to examine their own self-concepts and to become more receptive to what others say and feel. In addition, they begin to perceive how a group interacts, recognize how culture affects it, and develop skills in working with others. In summary, therefore, the goals of sensitivity training are understanding of self, understanding of others, insight into group process, understanding the influence of culture, and developing behavioral skills.[30]

After attending one of these sessions, the participant is supposed to be more open with his subordinates, willing to communicate with them and determined to use a leadership style to which they can respond. In many cases this is precisely what happens, and the manager is better off for having participated in the training or, as it is often called, T-group session. However, not everyone would agree. The technique also has its opponents who argue the other side, claiming that sensitivity training is of little, if any, value.

*Sensitivity train-
ing has great
potential value.*

Who is right? This is a difficult question to answer. Miner, for example, reports that a considerable amount of research has been directed at finding out whether the T-group approach really does change people. The answer is that it does. "Thus, potentially at least it can alter value structures on a broad basis and pave the way for widespread reorganization. Managers appear to become more sensitive, more open in their communication, more flexible, and more understanding of others."[31] On the other hand, surprisingly, there are many important aspects of sensitivity training on which virtually no research has been conducted. Dunnette and Campbell, for example, after conducting a comprehensive review of the literature, found little research on the effects of sensitivity training on an individual's ability to face up to and resolve personal conflict, analyze information or implement solutions to organization problems.[32]

Nevertheless, there is currently such a tremendous amount of enthusiasm and confidence in this technique that it will undoubtedly continue to be a major organizational development tool for a long time to come.

**TRANSACTIONAL
ANALYSIS**

Transactional analysis (TA) is a technique recently described by Berne in his best seller *Games People Play*.[33] Since then it has been further popularized by Harris[34] and James and

---

[30]Keith Davis, *Human Behavior At Work*, 4th edition (New York: McGraw-Hill Book Company, 1972), pp. 187–188.

[31]John B. Miner, *The Management Process: Theory, Research, and Practice* (New York: The Macmillan Company, 1973), p. 279.

[32]Marvin D. Dunnette and John P. Campbell, "Laboratory Education: Impact on People and Organizations," *Industrial Relations*, October 1968, p. 23.

[33]Eric Berne, *Games People Play* (New York: Grove Press, Inc., 1964).

[34]Thomas A. Harris, *I'm OK—You're OK* (New York: Harper & Row, Publishers, Inc., 1969).

Jongeward.[35] In essence, TA helps the manager communicate with and understand his people through an analysis of their behavior as well as his own.

Ego States

At the heart of TA is the concept of ego states.

At the heart of TA is the concept of *ego states*. Everyone has three ego states: the parent, the adult and the child.

The *parent ego state* contains the attitudes and behavior that a child receives from his parents. For better or worse the parents leave an indelible mark on the child by communicating to him their beliefs, their prejudices and their fears. Any time a person acts in a manner learned from his parents, he is said to be in the parent ego state. Generally this occurs when he acts officious or assumes a dominant role. (This is the way it is to be done.)

The *adult ego state* is characterized by attention to fact gathering and objective analysis. No matter what prejudices or emotions were communicated by his parents, a person who is in the adult state deals with reality from an objective standpoint and analyzes the situation as dispassionately or realistically as possible. (Let's look at the facts.)

The *child ego state* contains all the impulses learned as an infant. When a person is in this ego state, he can be described in terms such as curious, impulsive, sensuous, affectionate or uncensored. He is acting just the way he did as a child. A common illustration is people at a football game who are rooting and cheering. They are uncensored and impulsive. (We want a touchdown!)

These three ego states are often described by one-word adjectives. The parent state is referred to as *taught*, the adult state as *thought*, and the child state as *felt*. In addition, for purposes of analysis, the three are often diagrammed as in Figure 19–4.

Types of Transactions

Throughout a normal day people will move from one ego state to another. The manager's job is one of discerning which ego state the person is in and then responding appropriately. To do so requires an understanding of the three basic types of transactions: complementary, crossed and ulterior.

Complementary transactions are appropriate and expected.

Complementary Transactions.   Berne defines a complementary transaction as one that is "appropriate and expected and follows the natural order of healthy human relationships."[36]

---

[35]Muriel James and Dorothy Jongeward, *Born to Win* (Reading, Mass.: Addison-Wesley Publishing Co., 1971); and *Winning With People* (Reading, Mass.: Addison-Wesley Publishing Co., 1973).
[36]Berne, *op. cit.*, p. 29.

FIGURE 19-4   Simplified Ego State Structure

Sometimes an employee will ask the manager a simple question (adult ego state) and expect a truthful response (adult ego state), as in Figure 19–5.

It is not necessary however, that people remain in the adult state at all times. For example, a worker may feel sick and ask to go home. In this case he acts like a child requesting a favor from his parent (please, Daddy, may I?). In turn the manager assumes the parent role (you certainly may). Such a transaction is illustrated in Figure 19–6.

As long as the manager responds appropriately, there is a complementary transaction and communication and understanding are achieved.

Crossed Transactions.   Crossed transactions occur when there is not an appropriate or expected response. A diagram of the transaction can easily reveal this. Figures 19–7 and 19–8 are two examples, the first being one in which the manager errs, the second being one in which the subordinate creates the problem.

*Crossed trans-
actions are in-
appropriate or
unexpected.*

Ulterior Transactions.   Ulterior transactions are the most complex because they *always* involve more than two ego states. Usually the real message is disguised under a socially acceptable transaction. For example, a manager wants one of his subordinates to take a job in a branch office because he feels the man needs this experience if he is to succeed with the firm. However, the manager also believes the subordinate is unwilling to do so. He therefore sends him two messages, which can be seen in Figure 19–9. The verbal one is represented by a solid arrow, the ulterior one by a dotted arrow.

*Ulterior trans-
actions always
involve more
than two ego
states.*

FIGURE 19-5   A Complementary
Transaction

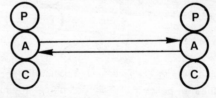

Employee:

Will there be any overtime
work this weekend?

Manager:

To the best of my knowledge
there will be.

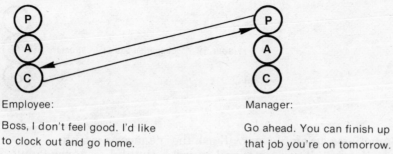

Employee:

Boss, I don't feel good. I'd like
to clock out and go home.

Manager:

Go ahead. You can finish up
that job you're on tomorrow.

FIGURE 19-6   A Complementary Transaction

The manager appears to be stating a fact, but he is really
appealing to the subordinate's child state by throwing him a
challenge and hoping he will respond appropriately. If the
subordinate says, "You're right, I want to stay here at the home
office," the manager has failed, for the individual has
answered the overt message only and responded on an adult-to-
adult basis. On the other hand, if the manager injures the
subordinate's pride (as he hopes to do), the man might say
"I think I can handle the job. I'd like to try it." In so doing,
he responds as a child (I can too do it. Just you watch!). The
point to be remembered is that when there are disguised
messages, the transaction is known as ulterior.

**TA and the
Manager**

TA is currently being used by a number of different firms,
including American Airlines, to help managers understand and
deal with their subordinates. As long as the manager realizes
that both he and his people have ego states and operate within
them, he is in a position to analyze what they say and how he
should respond. One of the things TA emphasizes is building
a strong adult ego state and encouraging others to do the same.
If the manager can do this, he will deal with his subordinates
in a forthright and objective manner. Naturally, there are times

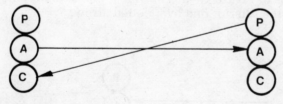

Subordinate:

I was on vacation last week and
didn't get a copy of the new policy
changes. Do you happen to have
an extra copy?

Manager:

What do I look like, the printing
office? If you want one, go up
to personnel and get one.

FIGURE 19-7   A Crossed Transaction

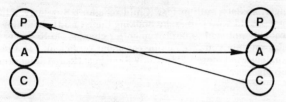

Manager:

Barry, according to the master
schedule it's your turn to stay late
tonight and clean up the work place.

Subordinate:

Oh, c'mon. I have a heavy date
tonight. Why don't you get
someone else, huh?

FIGURE 19-8   A Crossed Transaction

when the subordinates are justified in adopting other ego states.
For example, an employee may begin sulking because he has
failed to get a promotion (child state) and the manager offers
encouraging words (parent state). The important thing is to
refrain from using ulterior transactions or treating subordinates
as if they have no place in the decision-making process. If the
manager can do this, his people will respond more effectively.
In explaining how TA can help managers communicate change,
reduce resistance and encourage participative decision making,
American Airlines offers the following advice:

What can you do to minimize your own as well as others' resistance to change
and to improve efforts to improve? Remember that resistance to change
comes from the Parent or the Child. Sometimes resistance can be reduced
by providing or obtaining more data about the change. Involving people in
some aspect of the decision-making (thereby requiring the use of their Adult)
will also help to get them unhooked from their Parent or Child reactions.

The method you use in trying to improve something is also extremely
important. Telling people they *should* or *must* (Parent initiated "oughtman-
ship") improve something will probably hook their Child (and therefore
generate resistance.) For example, telling a group of employees, "You *must*
improve your customer service and also reduce costs" will likely generate only

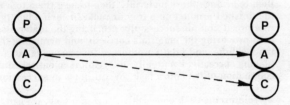

Manager:

Frank, there's been talk about
sending you to the branch office,
but I'm not so sure you're the
right man.

Subordinate:

You're right, I want to stay
here at the home office.

FIGURE 19-9   An Ulterior Transaction

anger, anxiety, guilt or fear (Child reaction). Similarly, telling people that they should worry (thereby hooking their Child) about this same problem will probably not lead to improvement or change. On the other hand, the more relevant data you give employees about service and cost performance problems, the more likely you will engage their Adults in problem-solving.[37]

ORGANIZATIONAL BEHAVIOR MODIFICATION

OB Mod employs learning theory.

Another technique that is currently receiving a great deal of attention is *organizational behavior modification* or, as Luthans calls it, OB Mod.[38] In essence, the technique attempts to modify behavior by rewarding correct conduct and punishing or ignoring incorrect conduct. In this way, the individual learns to do what is expected of him. Quite simply, the technique uses learning theory to train (or retrain) people to do things the way the manager wants them to.

Behavior Modification in Practice

Behavior modification has been used by many organizations. One area in which it has been very successfully employed is in handling mental patients and autistic children. A common approach has been to give the mental patients tokens for performing certain functions such as work around the hospital. These tokens can then be cashed in as payment for allowing them to engage in some activity they like such as watching an hour of television. This "token" approach serves to modify the behavior of the mental patients because it gets them to carry out certain tasks they would not otherwise perform.

Behavior modification is not confined to hospitals and clinics.

Behavior modification, however, is not restricted to hospitals and clinics. This same basic approach has been used in training the hard-core unemployed. In one case, report Beatty and Schneier, the trainer starts off by giving instructions to the recruits prior to the time they actually start the job. In this phase the trainer teaches:

. . . the skills required on the job by breaking the task into its component behaviors, using verbal instruction to demonstrate correct behaviors, and reinforcing correct behaviors. For example, consider a task requiring the trainee to *procure* materials from the proper place and in the proper amounts, then to *arrange* those materials, then to *feed* them to a machine, then to *place* the finished product on a tray or rack. In such a job, the trainee would be reinforced first for successfully procuring the materials, then reinforced for both procuring the materials correctly and arranging them correctly beside the machine, and finally reinforced for procuring, arranging, feeding, and placing correctly. Eventually, the reinforcement schedule would only reinforce completion of the entire task several times in succession.

By reinforcing each consecutive part of a task, we can "shape" behavior toward correctly performing the entire task.[39]

---

[37] Lyman Randall, *P-A-C- at Work*, American Airlines, 1971, p. 46.
[38] Fred Luthans, *Organizational Behavior* (New York: McGraw-Hill Book Company, 1973), p. 521.
[39] Richard Beatty and Craig E. Schneier, "Training the Hard-Core Unemployed Through Positive Reinforcement," *Human Resource Management*, Winter 1972, p. 13.

As the training continues, the reinforcement (money, praise) can be varied; i.e., the individual is rewarded only when he does the task right five times in a row or he is rewarded on a random basis. This reinforcement schedule will, of course, depend on the individual and the job. However, it should be remembered that this positive reinforcement only occurs if the person does the job *right*. If he does it wrong, he will be instructed again on the proper way, for the goal, of course, is to train him correctly. However, if he continues to do it wrong, the trainer will turn either to punishment (yell at him or threaten him with dismissal) or to extinction (ignore him). Neither of these two techniques will, by themselves, get the trainee to do the job right, but they may stop him from doing it wrong. In short, the trainer increases the probability that the individual will start doing the job right and will seek positive reinforcement over punishment or extinction.

The technique can be used for reducing tardiness.

Another objective for which behavior modification is being used is *reducing tardiness*. A hardware company in St. Louis, for example, has set up a lottery system for this purpose. If an individual is on time for work and takes only the allotted period for work breaks, he is eligible for a drawing at the end of the month. There is a prize worth about $25 awarded for every 25 eligible employees. Furthermore, at the end of six months, people with perfect attendance are eligible for a color television set drawing. In addition, the names of all winners, as well as those who were eligible, are printed in the company paper. Within 16 months of the program's installation, the firm's sick leave costs dropped by 62 per cent and the number of employees eligible for the monthly drawing rose from 151 (out of 530) in the first month to 219 in the sixteenth month.

One argument often made against OB Mod is that it is a manipulative technique. Certainly, if its use is limited to reducing tardiness, this is true, because the manager would be spending his time thinking up "gimmicky" approaches. In behavioral terminology, he would be offering his people contrived reinforcers that are external to the work environment. Although they are useful, the manager may well have to answer the question, what do I offer my people next when the lottery system for reducing tardiness proves ineffective? For this reason, OB Mod people attempt to rearrange the work environment more efficiently, using reinforcers that are *internal* to the job such as praising a person for work well done and ignoring him when work is poorly done.

Today the technique of behavior modification is being taken out of clinics and mental institutions and being applied to the management of humans in organizations.[40] Naturally, a great

---

[40]See, for example, Fred Luthans and Donald D. White, Jr., "Behavior Modification: Application to Manpower Management," *Personnel Administration*, July–August, 1971, pp. 41–47.

deal more needs to be done before its full value for management can be determined. However, it has had a promising start and appears to be an effective technique for helping organizations manage their human assets.

SUMMARY

In this chapter some of the latest tools and techniques for managing the firm's human assets have been examined. One approach, designed to get management in the right frame of mind, is human resources accounting. This technique suggests that the company evaluate its personnel and that this figure be reflected in the financial statements. After all, well-trained, well-motivated people are an asset. Another approach is to evaluate the personnel on a periodic basis by measuring causal, intervening and end-result variables. This technique gives management a reading on the kind of performance it can expect from its people in the near future.

A third technique, job enrichment, has been getting a lot of attention recently. It is currently being employed by a number of firms, including TI, AT&T and GM's Cadillac division. In essence, job enrichment places primary emphasis on Herzberg's motivators: advancement, growth and responsibility. Yet, despite wide acceptance, the technique has a number of vociferous critics who claim that it does not always work. Three of the primary reasons cited are: some workers do not find satisfaction in the work place; some people prefer boring, unpleasant jobs with good social interaction to enriched jobs that reduce the opportunity for such interaction; and some workers react to the technique with feelings of inadequacy and fears of failure.

Another technique that has also gained a great deal of popularity because of its potential for helping the manager carry out the decision-making, communication and control functions is MBO. In essence, it entails a meeting of superior and subordinate for deciding: (a) what the subordinate will do; (b) by what period of time; and (c) how performance will be evaluated. In addition to its participative decision-making feature, subordinates like the technique because it tells them what is expected of them, thereby reducing ambiguity and anxiety.

Sensitivity training is designed to make the manager more aware of his own actions and their effect on others, in addition to obtaining better insight into what makes his subordinates tick. Another approach, which is less psychological but just as valuable to the manager in communicating with his people, is transactional analysis. A number of companies, particularly

American Airlines, are using this technique to help their managers communicate more effectively with their subordinates.

Behavior modification is the newest of the techniques discussed in this chapter. In essence, it attempts to get people to do what management wants them to by discouraging incorrect behavior and rewarding correct behavior. Although used most widely by hospitals and clinics, today it is being adopted by business for handling numerous organizational challenges from training the hard-core unemployed to reducing employee tardiness.

This chapter has examined some of the latest tools and techniques for managing the firm's human assets. However, the company must be concerned with more than just the people within its walls. For over a decade now, business has been aware of an ever-growing demand on the part of the public for it to become socially responsible. The result has been a reevaluation, on the part of many firms, of the role they should play in the social arena. This will be the topic of Chapter 20.

REVIEW AND STUDY QUESTIONS

1. What is meant by the "great jackass fallacy"?

2. Why should a company think of its personnel as an investment? Should these people be accounted for in financial statements?

3. What is a causal variable? An intervening variable? An end-result variable? Of what value is this information to management?

4. In general, can a company improve its short-run earnings by switching from a System-4 to a System-1 management? Explain.

5. Why does a company, in moving from a System-1 to a System-4 management, not witness an immediate increase in earnings? Explain.

6. What is the primary goal of job enrichment? Will we see more of it throughout this current decade? Explain.

7. What are some of the arguments raised against job enrichment?

8. How does management by objectives work?

9. What are some of the problems one must be aware of in using MBO?

10. In what way can sensitivity training be of value to the manager?

11. How does TA help the manager communicate with and understand his people? Bring into your discussion the three basic types of transactions: complementary, crossed and ulterior.

12. How does behavior modification work? What are the basic steps or ideas in the process?

13. Behavior modification is nothing more than manipulation. Defend or oppose this statement.

SELECTED REFERENCES

Berne, E. *Games People Play*. New York: Grove Press, Inc., 1964.

"Business Tries Out 'Transactional Analysis,'" *Business Week*, January 12, 1974, pp. 74–75.

Cummings, L. L., and D. P. Schwab. *Performance in Organizations: Determinants and Appraisal*. Glenview, Ill.: Scott, Foresman and Company, 1973.

Drucker, P. F. *The Practice of Management*. New York: Harper & Row, Publishers, 1954.

Flamholtz, E. G. "Human Resources Accounting: Measuring Positional Replacement Costs." *Human Resource Management*, Spring 1973, pp. 8–16.

Ford, R. N. *Motivation Through the Work Itself*. New York: American Management Association, 1969.

Grote, R. C. "Implementing Job Enrichment." *California Management Review*, Fall 1972, pp. 16–21.

Harris, T. A. *I'm OK—You're OK*. New York: Harper & Row, Publishers, 1969.

Holloway, H. "Job Enrichment and the Bell System." *The Personnel Administration*, July–August 1971, pp. 28–30.

Hollingsworth, A. T. "Improving Managerial Decisions That Affect Human Resources." *Personnel Journal*, June 1973, pp. 446–450.

James, M., and D. Jongeward. *Born to Win*. Reading, Mass.: Addison Wesley Publishing Co., 1971.

Kegan, D. L. "Organizational Development: Description, Issues, and Some Research Results." *Academy of Management Journal*, December 1971, pp. 453–464.

Levinson, H. "Asinine Attitudes Toward Motivation." *Harvard Business Review*, January–February 1973, pp. 70–76.

Luthans, F., and D. D. White, Jr. "Behavior Modification: Application to Manpower Management. *Personnel Administration*, July–August 1971, pp. 41–47.

Luthans, F., and D. Lyman. "Training Supervisors to Use Organizational Behavior Modification." *Personnel*, September–October 1973, pp. 38–44.

Luthans, F., and R. Kreitner. "The Role of Punishment in Organizational Behavior Modification (OB Mod)." *Public Personnel Management*, May–June 1973, pp. 156–161.

Marguiles, N., and J. Wallace. *Organizational Change: Techniques and Applications*. Glenview, Ill.: Scott, Foresman and Company, 1973.

Myers, M. S. "Who Are Your Motivated Workers?" *Harvard Business Review*, January–February 1964, pp. 73–88.

Odiorne, G. S. *Management by Objectives*, New York: Pitman Publishing Corporation, 1965.

Paul, W. J., Jr., K. B. Robertson, and F. Herzberg. "Job Enrichment Pays Off." *Harvard Business Review*, March–April 1969, pp. 61–78.

Pyle, W. C. "Monitoring Human Resources—On Line." *Michigan Business Review*. July 1970, pp. 19–32.

Powell, R. M., and J. L. Schlacter. "Participative Management—A Panacea?" *Academy of Management Journal*, June 1971, pp. 165–173.

Reif, W. E., and F. Luthans. "Does Job Enrichment Really Pay Off?" *California Management Review*, Fall 1972, pp. 30–37.

Sirota, D., and A. D. Wolfson. "Job Enrichment: Surmounting the Obstacles." *Personnel*, July–August 1972, pp. 8–19.

Sokolik, S. L. "Organization Development: Its Meaning for the Professional Trainer." *MSU Business Topics*, Winter 1973, pp. 65–70.

Tosi, H., and S. J. Carroll, Jr. "Improving Management by Objectives: A Diagnostic Change Program." *California Management Review*, Fall 1973, pp. 57–66.

Walton, R. E. "How to Counter Alienation in the Plant." *Harvard Business Review*, November–December 1972, pp. 70–81.

CASE: A LIQUIDATION OF PEOPLE

When Jim Jackson became vice president of manufacturing at the Walters Corporation in 1972 the firm had been in a downward spiral. Profits had declined from $473,000 in 1965 to just over $250,000 in fiscal 1971. Return on investment during this period had dropped from 9.3 per cent to 4.0 per cent.

Within twenty-four months, however, Mr. Jackson turned the financial picture completely around. The accountant's report for these eight quarters revealed the following:

		Profit	ROI
1973	I	$290,000	4.3
	II	370,000	4.6
	III	420,000	4.9
	IV	550,000	6.1
1974	I	625,000	7.2
	II	750,000	8.1
	III	895,000	9.4
	IV	1,050,000	10.7

Then, to the president's dismay, Mr. Jackson submitted his resignation. He had been offered a job at twice his current salary and had decided to accept it. He would be leaving by the end of the month.

With only four weeks in which to find a replacement, the company quickly put out feelers to see who might fill the position. All reports seemed to indicate that Mr. Paul Robertson, factory manager for a large eastern firm, was the ideal choice. Mr. Robertson was invited in to see the facilities and financial reports. Toward the end of his visit he and the president had a chance to sit down and talk.

Paul, you've been here for three days now. Everyone is immensely impressed with your record and we'd like you to be our new vice president of manufacturing. What do you say?

I appreciate the offer, Mr. Canyon. However, quite frankly, I've decided not to accept. I just don't want to step in and spend the next two years rebuilding the firm.

Rebuilding? Why we have the best books in the industry.

True, on paper you look great. But what about the fact that over the last eighteen months half of your skilled work force has quit? These people are going to have to be replaced.

Sure we've lost some people. But Jim Jackson stepped into a tough position. He had to tighten things up. Before he came we were losing money. He made everyone start to pull their own weight.

And in the process he alienated the best employees. He's milked your human assets. I think you've gotten just about all the earnings you're going to get out of your current work force. The way I see it, you have a major rebuilding program on your hands. The man you think you're grateful to has actually liquidated your most important asset—your people.

Questions

1. If Mr. Robertson is correct in his analysis, how has the vice president of manufacturing liquidated the firm's human assets? Explain.

2. Why did the firm allow this to happen? Why did the president not take corrective action before this time?

3. What must the company do now? Explain.

CASE: DOING YOUR OWN THING[1]

One of the products manufactured by the Motorola Corporation is the Page Boy radio receiver. Slightly larger than a pen-and-pencil set, and weighing less than four ounces, the receiver allows doctors to be called from the golf course and executives to be found in the shop.

A number of companies manufacture these "pagers" but Motorola's approach is somewhat different. In the company's Fort Lauderdale plant, each of the assembly workers handling this product puts together and tests the entire unit. How well has it worked? Martin Cooper, vice president of operations for the corporation's Communications Division, says the approach has resulted in a "turned on group of individuals who enjoy their work and have a great deal of pride in their product." Motorola, however, is not the only company to use this approach. Non-Linear Systems, Texas Instruments and Hewlett Packard, among others, have also moved in this direction.

The key to success of the project rests with cost. Is it cheaper or more expensive to manufacture goods this way?

Motorola has found that individual assembly requires 25% more workers, as well as a more detailed training program. But [says a Motorola spokesman] the greater cost is just about offset by higher productivity, by the need for less inspection, and by lower repair costs. "Even more important is customer satisfaction"[says the spokesman]. In some plants, higher worker satisfaction has also led to lower turnover and less absenteeism.

In some plants the worker does not build the entire unit. For example, at Non-Linear Systems the company found that it was

---

[1]The data in this case can be found in "Motorola Creates a More Demanding Job," *Business Week*, September 4, 1971, p. 32.

too much of a challenge to ask each worker to assemble a digital voltmeter. It therefore assigned each worker a section of the instrument. Maytag does the same thing, having its people put together eight to ten major assemblies of a complete appliance.

Does the approach really motivate people and take away some of the boredom associated with the old assembly-line approach? Many people seem to think so and would agree with Michael Beer, a psychologist at Corning Glass Works, who contends that complete product assembly by one worker will some day be mandatory. If management does not voluntarily provide it, he contends, the unions will demand it.

Questions

1. What are the benefits that can be obtained from this assembly technique?

2. What are the disadvantages associated with this approach?

3. Do you agree or disagree with the statement regarding complete product assembly becoming mandatory? Explain.

CASE: TURNING PEOPLE ON[1]

Since 1970, Texas Instruments has been focusing its attention on maximizing the effectiveness of its employees. The name given to this program is "People and Asset Effectiveness," and the results thus far have been very gratifying. *Business Week* reports:

Net sales per employee rose from $14,600 in 1970 to $18,500 in 1972, while after-tax profits went from $510 to $870. Return on assets per person shot up from 5.6% to 10.1% over the three years.

The People and Asset Effectiveness program was devised to force TI planners to think hard about employees right down to the woman on the assembly line – and about their ability and willingness to produce.

And TI management expects the program to keep paying off. By the late 1970's, sales billed per person are expected to rise from this year's $18,500 to $30,000. Similarly, the goal for profits produced by each employee is $1,500 to $1,800 by that time, compared to last year's $870. That level of after-tax profits would result in a return on assets of 10% to 12%. Now, the strategy is to move "diagonally," increasing assets and productivity, toward the 1980s and TI's stated goal of $3-billion in annual sales.

What leads to such results? Frederick C. Ochsner, vice president and director of corporate personnel, says that it

---

[1]The data in this case can be found in "How Texas Instruments Turns Its People On," *Business Week*, September 29, 1973, pp. 88, 90.

is a host of things acting synergistically, including attitudes, team improvement programs, an open-door management policy and a nonstructured pecking order.

Ochsner is unwilling to say which of the programs has contributed most to TI's productivity gains. The key, he says, is flexibility. Some programs work well with one manager or supervisor or group of workers, some work well with others.

What makes it work, says Ochsner, is simple. "There are two things in life that people want," he explains. "They want to achieve and they want to be loved. And if you provide an atmosphere where these things can occur with a minimum amount of structure in the work flow, you are going to get what you want."

Questions

1. People are an organization's most valuable asset. Explain this statement.

2. What does Mr. Ochsner mean by "if you provide an atmosphere where these things can occur with a minimum amount of structure in the work flow, you are going to get what you want"?

3. Which of the techniques described in this chapter do you think TI might be using? Explain.

CASE: A CASE OF ELIGIBILITY

Absenteeism at the Pallering Corporation had been staggering. Between January and June of 1973 the average employee was showing up 15 minutes late for work three times a week. The management decided that something had to be done.

The problem was turned over to Jerry Peters of the personnel department. After pondering the situation for a few weeks, Jerry suggested that the management undertake an incentive program. Every worker who was on time during the month of August would be eligible for a cash award of $100. There would be three such awards in all, and the drawing would be held on September 4. Within five days of the time the award was announced, absenteeism declined to a lower level than it had ever been in the history of the firm. Furthermore, throughout the ensuing six months, the company continued to maintain this reward system and absenteeism remained lower than ever. In March of 1974 the firm abandoned the plan and absenteeism soared to an all-time high, but it returned to its former low level in April when the award was reinstituted.

Questions

1. Has the management actually modified behavior? Explain.

2. Why did absenteeism soar when the company abandoned the plan?

3. Why does absenteeism remain so low when the incentive award is made available? After all, isn't money only a temporary motivator?

CHAPTER 20

SOCIAL RESPONSIBILITY: A DEVELOPING CHALLENGE

GOALS OF THE CHAPTER
In the past decade business has found social responsibility to be a developing challenge. Specifically, firms are learning that they must be aware of, and responsive to, three social issues: equal opportunity, ecology and consumerism. The goal of this chapter is to examine these issues. In particular, attention will be focused on:

a. the doctrine of enlightened self-interest;
b. legislation designed to promote equal employment;
c. the role of the National Alliance of Businessmen in the social arena;
d. business' support of minority capitalism;
e. female discrimination in business;
f. air pollution and its challenge for business;
g. water pollution and its challenge for business;
h. noise pollution and its challenge for business;
i. ecological legislation designed to protect the environment;
j. current trends in liability laws; and
k. recent developments in the area of consumerism.

ENLIGHTENED SELF-INTEREST
By the 1960's, America was the most affluent nation the world had ever known. With this affluence, however, came a social awakening. People started asking questions about conditions in America and began demanding corrective action in areas such as equal opportunity, ecology and consumerism. Feeling that the business community had the resources and the know-how to handle these problems, and convinced that many companies had helped contribute to them, the public insisted that business become involved in social issues.

Such action was not in direct accord with many of business' objectives, i.e., profit, survival and growth. However, it was related by way of the doctrine of *enlightened self-interest*, which holds that by helping out the community, business is actually serving its own long-run interests. For example, since 1935, when the Internal Revenue Code permitted corporations to deduct up to 5 per cent of pretax income for charitable contributions, business firms have been extremely active in their support of various charities. Of course, not everyone has agreed with this action. Some stockholders have brought suits against their companies, contending that the contributions are in no way related to the running of the business. The courts, however, have consistently ruled for the firms, holding that such donations do indeed serve the interest of the company even though they provide no direct benefits. In addition, business can contribute to higher education. This issue was settled in 1953 by the New Jersey Superior Court when it ruled that a manufacturing firm could donate funds to Princeton University. The court held that support was not only a right but a duty, because by helping society the company was actually helping itself.

By helping society, business serves its own long-run interests.

By the same logic, expenditures to help improve community educational, health, and cultural facilities can be justified by the corporation's interest in attracting the skilled people it needs who would not move into a substandard community. Similarly, a corporation whose operations must inevitably take place in urban areas may well be justified in investing in the rehabilitation of ghetto housing and contributing to the improvement of ghetto educational, recreational, and other facilities. . . .

Indeed, the corporate interest broadly defined by management can support involvement in helping to solve virtually any social problem, because people who have a good environment, education, and opportunity make better employees, customers and neighbors for business than those who are poor, ignorant, and oppressed.[1]

The doctrine of enlightened self-interest extends further than merely pointing out the benefits of involvement. It is also based on the proposition that failure to assume social responsibility can jeopardize the organization's welfare. If business does not voluntarily do its share, the government will pass legislation and force it to become involved.

Statistics show that since the mid-1960's business has not only been aware of this social awakening in America but has also responded with positive action. What has accounted for this? Some say it has been newly enacted legislation. Others contend that the business community is merely trying to protect its image. Still others say that the businessman of today is more socially responsible than his predecessor. There is undoubtedly truth in all these statements. Yet, whatever the specific reason, many businesses have been developing programs to cope with the three most important social issues of the day: equal opportunity, ecology, and

[1]*Social Responsibilities of Business Corporations*, A Statement on National Policy by the Research and Policy Committee of the Committee for Economic Development, June 1971, pp. 27–28.

consumerism.[2] The remainder of the chapter will be devoted to an examination of these three areas.

EQUAL OPPORTUNITY

There are a number of important areas of equal opportunity currently providing a major challenge to business. In particular, these are: legislation, hiring of the hard-core unemployed, minority capitalism and female discrimination.

Legislation

One of the main reasons for business' attention to the area of equal opportunity has been legislation. The two most important laws enacted thus far have been the equal Pay Act of 1963 and the Civil Rights Act of 1964.

The *Equal Pay Act* was signed on June 10, 1963. Its purpose is to correct "the existence in industries engaged in commerce, or in the production of goods for commerce, of wage differentials based on sex."[3]

Specifically, the act forbids, "discrimination on the basis of sex for doing equal work on jobs requiring equal skill, effort and responsibility which are performed under similar working conditions."[4]

The law forbids discrimination in employment.

The *Civil Rights Act* was signed on July 2, 1964. Of its eleven major sections, Title VII is most important to business because it forbids discrimination on the basis of race, color, religion, sex or national origin. In addition, the Act established an Equal Employment Opportunity Commission (EEOC) composed of five members appointed by the President and approved by the Senate. Their job is to investigate complaints, seek to end violations through conciliation and ask the Attorney General to bring suit if such conciliation is unsuccessful.

These laws have been very helpful in providing for equal employment. One reason is that people have not been hesitant to use them. For example, in the first eighteen months of its existence, the EEOC received 14,000 complaints. In addition, minority group organizations such as the NAACP and CORE have been relatively active in using them to bring suit against firms for discriminatory practices. Equal employment, however, has proved to be more than a legal issue. Many firms have voluntarily responded to the challenge by eliminating or reducing their barriers for employment, thanks to a business program known as the National Alliance of Businessmen (NAB).

---

[2]Fred Luthans and Richard M. Hodgetts, *Social Issues in Business* (New York: The Macmillan Company, 1972).
[3]*Information on the Equal Pay Act of 1963*, pamphlet distributed by the Department of Labor, p. 1.
[4]*Ibid*, p. 2.

**Hiring of the
Hard-Core
Unemployed**

The NAB was formed in January, 1968 with Henry Ford II as chairman. It immediately established a program called JOBS (Job Opportunities in the Business Sector) and set out to find employment for 100,000 hard-core unemployed men and women by June 1969. Using a "community chest" type of drive, it established quotas for cities around the country and then canvassed each city, calling on businesses to pledge a specific number of jobs. In particular, it asked companies to review and modify their hiring policies so they could take on hard-core applicants. By the end of its first year of operation, the NAB had reached its goal and began setting even more challenging objectives. As a result, the organization was able to announce in its 1973 annual report that the JOBS program had found work for 1.3 million people since its inception.

Of course, since then not everything has been roses. The NAB has found it difficult to convince some companies, especially small ones, to employ its philosophy of "hire now, train later." These companies feel they are not sufficiently profitable to participate in the program. In addition, many participating firms have found that hard-core employees need

*Business has
helped hire the
hard-core
unemployed.*

special handling. Previously unable to keep a job, many hard-core employees really do not know what "work begins at 8 a.m." means. Some firms have tried to overcome this deficiency by assigning them a "buddy" or veteran employee who makes sure they get to work on time. Furthermore, there is the problem of training the hard-core, which in many cases averages around $3,000 per person. The government, through the Department of Labor, has tried to help solve this dilemma by awarding subsidy contracts to firms willing to undertake such training, but most companies have not been interested, preferring to do it themselves when at all possible.

How successful has this voluntary business venture been? Despite the many problems encountered, the program has proved extremely successful. Table 20–1 presents some of the survey results obtained from 76 firms in the alliance when they were asked about the policies and programs they had established in the area of hard-core employment. *Time* magazine, in referring to business' attempt to hire the hard-core unemployed, has reported that in recent years 60 per cent of new GM employees have been from minority groups. In New York City, approximately 50 per cent of Consolidated Edison's new employees are Puerto Rican or black. In addition, reported the magazine, the Bank of America in California had increased its minority-group personnel from 11 per cent in 1965 to 22 per cent by mid-1970.[5] Through voluntary programs business has begun putting increased emphasis on hiring of the hard-core unemployed.

---

[5]"The Executive As Social Activist," *Time*, July 20, 1970, p. 64.

**Minority
Capitalism**

In addition to hiring the hard-core unemployed, business has been focusing attention on the promotion of *minority-owned enterprises*. This program has taken two directions: helping set up new businesses and providing assistance to established ones.

In 1970, it was estimated that there were 150,000 minority-owned businesses in the United States, accounting for 1 per cent of all receipts.[6] In order to stimulate more of these enterprises, many firms have begun providing assistance in getting that all-important initial capital. At this stage there is also great emphasis placed on realism. Those who only *think* they want to start a business are screened out from the rest. The Colorado Economic Development Association (CEDA) does this by putting would-be minority entrepreneurs through a five-week business program that covers accounting, marketing, advertising, taxes and other related matters. By the end of the program, half of the people have dropped out. The rest usually reformulate their ideas, emerging with a much clearer picture of the type of business they want to establish. With these new ideas and CEDA's help in planning the business and the loan proposal, they are in a better position to approach banks for money. If they are successful in getting this initial capital, CEDA stays with them, providing managerial experience and helping them get off the ground. The results thus far reveal that

*Minority enter-
prise is
encouraged.*

---

[6]James M. Roche, "Making Free Enterprise Free," a talk delivered at the National Conference on Minority Enterprise, January 22, 1970.

**TABLE 20-1   Policies and Programs for Hiring the Hard-Core
Unemployed (76 firms responding)**

	Status (per cent)		
	Already in Progress	For the Future	No Plans in This Area
A policy on equal opportunity employment	100	0	0
A policy toward the hard-core unemployed	98	1	1
A program to insure nondiscrimination in employment	100	0	1
A program to hire hard-core unemployed	95	4	1
Revised employment tests	68	25	7
Lowered or modified educational requirements	87	6	7
Modified position on police records	78	11	11
Pre-employment training programs	69	14	17
On-the-job training programs	91	6	3
Recruiting in minority living areas	84	11	5
Recruiting in high unemployment areas	78	11	11

Source: Fred Luthans and Richard M. Hodgetts, "Government and Business: Partners in Social Action," *Labor Law Journal*, December 1969, p. 766.

only 10 per cent of these new businesses default on their loans. The success rests with the initial training and the emphasis on realistic proposals.[7]

Other firms have also provided similar assistance. For example, Hewlett Packard has guaranteed a $50,000 loan to a minority-owned electronics firm; Sun Ray Drug has funded black franchises in Philadelphia; and Menswear Retailers of America has arranged for a one-year credit on stock with suppliers for a newly founded clothing store.

Continued support must be forthcoming.

Business is also recognizing the importance of *continued support* to these enterprises. It is a well-known fact, for example, that black businesses cannot survive without going outside the ghetto. The same is true for virtually all other minority enterprises. They depend upon outside assistance. Much of this has been forthcoming in the form of customer orders. For example, former G. M. Chairman, James M. Roche, has commented:

Our varied needs and widespread operations lend themselves to an active search for existing minority business as new suppliers. They also enable us to develop new minority business that can supply quality goods on a competitive basis.

. . . We now purchase a variety of goods and services from young companies owned by minority citizens. For example, we buy glove compartment boxes in Watts in California, rubber production parts in Cleveland, and metal stampings in Detroit.[8]

G.M. has also deposited $5 million in black banks and placed $250 million in reinsurance business with black insurance companies.[9]

What will the future hold for minority enterprise development? A G.E. study has drawn the following conclusions about black business:

Despite some very obvious differences, the drive for 'black power' seems likely to follow some historical parallels with the emergence as a social force of other minority groups in an urban environment. On the economic front, the use of cooperatives to protect group interests and the growth of 'black capitalism' are interesting indicators that history may repeat itself, as group identity and cohesion assert themselves, before assimilation into the mainstream of American life.[10]

Perhaps the same general pattern will also emerge among other minorities during the decade. In any event, business is planning an active role in stimulating these enterprises.

---

[7]"Aid for Minority Businesses," *Business Week*, May 20, 1972, p. 102.
[8]Roche, *op. cit.*
[9]"A New Kind of Corporate Director," *Business Week*, May 20, 1972, p. 101.
[10]Ian Wilson, "How Our Values Are Changing," *The Futurist*, February 1970, p. 6.

**Female
Discrimination**

Although often overlooked in a discussion of equal employment, many women in the work force are discriminated against. This is particularly true in the areas of salary and management promotions. Business is finding, however, that the status quo in both areas is changing rapidly.

Salary Inequities.   The Labor Department has reported that the salary gap between men and women is getting wider. For

*Men receive
higher salaries
than women.*

example, at the beginning of the seventies women constituted 37 per cent of the work force but had an unemployment of 4.8 per cent compared with 2.9 per cent for men. In addition, the U.S. Bureau of the Census has estimated the average salary of year-round civilian, women workers in 1971 at $5,701 as compared with male employees who averaged $9,631.[11]

What accounts for the difference? The answer often rests with the interpretation of "equal pay for equal work" as provided for by the Equal Pay Act. Many employers have contended that women do not perform equal work, so they cannot receive equal salaries. However, in recent years working women have begun complaining and the U.S. Labor Department has started filing suits. The results have been astounding. Between 1965 and 1972, more than $43 million in back pay and court costs were awarded to 104,604 workers, most of them female, who were not receiving equal pay for equal work.

The most important decision came in 1970 when the U.S. Circuit Court upheld a decision against the Wheaton Glass Company of Millville, New Jersey. In its ruling the court said

*Women are
winning equal-
pay cases.*

that jobs did *not* have to be identical. If they were "substantially equal" the equal pay law applied. This meant that Wheaton had to pay its female inspector-packers over $900,000 in back pay. The U.S. Supreme Court refused to hear the appeal, thereby affirming the decision. Yet this is only one of the suits that have been brought. By late 1972, 400 equal-pay cases had been filed by the Labor Department. Of those that had been settled, the Department won 178 of 208 in the lower courts and 14 of the 30 "losers" on appeal. Some of the largest awards included:

Wheaton Glass	$901,062
G.C. Murphy	648,000
Pacific Telephone & Telegraph	593,457
Midwest Manufacturing	238,695
Daisy Manufacturing	209,905
Hayes Industries	206,214
American Can	149,927
RCA	100,432[12]

[11]Mary Hamblin and Michael J. Prell, "The Incomes of Men and Women: Why Do They Differ?" *Monthly Review* (Kansas Cit, Mo.: Federal Reserve Bank of Kansas City, April 1973), p. 5.
[12]"The Courts Back Women on Job Equality," *Business Week*, November 25, 1972, p. 44.

In addition to seeking redress through the courts, women are also employing *union power*, for they constitute a significant percentage of many unions. Twenty-one per cent of organized labor is female. The U.S. Labor Department has reported the ten unions with the greatest female membership as being:

	Total	Percentage of All Members[13]
1. Ladies' Garment Workers	353,870	80%
2. Clothing Workers	289,500	75%
3. Electrical Workers (IBEW)	276,510	30%
4. Teamsters	255,000	14%
5. Communications Workers	231,860	55%
6. Automobile Workers	193,130	13%
7. Service Employees	152,250	33%
8. State and County Employees	146,680	33%
9. Steelworkers	120,000	10%
10. Electrical Workers (IUE)	105,000	35%

If women continue to use this power, it is possible that many salary inequities will be greatly reduced by the end of the decade.

Management Promotions. By the end of World War II, it was evident that women were gaining a foothold in the business world. However, they have never really made significant gains in the management ranks. From 1950 to 1960, for example, the number of female executives increased from 8,875 to 25,457, but during the same period the *proportion* of female to male executives remained the same. Recent statistics show no great change in this condition. What keeps women from advancing in the organization? McCord has suggested the seven following factors:

The proportion of female to male executives has remained the same.

1. The occupations which offer prestige and power are not open to women.

2. There may be more confusion over the differences between the sexes and lack of understanding over the causes of sex-role stereotypes than there is actual discrimination.

3. Women generally do not receive the same education for business that men do.

4. Most companies know little about the identification and selection of women who are high-need achievers and have long-range career commitments.

5. Most women are hired into specific positions rather than into training programs or positions leading to general management.

6. Progression into higher levels of management is based on continuity of employment.

---

[13]"Women Workers: Gaining Power, Seeking More," *U.S. News & World Report,* November 13, 1972, p. 104.

7. Whether single or married, women in business are hampered by the male-orientated corporate life style.[14]

When one combines the fixed attitudes and outmoded notions of many male executives with the lack of clear-cut career patterns available to women seeking work at the managerial level, the importance of these seven factors in limiting the advancement of women in business becomes clear.

Steps being taken by business.

However, some firms are trying to rectify the situation, and in most cases the impetus is coming from the top. First, high-level executives are making it clear that women are to be considered for positions of responsibility. Second, recruiting practices are being modified to overcome traditional hiring barriers. Third, training programs are being established for those with supervisory potential but no prior business training. Fourth, there is a concerted effort being made to evaluate and promote both sexes on the same basis, whereas previously women were most frequently advanced on the basis of technical competence and men were often promoted on the basis of peer relations and anticipated long-range development. Of course, only time will tell whether business is *really* going to promote women up the management ranks, but it is definitely in the organization's best interest to take advantage of this virtually untapped human resource, and all signs indicate that management intends to do so.

ECOLOGY

In order to fully grasp the importance of the ecological challenge facing business, the reader should understand what is meant by the word ecology. Webster defines *ecology* as "a branch of science concerned with the interrelationship of organisms and their environments especially as manifested by natural cycles and rhythms, community development and structure, interaction between different kinds of organisms, geographic distributions, and population alterations."[15] The

The key word is interrelationship.

key to understanding ecology rests with the word *interrelationship*. All organisms must relate in some way to their environment. If they cannot co-exist with it, change occurs; the environment is altered or the organism dies. When such changes occur in nature's ecological balance, there can be side effects in other areas. As Ehrlich notes:

If we do something to an ecological system in one place, the whole system is affected. We must learn to look at the whole world and the people in it as a single interlocking system. It's impossible to do something somewhere that has no effect anywhere else.[16]

[14]Bird McCord, "Identifying and Developing Women for Management Positions," *Training and Development Journal*, November 1971, p. 2.
[15]*Webster's Third New Intercollegiate Dictionary*, volume 1 (Chicago: Encylopaedia Britannica, 1966) p. 720.
[16]"Playboy Interview: Dr. Paul Ehrlich," *Playboy Magazine*, August 1970, p. 56.

The entire world can thus be viewed as consisting of interlocking and interrelated ecosystems. If man starts making changes in these systems, havoc can result.

This section will review some of the ecological challenges facing business today. In particular, pesticides and pollution will be examined, since both serve to upset nature's ecological balance and thereby present a potential threat to mankind. Some of the current ecological legislation will then be reviewed.

Pesticides

Ecological concern is not new to America. For years, the nation has been aware of the need to conserve natural resources and protect endangered species. However, in the last decade ecology has witnessed a popular rebirth, and business has now become one of the prime targets. The issue that started it all was the use of pesticides.

Pesticides can be harmful.

Farmers have used chemical pesticides for years. In the early 1960's Rachel Carson wrote *Silent Spring*,[17] in which she charged that these chemicals such as DDT do not break down in the soil. Rather, they remain stable and dangerous for extended periods of time, posing grave danger to animals and humans alike. She further contended that these chemicals were being used with little or no investigation of their harmful effects; and there are many of them.

In Alamogordo, New Mexico, for example, a hog was accidentally fed seed that had been treated with a highly toxic mercury fungicide compound and it was subsequently slaughtered for consumption. The meat was eaten by three children who thereupon suffered serious brain damage. In another instance, scientists on the West Coast have discovered that pelicans eating fish with high residue levels of DDT lay eggs with extremely thin shells. The result is a premature cracking of the egg. Unless something is done, the pelican in this area faces extinction. Meanwhile, at Miami University, researchers have found a large percentage of terminal cancer patients with high concentrations of pesticide residues in their liver and brain tissues.[18]

Spurred on by such dangers, in mid-1972 William D. Ruckelshaus, head of the Environmental Protection Agency, banned nearly all uses of DDT in the United States. His decision rested with the finding that the pesticide was uncontrollable and capable of persisting in the soil for up to 17 years. However, the issue has certainly not been settled. Defenders of DDT warn that the insect killer is not only

[17]Rachel Carson, *Silent Spring* (Boston: Houghton Mifflin Company, 1962).
[18]Frank Graham, Jr., *Since Silent Spring* (Boston: Houghton Mifflin Company, 1970), p. 148.

important in preventing world starvation, but substitutes such as ethyl and methyl parathion are highly toxic and could prove even more dangerous.[19] Thus the pesticide issue continues to be a major ecological issue facing business.

Air Pollution

John Lindsay, former mayor of New York, once commented that he liked the city's air because he enjoyed seeing what he was breathing. There is no doubt that air pollution has increased dramatically over the past few decades, especially in a megalopolis such as New York. Two of the primary pollutants have been automobiles and industrial smokestacks.

Automobiles. The major cause of air pollution in America is the automobile. For some time now, the automakers have been trying to control the three main automotive emissions: carbon monoxide, hydrocarbons and nitrogen oxides. The basic approach has been engine modification. For example, in attempting to limit hydrocarbons and carbon monoxide, the major auto makers have turned to higher coolant temperatures

---

[19]Burt Schorr, "Agency Is Likely to Ban Most Uses of DDT In U.S. Today; Foreign Lands May Follow," *Wall Street Journal*, June 14, 1972, p. 38.

YOU DRIVE IT BACKWARD SO IT WILL TURN HYDROCARBONS INTO PURE GASOLINE.

(From *Keystone Motorist*, June, 1972.)

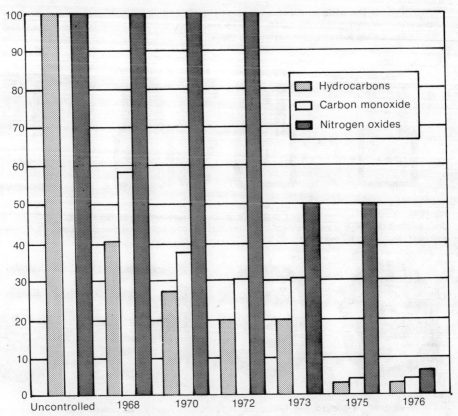

▲ *Percent emissions permitted by EPA*

FIGURE 20-1   Timetable for Cleaning Up Air Pollution (From National Academy of Sciences, National Research Council, as reported in "Detroit's Frantic Hunt for a Cleaner Engine," *Business Week,* December 9, 1972, p. 63. Reprinted with permission.)

The automobile is the major cause of air pollution.

and altered valve and retarded-spark timing. For limiting nitrogen oxides they have given major attention to reducing peak combustion temperatures through water injection or exhaust-gas recirculation and the use of a reducing-type catalyst for treating exhaust. Yet, whatever they do, the manufacturerers must hurry, for as seen in Figure 20-1, the deadline for cleaning up auto engines, barring a major change in governmental directives, is almost here.

This has led Detroit seriously to consider the use of non-piston auto engines such as the wankel or turbine (see Figure 20-2). The final outcome is yet to be decided, but one thing is clear— America is going to have less and less air pollution from automobiles during the coming decade.

Industrial Smokestacks.   If one ever drives into a big city on a cold winter day, smokestack pollution can be seen hanging over the metropolis. Among the worst of these industrial air polluters are the utilities, many of them hurling tons of sulphur dioxides into the air on a daily basis. By the early 1970's,

Utilities and refineries are also big air polluters.

Piston engine: The basis for the auto industry for the last 50 years. Antipollution rules are forcing auto makers to add costly gear to clean up emissions. But improvements are on the way that will help it hold a big part of the market into the 1980s

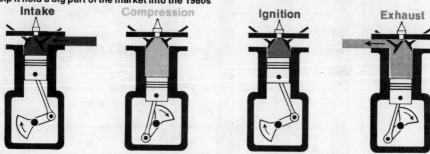

Wankel engine: Lighter, cheaper, more powerful for its size than the piston engine. Uncontrolled, though, it is even more of a polluter. But its compactness allows auto makers to fit extra pollution controls under the hood

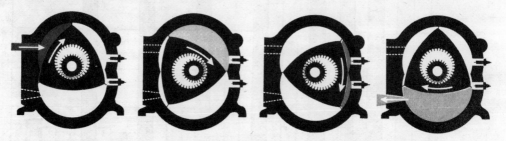

Turbine engine: A goal for the 1980s. But big problems have to be solved before it can win a mass market. Among them: high cost of materials and steep fuel consumption at a time when oil supplies are likely to be squeezed

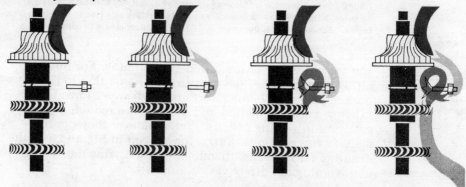

FIGURE 20-2   Auto Engines: Present and Future (From "Detroit's Frantic Hunt for a Cleaner Engine," *Business Week*, December 9, 1972, p. 61. Reprinted with permission from *Business Week* and the artist, Matt Greene.)

experts were placing the amount of air pollutants at 800 million tons annually, with utilities accounting for a significant percentage of this. Smelting and refining firms were also major contributors.

As a result, the government has taken steps to reduce industrial air pollution. In the case of utilities, this will require the purchase and installation of antipollution equipment. The Environmental Protection Agency estimates that:

> . . . electrical utilities will have to put forth 10% in additional capital to build . . . sulphur-removal systems and can look for an increase in generating costs of 7% to 30%. If the costs of controlling nitrogen oxides and particulates —two other major pollutants covered by the new plant standards—also are figured in, capital costs would shoot up 25% or more while generating costs would rise 15% to 40%. . . .[20]

The burden, of course, will eventually be borne by utility customers, but initial estimates indicate that the average power bill will rise less than 1 per cent.

Water Pollution   Many firms have used nearby lakes or streams as a drain pipe for carrying off their production wastes. As a result, some bodies of water, such as the Great Lakes, are said to be polluted beyond salvation. In other cases, companies have pumped liquid wastes into underground dumps. Unfortunately, sometimes these dumps have leaked and both underground and surface water have been polluted.

There is also the case of thermal, or warm-water, pollution, often brought about by hydroelectric plants. In order to generate electricity, the utility brings in cool water from a nearby lake or river. This is converted into steam to turn the plant's turbine engines. The steam is then passed through a condenser, cooled and turned back into water, and then returned to the lake or river. The problem is that many times this water is returned at 5 or 10 degrees above its original temperature. The ultimate effect can be a change in the basic ecosystem of the water. The aquatic life, unaccustomed to the warmer environment, may die.

Zero discharge is not a reality.   Presently, there is a great deal of pressure on business to cease any activity that may cause water pollution. This is all part of the current national goal of cleaning America's waterways by 1985. However, one should be aware that "zero discharge" will undoubtedly *not* become a reality because of the economics involved. As *Business Week* has reported:

> Like industry, the Administration fears the high cost of strict effluent limits. Russell Train, head of the Council on Environmental Quality, points out that cleanup costs rise exponentially with the degree of cleanliness sought. "The last 1% of treatment costs as much as the first 99%," he says. Preliminary CEQ data estimate the current water program, aimed at reducing pollution by about 85%, would eventually cost $60.8-billion. To achieve a 95% to 99% reduction would nearly double the tab to $118-billion. And to go the last effortful step to zero discharge would escalate the cost

---

[20]Burt Schorr, "What Price Clean Air?" *Wall Street Journal*, January 10, 1972, p. 24.

incredibly to $316-billion—or some $21-billion a year between now and 1985.[21]

How much will it cost to achieve the current goal of cleaning up pollution? McGraw-Hill's economics department has made estimates for various industries (see Table 20–2). Fortunately, the data reveal that although it will require a considerable outlay of funds, the cost is well within the reach of United States industry.

Noise Pollution

Excessive noise can damage hearing.

The amount of noise to which the average urban resident is subjected can be quite extreme. Car horns blast, pedestrians shout and overhead aircraft roar. In the past, little was done about all of this. Today, however, steps are being taken to reduce "noise pollution." One major reason for concern is medical research, which has established that people who are subjected to prolonged periods of noise at 85 decibels can suffer hearing damage. How loud is 85 decibels? The answer is louder than city traffic (60 decibels) but not so loud as the noise from a jet airliner (115 decibels).

The major aim of present action has been toward the abatement of aircraft noise. The Federal Aviation Agency has enacted a regulation that sets the maximum noise level for jet aircraft at between 102 and 108 decibels. Since many of these craft operate at 110 to 120 decibels, the airlines and aircraft manufacturers are going to have to come up with new design techniques.

Some aircraft engineers have been experimenting with the position, spacing and number of inlet vanes, outlet vanes and blades in an attempt to cut the whine of the fan during landing. Rolls-Royce has been considering the addition of a third engine shaft, thereby allowing the propeller to spin independently. NASA is also taking steps:

The agency will test a new engine design in all of the narrow-bodied jets. The front-end fans now used on these planes have two sets of rotating blades with stationary blades between. "If we can reduce this to a one-stage fan," [said a spokesman] "and increase the diameter of the engine by 6 in. to 8 in., takeoff noise should be lowered by 15 [noticeable decibels] and approach noise by about 19 [noticeable decibels]." That would drop the racket down to 100 [noticeable decibels] or lower.[22]

Aircraft, however, are not the only offenders. Some states, such as California, have ruled that no truck or car sold after 1972 can produce noise exceeding 88 decibels at a distance of 50

---

[21]"The Stormy Debate over 'Zero Discharge'," *Business Week*, February 5, 1972, p. 71.
[22]"Trying to Make Jets Whisper," *Business Week*, May 20, 1972, p. 56D.

TABLE 20-2 Cost of Cleaning Up Pollution

Industry	Total Investment Required [millions of dollars]*	Expenditures [millions of dollars]				Percentage of Total Capital Spending		
		1971 Actual	1972 Planned	Percentage Change, 1971 vs. 1972	1975 Planned	1971 Actual	1972 Planned	1975 Planned
Electric utilities	$6,190	$565	$1,027	+ 82%	$1,188	4.4%	7.2%	7.0%
Petroleum	2,690	527	542	+ 3	462	9.0	8.2	6.0
Paper	1,980	257	494	+ 92	224	20.6	29.8	14.5
Iron & steel	1,780	217	206	– 5	870	12.8	13.0	32.7
Nonferrous metals	1,670	111	269	+142	149	10.3	21.7	10.7
Chemicals	1,250	282	445	+ 58	419	8.2	12.2	10.7
Commercial**	1,200	234	224	– 4	315	1.3	1.1	1.5
Stone, clay & glass	780	112	173	+ 54	195	13.2	14.1	15.6
Machinery	560	95	381	+301	239	3.4	11.3	6.4
Food & beverages	550	101	158	+ 56	208	3.8	5.2	6.2
Mining	470	61	192	+215	157	2.8	6.8	5.4
Rubber	410	45	53	+ 18	100	5.4	5.0	8.0
Fabricated metals	400	89	119	+ 34	74	7.1	7.4	4.9
Instruments	260	60	74	+ 23	119	9.0	9.5	13.5
Electrical machinery	240	70	70	0	91	2.3	3.2	3.6
Gas utilities	220	49	79	+ 61	82	2.0	2.8	3.2
All business	**$22,760**	**$3,245**	**$4,906**	**+ 51%**	**$5,378**	**4.0%**	**5.3%**	**5.3%**

*Total required to meet pollution control standards in effect as of Jan. 1, 1972.
**Commercial category includes stores, insurance companies, and banks.

Source: McGraw-Hill Economics Department, as reported in "Spending Races to Catch Up to the Need," *Business Week*, May 13, 1972, p. 77. Reprinted with permission.

feet. In 1975 the limit drops to 83 decibels.[23] This reduction will have a significant effect on the average pedestrian, for a cutback of 10 decibels actually translates to a 50 per cent decrease in the individual's awareness of the noise.

Industrial plants are also trying to reduce noise pollution; for recent research reports that noise is becoming a major issue among workers. Yet there may be more to the problem than just anger over the possibility of impaired hearing. As the *Wall Street Journal* reports:

It has long been suspected that as many as 10 million workers may hear poorly due to excessive noise. Now some research links noise to such diverse ills as mental distress and heart disease. In Germany, a recent study of workers found that those subject to the most noise on the job suffered a higher incidence of heart disorders, circulatory problems and equilibrium disturbances. A number of medical men are certain that job noise is a factor in some neurotic and psychotic illnesses.[24]

Noise can also be a source of psychological distress.

Other research indicates that noise can prove to be a source of psychological distress contributing to symptoms such as instability, headaches, nausea, general anxiety and sexual impotency.[25]

Ecological Legislation

A number of ecological laws directly affecting business have been passed.

Thus far in this section the ecological issues facing business have been examined. Some of these problems are being met by voluntary action on the part of the business community. There are also many federal and state regulations that have been enacted in recent years calling for specific compliance. The two most important have been the Environmental Policy Act of 1969 and the Air Quality Standards Act of 1970.

The *Environmental Policy Act of 1969* established the Council on Environmental Quality. The council's basic duties are to assist the President in developing an annual environmental quality report, gather data on environmental trends and develop recommendations to promote environmental quality. In addition, the Act established the Environmental Protection Agency (EPA). The purpose of the agency is to coordinate all major federal pollution control programs for the purpose of achieving environmental quality.

The *National Air Quality Standards Act of 1970* represents one of the stiffest antipollution bills ever enacted. Some of its provisions are: (1) all new factories must have the latest pollution control equipment; (2) auto manufacturers must cut exhaust emissions by 90 per cent by 1975 and nitrogen oxides

---

[23]"The Din Over Muffling Noise," *Business Week*, April 8, 1972, p. 32n.
[24]Danforth W. Austin, "Factory Workers Grow Increasingly Rebellious Over Noise Pollution," *Wall Street Journal*, June 14, 1972, p. 1.
[25]*Ibid.*

by 90 percent by January 1, 1976; and (3) the federal government can set emission standards for ten major pollutants, from soot to sulphur dioxide. In addition, each state is given the authority to set factory-emission tolerances in accord with federal standards, and if they do not, the EPA, after thirty-days' notice to the respective state, can do so itself. Furthermore, the EPA can sue polluters directly, and if it is lax in this task, individual citizens have a right to sue both the agency and the polluter. Finally, violators of the act are subject to maximum fines of $25,000 per day or one year in jail.

These are only a few of the many environmental control acts now in existence. What does the future hold? *Business Week* contends that tougher legislation is a certainty. More specifically, Davis and Blomstrom predict:

Tax incentives for pollution control equipment (such as faster depreciation or tax credits

Matching grants or subsidies for installation of pollution control equipment

Denial of government contracts and other privileges to violators (or perhaps privileges to nonpolluters, similar to veterans' preference in government employment)

Research grants for development of new control methods, and demonstration grants to test them in service

Fixed charges for pollution emissions (such as a certain number of dollars for each ton of noxious fumes from a smokestack or each gallon of a chemical waste dumped into a river), an approach effective in reducing pollution of certain European rivers[26]

CONSUMERISM Since the late 1960's, consumerism has proved to be a major social issue facing business. Kotler has defined consumerism as *a social movement seeking to augment the rights and power of buyers in relation to sellers.*[27] This augmentation is taking two major forms: (a) buyers are demanding more information about the products and services they are purchasing; and (b) buyers are insisting on safer products.

Consumer Information and Assistance It is no surprise that research reveals that many people, when they lack knowledge about a product, tend to equate price with quality. After all, how does one go about deciding which of five brands of aspirin is *really* the best buy?

Legislative Protection. In recent years, legislation designed to make the consumer more knowledgeable has been enacted.

---

[26]Keith Davis and Robert L. Blomstrom, *Business, Society, and Environment: Social Power and Social Response*, 2nd edition (New York: McGraw-Hill Book Company, 1971), p. 348.
[27]Phillip Kotler, "What Consumerism Means for Marketers," *Harvard Business Review*, May–June 1972, p. 49.

*The Truth in
Packaging Act
sets forth
mandatory label-
ing provisions.*
One of these laws is the *Truth in Packaging Act*, which sets
forth the following mandatory labeling provisions:

1. The identity of the commodity shall be specified on the label.

2. The net quantity of contents shall be stated in a uniform and prominent
   location on the package.

3. The net quantity of contents shall be clearly expressed in ounces [only]
   and, if applicable, pounds [only] or in the case of liquid measures in the
   largest whole unit of quarts or pints.

4. The net quantity of a "serving" must be stated if the package bears a
   representation concerning servings.[28]

In addition, there is the *Truth in Lending Act*. This bill
regulates the extension of credit to individuals and is
primarily concerned with ensuring that the person knows the
charges, direct and indirect, associated with the loan. On open-
end accounts such as revolving charges, for example, the
individual must be provided with the following information on
his monthly statement:

1. the amount owed at the beginning of the period,
2. the amount and date of new purchases,
3. any payments made,
4. the finance charge in dollars and cents,
5. the annual percentage rate,
6. the balance upon which the finance charge is calculated, and
7. the closing date of billing and the accompanying unpaid balance.[29]

Business Assistance.   The business community is taking action
of its own to make the consumer more knowledgeable. For
example, General Foods and Lever Brothers have sponsored
consumer clinics in which customers are taught how to use
the firm's product. If something should go wrong, many firms
have established departments or offices to expedite the matter.
*Consumer
complaint depart-
ments have been
established.*
For example, Whirlpool offers its customers a 24-hour "cool
line." If the individual has a complaint or a question about
service, he can call this number toll free, anytime from anywhere in the country. Other companies have established
consumer complaint departments, which assign a problem to a
specific individual, and he stays with it until the customer is
satisfied. Corning Glass has extended this idea and appointed
a manager of consumer interests, whose job it is to represent
the consumer and make sure the complaint does not get lost.
In this way, the customer has an in-house agent.

Product Safety   Another major issue in consumerism is that of product safety.
Two areas currently receiving major attention are auto safety
and general product safety.

---

[28]Stewart H. Rewoldt, James D. Scott, and Martin R. Warshaw, *Introduction to
Marketing Management*, revised edition (Homewood, Ill.: Richard D. Irwin,
Inc., 1973), p. 270.
[29]"What You Must Tell Your Customers," *Nation's Business*, June 1969, pp.
42–44.

Auto Safety.   Ever since Ralph Nader wrote *Unsafe At Any Speed*,[30] auto safety has been an issue of concern. The last decade has seen a dramatic increase in auto safety legislation. In all fairness to the manufacturers, however, it must be noted that prior to this public outcry, sales indicated that people were not willing to pay for safety features. Now, of course, much of that is changed.

Some of the new features being installed on autos include seat belts, shoulder belts, energy-absorbing steering columns, padded dash boards and bumpers capable of withstanding minor collisions. In addition, there is still serious consideration being given to the air bag, although many of the auto makers are hesitant about employing the device. *Business Week* reports:

Many new auto safety features are being added.

> Detroit is resisting because the air bag is the single most complex subsystem ever considered for the automobile, and there are legitimate doubts about it. Though designed to save lives, it has the potential, however small, of causing deaths. The auto makers, likely to be charged with responsibility for any failures, are understandably reluctant to rush into production with a radically new and largely unproved device.[31]

If the air bag should prove unreliable in just one case, death could result, and there is the possibility of a law suit. For this reason, many manufacturers contend that lap and shoulder belts are just as safe and much more reliable than air bags.

In any event, the Department of Transportation and the auto makers are working toward a "safe" car. Some of its characteristics will include: (a) occupant survival if the auto hits a solid barrier at 50 mph or rolls over at 70 mph; (b) no damage to the car body in any collision of 10 mph or less; (c) sufficient side support to withstand a 30-mph side collision; (d) improved steering, braking and handling; and (e) a spill-proof gas tank.[32] In the meantime, one can take heart in the fact that even when the effects of lower national speed limits is discounted, auto deaths are beginning to fall below official predictions. With the present emphasis on safety, this trend should continue.

A "safe" car is being designed.

General Product Safety.   Many firms, spurred on by government legislation and the possibility of costly lawsuits, are placing great emphasis on product safety. Some are establishing product safety committees to evaluate current products. Others are providing safety tips with emphasis on certain short-cuts that are potentially dangerous and should be avoided. For

---

[30]Ralph Nader, *Unsafe At Any Speed* (New York: Grossman Publishers, 1965).
[31]"The Air Bag Faces a Showdown Fight," *Business Week*, August 14, 1971, p. 74.
[32]"The Crash Program That Is Changing Detroit," *Business Week*, February 27, 1971, p. 82.

example, the Hoover Company makes it a practice to tell the operator *not* to pick up puddles of water with the vacuum.

Legal Aspects.   In recent years, liability laws have undergone drastic changes. Two areas of particular importance for business have been *negligence* and *strict liability.*

Privity of contract has been pushed aside.

Under old English law businesses were liable for negligence only to the person who bought the good. This is known as *privity of contract.* Today the courts have pushed aside this doctrine and an individual does not have to prove a direct contractual relationship. A person who buys a defective car need not sue the dealer; he can sue the auto maker directly. This means that manufacturers are now much more prone to suit than before.

Forty states have strict liability laws.

Strict liability means that a manufacturer can be held responsible for products that injure the buyer or user; direct negligence need not be proved. If a company places a product on the market, it must stand behind the item. By 1970, forty states had enacted strict liability laws, and it is likely that by the end of the decade all will have them.

Safety Checklist.   With the courts making it easier to sue manufacturers for damages, many firms are finding it necessary to review the entire area of product safety. Carl Clark, Chief of the National Commission Task Group on Industry Self-Regulation, has suggested that manufacturers use the following safety checklist:

1. Review working conditions and competence of key personnel.

2. Predict ways in which the product will fail and the consequences of these failures at the design stage.

3. Select raw materials that are either pretested or certified as flawless.

A manufacturer's safety checklist.

4. Make use of trade association research and analyses concerning product safety.

5. Insist that product safety factors be tested by an independent laboratory.

6. Document any production changes that might later affect safety problems.

7. Encourage the product safety staff to review advertising or safety aspects.

8. Inform salesmen of the product's safety features and under what conditions they will fail.

9. Provide information to the consumer on product performance.

10. Investigate every consumer complaint.[33]

---

[33]"Consumerism: The Mood Turns Mean," *Sales Management*, July 15, 1969, p. 40.

This list can be valuable to manufacturers in light of the fact that in late 1972 the *Wall Street Journal* reported:

Products that don't work as they should, which now rival automobile accidents as the nation's No. 1 cause of litigation, were responsible for an estimated 500,000 court cases last year, compared with 100,000 five years ago, and many expect the annual total to reach one million by 1985.

The percentage of cases in which juries rule in favor of plaintiffs has also risen in recent years—to 52% this year from 49% in 1965, according to surveys by Jury Verdict Research, Cleveland. And the amount of the average award has increased substantially, going to $67,290 in 1969 from $11,644 in 1965 in household chemical cases, for example, and to $77,763 from $38,112 over the same period in cases involving automobiles and trucks. Though more recent figures aren't available, Jury Verdict Research say the increases appear to have continued.[34]

SUMMARY

In this chapter the three major areas of social responsibility for business have been examined: equal opportunity, ecology and consumerism. The challenges facing the business community in each of these areas were also described.

Business is taking many steps in dealing with these issues. Some of these actions are a result of legislation, but many are voluntary in nature. The NAB is a good example. Why is business undertaking programs of its own? Part of the answer rests on the doctrine of enlightened self-interest. Part of it is a result of a developing social conscience. As the *Wall Street Journal* has noted, firms are realizing that it is not enough to make a good, sell it at a fair price and earn a respectable profit.

. . . For an increasing number of companies, the answer—in theory, at least—is to help clean the air and water, to provide jobs for minorities, to contribute money and talent to the solution of urban problems, to be more helpful to consumers and, in general, to help enhance the quality of life for everyone. At long last, it seems, the corporation is developing a social conscience.[35]

REVIEW AND STUDY QUESTIONS

1. What is meant by the doctrine of enlightened self-interest?

2. In what way has the Equal Pay Act of 1963 been of value in promoting equal opportunity?

3. In what way has the Civil Rights Act of 1964 been of value in promoting equal opportunity?

4. What role has the National Alliance of Businessmen played in the social arena? What contribution has it made?

[34]Richard A. Shaffer, "More Customers Press Lawsuits Against Firms Selling Faulty Products," *Wall Street Journal,* November 3, 1972, p. 1.
[35]Charles N. Stabler, "For Many Corporations, Social Responsibility Is Now A Major Concern," *Wall Street Journal,* October 26, 1971, p. 1.

5. How has the business community helped promote minority capitalism? Give two examples.

6. What are the two most common forms of female discrimination? Explain each.

7. What is meant by the word "ecology"?

8. What is the major cause of air pollution in America and what is business doing about it?

9. Why is "zero discharge" considered unrealistic? Explain.

10. What effect can noise pollution have on people? Give an example.

11. What are the major provisions of the Environmental Policy Act of 1969?

12. What are the major provisions of the National Air Quality Standards Act of 1970?

13. What is meant by the term "consumerism"?

14. What are the major provisions of the Truth in Packaging Act?

15. What are the major provisions of the Truth in Lending Act?

16. What new changes are occurring in liability laws and what effect are they having on business? Explain.

SELECTED REFERENCES

Aaker, D. A., and George S. Day. "Corporate Responses to Consumerism Pressures." *Harvard Business Review*, November–December 1972, pp. 114–124.

Ackerman, R. W. "How Companies Respond to Social Demands." *Harvard Business Review*, July–August 1973, pp. 88–98.

Andrews, K. R. "Can the Best Corporations Be Made Moral?" *Harvard Business Review*, May–June 1973, pp. 57–64.

Bauer, R. A., and Dan H. Fenn, Jr. "What *Is* a Corporate Social Audit?" *Harvard Business Review*, January–February 1973, pp. 37–48.

Boyle, M. B. "Equal Opportunity for Women is Smart Business." *Harvard Business Review*, May–June 1973, pp. 85–95.

Bralove, M. "Costly Lawsuits Spur Companies to Step Up Efforts to End Bias." *Wall Street Journal*, August 2, 1974, pp. 1, 15.

Brothers, J. "Are You a Male Chauvinist Boss?" *Supervisory Management*, December 1972, pp. 2–8.

Carson, R. *Silent Spring*. Boston: Houghton Mifflin, 1962.

Conderacci, G. "Criticism Increases as the Auto Makers Press Claims of Cars' Gasoline Economy." *Wall Street Journal*, July 18, 1974, p. 32.

Davis, K., and R. L. Blomstrom. *Business, Society, and Environment: Social Power and Social Response*. New York: McGraw-Hill Book Company, 1971.

Elbing, A. O., Jr. "The Value of Business: The Responsibility of the Business-man." *Academy of Management Journal*, March 1970, pp. 79–89.

Fretz, C. F., and J. Hayman. "Progress for Women—Men Are Still More Equal." *Harvard Business Review*, September–October 1973, pp. 133–142.

Graham, E. "Many Seminars Are Held to Aid Women in Firms; Then What Happens?" *Wall Street Journal*, April 26, 1973, pp. 1, 10.

Graham, F., Jr. *Since Silent Spring.* Boston: Houghton Mifflin, 1970.

Hackamack, L. C., and A. B. Solid. "The Woman Executive." *Business Horizons,* April 1972, pp. 89–93.

Henderson, H. "Ecologists Versus Economists." *Harvard Business Review,* July–August 1973, pp. 28–36, 152–157.

Holley, W. H., Jr. "Successful Employment of the Disadvantaged." *Personnel Journal,* March 1973, pp. 193–197, 208.

"How a Social Conscience Shapes Banking," *Business Week,* September 15, 1973, pp. 140–141.

Jones, E. W., Jr. "What It's Like to Be a Black Manager," *Harvard Business Review,* July–August 1973, pp. 108–116.

Luthans, F., and R. M. Hodgetts. *Social Issues in Business.* New York: The Macmillan Company, 1972.

Luthans, F., and R. M. Hodgetts. "Government and Business: Partners in Social Action." *Labor Law Journal,* December 1969, pp. 763–770.

Nader, R. *Unsafe At Any Speed.* New York: Grossman Publishers, 1965.

Novick, D. "Cost-Benefit Analysis and Social Responsibility." *Business Horizons,* October 1973, pp. 63–72.

Richman, B. "New Paths to Corporate Social Responsibility." *California Management Review,* Spring 1973, pp. 20–36.

Sawyer, G. C. "Social Issues and Social Change: Impact on Strategic Decisions." *MSU Business Topics,* Summer 1973, pp. 15–20.

Shaffer, R. A. "More Customers Press Lawsuits Against Firms Selling Faulty Products." *Wall Street Journal,* November 3, 1972, pp. 1, 22.

Stabler, C. N. "For Many Corporations, Social Responsibility Is Now a Major Concern." *Wall Street Journal,* October 26, 1971, p. 1.

Webster, F. E., Jr. "Does Business Misunderstand Consumerism?" *Harvard Business Review,* September–October 1973, pp. 89–97.

CASE: MALE CHAUVINIST PIG

Cal Havin, president of a large eastern insurance firm, was quite distressed. He had thrown a party at his home over the weekend, and during the festivities he was cornered by one of his wife's friends who spent the better part of an hour bending his ear about "women's lib." Most of what she said was of little interest to Cal. However, she did catch his interest when she asked him how many women managers he had. Cal had to admit he did not know. "Oh, but if you had any, Cal, you'd remember," she said. "Men don't forget things like that."

Cal was incensed. The first thing Monday morning he asked for a report and found that there were indeed women in the management ranks of the company. However, he did have to admit that they only represented 1 per cent of all the managers and that they held low-level jobs.

This started Cal thinking about the role of women in management. His first step was to gather some articles and books on the subject. Over the next two weeks he perused these at his leisure. When he was finished, he concluded that the only way to ensure women equal advancement opportunities was to give the matter a push from the top. Before doing so, he decided to find out how much the top managers really knew about women in business. He therefore gave them the following true-false quiz:

T F   1. Life is much more difficult for a family if the mother works.

T F   2. Women like to work for men.

T F   3. Men do not like to work for women.

T F   4. Women managers have great difficulty with male subordinates.

T F   5. Most women have proved too emotional to handle positions of great responsibility.

T F   6. Women are absent from work much more than their male peers.

T F   7. Because they lack the long-range potential of men, women should be paid less.

T F   8. Women are better suited than men for dull, repetitive work.

T F   9. Women can be good homemakers or successful workers but not both.

T F   10. If most women worked, children would suffer greatly.[1]

On the average, eight of the ten questions were marked "true" by the managers. In reality, all ten statements are false.

Questions

1. What do the results of the quiz show?

2. How difficult will it be to ensure women equal opportunity in this company, especially at the management ranks? Explain.

3. What initial steps would you recommend Cal initiate? Be specific.

CASE: LET THE SELLER BEWARE[2]

Mrs. Velma Toth of Dayton, Ohio was pouring coffee for her husband when the pot cracked and scalding coffee burned his leg. The Toth's sued Corning Glass Works and were awarded $6,000 on appeal.

Bob Anderson, of Seattle, was opening a bottle of champagne when the plastic stopper prematurely shot out of the bottle

---

[1]These questions have been adapted from "Is Your Chauvinism Showing?" *Hospital Supervisor's Bulletin*, October 31, 1972, p. 5.
[2]The data in this case can be found in Richard A. Shaffer, "Seller Beware," *Wall Street Journal*, November 3, 1972, pp. 1, 22.

and struck him in the eye, thereby blinding him. He sued the manufacturer and won $70,000.

John McPhee, Jr., of Prairie du Chien, Wisconsin, was sawing logs when a sliver jammed the machine. He put the apparatus in neutral and crawled inside to remove the piece of wood when the machine suddenly slipped into gear causing him great bodily harm. A federal court jury awarded him $500,000 in damages.

These stories all lend credence to the statement, "Today, a poorly made product isn't passed off with the remark, 'I've got a lemon.' More likely, the words heard are 'I'll sue'."

The future promises more of the same, since not only are more people going to court and winning, but also the courts are extending the benefits of strict liability to injured bystanders as well as to those who are actually using the faulty merchandise. Consider the following case of Mr. and Mrs. Frank Codling of Glenmont, N.Y., who were injured when their Buick was hit by a Chrysler after the Chrysler's power steering had failed.

The traditional view would be that Chrysler owed the Codlings nothing because they weren't driving the defective car. But an appellate judge ruled that they could indeed collect from Chrysler—some $350,000—because, quoting an earlier California decision, "if anything bystanders should be entitled to greater protection than the consumer or user where injury to bystanders from the defect is reasonably foreseeable. Consumers and users, at least, have the opportunity to inspect for defects and to limit their purchases to articles manufactured by reputable manufacturers and sold by reputable retailers, whereas the bystander ordinarily has no such opportunity.

These actions are leading many to conclude that the old adage "let the buyer beware" has now changed to "let the seller beware."

Questions

1. How much responsibility should a manufacturer assume for the goods he produces? Explain.

2. Do you think the awards made in this case were exhorbitant or fair? Explain.

3. How can a manufacturer protect himself from such law suits? Be specific.

CASE: SHOW AND TELL[1]

In late 1972, the Federal Trade Commission (FTC) ordered a dozen automobile makers to back up more than 100 advertising

---

[1]The data in this case can be found in "FTC Orders 12 Auto Makers To Back Up Advertising Claims," *Lincoln Star*, Lincoln, Nebraska, December 15, 1972, p. 28.

claims. The FTC made it clear that it was merely gathering information and not filing complaints or suggesting that the manufacturers were guilty of violating federal regulations. However, the Commission was interested in receiving documentation from the respective firms, within sixty days, to support some of their claims, such as:

a. the Volkswagen squareback sedan gets about 24 miles to the gallon;

b. in contrast to the average domestic compact car, Volkswagen saves its owner over 200 gallons of gasoline in a normal driving year;

c. each one of the Volvo's steel pillars, which hold up the car roof, is strong enough to support the weight of the entire car;

d. Ford Pinto's four-speed transmission needs no lubrication over the life of the car;

e. the guard beams in GM's Vega provide more side impact collision protection than is available in any other comparable economy car;

f. the electronic ignition system in Chrysler cars never needs retiming; and

g. American Motor's Gremlin is wider, heavier and has more horsepower than any comparably priced car.

Other firms that were asked to provide documentation included Toyota, Fiat, Subaru, Renault, Saab and British Leyland Motors.

Questions

1. If any of the manufacturers find they cannot prove their advertising claim, should they be forced to withdraw the advertisement from circulation? Explain.

2. How accurate should an advertisement be? Is there any room for exaggeration?

3. How do you interpret the FTC request? Is it strictly a matter of wanting to obtain general information or is the Commission really getting ready to crack down?

CASE: A CASE OF DISCRIMINATION?[1]

James Cofield, Jr. received an MBA from Stanford in June, 1970. By that time he had been an intern at the First National City Bank of New York, worked for a major brokerage house, and been an administrative assistant at Winston-Salem State College.

However, when he applied for a job with Goldman, Sachs & Co., a Wall Street securities firm, he was turned down. Mr. Cofield

---

[1]The data in this case can be found in Ed Henry, "MBA Grad Charges Goldman Sachs Denied Him Job Due to Race," *Wall Street Journal*, June 1, 1972, p. 8.

charged that he was rejected because he was black. Specifically, he contended that during a recruitment interview at Stanford he was advised by a representative of the firm "that his application (for employment) couldn't be given further consideration because of the negative view held by a senior partner regarding blacks."

A spokesman for the brokerage denied that charge, stating that the entire matter was a misunderstanding. The brokerage had hired blacks in the past, he explained, but Mr. Cofield wanted to go into the "risk capital" business and the firm felt he would have a better opportunity to do this with another company.

Mr. Cofield took the matter to university authorities who eventually barred Goldman Sachs recruiters from the campus. In addition, he went to the New York State Human Rights Division which found "probable cause" that the brokerage engaged in unlawful discrimination. The Equal Employment Opportunity Commission also investigated and said it found:

. . . 'no concrete evidence to support the respondent's (Goldman Sachs') statements that they have actively recruited for executive personnel among minority groups.' Instead it found 'reasonable cause to believe that (the) respondent violated Title VII of the Civil Rights Act of 1964, as alleged.'

It stated that of a total of 1,425 individuals employed by the firm, only 126 were minority group members, as of 1970. Of these, three were employed as 'sales workers,' one as a professional and none in an 'official or managerial' capacity, the EEOC said.

Questions

1. Based on the data in the story, is this a case of discrimination? Explain.

2. Is employment discrimination as frequent as it was ten years ago? Why or why not?

3. What action would you recommend be taken if the brokerage is guilty? Explain.

CHAPTER 21

INTERNATIONAL MANAGEMENT: CHALLENGES AND OPPORTUNITIES

GOALS OF THE CHAPTER The United States is the most important nation in the international arena. This is true for two reasons. First, she does more exporting and. importing than any other country in the world (see Table 21–1). Second, some of her largest business firms conduct a substantial amount of trading with foreign countries (see Table 21–2) and keep a large percentage of their assets overseas. The modern American business

TABLE 21–1 International Trade Among Industrialized Countries (in billions of dollars)

Country	1972			1971		
	Exports	Imports	Balance of Trade	Exports	and Imports	Balance of Trade
United States	47.43	53.92	−6.49	44.14	45.60	−1.46
Canada	19.18	18.08	1.10	17.68	15.46	2.22
Belgium	14.80	14.38	0.42	12.30	12.67	−0.37
France	24.77	25.87	−1.10	20.52	21.24	−0.72
West Germany	45.17	38.84	−6.33	39.04	34.34	4.70
Italy	17.74	18.19	−0.45	15.12	15.98	−0.86
Netherlands	16.16	16.52	−0.36	14.02	15.19	−1.17
aEFTA	54.84	61.70	−6.86	48.41	55.84	−7.43
Japan	26.70	21.74	4.96	24.01	19.70	4.31
Total	266.80	269.21	−2.41	235.24	236.04	−0.80

aEFTA (European Free Trade Association) at this time was made up of Austria, Denmark, Finland, Norway, Portugal, Sweden and Great Britain.

Source: Organization for Economic Cooperation and Development, *Main Economic Indicators*, 1973.

TABLE 21-2   Some of the Large American Firms Operating in the
International Arena in 1971

Company	Total 1971 Sales Billions of Dollars	Foreign Sales as Percentage of Total	Number of Countries in Which Subsidiaries Are Located
General Motors	$28.3	19%	21
Exxon	18.7	50	25
Ford	16.4	26	30
General Electric	9.4	16	32
IBM	8.3	39	80
Mobil Oil	8.2	45	62
Chrysler	8.0	24	26
Texaco	7.5	40	30
ITT	7.3	42	40
Standard Oil of California	5.1	45	26

Source: Business Week, August 18, 1973, p. 26.

executive is thus concerned not only with domestic management but with international management as well.

The first goal of this chapter is to examine the possible advantages and disadvantages of "going international." The second objective is to analyze the methods used in organizing, controlling and staffing these overseas operations. The third goal is to scrutinize the role of the multinational corporation in the international economic arena. In particular, attention will be focused on:

a. why an American business firm will consider entering a foreign market;
b. the possible advantages and disadvantages of going overseas;
c. how a joint venture works;
d. the various forms of organization structure used in foreign operations;
e. the degrees of control a parent company can exercise over a subsidiary;
f. how a business firm will attempt to staff its overseas operations;
g. the role of monetary incentives in motivating personnel to accept overseas assignments;
h. upward mobility in foreign subsidiaries; and
i. the economic power and international responsibility of the multinational corporation.

ENTERING FOREIGN MARKETS

Why do American businesses enter foreign markets? There are numerous answers, including: (a) a high-level executive pushes for it; (b) an outside group approaches the firm with a proposal such as an overseas joint venture; (c) the firm fears it will lose business if it does not move into the foreign market; (d) domestic competitors are expanding into certain areas abroad and the firm decides to get on the bandwagon; and (e) strong domestic competition makes foreign expansion desirable.

**Identifying
the Firm's
Basic Mission**

*What business is
the firm in?*

Regardless of the reason, the first step a firm must take is to examine its operations. What kind of company is it? What is its real business? These are the same type of questions that were raised in Chapter 7 when strategic planning was examined. This time, however, the focus is on international expansion. In answering the question, how do you define your mission?, Jacques G. Maisonrouge, President of IBM World Trade, has stated:

> We want to be in the problem-solving business—this is our mission. Our business is not to make computers. It is to help solve administrative, scientific, and even human problems. If your mission is broad enough, you do not find one day that a competitor's new product has outmoded all your equipment.[1]

Meanwhile, Fred J. Borch, Chairman of the General Electric Corporation, has answered the question this way:

> We no longer define it as energy, electricity, and so on. That is a limiting factor. Rather, it is those areas of opportunity where our talents (whether they are technological, manufacturing, or marketing) can make a contribution that fits both our societal objectives and our growth objectives—those we give serious condition to. There is no limit to where our talents can take us.[2]

Both responses indicate that the firms see their mission as global in nature. Problem-solving (IBM) and societal and growth objectives (GE) are not restricted to national boundaries. If a firm feels foreign expansion is within the scope of its basic mission, it can begin evaluating the possible advantages and disadvantages of going overseas.

**Evaluating
the Possible
Advantages**

Expansion into a foreign market can have many advantages, some of which are profit, stability and a foothold in the Common Market or some similar economic union.

*Profit is
important.*

Profit.   One of the biggest attractions in going international is the possibility of increased *profit*. McKinsey & Company have found that among 100 major U.S. firms they examined, more than half had doubled their overseas profits during the decade of the fifties and their ROI was higher in the foreign than in the domestic market. And during the sixties, although the returns were somewhat lower, they were still considered quite good. Now, with current dollar devaluation, overseas ventures in the seventies are very promising indeed.[3] A second profit feature is the favorable tax rate, in contrast to that of the United States imposed by certain foreign countries. A third is the low wages paid overseas.

---

[1]Gene E. Bradley and Edward C. Bursk, "Multinationalism and the 29th Day," *Harvard Business Review*, January–February 1972, p. 45.
[2]*Ibid.*
[3]See "Foreign Ventures Fetch More Profit for Firms Based in United States," *Wall Street Journal*, November 1, 1973, p. 1.

WALL STREET JOURNAL

"Would you have a list of countries where you don't expect the dollar to bounce?" (Courtesy of Joseph Serrano)

Stability.   A second major advantage of foreign expansion is *stability*. Many firms are capable of manufacturing far more units than they can sell domestically, and a foreign market provides a source of demand for the goods. This can be done through direct export to an agent abroad or through an overseas branch or subsidiary. However, because of rising nationalism, a more common approach is to set up operations abroad and attempt to stabilize sales and production by working directly in both the foreign and domestic markets.

A foreign source of demand.

Common Market and Other Economic Unions.   Foreign production, especially in countries such as France, West Germany, Italy, Holland, Belgium and Luxembourg, can be beneficial also because it gives the company a foothold in the *Common Market*. In 1957, these six countries created the European Economic Community (EEC), or the Common Market as it is often called. The goal of the EEC is to reduce trade barriers between the members. By 1967, duties charged on industrial goods circulating within the Common Market were 20 per cent of what they had been. By mid-1968, they were eliminated entirely. In addition, during the current decade Great Britain, Ireland and Denmark have been given membership in the group.

The significance of the Common Market becomes clearer when EEC statistics are examined. During the decade of the

sixties, growth among the member countries ranged from 4.7
to 5.7 per cent annually. In the same period, the annual
percentage increases for the United States and Britain (which
was not yet a member) were 4.2 and 2.7 per cent respectively.

*The EEC has
made great
economic strides.*
Furthermore, during this decade the standard of living among
EEC member countries rose 74 per cent whereas Britain's
climbed only 31 per cent. Thus, although at the beginning of
the decade Britain had a higher standard of living than any
of the six Common Market countries, by 1970 she had been
surpassed by all of them except Italy.[4]

In addition to eliminating interior barriers, the EEC intends to
put a tariff wall around its members to protect them from outsiders. The result, hopefully, will be a united European market
that can compete successfully with American firms. By entering
the Common Market, however, U.S. firms can take advantage of
these developments. Servan-Schreiber points out that American
companies are not only doing this but they are also getting
Europeans to help them. In his famous book, *The American
Challenge,* he put it this way:

During 1965 the Americans invested $4 billion in Europe. This is where the
money came from:
1. **Loans from the European capital market (Euro-issues) and direct credits
   from European countries—55 per cent;**

2. **Subsidies from European governments and internal financing from local
   earnings—35 per cent;**

3. **Direct dollar transfers from the United States—10 per cent.**

Thus, nine-tenths of American investment in Europe is financed from European
sources. In other words, *we pay them to buy us.*[5]

This basic idea is not limited to the Common Market. There
are other economic unions that have also been formed for
similar reasons, including the European Free Trade Association
(Austria, Denmark, Finland, Portugal and Sweden), the Central
American Common Market (Costa Rica, Guatemala, Nicaragua,
Honduras and El Salvador) and the Latin American Free Trade
Association (most of the South American countries and Mexico).

**Evaluating the
Possible
Disadvantages**
There are also possible disadvantages associated with going
international. Some of these include: (a) lower than anticipated
profits; (b) need to understand foreign customs and culture;
(c) company-government relations and red tape; and (d) risk,
expropriation and the pressure, especially in underdeveloped
countries, to bring in foreign partners.

---

[4]"Falling Behind Again," *The Economist,* August 14, 1971, pp. 54–55.
[5]J.-J. Servan-Schreiber, *The American Challenge* (New York: Atheneum House,
Inc., 1968), p. 14.

Lower Than Anticipated Profits.   The primary disadvantage in expanding abroad is the possibility that the expected market will not materialize either because the raw materials or personnel are not available in the necessary quantities or the price for the good cannot be obtained. In either case, the result is *lower than anticipated profits.* This has often been true, for example, in Latin America:

Profits may not materialize.

> U.S. corporations now have nearly $12 billion of direct capital investment in Latin America. It is estimated by the Council of the Americas that U.S.-owned enterprises account for one third of its exports, one fifth of its tax revenues, and at least one tenth of its GNP.

> But in the 1960's the return on that investment averaged 12.7% — far less than in Asia and even less than in Africa.[6]

Customs and Culture.   Another disadvantage may be the new market itself. Precisely what does the company know about the country and its people? Does it understand the *customs* and the *culture*? What are the religious beliefs of the people? How do these affect their moral and ethical standards? What about the family — is it basically a matriarchal or patriarchal society? Are the people well educated or virtually illiterate? What are the social relationships and the value systems to which these people subscribe? If the company can answer these questions, it has a basic idea of how to interact with the people.

Customs and culture may be major stumbling blocks.

Yet as Fayerweather, an expert in international marketing, points out, there are still other attitudes among each population that are not covered by these questions.

> Notable . . . are the artistic tastes of the people, which are important factors. . . . That these tastes differ among societies is readily apparent to anyone comparing the dance, painting, music, and other art forms found in various countries. Likewise there are temperamental differences among peoples: the Latins are given to acting on impulse, while the Germans are more solid and rational. There are also a host of specific elements in the life of each country that are significant in some way — white is for mourning in China, a cow is sacred in India, and so on.[7]

In short, if a company is going to set up a business in a foreign country, it needs to know something about the people. This can be a time-consuming problem, especially if the firm is in a hurry. The last thing the manager wants to do is violate social custom, but he does want to get action. In a country like Japan where negotiations often move very slowly, the American businessman may find himself extremely frustrated. In fact, some companies have cancelled their plans to expand into overseas markets because they have found themselves unable to adapt to the norms and customs of doing business in the foreign country.

---

[6]Sol M. Linowitz, "Why Invest in Latin America?" *Harvard Business Review,* January-February 1971, p. 129.
[7]John Fayerweather, *International Marketing,* 2nd edition (Englewood Cliffs, N.J.: Prentice-Hall, 1970), p. 26.

Company-government Relations.   In many countries, especially those that are in the process of developing themselves industrially, the company must show the government that its proposed business venture will be beneficial to both parties. However, if the government has a master plan (and many do) and there is another business firm already manufacturing the good or providing the proposed service, the company may not be allowed to start up. This can be true even if the firm that is already licensed by the government is less efficient than the one seeking entry into the market.

Government red tape may be too great.

Furthermore, even if the initial proposal appears feasible, the company must often begin wending its way through a mass of red tape. The finance minister wants to know how much money the firm will bring into the country and how operations will affect the nation's balance of payments. The minister of power wants to know how much electricity will be needed by the proposed plant. Bringing all of these government officials together and obtaining final permissions for the proposed project may take so much time that the company will simply abandon the undertaking.

Risk, Expropriation and Foreign Partners.   If it does proceed, the company may find that the government has the authority to set the price of the good and adjust it as it sees fit, permitting the firm a "reasonable" return but no more. Many companies often dislike this idea because they feel the return does not justify the risk associated with the investment and the possibility of expropriation. There are numerous illustrations of rising nationalism leading to a takeover of American business. For example, in 1969, Gulf Oil's Bolivian subsidiary was nationalized, while Chile, under socialist President Salvador Allende, took over the affiliates of Anaconda and Kennecott Copper. Predicting such events is difficult. Some managers believe the government only expropriates or nationalizes small companies because the big ones present too formidable an obstacle. Others hold the opposite point of view, contending that large businesses stand the best chance of being seized. Actually, size may not be a very accurate determination of risk. Gulf Oil's subsidiary was doing only $26 million worth of business a year in Bolivia while the copper companies in Chile were helping to supply 70 per cent of that country's exports. Yet both were nationalized.

Expropriation is possible.

To reduce the possibility of expropriation, many firms take in native partners and operate the business as a joint venture. In some countries the government actually requires such action. On the positive side, the nationals can be useful in helping cut red tape. In addition, their awareness of local customs and marketing channels can be a great advantage. On the negative side, however, most businesses dislike turning over substantial (and possibly controlling) interest to an outside party.

Nevertheless, today most firms must be willing to establish some kind of balance between their own success and the welfare of the country if they hope to succeed in an overseas market. As Cateora points out:

> Unless the multinational investor of the 70s concerns himself with the host country's local economy, the growing animosity to U.S. dollars throughout the world will continue to show itself in government-initiated domestication and expropriation of U.S. investments. In order to avoid the economic pitfalls of these two policies, global investment strategies will have to include a social awareness of local needs and wants. The investment must be aimed toward becoming a fully-integrated part of the domestic economy. Such predetermined domestication seems to be the most workable policy for the coming years in light of the evolving hostile political atmosphere found in many countries around the world.[8]

One way of attaining this goal is through a joint venture.

Understanding the Joint Venture

When a firm establishes a *joint venture*, it takes in local partners who provide money and/or managerial talent. In foreign countries, nationalistic pressure, coupled with the desire of local capitalists who are eager to profit from industrial growth, has led to an increase in the use of this organization form.

Foreign partners can be useful.

On the positive side, the joint venture combines American technical expertise and foreign understanding of how to cut government red tape and market the product. Many companies have used this approach, including Du Pont, which holds a 49 per cent interest in a Mexican chemical plant, and Merck, which has a 50 per cent interest in an Indian pharmaceutical operation.

However, loss of control can be dangerous.

On the negative side, however, is the issue of control. Some countries insist that their people hold at least a 51 per cent interest in the venture. This idea is not agreeable to many American firms, including IBM, and there are some very valid reasons for opposing joint ventures. First, the local partners are sometimes more interested in their short-run profit than in the company's long-term gains. Second, the nationals may lack managerial skills but, as controlling partners, make decisions that may prove quite costly to the firm. Third, the partners may have a disagreement over policy. Fourth, custom or culture may dictate that the nationals find jobs for their families in the company. In all these instances, the firm stands to suffer. As a result, many businessmen say they will accept a joint venture only when it is forced upon them. Others simply stay out of countries where this organization form is required. IBM's strategy, for example, is to enter nations that do not require joint ventures, work closely with government officials

---

[8]Philip R. Cateora, "The Multinational Enterprise and Nationalism," *MSU Business Topics*, Spring 1971, p. 55.

and adopt a very low profile. In so doing, the company virtually blends into the business environment of the host country.

> . . . IBM has done a fine job of blending into France. The French government has a very active policy aimed at stimulating exports. IBM has brought its practices into line with this policy and is consistently that country's No. 1 or 2 exporter. IBM has done this in very clever ways, and the French government gives it much credit for favorably affecting France's balance of trade. (In Europe, IBM has about 65,000 employees, 10 manufacturing plants, and 4 research centers. The company has conscientiously tried to fit into the business climate in every country it has entered.)[9]

The giant computer firm has thus overcome any charges of exploitation, one of the prime reasons for the rise of joint ventures, while simultaneously refusing to give up any control of its operations.

Despite the disadvantages, the American businessman is finding that joint ventures are becoming more common today than ever before. Firms that are thinking of going international must be aware of the potentials and pitfalls involved in this organization form and, especially in underdeveloped countries, be prepared to accept them.

Making the Final Decision

Size of the market.

After evaluating the pros and cons, the company's top-level managers will make the final decision. Naturally, the major criterion is going to be profit, but there are many qualitative judgments that will be reflected in the decision. First, how large is the market? Domestic consumers are very different from foreign ones. In America, a large percentage of the population is middle class. In England, the largest group is the working class, whose incomes would put them in the upper-lower or lower-middle levels in America. In India, most people are at the lowest levels of the income scale (less than $2,000). The question of economic growth and stability is thus an important one.

Political stability.

Second, is the government stable or are political upheavals more the rule than the exception? It will take time to recoup any investment and the company must forecast such developments in the political arena. Some areas of the world are considered very risky. Linowitz, for example, reports that ". . . comparatively low yield, the increased governmental problems, inflation, and the new outbursts of economic nationalism are leading U.S. companies to reexamine their plans for further large-scale investments in South and Central America."[10]

---

[9]James K. Sweeney, "A Small Company Enters the European Market," *Harvard Business Review*, September–October 1970, p. 129.
[10]Linowitz, *op. cit.*, pp. 129–130.

Marketing channels.

Third, if the market and political conditions look favorable, is the company going to export goods to the country or set up facilities there? If it is going to export, marketing channels must be established. If it is going to set up facilities in the foreign country, a plant site must be chosen by matching the needs of the firm with the locations available. Perhaps the company needs to be located near a river or a source of raw materials. In any event, one site will be more advantageous than the others, and the company will want to select it as the final choice.

Review of market investment.

Fourth, and finally, a review of the market investment will be necessary. How much money will this venture entail and how long will it take to reach the break-even point? Also, if there are local partners, will they be putting up any of the money or will the venture be financed entirely by the firm? The answers to these questions will determine the ultimate fate of the project, for it will come down to a question of risk versus reward.

If the company decides to go ahead, attention must then be focused on the management of the enterprise. What type of organization structure will be best? What kind of control will the company want to exercise? How should the company go about staffing the operation?

MANAGEMENT OF FOREIGN OPERATIONS

Exporting or licensing?

The simplest way, organizationally speaking, for a company to handle its foreign operations is by exporting the goods to agents and distributors abroad. Sometimes, of course, because of strong nationalistic feelings, import restrictions and/or foreign exchange problems, the company is forced to become more deeply involved. For those wishing to keep the involvement at a minimum, licensing may be the answer. Under a licensing agreement, a manufacturer will permit a product on which it holds patents or trademarks to be produced in a foreign country. In turn, the licensee will make royalty payments to the company for each unit it manufactures. To ensure that the product is made correctly, many firms will train the licensee in production methods and manufacturing management. There is thus some involvement on the part of the company.

Overseas assembly.

Another approach, which entails still more involvement, is to manufacture the goods at home and then ship them overseas for assembling. Many firms have used this approach, but over time it is common to find them turning more and more to foreign manufacture. In the final stage, it is likely that the entire product will be manufactured overseas and the firm will begin exporting to nearby countries.

Organization Structure

There are many types of organization structure that can be employed in the management of foreign operations. In essence, the structure will depend on the firm's degree of involvement and its desire for control.

Branch Organizations, Subsidiaries and International Corporations.

The simplest form is the *branch organization*, which is an integral part of the company structure. In essence, a branch is simply an outpost or detachment that is placed in a specific location for the purpose of accomplishing certain goals on a local level. It is quite common to find branch offices responsible primarily for selling, and the branch manager as a sales manager who supervises salesmen, handles orders and resolves local problems. In the area of control, there is great disparity. Some branch offices are highly autonomous and others are under close supervision of the parent company.

A branch organization is an integral part of the company structure.

A *subsidiary* differs from a branch in that it is a separate company, organized under the laws of the foreign country for the purpose of carrying out tasks assigned by the parent firm. By definition, a subsidiary is controlled (at least 51 per cent ownership) by the parent, although it may not be completely owned by the parent.

A subsidiary is a separate company.

Some subsidiaries are highly dependent on the parent for operating instructions. Subsidiary department heads, for example, might report directly to their functional counterpart in the home office, the plant manager to the vice president of manufacturing, the head of sales to the vice president of marketing. Although those in the home office may not be best equipped to make decisions for the subsidiary a thousand miles away, the organization structure does provide for close coordination of foreign and domestic operations.

On the other hand, many subsidiaries are highly autonomous. Some, for example, have a free hand in conducting small local operations or carrying out narrow functions in a limited market. Others are full-scale companies with a great deal of autonomy across a wide area. An example is the IBM World Trade Corporation, which conducts all of the firm's business outside the United States, either directly or through subsidiaries.

When foreign operations begin increasing in size and encompass three or four subsidiaries in a number of different countries, it is common to find the parent company establishing an *international division* in the home office. It will usually be handled by a vice president of international operations, and the managers of the subsidiaries will report directly to him. He will have a staff to advise him on matters relating to marketing, production and finance. Another variation of this, as seen in the case of IBM, is to organize an *international* or *world trade corporation*. Although similar to the international division, it is a separate entity, often incorporated abroad, with its own president and board of directors. The board will include the

An international division will manage a number of subsidiaries.

head of the subsidiaries as well as members of top management in the parent company. The head of the international corporation will report directly to the parent company president, as seen in Figure 21–1.

Control

The parent firm can exercise heavy, intermediate or light control over the subordinate.

The key criterion in organizing foreign operations is usually that of control: how closely does the parent wish to monitor overseas activities?

There are three degrees of control a parent firm can exercise: heavy, intermediate and light. Each has advantages and limitations.

Heavy Control.   When a subsidiary is required to keep the home office aware of all operations and activities and seek permission before undertaking any important actions, the parent is exercising *heavy control.* On the positive side, such control ensures that the subsidiary is operating in accord with home office policies. In addition, this approach makes it easier for the parent to integrate and coordinate its world-wide operations. If a problem arises, the home office is in a good position to help solve the issue because it understands, through continual monitoring of operations, what is going on.

On the negative side, heavy control can be expensive and far less effective than the home office would like. In addition, there may be costly delays while the parent company ponders

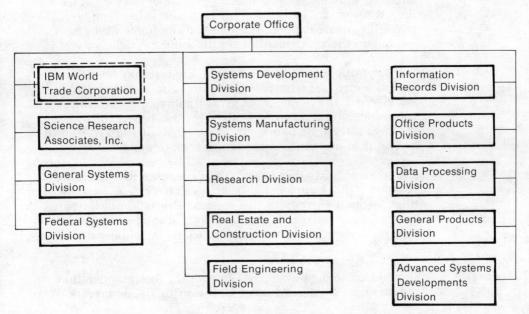

FIGURE 21–1   IBM Divisions and Subsidiaries (From 1972 Annual Report)

a decision. Also, the subsidiary manager and his staff may quit or ask to be transferred home, feeling that they are merely rubber stamps who are not allowed to exercise any personal initiative.

Intermediate Control.   When the subsidiary submits continued reports to the home office but has the freedom to make important decisions without obtaining permission in advance, the parent is exercising *intermediate control*. On the positive side, the reporting system helps the home office monitor activities and provide assistance to the subsidiary. In addition, the freedom to make decisions helps the subsidiary manager and his staff deal quickly with operational problems. This freedom of action can be a great morale booster for the overseas staff.

On the negative side, the manager is expected to be an operating executive and a paperwork specialist, and it may be difficult to find a man who is qualified to fill both roles. Also, the home office may be setting the goals for the subsidiary while the manager's job is to attain them. There may be difficulty here, however, because the subsidiary is not being allowed sufficient input into the plan.

Light Control.   When a subsidiary is allowed virtually complete freedom, having to provide the home office with only a minimum of information, the parent is exercising *light control*. There are several advantages to this type of control. First, the manager can devote his full attention to running the subsidiary and making money for the firm. Second, by reducing all the paperwork, the number of personnel can be cut back and the overhead cost reduced. Third, morale is likely to be high when the overseas people realize that the home office is relying on their judgment to get the job done right.

Light control has its disadvantages. First, it may be difficult to find a manager who is qualified to handle such a demanding job. Second, the home office gives up any chance to fully coordinate and integrate world-wide operations. Third, if a problem arises, the parent company may not learn of it until a great deal of damage already has been done.

Experience shows that heavy control is often too inflexible, whereas light control is too lacking in checks and balances. For this reason, many companies use some variation of intermediate control. The manager makes decisions at the local level but continually reports to the home office on subsidiary operations.

Staffing

In addition to organizing and controlling foreign operations, a company must concern itself with staffing the enterprise. Who should head up the subsidiary? What qualifications will the organizational personnel need to have?

Choosing the Right People.   Many of the questions about staffing will be answered when the company decides whether to set up a branch or a subsidiary. Others will be resolved when the issue of control over operations is determined. Of those questions remaining, some can be handled quite easily. For example, if the firm has been exporting to a foreign country and now decides to set up a subsidiary there, the export manager may be the natural choice for subsidiary head. If the company has an operation in Venezuela and decides to open one in Colombia, it may simply transfer personnel. After all, these people probably speak the language and undoubtedly know a great deal about South American culture and custom. Their skills are thus transferable.

Careful staff selection is necessary.

In staffing subsidiaries in underdeveloped countries, many firms have formulated guidelines based on past experience. Many, for example, like to employ bachelors because the man has only his personal adjustment to worry about; a married man would have to consider his wife and children as well. On the other hand, one American oil company operating in the Middle East has found that the best risks are middle-aged men with grown children. Economic conditions of the country and the specific operations of the firm can thus have an effect on who is most suitable for the job. So, too, can the geographic terrain. Companies with desertlike surroundings find that people from Texas or California tend to be better risks than those from New England. By employing such guidelines, the firm can often pick those most suitable for the job.

Not all the personnel, however, are going to be Americans. Many firms realize that unless some nationals are recruited, the company may find the going rough. Not only are there cultural and social problems, but there is also the issue of nationalism. Foreign governments may insist that the company hire local people. For both of these reasons, it is common to find multinational firms attempting to recruit local people with either good business judgment or political connections.

Monetary Incentives.   Once the "right" people have been chosen, there is the problem of getting them to accept overseas assignments. In addition to travel, many firms offer *monetary incentives*. Besides their base salary, these people may be given housing subsidies and basic allowances. In recent years, these extras have risen dramatically. Table 21–3 shows the total compensation recommended by a leading consulting firm to move a $36,000 a year executive family of four to a job overseas.

These allowances are, of course, quite costly. For this reason, many firms will hire local managers when possible. Not only

TABLE 21-3   Cost of Keeping a $36,000 Man Overseas

	Hardship Bonus	Cost of Living Allowance	Housing Allowance	Education Allowance	Total[1] Compensation
Bonn	$5400	$ 9372	$3012	$2202	$55,986
Brussels	5400	8868	3264	4179	57,711
Hong Kong	5400	2076	8328	2250	54,054
London	5400	2568	2496	3450	49,914
Madrid	5400	2244	4212	2939	50,795
Milan	5400	5220	1224	3750	51,594
Moscow	5400	4620	24	4171	55,615[2]
Paris	5400	10,200	5472	4790	61,862
Sao Paulo	5400	72	4092	3350	48,914
Stockholm	5400	9204	2136	2550	55,290
Tokyo	5400	10,200	15,636	3747	70,983

[1]Figures based on current exchange rates; amounts paid annually before U.S. taxes.
[2]Includes an extra $5400 hardship allowance.
Source: *Business Week*, May 19, 1973, p. 83. Reprinted by special permission.
Copyright 1973 by McGraw-Hill, Inc.

Foreign managers are paid less.

can they save the basic allowance and housing subsidy, but the pay scale for foreign managers is often much lower. For example, a French manager running a French subsidiary will receive far less than an American doing the same job. Such discrepancies are still a source of dispute with many foreign personnel. The situation can become even more difficult if one considers the French student who comes to the United States, receives a degree in business administration, and then takes a job in New York City with a multinational firm. In this capacity he will receive an equivalent American salary. However, what will happen if two years later he is sent to France to assist the manager in running the subsidiary there? He will be earning more money than his superior. What should the company do?

Currently, this entire area of wages and compensation is under examination. Multinational firms have established various schemes for resolving the matter. However, the answer still seems to depend on an individual analysis of the merits of the particular situation. Quite often, paying a competitive wage seems to be the only satisfactory solution.

Upward Mobility.   Another advantage in going overseas is
Rapid promotion is possible.
rapid promotion. Most executives admit that the man overseas can move up the subsidiary ranks much faster than he would move up the ranks at home, because although many American personnel will stay overseas for two or three years, most like to get back to the home office, having done their job in the field. This opens up opportunities for the lower-level managers to advance. Thus, for the individual who is adaptable to foreign habitats and can deal with the emotional strains of "going international," there is the promise of upward mobility.

THE MULTI-NATIONAL CORPORATION

In recent years, a good deal of attention has been focused on the multinational corporation, although there is disagreement on how to apply the term. Some individuals say a multinational company is, quite simply, one that operates in more than one country. Others employ a much larger number of criteria. Maisonrouge of IBM, for example, contends that five basic criteria must be present for a firm to qualify for multinational status:

1. The company must do business in many countries.

2. The foreign subsidiaries must be more than mere sales organizations. There must be some services, such as R&D and manufacturing, carried on.

Criteria for multinationalism.

3. Nationals should be running the local companies since they understand the people and the environment better than anyone else.

4. There must be a multinational headquarters staffed by people from many different countries.

5. The company's stock must be owned by people in many different countries.[11]

Most individuals are inclined to accept far less rigid criteria and would tend to agree with the group of authors who identified a multinational company as *"any firm that has a large portion of its operations devoted to activity that is not limited to one country."*[12] This definition allows for various interpretations while conveying the most widely accepted meaning of the term.

International Economic Power

American firms have invested large sums of money in foreign enterprises. As seen in Figure 21–2, the greatest amount has been invested in Canada. Next comes Europe, especially Common Market countries. The third largest share of revenue has gone into Latin America.

These investments have made the multinational firm a power in the international economic arena. This is especially true for the large American business firms (see Table 21–2). Everywhere giant U.S. companies have significant economic control. In fact, over a decade ago, American companies in France already controlled virtually two-thirds of the country's farm machinery, telecommunications equipment and film photographic paper production, in addition to 40 per cent of the nation's petroleum market. In Europe they controlled 15 per cent of all consumer goods which were being manufactured, 50 per cent of all semi-conductors, 80 per cent of all computers and 95 per cent of the integrated circuits market. No wonder Servan-Schreiber predicted that, "Fifteen years from now it is

U.S. firms have international economic power.

---

[11]Bradley and Bursk, *op. cit.*, p. 39.
[12]Richard D. Hays, Christopher M. Korth and Manucher Roudiani, *International Business: An Introduction to the World of the Multinational Firm* (Englewood Cliffs, N.J.: Prentice–Hall, 1972), p. 260.

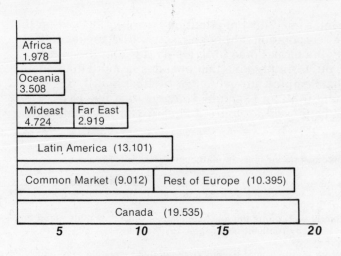

FIGURE 21-2 U.S. Direct Investment Abroad as of 1969, Excluding South Africa (From *Survey of Business,* U.S. Department of Commerce, October 1970, p. 28.)

BILLIONS OF DOLLARS

quite possible that the world's third greatest industrial power, just after the United States and Russia, will not be Europe but *American industry in Europe.*"[13]

General Electric is a good example of American success abroad. Its total and international sales picture for 1968–1973 inclusive is shown in Table 21–4. International sales are increasing at a faster rate than domestic sales, and this picture is not uncommon for the multinational firm.

Becoming Truly International

With economic power comes responsibility. As the multinational corporations grow ever larger, they face the problem of rising nationalism. Is American business trying to dominate foreign countries? Some people seem to think so and believe that the challenge of the next decade will be one of integrating

[13]Servan-Schreiber, *op. cit.,* p. 3.

TABLE 21–4 General Electric Financial Data (in millions)

	Total Sales	International Sales	Net Earnings on International Sales
1973	$11,575	$2,318	$151
1972	10,240	1,830	99
1971	9,425	1,584	86
1970	8,727	1,393	66
1969	8,448	1,201	48
1968	8,382	1,154	33

Source: 1973 Annual Report

With economic power comes responsibility.

nationals into the top ranks of these giant organizations so that management's point of view becomes *international* in focus. Unfortunately, some developments show little progress in this direction. For example, *The Sunday Times*, reporting on Ford's operations in the United Kingdon has indicated that the company is very tightly controlled by Americans.[14] Simmonds, after conducting research among the 150 largest U.S. industrial corporations, found that one-fifth of all the employees but only 1.6 per cent of the top management was foreign.[15] Americans tend to dominate the top ranks. If this problem is to be surmounted, business will have to take concerted steps to integrate nationals into top management.

Ensuring that top corporate management in the international corporation does become truly international requires planned action. There are many ways to start. Noteworthy steps include: international executive development programs that concentrate on top management problems, rotation of younger foreign executives through corporate headquarters, decentralization of staff functions to foreign sites, or adoption of policies that treat all executives as internationalists regardless of origin.[16]

Only in this way can multinational corporations prove beyond a doubt that they are truly interested in the economic future of the country in which they have operations. This is extremely important for major U.S. firms that hope to continue expanding overseas.

One country in which nationals have been recruited for management of U.S. firms is Brazil. Watson, for example, has reported that factors such as the cost of sending an American abroad; the current pool of well-trained Brazilians; and the maintenance of high morale among local managers who saw the opportunity for promotions to the upper levels of the subsidiary have all been determining factors in using Brazilians rather than Americans to manage U.S. enterprise there.[17] In addition, not only are Brazilians holding managerial jobs in American subsidiaries, but they are also filling high-level positions in areas such as finance, accounting and personnel (see Tables 21–5 and 21–6).

Another good illustration is found in the case of IBM, whose World Trade subsidiary president has stated the company's future plans as follows:

It has been our constant desire to grow, and to grow by being present in every feasible market, that has led IBM to where it is today. Wanting growth

---

[14]John Barry, "Ford's Top Britons Quit As U.S. Grip Tightens," *The Sunday Times* (London) November 21, 1965.
[15]Kenneth Simmonds, "Multinational? Well, Not Quite," *Columbia Journal of World Business*, Fall 1966, pp. 115–122.
[16]*Ibid*, p. 122.
[17]Charles E. Watson, "The 'Brazilianization' of U.S. Subsidiaries," *Personnel*, July–August 1972, pp. 54–56.

TABLE 21-5   Number and Percentage of Brazilian, American and Third-Country Nationals in Managerial Positions of U.S.-Owned Subsidiaries in Brazil

Manager's Nationality	(18 Firms Sampled) 1950		(51 Firms Sampled) 1960		(69 Firms Sampled) 1970	
	No.	%	No.	%	No.	%
Brazilian	29	46.0	94	40.8	288	64.2
American	32	50.8	120	52.3	112	24.8
Third-Country	2	3.2	16	6.9	50	11.0
	63	100.0%	230	100.0%	450	100.0%

Adapted from Charles E. Watson, "The 'Brazilianization' of U.S. Subsidiaries," *Personnel*, July-August 1972, p. 57.

has nothing to do with imperialistic motives. Rather, it is one of the conditions necessary to remain dynamic, to remain young, and to maintain a sound level of excellence. Through time, I am sure, we will have substantial changes in the structure of the company, but one thing that will remain is our desire to grow, our desire to develop the non-U.S. markets, and to be present, as much as we can, in all the countries of the world.[18]

American management has been very successful in its foreign operations. It possesses not only technical know-how but organizational skills as well. The future, however, demands that American multinational corporations begin to pay closer attention to the countries and people with whom they are doing business. Servan-Schreiber has said that American society, in contrast to European, "wagers much more on human intelligence than it wastes on gadgets."[19] The corporations will have to do the same in foreign countries. All the world is aware of American management ability. The question now is whether American management has the foresight to use this ability for the betterment of *all* mankind.

[18]Bradley and Bursk, *op. cit.*, p. 45.
[19]Servan-Schreiber, *op. cit.*, p. 253

TABLE 21-6   Nationality of Highest-Level Person With Responsibility for Various Functions

Manager's Nationality	Highest-Level Position		Finance		Accounting		Personnel	
	No.	%	No.	%	No.	%	No.	%
Brazilian	24	34.7	40	63.5	57	86.5	59	98.3
American	34	49.3	12	19.0	4	6.0	1	1.7
Third-Country	11	16.0	11	17.5	5	7.5	0	0.0
	69	100.0%	63	100.0%	66	100.0%	60	100.0%

Adapted from Charles E. Watson, "The 'Brazilianization' of U.S. Subsidiaries," *Personnel*, July–August 1972, p. 57.

SUMMARY   In this chapter the area of international management has been examined. American firms account for a significant percentage of all international business. The student of management thus needs a working knowledge of this area.

In deciding whether or not to "go international" a firm must evaluate many factors. First and foremost is its basic mission. Precisely what business is it in? If the management decides the international arena is within its sphere of operations, it can begin analyzing the possible advantages and disadvantages associated with such an undertaking. On the positive side are profit, stability and the possibility of a foothold in an economic union such as the Common Market. On the negative side are financial setbacks, foreign customs and culture, company-government relations, risk, expropriation and the possibility of having to bring in foreign partners, which, for many businessmen, constitutes the biggest drawback. IBM, for one, flatly refuses to enter into a joint venture, although because of rising nationalism, they are becoming a common phenomenon.

If a company decides to go ahead with a foreign operation, it must find an appropriate organization structure. This will, of course, depend on the amount of involvement it is willing to undertake. For some firms a branch organization will do; for others a subsidiary is necessary. The next question will be one of control. Which is best: heavy, intermediate or light? Most firms opt for intermediate. Then comes staffing. This will entail identifying qualified people and offering them sufficient monetary incentive and upward mobility to get them to go abroad.

The last section of this chapter examined the multinational corporation. Most of these firms are American, and they carry a good deal of economic power in the international arena. However, with this power comes responsibility, and the challenge of the next decade will be to incorporate foreign nationals into the upper ranks of management so that the interests of all countries are properly served. In so doing, the multinational firms will become truly *international* in nature.

REVIEW AND STUDY QUESTIONS

1. Why do American businesses enter foreign markets? Explain.

2. What are the advantages of "going international"? What are the disadvantages?

3. What is the Common Market? What are its goals? How successful has it been?

4. According to Servan-Schreiber, what is the "American challenge"?

5. How does a joint venture work?

6. How does a branch office differ from a subsidiary?

7. What are the advantages associated with heavy control of foreign subsidiaries? Loose control?

8. Why do most firms use intermediate control with their overseas subsidiaries?

9. What are some of the things a firm should look for in the people it chooses for overseas operations?

10. How lucrative are the financial incentives management gives to the people it sends overseas? Explain.

11. Is the chance for upward mobility of an individual in a foreign subsidiary better or worse than it would be in the home office?

12. What is a multinational corporation?

13. How powerful are American multinational corporations in the international economic arena?

14. How international are the top management ranks of multinational corporations? Explain. Why do you think this is the case?

SELECTED REFERENCES

Bradley, G. E., and E. C. Bursk. "Multinationalism and the 29th Day." *Harvard Business Review*, January–February 1972, pp. 37–47.

Cuddy, D. J. "Planning and Control of Foreign Operations." *Managerial Planning*, November–December 1973, pp. 1–5.

Daniels, J.D., and J. Arpan. "Comparative Home Country Influences on Management Practices Abroad." *Academy of Management Journal*, September 1972, pp. 305–315.

Fayerweather, J. *International Marketing*, 2nd edition. Englewood Cliffs, N.J.: Prentice-Hall, 1970.

Franko, L. G. "Who Manages Multinational Enterprises?" *Columbia Journal of World Business*, Summer 1973, pp. 30–42.

Hays, R. D., C. M. Korth, and M. Roudiani. *International Business: An Introduction to the World of the Multinational Firm*, Englewood Cliffs, N.J.: Prentice-Hall, 1972.

Kuin, P. "The Magic of Multinational Management." *Harvard Business Review*, November–December 1972, pp. 89–97.

Linowitz, S. M., "Why Invest in Latin America?" *Harvard Business Review*, January–February 1971, pp. 120–130.

Miller, E. L. "The International Selection Decision: A Study of Some Dimensions of Managerial Behavior in the Selection Decision Process." *Academy of Management Journal*, June 1973, pp. 239–252.

Robbins, S. M., and R. B. Stobaugh. "The Bent Measuring Stick for Foreign Subsidiaries." *Harvard Business Review*, September–October 1973, pp. 80–88.

Schollhammer, H. "Organization Structures of Multinational Corporations." *Academy of Management Journal*, September 1971, pp. 345–365.

Servan-Schreiber, J.-J. *The American Challenge*. New York: Atheneum House, Inc., 1968.

Simmonds, K. "Multinational? Well, Not Quite." *Columbia Journal of World Business*, Fall 1966, pp. 115–122.

Sweeney, J. K. "A Small Company Enters the European Market." *Harvard Business Review,* September–October 1970, pp. 126–132.

Welch, W. H. "The Business Outlook for Southeast Asia." *Harvard Business Review,* May–June 1973, pp. 72–84.

Widing, J. W. Jr. "Reorganizing Your Worldwide Business." *Harvard Business Review,* May–June 1973, pp. 153–160.

Young, D. "Fair Compensation for Expatriates." *Harvard Business Review,* July–August 1973, pp. 117–126.

CASE: TWENTY QUESTIONS[1]

Before "going international," there are many questions a business should be able to answer. Some of these are:

1. **Will our sales force in the new market respond best to straight salary, or to some combination of straight salary and commission?**

2. **How will our middleman respond to alternative policies we might employ?**

3. **Will the local partners be interested in long-term capital gain or in current income and prestige?**

4. **Will the government want to give us a maximum of elbow room to operate because they want to show that they welcome foreign investment?**

5. **Or, will the government want to impose controls to assure, for example, that the positive balance of payments effect of the investment is maximized, that the number of foreign nationals in the operation is held down to some minimum, and that at least x per cent of the purchases of raw materials, components and supplies will be from local sources?**

Questions such as these are useful to the firm in developing its alternative strategies, reducing risk and uncertainty and obtaining the greatest return on its investment.

Questions

1. In addition to the above, what other questions must be answered by a firm that is thinking about going international? Be explicit.

2. How does a firm go about getting answers to these questions?

3. Are there any questions to which the firm will not be able to obtain answers? Explain.

CASE: YANKEE GO HOME[2]

In late 1971, Avnet Inc., distributor of Garrard stereo component systems in the United States bought a 70 per cent interest in a

---

[1]The questions in this case can be found in Richard H. Holton, "Marketing Policies in Multinational Corporations," *California Management Review,* Summer 1971, p. 61.

[2]The data in this case can be found in Eric Morgenthaler, "Mexico Takes Hard Look at Foreign Plants, Discouraging Investment by U.S. Concerns," *Wall Street Journal,* March 21, 1973, p. 40.

small Mexican electronics company that manufactured Garrard components for the Latin American market. It appeared to be a logical move. However, in late 1972, the Mexican government put new tax and investment codes, tough on foreigners, into effect. The company was left with two alternatives: take a minority position in the venture or sell out completely. It chose the latter.

In March, 1972 General Portland Inc., a Dallas-based cement manufacturer, was negotiating the purchase of a 49 per cent interest in a Mexican cement plant. By October the deal was virtually ready to be closed when suddenly a Mexican government-controlled company entered the picture and indicated that it wanted to obtain half of General Portland's 49 per cent. The American firm backed out of the deal.

Both of these stories indicate the position currently being taken by the Mexican government. Although foreign investment is welcomed, the government prefers that outsiders take a minority position. This is further encouraged by legislation.

Late last year, comprehensive laws on foreign investment and technology were introduced and passed. Although they distress many businessmen already operating here, the brunt of their weight will be felt by new investors entering Mexico.

The laws state for the first time that, with certain exceptions, foreigners must maintain only a minority position in Mexican ventures and that their control of management must not exceed their stock interests. . . . New business projects are subject to the scrutiny of a new cabinet-level body, with authority to reject any foreign ventures deemed against Mexican interests.

There is also more regulation of technology-sharing and patent agreements. A national registry for the transfer of technology will examine all such agreements and can reject them when they are determined to be disadvantageous to Mexico. What's more, any disputes arising under such contracts must be settled in Mexican courts.

Questions

1. Are such laws harmful to Mexico because they discourage foreign investments?

2. What is the logic behind this new legislation?

3. Do you think during this decade more countries will follow the same approach or is Mexico unique in this regard? Explain.

CASE: DEVELOPMENTS FROM ABROAD[1]

American innovation and know-how is one of its most exportable commodities. However, the Europeans have

[1]The data in this case can be found in Ralph Z. Sorenson II, "U.S. Marketers Can Learn From European Innovators," *Harvard Business Review*, September–October, 1972, pp. 92–93.

apparently been more successful than their American competitors in a number of fields. Consider the following:

a. glass—the major modern breakthrough in glass making, developed in England, is the float glass method whereby the product can be cooled without having to be polished.

b. power equipment—a Swiss firm is the world leader in large turbo-generators while the Austrians are out in front in diesel engine technology.

c. farm and earth-moving equipment—the integrator tractor loader was developed in Germany, the 360-degree excavating shovel in France and the side-adjustable backhoe in England.

d. electrical appliances—the Italians have developed a number of low cost, compact electrical appliances including refrigerators, stoves and washing machines.

e. consumer goods—here the list gets quite long and includes, among others, Wilkinson Sword razor blades (England), cordless rotary-head electric shavers (Holland), throwaway BIC ballpoint pens (France) and throwaway lighters (Italy).

f. drugs—the two best-selling prescription drugs in the U.S. during the 1960's were developed by a Swiss pharmaceutical firm.

g. automobiles—front wheel drive, radial tires, disk brakes, electronic fuel injection and the Wankel rotary engine are all European inventions.

h. chemicals—six of the world's eight largest chemicals groups are in Europe helping to account for firsts in the area of plastics, dye stuffs and synthetic fibers.

i. steel—electric furnaces, the basic oxygen furnace and the development of minimills were all pioneered in Europe.

j. construction—systems and modular-building techniques were also initiated in Europe.

Questions

1. If the Europeans are so inventive, why are American firms trying to compete with them overseas? Isn't it a hopeless task?

2. Is American ingenuity declining? Explain.

3. The data in this case is misleading because many of the European firms inventing these products may well be American controlled. Defend or oppose this statement.

CASE: A BIG WINDFALL[1]

American firms operating overseas in 1972 had a very profitable year, and 1973 promised to be even more lucrative, according

[1]The data in this case can be found in "Foreign Ventures Fetch More Profit for Firms Based in United States," *Wall Street Journal,* November 1, 1973, p. 1.

to reports issued late in 1972. Some businesses were looking for 30%, 40% and even 50% profits on their foreign operations. In explaining these optimistic projections, *Business Week* noted:

You can run your finger down the list of the 500 biggest industrial firms in the U.S., stop at most any one of them, and find an international success story this year. Union Carbide earned $44.7 million abroad in 1971 and $62.9 million in 1972; this year, the company says, should prove another winner. Hercules Inc., a big Delaware chemicals concern, says it is "doing just fabulously abroad." All three big automobile makers report sharply rising foreign earnings. Though International Business Machines Corp. won't talk publicly about this year's foreign earnings, analysts think they are partly responsible for what looks like a rich year for IBM. "IBM is very, very healthy overseas," one analyst says.

Polaroid, for the third straight year, expects its foreign sales to rise by more than 30% from prior-year sales. Profits? They're "increasing at rates exceeding the sales gains," says Thomas H. Wyman, senior vice president and general manager. Polaroid sold one-third of its cameras and one-fourth of its film overseas in the first nine months of 1973.

International Harvester's foreign profits nearly doubled in 1972 to $86.6 million from $45.2 million in 1971. As a proportion of overseas assets, this meant an increase to 22.3% from 12.6% against a rise in the domestic return on assets to 6.5% from 4.4%.

The story for small firms operating abroad was pretty much the same.

Furthermore, not only were these overseas businesses earning more money than ever before, but they were also unaffected by the 1972 dollar devaluation. In fact, even if they made no more money in 1973 than they did in 1972, they would wind up with more dollar profits simply because foreign currency was now buying more dollars than it did before the devaluation. Companies with overseas operations were finding themselves in for a big windfall in 1973.

Questions

1. Companies operating overseas should expect to make a greater return on investment than those operating in the United States because they have to underwrite a greater risk. Explain this statement.

2. What types of responsibilities do firms operating overseas have to the host nation? Will these responsibilities change if the profit picture suddenly changes and many of the firms reported in this case find their returns dropping to 7 to 10 per cent? Explain.

3. Will the future find more or less American firms setting up overseas operations? Give your reasoning.

CHAPTER 22

MANAGEMENT IN THE FUTURE

GOALS OF THE CHAPTER

Having discussed past and present developments in the field of management throughout the last 21 chapters, it is now possible to forecast what the future will hold. The first goal of this chapter, however, is to synthesize what has already transpired. After all, the future is partially determined by the past. The second goal is to review developments in modern management theory, and the third is to examine other developments on the horizon that will continue to gain in importance over the next two decades. In particular, attention will be focused on:

a. the contribution of early classical management theory;
b. the three major schools of management thought;
c. developments currently taking place in modern management theory;
d. the rise of corporate democracy;
e. the current scramble for young executive talent; and
f. the continuing trend toward professionalism in management.

THE PAST IS PROLOGUE

In management theory, as in history, the past helps determine the events of the future. What has gone before sets the stage for what will follow. In the first section of this book, early management thought was examined. At that time it was noted that scientific management, administrative management and the human relations movement all made major contributions to the development of modern management theory. Although early classical theorists had their shortcomings, they did help uncover some important principles and theories that are still useful today. Filley and House have concluded that:

In our review, many critical propositions derived from classical management theory have stood the test of research evaluation rather well. They suffer not so much from what they say as from what they fail to say. For example . . . the principle of unity of command is a pragmatic convenience, not a necessity. Similarly, optimum spans of supervision *do* exist, but their determination depends upon a number of variables which are only now becoming clear.[1]

The classical theorists thus made some important contributions to management.

Three distinct schools of thought have emerged. There was, however, much more to be learned about the field. As research increased and the boundaries of management knowledge expanded, three distinct schools of thought emerged. The first, representing a continuation and expansion of Fayol's work, is the management process school. Chapters 7 to 9, which examined planning, organizing and controlling, established the basic framework of this school of thought. The second school of thought, often traced directly to Taylor and his scientific management associates, is the quantitative school. Chapters 10 and 11, which examined the fundamentals of decision making and some of the tools and techniques being employed by the modern manager in choosing from among alternatives, introduced the basic philosophy of this school. The third school of thought, which is concerned with applying psycho-sociological concepts in the work place, is the behavioral school. Chapters 12 to 14, which examined the areas of communication, motivation and leadership, presented the concepts subscribed to by the advocates of this school.

By the 1970's, management theory could be represented as in Figure 22–1.

However, there are other developments on the horizon, and it is highly likely that by 1980 Figure 22–1 will need to be revised. In particular, the emerging systems and situational schools will both play significant roles in this development.

---

[1]Alan C. Filley and Robert J. House, *Managerial Process and Organizational Behavior,* (Glenview, Ill.: Scott, Foresman and Company, 1969), p. 483.

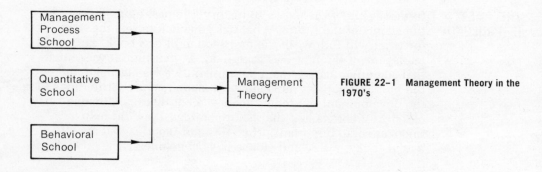

FIGURE 22–1   Management Theory in the 1970's

THE FUTURE OF MODERN MANAGEMENT THEORY

Modern management theory is advancing on a number of fronts.

Systems theory.

At the present time, modern management theory is advancing on a number of fronts, including: (a) continued emphasis on systems theory; (b) the development of modern organization structures; (c) increased research on human behavior in organizations; and (d) greater attention to the management of change.

New developments in *systems theory* were examined in Chapters 15 to 18. Some individuals believe that this systems area is a school of thought in itself because it is capable of synthesizing the views of all other schools from a pragmatic standpoint. The very description of systems management illustrates this.

> *Systems management* involves the application of systems concepts to managing organizations. The viewpoint is pragmatic; the method is synthesis (the art of building an organization as a system through the assemblage or combination of parts); and the task is to coordinate operations into an integrative whole. Systems management is vitally concerned with the appropriate design of the organization to achieve maximum operational efficiency as well as enhancing the well-being of human participants.[2]

At present, however, the systems concept appears to be less of a base for a school of thought and more of an integrative idea for the manager to employ in carrying out his job. More and more managers today are viewing the organization as an open system, subject to developments in the external as well as internal arena. Although the computer is the best known development in the systems area, its impact within the organization has not been as dramatic as many writers had predicted. Rather, external developments such as changing technology and increased competition have been more severe, because they have forced many organizations to abandon their mechanistic structures and adopt more organic ones.

Modern organization structures.

The result, as seen in Chapter 18, has been the development of *modern organization structures*. In contrast to their mechanistic-bureaucratic counterparts, modern organization structures are less predictable and orderly. On the other hand, they are very well suited to meet the needs of many modern businesses. In predicting what organizations of the future will look like, Kast and Rosenzweig have offered the following descriptions:

1. Organizations will be operating in a turbulent environment where they will have to withstand continual change and adjustment.

2. Organizations will increase in size and complexity.

3. Greater emphasis will be placed upon persuasion rather than coercion in getting employees to participate in organizational functions.

_____

[2]Richard A. Johnson, Fremont E. Kast and James E. Rosenzweig, *The Theory and Management of Systems*, 3rd edition (New York: McGraw–Hill Book Company, 1973), p. 504.

4. The influence of employees at all levels of the organization will increase, thereby resulting in power-equalization.

5. There will be an increase in the number and influence of scientists and professionals within organizations.

6. The goals of complex organizations will increase and emphasis will be given to satisficing a number of them rather than maximizing any one.[3]

Human behavior research.

Management is also finding that in order to manage its human assets it has to focus increased attention on the demands of the employees for meaningful work and increased responsibility. These demands, as well as their effect on the national and international arenas, were examined in Chapters 19 to 21. Today, the business organization is more than a profit-making institution, and its responsibilities cannot be limited solely to that function. It is a place where individuals come together and, in a give-and-take process, interact with each other and the organization itself (formal objectives, plans, policies, procedures and rules) in producing a good or providing a service to some segment of society. In an attempt to achieve the necessary coordination and cooperation of its personnel, management is trying to understand the needs and values of its people through *increased research on human behavior in organizations*. This includes techniques such as MBO, job enrichment, TA and behavior modification. The future will hold more of the same as behaviorists attempt to answer the question, how can man and the organization be brought together in a harmonious, meaningful and rewarding relationship?

The *management of change* is actually part and parcel of the three areas that have just been described in this section. With the business environment in a continual state of flux, organizations are discovering that they have to live with change on a daily basis. However, as noted earlier in the book, change frightens many people. In overcoming this problem, management is taking a systems approach to bringing together the people and the work. As Kast and Rosenzweig point out:

In order to ensure the effective coordination of many of the diverse organizational activities, it will be necessary to establish linking departments and individuals such as program or project managers. Emphasis will be placed on horizontal as well as hierarchical relationships. There will be less concern with strict departmentalization of activities and a more free-form fluidity with people assigned to individual programs and projects where their capabilities and knowledge can be utilized.[4]

In short, management will continue to develop techniques and tools for managing change.

---

[3]Fremont E. Kast and James E. Rosenzweig. *Organization and Management*, 2nd edition (New York: McGraw-Hill Book Company, 1974), pp. 617–618.
[4]*Ibid*, p. 618.

How then will management theory integrate all these ideas? Many people feel the answer is to be found in a situational or contingency theory of management in which the manager draws on functional, quantitative, behavioral and systems concepts as needed. Certainly this is the direction in which modern management theory seems to be moving. It should be realized, however, that despite what the situational theory people say about a "new" school of thought, this is really nothing more than the formalization of ancient managerial thinking. After all, did not Machiavelli recommend pragmatism via his four principles of leadership? Is this not situational or contingency theory? In short, the systems and situational schools may emerge on their own, but the basic thinking is already contained in management theory. Effective administrators are already using *both* systems and contingency concepts in attaining organizational objectives. Thus, a better term for this type of management theory may well be *eclectic*. The manager, having no allegiance to any of the schools, draws the best features from each and employs them pragmatically.

OTHER DEVELOP-MENTS ON THE HORIZON

Although the previous section synthesizes much of what has been said in this book and provides insight into what can be expected to occur over the next few decades, there are three other developments that also merit closer examination. The three have been alluded to previously, but have not been given sufficient attention as of yet. They are: (a) the trend toward corporate democracy; (b) the current scramble for young executive talent; and (c) the continuing trend toward the professionalism of management.

Corporate Democracy

One of the most pronounced trends in industry today is that of corporate democracy. Employees are indicating that they want some code of fair play enacted.

Current Research Findings.   This has been clearly seen in the results of a recent questionnaire survey, entitled "Management Privileges and Obligations," conducted by the editors of the *Harvard Business Review*. In all, 9800 subscribers and 278 second-year MBA students at the Harvard Business School were polled in an attempt to obtain opinions to questions such as:

1. How arbitrary can a boss be with an employee in the name of efficiency and corporate necessity?

2. At what point does the action he can take, legally speaking, become, from a practical standpoint, nonpermissible?

3. If an employee has a grievance, what kind of corrective procedures should be available to him?[5]

---

[5]David W. Ewing, "Who Wants Employee Rights?" *Harvard Business Review*, November–December 1971, pp. 22–23.

Some of the survey results were the following:

1. Even when done with the best interests of the organization in mind, firing managers without giving them an opportunity to defend themselves is opposed.

2. An employee who is about to be fired is entitled to find out the allegations made against him.

3. A subordinate can disobey a superior if the order violates his ethical principles (although the respondents were mixed in their views where the action might hurt company sales).

4. Management no longer has an unlimited prerogative to arbitrarily transfer employees.

5. Executives, especially young ones, are fairly tolerant of "mod dress."[6]

These findings were obtained by giving the respondents case situations and then offering them alternative solutions. In the case of the mod dresser, for example, the individuals were told that a capable young manager in a financial service company had come back from a month's vacation with a beard and long sideburns. He also started showing up at work in bell-bottom trousers and bright-colored sports shirts. This was a major change in dress habits for the man and in direct contrast to the conservative suits worn by the other managers. How should the situation be handled? The respondents answered as follows:

His superior should sit down with him, tell him that some people object to his appearance, and that we'd like to have him stay with us but not if he looks like a hippy.	52%
How he looks is his own business unless it irritates people, in which case I would tell him either to change his ways or begin hunting for another job.	30%
What the kid wears and how he looks is his own business.	18%
He should be dismissed outright. He's worked with us long enough to know better.[7]	.1%

Today's young managers are more liberal.

Although the above responses represent a rather liberal point of view, the responses to the entire questionnaire were generally conservative. However, a point to be noted is that when the respondents were analyzed according to age, the younger ones proved much more liberal and permissive than the older ones. Thus, it appears that as these individuals move into positions of responsibility, the posture of their companies will change. Of course, young managers may become more strict with their subordinates as they grow older. However, the editors of the *Harvard Business Review* concluded that ". . . even when this is allowed for, a basic shift seems to be in the making. It is extremely doubtful that the conservative senior respondents were as open-minded to dissident

[6]*Ibid.*, p. 23.
[7]*Ibid.*, p. 31.

action when they were young as are the younger managers today."[8]

Specific Action.   If the Harvard survey is accurate and managers are becoming more interested in employee rights, what specific kinds of action are going to have to be undertaken to meet these demands? Hanan sees three necessary developments: creation of an ombudsman's office to handle complaints and inquiries; an employee bill of rights; and tenure agreements tied to middle-management position descriptions.[9]

An ombudsman handles complaints.

An *ombudsman* is an individual who handles complaints by making inquiries and investigating problem areas. Some states, for example, have appointed an ombudsman to handle complaints from citizens regarding corruption or inefficiency in state agencies and departments. The individual's job is to cut through red tape and get positive action initiated. The same approach is being used in some corporate settings, where the ombudsman (generally a top-ranking officer) listens to complaints and acts as an impartial judge.

The ombudsman's domain is developing to include all grievances which adversely affect an individual or a small group of individuals. An ombudsman may function alone as a one-man office. Or he may head an Office of Management Counsel to represent individual interests before the organization. In this enlarged role, the ombudsman's office acts as an impartial tribunal of quasi-judicial review.[10]

An employee bill of rights enumerates management's responsibilities to the workers.

An employee *bill of rights* spells out some of the obligations management has to the workers. This is in direct contrast to the booklet many companies give their new people which relates what the firm expects of them. Some managers, for example, like to comment on the pamphlet they received when they first joined the company, which contained twenty-five pages of duties and obligations and one page of employee rights. As one middle manager stated it, "You learn your responsibilities as soon as you join a company. But you earn the knowledge of your rights one by one over many years. They don't exist anywhere; you have to sense them out. If you sense wrong, or if you sense too much too soon, that's it: you suddenly have another responsibility—to find a new job."[11] The bill of rights (see Chart 22–1) is less a protective device and more a recognition by the company of the freedoms the employees have a right to exercise. Modern organization man feels corporate life entails some sacrifice of personal liberty, but there is a limit to how far the company may go.

---

[8]David W. Ewing, "Who Wants Corporate Democracy?" *Harvard Business Review,* September–October 1971, p. 14.
[9]Mack Hanan, "Make Way for the New Organization Man," *Harvard Business Review,* July–August 1971, pp. 135–137.
[10]*Ibid.,* p. 135.
[11]*Ibid.,* p. 136.

CHART 22-1   Sample Corporate Bill of Rights

Article 1

Management shall in no way abridge the right of an employee to express his social, economic, political or religious beliefs within or outside the confines of the organization.

Article 2

The offices, papers and personal effects of an employee should be secure from unreasonable searches and seizures.

Article 3

No employee shall have to answer for a malfeasance or misfeasance unless management presents to him in writing the exact nature and cause of the accusation.

Article 4

If an employee is involved in a dispute, he shall be entitled to a public hearing within the organization; have a right to be confronted by those bringing complaint against him; bring in witnesses favorable to his position; and be assisted by the company ombudsman or other counsel for his defense.

Article 5

No employee shall be dismissed from his job without due process of deliberation.

Adapted from Mack Hanan, "Make Way for the New Organization Man," *Harvard Business Review*, July–August 1971, p. 136.

Tenure agreements for middle managers are, quite simply, employment contracts. They have three very important advantages. First, they acknowledge the individuality of the manager by signifying that, of his own volition, he is willing to perform some service for the corporation and, in turn, will receive some reimbursement. The point to be noted is that the manager himself chooses to accept the contract, it is not forced upon him. Second, this guarantee of employment allows the manager to begin laying out his career self-development plans. Third, tenure implies accomplishment and proof of contribution. The manager no longer has to wait for years before being ensured of a permanent place in the organization. He is rewarded on the basis of accomplishment, not seniority.

Tenure agreements are employment contracts.

The rise of corporate democracy is actually inevitable. In the late 1950's, Whyte wrote *The Organization Man* in which he contended that corporate bureaucracies were molding people into company men.[12] The Protestant Ethic, characterized by rugged individualism and thriftiness, was being

[12]William H. Whyte, Jr. *The Organization Man* (New York: Doubleday, Anchor Books, 1957).

replaced by a social ethic that put primary emphasis upon conformity to group norms and the need to belong. Today, it appears that Whyte's fears will not materialize. If anything, industry is putting greater emphasis on individuality. The old organization man is being replaced by a new one who demands freedom of expression as well as personal involvement in organization affairs.

Scramble for Young Executive Talent

There will be a decline in the number of available young executives.

When a rookie football player receives a $500,000 no-cut contract or a college basketball star is given a $2 million deal by the pro team that drafted him, no one is really surprised. After all, athletic talent is in short supply. So too, however, is young executive talent, as many firms are finding out. Four of the major reasons are:

1. the low birth rate of the 1930's;

2. the unprecedented expansion in the size of the average corporation in recent years;

3. the increasing complexity of the management process; and

4. the increased demand for executive talents in other fields, most notably government and education.[13]

Specifics of the Issue.   The *low birth rate* during the depression years has caused a decline in the number of available young executives. The following, for example, illustrates actual and forecasted statistics for males between the ages of 35–44 for the years 1950–1990.

1950 (actual)	10,706,000
1960	11,873,000
1970	11,323,000
1975 (forecast)	11,130,000
1980	12,467,000
1990	18,380,000
2000	20,870,000[14]

It will take until almost 1980 for this segment of the population to return to its former peak (1963).

Of course, some companies are supplementing these statistics by adding the number of women in the 35–44 age category.

---

[13]Arch Patton, "The Coming Scramble for Executive Talent," *Harvard Business Review*, May–June 1967, p. 155.
[14]*Statistical Abstract of the United States: 1973*, 94th Annual Edition (Washington, D.C.: U.S. Government Printing Office, 1973), p. 7.

The Bureau of the Census reports the actual and expected population statistics for this group as:

1950 (actual)	10,931,000
1960	12,349,000
1970	11,833,000
1975 (forecast)	11,590,000
1980	12,903,000
1985	18,524,000
1990	20,812,000[15]

The problem, of course, as seen in Chapter 20, is that many firms feel women do not make effective executives. As long as this thinking continues to prevail, there will be a shortage of young executive talent for some time to come.

Company growth is creating managerial positions.

Company growth is a second problem. As the size of business organizations increases and technology upgrades jobs, there will be a greater need for management personnel. However, it will take until well into the 1980's before the percentage of men *and* women in the 35–44 age category surpasses that of the labor force in general, as seen in Table 21–1.

So, too, is increasing complexity.

Increasing complexity is a third stumbling block. As competition mounts and more firms go international, the operations and functions performed at the executive level will grow dramatically. This, in turn, will put pressure on the organization to train or hire increasing numbers of competent young executives.

Business firms are not alone in their quest for these people. Other groups such as government and educational institutions are also interested in hiring executive talent. When one couples this information with the fact that many managers feel no great loyalty to their present firm when they receive a better offer from the competition, the gravity of the situation becomes clearer.

Dealing with the crisis.

Handling the Crisis. There are a number of ways for management to deal with the current situation. One, quite simply, is to try operating with *fewer* management people. Job enrichment is one technique that would help. Another is wider spans of control that would permit a smaller manager-worker ratio.

A second, and supplemental, method is to take steps to maintain the services of young executives currently with the firm. This will not only save the company time and money in recruiting endeavors, but will also force it to answer the question, how can we motivate our young people to remain with us?

---

[15] *Ibid.*

TABLE 22–1 Growth of Total Labor Force in General and Individuals 34–44 Years of Age In the Work Force in Particular

Year	Total Labor Force (in thousands)	Percentage Change	Number of Males 35–44 Years of Age	Percentage Change	Number of Males and Females 35–44 Years of Age	Percentage Change
1960 (actual)	72,104		11,454		16,779	
1970	85,903	19.0	10,818	–5.5	16,788	0
1980 (projected)	101,809	18.6	11,851	9.7	18,720	11.5
1990	112,576	11.0	17,398	47.0	27,617	32.0

Source: *Manpower Report of the President* (Washington, D.C.: U.S. Government Printing Office, 1973). p. 220.

A third approach will continue to be executive training programs. By developing people from inside the organization, a business can reduce its reliance on external market pressures. At the same time, it will attract outside talent who realize the firm is interested in preparing its people for top-level jobs.

Previously many firms have conducted income and expense forecasts to see where the company will be financially in five years. The future will see greater use of *manpower forecasting* with consideration given to questions such as: What are our manpower needs likely to be over the next decade? How can we obtain the necessary personnel? What types of training will be required? How can we assure ourselves of keeping these people? Attention to such questions will help the modern organization meet the challenge of obtaining young executive talent.

Continuing Trend Toward Professionalism

At the present time there is a continuing trend toward the professionalization of management. Although many definitions have been given to the word *profession*, the following represents one of the most comprehensive:

> A profession is a vocation whose practice is founded upon an understanding of the theoretical structure of some department of learning or science, and upon the abilities accompanying such understanding. This understanding and these abilities are applied to the vital practical affairs of man. The practices of the profession are modified by knowledge of a generalized nature and by the accumulated wisdom and experience of mankind, which serve to correct the errors of specialism. The profession, serving the vital needs of man, considers its first ethical imperative to be altruistic service to the client.[16]

There are five criteria for a profession.

The major criteria for a profession are: knowledge, competent application, social responsibility, self-control and community sanction.[17] Before discussing these it should be noted that management differs from many of the other professions, especially the traditional ones of theology, law and medicine, in that one cannot rigidly apply a set of conditions. With this in mind, it is possible to show that management is indeed moving toward professionalism.

Management Knowledge. As seen throughout this book, there has been a tremendous increase in *management knowledge* over the last twenty- five years. As Andrews points out, "No responsible critic . . . will deny that management practice now rests on a developing body of knowledge being systematically extended by valid research methods."[18] Thus, management meets this first criterion.

---

[16]Cited by Morris L. Cogan in Howard W. Vollmer and Donald L. Mills, *Professionalization* (Englewood Cliffs, N.J.: Prentice–Hall, 1966), p. 10.
[17]Kenneth R. Andrews, "Toward Professionalism in Business Management," *Harvard Business Review*, March–April 1969, pp. 50–51.
[18]*Ibid.*, p. 52.

Competent Application. Many professions such as medicine and law ensure *competent application* by certifying their people for practice. Although this is not the case in management, the surveillance of junior managers by higher-level executives serves the same purpose. Furthermore, " . . . the diversity of business practice, the market mechanism rewarding successful and penalizing unsuccessful entrepreneurship, and the organization means for supervising competence in management all make it impracticable and unnecessary to erect educational requirements in imitation of the formality of law, medicine, and the ministry."[19]

Social Responsibility. This topic was covered in depth in Chapter 20. Today, more than ever before, business is aware of the importance of assuming a social role. Although profit is not a dirty word, business is making it increasingly clear that it is pursuing multiple objectives and profit is but one of these.

Other objectives are the provision of goods and services to the customer and the integration of the firm into the everyday life of the community. In this decade many businesses have been formulating *social responsibility* philosophies in way of meeting this criterion.

Emergence of Self-Control. Federal and state agencies have been established to regulate business and ensure compliance to prescribed norms. At the national level, for example, are the Federal Drug Administration, Federal Trade Commission and the Antitrust Division of the Department of Justice. It should be realized, however, that business also exercises degrees of *self-control* as reflected by industry codes of conduct. For example, the National Association of Purchasing Agents has an extensive code, one of its standards being "to buy and sell on the basis of value, recognizing that value represents the combination of quality, service and price which assures greatest ultimate economy to the user." The American Association of Advertising Agencies has an analogous set of standards, one of them being "Advertising shall tell the truth and shall reveal material facts, the concealment of which might mislead the public." Codes such as these will undoubtedly increase in number throughout the ensuing decades. Why? The answer is twofold. First, the public is demanding higher ethical standards. Second, business managers not only believe ethics is good business but also feel that an industry code can have many advantages.

First, it would be a useful aid when businessmen wanted impersonally to refuse an unethical request. Rather than merely turn down an individual, it would be much easier if the executive could point to a code and thus have a nonpersonal basis for refusing. A second advantage would be that a code

---

[19] *Ibid.*, p. 53.

would help businessmen clearly define the limits of acceptable conduct. Third, it would raise the ethical level of the industry. Fourth, it would, in situations where severe competition existed, reduce cut-throat practices.[20]

There is thus the emergence of self-control.

Community Sanction.   The final attribute of a profession, *community sanction*, is also present in management today. Many groups are not held in esteem by the public. Electricians who are called in to install a new outlet and then charge the home owner $67.50 do little to win community acceptance. Plumbers who fix a sink in five minutes but have a minimum house-call fee of $27.50 leave people angry and disillusioned. Fortunately, however, the management profession does not suffer from such stigmas. "The depression which appears to afflict our society in the presence of . . . rebellious youth, the problems of the cities, and the balance of international payments has not extended to disillusion about the management of our enterprise system."[21] In fact, in many areas such as poverty, housing and hard-core employment, the public realizes that American management has the technical skill and the organizational expertise to help overcome the problems. If anything, community sanction of management is stronger than ever.

Future Developments.   Of course, management still has a way to go before it will qualify as a profession. However, significant steps have been taken, and this decade will see even greater progress. In particular will be the continuing development of management curricula, including: (a) the growth of new methods of quantitative analysis associated with the computer; (b) the study of organizational behavior; (c) better concepts for analyzing, understanding and reacting responsibly to the social, economic, technical and political environment of business; and (d) the study of policy formulation.[22] This, in turn, will lead to more sophisticated management practices, better self-regulation and more attention to "people" problems in both the domestic and international arenas.

JUST A BEGINNING

Managerial knowledge is a good beginning.

The purpose of this text has been to identify, define and place in proper perspective the concepts most important to the modern manager. However, this knowledge alone will not solve all the organization's problems; it will merely provide a basis for formulating intelligent approaches to dealing with each specific situation. From here the manager will have to employ

[20]Fred Luthans and Richard M. Hodgetts, *Social Issues In Business* (New York: The Macmillan Company, 1972), p. 66.
[21]Andrews, *op. cit.*, p. 56.
[22]*Ibid.*, p. 59.

the method which he believes will work best. As Getty, the oil billionaire, has noted:

> . . . to argue that business management is a science, in the sense that chemistry is a science, is to misunderstand the functions of management and to disregard its most significant element: people. Management—the fine art of being boss— is nothing less than the direction of human activities, obtaining results *through* people. Formal business education can only form a basis on which man can build. . . . But no theory in the world holds that a man with one, two or even three degrees in business administration can repair a cracking corporate structure merely because he has a collection of sheepskins hanging on his office wall. Getting results through people is a skill that cannot be learned in a classroom.[23]

When one couples this information with the fact that modern organizations are in a state of flux and the environment promises to become more, not less, dynamic, management may appear to be a profession that should be pursued by only the most daring (or foolhardy). On the other hand, there is much information available to the manager in wending his way through the maze of modern organizational problems, and the rewards and challenges promise to make it an exciting career for those who have the potential and the desire.

SUMMARY Management has come a long way since the days of the early classical theorists. It has had contributions from many people in many fields, including psychology, sociology and anthropology, and management thought has not developed in one basic direction. Rather, it has branched out into three schools: management process, quantitative and behavioral. Today, however, these three schools are being supplemented by the emergence of two other schools: systems and situational.

What does the future hold? In one respect it will be more of the same: continued emphasis on systems theory; the development of modern organization structures; increased research on human behavior in organizations; and greater attention to the management of change. In addition, however, there are other developments on the management horizon which also merit mention. These are: corporate democracy; the scramble for young executive talent; and the continuing trend toward professionalism.

Managers of the future will need to be aware of these developments. However, this knowledge, in and of itself, is no guarantee of success. The challenges of management are too great to be solved by a simple panacea such as mere knowledge of effective management processes and practices. On the other hand, for those who have the ability and the desire, the

---

[23]J. Paul Getty, "The Fine Art of Being the Boss," *Playboy,* June 1972, p. 146.

opportunities and rewards in the field of management promise to be very great indeed.

**REVIEW AND
STUDY
QUESTIONS**

1. What contributions did the classical theorists make to management theory?

2. What are the three major schools of management thought? Briefly describe each.

3. Why is the systems approach defined as eclectic?

4. What is the situational or contingency school of thought?

5. How are the systems and contingency approaches eclectic in nature?

6. The future will see a continued emphasis on corporate democracy. Explain this statement, incorporating into your answer the results found by the editors of the *Harvard Business Review* in their research on this subject.

7. What is a corporate ombudsman? How can he be useful to the employees?

8. What is an employee bill of rights? Explain.

9. Why is there currently a scramble for young executive talent?

10. What does the term "profession" mean?

11. What are the major criteria for a profession? Explain.

12. Is management a profession? Give your reasoning.

**SELECTED
REFERENCES**

Andrews, K. R. "Toward Professionalism in Business Management." *Harvard Business Review*, March–April, 1969, pp. 49–60.

Bowen, C. P., Jr. "Let's Put Realism Into Management Development." *Harvard Business Review*, July–August 1973, pp. 80–87.

Drucker, P. F. "New/Old Top Management Aid: The 'Executive Secretariat'," *Harvard Business Review*, September–October 1973, pp. 6–8.

Estafen, B. D. "Methods for Management Research in the 1970's: An Ecological Systems Approach." *Academy of Management Journal*, March 1971, pp. 51–64.

Ewing, D. W. "Who Wants Corporate Democracy?" *Harvard Business Review*, September–October 1971, pp. 12–28, 146–149.

Ewing, D. W. "Who Wants Employee Rights?" *Harvard Business Review*, November–December 1971, pp. 22–35, 155–160.

"Executive Recruiting: A Growth Business." *Business Week*, January 27, 1973, pp. 58–59.

Foss, L. "Managerial Strategy for the Future: Theory Z Management." *California Management Review*, Spring 1973, pp. 68–81.

Fulmer, R. M. "The Management of Tomorrow," *Business Horizons*, August 1972, pp. 5–13.

Fulmer, R. M., and L. W. Rue. "Competence: The Cohesive of Future Organizations." *Personnel Journal*, April 1973, pp. 264–273.

Hanan, M. "Make Way for the New Organization Man." *Harvard Business Review*, July–August 1971, pp. 128–138.

Hellriegel, D., and J. W. Slocum. *Management: A Contingency Approach.* Reading, Mass.: Addison-Wesley Publishing Company, 1973.

Johnson, R. A., F. E. Kast, and J. E. Rosenzweig. *The Theory and Management of Systems*, 3rd edition. New York: McGraw-Hill Book Company, 1973.

Mee, J. F. "The Manager of the Future." *Business Horizons*, June 1973, pp. 5–14.

Nanus, B., and R. E. Coffey. "Future-Oriented Business Education." *California Management Review*, Summer 1973, pp. 28–34.

Napier, H. S. "Deputy President: Top Management in 1982." *Personnel Journal*, August 1973, pp. 714–719.

Patton, A. "The Coming Scramble for Executive Talent." *Harvard Business Review*, May–June 1967, pp. 155–171.

Scott, B. R. "The Industrial State: Old Myths and New Realities." *Harvard Business Review*, March–April 1973, pp. 133–148.

Whyte, Jr. W. H. *The Organization Man.* New York: Doubleday, Anchor Books, 1957.

CASE: ONE MAN'S OPINION[1]

In a recent *Harvard Business Review* survey, respondents were provided with a short background on a 34 year old manager in a chemical firm, who for the past three years had worked on ecological and water pollution problems. Prior to this, he had spent several years studying the possible toxic effects of a food additive which was produced by the company. At this point, the company transferred him to a purchasing division and assigned him to a project involving a new computer system for ordering and stocking manufacturing materials. However, the man objected, pointing out that he was interested in the human-environmental effects of chemistry. His superiors, on the other hand, contended that he needed this new experience to broaden his interests. Besides, he was supposed to do what he was told.

Survey respondents were asked to indicate which of the three general views expressed their reaction to the case. The alternatives and the accompanying responses were the following:

The company erred, should admit it and correct the mistake by giving the man an assignment which is acceptable to him.   **54%**

The firm erred but the decision has been made and management should stick with it and give the man at least a short exposure to the new experience.   **35%**

Management was acting within its prerogatives and should expect complete cooperation from the man as long as he is useful in this new job.   **11%**

---

[1]The data in this case can be found in David W. Ewing, "Who Wants Employee Rights?" *Harvard Business Review*, November–December, 1971, pp. 34–35.

Questions

1. With which of the three alternatives do you agree? Why?

2. How does this case relate to "corporate democracy"? Explain.

CASE: THE NONCONFORMISTS[1]

Many of today's young managers can best be described by the term "nonconformist." Consider the case of James W. Hughes of the Equitable Life Assurance Society. Recently he was offered a transfer from Dayton to New York. In addition to a big raise, the move would have eventually been worth $5000 a year. However, Mr. Hughes turned down the offer because he felt commuting to and from work in New York City would take him away from his family more each day. In the past, such a decision might well have meant the end of a young manager's career with the firm. However, in this case:

The people at Equitable weren't too surprised by the decision. More than half of its workers today reject proferred transfers, compared with about 10% a decade ago—even though practically every move involves both a raise and a promotion, says Patrick J. Scollard, vice president and personnel director. Young managers "aren't willing to accept the company above all else," he says.

Other executives echo these sentiments. The national sales manager at Pet Foods division of General Foods Corporation, for example, says, "Today, many people are less willing to move—and more willing to tell the company how they feel." Furthermore, refusal to accept a transfer is no longer the end of the line. At the Exxon Corporation, a young executive refused a transfer overseas and his father, a retired company executive, told him that his career was "as good as dead." Since that time, however, the man has had two promotions.

This nonconformity carries over to the work itself. Today many firms are finding that they are having to cut their training periods and get the individual started on his career. The young manager wants meaningful work and responsibility, not training. As a vice president at First National City Bank in New York explained, "Shortening our training program gave us a real selling point. Good people want responsibility early." A young employee at the bank, who turned down offers from two competitors to join Citibank, agreed, "At the other two banks, it would have been at least a year before I could get into a line position. Here, I was working on a real problem by 2 p.m. of the first day."

---

[1]The data in this case can be found in Roger Ricklefs, "Young Managers Today Less Eager to Adapt, So Firms Alter Policies," *Wall Street Journal*, May 16, 1973, pp. 1, 34.

Questions

1. Are the trends described in this case going to continue throughout the seventies? Explain.

2. Aren't these trends dangerous for business? Aren't the managers getting too powerful with their nonconformist attitude?

3. What advantages do you see accruing to business by allowing managers to refuse assignments and putting people into positions of responsibility early in their career? Explain.

CASE: EXECUTIVE RECRUITING[1]

When an opening occurs in a top-management position, many firms will promote one of their current personnel—but not always. Today some firms are turning to outside executive recruiting agencies to help fill the position. If nothing else, the practice keeps company managers on their toes because they realize their promotions are not automatic.

Executive recruiting agencies have been doing quite a good business lately. For example, in July 1972 they helped Arthur Taylor move from executive vice president at International Paper to president at CBS. In November they were responsible for John Hanley's move from executive vice president and number three man at Proctor & Gamble to chief executive officer at Monsanto Chemical. In January 1973 they helped Robert Jensen shift from president of the Howmet Corporation to the same position at General Cable.

Executive recruiting is not a new practice, but dates back to the late 1940's. It is presently a very lucrative business because it often entails placing executives very high up in the structure and the standard "placement fee" is 25 per cent of the new executive's first-year salary.

"Currently, some 25% of our assignments involve presidents and chief executives," says George Haley of Haley Associates. Right now . . . he and his six recruiters are working on 10 searches where the annual salary involved is more than $100,000. Four of those jobs have pay packages that come to more than $200,000. "Ten years ago," says Haley, "we would have been happy for a $50,000 assignment. Now, our average assignment is filling a job that pays $78,000 a year."

These recruiters do more than just locate likely candidates. The first time a new executive and his boss get together they may discuss the job in very general terms. In reality, the boss may be expecting quite a bit from the new man. For this reason, some executive recruiters feel a responsibility to get the two men together for a "shakedown exercise," in which both nail

---

[1]The data in this case can be found in "Executive Recruiting: A Growth Business," *Business Week*, January 27, 1973, pp. 58–59.

down exactly what they are expecting from each other. In short, the recruiter has a moral obligation to both the client and the candidate.

Will the future see more of the executive recruiter? With the great demand for executive talent, the answer appears to be "emphatically yes."

Questions

1. What criteria should a company use in deciding whether or not to hire a man for a top-level position? Explain.

2. In the current scramble for executive talent, what kinds of benefits must a company be willing to offer?

3. Is executive recruiting unethical? After all, isn't the recruiter "raiding" another company's management ranks? Explain.

CASE: TELLING IT LIKE IT IS[1]

The Food and Drug Administration released its 12-part voluntary nutrition-labeling standards in early 1973. The following month the Del Monte Corporation, a San Francisco-based firm, announced that it would start labeling the nutritional content of 34 of its major products, which constituted over half of its canned food volume. Furthermore, the company indicated that it would expand the program to cover 120 basic items before the next canning season got under way. *Business Week* reported the following:

Del Monte's approach to nutrition labeling typifies the company's new look and aggressiveness. As the next great frontier in consumerism's drive for more and better product information, nutrition labeling is a natural extension of two other recent major labeling advances: "open dating," which tells the food buyer how fresh the product is and "unit pricing" of items by the quart, pound or other standard measure, rather than by the package. Nutritional labeling, in turn, promises to lead to two more major consumerist goals: grade labeling and "percentage labeling"—for instance, the percentage of beef in beef stew.

Questions

1. Is Del Monte socially responsible or are they just trying to get on the bandwagon early?

2. On the basis of the case data, is it possible to comment on the professionalism of the firm's management? Explain, elaborating upon the criteria you believe should be present before the term "professionalism" can be employed.

[1]The data in this case can be found in: "Del Monte Living With New Labeling Rules," *Business Week*, February 3, 1973, pp. 42–45.

GLOSSARY OF TERMS

The following glossary contains definitions of many of the concepts and terms used in this book. For the most part, the terms correspond to those given in the text and represent ones which the reader is most likely to encounter in the business world. In addition, a few extra definitions not included in the book have been added in order to provide the most comprehensive and most useful glossary possible.

Absoluteness of Responsibility — A manager cannot escape responsibility for the activities of his subordinates. He may delegate authority to his people but he cannot delegate all the responsibility.

Acceptance Theory of Authority — Popularized through the writings of Chester I. Barnard, this theory states that the ultimate source of authority is the subordinate who chooses to either accept or reject orders given to him by his superior.

Activity — An operation required to accomplish a particular event in a PERT network.

Ad Hoc Committee — A committee that is appointed for a specific purpose and, once the job is completed, is then disbanded.

Administrative Man — A term used to describe an individual who employs satisficing behavior by looking for a course of action that is satisfactory or good enough, in contrast to an individual who attempts to select the best alternative from among all those available. (See *Economic Man*.)

Aggression — One of man's frustration reactions, it consists of attacking, either physically or symbolically, the barrier preventing goal attainment.

Analog Computer — A measuring machine used principally by engineers in solving job-related problems.

Authority — The right to command.

Automation — The technique of making an apparatus, a process or a system operate automatically.

Avoidance—One of man's frustration reactions, it entails withdrawing from a situation that is too frustrating to endure.

Balance Theory—A theory used in the study of communication to explain how people react to change. In essence, the theory places primary attention on the consideration of three relationships: (a) the attitude of the receiver toward the sender, (b) the attitude of the receiver toward the new change and (c) the receiver's perception of the sender's own attitude toward the change.

Basic Socio-Economic Purpose—The reason for an organization's existence.

Behavioral School—A modern school of management thought consisting of those individuals who view management as a psycho-sociological process. Advocates of this school are very concerned with topics such as needs, drives, motivation, leadership, personality, behavior, work groups and the management of change.

Benevolent-Authoritative Leadership Style—A basic leadership style in which management acts in a condescending manner toward the subordinates and decision making at the lower levels occurs within a prescribed framework.

Black Box Concept—The inner workings that take place between the input and the output. As applied to human behavior, there may be the introduction of a new wage incentive payment scheme (input) and a 10 per cent increase in productivity (output). The reason for the change may be the wage plan or it may be accounted for by some other cause. The answer rests in the black box or transformation process which occurs between the input and the output.

Branch Organization—Often employed in foreign operations, it is simply an overseas office set up by the parent company.

Break-Even Point—The volume of sales sufficient to cover all fixed and variable expenses but no profit.

Budget—A type of plan that specifies anticipated results in numerical terms and serves as a control device for feedback, evaluation and follow-up.

Carrying Costs—Costs associated with keeping inventory on hand, including sundry expenses such as storage space, taxes and obsolescence.

Centralization—A system of management in which major decisions are made at the upper levels of the hierarchy.

Certainty Decisions—Decision situations in which the manager knows all the alternatives and the outcomes of each.

Civil Rights Act—Legislation that forbids discrimination based on race, color, religion, sex or national origin and provides, through the Equal Employment Opportunity Commission, an agency for dealing with complaints or charges of discrimination.

Closed System—A system that does not interact with its external environment.

COBOL—A computer programming language designed especially for business, the word is derived from "common business oriented language."

Common Market—A European economic community formed in 1957 by France, West Germany, Italy, Holland, Belgium and Luxembourg. Today Great Britain and Ireland are also members.

Communication Process—The conveying of meaning from sender to receiver.

Completed Staff Work—Staff work whose completed recommendation or solution can be either approved or disapproved by a line executive without the need for any further investigation.

Comprehensive Budgeting—A budgeting process that covers all phases of operations.

Comprehensive Planning—Planning that incorporates all levels of the organization: top, middle and lower.

Compulsory Staff Service—A concept developed centuries ago by the Catholic Church that requires superiors to solicit the advice of their subordinates before making any decision.

Computer Program—A set of instructions that tell the computer what to do.

Consultative-Democratic Leadership Style—A basic leadership style in which management has quite a bit of confidence and trust in the subordinates and, except for major decisions, a great deal of decision making is carried out at the lower levels.

Contingency Model of Leadership Effectiveness—A leadership model developed by Fred Fiedler that postulates that a leader's effectiveness is determined by three variables: (a) how well the leader is accepted by his subordinates, (b) the degree to which the subordinates' jobs are routine and spelled out in contrast to being vague and undefined and (c) the formal authority provided for in the position the leader occupies.

Controlling Process—The process of determining that everything is going according to plan. In essence, controlling consists of three steps: (a) the establishment of standards, (b) the comparison of performance against standards and (c) the correction of deviations that have occurred.

Critical Path—The longest path in a PERT network, beginning with the first event and ending with the last one.

Decentralization—A system of management in which a great deal of decision-making authority rests at the lower levels of the hierarchy.

Decision Making—The process of choosing from among alternatives.

Decision Theory—A term used to describe how managers make decisions under conditions of certainty, risk and uncertainty.

Decision Tree—An operations research tool that permits: (a) the identification of alternative courses of action in solving a problem, (b) the assignment of probability estimates to the events associated with these alternatives and (c) the calculation of the payoffs corresponding to each act-event combination.

Delphi Technique—A method for forecasting future developments, especially technological discoveries.

Delegation of Authority—The process a manager employs in distributing work to his subordinates.

Departmentalization—The process of grouping jobs on the basis of some common characteristic, i.e., function, product, territory, customer, process.

Derivative Departments—Departments that are formed when the activities of a major department are subdivided. For example, derivative production departments might include manufacturing and purchasing. (See Figure 8–3 in the text.)

Differential Piece Rate System—An incentive wage system formulated by Frederick W. Taylor that paid a fixed rate per piece for all production up to standard and a higher rate for all pieces if the standard was met.

Digital Computer—A counting machine that by use of electrical impulses can perform arithmetic calculations far in excess of human capacity. This computer is widely used by business firms.

Discounted Cash Flows—The statement of future cash flows in terms of current dollars.

Division of Work—Breaking down a job into simple routine tasks so that each worker can become a specialist in handling one particular phase of the operation. The result is often increased efficiency.

Domestic System—The basic stage of a materially productive civilization in which individuals, assured of their own survival, begin specializing in some area, such as fabricating textiles and then selling them at the local fair for whatever they will bring. This system was predominant in England in the early eighteenth century.

Economic Man—A term used to identify a person who makes decisions that maximize his economic objectives.

Econometrics—A mathematical approach used in economic forecasting.

EDP—Electronic data processing.

Enlightened Self-Interest—A doctrine that states that by helping out the community, business is actually serving its own long-run interests.

Entropy—The tendency of a closed system to move toward a choatic, random or inert state.

EOQ Formula—An economic order quantity model useful to the manager in determining how many units to reorder in replenishing his inventory.

Equal Pay Act—Legislation designed to correct the existence of wage differentials based on sex in industries engaged in commerce or the production of goods for commerce.

Equity or Social Comparison Theory—A theory that contends that people are motivated not only by what they receive but also by what they see, or believe, others are receiving. Individuals compare their rewards with those of others in judging whether or not they are receiving equitable remuneration.

Esprit de Corps—One of Fayol's principles of management, it means that "in union there is strength."

Event — A point in time when an activity is begun or finished. (See *PERT* and *Activity*.)

Exception Principle — A manager should concern himself with exceptional cases and not routine results.

Expectancy — The probability that a specific action will be followed by a particular first-level outcome. (See *First-Level Outcome*.)

Expectancy Theory — A theory of motivation that holds that an individual will be a high-performer when he: (1) sees a high probability that his efforts will lead to high performance, (2) sees a high probability that high performance will lead to specific outcomes and (3) views these outcomes to be, on balance, positively attractive to himself.

Expectancy-Valence Theory — A motivation theory formulated by Victor Vroom which states that motivation is equal to the summation of valence times expectancy. (See *Instrumentality, Valence* and *Expectancy*.)

Expected Time — A time estimate for each activity in a PERT network calculated by using the following formula:

$$t_E = \frac{t_O + 4t_m + t_p}{6}$$

where t_E = expected time
t_O = optimistic time
t_m = most likely time
t_p = pessimistic time

Exploitive-Authoritative Leadership Style — A basic leadership style in which management has little confidence in the subordinates and decision making tends to be highly centralized.

Exploratory Forecast — A technological forecasting technique that assumes that future technological progress will continue at the present rate. This technique moves from the present to the future and considers technical factors most heavily.

Extrapolation — The simplest form of economic forecast, it consists of merely projecting current trends into the future.

Factory System — The final stage in the evolution of a materially productive civilization (see *Domestic System* and *Putting-Out System*) characterized by the introduction of power-driven machinery. Instead of work being done in the home, the workers now come to one central site where the machinery is located, namely, the factory.

First-Level Outcome — A factor that brings about a second-level outcome. For example, in many companies, productivity (first-level outcome) leads to promotion (second-level outcome).

Fixed Costs — Costs that will remain constant (at least in the short-run) regardless of operations. Property taxes and administrative salaries are illustrations.

Flat Organization Structure — An organization structure in which there is a wide span of control with only a small number of levels in the hierarchy.

Forecasting — A method of projecting future business conditions for the purpose of establishing goals and budgets.

Formal Organization — The officially designated jobs and relationships in an organization as seen on the organization chart and reflected in the job descriptions.

Formal Theory of Authority — A theory that holds that the source of authority is found in the right of private property provided for in the Constitution and flows down the organization structure from the president to the lowest worker. As such, the theory supports the hierarchical structure of the organization. (For a marked contrast, see *Acceptance Theory of Authority*.)

FORTRAN — A computer programming language designed for scientific work, the word is derived from "formula translation."

Free-Form Organization Structure — See *Organic Organization Structure*.

Functional Authority — Authority in a department other than one's own, as seen in the case of the comptroller who can order production personnel to provide him with cost per unit data.

Functional Departmentalization — A department organized along the lines of major activities. In a manufacturing firm so organized, it is not uncommon to find marketing, production and finance departments reporting directly to the president.

Functional Foremanship — A concept developed by Frederick W. Taylor whereby the functions of the foreman were divided into eight separate subfunctions and each one assigned to an individual foreman. In this way, each foreman could concentrate his attention on one aspect of the job, i.e., inspection, repair, discipline, rather than having to carry out all eight. Taylor believed that such a division of work would result in increased efficiency.

Fusion Process — The process by which the individual and the organization, when they come together, tend to influence each other's objectives.

Gain Sharing — A wage incentive payment plan designed by Henry Towne in which each individual was given a guaranteed wage. Then, a standard of work was set for each department, the costs of production were determined and, if any department had a gain because of increased efforts, this would be shared between the workers in the department and the management on a fifty-fifty basis.

Game Theory — Theory used in operations research to study conflict-of-interest situations.

Gangplank Principle — Developed by Henri Fayol, this principle holds that individuals at the same level of the hierarchy should be allowed to communicate directly, provided they have permission from their superiors to do so and they tell their respective chiefs afterwards what they have agreed to do. The purpose of the principle is to cut red tape while maintaining the integrity of the hierarchy.

Gantt Chart — A chart on which progress on various parts of an undertaking are compared with time.

Grapevine — The informal communication channel in an organization.

Gross National Product (GNP) — The value of goods and services produced in a year.

Hawthorne Effect—The novelty or interest in a new situation which leads, at least initially, to positive results.

Hawthorne Studies—Studies that provided the impetus for the human relations movement. Conducted at the Western Electric plant in Chicago, Illinois, the research had four major phases: (a) illumination experiments, (b) relay assembly test room experiments, (c) massive interviewing program and (d) the bank wiring observation room study.

Heuristic Programming—An operations research technique that employs both rules of thumb and the use of trial-and-error.

Hierarchy of Objectives—Short-run objectives are related to intermediate-range objectives which, in turn, tie in to long-range objectives. There is thus an interrelated hierarchy of objectives throughout the organization.

Human Resources Accounting—A recent development in management which attempts to: (a) view the acquisition of organizational personnel as an investment and (b) obtain a regular evaluation of these assets.

Human Relations Philosophy—A philosophy that holds that the business organization is a social system and that employees are largely motivated and controlled by the human relationships in that system.

Human Resources Philosophy—A philosophy that holds that individuals do not want merely to be treated well (see *Human Relations Philosophy*); they want an opportunity to contribute creatively to organizational problems (see *Theory Y*) by being used well.

Hygiene Factors—Identified by Frederick Herzberg in his two-factor theory of motivation, the term refers to factors that will not motivate people by their presence but will cause dissatisfaction by their absence. Some of the hygiene factors he identified include money, security and working conditions.

Industrial Psychology—A subfield of psychology concerned with applying psychological knowledge to the selection, training and development of organizational personnel.

Informal Group Norms—Sentiments to which individuals must adhere if they wish to be accepted as members of a group. In the bank wiring observation room, for example, these included: (a) you should not turn out too much work; (b) you should not turn out too little work; (c) you should not tell a superior anything that will react to the detriment of an associate; (d) you should not attempt to maintain social distance or act officious and (e) you should not be noisy, self-assertive and anxious for leadership.

Informal Organization—The unofficially designated relationships in an organization not shown on the organization chart and often not reflected in the job descriptions.

Information Design—A process of filtering the number and kinds of reports and other data being sent to managers to prevent their being inundated with irrelevant information.

Institutional Level—Upper level of the organization concerned with relating the overall organization to its environment.

Institutional Managers—Top level managers concerned with surveying the environment and developing cooperative and competitive strategies that will ensure the organization's survival. These managers tend to have a philosophical point of view.

Instrumentality—The relationship an individual perceives between a first- and second-level outcome. (See *First-Level Outcome* and *Second-Level Outcome*.)

Intermediate-Range Planning—The setting of subobjectives and substrategies that are in accord with the long-run objectives and strategies of the strategic plan.

Intervening Variables—Internal, unobservable, psychological processes that account for human behavior. These variables cannot be measured directly; they must be inferred. Motivation is an example.

Job Description—Description of the authority and responsibilities that accompany a job.

Job Enlargement—Increasing the number of tasks being performed by an individual in an attempt to make the work more psychologically rewarding.

Job Enrichment—Popularized by M. Scott Myers, this involves building motivators (see *Motivational Factors*) into the job in an effort to allow the worker to satisfy some of his higher-level needs.

Joint Venture—An enterprise undertaken by two or more parties. In foreign trade, it often consists of a foreign corporation, such as a U.S. business firm, and a local partner.

Key Area Control—A control technique by which a firm measures its performance in a number of vital areas. At General Electric, for example, these areas include profitability, market position, productivity, product leadership, personnel development, employee attitudes, public responsibility and integration of short- and long-range objectives.

Lag Indicators—Series of economic indicators which often follow changes in the economic cycle.

Laplace Criterion—A basis for decision making in which the manager applies equal probabilities to all states of nature.

Law of Triviality—Formulated by C. Northcote Parkinson, this law states that the time spent on any agenda item will be in inverse proportion to the sum involved.

Lead Indicators—Series of economic indicators which often precede changes in the economic cycle.

Leadership—A process of influencing people to direct their efforts toward the achievement of some particular goal(s).

Learned Behavior—Behavior based on some form of reinforcement (or lack of it).

Life Cycle Theory of Leadership—A leadership theory developed by Paul Hersey and Kenneth Blanchard that contends that as the maturity of the followers increases, appropriate leadership behavior requires varying degrees of task and relationship orientation.

Line Authority—Direct authority, as in the case of a superior who can give orders directly to a subordinate.

Line Department—A department concerned with attaining the basic objectives of the organization. In a manufacturing firm, production, marketing and finance would be line departments.

Linear Programming—A mathematical technique for determining optimum answers in cases in which a linear relationship exists between the variables.

Management—The process of getting things done through people.

Management Audit—An evaluation of how well the management has operated the organization. Some criteria often employed in this evaluation include production efficiency, health of earnings, fairness to stockholders and executive ability.

Management by Objectives—A process in which superior and subordinate jointly identify common goals, define the subordinate's areas of responsibility in terms of expected results, and use these measures as guides in operating the unit and evaluating the subordinate's contribution.

Management Functions—The activities a manager must perform in carrying out his job. The most commonly accepted are planning, organizing and controlling.

Management Process School—Modern school of management thought whose adherents believe that the way to study management is through a systematic analysis of the managerial functions, i.e., planning, organizing and controlling.

Management Science—See *Operations Research.*

Management Systems—Basic leadership styles identified by Rensis Likert. In essence, there are four: exploitive-authoritative, benevolent-authoritative, consultative-democratic and participative-democratic.

Managerial Grid—A two-dimensional leadership model that permits simultaneous consideration of "concern for production" and "concern for people."

Marginal Cost—The costs incurred by selling one more unit of output.

Marginal Physical Product—The extra output obtained by adding one unit of that product while all other factors are held constant. For example, the extra output obtained by adding one unit of labor while holding all other inputs constant.

Marginal Revenue—The additional revenue obtained by selling one more unit of output.

Matrix Structure—A hybrid form of organization containing characteristics of both project and functional structures.

Maximax Criterion—A basis for decision making in which the manager determines the greatest payoff for each strategy and then chooses the one that is most favorable. In so doing, he maximizes his maximum gain.

Maximin Criterion—A basis for decision making in which the manager determines the most negative payoff for each strategy and then chooses the one that is most favorable. In so doing, he maximizes his minimum gain.

Mechanistic Organization Structure—An organization structure that is often effective in a stable environment where technology does not play a significant role.

Microchronometer—A clock with a large sweeping hand capable of recording time to 1/2000 of a minute. Developed by Frank Gilbreth, the clock is still of use today in photographing time and motion patterns.

Milestone Scheduling—A scheduling and control procedure that employs bar charts to monitor progress. In essence, it is very similar to a Gantt chart but its use is not restricted to production activities.

MIS—Management information system.

Monte Carlo Technique—An operations research technique that makes use of simulation and random numbers in arriving at optimal solutions.

Mooney and Reiley's Principles of Organization—According to James D. Mooney and Alan C. Reiley, the first principle of organization is coordination, which is implemented through the chain of command (process) and results in the definition of duties for all individuals in the hierarchy (effect). Taking this principle-process-effect concept and employing a framework developed by Lewis F. Anderson in which every principle, process and effect has its own principle, process and effect, the two authors were able, via deductive reasoning, to develop a logically complete three-by-three matrix.

Motion Study—The process of analyzing work in order to determine the preferred motions for completing the job most efficiently.

Motivational Factors—Identified by Frederick Herzberg in his two-factor theory of motivation, the term refers to those factors that will build high levels of motivation and job satisfaction. Some of the motivational factors he identified include recognition, advancement and achievement.

Multinational Corporation—Any firm that has a large percentage of its operations devoted to activities not limited to one country.

Need Hierarchy—A widely accepted framework of motivation developed by Abraham H. Maslow. In essence, the theory states that:

1. There are five levels of needs. In order of importance they are: physiological, safety, social, esteem and self-actualization.
2. Only those needs not yet satisfied influence behavior.
3. When one level of needs has been satisfied, the next higher level emerges as dominant and influential.

Non-Zero-Sum Games—Games in which gains by one side do not automatically result in equal losses to the other side.

Normative Forecasting—A technological forecasting technique that begins with the identification of some future technological objective and works back to the present, identifying problem areas that will have to be surmounted along the way. This approach considers both technological and nontechnological factors.

Normative Reality—Interpretive reality as manifested by personal opinion.

Ombudsman—An individual who handles complaints by making inquiries and investigating problem areas.

Open System—A system that is in constant interaction with its external environment.

Operational Planning—The setting of short-run goals and targets that are in accord with the subobjectives and substrategies of the intermediate-range plan.

Operations Research—The application of mathematical tools and techniques to the decision-making process.

Optimistic Time—See *Expected Time.*

Optimization—The combining of elements in just the right balance, often times to secure maximum profit.

Organic Functions—Activities that must be carried out if an organization wishes to remain in existence. In a manufacturing firm, for example, these would include marketing, production and finance.

Organic Organization Structure—An organization structure that is often effective in a dynamic environment where technology plays a significant role. These structures can take any design and hence are also known as free-form structures.

Organization Chart—A diagram of an organization's departments and their relationship to each other.

Organizational Level—Middle level of the organization concerned with coordinating and integrating work performance at the technical level. (See Chapter 15.)

Organizational Managers—Middle managers whose goal is to bring together the technical and institutional levels in some harmonious fashion. These managers tend to have a political or mediating point of view. (See Chapter 15.)

Organizational Behavior Modification—A behavioral technique designed to modify behavior by rewarding correct conduct and punishing or ignoring incorrect conduct.

Organizing Function—The assignment of duties and the coordination of efforts among all organizational personnel to ensure maximum efficiency in the attainment of predetermined objectives.

Participative-Democratic Leadership Style—A basic leadership style in which management has complete confidence and trust in the subordinates and decision making is highly decentralized.

Payback Period—The time it takes for an investment to pay for itself.

Perception—A person's view of reality.

Personal Power—Informal authority that is created or sustained by factors such as experience, drive, association with the right groups and education.

Pessimistic Time—See *Expected Time.*

Planning Function—The formulation of objectives and the steps that will be employed in attaining them.

Planning Organization—An organization designed specifically to help a company develop a comprehensive and logical approach to planning at all levels of the hierarchy.

Plural Executives—Committees that have the authority to order their recommendations implemented.

Policy—A general guide to thinking and action.

Premium Plan—A payment plan devised by Frederick Halsey in which every worker was guaranteed a daily wage and, using the individual's past performance as a base, a premium was offered for all work above this amount. The premium constituted 33⅓ per cent of what the worker saved the company in wages.

Primacy of Planning Principle—At least initially, planning precedes all the other managerial functions.

Principle-Process-Effect—A framework for analysis developed by Lewis F. Anderson and employed by James D. Mooney and Alan C. Reiley in formulating principles of organization. (See *Mooney and Reiley's Principles of Organization.*)

Principles of Management—General guidelines (although in the case of the classical theorists, these were not viewed as being very inflexible) useful to the manager in carrying out his activities.

Principles of Scientific Management—As set forth by Frederick W. Taylor, there were four:

a. Develop a science for each element of a man's work, which replaces the old rule-of-thumb method.
b. Scientifically select and then train, teach, and develop the workman, whereas in the past he chose his own work and trained himself as best he could.
c. Heartily cooperate with the men so as to ensure that all the work being done is in accordance with the principles of the science that has been developed.
d. There is almost an equal division of work and responsibility between the management and the workmen. The management takes over all work for which it is better fitted than the workmen, whereas in the past almost all of the work and the greater part of the responsibility were thrown upon the men.

Probability—The likelihood that a particular event will occur.

Procedure—A guide to action that relates the chronological steps entailed in attaining some objective such as allowing a person to returr faulty merchandise.

Product Departmentalization—A department that is organized along product lines. General Electric, for example, uses this approach, as seen by its consumer product group. So, too, do General Motors, Ford Motor, Chrysler and a host of other large organizations.

Productivity—Output/input.

Profession—A vocation whose practice is founded upon an understanding of some department of learning or science, or upon the abilities accompanying such understanding. Major criteria include: (a) knowledge, (b) competent application, (c) social responsibility, (d) self-control and (e) community sanction.

Profit—The remainder after expenses are deducted from revenues.

Program Evaluation and Review Technique (PERT)—A sophisticated time-event network series that permits a manager to evaluate and control the progress of a complex undertaking. (See *Event* and *Activity*.)

Program Planning Budgeting System (PPBS)—A control technique used to tie a budget to its objective and not to a time framework.

Project Authority—Authority exercised by the project manager over the personnel assigned to him for the project. In contrast to functional authority, project authority flows horizontally. (See Chapter 18.)

Projection—One of man's frustration reactions, it involves blaming others for one's own shortcomings.

Psychology—The study of human behavior.

Putting-Out System—The second stage in the evolution of a materially productive civilization (see *Domestic System*) initially characterized by an entrepreneur's agreeing to take all the output an individual (or family) can produce at a fixed price. This eventually progressed to the stage where the entrepreneur provided the workers with the raw materials and paid them on a piece-rate basis for the finished goods.

Quantitative School—A modern school of management thought consisting of those individuals who view management as a system of mathematical models and processes. Advocates of this school are greatly concerned with decision making. This school had its genesis with the scientific management movement.

Queuing Theory—An operations research technique used for balancing waiting lines and service.

Rabble Hypothesis—The belief that the workers are a disorganized group of individuals, each one acting in his own self-interest.

Responsibility—The obligation of a subordinate to perform assigned tasks.

Return on Investment—A control technique used to determine how well a firm is managing its assets. In essence, the ROI computation is:

$$\frac{\text{Earnings}}{\text{Sales}} \times \frac{\text{Sales}}{\substack{\text{Total} \\ \text{Investment}}}$$

Revery—Daydreaming.

Risk Decisions—Decision situations in which the manager has some information on the outcomes of each alternative and can formulate probability estimates based on this knowledge.

Rule—An inflexible guide to action such as a "No Smoking" sign.

Saddle Point—A term used in game theory to identify an ideal strategy.

Sales Forecast—A method used for projecting future sales. Some of the common techniques used in attaining this objective include survey of current sales information, the jury of executive opinion, the grass-roots method and user expectation. (See Chapter 7 for a description of each of these techniques.)

Satisficing—Striving for a level that is satisfactory or good enough.

Scalar Chain — The chain of command that runs from the top of an organization to its lowest ranks.

Scientific Management — A system of management, popularized by Frederick W. Taylor and others in the early twentieth century, that sought to develop: (a) ways of increasing productivity by making work easier to perform and (b) methods for motivating the workers to take advantage of these labor-saving devices and techniques.

Scientific Method — A logical problem-solving process used in identifying the problem, diagnosing the situation, gathering preliminary data, classifying the information, stating a tentative answer to the problem and testing the answer.

Second-Level Outcome — The effect brought about by a first-level outcome. For example, in many companies productivity (first-level outcome) leads to promotion (second-level outcome).

Sensitivity Training — A form of training designed to make managers more aware of their own feelings and those of others.

Sensory Reality — Physical reality such as a house or a chair.

Simulation — As used in a business setting, these are often mathematical models designed to provide answers to "what if" questions.

Situational Theory — A theory that views leadership as multi-dimensional, consisting of the leader's personality, the requirements of the task, the expectations, needs and attitudes of the followers, and the environment in which they are operating.

Slack Time — The time difference between scheduled completion and each of the paths in a PERT network.

Social Responsibility — The obligations business has to society, especially in the areas of equal opportunity, ecology and consumerism.

Sociology — The study of group behavior.

Soldiering — A term used by scientific managers, especially Frederick W. Taylor, to describe the workers' practice of restricting output.

Span of Control — The number of subordinates who report to a given superior.

Staff Authority — Auxiliary authority as seen in the case of individuals who advise, assist, recommend or facilitate organizational activities. An example is the company lawyer who advises the president on the legality of contract matters.

Staff Department — A department that provides assistance and support to line departments in attaining basic objectives of the organization. In a manufacturing firm, purchasing and accounting would be staff departments.

Staff Independence — A concept developed centuries ago by the Catholic Church whereby advisors are neither appointed by the person they advise nor removable by him, thereby avoiding the yes-man pitfall.

Status — Attributes that rank and relate individuals in an organization.

Strategic Planning — The determination of an organization's major objectives and the policies and strategies that will govern the acquisition, use and disposition of resources in achieving these objectives.

Subsidiary—A company owned partially or completely by another.

System—A combination of parts forming a complex or unitary whole.

Tall Organization Structure—An organization structure in which there is a narrow span of control with a large number of levels in the hierarchy. (For a contrast, see *Flat Organization Structure.*)

Task and Bonus System—A payment plan developed by Henry Gantt that guaranteed each worker a day's wage and a bonus if the man accomplished the task assigned to him for that day.

Technical Level—Low organizational level concerned primarily with the production and distribution of goods and services.

Technical Managers—Low-level managers concerned with turning out goods and services as economically as possible. These managers tend to have an engineering point of view.

Tenure Agreements—Employment contracts.

Territorial Departmentalization—A department that is organized along the lines of geographic location. An example is found in the company with four major divisions: eastern division, midwestern diversion, western division and foreign division.

Theory X—A set of assumptions that holds that people: (a) dislike work; (b) have little ambition; (c) want security above all else and (d) must be coerced, controlled and threatened with punishment in order for them to attain organizational objectives.

Theory Y—A set of assumptions that holds that: (a) if the conditions are favorable, people will not only accept responsibility, they will seek it; (b) if people are committed to organizational objectives, they will exercise self-direction and self-control and (c) commitment is a function of the rewards associated with goal attainment.

Therblig—A term used in time and motion study to identify a basic hand motion such as "grasp" or "hold." The word is formed by spelling Gilbreth backwards with the "t" and "h" transposed.

Three-Dimension Leadership Model—A leadership model developed by William J. Reddin that stresses the importance of three factors: (a) task orientation, (b) relationships orientation and (c) effectiveness.

Time Study—A method of determining the time it takes to perform a particular task. The procedure often involves the use of a stopwatch for timing all the various elements associated with the task, e.g., the time for picking up a piece of material, positioning it or inserting it into the machine. Time study was widely used by the scientific managers in determining a fair day's work and is still employed in industrial settings today.

Time-Event Analyses—Control techniques that permit the manager to monitor and evaluate elapsed time and attained progress on an undertaking.

Trait Theory—A theory of leadership that attempts to relate success to an individual's personal characteristics or traits.

Transactional Analysis (TA) — A technique designed to help the manager communicate with and understand his people through an analysis of their behavior as well as his own.

Transformation Process — See *Black Box Concept.*

Two-Way Communication — Transmission of information and ideas both up and down the hierarchy.

Uncertainty Decisions — Decision situations for which the manager feels he cannot develop probability estimates because he has no way of gauging the likelihood of the various alternatives.

Unity of Command — A management principle that states that a subordinate should report to only one superior.

Unity of Direction — See *Unity of Management.*

Unity of Management — One of Fayol's classical principles, it calls for one manager and one plan for all operations having the same objective. Another term often given to this is unity of direction.

Valence — A person's preference for a first-level outcome. (See *First-Level Outcome.*)

Variable Costs — Costs that change in relation to output. Labor salaries and cost of materials are examples.

Zero-Sum Games — Games in which gains by one side are offset by losses to the other side.

NAME INDEX

Aaker, D.A., 522
Ackerman, R.W., 522
Ackoff, R. L., 271
Adler, A., 315
Albers, H.H., 49, 108, 109, 122, 286
Alford, L.P., 59
Alutto, J.A., 185
Ament, R.H., 431
Anderson, B.F., 97
Anderson, L.F., 50
Andrews, K.R., 522, 564, 566, 568
Annas, J.W., 335
Anthony, R.N., 216
Apgar, M., IV, 153
Argyris, C., 97, 322, 474
Arkwright, R., 14
Arnoff, E.L., 271
Arpan, J., 548
Athanassiades, J.C., 303
Austin, D.W., 516

Babbage, C., 24, 25, 36, 403
Babcock, J.D., 413, 414, 417
Bagley, F.R.C., 16
Baker, J.D., 416
Bakke, E.W., 182
Balderson, C., 59
Baldwin, R.A., 417
Bamforth, K.W., 95, 435
Barnard, C.I., 56, 58, 60, 115, 172
Barnes, L.B., 244, 353
Barry, J., 545
Bassett, W.R., 60
Bauer, R.A., 522
Beatty, R., 490
Behling, O., 335
Belasco, J.A., 185
Bell, G.D., 119, 120
Bennis, W., 469
Berlo, D.K., 278, 303
Berne, E., 485, 486, 494
Besse, R.M., 129

Blake, R.R., 350, 351, 352, 353, 361
Blanchard, K.H., 291, 316, 358, 361
Blankenship, L.V., 185
Blau, Peter M., 88, 450
Blomfield, D., 60
Blomstrom, R.L., 517, 522
Bockman, V.M., 335
Boettinger, H.M., 434, 443
Boulden, J.B., 408, 416
Boulding, K., 370, 386
Boulton, M., 22
Bowen, C.P., Jr., 568
Boyd, B.B., 303
Boyle, M.B., 522
Bradley, G.E., 530, 543, 546, 548
Bradspies, R.W., 217
Brady, R.H., 411, 484
Bralove, M., 522
Brand, C.E., 16, 17
Brecht, R.P., 59
Bright, J.R., 431
Briloff, A.J., 211
Brooks, H., 428, 443
Brothers, J., 522
Brown, R.V., 122, 271
Buchele, R.B., 217
Buffa, E.S., 408, 416
Burns, R., 437, 443
Bursk, E.C., 530, 543, 546, 548
Burton, J.C., 217
Butler, A.G., Jr., 468
Byrd, C., 342
Byron, G.F., 361

Campbell, J.P., 335, 485
Carlisle, H.M., 463, 464, 468
Carne, E.B., 425, 443
Carroll, S.J., Jr., 494
Carson, R., 509, 522
Carzo, R., Jr., 171
Cateora, P.R., 535
Chambers, J.C., 153

589

Chandler, A.D., Jr., 161, 185, 439
Chaney, F.B., 361
Charles, A.W., 335
Child, J., 185, 468
Church, A.H., 60
Churchman, C.W., 271
Cicero, J.P., 468
Clark, P.A., 185
Clarke, A.C., 410, 416
Cleland, D.I., 386, 451, 452, 457, 458, 468
Coffey, R.E., 569
Cogan, M.L., 564
Conderacci, G., 522
Cook-Taylor, R.W., 36
Cuddy, D.J., 548
Cummings, L.L., 325, 327, 494
Curcuru, E.H., 186
Cyert, R.H., 154

Dale, E., 108, 109, 169, 179, 180, 186, 404, 411, 414, 468
Daniels, J.D., 548
Davis, K., 293, 294, 303, 335, 342, 343, 359, 361, 484, 517, 522
Day, G.S., 522
Dearden, 412, 416
Derman, J., 416
DeVitt, W.H., 325
Dewhirst, H.D., 303
Dickson, G.W., 399, 400, 401, 402, 416
Dickson, W.J., 73, 77, 78, 82
Diocletian, 9
Dory, J.P., 429, 433, 443
Drever, J., 82
Drucker, P.F., 139, 153, 154, 171, 186, 217, 244, 483, 494, 568
Dubin, R., 97
Dunnette, M.D., 335, 485
Durant, W., 6, 8
Dutton, H.P., 60

Eastlack, J.O., Jr., 154
Eckerman, A.C., 335
Edie, L.D., 82
Ehrlick, P., 508
Elbing, A.O., 122, 522
Emerson, H., 34, 37
Ernst, M.L., 416
Estafen, B.D., 568
Evans, M.G., 361
Ewing, D.W., 557, 568, 569

Fansweet, S.J., 156
Fayerweather, J., 533, 548
Fayol, H., 42–49, 52, 54, 58, 59, 89, 91, 107, 108, 122, 193, 196

Fein, M., 482
Fenn, D.H., Jr., 522
Ferguson, R.O., 254, 271
Fiedler, F.E., 354, 361
Field, G.A., 416
Filley, A.C., 343, 361, 554
Flamholtz, E.G., 476, 494
Foltz, R.G., 303
Ford, C.F., 186
Ford, R.N., 481, 483, 494
Foss, L., 568
Foster, R.N., 431
Franko, L.G., 548
Fretz, C.F., 522
Fromm, E., 321
Fruchter, B., 352
Fulmer, R.M., 568
Fusfeld, A.R., 431

Gantt, H.L., 34, 37, 115
Garrett, R.W., 272
Gellerman, S.W., 335
George, C.S., Jr., 13, 14, 16, 22, 35, 56, 154
Gerstner, L.V., Jr., 154
Getty, J.P., 567
Gibbons, C.C., 217
Gilbreth, F., 33, 37
Gilbreth, L.M., 33, 37
Gilman, N.P., 37
Gilmore, F.F., 154
Goetz, B.E., 214
Golembiewsi, R.T., 186
Golightly, H.O., 154
Gordon, P.J., 269
Gordon, T.J., 431
Graham, E., 522
Graham, F., Jr., 523
Greene, C.N., 332, 335
Greenlaw, P.S., 122, 244, 272
Greenwood, W.G., 215
Greiner, L.E., 19, 244, 353
Groner, A., 423
Grote, R.C., 481, 494
Gulick, L., 89, 90
Guth, W.D., 226, 227, 244

Hackamack, L.C., 523
Haimann, T., 108, 109, 341
Hain, T., 477, 478
Haire, M., 468
Hakel, M.D., 335
Hall, J., 303
Hall, R.H., 119
Halpin, A.W., 350
Hamblin, M., 506
Hamilton, I., Sir, 90
Halsey, F., 27
Hammon, R., 16
Hammurabi, 6

Hampton, D.R., 319
Hanan, M., 559, 560, 569
Harper, R.F., 7
Harris, T.A., 485, 494
Hartman, R.I., 416
Hartness, J., 82
Harvey, E., 439
Hathaway, H.K., 41
Hay, L.E., 416
Hayman, J., 522
Hays, R.D., 543, 548
Healey, J.H., 186
Heller, F.A., 361
Hellriegel, D., 186, 569
Henderson, H., 523
Henning, D.A., 199
Henry, E., 526
Hersey, P., 291, 316, 358, 361
Herzberg, F., 323, 324, 325, 326, 335,
    481, 494
Hicks, H.G., 108, 109
Hickson, D.J., 441, 443
Hill, J.W., 330
Hodgetts, R.M., 183, 227, 228, 266,
    407, 432, 451, 455, 468, 502, 504,
    523, 566
Hofer, C.W., 412, 416
Holley, W.H., Jr., 523
Hollingsworth, A.T., 494
Hollingsworth, H.L., 82
Holloway, H., 494
Holton, R.H., 549
Homans, G.C., 78
Hopeman, R.J., 207
House, R.J., 154, 171, 186, 343, 554
Hoxie, R.F., 37
Hulin, C.L., 335
Hurt, J.G., 330
Hunt, R.G., 443
Hyatt, J.C., 37

Ives, B.D., 244

James, M., 486, 494
Janson, R., 481
Jay, A., 11, 16
Jenkins, W.O., 342
Jevons, W.S., 25
Johnson, R., 386, 555, 569
Jones, C.H., 408, 409, 411, 417
Jones, D.M.C., 475
Jones, E.W., Jr., 523
Jones, H.R., Jr., 186
Jongeward, D., 486

Kahn, R.L., 289, 376
Kakar, S., 37
Kalman, J.C., 154

Kast, F.E., 370, 386, 468, 469, 555,
    556, 569
Katz, D., 289, 376
Kaufmann, F., 244
Kegan, D.L., 494
Keller, R.T., 440
Kelly, J., 122
Kennevan, W., 395
Kerlinger, F.N., 96
Kilbridge, M.D., 482
King, W.R., 386, 417, 451, 452, 458,
    468
Kleber, T.P., 484
Klein, F.C., 143
Knowles, H.P., 320
Koester, R., 410
Koontz, H., 9, 106, 108, 109, 116, 122,
    203, 217, 233, 251, 341, 479
Korth, C.M., 543, 548
Kotler, P., 517
Kreitner, R., 328, 494
Kuin, P., 548

Landsberger, H.A., 92, 97
Langer, W.C., 296
Lawler, E.E., III, 327, 330, 331, 335
Lawrence, P.R., 439, 442, 443, 463
Leavitt, H., 412
Leitch, D.P., 244
Lessing, L., 379
Levinson, H., 474, 494
Lewin, K., 81
Likert, R., 288, 290, 345, 346, 348,
    349, 361, 468, 474, 475, 479
Lindsay, C.A., 335
Linowitz, S.M., 533, 536, 548
Lippet, R., 81
Litschert, R.J., 154
Lloyd, J.H., 417
Logan, H.H., 186
Lord, R.J., 429, 443
Lorsch, J.W., 433, 439, 442, 443, 463,
    465, 466, 468
Luthans, F., 79, 82, 116, 183, 227,
    228, 303, 328, 368, 373, 384, 386,
    400, 407, 410, 481, 483, 490, 494,
    502, 504, 523, 566
Lyman, D., 494

Machiavelli, Niccolò, 11, 16
MacKinnon, N.L., 482
Macleod, R.K., 217
Magee, J.F., 271
Maier, N.R.F., 186
Malcolm, D.G., 271
Mann, F.C., 435
Marguiles, N., 494
Marks, B.A., 244
Marks, E., 335
Martin, R., 217

Martindell, J., 215, 217
Maslow, A., 225, 312, 316, 317, 318, 322, 325, 326
Mason, R.H., 149, 154
Mausner, B., 323, 335
Mautz, R.K., 217
Mayo, Elton, 70–81, 91, 94, 95, 97, 115
McClelland, D.C., 316, 319, 333
McCord, B., 508
McDonald, J., 260, 271
McDonald, P.R., 154
McFarland, D.E., 341, 403, 450, 468
McGregor, D., 318–322, 399
McKenna, S., 338
McLean, E.R., 417
Mee, J.F., 60, 569
Megginson, L.C., 92
Merrill, C.F., 60
Mesthene, E.G., 443
Metcalfe, H., 37, 60
Meyer, M.W., 439, 442
Michaels, E.G., III, 217
Miles, R.E., 93, 185, 335
Miller, D.W., 122
Miller, E.L., 548
Mills, D.L. 564
Miner, J.B., 106, 107, 118, 119, 122, 171, 186, 485
Mintzberg, H., 395, 417
Mockler, R.J., 217, 468
Mooney, J.D., 10, 16, 49, 51, 52, 54, 59, 60
More, T., Sir, 16
Morgenthaler, E., 549
Morse, J.J., 465, 466, 468
Moss, S., 302, 303
Mossberg, W., 337, 339
Most, K.S., 154
Mouton, J.S., 350, 351, 352, 353, 361
Mullick, S.K., 153
Münsterberg, H., 66–70, 69, 82, 115
Münsterberg, M., 82
Muse, W.V., 122
Myers, C.E., 37, 82, 325, 480, 481, 494

Nader, R., 519, 523
Nanus, B., 569
Napier, H.S., 569
Nebuchadnezzar, 7
Netschert, B.C., 426, 443
Neumann, F.L., 217
Newman, W.H., 108, 109, 181
Nichols, R.G., 289, 299, 300, 303
Nielander, W.A., 301
North, H.Q., 443
Novick, D., 523

Odiorne, G.S., 483, 494
O'Donnell, C., 9, 106, 108, 109, 122, 203, 233, 251, 341, 479

O'Donnell, L., 337
O'Hanlon, T., 460
O'Reilly, A.P., 335
Owen, R., 23

Packard, V., 315
Paranka, S., 271
Parkinson, C.N., 168, 186
Parsons, T., 379, 386
Pascussi, J.H., 460
Patton, A., 561, 569
Paul, W.J., Jr., 481, 494
Petit, T.A., 380, 381, 382, 386
Pheysey, D.C., 441, 443
Phillips, D.C., 386
Phillips, T.R., 8, 9, 16
Poffenberger, A.T., 82
Pollay, R., 272
Porter, L.W., 327, 330, 331, 335
Powell, R.M., 494
Prell, M.J., 506
Pugh, D.S., 441, 443
Pyke, D.L., 443
Pyle, W.C., 475, 494

Ramaswamy, T.N., 16
Randall, L., 490
Reddin, W., 355, 361
Reif, W.E., 481, 482, 483, 494
Reiley, A.C., 10, 16, 49, 51, 52, 54, 59, 60
Reiman, B.C., 468
Rewoldt, S.H., 518
Rezler, J., 443
Richards, M.D., 122, 244, 272, 301
Richman, B., 523
Ricklefs, R., 336, 570
Roach, D., 335
Robbins, S.M., 548
Roberts, K.H., 335
Robertson, K.B., 481, 494
Robinson, W., 60
Roche, J.M., 504, 505
Roche, W. J., 482
Roethlisberger, F.J., 73, 77, 78, 82, 97
Roman, D., 428, 443
Rosenzweig, J.E., 370, 386, 468, 469, 555, 556, 569
Ross, R., 279, 280
Roudiani, M., 543, 548
Rowntree, B.S., 82
Rue, L.W., 569

Sales, S.M., 359
Samuelson, P., 236
Sargent, L.F., 254
Sawyer, G.C., 523
Saxburg, B.O., 320
Sayles, L., 383

Schachter, S., 315
Schaffer, R.A., 521
Schlacter, J.L., 494
Schmidt, W.H., 344, 361
Schneider, C.E., 490
Schoderbek, P.P., 217, 413, 414, 417, 482
Schollhammer, H., 548
Schonberger, R.J., 217, 373
Schorr, B., 510, 513
Schwab, D.P., 325, 327, 494
Scott, B.R., 569
Scott, J.D., 518
Scott, W.D., 37
Scott, W.G., 108, 109, 342
Segura, E.L., 154
Seiler, J.A., 386
Servan-Schreiber, J.-J., 532, 544, 546, 548
Shaffer, R.A., 523
Sheldon, O., 60
Shell, R.L., 244
Shepard, J.M., 97
Shetty, Y.K., 463, 464, 468
Sigband, N.B., 303
Sihler, W.W., 245
Simmonds, K., 545, 548
Simmons, J.K., 399, 400, 401, 402, 416
Simon, H.A., 88, 90, 97, 224, 230, 231, 245, 250, 272
Sirota, D., 494
Sisk, H.L., 108, 109
Slocum, J.W., Jr., 186, 569
Smallwood, J.E., 154
Smith, A., 14, 15, 16
Smith, P.A., 335
Snyderman, B., 323, 335
Sokolik, S.L., 494
Sorenson, R.Z., II, 550
Spranger, E., 226
Spriegel, W.R., 37
Stabler, C.N., 521, 523
Stalker, G.M., 437, 443
Starke, F.A., 335
Starr, M.K., 122
Steiner, G., 130, 141, 154
Stelzer, D.F., 244
Stewart, J.M., 451
Stobaugh, R.B., 548
Stoller, D.S., 396
Strauss, G., 322
Summer, C.E., 108, 109, 181, 319
Sun Tzu, 8
Swager, W.L., 443
Swart, J.C., 417
Sweeney, J.K., 536, 549

Tagiuri, R., 226, 227, 244
Tannenbaum, A.S., 217
Tannenbaum, R., 344, 361
Taylor, F.W., 28–33, 37, 45, 52, 67, 87, 91

Teel, K.S., 361
Terry, G., 108, 109, 110, 113
Tersine, R.J., 386
Thompson, S.E., 67
Thune, S.S., 154
Thurber, J.A., 186
Toffler, A., 444
Tosi, H., 361, 494
Towne, H.R., 26
Townsend, R., 98
Trist, E.L., 95, 435
Tubbs, S.L., 302, 303
Turner, C.E., 80

Urwick, L.F., 51–56, 59, 60
Utterback, J.M., 444

Van Horn, R.L., 396
Vancil, R.F., 144
Vandell, R.F., 272
Vergin, R.C., 412
Virts, J.R., 272
Voich, D., Jr., 108, 109
Vollmer, H.W., 564
Von Bertalanffy, L., 386
Vroom, V., 325, 328, 335

Wadia, M.S., 122
Walker, J., 183, 407
Wallace, J., 494
Walter, G.A., 335
Walton, R.E., 480, 494
Warren, E.K., 108, 109, 181
Warshaw, M.R., 518
Waters, L.K., 335
Watson, C.E., 545, 546
Watt, J., 22
Ways, M., 468
Weber, M., 450
Webster, F.E., Jr., 523
Weiner, J.B., 461
Welch, W.H., 549
Weston, J.F., 217
Wheelwright, S.S., 154
Whisler, T.L., 412
White, D.D., Jr., 491, 494
White, R.K., 81
White, R.W., 316
Whyte, W.H., Jr., 560, 569
Wickesberg, A.K., 303
Widgery, R.N., 298
Widing, J.W., Jr., 549
Wilemon, D.L., 468
Williams, L.K., 245, 435
Williams, R.W., 209
Williams, W., 82
Wilson, I., 132, 154, 505
Wolfbein, S., 425

Woodward, J., 438, 441, 442, 444
Woolf, D.A., 122
Worthy, J.C., 170
Wortman, M.S., Jr., 117, 122, 368, 386
Wren, D.A., 16, 49, 51, 60, 108, 109
Wright, C.D., 37

Yanouzas, J.N., 171

Young, D., 459
Young, S.D., 386, 378, 468
Yukl, G., 361

Zani, W.M., 395, 397, 417
Zipf, A.R., 410
Zwerman, W.L., 439, 442, 444

SUBJECT INDEX

Ability, technical vs. administrative, 43
Abstraction, in communication, 284
Acceptance theory of authority, 57–58, 316–317
Achievement, need for, 316–317, 319
Adaptive structures, 449. See also *Free-form organizations; Matrix structure; Organic structures; Project organizations.*
Administration. See also *Management.*
  principle of, 43
Administrative ability, vs. technical ability, 43
Administrative costs, 251
Administrative man, 88, 239
Aggression, MIS and, 400
Air pollution
  from automobiles, 510–511
  from industrial smokestacks, 511–513
Analysis
  financial, 241–243
  marginal, 236–239
  morphological, 429
  time-event, 204–208
  transactional, 485–490
Art of War, The, 8–9
Assets, human
  evaluation of, 474–479
  management of, 473–493
Auditing
  external, 214
  internal, 214
  management, 214–216
Authority. See also *Decision making.*
  acceptance theory of, 57–58, 316–317
  and power, 183–184
  and responsibility, 171–178
  centralization of, 46
  decentralization of, 178–181
  defined, 44, 50

Authority (*Continued*)
  delegation of, 181–182
  formal theory of, 171–172
  functional, 176–178
    vs. project, 457
  legal, 455
  line, 173–174
  of knowledge, 172–173
  of situation, 172
  project, 454–455
    vs. functional, 457
  reality, 455
  sources of, 171–173
  staff, 174
  types of, 173–178
Automation, in business, 403
Avoidance
  change and, 287
  MIS and, 400–401

Balance theory, 297–299
Basic decisions, 229–230
Basic mission, 131
  in international expansion, 530
Behavior
  dysfunctional, 399
  learned, 327–328
  needs and, 311–312
  of leader, 344–359
  reinforcement of, 328
Behavior modification, organizational, 490–492
Behavioral school
  contributions of, 277–366
  human behavior branch of, 116–117
  social systems branch of, 116–117
  weaknesses of, 120
Bethlehem steel experiments, 29–31
Bill of rights, employee, 559–560
Black box, 88–89
Branch organization, 538

Break-even point, 201–203
Budget(s)
    alternative, 201
    balance sheet, 200–201
    capital expenditure, 200
    cash, 200
    comprehensive, 180–200
    flexibility of, 201
    material, 200
    production, 200
    revenue and expense, 200
    supplemental monthly, 201
    time, 200
    types of, 200–201
    variable expense, 201
Bureaucracy, 450
Business
    role of in ecology, 508–517
    role of in equal opportunity, 502–
        508
    socio-economic purpose of, 131

Capitalism, minority, 504–505
Cash flow, discounted, 242–243
Central American Common Market,
    532
Centralization, of authority, 46
Certainty decisions, 230, 232
Change, resistance to, 287
Civil Rights Act, 502
Clerical costs, 251
Cliques, social, in Hawthorne
    studies, 77
COBOL, 404
Commanding, 48
Committees
    ad hoc, 167
    advantages of, 167–168
    disadvantages of, 168–169
    effective use of, 169
    standing, 167
Common Market, 531
Communication
    abstraction in, 284
    bad listening habits in, 299–300
    cluster chains of, 292–293
    commandments of, 300–301
    common barriers to, 281–288
    credibility of, 297–299
    diagonal, 291
    downward, 289–290
    face-to-face, 295
    formal channels of, 288–291
    gossip chain of, 293
    inference in, 284, 286
    informal channels of, 291–294
    interpersonal, 278–288
    lateral, 291
    oral, 295–296
    perception problems in, 281–285
    process of, 278–281

Communication (*Continued*)
    single strand, 293
    technology of, 425
    through grapevine, 292
    two-way, 296
    upward, 290–291
    written, 294–295
Competence, need for, 316
    of personnel, 138
Compulsory staff service, 10
Computers
    analog, 403
    and organization structure, 412–
        413
    and personnel, 413–414
    and unemployment, 411–412
    digital, 403–404
    drawbacks of, 410–411
    elements of, 410–411
    impact of, 411–414
    modern, 403–404
    power of, 403
    programming of, 404–406
    simulations with, 408–409
    uses of, 406–410
Consideration–initiating structure
    continuum, 350–351
Consumerism, 517–521
Contingency organization design
    forces influencing, 463–464
    structure of, 464–466
    trend toward, 463
Contract, privity of, 520
Control
    Babylonian methods of, 8
    description of, 48
    feedback, 195–196
    financial, 13
    inventory. See *Inventory control.*
    key area, 213–214
    managerial, 6
    of overall performance, 209–215
    principles of, 54
    process of, 193–222
    production, 8
    requirements for, 196–198
    span of. See *Span of control.*
    standards of, 194
        deviations from, 195
        performance compared with, 194–
            195
    techniques of, specialized, 203–209
        traditional, 198–203
Coordination
    description of, 48
    effective, 50
    principles of, 50, 53–54
    processive, 50
    through committees, 167–168
CORE, 502
Corporate democracy
    current research findings on, 557–
        559
    specific action of, 559–561

Corporations, international, 538
multinational, 543–546
Costs, clerical, 251
Customs, foreign, 533

Decentralization of authority, 179–
181. See also *Decision making.*
Decision(s)
basic, 229–230
certainty, 230, 232
nonprogrammed, 230, 231
organizational, 228–229
personal, 228–230
programmed, 230, 231
rational, 225–226
risk, 232–234
routine, 229–230
types of, 228–231
uncertainty, 234–236
Decision making. See also *Authority.*
conditions of, 232–236, 239
effect of personal values on, 226–
228
mathematical models for, 114–115
modern quantitative, 249–276
process of, 224–225, 249–273
rationality in, 225–226
techniques of, 231, 236–243
Decision trees, 267–268
Delegation of authority
defined, 181
improvement of, 181–182
Delphi technique
forecasts using, 431
steps in, 429
process of, 429–431
worksheet, 430
Democracy, corporate, 557–561
Departmentalization
by customer, 166
by equipment, 166
by process, 166–167
by simple numbers, 166
by time, 166
common forms of, 162–167
functional, 162–163
product, 163–165
territorial, 165–166
Discipline, organizational, 44
Discounted cash flow, 242–243
Discourses, The, 11
Discrimination, against women. See
Women, discrimination against.
Distortion, change and, 287
Division of labor, 14–15, 44
Domestic system, 12
Dysfunctional behavior, 399

Ecology, role of business in, 508–517
Econometrics, 135
Economic man, 87–88, 239

Economic order quantity formula, 253
Economic unions, 531
EDP. See *Electronic data processing.*
Efficiency, Emerson's twelve princi-
ples of, 35
Ego states, in transactional analysis,
486
Electronic data processing, 413–414.
See also *Computers.*
Employee bill of rights, 559–560
Employment, equality in, 502
Energy
alternate source of, 427–428
efficent use of, 426–427
shortage of, 426
Enlightened self-interest, 500–501
Entropy in systems, 375
Environmental evaluation, external,
133–137
internal, 137–138
Equal employment, 502
Equal Employment Opportunity
Commission, 502
Equal opportunity, role of business
in, 502–508
Equal Pay Act, 502
Equity
organizational, 47
theory of, 332–333
European Economic Community, 531
Executive, plural, 167
Executive opinion, jury of, 137
Executive talent, lack of, 561–564
Expectancy theory, 327–333
Expectancy-valence theory, 328–330
Exporting
between industrialized countries,
528
vs. licensing, 537
Expropriation, risk of in going
international, 534–535
Extrapolation, 134

Factory system, 13
Fallacy, great jackass, 473–474
Feedback, 195–196, 280
Female discrimination. See *Women,
discrimination against.*
Financial analysis, 241–243
Financial plan, 144
Financial statements, 145–147
Forecasting
econometrics method of, 135–136
economic, 134–136
effect of governmental action on,
136
envelope, 429
environmental, external, 133–137
internal, 137–138
lag indicators in, 135
lead indicators in, 135
methods of

Forecasting (*Continued*)
    methods of, econometrics, 135–136
      grass-roots, 137
      jury of executive opinion, 137
      lead and lag, 134–135
    nontechnical factors in, 432
    normative, 429
    sales, 136–137
    technical factors in, 432
    technological, 423–433
    use of Delphi technique in, 431
    user expectation of, 137
Foremanship, functional, 45
Formal theory of authority, 171–172
FORTRAN, 404
Free-form organization. See also
    Organic structures.
    challenges of, 462–463
    examples of, 460–463
    strategic planning in, 459–460
Frustration reactions, MIS and,
    399–401
Functional definition, 50
Functional effect, 50
Functional foremanship, 45
Functionalism
    applicative, 50
    defined, 10
    determinative, 50
    interpretative, 50
Functions of the Executive, 56

Gain sharing, 27
Game theory
    described, 260
    maximin concept of, 262
    minimax concept of, 262
    saddle point in, 261–264
Games
    non-zero-sum, 265–266
    zero-sum, 261–264
Gangplank principle, 46
Gantt chart, 34
    example of, 204–205
General systems theory, 370–372, 555
Government, effect of on business,
    136
"Great jackass fallacy", 473–474
Group dynamics, 76–77

Hammurabi, Code of, 607
Hawthorne effect, 79
Hawthorne studies, 75–92
    of bank wiring observation room,
      75–79
    of illumination experiments, 72–73
    of massive interviewing program,
      74–75
    of relay assembly test room, 73–74
    scientific method in, 91–92

Heuristic programming, 269–270
Human behavior research, 556. See
    also *Communication; Hawthorne
    studies; Leadership; Motivation.*
Human element in work place, 65–68
Human relations philosophy, 92
    vs. human resources philosophy, 93
Human resources accounting
    human replacement costs in, 476
    leadership style and, 477–479
    periodic evaluations of, 475–479
    personnel as investment in, 475
Human resources philosophy, 23–24
    vs. human relations philosophy, 93
Human Side of Enterprise, The, 318
Hygiene factors, 322–324

Immaturity-maturity theory, 322–323
Indifference, zone of, 58
*Industrial and General Administra-
    tion,* 42
Industrial Revolution
    domestic system in, 12
    factory system in, 12
    putting-out system in, 12–13
Inference, in communication, 284, 286
Informal organization, 182–184
Information design, 203–204
Initiating structure–consideration
    continuum, 350–351
Initiative, administrative, 47
Instrumentality, 328–330
International corporations, 538
International divisions, 538
International management
    advantages of, 530–532
    and entry into foreign markets,
      529–531
    control of, 538–540
    disadvantages of, 532–535
    monetary incentives of, 541–542
    of foreign operations, 537–542
    of multinational corporation, 543–
      546
    organization structure of, 531–539
    staffing of, 540–541
    upward mobility within, 542–543
Interviewing, nondirective, 75
Inventory control, 8
    economic order quantity formula of,
      253–254
    trial and error approach to, 252–253
Investment, return on. See *Return
    on investment.*
Isoprofit line, computation of, 259

"Jackass fallacy," 473–474
Job enrichment
    described, 480
    in action, 480–481
    under attack, 481–483

Job Opportunities in the Business
  Sector, 503
JOBS, 503
Joint ventures, 535–536
Jury of executive opinion, 137

Key area control, 213–214

Labor, division of, 14–15, 44
Lag indicators, 134–135
Language, effective use of, 284, 297
Laplace criterion, 235
Latin American Free Trade Association, 532
Law of triviality, 168
Lead indicators, 134–135
Leader
  adaptive, 359
  authoritarian, 345
  behavior of, 344–359
  democratic, 345
Leader-member relations, 354
Leadership
  adaptive, 359
  behavioral aspects of, 345–348
  contingency theory of, 354–355
  continuum of, 344–345
  defined, 341–342
  effectiveness of, 341–360
  implementation program of, 353
  life cycle theory of, 357–359
  Likert's systems of, 345–350
  managerial grid of, 351–354
  nature of, 341–359
  Ohio State research on, 350–351
  principles of, 11–12
  situational theory of, 343–344
  styles of, 7, 345–360
    changes in, 477–479
    modern, 482
    traditional, 482
  three-dimensional, 355–357
  trait theory of, 342–343
  two-dimensional, 350–354
Liability, strict, 520
Licensing, vs. exporting, 537
Line
  and staff, conflicts between, 174–
    176
    improving relations between, 176
  authority of, 173
  departments, 177
Linear programming
  characteristics of, 254
  defined, 254
  graphic method of, 254–260
  limitations of, 260
  use of isoprofit line in, 259–260
Listening, bad habits of, 299–300
Logic, in communication, 284
Loss, and profit, 209–211

Management
  as a process, 110
  as a profession. See *Professionalism.*
  by objectives, 483
    common errors of, 484
  classical, deficiencies of, 89–91
  defined, 5
  functions of, 48, 57, 108–109
    universality of, 111, 119–120
  in the future, 553–567
  information system, 394–402
    behavioral effects of, 398–402
    blueprint of, 396–398
    design of, 395–398
    major determinants in, 395–396
    operating management in, 401
    operating personnel in, 401
    organization and, 401–402
    technical staff in, 401–402
    top management in, 402
  international. See *International
    management.*
  of change, 556
  of foreign operations, 537–546
  of human assets, 473–493
  of military, 8–9
  philosophy of, 112, 180
    changes in, 96
  principles of, 44–47, 89–91, 110–
    111, 118–119
  recent developments in, 391–572
  scientific. See *Scientific
    management.*
  technology and, 433–438
  theory of, 117–118
    current status of, 368–370
    future direction of, 368–369, 383–
      384, 555–557, 566
  values of, 131
    changes in, 132
Management process school, 127–222
  as seen by various authors, 108–109
  framework of, 107, 110
  philosophy of, 112
  principles of, 110–111
  universal functions of, 111
  weaknesses of, 118–120
Management science, 113. See also
  *Operations research; Quantitative
  school.*
Managerial grid, 351–353
Managers
  in managerial system, characteristics
    of, 381–382
  institutional, 381–382
  organizational, 382
  technical, 381, 382
Marginal analysis, 236–239
Marginal physical product, 237–239
Marginal revenue, 239–241
Marketing plan, 145
Material resources, 137–138
Matrix structure, 452–459
  advantages of, 458–459
  described, 452, 454–458

Maximax criterion, 235
Maximin criterion, 235, 262
MBO. See *Management, by objectives.*
Means-end hierarchy, rationality and, 225–226
Mechanistic structures
key dimensions of, 437–438
research on, 438–441
Milestone scheduling, 207, 208
Minimax criterion, 235–236, 262
Minimum wage, 7
Minority capitalism, 504–505
MIS. See *Management, information system.*
Monte Carlo technique, 267
Morale, 47
Morphological analysis, 429
Motion study, 22, 29–31, 33. See also *Scientific management.*
Motivation
committees and, 167
equity theory of, 332–333
expectancy and, 328–332
immaturity-maturity theory of, 322–323
managerial assumptions about, 318–322
modern theories of, 311–340
money and, 333
need hierarchy of, 312–318
needs and behavior affecting, 311–312
two-factor theory of, 323–326
Motivators, 324

NAACP, 502
NAB, 502–503
National Alliance of Businessmen, 502–503
National Association for the Advancement of Colored People, 502
Needs
and behavior, 311–312
and motivation, 311–312
esteem, 315–316
Maslow's hierarchy of, 312–318, 326
of the individual, 317–318, 322, 327
physiological, 313
safety, 314
self-actualization, 316
social, 314–315
New Lanark experiment, 23
Niche, organizational. See "Propitious niche".
Noise pollution, 514, 516.
Nondirective interviewing, 75
Nonprogrammed decisions, 230, 231
Non-zero-sum games, 265–266
Normative reality, 282–284
Norms, behavioral, 78

Objectives, of business
intermediate-range, 140–141
long-range, 140–141
short-range, 141–148
OB/Mod, 490–492
Ombudsman, 559
On the Economy of Machinery and Manufacture, 25
Onward Industry!, 49
Open system, 373–396
adaptive mechanisms in, 374–375
and entropy, 375–376
contrived adaptivity of, 376
maintenance mechanisms in, 375
Operations, foreign, management of, 537–546. See also *International management.*
Operations research
defined, 250–251
essentials of, 251
Optimization, 113–114
OR. See *Operations research.*
Order, principle of, 47
Organic structures. See also *Free-form organization; Matrix structure; Project organization.*
of the future, 555–556
key dimensions of, 437–438
research on, 438–441
Organization(s). See also *Structure(s).*
as open system, 373–376
branch, 538
committee, 167–168
formal, 57
free-form. See *Free-form organization.*
informal, 182–184
line-staff, 174
modern structures of, 449–472
planning. See *Planning organization.*
project. See *Project organization.*
matrix. See *Matrix structure.*
structure of, 464, 466
technology in, 438–441
total systems design of, 377–379
Organizational behavior modification, 490–492
Organizational decisions, 228–229
Organizing
defined, 48
guidlines for, 48
principles of, 50–51
process of, 161–192

Payback period, 242
Perception, problems of in communication, 281–284
Performance, and rewards, 330–332
Personal decisions, 228–230
Personal observation, 203

Personnel
as investment, 475
competence of, 138
effect of technology on, 433–438
management of, 473–493
PERT. See *Program evaluation and review technique.*
PERT/COST, 207
PERT network, 205–207
Pessimistic revery, 72, 79
Pesticides, 509–510
Philadelphia textile study, 71–72
Physical product, marginal, 237–239
Piece-rate work, 12, 13
Plan, premium, 27–28
Planning. See also *Decision making; Forecasting.*
advantages of, 150–151
comprehensive, 128–130
description of, 48
environmental evaluation in,
external, 133–137
internal, 137–138
financial, 144
functional, 142–148
marketing, 142–143
operational, 141–148
principles of, 52–53
production, 143–144
strategic, 130–138
Planning organization
metamorphosis of, 149–150
time phases of, 149
Plural executives, 167
Policy(ies)
defined, 229–230
open-door, 181
uniform, 179
vs. procedures, 229
Pollution
air, 510–513
cost of cleaning up, 515
noise, 514, 516
water, 513–514
Power
and authority, 183–184
informal, sources of, 183
of position, 354
PPBS, 208–209
Premium plan, 27–28
Prince, The, 11
Principle-process-effect thesis
Mooney and Reiley's, 50–51
Urwick's, 52–55
Principles of Organization, 49
Principles of Scientific Management, The, 67
Privity of contract, 520
Probability
estimates of, 232
objective, 232–233
subjective, 233
Procedures
defined, 229
vs. policies, 229

Product safety
checklist for, 520
general, 519–520
legal aspects of, 520–521
of air bags, 519
of automobiles, 520
Production plan, 143–144
Professionalism, of management
and knowledge, 564
and self-control, 565–566
and social responsibility, 565
application of, 565
community sanction of, 566
future developments in, 566
Program evaluation and review technique
cost applied to, 207
critical path of, 206
expected time of, 205–206
limitations of, 207
slack in, 207
strengths of, 207
time-event network of, 205–207
Programmed decisions, 230, 231
Programming
heuristic, 269–270
linear. See *Linear programming.*
Program-planning-budgeting system, 208–209
Project organization
advantages of, 451
aggregate, 453
criteria for, 451
defined, 451
design of, 452
pure, 453
Projection, 400
"Propitious niche"
development of, 139
planning and, 138–140
Psycho-technical problem, 67
Psychology
industrial, 66–70
scientific, 67
Purpose of business, socio-economic, 131
Putting-out system, 12

Quantitative school, 223–276
characteristics of, 112–113
contributions of, 115
mathematical models used in, 114–115
use of optimization in, 113
use of suboptimization in, 113
Queuing theory, 266

Rabble hypothesis, 94–95
Rationalism, irrationality of, 88
Rationality, and means-end hierarchy, 225–226

Reality
    normative, 282–284
    sensory, 282–284
Reinforcement of behavior, 328
Rejection
    change and, 287
Research methodology. See
    Scientific method.
Resistance to change, 287
Responsibility
    and authority, 44, 177–178
    defined, 44
    functional, 456
    Hammurabi on, 7
    social. See Social responsibility.
Return on investment
    as control technique, 212–213
    calculation of, 145, 212
Revery, pessimistic, 72, 79
Rewards
    inputs and, 323–333
    performance and, 330–332
Risk decisions, 232–234
Risk preference, 233–234
ROI. See Return on investment.
Roman empire, reorganization of by
    Diocletian, 9
Routine decisions, 229–230

Saddle point, 262–263, 264, 265
Satisfaction, effect of on performance,
    330–332
Satisficing, 88. See also Administra-
    tive man.
Scalar chain, 46
Scalar process, 50
Scenario writing, 429
Scientific management, 21–40
    defined, 32
    in bricklaying, 33
    in labor and fatigue studies, 25–26
    in metal-cutting experiments, 31
    in New Lanark experiment, 23–24
    in pig-iron experiment, 29–30
    in shoveling experiments, 30–31
    in Soho foundry, 22–23
    incentive payment plans in, 27–28,
        31, 34
    principles of, 32
    psychology and, 66–67
    shortcomings of, 87–89
    task system in, 30
    time and motion study in, 22, 29–
        31, 33
Scientific method
    in Hawthorne studies, 91–92
    steps of, 95–96
Scramble for young executive talent,
    561–564
Sensitivity, in communication, 296
Sensitivity training, 484–485
Sensory reality, 282–284

Simulation, 408–409
Social cliques, in Hawthorne studies,
    77–78
Social comparison theory, 332–333
Social responsibility, 500–527
    consumerism and, 517–521
    ecology and, 508–517
    enlightened self-interest and,
        500–501
    equal opportunity and, 502–508
    legislation defining, 502, 516–
        518
Socio-economic purpose, of
    business, 131
Soldiering, systematic, 29
Span of control
    and classical theorists, 169
    defined, 90, 169
    flat structures in, 170–171
    narrow, 169–170
    tall structures in, 170–171
    wide, 170
Staff
    and line, conflicts between, 174–
        176
        improving relations between, 176
    compulsory service of, 10
    departments, 177
    stability of, 47
Staff authority
    defined, 174
    Catholic Church's use of, 10
Staff independence, 10
Staff principle, 10
Status, effect of on communication,
    286–287
Strategy. See also Planning.
    and structure, 161–162
    military, 8
Strict liability, 520
Structure(s). See also
    Organization(s).
    adaptive, 449
    bureaucratic, decline of, 449–450
    flat, 170–172
    from strategy to, 161
    impact of technology on, 438–442
    matrix. See Matrix structure.
    mechanistic. See Mechanistic
        structures.
    modern organization, 449–472
    of organization, 463–466
    organic. See Organic structures.
    tall, 170–171
Synergism, in strategic planning, 459–
    460
System(s)
    applied concepts of, 372, 373
    closed, 375
    entropy in, 375
    general theory of, 370, 555
    levels of, 370–371
    managerial, 379–381
    open. See Open system.

System (*Continued*)
  point of view of, 382–383
  school of management, 370–373
  social, 376
  totally adaptive organization,
    376–379
Systems management, 555
Systems school, 370–373
Systems theory, 370, 555

TA. See *Transactional analysis.*
Task-and-bonus system, 34
Technical ability, vs. administrative
  ability, 43
Technology
  advances in, 424–428
  and group cohesiveness, 433–436
  and power production, 426–428
  and psycho-social system, 434–435
  and tension, 433–434
  automated, 423
  communication and, 425–426
  cybernetic, 423
  effect of, on personnel, 433–438
    on structure, 438–442
  effectiveness of, 434–435
  handicraft, 423
  historical perspective on, 423
  impact of on forecasting, 428–433
  mechanistic, 423
  mechanized, 423
  of communication, 425
Tenure agreements, 560
Testing, vocational, 67–69
Theory of Political Economy, The, 25
Theory X, 318–321
Theory Y, 321–322
Therblig, 33
Time and motion study, 22, 29–31, 33
Time-event analyses, 204–208
Transactional analysis, 485–490
  ego states in, 486
  managers' use of, 488–490

Transactions
  complementary, 486–487, 488
  crossed, 487, 488, 489
  ulterior, 487–488, 489
Transformation process, 88–89
Triviality, law of, 168
Truth in Lending Act, 518
Truth in Packaging Act, 518
Twelve Principles of Efficiency, The,
  34
Two-factor theory of motivation,
  323–326

Uncertainty decisions, 234–236
Unemployed, hard-core, hiring of,
  503
Unity of command, 44–45, 89–90
Universality of management functions,
  111, 119–120
Unsafe at Any Speed, 519

Valence, and expectancy, 328–330
Values, of management, 131–132
  according to Spranger, 226–228
  changes in, 132
Vocational testing, 67–69

Wage, minimum, 7
Waiting-line theory, 266
Water pollution, 513–514
Wealth of Nations, The, 14
Women, discrimination against, 502,
  506–508
Work place, human element in, 65–86
Work standards, 22, 29
World Trade Corporation, 538

Zero-sum games, 261–264
Zone of indifference, 58